Copyright © 2014 Ligia Balu

Ligia Balu - Author and Publisher

All Copyrights Reserved.

No part of this book may be reproduced, sorted, or transmitted in any form or by any means, electronic or mechanical, including photocopying, recording, or by information storage or retrieval system, without permission in writing from the publisher and from the author except for the inclusion of brief quotations in a review.

Price $ 39.95

ISBN: 0-9651186-1-4

Printed in the United States of America

Book of Astrology by LIGIA BALU

COMPLETE ASTROLOGY - How to Find Your Soul-Mate, Stars, and Destiny Volumes 1, 2 & 3

Visit: www.ligiabalu.com

How to Find Your Soul-Mate, Stars, and Destiny

Forward

Astrology means the study of the stars. It is an ancient course of study dating to prehistoric times which concentrates on the correlation between celestial events and human events. *How to Find Your Soul-Mate, Stars and Destiny* is based on traditional research and offers a basic introduction to this age old science. It is important to know how to find one's soul mate and destiny, and one important aspect of that search is a better understanding of one's self. Understanding ourselves and our motivations sets us on a path of better understanding the other persons in our lives and those persons we come in contact with. If you are very careful in your decision making, when you learn to match the signs by hour, days, months, and years with your own sign, you are less likely to make mistakes in choosing your love, soul mate, and destiny for life. This is a unique book designed for the reader to prevent unnecessary mistakes in life: broken hearts, broken families, lost loves, lonely times, crying and screaming over loved ones. Through the study of Astrology, you the reader, may come to a better understanding of the problems you have suffered in life. Perhaps you have found yourself asking why other people appear happy together and why other people appear to have so few problems. Perhaps you have asked yourself, "Why not me? What is wrong with me? Why can't I be happy? I have many good qualities just like other people. Why am I attracted to the wrong person? Why do bad things happen to me?" By thoroughly understanding not only your conscious self but your subconscious reasoning (often referred to in Astrology as the unconscious), you may finally find the answers you have been searching for. Just as effectively, you can study and begin to understand persons born to other signs as well. Why does a person act or behave the way they do, either obstinate, or changeable, or impulsive? Perhaps a basic answer to that question can be found in the nature of the Sun sign.

The Zodiac refers to the "Circle of Animals" or the "Circle of Life" and is the name for the belt of constellations viewed in the celestial heavens. It is made up of twelve signs: Aries, Taurus, Gemini, Cancer, Leo, Virgo, Libra, Scorpio, Sagittarius, Capricorn, Aquarius, and Pisces. These are referred to as the Sun signs or the sign which the Sun was in on the date a person was born. The Sun, as the most important celestial body, is considered the greatest influence in one's personal horoscope. A further understanding of Astrology, however, depends upon an understanding of one's Moon sign, Ascendant, Houses, Planets, and the Aspects these Planets make to one another. Each of these influences the person as well which is why two people with the same Sun sign can be so different. *STARS AND DESTINY* provides the reader with an explanation of each of these influences. And because each person is different, *STARS AND DESTINY* presents both the positive and the negative characteristics of each of these influences. And it is the combination of these positives and negatives that produce the individual. And it is left to each individual to determine how to react to these positives and negatives. In other words, one person may use assertiveness to develop leadership qualities while another becomes aggressive, obstinate, and even hostile. Life is a long road of self-improvement, but the basics remain the same. How one person reacts and relates to another depends to a large degree on each person's security and self-esteem. That is what this book strives to explain: Why we are the way we are.

Over the last twenty years, in my journey through life, many friends, co-workers, acquaintances, and others who chose the wrong soul mate for better or for worse have called me for counseling. Because love can be blind, these situations often change into disaster. I have observed over time that these decisions lead to misunderstandings, disappointments, tragedies, divorce, and loneliness. What suffers the most is the creation of love. The resulting lonely time is not a life to live. Life is short, and this is no way to find happiness or to be content. A broken heart can lead a person to believe that all men and/or women are the same, and it is no use to continue looking for the right one. This attitude can result in the person choosing to be alone for a long time or to attempt to protect themselves and the creations of love: their children. Rather than trying again to find the right partner, they choose to remain alone when it, otherwise, would be possible to be happy and never lonely. It may be difficult to believe, but Astrology can help people learn the lessons they need to know in order never to be lonely. The simple truth comes from God above. God doesn't like to see us alone. He never intended people to go through life by themselves, but instead, He planned for each of us to discover our true soul mates and to go through life - and eternity - together. This is simple logic because the soul mate is the other half of ourselves.

In life, it is easy to make mistakes especially if one is attracted to the wrong person in the wrong place for the wrong reasons. We are all really looking for love rather than to be left lonely and by ourselves. Why have the men and women in your life been mistakes? When thinking about love, remember it is the most powerful force in life. It is nice to have someone to share your life with. Success is an empty bag when you have no one to share it with. You ask yourself, "What is wrong with me?" Nothing is wrong with you. You have just been attracted to the wrong person. It is difficult to find Mr. or Mrs. Right when you are attracted to Mr. or Mrs. Wrong. Once in this relationship, you struggle to make it work. Many times, when we are caught up in these wrong relationships, we miss the opportunity to meet Mr. or Mrs. Right. Why do we struggle so much when there is a way to make life easier and never to be alone again? Take time for yourself. Study not only yourself but the others around you. Of the people you meet, select one for your destiny with whom to share love and life. Astrology provides you with this necessary information. What is required is the time and effort to grasp a fuller understanding of yourself. When you truly understand yourself, you better understand what it is you want, what you are looking for, and what makes you happy. You are a unique individual with a specific combination of characteristics, personality traits, likes, and dislikes. What you must also accept is that others have particular tendencies which you must either accept and learn to live with or make the decision to find that special person with whom you are the most compatible. Love is the magic which propels us all to initiate this search throughout the universe for our true soul mate and love match. I like to see people happy and to see less sorrow and loneliness. Lift is short. Today we are here, and tomorrow we are not. Learn to live each day to its fullest.

How to Find Your *Soul-Mate*, *Stars*, and *Destiny*

House Rulerships

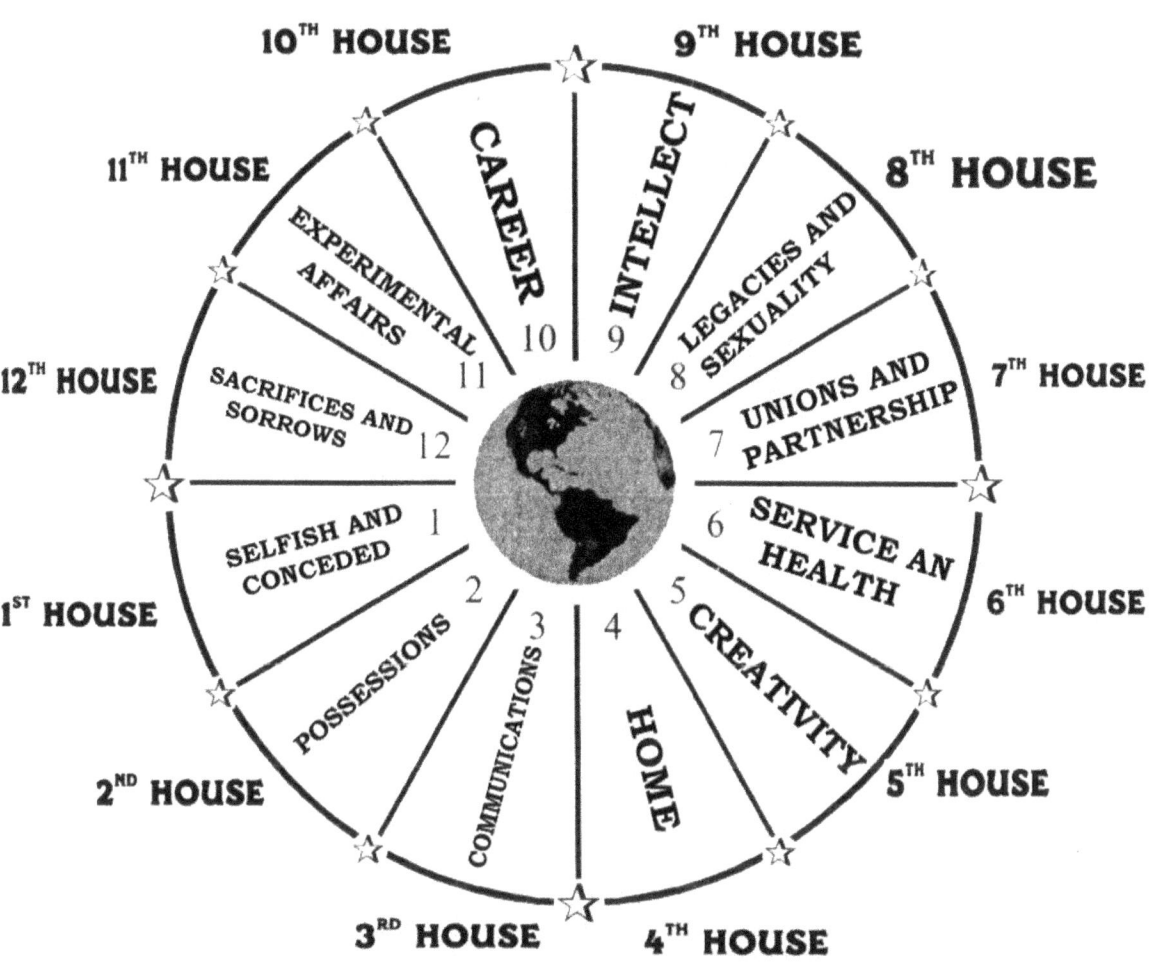

How to Find Your *Soul-Mate, Stars,* and *Destiny*

Combinations of Elements - Our Mission on The Earth

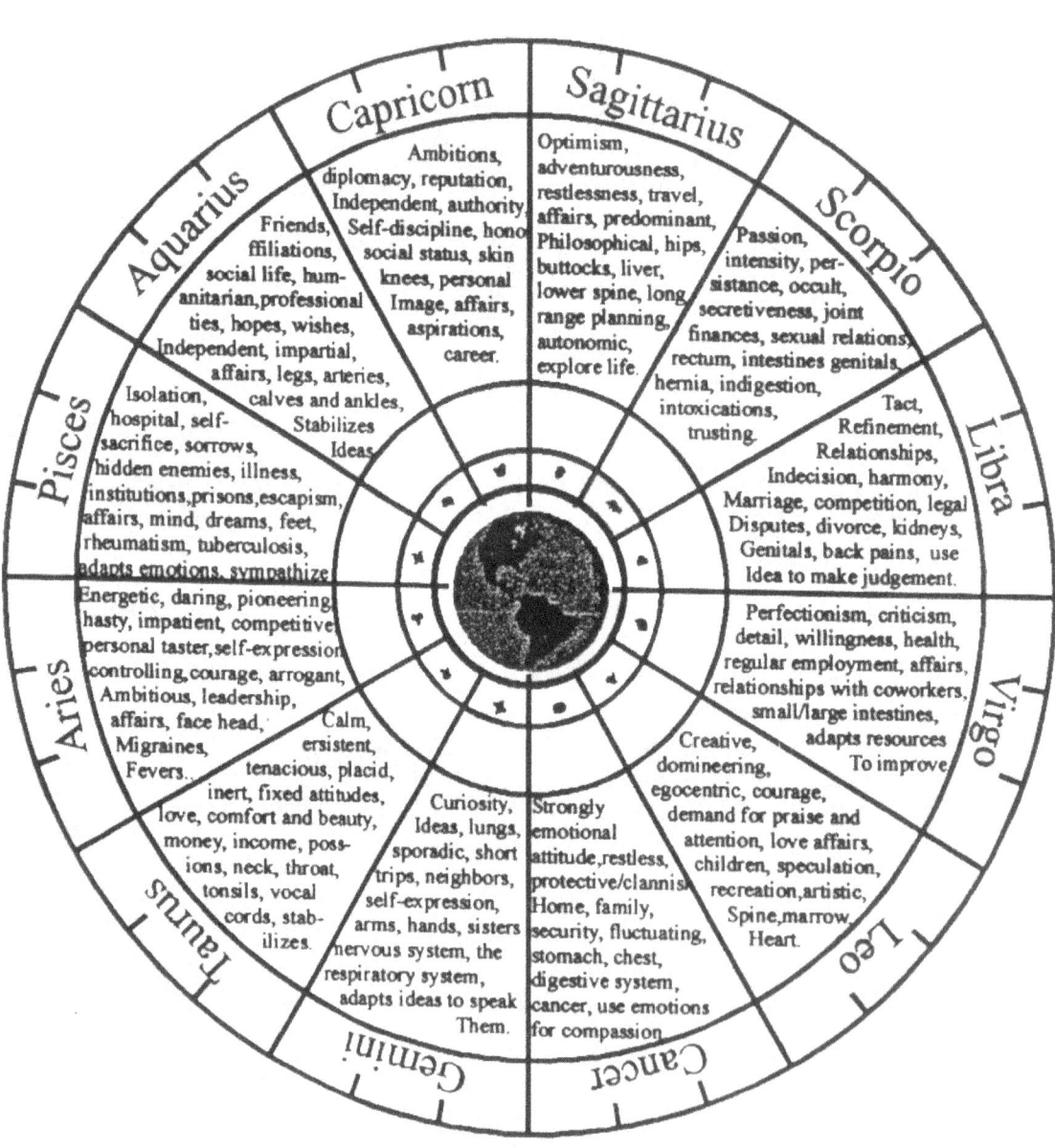

The Meaning of Life on Earth

The Metempsychosis or Transmigration of Everyone's Souls, Their Soul-Mates, Stars, and Destinies

How to Find Your Soul-Mate, Stars, and Destiny

Ligia Balu, Author

Ligia Balu blends the wisdom of the ancient astrologers together with her insight of discovering your *destiny*, fulfilling your *fantasies*, and finding your *soul-mate*. This book provides the stepping stones to unlocking the mysteries of *Astrology*. Through **Ligia Balu's** sensitivities, the reader comes to understand the influence of the stars on our very lives.

Ligia Balu explains not only how the stars lead us to our destinies but why we make the decisions we do, why we are attracted to certain people and certain situations, and why we face the challenge in our daily lives of overcoming our individual problems.

Ligia Balu provides us with an understanding of ourselves and of other people. She explains how to recognize your *soul-mate*, how to become more compatible with others, and most importantly, how to be happier and more content through an understanding of your own destiny. The stars lead us and guide us, influencing us daily, and challenging us with obstacles that mold us into the people we become. Learn to read the future and how to make better decisions through the stars.

Ligia Balu takes her readers on the grand adventure of inner exploration through an understanding of the vastness of the Universe. Sensitive by nature, she explores with her readers the dilemmas of everyday life that face us all. She brings to her readers the needed information for finding the *soul-mate* of our dreams. She explains why some Sun signs are compulsively drawn to others even when it is against all logical explanation while other Sun signs seldom waver from a logical course of action and rarely experience spur of the moment activities.

LIGIA BALU takes her readers on a guided tour of the mysteries of the Universe and explains why:

SAGITTARIUS are impulsively drawn to the stubborn ARIES.

LEO and CAPRICORN disagree about money.

CANCER women are patient with GEMINI men.

TAURUS develop either love or hate relationships with SCORPIO.

VIRGO women never approve of how SAGITTARIUS men spend money.

GEMINI may upset the boat for AQUARIUS.

LIBRA can be easily unbalanced by SCORPIO moods.

PISCES women find excitement with ARIES men.

SCORPIO has trouble understanding the flaky AQUARIUS.

ARIES men with an ARIES women spells competition.

SCORPIO can exact retribution from SAGITTARIUS.

CAPRICORN men delight in PISCES women if they can rule the magic.

There is a relationship between the causes and effects, a relationship born of fatalistic attractions in an order established by Ethereal reasoning. The Sun, Moon, Planets, and Stars are celestial bodies adding to and influencing our daily lives and spiritual beings. Through an intangible electromagnetic force this influence rides like waves of energy pulsating and dispensing impending causes and effects and leading us on a journey through life and understanding. This law can appear to be a terrible experience for some people because, quite often, a person is destined to suffer during either part or all of his life. No matter how hard this person attempts to avoid this suffering it seems that whatever is destined will be accomplished. While this law of cause and effect can seem like a terrible injustice, it is respectful and Holy in that it also serves a purpose. In its mystery, this law is superior to our ability to fully understand it or its reason for being. The law precedes our development and in no way fits comfortably into our way of thinking.

The aspects of the sky during our birth, our dreams, and even during our human misgivings, indicate a very strange but real connection between our perception of life and this Ethereal influence which surrounds us. Through the Universe designed by God comes these guides offering us warnings that we are destined for these experiences, and that the suffering serves a purpose in our lives.

Ancient scholars living in remote and desolate areas of the old world studied this phenomena. These scholars devoted their lives to studying God's purpose for man. Their lives were difficult, and they maintained minimum contact with the outside world. They turned their thoughts to studying the mysteries of the Universe and the secrets of the world. From time to time, they shared these secrets with a few chosen people who sought them out. They taught that all of our present lives are linked to our past lives.

This transmigration of the souls, as it iscalled, was studied by Pythagora, the Greek philosopher. Pythagora explained that the visible Universe, the sky with all its stars, are only passing stages of the soul of the whole world. Matter is concentrated then dissolved and seeded in all of the Cosmic and imponderable space. Every solar whirlpool contains a part of the Universal soul which is developing within itself during the millions of centuries and which contains an impressive, impulsive force and measure. When considering these Powers, the species of the live souls, which appear one by one on the stage of our little World, are given by God and descend from the Father. They are coming from an unalterable and superior spiritual order, conforming to a preceding material evolution, and belongs to a dead solar system. Some of these invisible, endless powers are guiding the existence of this World, and others are waiting, in a cosmic divine dream-like sleep. They blossom to re-enter into later generations according to the Divine law.

The Planets are The Daughters of The Sun,

born of the Sun, and each is in tune with the attractive forces with its inherent material rotating. Each possesses a semiconscious soul which rises from the solar heart, and each possesses a specific character relating to its special evolutionary role. As every Planet is a different expression of God's will, it has a specific function in the chain of the Planets and, therefore, in the chain of events. The ancient scholars identified the characteristics associated with each of these Planets and with those of the gods--characteristics which represent divine faculties of the action and reaction in the Universe.

The ancients identified the four elements as the fundamental indicators of the four graduated stages of the material world. The first element, the densest and roughest one, is the most unmanageable to the Spirit while the last element, the finest one, has the closest relationship with the Spirit. Earth represents the solid state, water the liquid state, air the gaseous state, and fire the imponderable state. There is another fifth element, the Ethereal one, which represents such a subtle force that it does not exist in the material state. This is the original Cosmic Fluid, the Astral Light or the Soul of the World.

What is the human soul but a part of the Great Soul of the World, a sparkle from the Divine Spirit--a coin for immortality. Everyone of us has within himself GOD, but to find Him, we need to develop ourselves. We must build a moral foundation upon which we can remain next to Him.

How to Find Your *Soul-Mate, Stars,* and *Destiny*

The Creator made man to have His face and to be like Him; however, Man does not accomplish this until after many incarnations. These successive lives are given to man so that he can improve himself and atone for previous sins thus helping him to differentiate the good from the bad and the light from the darkness.

Only these cycles can explain terrible injustices and unfairness which are suffered by some people, great happiness which is given to other people, sudden deaths, twin souls searching for each other all their lives, enemies and friendships, and unexplainable passions. Is there a Director behind the scenes whose existence we cannot explain? Are we not the same actors just performing in different plays? Is it not possible for one to have moments of lucid retrospective, which seems to be reminiscences of a previous life?

And what happens to the soul at the time of death of the body? When death approaches, the soul may have misgivings about separating from the body, and in some instances, pictures of the life flashes before it in rapid succession and frightful clearness. The approaching death disturbs the soul as it slowly loses consciousness.

In a saintly and pure soul, there is a Spiritual Awakening that occurs during this gradual detachment from the body. Through introspection this soul perceives the existence of another world before the body's last dying breath. It hears a remote call and responds to a pale, invisible beam of light. This soul feels happiness when it is at last released from the dying body. There is a feeling of escaping and being caught up in the middle of that great light that takes it to the spiritual world where it will belong from now on.

Most likely this does not happen with the many people whose lives were a fight between the material and any superior aspiration. In these cases, the soul may awake as if in a nightmare with no guiding hand to lead it. With no voice to cry out, this soul remembers the suffering and may exist in fear and darkness. It longs for its earthly body which it may still see and which holds an unbearable attraction to it. This soul was living only by its body and for its body, and at death, it searches through the cold body and the dead brain matter, but it cannot find itself. Whether dead or alive, it does not know, and while it wishes to see and understand, it does not. The darkness is all encompassing as is chaos and obscurity. This soul may cling to the phosphorescence of its mortal remains which is frightening but attracting it at the same time. Then the ugly dream and chaos begins again. This state may continue for several months or years depending upon the forces of the material instincts of the soul. Whether good or bad, this soul becomes, little by little, conscious of the new stage of existence. It leads itself, finally free from the body, to drift and fly between the hollows of the Earth's atmosphere as if it is carried upon electrical rivers and where it will see other lost souls. In this way a journey begins like a dizzy and fiery flight. It will climb higher and higher in an effort to escape the Earth's atmosphere and travel to a region of the solar system where it will find guides who, in some cases, are friends and relatives from the former life. The Earth slowly disappears like in a dream, and a new sleep which is like a delicious swoon wraps the soul like a sweet caress. The soul sees only its flying guide which carries it into the deepest infinity of space. It reawakens on a star where the mountains, flowers, and vegetation provide a sweet embrace. The soul is surrounded by lightening creatures, both men and women, who overlook and initiate it into the mystery of this new life. Here, the aspect of the body does not become the mask of the soul. The transparent soul appears in its true shape as if shining in the daylight. The soul's psyche, led by a sublime wisdom, finds the Divine Country in which it attempts to understand the Symphony of the

How to Find Your Soul-Mate, Stars, and Destiny

Universe. The soul rests on the golden beaches of this star paradise, and it rests under the transparent veil of a dream filled with sublime light, perfumes, and melodies.

This celestial life of the soul can last for hundreds of thousands of years depending upon its scale and impulsive force. Only the most perfect soul or the most sublime; however, can prolong this existence endlessly. Other souls are recalled by the law of reincarnation to suffer new trials in order to forget previous sins. Exactly like the human life, the spiritual life has a beginning, an apogee or culmination, and a decline. When the spiritual life is ending, the soul is trapped in a whirlpool of melancholy, but an undefinable force is attracting it again to the pain and suffering of the Earth. This desire is filled with terrible misgivings of leaving the Earthly life. But the day has arrived, and the law must be accomplished. A veil-like mist covers the face, and the soul can no longer see its companions through this veil which becomes thicker and thicker. The soul hears their sad farewells, and the tears of the people who loved him are penetrating him like a celestial dew, leaving it thirsty for a now unknown happiness. Then the soul solemnly swears and makes promises to remember the truth from a world of love or lies and pain from a world of hate.

When the soul awakens again, it is in the heavy atmosphere of the Earth, in the abyss of birth and death, not having yet lost its heavenly memories. It is here that its guide introduces the soul to its new mother who is carrying the child's seed. Then, the most impenetrable mystery of life on Earth, the mystery of reincarnation and maternity transpires. This mysterous fusion is carried out slowly, organ by organ, fiber by fiber. Step by step, the soul loses its Divine Self-Conscience, and the Light becomes dimmer and dimmer. With birth, that horrible pain pushes the soul, and a bloody convulsion uproots it from the Eternal Soul and places it in a newborn body. The new-baby arrives into this world and is yelling frightfully. The Celestial Memory has entered the deep recesses of the unconsciousness.

The Law of Reincarnation and Deincarnation is the true sense of live and death. This law represents the main mode of the soul's evolution and enables us to watch the past or the future and into the depth of Nature and Divinity. This law shows us the rhythm and the measure, the immortality and the goal. From the Spiritual point of view, it shows us that the correspondence of Devine life and death - as birth on Earth is like a Devine death - and the death is like a revival. The alternation of these two lives is necessary for the development of the soul, and each is the consequence and the explanation of the other. According to this Law, the facts from a specific life have an influence on the next life.

These lives follow one by one, but they do not seem to be alike, and yet they are linked by an undefeatable logic. Each of these lives has his or her own law and his or her different destiny. According to the Law of Repercussion, the events in a specific live have a punishing or rewarding influence on the next life. The individual will be reborn owning the instincts and the talents molded in his previous incarnation, and the quality of his next existence will be determined, in most cases, by the quality of his choices made in his previous life.

Pytagora taught that the apparent injustices of destiny, misery, suffering, and misfortunes, can be explained by the fact that each existence is the reward or punishment for the previous life.

There are No Words or Actions Without an Echo in Eternity.

When the soul finally wins over the material, then it finds itself at the beginning and ending of all things. By development of all its Spiritual Faculties, the soul then enters into a Divine Stage and in full agreement with the Holy Will. According to this, when the soul arrives at that progressed state, it does not go back but becomes immortal in a place where there is no pain and no sadness, but only endless love.

A sinful life will only allow a painful next life; an imperfect life will only allow a hardworking next life; and that is the way morality, while imperfect during a single life, can be perfectly achieved in successive lives.

What is the Ultimate Goal of man and of mankind, according to this doctrine? After so many lives, deaths, reincarnations, leisure, and painful awakens is there an end for the infinite soul?

Yes, undoubtedly yes! Only through the development of all his spiritual faculties, will the soul finally matter. He will find within himself the beginning and ending of all things. Only then will he enter into the Divine stage in full agreement with the Holy Will. We know that once the soul has arrived at this Superior Stage, it cannot go back. He will be immortal forever.

The above is an explanation of why some people have "lucky" stars, why some people suffer and why, after a sad or happy time on Earth, nobody will encounter a final death. Then, when our missions on Earth come to an end, and when our souls are lost in the land where:

"THERE IS NO PAIN, NO SADNESS, NO TEARS, BUT ONLY AN ENDLESS HAPPY, LOVING LIFE FOREVER AND EVER." Only then shall we encounter the GREAT GATE, written upon it:

"IDEALS, DREAMS, LOVE, FORGIVENESS, FORGETFULNESS, PEACE"

How to Find Your *Soul-Mate, Stars,* and *Destiny*

Table of Contents
Volume 1

Introduction to Astrology 1
- The Horoscope 2
- The Zodiac 3
- The Heavenly Houses 7
- Duality 18
- Triplicities 18
- Quadruplicities 19
- Polarities 20
- Sidereal Astrology 23
- Synastry 24
- Birth Chart 25
- Predicitions 28
- The Stages of Life 29
- Conclusion 31
- Astrological Months 32
- The Twelve Sun Signs of The Zodiac 35
- Zodiac Anatomy 40

Aries Astrology 43
- Aries Personality 46
- Aries Character 50
- Aries Destiny 54
- Aries Occupation 57
- Aries Marriage 60
- The Aries Man 62
- The Aries Woman 63
- Aries Love Life 65
- Aries Children 66
- Relationships with Other Signs 67

Aries Sexuality	69
Aries Sexuality - Man	70
Aries Sexuality - Woman	72
Aries Health	73
History of Aries	75
The Aries Thebaic Calendar	76
Aries Self-Expression	91
Celebrity Birthdays	94

Taurus Astrology ... 101

Taurus Personality	103
Taurus Character	108
Taurus Destiny	111
Taurus Occupation	113
Taurus Marriage	115
The Taurus Man	117
The Taurus Woman	118
Taurus Love Life	119
Taurus Children	120
Relationships with Other Signs	121
Taurus Sexuality	122
Taurus Sexuality - Man	122
Taurus Sexuality - Woman	125
Taurus Health	126
History of Taurus	127
The Taurus Thebaic Calendar	129
Taurus Self-Expression	143
Celebrity Birthdays	146

Gemini Astrology ... 153

Gemini Personality	155
Gemini Character	158
Gemini Destiny	161
Gemini Occupation	164
Gemini Marriage	165
The Gemini Man	166
The Gemini Woman	167

- Gemini Love Life 168
- Gemini Children 170
- Relationships with Other Signs 171
- Gemini Sexuality 172
- Gemini Sexuality - Man 174
- Gemini Sexuality - Woman 175
- Gemini Health 177
- History of Gemini 178
- The Gemini Thebaic Calendar 179
- Gemini Self-Expression 193
- Celebrity Birthdays 196

Cancer Astrology 203
- Cancer Personality 205
- Cancer Character 208
- Cancer Destiny 211
- Cancer Occupation 213
- Cancer Marriage 214
- The Cancer Man 215
- The Cancer Woman 217
- Cancer Love Life 219
- Cancer Children 220
- Relationships with Other Signs 222
- Cancer Sexuality 224
- Cancer Sexuality - Man 225
- Cancer Sexuality - Woman 227
- Cancer Health 228
- History of Cancer 229
- The Cancer Thebaic Calendar 231
- Cancer Self-Expression 245
- Celebrity Birthdays 248

Leo Astrology 255
- Leo Personality 258
- Leo Character 261
- Leo Destiny 264

Leo Occupation	266
Leo Marriage	267
The Leo Man	269
The Leo Woman	271
Leo Love Life	272
Leo Children	274
Relationships with Other Signs	275
Leo Sexuality	276
Leo Sexuality - Man	278
Leo Sexuality - Woman	279
Leo Health	281
History of Leo	282
The Leo Thebaic Calendar	284
Leo Self-Expression	299
Celebrity Birthdays	302

Virgo Astrology 309

Vigro Personality	311
Vigro Character	314
Vigro Destiny	317
Vigro Occupation	318
Vigro Marriage	320
The Vigro Man	321
The Vigro Woman	322
Vigro Love Life	323
Vigro Children	325
Relationships with Other Signs	326
Vigro Sexuality	327
Vigro Sexuality - Man	329
Vigro Sexuality - Woman	330
Vigro Health	332
History of Vigro	333
The Vigro Thebaic Calendar	335
Vigro Self-Expression	350
Celebrity Birthdays	353

Libra Astrology 359
- Libra Personality 361
- Libra Character 364
- Libra Destiny 367
- Libra Occupation 369
- Libra Marriage 371
- The Libra Man 372
- The Libra Woman 374
- Libra Love Life 376
- Libra Children 377
- Relationships with Other Signs 378
- Libra Sexuality 380
- Libra Sexuality - Man 381
- Libra Sexuality - Woman 383
- Libra Health 384
- History of Libra 385
- The Libra Thebaic Calendar 387
- Libra Self-Expression 402
- Celebrity Birthdays 405

Scorpio Astrology 411
- Scorpio Personality 414
- Scorpio Character 417
- Scorpio Destiny 420
- Scorpio Occupation 422
- Scorpio Marriage 423
- The Scorpio Man 424
- The Scorpio Woman 426
- Scorpio Love Life 427
- Scorpio Children 428
- Relationships with Other Signs 430
- Scorpio Sexuality 431
- Scorpio Sexuality - Man 432
- Scorpio Sexuality - Woman 434
- Scorpio Health 435
- History of Scorpio 437

THE SCORPIO THEBAIC CALENDAR	438
SCORPIO SELF-EXPRESSION	452
CELEBRITY BIRTHDAYS	455

SAGITTARIUS ASTROLOGY ... 461

SAGITTARIUS PERSONALITY	464
SAGITTARIUS CHARACTER	466
SAGITTARIUS DESTINY	469
SAGITTARIUS OCCUPATION	470
SAGITTARIUS MARRIAGE	472
THE SAGITTARIUS MAN	473
THE SAGITTARIUS WOMAN	475
SAGITTARIUS LOVE LIFE	477
SAGITTARIUS CHILDREN	478
RELATIONSHIPS WITH OTHER SIGNS	480
SAGITTARIUS SEXUALITY	481
SAGITTARIUS SEXUALITY - MAN	483
SAGITTARIUS SEXUALITY - WOMAN	485
SAGITTARIUS HEALTH	486
HISTORY OF SAGITTARIUS	487
THE SAGITTARIUS THEBAIC CALENDAR	489
SAGITTARIUS SELF-EXPRESSION	504
CELEBRITY BIRTHDAYS	507

Volume 2

CAPRICORN ASTROLOGY ... 513

CAPRICORN PERSONALITY	516
CAPRICORN CHARACTER	519
CAPRICORN DESTINY	521
CAPRICORN OCCUPATION	523
CAPRICORN MARRIAGE	524
THE CAPRICORN MAN	526

THE CAPRICORN WOMAN	528
CAPRICORN LOVE LIFE	530
CAPRICORN CHILDREN	531
RELATIONSHIPS WITH OTHER SIGNS	532
CAPRICORN SEXUALITY	534
CAPRICORN SEXUALITY - MAN	535
CAPRICORN SEXUALITY - WOMAN	537
CAPRICORN HEALTH	538
HISTORY OF CAPRICORN	539
THE CAPRICORN THEBAIC CALENDAR	541
CAPRICORN SELF-EXPRESSION	555
CELEBRITY BIRTHDAYS	558

AQUARIUS ASTROLOGY 565

AQUARIUS PERSONALITY	568
AQUARIUS CHARACTER	571
AQUARIUS DESTINY	574
AQUARIUS OCCUPATION	576
AQUARIUS MARRIAGE	577
THE AQUARIUS MAN	579
THE AQUARIUS WOMAN	580
AQUARIUS LOVE LIFE	582
AQUARIUS CHILDREN	583
RELATIONSHIPS WITH OTHER SIGNS	585
AQUARIUS SEXUALITY	586
AQUARIUS SEXUALITY - MAN	588
AQUARIUS SEXUALITY - WOMAN	589
AQUARIUS HEALTH	591
HISTORY OF AQUARIUS	592
THE AQUARIUS THEBAIC CALENDAR	593
AQUARIUS SELF-EXPRESSION	608
CELEBRITY BIRTHDAYS	611

PISCES ASTROLOGY 617

PISCES PERSONALITY	620

Pisces Character	622
Pisces Destiny	625
Pisces Occupation	626
Pisces Marriage	628
The Pisces Man	630
The Pisces Woman	631
Pisces Love Life	633
Pisces Children	635
Relationships with Other Signs	636
Pisces Sexuality	637
Pisces Sexuality - Man	639
Pisces Sexuality - Woman	640
Pisces Health	642
History of Pisces	643
The Pisces Thebaic Calendar	645
Pisces Self-Expression	659
Celebrity Birthdays	662

Love-Signs - Introduction to Relationships and Compatibilities 667

Aries Love Signs	670
Taurus Love Signs	702
Gemini Love Signs	730
Cancer Love Signs	756
Leo Love Signs	779
Virgo Love Signs	800
Libra Love Signs	818
Scorpio Love Signs	833
Sagittarius Love Signs	845
Capricorn Love Signs	855
Aquarius Love Signs	862
Pisces Love Signs	867

The Twelve Houses of The Souls 871

Planets in The First House Ruled by Aries	883
Planets in The Second House Ruled by Taurus	893

How to Find Your *Soul-Mate*, *Stars*, and *Destiny*

Planets in The Third House Ruled by Gemini 903
Planets in The Fourth House Ruled by Cancer 912
Planets in The Fifth House Ruled by Leo 921
Planets in The Sixth House Ruled by Virgo 931
Planets in The Seventh House Ruled by Libra 940
Planets in The Eighth House Ruled by Scorpio 949
Planets in The Ninth House Ruled by Sagittarius ... 959
Planets in The Tenth House Ruled by Capricorn 968
Planets in The Eleventh House Ruled by Aquarius 977
Planets in The Twelfth House Ruled by Pisces 986
House of The Sky 995

Volume 3

The Influence of The Planets 999
Mercury 1001
Venus 1008
Mars 1015
Jupiter 1022
Saturn 1029
Uranus 1036
Neptune 1043
Pluto 1050

The Moon Signs 1057
Moon in Aries 1058
Moon in Taurus 1059
Moon in Gemini 1060
Moon in Cancer 1061
Moon in Leo 1062
Moon in Virgo 1063
Moon in Libra 1064
Moon in Scorpio 1065
Moon in Sagittarius 1066
Moon in Capricorn 1067

Moon in Aquarius 1068
　　　Moon in Pisces 1069

Moon Signs Tables 1073

Aspects 1136

　　　Major Aspects 1105
　　　Minor Aspects 1111
　　　Sun 1114
　　　Moon 1122
　　　Mercury 1132
　　　Venus 1140
　　　Mars 1148
　　　Jupiter 1155
　　　Saturn 1161
　　　Uranus 1166
　　　Neptune 1169
　　　Pluto 1171

The Ascendant Your Rising Sign 1175

　　　Aries Ascendant 1176
　　　Taurus Ascendant 1177
　　　Gemini Ascendant 1178
　　　Cancer Ascendant 1179
　　　Leo Ascendant 1180
　　　Virgo Ascendant 1181
　　　Libra Ascendant 1182
　　　Scorpio Ascendant 1183
　　　Sagittarius Ascendant 1184
　　　Capricorn Ascendant 1185
　　　Aquarius Ascendant 1186
　　　Pisces Ascendant 1187

The Planets are The Daughters of The Sun 1189

Constructing The Birth Chart 1191
The Hour of Your Birth 1195
Tables 1201
Mercury 1201
Venus 1217
Mars 1233
Jupiter 1241
Saturn 1244
Uranus 1247
Neptune 1249
Pluto 1251
Sun 1253
Rising Signs A.M. Births 1259
Rising Signs P.M. Births 1263
Chinese Astrology 1269
Table of Years from Europe which Corresponds to The Chinese Signs 1270
The Rat 1274
The Ox 1285
The Tiger 1297
The Rabbit 1310
The Dragon 1322
The Snake 1334
The Horse 1346
The Goat 1358
The Monkey 1370
The Rooster 1382
The Dog 1494
The Boar 1406
Numerology 1417

How to Find Your *Soul-Mate*, *Stars*, and *Destiny*

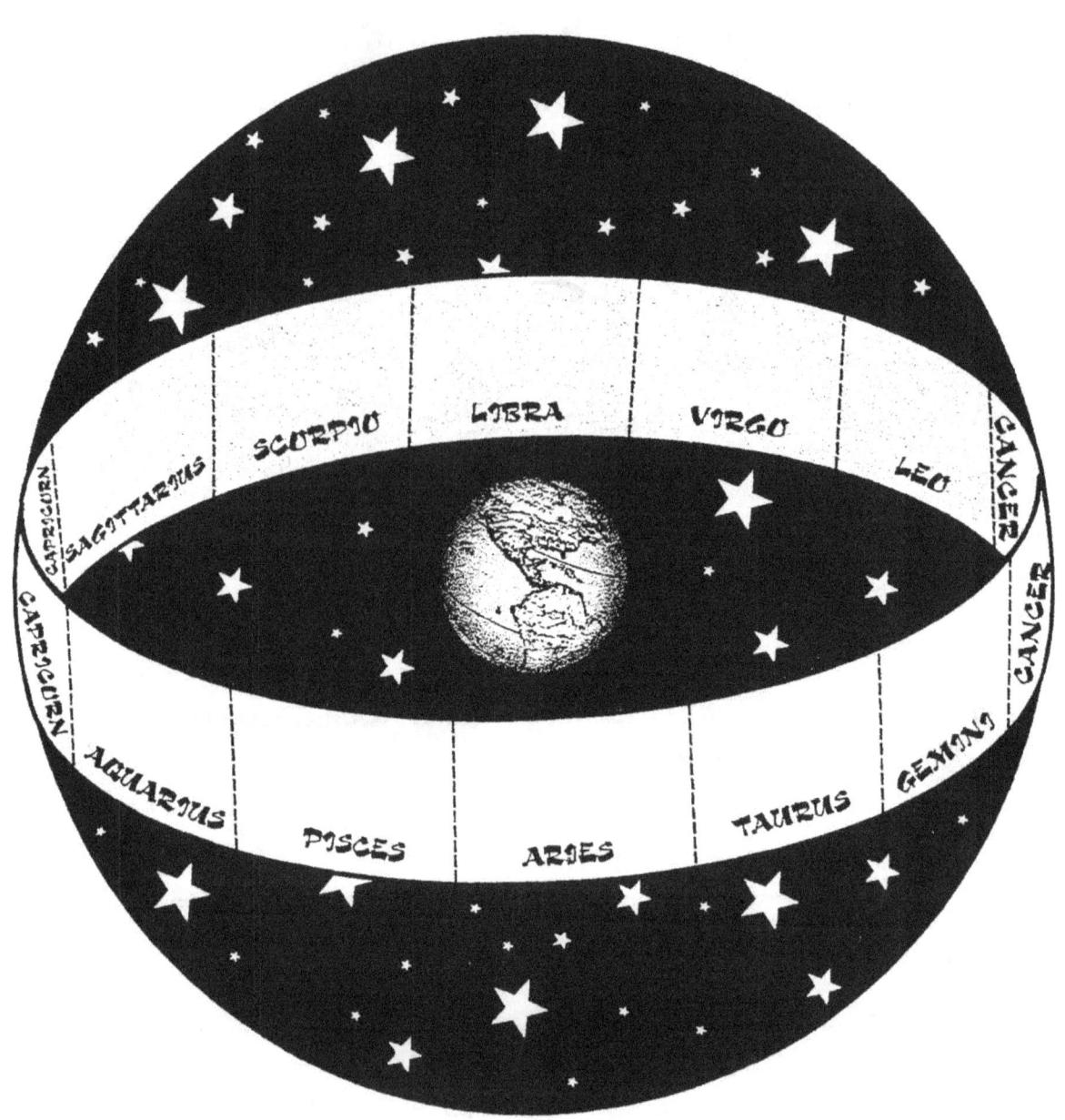

Introduction to Astrology
How to Find Your
Soul-Mate, Stars, and
Destiny

The science of astrology encompasses many precepts of the Universe including the relationship existing between the movements of the Moon, the Sun, the Planets, and the occurrences in the everyday lives of people. Historically, astrology was considered by some a science and by others a pseudo-science, witchcraft, artistic theory, or as a celestial theology. In more recent times, there are those who began to give it more serious consideration, elevating it to the level of pure science. The phenomena of this relationship between the stars and people's lives have even been studied at many well-known universities.

Imagine the primitive civilizations when man faced the challenge of comprehending the tides, the changing Moon and Sun, the eclipses, seasons, and equinoxes. These primitive peoples developed not only the first calendars, but also, the rudiments of astrology and astronomy. The Summerians and the Babylonians, the Maya and the Chinese, developed calendars based on the changing Moon and Sun. They could perform meteorological forecasts or foresee the nebula, the new stars, and the comets.

The early astrologers were the wizards of this science. These wizards were consulted to prevent drought, famines and floods. They foresaw battles, victories, defeats, natural disasters and times of prosperity. Many also played a role in determining the destinies of royal families and of powerful people the world over.

During these early times, the Moon was considered supernatural which gave the new science of astrology a celestial character. The personified divinities of the Moon, the Sun, and stars held specific significance and power. This scientific study intensified ushering in the age of the benevolent astrologer who could foresee atmospheric conditions, good or bad days, and the will of the gods. In many societies, these decisions makers became the high priests whose power influenced the day-to-day activities of others.

The development of astrology was not without its Greek influence. After conquering Chaldeea, Alexander the Great brought magicians and astrologers from Babylon to Greece where they influenced the philosophers who were all ready questioning the origin of the Universe. Astrology was considered a divine science by Empedocle, Plato, and Aristotle. These Greek philosophers were the first to ponder how the stars influenced an individual's date of birth. And from this comes the adage, "To be born under a good star".

The Greek influence reached Rome where astrologers were an elevated class of scientists. Claudius Ptoloemeus, while living in Alexandria during the second century, authored two important books: *Almagestell* and *Tetrabiblonly*.

THE HOROSCOPE

The horoscope is the determination of the position of the stars and planets in relation to time, or an event, at a certain longitudinal and latitudinal point of the Earth. The individual horoscope is represented as a sphere around which all the sky bodies are moving. According to their position at the moment of birth, each individual encounters varying influences. It is important to know the time of birth (even the minutes and seconds) in order to determine the position of the stars.

In addition to providing a philosophical explanation or a scientific theory, we can consider the importance of the stars in the same manner as our ancestors. Consider the affirmation, "The nineteenth century was the progress century: many discoveries allowed humanity to go forward and improve. The twentieth century is the technology century, the time when all the inventions have been applied; the twenty-first century will be magicians' and poets' century." The term magician is used because there will be a rational explanation of what was once thought of as phenomenon. The term poet refers to the hope that future technology will be saved by poetry, that is, it will save people from total alienation. Einstein referred to astrology as a, "science, a source of life for humanity,".

How to Find Your Soul-Mate, Stars, and Destiny

The Zodiac

What kind of person are you? Often, we take our own character for granted considering ourselves as normal as the next person until someone has the audacity to criticize us. Whether it's criticism or praise, how helpful is it?

It does help to know our strengths and weaknesses, but our sensitive nature often times does not allow us to find ourselves. Our tired minds and busy schedules just as often prevent or distract us from discovering our inner person, our other intellect, our potentials, and our connection with the Universe.

Everybody has a psychic power or ability, but it depends on how we choose to use it or to ignore it. How does one find this power, connect with it, and utilize it to benefit themselves and the lives of others?

The study of the Zodiac is one of the most popular methods of coming to terms with our complicated lives. Have you ever wondered, "Why did I do that?" By the time the question is asked, it is too late to alter the action or the outcome. The motto, "know thyself", appears obvious, but consider that it was the foundation of the wisdom of the ancient Greek philosophers and was adopted by not only the "mystery religions" of Greece, Rome and the Middle East, but also remains tantamount in all serious schools of mind training or mystical training as, for example, those of India based on yoga and those of the West founded on the Kabala.

Various classification systems of the personality exist. One system divides men into three types according to whether they most often follow the impulses received from their muscles, leading to physical action, or from their digestive organs, resulting in emotion, or from the brain and nerves, resulting in cognitive processes. Another system portrays character as determined by the endocrine glands and gives us such labels as ‚pituitary', ‚thyroid', or ‚hyperthyroid' types. These various systems are not necessarily inclusive or in conflict. Often, they are different methods of saying the same thing. Heredity and environment both contribute to mold our character. And genetics, it is being proven, plays an ever important role in determining our natures.

The disadvantage of these systems of classification is the need to place oneself in a category. For example, a person may be reluctant to admit that he acts to please his emotions. So, he deceives himself for years by attempting to fit into the ‚best' type. Of course, there is no best. Each category has its strength and weaknesses. But when the classification process is simply guesswork or is done to flatter one's ego, then the result is easily self-deception.

Consider the advantages of the signs of the Zodiac. The problem of deciding the classification is removed. If the date of birth is known, the sign is automatically determined. The only guessing required, in some instances, is the hour.

Can anything be that easy? Can the entire population of the world be divided, uncontroversially, into twelve types? Truthfully, the Zodiac was never designed in that manner. There exists a wide range of personality types within each sign. Why? Because each sign is influenced to some extent by one or two of the other signs.

How to Find Your Soul-Mate, Stars, and Destiny

Consider it this way. A single sign is inadequate to explain the differences between people because very few people are born under only one sign. A horoscope means „a consideration of the hour'. Thus, besides the day and month of birth, the time including the hour and minute down to the nearest five minutes and preferably the exact minute are important.

The birth month determines which sign of the Zodiac was occupied by the Sun. The day and hour determine what sign was occupied by the Moon, and the accurate minute indicates which sign was rising on the eastern horizon. Referred to as the Ascendant, this rising sign is considered one of the most important aspects of the horoscope.

Take for example, if you were born at one in the morning, the Sun is not important so the month of birth will not be important. What is important is the Ascendant and perhaps one or two of the planets. On any given day and hour, the Ascendant is the same at any given place. However, the Moon and the planets are different from day to day, moving at different speeds. Because of this, the planets are noted in an astronomical table referred to as an ephemeris. It is from the information gained from these tables that the inner most nature of a person is determined.

The Sun signifies the heart. The Moon signifies a person's mannerisms, behaviors and even his gestures. For that reason, the Romans referred to the Emperor Augustus as a Capricorn, meaning that he had the Moon in Capricorn. An astrologer might call Disraeli a Scorpio considering that he had Scorpio rising, but others would refer to him as a Sagittarian based on the Sun, while the Romans would have determined that he was a Leo because his Moon was in Leo.

The Sun becomes a principal influence if a person is born near sunrise, sunset, noon or midnight. Therefore, when a person doesn't appear to fit into his sign, perhaps it would be worthwhile to read the other indicators to determine if one of them is rising or occupied by the Moon. It also appears that the influence of the Sun develops as one grows older making it easier to guess the month of birth in people over forty. Younger people are supposedly influenced mainly by their Ascendant which characterizes both the body and the physical personality.

The planets are of importance also. For example, if Mars, the planet of war, was rising at birth, the person will be active and energetic but not necessarily aggressive. Mars in the south is aggressive, and Mars setting is apt to attack in self-defense often without good reason. People influenced by Venus are known to exert charm, Jupiter rising looks for wealth and rank, Mercury talks a lot and likes to make many friends. But each planet can rise in every sign, meaning that the sign of one's birth can be complicated by three or four planets rising or soothing simultaneously, besides being partly canceled out by the signs containing the Sun and Moon.

This illustrates how complicated a horoscope can be and explains the differences in personalities. But does it explain why the signs of the Zodiac would have an effect on a person's character at all? Astrologers describe the physical influence over the Earth such as the Moon's gravitational pull on the tides. This may also hold true of the planets which are physical bodies and have a gravitational pull, but the signs of the Zodiac are not physical bodies and don't have a gravitational field. Therefore, they are more difficult to explain. Stars are arranged in irregular distribution across the sky, and each must have a small gravitation effect as well; but this offers no explanation because the stars are not divided into twelve regions like the signs, nor are they confined to the belt called the Zodiac.

What does appear to be important is the minute of birth. If this matters, it suggests that the signs of the Zodiac do have an influence. But consider the word „influence'. Perhaps in the world of physical bodies the signs of the Zodiac have no influence, but it does not follow that they have no meaning. And what is the definition of „meaning'? But where the Zodiac has meaning and implies knowing, its concept has seeped into the universal consciousness of our minds, and it is there that its influence lies although it has no physical properties. And so the mystery remains.

The Zodiac, this idea in the mind of the human race dating back to the ancient mystics, while not a physical property, is related to a band around the sky wherein lies our destiny. Every person on this planet is born with a star. A star that directs you in your life. With luck, you are born under a good star. Every twenty four hours has seven bad hours. You never know when the seven bad hours appear. If you say something, or make a good or bad decision, or joke around about something, you would be surprised how by accident or mistake you reach the bad hour and it comes true exactly as you said or as you wished in your life or someone else's life. If you don't like what you said, or you don't mean it, the words of the bad hour follow you for the rest of your life. So be careful what you ask for. The stars are the magnet of the destiny, the present, the future, and the past.

The central line of the Zodiac is called the Ecliptic. Along this line the Sun passes taking just under 365 days to complete the circle. It is the same every year and perfectly straight. Its most northerly point is the Summer Solstice, where the Sun is in the longest day, and this is in the constellations of Gemini.

The most suitable method for following the course of the Zodiac is to use the Moon which when full is opposite the Sun. The full Moon at the Summer Solstice marks where the Sun will be at the Winter Solstice and vice versa. However, the Moon does not follow exactly the same path and can be over five degrees north or south of the central line. This means that the Moon passes sometimes below and sometimes above the stars in the Zodiac.

A sign of the Zodiac most definitely appears different with a planet in it as the planet is usually brighter than any of its stars. Planets, like the Moon, vary in brightness from time to time, according to the angle at which they are seen. Mars in the south at midnight is very bright and red because it is opposite the Sun and therefore fully illuminated, just like the full Moon, but two months later it is much dimmer and not so red.

A brilliant planet in the west or southwest after sunset is usually Venus or sometimes Jupiter. Venus is always either the evening star or the morning star, and when very close to the Sun, invisible all together. Mercury is usually invisible except in clear climates and with no city lights.

Saturn is white and appears in the east just before sunrise and, as the months pass, progresses slowly across the sky from east to west, rising roughly four minutes earlier everyday until after a year, it is seen for a week or two in the west at dusk and then is lost in the sunset glow. At that time, it is in conjunction with the Sun and can not be seen.

The twelve constellations of the Zodiac take their turns being visible after sunset in the east and at midnight in the south, but this happens at the time of year when the Sun is in the opposite sign. Aries the Ram, for example, holds this position in October, Taurus in November, and Gemini in December. But a constellation cannot be seen at all when it holds the Sun. It is useless to look for Aries in April and May or for Taurus in May and June. Just after the Sun has passed through it, your constellation is only visible in the early morning.

To find a particular constellation, start with a bright and obvious group. The best known of all constellations is the Wain, Plough or Big Dipper, which is north of the Zodiac and the only sign of the twelve which can be found from it is Leo, or, by passing through Arcturus, Virgo.

How to Find Your *Soul-Mate, Stars,* and *Destiny*

Across the equator and a little south of the Zodiac is Orion, under the feet of Taurus and Gemini. This is one of the brightest areas of the sky. The ancient Egyptians used Sirius as the fixed point of their calendar perhaps because it rose in time to announce the annual inundation of the Nile.

Aries, the Ram, is not an obvious constellation. It is most easily found either from Taurus to its left or from the great square of Pegasus on its opposite side. The only noticeable part of it is the three stars of the head marking its eye, nostril and mouth. Aries rises at sunset at the end of October and reaches the south at midnight in the same period.

Taurus does not resemble a bull, but it has two obvious features, the Pleiades and Hyades. The Pleiages is a large but tight cluster of little stars with six being clearly distinguishable. The Hyades follows forming a V of five stars, some of which are double, and the upper one on the left is a large red one called Aldebarin or the Forecaster. There are two other fairly bright stars on the tips of the horns, El Nath and Al Hecka which extend to the northeast between Capella and Orion's head.

The forepart of the Bull is shown on star atlases, the hind part being omitted to leave room for Aries since Greek times. Perhaps this is due to the triangle of the Hyades which could be compared to the Bull's face with the horns rising up as far as El Nath and Al Hecka. But the name is plainly not derived from the shape; for the plowing season in Babylon was marked by the Moon being full in this constellation; and the Babylonian Plough, drawn by an ox, was not the Wain, but our small constellation Triangulum, over the head of Aries. The Pleiades represented a tuft of hair on the shoulder which most bulls do not have. And in any case the Babylonian bull was smaller than ours, otherwise the earliest Babylonian Zodiac could not have contained eighteen signs instead of twelve.

Of the two stars in the upper part of Orion, Betelgeuze, the larger and redder, means „shoulder of the giant', and Bellatrix means „female warrior'. They mark his shoulders and not his face which is the small triangle of stars between and above them. His belt, three equal stars in a straight line, is a very useful reference point. His sword, containing the famous nebula, hangs below it on the left side, and the brighter of his two feet is called Rigel, or Rijl, which is Arabic for foot.

Gemini, the Twins, is one of the few constellations obtaining its name from its shape. It originally consisted of only two stars which were very bright and of equal magnitude. The constellation as a whole now forms an oblong with an extra star (Propus) protruding at the upper right hand corner. The feet extend southward towards Orion's shoulders and the brightest star in the feet is called Alhena.

Cancer, the Crab, the smallest and most inconspicuous constellation in the Zodiac, has as its principal features two Asses eating out of the Manger. The Manger has also been called the Beehive. Its astronomical name is Praesepe. It is a large cluster of dim stars, and the Asses, called the North and South Aselli, are obliquely above it. However, people born under Cancer are no more foolish and selfish than others.

Leo the Lion is a large, obvious constellation with a vague resemblance to a large animal. The Babylonians called it the Great Dog, but it is probably Egyptian in origin.   Virgo   is positioned on the equator, rising due east and due west.

The Heavenly Houses

The sky is gauged by astronomers from the spring equinox of the northern hemisphere. It seems natural that the positions of the Moon and Planets are described in reference to the fixed stars. The proper measuring stars became Spica, Antares, Aldebaran and Regulus. The first guess at the proper way of measuring was used by the Greeks. However, for centuries there was a great deal of confusion and a number of different Zodiacs were used by different astrologers. Thus, the confusion continues with the dates of the twelve signs used in newspapers being different.

Remember, the significant aspect of the horoscope is not the position of the Sun or Moon, but the Ascendant, rising on the eastern horizon at the moment. Before it was noted which sign was rising, the actual stars were of importance. This is complex, considering that it requires either actual observation without clouds at night or a series of complex computations. For example, the stars rising along the eastern half of the horizon vary with every half-degree of latitude. It would appear difficult to analyze the influence of that number of stars. For that reason, perhaps, the signs of the Zodiac were given a similar influence regardless of the number of stars involved.

A guide to designating the characters of the signs of the Zodiac would be the ruling Planets. Mars, for example, is a masculine planet and the god of war, and, therefore, Aries and Scorpio were considered the most positive and aggressive signs. Venus, the feminine Planet, stands for peace, love, beauty, art and friendship, clothes and cosmetics, and these concepts are associated with Libra and Taurus along with natural beauty.

Mercury represents the communication and circulation of ideas (speech, writing, gossip and news) as well as learning, teaching, methods and the circulation of other things such as transport, correspondence, and may include stolen properties.

Jupiter represents growth and „the bigger the better' attitude while Sagittarius is associated with ambition, snobbery, aspiration, idealism and/or religious devotion. Pisces may represent self-indulgence but, conversely can also be a kind or tolerant acceptance of everyone, a tendency to think the best.

Saturn, with its principle of contraction, has a disagreeable nature suffering with limitations or restrictions. However, considering that concentration is essentially an abstract form of thinking, Saturn is considered a beneficial Planet to be born under in that it provides the ability to control one's mind.

There are exaltations in certain signs that also affect the character of the sign although not to the same degree as does rulership. Saturn, in this regard, is exalted in Libra, the constellation of justice adding dimension to the Venusian leanings toward art, peace, fine clothes, and sales. Jupiter's exaltation is in Cancer, the sign of the Moon which is feminine and associated with growth. Mercury is exalted in the sign of Virgo, while Venus is in the Fishes, the sign of pleasure. It would appear that the least desirable exaltation is that of Mars in the Saturnian sign of Capricorn because energy under restriction wouldn't be advisable; however, compressed energy achieves a great deal such as a vacuum of air suddenly released.

How to Find Your Soul-Mate, Stars, and Destiny

Medieval astrologers assigned the Twelve Houses of the horoscope which originally were designed to enable astrologers to forecast the sphere of life of a coming event. These twelve houses are described:

Characterisitcs of The Twelve Houses

1st: Personality, Character, Leadership, Enterprise, Physique, Attitude

2nd: Money, Prosperity, Property, Resources, Peace, Liberty, Emotions

3rd: Family, Relationships, Short Journeys, Messenger, Politics

4th: Home, Parents, Security, Real Estate, Second Half of Life, Moody

5th: Children, Pleasure, Theaters, Speculation, Love Affairs, Domineering

6th: Health, Servants, Employment, Meticulous Military Service

7th: Marriage, Other Partners, Enemies, Competition, Tempermental

8th: Death, Inheritance, Sexual Relationships, Proud, Sensual, Scientific

9th: Religion, Long Journeys, Education, Religion, Philosophical Views

10th: Status, Profession, Reputation, Supervisors Business Dealings

How to Find Your Soul-Mate, Stars, and Destiny

11th: Friends, Helpers, Affiliations, Diplomacy, Social Life, Desires, Flaky, Selfish, Egotist

12th: Secret Enemies, Imprisonment, Illness, Martyr, Artistic, Indecisive, Sacrifice, Sorrow

There has also been noted a relationship between the signs of the Zodiac and that of human life. Naturally, these phases are not of equal length because change comes more readily during youth. The first phase corresponds to Aries who, like a baby, demands what it wants immediately even if it requires yelling regardless of the effect on others. Consider how many dictators were born under the sign of Aries.

The second phase regards relationships. In this phase, Taurus, the second sign, ruled by Venus, begins to be aware of relationships and love. Gemini, the phase of play, represents family and the age of first friendships outside the home. Cancer, ruled by the Moon, suggests mother, home, and the age of adolescence. It is a changing, emotional phase like the Moon, but like an adolescent is not independent, often reflecting the opinions of others.

Leo, ruled by the Sun, represents the first phase of adulthood, but its desires are not yet achieved. Virgo, the Virgin or the Servingmaid is the youthful, willing helper who is prepared to learn. Libra, the Balance phase enhances finding its proper place in the world, equality, and polarity in marriage. Scorpio, ruled by Mars, works toward achievement with energy and conflict if necessary. Sagittarius is either the ambitious or conversely the religious attempting to find wisdom. Capricorn, the Goat, is the phase of enjoying one's achievements. Aquarius is the phase of understanding. And Pisces, at last, is concerned with pure enjoyment but with ultimate meaning.

Consider, each person is born with a destiny. A destiny determined by the character given to the individual by the stars. Astrology is the study of the stars, and the corresponding effects on individual lives based on an ongoing compilation of data and research, an ongoing evolution of understanding based upon research first begun by ancient civilizations, and it continues to mystify and influence us.

This destiny is enhanced by cosmic influences projected upon the newly born by a "fixed electromagnetic condenser", the Zodiac, and mobile condensers, the wandering Planets, the Sun, and the Moon. These cosmic influences leave marks on the human body, along the force lines, that are sensitive during the entire life of the individual. This sensitivity develops in each individual becoming the „Destiny'. With harmony between the actual projection of the sky condensers and the imprints created since birth, the events will be happy or lucky; conflict between these events result in unpleasant or dramatic happenings. And these electromagnetic occurrences produce havoc or harmony within the communications of the basic elements of the body.

There is the thought that when God made people, he made them with a little map and a little star. The individual has to follow both. When each person is born, their little star is born too, at the same time. When the person dies, the star dies at the same time. The person becomes the servant to both the star and the map until the end. A person cannot do in life what he or she wants to do but what the star and the map allow him to do. How do you bring God into your heart? By the same method, the ancients brought the Sky closer to the Earth to form an intimate and absolute unity.

The Zodiac was assigned names by the ancients, the old Magi, who imagined the shapes in the night sky of the stars as being similar to the different shapes of people and of animals. Our information today indicates that the twelve signs of the Zodiac were completed hundreds and hundreds of years before the birth of Chirst: Aries, Taurus, Gemini, Cancer, Leo, Virgo, Balance, Scorpio, Sagittarius, Ram, Aquarius, and Pisces.

The Planets, thought of as living creatures in motion in the sky, had weaknesses, like humans, and preferences for certain Zodiac signs. The Sky Houses, however, were different from the Planets and the signs. The Sky Houses consist of six houses above the Earth and six under ground. These six Houses were unconditionally motionless. The old Magi established that the Houses numbered one and eight, were governed by Mars, controlling the temperament and death; the second and the seventh, were governed by Venus, controlling fortune; Mercury governed the third and sixth House with writing and servitude; ninth and twelfth were under Jupiter, taking care of the voyages, ideas, and isolation. The tenth and eleventh, governed by Saturn, controlled social situations. The planets Saturn and Mars were limiting, Jupiter and Venus were good or lucky, and Mercury and the Moon were very moody. The same remains true today for the Planets as well as the Zodiac.

The Planets are very sensitive, like people. They are influenced by the Zodiac. This can be good or bad. According to the Planets' positions in the sky, the ancients arrived at conclusions, made predictions, and gave advice. The Zodiac, a reflection of the Earth, shows how everything is happening on our planet. The ancient people believed that the human body was protected in the Orion Zodiac.

The ancients imagined a huge body with the head corresponding to the first House of the sky, i.e., Aries and the legs corresponding to the last House, number twelve, which is Pisces. The throat and neck are under the sign of Taurus; the fourth House, Cancer, corresponds to the chest and lungs; Leo, the fifth, is the heart and spine; Virgo, the sixth, the internal organs; Balance, the seventh, the kidneys; the eighth is Scorpio with the sexual organs; the ninth is Sagittarius, the hips and upper legs; the tenth is the Goat with knees and joints; the eleventh is Aquarius, the lower legs and feet; and the twelfth is Pisces with the feet. These were the symbols of the ancient astrologers.

Astrology has occupied the minds of kings, Popes, presidents, scholars, and philosophers. No science has been more appreciated or more ridiculed than astrology. The more one learns, the more one becomes enthralled with the mystery of the stars, Planets, and the Zodiac. There are those people born more gifted, with knowledge and sensitivities, who like to practice and to develop the ability and the power of this gift from God. These people are those who appreciate and make the astrologies and horoscopes. This is especially true of people born between January 20 and February 20. The ones born between October 20 and November 20 have an interest in stars in general. Those born under the sign of Aries, between December 20 and January 20, have a speculative interest; and those born under the sign of Pisces are passionate in astrology and psychic ability. Generally, individuals born in Spring or Summer, under the remaining signs, have a curiosity but a selfish nature, like Taurus, April 20 to May 20, taking mostly into consideration their own fate. Gemini, May 20 to June 20, reflect those of an intellectual nature and interest. The Cancer individual, born June 20 to July 20, will always love astrology as they do any science that provides information from the past.

These people who have more abilities, who deal with the cumulative knowledge and mysteries of the Universe, appear to be on another level as compared to more average people. Perhaps this is because they have evolved from successive existences, making them ever more sensitive with powers of the mind.

Psychiatrists have been observing and studying the personalities of not only the genius but also the criminal and the psychotic. They have developed methods and treatments, but the conclusions remain elusive. We're aware that the genius may also exhibit abnormal behavior. This is of a celestial influence, the electromagnetic imprint on the new born. This break in the balance of the Horoscope is completely abnormal. The Moon represents the factor of receptivity that can lead to psychosis, madness, when the factor is dissonant and to genius when the factor is harmonious. If a sector of the sky is under a violent sign or has a large crowd of planets, this indicates a prominent predisposition for a frantic instinctual life. If a break occurs in a particular part of the Horoscope, by a planetary low tide, it will create a blockage in the instinctual flow by sublimation. If the individual cannot achieve through his instincts, he will become a teacher or a great artist. In other words, he will play in public what he cannot play in his intimate life. Women who become nuns always have contradictory instinctual factors.

There are areas of the Zodiac that don't receive as much magnetism. This creates an unbalance. Violent criminals have a few planets, a few Celestial condensers under the violent sign of Aries, in a weak, miserable, isolated House, the secret twelfth House of the Sky. People with double personalities are usually born between two Zodiac signs. Or consider the Horoscopes of two people, victims of a passionate connection, and you'll immediately notice a difference of potential between certain Zodiac signs in a particular area of the Horoscope.

Have you ever tried to understand an attraction or a rejection of another person. Remember, there are those who bring good luck or who bring bad luck. An agreement among good planets leads to good luck, chance and possibilities. When a negative planet influence encounters a positive planet in a particular spot of the Horoscope, it is absolutely fatal resulting in a loss or misery brought on by someone else. These negatively influenced individuals can enter your life and cause trouble without warning.

Like Celestial bodies, people receive and send impulses. People who can heal have the ability to control their own magnetism, and even their presence is pleasant and soothing. In contrast, other people who create confusion, bother us by sending out impulses faster.

In studying the birth skies, it can be seen that the good times in life are the reenacting of an imprint or imprints that occurred at birth. These imprints can arrive at harmony with the stars' movements at some time during life. A series of good or bad events can occur when the planets are grouped in a cluster at a particular time. Some people receive a „chance' during the first part of life, others during the second part of life. The former were born during the day when the majority of the planets were above the horizon while the latter were born at night when the planets were below the horizon. The happiest part of life is the second „chance', particularly for those born at midnight. Later in life, some people become rich, others lose everything. This happens when their Planet changes directions at birth.

When studying the Horoscope, it can be observed that sometimes the majority of the Planets are situated on one side, for example, the East side. This means that the person will live half their normal life expectancy or the second part of their life can become meaningless. Then again, if the Planet Saturn is rising before it is continuously descending, a person has a continuous descending rhythm.

Wise people keep a low profile, perhaps inferior to what they deserve, in order to maintain balance and the best situation over a length of time. Others attain material wealth but also a moral misery, depression and deception with families which have continuous unfortunate events occurring, like a curse, even from generation to generation. A horoscopic genealogy can show a fatal event happening during many generations with some changes and transformations; one person dies, depressed, another one is sick or loses his situation or money, but all the time someone sooner or later dies. In this situation, no one can do anything about it. Some people choose to have children later in life, and if you watch these children's Horoscope, you'll see they were created under a certain influence and constellation in order to correspond to a certain familiar destiny and in order to close the circle of events of their families.

Children born around seven months are destined to create a balance with their brother's life. Many times these children can become very psychic and gifted. Born at nine months, a person's existence corresponds with the one in the sky, under a certain star influence, in conjunction with the Birth-Sky of their parents or ancestors. The children who die at birth, or soon after, cannot adapt to the Celestial heredity.

The combination between different nationalities are interesting because each of the partners comes with his own Celestial possibilities. Combinations between relatives can create birth defects, or even block the possibility of having children because the Celestial possibilities are minimal having been used by the rest of the family.

The movement of the Planets, in their celestial clusters and separate from each other, influence people's rhythm. Some people give and receive good energy, others negative energy. Remember, the good energy can bring good luck, the bad energy bad luck!

Astrology, when understood, makes crystal clear the understanding of the manifestations of Nature through human and mundane affairs. Even ordinary people with average education can benefit and learn astrological insights. Granted, true skill is best acquired by those who have an inborn love of all that is mystical and who possess an active sense of intuition. The temperament of the metaphysically gifted rather than formal schooling is the prerequisite for those wishing to become adept in this science.

Astrology has been garnered from the records of astral phenomena and reduced to a science by observing the effects of Planetary influence, commencing with the history of man. These observations have been compiled and recorded by some of the brightest intellects known, both ancient and modern. Astrology explains the inequalities of humanity shedding light upon the path leading to improvement in living conditions and relations with others. Much pleasure, satisfaction, and knowledge can be gained through the study of astrology. The insights gained provide people with broader views and more tolerant attitudes making them more charitable toward their fellow man.

The study of astrology continues becoming more and more scientific. As the number of serious students increases so does the evidence of its usefulness. Note that no one can claim to possess a proper understanding of astrology until he can cast and delineate the horoscope of birth and design and read a progressed chart.

The word horoscope is a derivative of „hora', an hour, and „scope', to view. It is a view of the heavens at a certain hour as measured by the Sun. Originally the word referred only to the

How to Find Your Soul-Mate, Stars, and Destiny

Ascendant, but now it refers to a more general reference to a whole figure or map of the heavens at birth and is some times referred to as a nativity.

Some say that the purpose of astrology is to learn by Planetary indications that were affecting the Earth and its atmosphere at the time of birth and to endeavor to develop in this nature qualities which will insure an exalted expression of life. A well-cast horoscope can become a guide regarding changes, health, marriage, business and important affairs of life and relationships.

Why would any person be interested in Astrology? For starters, the study of astrology pre-dates all the other known sciences as well as present day organized religions. Every prehistoric and ancient culture left behind artifacts and proof that the study of the stars which later developed into astronomy and astrology were important to these societies. Astrology appears to have begun many of thousands of years ago in the very cradle of civilization and has been added to and influenced by scholars of every culture. And a science that was once available only to dignitaries and heads of state is now of use to each and every person. The language of astrology pervades our daily lives from the names of the days of the week to the names of the Planets and stars.

Modern societies put satellites in the sky and those satellites communicate with Earth. In much the same manner, the celestial bodies, the Sun and Moon, the Planets and the stars communicate with Earth. People can't see this happening, but it is accepted, felt intuitively, and proven scientifically that a correlation and an interrelation does exist. There is, in other words, an interaction between all of life, nature and mankind, and the Universe beyond. And whether it is the Moon's pull on the Earth's tides, or the Sun's radiation, or the unseen and unfelt rhythms and waves of the Planets in their transits, this interaction is continuous and pervasive. Our days and nights, our seasons and the weather all depend upon this interaction--this movement of our Planet, Earth, through its course in space and the Earth's correlation to the other rotating bodies.

Astrophysics is a science that applies the principles of physics to many fields of astronomy and which provides the basis for one of the concepts of astrology. Astrophysicists attempt to determine the physical nature and the origin and development of the solar system, stars, galaxies, and the universe. They conduct many studies with optical telescopes which enable them to observe cosmic objects that give off electromagnetic waves in the form of visible and infrared light. Radio telescopes are used to study radio waves that are emitted or reflected by Planets, stars, and galaxies. And various cosmic objects give off gamma rays, X-rays, and ultraviolet light. Other special detectors are used to study electromagnetic waves that are largely absorbed by the Earth's atmosphere and so cannot be detected by telescopes. These scientists estimate the motion of a star or galaxy by measuring the shift in the wavelengths of its light on the spectrum. Cosmic ray research also helps scientists understand the nuclear processes that occur within certain stars.

Research by biologists has proven that any number of Plants and animals respond to the interrelationship of the cycles of the Moon to the Earth and Sun. Worms react to the new Moon and the full Moon as do sea urchins, the fiddler crab, oysters, chickens, and hamsters. Even the migratory pattern of birds in flight appears to be influenced by the stars in the sky. There are natural rhythms which humans respond to as well, as if to some natural and internal clock. Behavioral scientists refer to these natural rhythms as a person's biological clock or bio-rhythms.

This gradual recognition by scientists that there exists a correlation and significant relationship between celestial bodies and life on Earth has helped to bring the study of astrology into proper perspective. The earliest astrologers, however, didn't appear to need this scientific affirmation of their observations and conclusions. They studied not only the heavens but the behavior of people and noted their findings before the advent of written histories. And what was a mystery to these ancient scholars remains in many ways just as much a mystery to modern scientists. The importance of astrology has also been recognized by notable psychologists such as Carl Jung who conducted his own studies into the behavior of people based on a comparison of their Birth Charts.

The earliest thinking people watched the stars, plotted the courses of the Planets and began timing events based upon the patterns of the stars in the sky. By plotting and anticipating the heavens, agrarian cultures knew when to expect flooding, when to plant their crops, and the best time for harvesting. Based on the luminaries, the Sun and the Moon, and the pattern of the Planets and the stars, the first calendars were devised. For centuries, early astrologers found favor with kings, queens, pharaohs, rulers, and leaders and advised them concerning matters of state, decisions, and events of importance. Astrology and astronomy, in those days, were linked for this purpose, and this link produced noted astrologers.

This preoccupation with astrology has had its own history of interest and disinterest, favor and disfavor. First it was accepted and favored by the early churches, numerous Popes, and religious leaders, and then it was suppressed, forbidden, and banned. Then moving almost as if in a cyclical pattern, astrology became once again an accepted study and practice becoming a subject matter which today is offered in many university classes and through astrological societies. And even the most skeptical of people and others who know very little about this science and study will know their Sun signs and the signs of their family members, lovers, and friends. Ancient scholars gazed at the stars and detected the constellations which make a wide belt or arc in the sky. The same ancient scholars named these constellations, and it is from these that the names of the twelve signs of the Zodiac are based. It might seem to many that individual lives make an arc as well, and when a person looks back it seems notable that each event is connected and leads to the next.

These very early astronomers and astrologers based their assumptions and calculations on the then accepted fact that the Sun moved around the Earth. In fact, the early Church and religious leaders considered it heresy to even suggest that the Earth actually moved around the Sun which resulted in it taking a number of years for this concept to be accepted. But for the casting of an individual horoscope or a Birth Chart, this earlier assumption is still practiced. There is a reason for that. The Birth Chart actually represents a picture of time taken at the exact moment of birth of an individual. The picture is taken from Earth and places the luminaries and the planets on the chart in relative degrees of each other. The person's Sun sign correlates with the constellation the Sun is moving through at the time of birth. The Ascendant, or rising sign, is the planet on the horizon at the time of birth. And each of the other planets fall into place around the 360 degree chart. The science of astrology is then the practical use of astronomy which links luminaries and planets with our daily lives. And it is by ascertaining the Birth Chart that an astrologer can give insight to the individual about personality and character traits, strengths, weaknesses, emotions, and predispositions to certain decision making processes and actions. How a person responds and interacts with parents, family, and other people and personal relations is indicated. What makes a person feel most secure and happy is indicated. And, of course, what kind of person this individual is attracted to may well be indicated by the Birth Chart. Has the person's life been filled with good luck or with difficult times and obstacles? Many times, how a person reacts to obstacles determines their luck. What modern astrology attempts to do is give the individual enough information for that person to understand his or her own character traits better. If you understood why you make the decisions you make, would you then make better decisions?

Many people want to know if astrology can predict the future for an individual. This is not the function of astrology. Free will being what it is, each person is free to either succumb to negative traits or to overcome even the harshest of obstacles in order to lead a better life. What astrology can tell a person is when the Planets may be properly aligned for making decisions, taking actions, or holding off on actions. That picture of the sky at the moment of the individuals birth can portray for the person the basic nature inherent in his or her make up. How that person uses this information to live life is still up to that person. The modern interest in astrology is indicative of the fact that people want to know more about themselves and to understand themselves better. And neither does it hurt to know other people better. By comparing Birth Charts, individuals can learn in what areas of life they are compatible with their lover and what other areas may cause stress or tensions. What is of importance to astrologers, then, is the positions of the Planets.

The idea of the arc, or celestial sphere, was first perceived as a dome rising above the flat Earth. This arc appeared to early observers to revolve around the Earth once a day. In drawing up a Birth Chart, the most relevant information is the position of the Planets to this arc or celestial sphere. It is the projection of the Earth's equator to this celestial sphere that marks the celestial equator, and the direction of the Earth's axis indicates the two poles of the sky with the north pole being marked approximately by Polaris. The yearly path of the Sun in the sky is referred to as the ecliptic and may be defined as the projection of the plane of the Earth's orbit to the celestial sphere which intersects at the vernal equinox and the autumnal equinox. The solstices represent those times when the Sun reaches its maximum north or south point on the celestial equator. Presently, those dates are approximately June 22 for the Summer Solstice and December 22 for the Winter Solstice. These dates or times were significant to early astrologers to whom fell the duty of compiling and organizing the first calendar. Because of the Earth's rotation around the Sun, the Sun appears to make one trip around the ecliptic in the same time span passing through each of the signs of the Zodiac in a year's time.

Ancient lore applied to modern life? Does it work? What the modern astrologer attempts to do is utilize the combined knowledge of the past and to apply it to modern precepts. And, yes, for all practical purposes, this application does appear to work. Why else do so many people open an astrology book, read about themselves, and come away with the feeling that the information applies to them and to their lives. Why then, one might ask, are there variations within each Sun sign? Why are so many people within the same Sun sign so different from one another? The Sun sign is indicative of a set of characteristics and personality traits. But it is the entire chart and the positions of the Planets that actually point to the individual differences and make each person unique. As the rising sign changes within a matter of minutes, each Birth Chart is uniquely different as well. Astrology is a complicated but precise science.

It is a study based on centuries old observations combined with modern observations. The basis of this science is numbers. In other words, astrology is a mathematical based science with predictions of future planetary positions determined by astronomy and calculations. Within astrology, the very precepts of the study is a numerical division which starts with the twelve signs of the Zodiac and then enumerates them into further divisions. These twelve signs are first divided into dualities, or two groups of masculine and feminine. They are also divided into four triplicities each representing a different element. Next, the twelve signs are again divided into three groups of four signs each, called quadruplicities, which denote a quality. Last, the twelve signs are divided into six groups containing two signs each and called a polarity.

And like any discipline or field of study, astrology has its own language, that is, certain words pertain to particular concepts. To come to an understanding of even the most basic astrological thoughts means taking the time to become familiar with this special blend of math and language. One significance of these divisions is that no two signs have the same designations which in effect makes each sign distinctive one from the others. Therefore, the Fire signs are different from each other even though they possess the same characteristics of being a Fire sign. The differences become more apparent in the following analysis which delineates each sign into separate groups.

Duality

Each of the twelve signs of the Zodiac is designated a duality which is either masculine or feminine, and this distinction was given to the signs by early astrologers some two thousand years ago. Using the language of astrology, a masculine sign is direct and energetic while a feminine sign is receptive and magnetic. In modern terms, the masculine signs are said to be outgoing and active while the feminine signs are thought of as self-controlled with inner strength.

Masculine	Feminine
Aries	Taurus
Gemini	Cancer
Leo	Virgo
Libra	Scorpio
Sagittarius	Capricorn
Aquarius	Pisces

Triplicities

The triplicities denote the elements of Fire, Earth, Air, and Water which symbolizes the fundamental characteristics of the signs. The Fire signs are said to be active, enthusiastic and fiery. The Earth signs are thought of as practical and stable. The Air signs are the intellects and communicators of the Zodiac while the Water signs are more emotional and intuitive. The element of the Sun sign influences how a person reacts to everyday stimulus. Are you fiery and impulsive? Do you intellectualize your feelings? Do you feel deeply and react to the world through your emotions? Or do you apply logic and rationalization to your decisions?

FIRE: ARIES, LEO, SAGITTARIUS
EARTH: TAURUS, VIRGO, CAPRICORN
AIR: GEMINI, LIBRA, AQUARIUS
WATER: CANCER, SCORPIO, PISCES

QUADRUPLICITIES

The three quadruplicities each contain four signs and denote a quality of either Cardinal, Fixed, or Mutable which signify the Sun sign's interrelation and interaction with others. The Cardinal signs possess an inclination to lead others and exhibit initiative and an enterprising, outgoing spirit. The Fixed signs are more fixed in their opinions and resistant to change, and these people follow through and complete projects. The Mutable signs are the most flexible, adaptable, tolerant and versatile and are more easily capable of adjusting to change and to different people, ideas, and situations. Now then, are you resistant to change and like to have your own way, or are you open to the ideas of other people and receptive to different thoughts, opinions and lifestyles?

CARDINAL: ARIES, CANCER, LIBRA, CAPRICORN
FIXED: TAURUS, LEO, SCORPIO, AQUARIUS
MUTABLE: GEMINI, VIRGO, SAGITTARIUS, PISCES

POLARITIES

The polarities which contain two signs each signify the opposites in the Zodiac. Each sign has its opposite on the other side of the Zodiac wheel. This is not a necessarily bad designation because quite often opposites find that they are capable of blending their positive traits in order to overcome their negative traits.

ARIES & LIBRA: Aries, the most personal sign, is very self-oriented while Libra remains interested in partnerships and the other person.

TAURUS & SCORPIO: The sign of Taurus represents personal possessions, while Scorpio represents legacies and shared possessions.

GEMINI & SAGITTARIUS: Gemini is the sign of intellect and self-expression, while Sagittarius is the philosopher with an expansive nature.

CANCER & CAPRICORN: Cancer is interested in home and family, while Capricorn represents public life and ambition.

LEO & AQUARIUS: Leo is powerful with a creative and dramatic flair, while Aquarius is the independent thinker and humanitarian.

VIRGO & PISCES: Virgo is known for hard work, diligent efforts and a critical, analytical mind,. while Pisces is emotional, intuitive, and prone to dreaming.

All of the above is pretty simple math and if that was all there was to astrology, each and everyone of us could follow it quite easily. But these designations comprise only the basics, and just the beginning of the complexities entailed in this remarkable study of humankind based on the observations of the heavens. That brings us back to the subject of the planets and how they influence our daily lives and behavior. For it is the movement of the luminaries, the Sun, the Moon, and the Planets, as observed from Earth, which most influence astrological precepts and concepts.

How to Find Your Soul-Mate, Stars, and Destiny

Each Sun sign in the Zodiac is ruled by a Planet (The Sun and Moon are often included in discussions of the Planets.). Each Planet is associated with particular characteristics which are bestowed upon the individuals of that Sun sign, but that is not the only job of the Planets. Each Planet also rules a House of the Zodiac and there are twelve Houses. Each Planet is also placed on a person's Birth Chart by degrees according to its location in the sky at the moment, of that person's birth. These locations of the Planets on the Birth Chart form aspects, or angles, which are either beneficial or strenuous to each other. The locations of the Planets are determined by astronomy and can be found in an ephemeris which lists their positions for each day of each year. The Planets are also considered to be in detriment, in exaltation, or in fall in particular signs. A Planet is most powerful when in exaltation and loses its power or is less influential when it is in fall or in detriment. Two Planets are in mutual reception when each falls in the sign ruled by the other which strengthens them and allows them to benefit the individual. On the Birth Chart, the Sun is considered the most powerful Planet followed by the Moon, Mercury, Venus, Mars, Jupiter, Saturn, Neptune, and Pluto. The influences of Neptune and Pluto, because of their distances from the Earth, are considered to be generational in effect. Take all of that into consideration and then place the nodes of the Moon on the Birth Chart, and a person will have an overall picture of the information. From all of this, it is quite readily seen why a person would seek out a professional astrologer not only to draw up the chart but also to have it analyzed and interpreted. This has been made easier with the use of computer programs which do just that.

The next step for the professional astrologer would be to progress the Birth Chart which would allow the determination of favorable periods in an individuals life. Also, a comparison of two Birth Charts can provide information regarding the compatibility of two people. The study of astrology is both fascinating and intriguing. It allows for and enhances the uniqueness and individuality of the human experience. And it allows each individual the opportunity for self exploration and understanding as well as for personal growth and development. In essence, it provides the colors with which the Creator painted the skies.

Astrology is, therefore, a math, science, and language based study with very strong cultural inferences. No doubt there are many people who do not consider it a pure science in that it is also closely associated with spiritualism and has been, in one way or another and at one time or another, closely associated with the major religions of the world. And in this respect, astrology is not only spiritual but historical as well, as evidenced by the numerous archeology and anthropology findings which indicate and prove man's earliest interest in the stars and heavens.

It should be mentioned that astrology appears to be influenced by the culture and the period in which it is being studied. In many instances, modern astrology, much like modern translations of the Bible, seem to be watered down versions which are deemed suitable for the acceptance and understanding of the masses (which also makes it more commercial). It is notable that the language becomes richer when reading earlier astrologers just as the language in earlier translations of the Bible is more meaningful and more poetic. In fact, a comparison of the word usage in both earlier astrology writings and older Biblical translations reveal numerous similarities. Words such as afflictions, obstacles, adversities, determination, patience, and endurance are most obvious as are many others. Modern astrologers appear to have a tendency to pointedly down play such words as afflictions and adversities preferring words like stress and tensions. However, in real life there remains more than a fair share of serious problems which each individual must deal with. As well, there are also numerous Biblical references to the stars, Planets, skies and luminaries.

How to Find Your Soul-Mate, Stars, and Destiny

One example of this is found in the modern translations of the Dead Sea Scrolls, which have only recently been made available for translation for the general public. From these translations comes the story of Maskil, leader of a strict Jewish sect known as the Essenes, who in about 30 B.C., left his desert compound to speak to the Sons of Dawn, disciples who were serving a two-year novitiate before being accepted as Sons of Light and allowed to enter the community. Maskil, it seems, was taking a risk because he was carrying with him a doctrine which he didn't want to fall into the hands of the Sons of Darkness. Thus, he wrote his speech in code and encrypted it on a scroll with only the title being readable, "Words of the Sage to the Sons of Dawn". Using a painstaking technique of counting letters and comparing their frequency in the text to known Hebrew texts, this scroll and others has been translated. One, dating to the second century B.C. explains the Book of Moses while another from the same period is a calendar setting out a system for following the phases of the Moon. The calendar appears to have been a draft which attempts to find a pattern between lunar months and the solar year. It seems that a precise calendar was crucial to the Essenes because the regular movement of the heavenly bodies was believed to be a divine sign that, if properly understood, enabled a man to live in step with the designs of the heavens above. The "Words of the Sage", hidden in a desert cave for over 2,000 years only to be found by a Bedouin shepherd, spoke of the creation of the universe, how its branches reach to the heavens and its roots to the abyss below. The Maskil spoke of man, created from the dust of the Earth.

And in like manner, the study of the stars and astrology has been intertwined in one manner or another in the history of all cultures. That it has touched the lives of so many people from great kings to infamous scholars is perhaps the most remarkable story of all. It is all pervasive, and whether anyone likes it or not, it is shrouded in a rich spiritualism and mysticism. For it appears to be our intuitions that draw us to the study of astrology more so even than our intellects. How then did it come to be a science taken less seriously than the other sciences? Again, that question leads one to religion and science. It appears that a few influential and powerful religious leaders decided the study of astrology should be shunned. Then along came the Age of Science and the skeptics who felt they could prove anything that was observable and astrology wasn't observable. All of which brings us to modern times when even famous physicists are attempting to mathematically prove that there is a God. Believers have never needed mathematical proof of a Supreme Being any more than serious students of astrology needed to be told how to think. What free will grants is the ability for each person to make that determination and his or her own decisions.

The test of any great thought has always been its longevity, and astrology has been with humankind throughout the ages. The earliest man and woman gazed at the stars in wonder just as people do to this day. It is little wonder then that we all want to know what is beyond our reach in the heavens above. And it is little wonder that the stars and Planets compel us and draw us to study and observe them. Our probings into the vast unknown of the universe, and the galaxies beyond our own, are only indicative of the curiosity that beset humankind from the very beginnings of time. And this very curiosity is indicative of the influence the Planets and luminaries have upon each and every one of us.

Sidereal Astrology

It needs to be mentioned that, like any science, astrology has branched and formed different areas of study. One branch of astrology is Sidereal. The Sidereal astrologers reflect that the Earth slowly shifts position and the stars slowly shift their positions in relation to Earth. Therefore, dates of the Sun's entrance into each sign should change along with the Earth's shift in position. This concept is seen by the Sidereal astrologers as being more scientific because it is based on the actual positions of the constellations in the Zodiac. They point out that the dates established by Claudius Ptolemy in the second century A.D. have changed by approximately twenty-five days.

Traditional astrologers, however, feel that the Zodiac never actually corresponded to the actual constellations but rather to the movement of the planets. Traditional astrologers continue to use the groupings that have been around for thousands of years. That is, the signs of the Zodiac are divided into twelve equal segments of thirty degrees each.

In studying astrology, the casual reader will also come across various methods for drawing up the Birth Chart. Again this personal preference is left up to the individual person and to the professional astrologer being consulted.

Synastry

Synastry is the practice of comparing two or more Birth Charts for indications of compatibility. While numerous generalizations have been made about compatibility based on Sun signs alone, Synastry offers a more detailed perspective on matters of partnerships, associates, friends, lovers, and spouses. The practice of Synastry provides basic factors and driving forces to the nature of the relationship.

In comparing two Birth Charts, one major indicator is whether one person's Sun sign is the same as the other person's Ascendant sign. Another factor is whether the first person's Sun sign is on the cusp of the Seventh House on the other person's chart. Or, is one person's Sun in the same sign as the other's Midheaven. Another strong indication would be to consider whether the Sun sign is in the opposite sign of the other person's Ascendant. On the other hand, stress can occur within the relationship when the Sun and Ascendant have an aspect which is square, and this square can provide that area of life which the couple either disagree about or that provides obstacles to overcome. A trine or sextile aspect between the Sun and Ascendant produces a pleasant and easy going relationship, but it can also produce a relationship that becomes dull. Negative situations can occur when the Sun and Ascendant are in semi-sextile aspects because signs which are next to each other are so different. This, of course, is strengthened or weakened by other aspects in the two respective Charts, and is also negated in a relationship between Capricorn and Aquarius. Another factor considered negative is a quincunx aspect with the exception of relationships between Aries and Scorpio, Taurus and Libra, and Leo and Pisces.

The next consideration in Synastry is a comparison of the relationship of the Planets and their aspects in the two individual Charts. Traditionally, only the major aspects and quincunx are used for this comparison. Again, what is being examined is the interrelationship of the Planets and no one aspect should be considered out of context with the entire picture. Particularly positive Planetary relationships between two Charts are when the two Suns form a conjunction, the woman's Sun conjuncts with the man's Moon, the woman's Moon conjuncts with the man's Sun, the ruling planets form positive aspects, or ruling planets make strong aspects to the other person's Sun and Moon. Next, comes the comparison of each person's Houses. And, after all that is completed, the two Charts can be progressed (examined) for indications of future compatibility.

Is all of this helpful to the people involved? Evidently enough people think so to keep astrologers busy calculating and drawing up Birth Charts. And this same process can be used for business and even political advice.

BIRTH CHART

Astronomers have discovered that stars get their energy through the transformation of mass into energy. Humans, comparatively, transform energy into actions. What is it exactly that impels and compels people to decide to take particular actions? Some people act on impulse while others use rational and logical thought. There are those people who intellectualize their actions and others whose actions are a reaction to their emotions or their intuitions. It required centuries for the behavioral scientists and psychologist to be taken seriously, and it may require more time for it to catch up to the precepts of astrology. And even genetics are proving that people are born with certain characteristics.

Astrology addresses the differences in the make-up of individuals which makes each of us unique. Add to that our cultural, economical, social, and familial differences, and there is produced a rich mosaic of people. The fact that each person is an unique individual is reflected in the Birth Chart. A horoscope is a picture of the heavens, referred to as the Zodiac, and can be drawn up for any particular time such as when decisions must be made, when a person is entering a new relationship, at the beginning of a business venture, or a career change. The Birth Chart, as already mentioned, is a picture of the heavens drawn up to represent the time of birth. This is also called a Natal Chart and is somewhat different than a Solar Chart. The Solar Chart, used by many astrologers, can be drawn up if a person doesn't know the exact time of birth. It represents the day a person was born and will be the same for everyone sharing that birth date. The Solar Chart is, of course, less personal than the Natal Chart.

It is the time of birth that allows the astrologer to determine the Ascendant or Rising Sign and this information is a determining factor in the Birth Chart because it falls on the cusp of the First House on the Chart. From there, the Chart is made up of Planets, Signs, and Houses. The Planets represent the forces that act while the Signs determine how the Planets will act, and the Houses represent where in life the Planets will have an influence. Another important factor is the ruling Planet. This is the Planet that rules the Sign in a person's First House. Also of significance, is the Planet, called a dispositor, that rules a person's Sun Sign and strengthens the power of the Sun in the Chart. A person's emotional life may be indicated by the position of the dispositor or ruler of the Moon. Next, the astrologer looks at what Planets fall in the Angles of a Chart which enhances their power and strength. The four Angles are the Ascendant (cusp of the First House), the Nadir (cusp of the Fourth House), the Descendant (cusp of the Seventh House), and the Midheaven (cusp of the Tenth House). Next, it is determined if a person has Planets in their Dominion, that is, Planets that are in the sign that they rule. A Planet in its Home Sign is more powerful especially in relation to the House which it is in. Then too, Planets are considered in mutual reception if each one occupies the Sign that the other one rules. For example, if Mars is in Libra (ruled by Venus) and Venus is in Aries (ruled by Mars). This means that the two Planets are cooperating and each is strengthened. The Planets and the Signs each rules are listed below in order of significance to the Chart.

How to Find Your *Soul-Mate, Stars,* and *Destiny*

Sun — Rules Leo, is exalted in Aries, is indetriment in Aquarius, and is in fall in Libra.

Moon — Rules Cancer, is exalted in Taurus, is indetriment in Capricorn, and in fall in Scorpio.

Mercury — Rules Gemini and Virgo, is exalted in Virgo, is indetriment in Sagittarius, and in fall in Pisces.

Venus — Rules Taurus and Libra, is exalted in Pisces, is indetriment in Aries, is in fall in Virgo.

Mars — Rules Aries (and traditionally Scorpio), is exalted in Capricorn, is indetriment in Libra, and in fall in Cancer.

Jupiter — Rules Sagittarius (and traditionally Pisces), is exalted in Cancer, is indetriment Gemini, is in fall in Capricorn.

Saturn -- Rules Capricorn (and traditionally Aquarius), is exalted in Libra, is indetriment in Cancer, is in fall in Aries.

Uranus -- Rules Aquarius, is exalted in Scorpio, is indetriment in Leo, is in fall in Taurus.

Neptune -- Rules Pisces, is exalted in Leo, is indetriment in Virgo, is in fall in Aquarius.

Pluto -- Rules Scorpio, and is indetriment in Taurus.

PREDICTIONS

Serious astrologers do not claim to be able to predict the future. What they do is ascertain the upcoming trends and indicate possible areas of stress and obstacles or possible times when opportunities or changes may present themselves. And while various astrologers put to use different methods for arriving at this information, a reliable astrologer is likely to be familiar with more than one method.

One of the most frequently used methods of determining future trends is the Progressed Chart. Progressed aspects, as mentioned, are indicative of general trends in a person's life. Lunar aspects affect the life for two to three months, and planetary transits last for a few weeks or a few days depending upon the particular planet. Years in which the progressed Sun progresses into the next sign are considered important in the life of the person.

One way to progress a chart is to use the one day for one year system. This involves noting the Birth Date and then counting forward the number of days which corresponds to the year in question. For example, if a person was curious about events to transpire when he or she was age forty, the astrologer would count forward forty days from the date of birth and then cast a new Chart. This system is related to the theory that there exists a relationship in the make up of the person between the Earth's daily rotation on its axis and its annual revolution around the Sun. It is theorized that the days after birth represent the development of the psyche of a person during the corresponding years. Another method to progress the Chart is to use the perpetual noon-date or the date directly related to the date and time of birth. Using this method, the Planetary positions at noon on the day in question are taken to relate to noon on the perpetual noon-date and to conditions for the twelve months afterwards. This is correlated to the amount of time between the birth time and noon on the birth date. The one-degree method of progression involves progressing a Planet from its position at birth, one degree for each year of life.

Followers of horary astrology use a different method altogether. These astrologers cast a Chart for the moment in time when the question is asked. In other words, a person asks the question, and the astrologer believes that when the question is asked is indicative of a relationship of what will happen, i.e., events are felt to take on the nature of the time at which they occur.

Another method is to study the transits of the Planets in comparison to the positions of the Planets in the Birth Chart. Planetary positions can be ascertained by checking an ephemeris for the date in question. Then compare these transits with the Birth Chart to find out what aspects are formed. Positive aspects formed with the transits of Jupiter, for example, are considered beneficial and enjoyable and a good time for action or travel. On the other hand, aspects formed with Saturn would indicate a time to hold off on major decisions. Mars is thought of as adding energy to another Planet (which is good but it can also make the person accident prone) while the transits of Venus bring about an enjoyable social life, and Uranus and Pluto indicate changes.

One other method is the Solar Return Chart. This involves a horoscope which is drawn up for the exact moment that the Sun is passing through the degree of the sign it was in at the moment of a person's birth. The Solar Return Chart is compared with the Birth Chart in order to determine any aspects formed between the two charts. This is considered a most useful method for spotting trends in the upcoming year. Similar to the Solar Return Chart is the Lunar Return Chart which is used to determine trends in the forthcoming month.

Modern astrologers are also observing and analyzing what is referred to as midpoints. This system dates back to the 13th century and focuses on the degree of the ecliptic which falls halfway between any two Planets, the Ascendant, or the Midheaven. This is considered a sensitive area in that it is the point at which the magnetic forces of the two Planets meet and connect. This midpoint, it is felt, is activated by the transits of the Planets or by Planetary progressions. It goes without saying that this system requires a thorough understanding of transits and progressions, but it is useful in that unexpected and often uncharted occurrences happen at these points.

The Stages of Life

One of the interesting corollaries often mentioned in astrology texts is the relationship between the signs and the stages of life. These do not form a direct connection to the individual Birth Chart, but as one becomes more familiar with astrology and the descriptions of the Sun signs and how they relate to real people, the Stages of Life Concept gains significance in its applicability.

ARIES - The first stage of life, that of the newborn baby in its cradle, is often used in portraying the characteristics of Aries. The baby is capable of thinking only of itself and its immediate needs, wanting what it wants at once and being quite prepared to yell and to demand what it wants if necessary. The baby is incapable of considering the effects of its demands on other people.

TAURUS - The second stage of life corresponds to Taurus and implies a time in life when the infant is learning to interact with others and to form its first relationships. This child is aware of others and becoming aware of feelings. The child is also learning and discovering the ability to do things for oneself. Thus, Taurus likes to work.

GEMINI - Is considered the playful child who learns to make friendships outside of the home. This is also the time of life when one is learning and developing intelligence.

CANCER - Corresponds to the adolescent who is changeable, susceptible to suggestions, and emotional. He is not quite ready to be independent, and home and mother are important. Often Cancer reflects the opinions of others (peers) rather than the individual.

LEO - Is the first stage in an individuals life when effort is being made to be independent and grown up, and ambitions are becoming important. This person may be overly impressed with himself.

VIRGO - Next is Virgo who is associated with the Serving-maid who is willing to help others and to learn a skill through training and effort.

LIBRA - Is associated with that stage of life when one is attempting to find the proper balance and place in the world through relationships and partnerships.

SCORPIO - Represents the active stage of a persons life which requires applying energy to endeavors and overcoming any obstacles along the way.

SAGITTARIUS - Might be that worldly, ambitious person or the person who strives to achieve wisdom and spirituality.

CAPRICORN - Represents achievements in life and realizing one's ambitions.

AQUARIUS - Is associated with loftier ideals and a person who is no longer striving for achievement but is reflecting on life.

PISCES - Is that stage of life that reflects the ultimate meaning in the previous stages, and it is said that Pisces individuals are old souls who have evolved through the other signs and are ready for rebirth or the beginning of the next wheel or cycle of life.

THESE CHARACTERISTICS, of course, do not apply directly to the signs but are used as references in regard to the general nature of the Sun Signs.

Conclusion

That astrology is a complex study should be apparent. An effort has been made to introduce many of the concepts which will be discussed within this book, and, hopefully, this general overview will add to the understanding of the efforts being made within the field of astrology.

Many within this field accept it as part of what is referred to as the collective mind or the collective human experience. And this explanation may go a long way in explaining the lasting interest in astrology which has endured through the ages. There is also discussion of the unconscious aspect of the human experience which alludes to that part of the mind which is unaware of itself and cannot be controlled by conscious effort. The psychologist Carl Jung, with his interest in astrology, offered his own explanation of this collective experience.

Perhaps the most basic concept found within astrology is the idea that nothing exists which is not in some way related or interrelated to some other part of the universe. That is to say that no one part of the universe is ever independent or cut off from the rest of the universe. There is a link, however subtle, between the forces of nature and the dependency that life on Earth has to not only the Sun and the Moon but in some degree to the other Planets as well. And this interrelation ties in most directly with the rhythms, the waves, and the movements of these heavenly bodies through space. Did atoms not exist before they were discovered? Or were quarks some unknown mystery before the physicist learned to quantify them? What leads even the greatest of these scientists and thinkers to want to know more? And what leads everyday people to also want to know more and to discover some explanation for the reasoning behind what makes the world go round?

Astrology, in conclusion, is not an entertainment made up merely for distraction, but rather. But rather considering its age alone, it is a science that has been studied, added to, and evaluated throughout the time of men and women on Earth. It is a fascinating discovery and correlation of events, times, and people. That its scope includes the entire universe as we know it today adds to its fascination. And that it is only as old as our knowledge of the universe adds to its perplexities. It is a field of study which undoubtedly will continue to grow and expand.

Astrological Months

The twelve Zodiac constellations do not correspond with the so-called constellations any more. When we talk about "the Virgo" it does not mean that the respective Planet is in the Virgo constellation. The signs of the Zodiac are astrologically classified (1) according to their nature as: Cardinal, Fixed, and Mutable; (2) according to gender: masculine and feminine; and (3) according to the four fundamental elements as: Earth, Air, Fire and Water.

The Classifications of The Signs According to Their Respective Elements are:

- **Earth:** Taurus, Virgo, Capricorn
- **Fire:** Aries, Leo, Sagittarius
- **Air:** Gemini, Libra, Aquarius
- **Water:** Cancer, Scorpio, Pisces

The Signs Correspond to The Following Periods of The Year:

Aries:	March 21 to April 20
Taurus:	April 21 to May 20
Gemini:	May 21 to June 21
Cancer:	June 22 to July 22
Leo:	July 23 to August 22
Virgo:	August 23 to September 22
Libra:	September 23 to October 22
Scorpio:	October 23 to November 21
Sagittarius:	November 22 to December 20
Capricorn:	December 21 to January 19
Aquarius:	January 20 to February 18
Pisces:	February 19 to March 20

When referring to a sign, we must first consider the month that sign represents because nature shows the psycho-temperamental characteristic of a respective person and also his evolution. From, the moment of birth, the person follows nature's path. For example, the Sun moves from the Spring equinox towards the Summer Solstice. This is a cosmic impulse of the life giving Plan et. Many writers and poets describe this as the moment of triumph, the awakening of nature.

The Planets are The Daughters of The Sun by Science, Pain, Love, or by Death

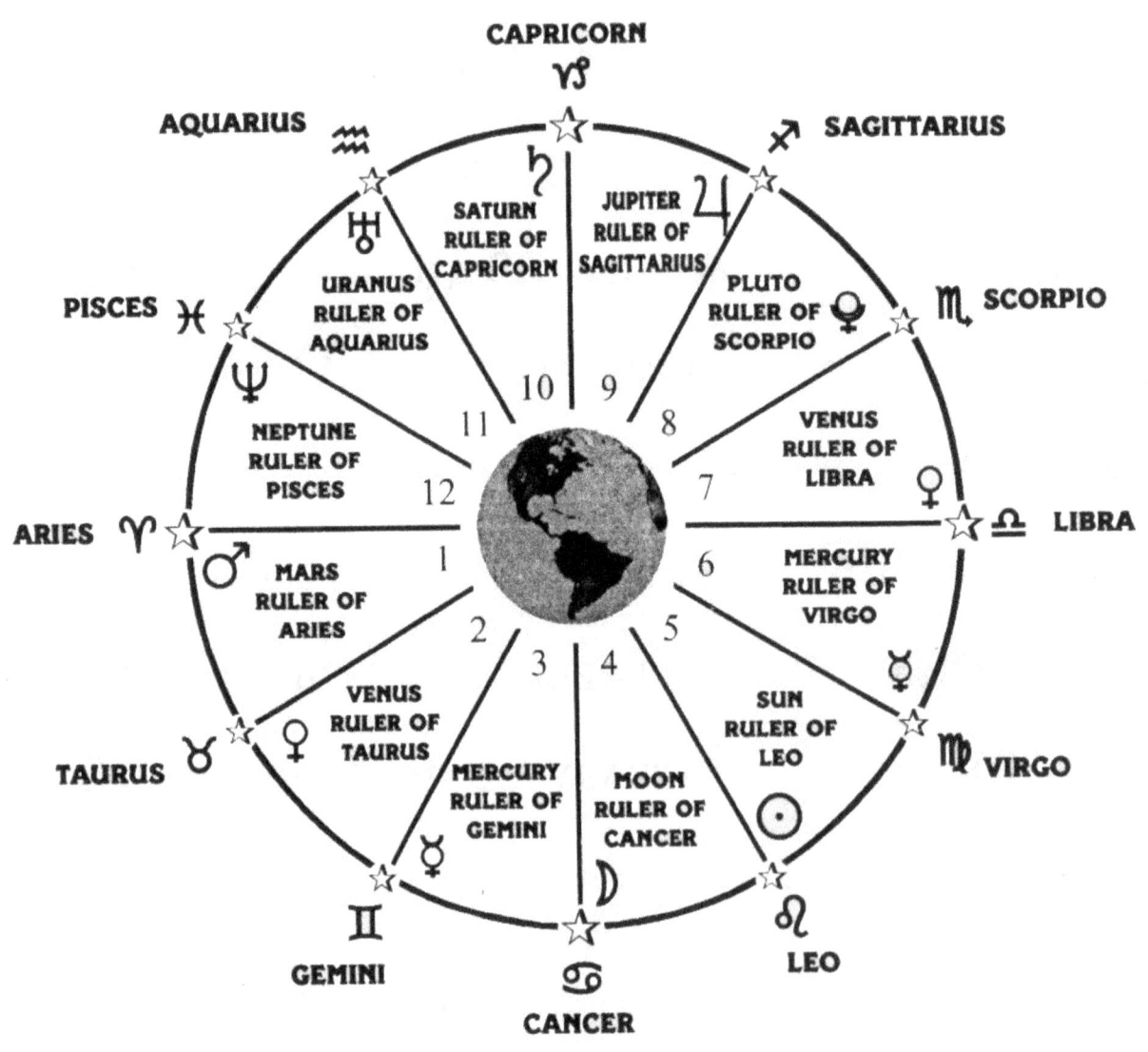

How to Find Your *Soul-Mate, Stars,* and *Destiny*

The Twelve Sun Signs of The Zodiac

Aries: March 21 -- April 20

Cardinal, Fire sign; Positive; Masculine; Ruled by Mars; Aries rules the head; Symbolized by the Ram; Glyph represents a ram's horns; indicates sandy, hilly, dry or arid settings, fireplaces, ceilings, tools, furnaces; sayings: "the untamed fire of impulse,"; keywords: "I AM", representing the birth of awareness; traits: dynamic, ambitious, active, ardent, headstrong, impatient, courageous, enthusiastic, imaginative, energetic, excitable, proud, impulsive, rash, undomestic, hasty, sharp spoken, passionate, quick tempered, self-centered, quick with ideas, aggressive, enterprising, executive, pioneering, confident, independent, ingenious, scientific, explorative, forceful, strong willed, urgent, generous, seeking affirmation and admiration; Color: red; Metal: copper; Stone: diamond.

Taurus: April 21 -- May 20

Fixed, Earth sign; Feminine; Receptive; Ruled by Venus; Taurus rules the throat and cerebellum; symbolized by the Bull; Glyph represents the bull's head and horns; indicates banks, safety deposit boxes, money boxes, jewel cases, stables, dairies, tack rooms, pastures, fields, and round items such as rings, coins, wheels; sayings: "Mad as a bull"; keywords: "I HAVE"; traits: possessive, permanency, artistic, gentle, loyal, domestic, proud, self-indulgent and self-interested, sensual, amorous, patient but hot tempered when angry, persistent, thorough, conservative, retentive, discriminating, determined, can be stubborn and obstinate, materialistic, hard working, diligent, steady, kind, trustworthy, self-reliant, composed, practical, sympathetic, careful, fearless, enduring; Color: pink and pale blue; Metal: copper; Stone: sapphire.

Gemini: May 21 -- June 21

Mutable, Air sign; Masculine; Positive; Ruled by Mercury; Gemini rules the hands, shoulders, arms, and lungs; symbolized by the Twins; Glyph represents the two figures of the Twins; indicates letters, communications, messengers, news, newspapers and magazines, neighbors, relatives, short journeys, lecturing, debating, teaching, advertising, reporting, clerical assignments, story telling, merchandising, printing, education; sayings for Gemini: "Here today, but gone tomorrow," "Too many irons in the fire,"; keywords: "I THINK"; traits: communicative, adaptable, versatile, sensitive, eloquent, generous, likes traveling, undomestic, companionable, changeable, congenial, sociable, temperamental, mood-swings, inventive, curious, tricky, dexterous, literary, expressive, intellectual, idealistic, restless, impulsive; Color: yellow; Metal: mercury; Stone: agate.

Cancer: June 22 -- July 22

Cardinal, Water sign; Feminine, Receptive; Ruled by the Moon; Cancer rules the breasts and stomach; symbolized by the Crab; Glyph is drawn from the human breasts representing motherhood; indicates lakes, rivers, streams, springs, marshy lands, homes, stables, mangers, taverns, public places, kitchens, water receptacles, cellars; sayings: "The restless tides of the oceans," "Clings like a crab," "By the light of the silvery Moon,"; keywords: "I FEEL"; traits: protective, sensitive, imaginative, sympathetic, kind, emotional, shrewd, active, intuitive, moody, artistic, dreamy, maternal, romantic, domestic, impressionable, psychic, restless, changeable, versatile, receptive, drawn to history and ancestors, cautious, reserved, brooding, self-centered, selfish, possessive, vain; Color: green; Metal: silver; Stone: pearl.

Leo: July 23 -- August 22

Fixed, Fire sign; Masculine, Positive; Ruled by the Sun; Leo rules the back, spine, and heart; symbolized by the Lion; Glyph represents two incomplete circles of the Sun joined by the Moon, i.e., power derived from the intellect and the emotions; indicates rounded hills, wilderness, deserts, forests, forts, palaces, clubs, theaters, playgrounds, ballrooms, amusement parks, sports and games of chance, social gatherings and functions, fireplaces, furnaces, sun porches; sayings: "All is fair in love and war," "Lionhearted," "Fire of the heart,"; keywords: "I WILL"; traits: idealistic, proud, magnetic, loyal, philanthropic, creative, impressive, powerful, ambitious, commanding, generous, fixed opinions, challenging, bold, domineering, autocratic, hopeful, sociable, magnanimous, outspoken, ardent, arrogant, self-centered; Color: gold and orange; Metal: gold; Stone: ruby.

Virgo: August 23 -- September 22

Mutable, Earth sign; Feminine, Receptive; Ruled by Mercury; Virgo rules the nervous system and intestines; symbolized by the Virgin; Glyph represents the Virgin; indicates gardens, fields, grain mills and elevators, pantries, restaurants, storage for fruits and vegetables and grains, file cabinets, shelves, and storage for books, papers, maps, charts and plans; sayings: "He serves most who serves best," "Virtue is its own reward,"; keywords: "I ANALYZE"; traits: kind, domestic, ingenious, witty, studious, intellectual, methodical, detail-oriented, analytical, serious, active, concise, discreet, sensitive, perceptive, intuitive, industrious, calculating, anxious, worries, skeptical, critical, quick-tempered, discontent, fearful of disease and poverty, indecisive, contemplative; Color: blue and gray; Metal: mercury; Stone: sapphire.

Libra: September 23 -- October 22

Cardinal, Air sign; Masculine, Positive; Ruled by Venus; Libra rules the lower back, buttocks, and kidneys; symbolized by the Scales; Glyph represents the Scales in perfect balance; indicates windmills, barns, cut wood, harbors, shipyards, mountain tops, hills, trees, hunting grounds, sandy soil, domed buildings, courthouses, lofts, closets, guest rooms, pianos, scales, weights, measures, dresser tops, jewel cases; sayings for Libra: "Tell it to the judge," "Blessed are the peace makers,"; keywords: "I BALANCE"; traits: refined, impartial, diplomatic, thoughtful, gracious, modest, decorous, artistic, adaptable, persuasive, sociable, peace loving, judicial, affectionate, charming, kind, understanding, harmonious, well balanced, romantic, idealistic, tactful, indecisive, reckless, gullible, procrastinating, susceptible, impressionable, illusive, vain; Color: blue and purple; Metal: copper; Stone: opal.

Scorpio: October 23 -- November 21

Fixed, Water sign; Feminine, Receptive; Ruled by Pluto; Scorpio rules the genitals; symbolized by the Scorpion; Glyph represents the Scorpion stinger connected to the reproductive organs; indicates surgeons, chemists, detectives and investigators, researchers, lowlands, gardens, vineyards, slaughter houses, meat markets, laboratories, funeral homes; sayings: "The eye of an eagle,"; keywords: "I DESIRE"; traits: intense, passionate, active, energetic, positive, fearless, tenacious, penetrating, thoughtful, eloquent, devoted, secretive, emotional, subtle, persistent, obstinate, imaginative, possessive, jealous, quick-tempered, revengeful, temperamental, sarcastic, vindictive; Color: crimson and maroon; Metal: Plutonium; Stone: topaz.

Sagittarius: November 22 -- December 20

Mutable, Fire sign; Masculine, Positive; Ruled by Jupiter; Sagittarius rules the liver, hips, and thighs; symbolized by the Archer; Glyph represents the arrow of the Archer; indicates high or elevated places, around fire; stables; arrows, spears, swords, needles, obelisks, poles, canes, rope, long tools, race horses, incense burners; sayings for Sagittarius: "For he's a jolly good fellow," "A good sport,"; traits: energetic, optimistic, zealous, proud, lucky, tolerant, open minded, sincere, honest, prophetic, humane, foresight, out spoken, freedom loving, exploratory, jovial, progressive, curious, amiable and friendly, speculative, risk taker, idealistic, daring, impatient, undomestic, self indulgent, charitable, assertive, defiant, stubborn, independent, sport loving; Color: dark blue and purple; Metal: tin; Stone: turquoise.

Capricorn: December 21 -- January 19

Cardinal, Earth sign; Feminine, Receptive; Ruled by Saturn; Capricorn rules the bones, joints, and knees; symbolized by the Goat; Glyph represents the beard of the Goat; indicates leather, logs, older trees, lumber, cement, brick, mortar, goats, plaster, bones, skeletons, docks, hemlock, frost, snow, ice; sayings for Capricorn: "Watch and wait," "What is worth doing is worth doing well,"; keywords: "I USE"; traits: prudent, aspiring, steadfast; dignity, cautious, patient, disciplined, determined, practical, well organized, service, leadership, ambitious, forceful, economical, conservative, thrifty, scrupulous, trustworthy, stubborn, domineering, good friends and bad enemies, brooding, egotistical; Color: green and brown; Metal: lead; Stone: garnet.

Aquarius: January 20 -- February 18

Fixed, Air sign; Masculine, Positive; Ruled by Uranus; Aquarius rules the circulatory system, calves and ankles; symbolized by the Waterbearer; Glyph represents waves as in the water pouring between Heaven and the Earth, electrical energy, and universal wisdom; indicates hilly terrain, springs, roofs, highways, cups, vases, pitchers, smoke, steam, vapor, rain, fog, bridges and ferries, railroads, vehicles and airplanes, electricity and electrical engines, telephones, radios, ladders, and stairs; sayings: "The waters of life," "A stranger in a strange land,"; keywords: "I KNOW"; traits: idealistic, truth seeker, humanitarian, sincere, assertive, independent, progressive, analytical, inventive, intellectual, tolerant but fixed in opinion, domestic but changeable, kind, well-liked, gentle, altruistic, anxious, unconventional, temperamental, sociable, considerate, intuitive, scientific, earnest, futuristic, can be radical, irrational, scattered, skeptical, and gullible; Color: aquamarine and sky blue; Metal: Uranium; Stone: amethyst.

Pisces: February 19 -- March 20

Mutable, Water sign; Feminine, Receptive; Ruled by Neptune; Pisces rules the feet; symbolized by the Fish (two fish going in opposite directions); Glyph represents the two fish tied together or two crescent moons--one for emotions and one for reality, i.e., a higher consciousness limited by the restrictions of a physical body and the temptations of the world; indicates: oceans, fish, nets, fishing, boats, canneries, bodies of water, aquariums, under water ventures, oil and petroleum, spiritualism, and churches; sayings for Pisces: "A fish out of water," "Two ships passing in the night,"; keywords: "I Believe,"; traits: idealistic, hospitable, loyal, self-sacrificing, refined, perceptive, emotional, sensitive, romantic, intuitive, mystical, impressionable, changeable, moody, devoted, psychic, secretive, compassionate, versatile, tempted by pleasures, dreamy, submissive; Colors: sea green, lilac, lavender; Metal: platinum, tin; Stone: aquamarine, moonstone.

ZODIAC ANATOMY

SIGNS	PARTS OF THE BODY	ORGANS	GLANDS	SYSTEM
ARIES	Head, Face	Blood, Brain	Pituitary	Muscular
TAURUS	Neck	Throat	Thyroid	Metabolic
GEMINI	Shoulders, Arms, Hands	Lungs, Nerves	Thymus	Central Nervous System
CANCER	Breasts	Stomach, Uterus	Mammary, Salivary	Digestive (Upper)
LEO	Upper Back	Heart, Upper Spine, Blood Marrow	Spleen	Cardiac
VIRGO	Abdomen	Small Intestines	Pancreas	Digestive (Lower)
LIBRA	Small of the Back	Kidneys, Genitalia	Adrenals	Endocrine
SCORPIO	Genitalia, Intestines	Colon, Internal Genitalia	Glands	Reproduction Renal
SAGITTARIUS	Buttocks, Hips, Calves	Lower Spine	Liver	Autonomic Nervous System
CAPRICORN	Knees, Skin	Joints, Bones, Teeth, Hair	Gallbladder, Sebaceous Glands	Skeletal
AQUARIUS	Ankles, Legs	Nerves	Parathyroid	Circulatory
PISCES	Feet	Body Fluids	Lacrimal, Lymph, Pineal	Lymphatic

Date With Destiny

Share With Me Your Fantasy

Date With Destiny

Share With Me Your Fantasy

Aries

March 21 - April 20
Man - Woman - Child - Character - Relationships - Compatibilities - Love Signs

The word Aries is taken from the Latin word for Ram and is often depicted as such. But Aries was also the Greek god of war, and many of the personal characteristics of individuals born to this Sun sign resemble this mythological and legendary ruler of war and conflict. Aries was an erotic lover who had numerous affairs. He was both brave and insolent, youthful, and impulsive.

HOW TO FIND YOUR SOUL-MATE, STARS, AND DESTINY

Aries is the first Sun sign of the Zodiac, and because of this, is often referred to as the baby of the Zodiac. Like a baby, Aries can be self-centered, demanding, and delighting in immediate gratification. This is a brave, courageous, and daring person who is unafraid of standing up for personal rights and freedoms. But Aries is at other times considered rash, crude, pushy, and overly aggressive. This is the demanding egotist who is Aries.

The first sign of the Zodiac, Aries, is under the control of Mars. It is the Cardinal sign of Fire, which represents the Earth as it was before Genesis, i.e., during the time when fire, the chaos and other elements were ravishing the Universe. Mars is the sign of force coordinating the other natural forces. It represents action and direction. It begins each year as the Sun reaches the Equator at the Spring Equinox, bringing forth the cosmic impulse of the life-giving planet. Many philosophers and writers refer to this as the moment of triumph, of the awakening of nature. This constellation is divided into two groups: A fixed group of stars forms the shape of the Aries; a part of the head, neck, the right horn and the front legs belong to the Aries area, the Ram, with the rest of the body inside the area of the Taurus.

The symbol of the Ram can represent a battering ram thrusting forward, ever rambunctious and even rampaging on its journeys. Aries rules the head and is noted for its headstrong impulsiveness which may often compel its natives to plunge into endeavors and situations without considering the outcomes or consequences of their actions. Their overpowering self-assertiveness can prevent them from judging well the reactions of other people. If the Ram persistently butts up against too much opposition, losing his energies, he can become as the sheep, losing direction and meandering from place to place.

Aries, being the first Fire sign, represents action, direction, energy, and courage. The Aries individual possesses a strong belief in his or her own value or self-worth. People born under the sign of Aries are known for being dynamic with swiftness of action and thought and with an extremely strong will. They possess an exceptional ability to organize and to coordinate. They rarely lose courage and are gifted with an excellent character. They fight back adversity, retain courage in difficult moments, and reshape their existence, paying with their own life if necessary. However, it is quite possible for the Aries person, at times, to reach their purpose or to obtain their goal, and, as will be explained later in this text, this is not always very favorable to them.

Then too, Aries natives are authoritarian and impulsive. They want everyone else in their lives to shape according to their will, but, at the same time, it can be said that they are capable of making great sacrifices for their loved ones. And even when their finances are moderate, they can also be generous to a fault. They are ready to forgive but not to forget inequities, attempting with all their effort to turn a negative experience into a future profitable one.

The Aries soul wonders toward metaphysical thought, and if this gift is developed through meditation and self-improvement, it can inspire the individual. The clairvoyant and psychic powers often being so phenomenally great that the Aries can readily read the minds and thoughts and know the motives of others without the exchange of a single word. When in a highly developed state, many mysteries of the spirit world are revealed to them. Aries people are surrounded with occult, magnetic and solar forces which, when realized, can be so great that these people have the power to banish the misgivings and doubts of others. Many gifted psychics, mind readers, telepathists and spiritual advisers have been Aries individuals.

However, it must be remembered that the first-sign Aries can be impractical and impulsive, and although his or her moral code may at times be flexible, they are most generally honest, helpful and courageous. Many famous pioneers and explorers were born under this sign. If the individual is involved in a medical career, he becomes scrupulous, careful and very conscientious.

Some astrologers view Aries as having the ability to develop his or her positive traits or submitting and falling prey to their less than positive traits. The individual Aries has the propensity or opportunity to choose either direction. Aries, as the first sign of the Zodiac, has not only the freedom but the strength and youthful energy to walk either path, choosing his directions as he pleases. Aries, representing the cosmic principle of action, evokes the will to begin, to seek, to take the initiative. This sign signifies the drive to expand, ‚to be', to experiencing becoming what one all ready is, all that one is, to externalize and explore all possibilities, keeping nothing latent, but, rather, exploring and tasting every emotion, pleasure, sensual sensation, and adventure. Aries is considered a mental sign because an individual must have a strong intellect in order to make decisions and to select a path or to venture into an unknown future. To the Aries individual comes the realization that ideas are the most potent force known to man. This person, preferring words to a sword, can be the inspired thinker who compels others to action. To the Aries individual, words are the most effective implements of his or her will power.

Aries has been called the birthplace of divine ideas. As the first sign, Aries initiates ideologies and causes. Metaphysically, it signifies the entrance into a higher state of increased self-realization and spiritual illumination. Man, as a thinking creature, has over the ages utilized this visionary power of Aries to explore and conquer the Universe. The dynamism, the speed and strong will are the features of the native Aries, influenced by Mars. In certain situations Aries becomes distracted and is just as happy that they passed the difficulties, perhaps not even being curious about the results. There are times when Aries needs others to take over what they started. Aries live for the present. They don't want to worry about the future. Their ideas is, "to try to solve today the problem of the moment." Aries can not wait--they want everything "now".

Aries Personality

Aries are open, outspoken, enthusiastic, and intensely individualistic. Enterprising and ambitious, they are often versatile, but headstrong with a tendency to be impulsive. They have a forceful nature and make determined efforts, but they can also be fiery and quick-tempered. With their strong ambition and drive, their desire to lead is compelling. This is a fiercely independent person who can be the first to take the side of the underdog or to accept unpopular viewpoints.

Aries are outgoing, extroverted, self-assured, active, combative, enterprising and industrious; and they strive to appear self-possessed and self-confident under all conditions. They possess both physical and moral character and a supreme courage that carries them forward in their existence and their survival of all situations both good and bad. They strive to achieve practical goals and tangible rewards and with the influence of Mars are predictably people of swift, expeditious, decisive conduct and movements. This person is most generally concerned with intellectual pursuits rather than spiritual values. Aries are outspoken and frank to a fault, and while they are basically amiable and friendly, they are hasty to jump to conclusions and to make decisions. The keen and alert Aries intellect is swift to grasp and to initiate new ideas. This attribute aids the Aries individual in his or her desire to be noticed and to stand out in a crowd. These desires are also augmented by a quick wit, alluring charm, inspiring conversation, and open generosity. They are well aware of their strong beliefs, and often declaring their superiority, which when coupled with their impatience and enthusiastic desire to lead, can appear arrogant and dogmatic.

They can also appear rash and reckless, qualities that are exhibited in unconscious impulses and compulsive behavior. Sometimes this is the first impression they make on others because Aries has the innate ability to think extremely fast, to grasp ideas and to size up situations, to weigh pros and cons, to estimate chances, and to calculate risks rapidly. Often times, although he appears rash, his plans have been calculated and well planned beforehand. Aries are willing to act independently, initiate plans, take the first step, attempt new methods, innovate, change, and improvise. Any action taken is likely to be direct and forceful, and Aries are often scornful of the slow-moving diplomatic methods, much preferring to plunge into endeavors with eagerness and energy. Little concern is given to obstacles that would prevent others from proceeding, as the Aries sizes up the situation, lays out a plan, and plows around or through any walls, fences, oppositions or rules that he considers made for others and not for him.

The Vernal Equinox, the beginning of the new cycle of seasons, compels Aries to begin, to seek the new, to take the lead, to break new ground and to pioneer by example. There is a fresh but impatient dynamism to Aries. This beginning youthful sign with its boundless and ardent energies also lacks reasoning and maturity. There is an almost childlike innocence, a trusting quality with great appeal and charm, but one which at times works against the individual. This is the underlying cause of major disappointments, disillusionment and failures in the Aries life. These setbacks can often hurt the Aries ego, resulting in deep depression. However, the Aries nature is resilient. It rebounds from defeat, recovers from depression, and turns to new endeavors and enterprises with inspired and renewed enthusiasm, optimism, and energy.

Aries espouses great intensity, even if it is at times short lived. They require recognition and appreciation which fuels their drives, renews their energies, and satisfies their egos. At first, Aries may appear self-centered, striving to increase their self-esteem and improve other people's regard or impression of them. At the same time, the more positive attributes of Aries include generosity, courage, spontaneity and idealism. Aries are extremely generous with their time, effort and money. They are sympathetic, giving advice and listening, and taking steps to help those who are less well off. Aries loves to solve the problems of others, but in return will require recognition for his or her efforts, unquestionable loyalty and ongoing patronage reminiscent of slavery.

The Aries moral and physical courage motivates these individuals to be protective and supportive of those being persecuted or unfairly treated. Aries can act with spontaneity, without premeditation or much thought given to the results of their actions. This leads to their genuine idealism which is unconcerned with spiritual or abstract values. This idealism motivates them to take definite steps to achieve results to benefit themselves and others.

Psychologically, this youthful sign, being the first in the Zodiac and known as the infant of the Zodiac, is innately endowed with deep-seated insecurities and a sense of inadequacy. The fundamental youthfulness of the Aries nature can result in extravagant shows of opinionated knowledge and elaborate exhibitions of self-assurance that displays their arrogance. However, some Aries are unconsciously flawed by anxiety to such a degree that the person will abandon a task or endeavor out of fear of failure and then suddenly direct his or her attention and energies in an entirely new direction. Another anxiety is the fear of rejection. This may be the unconscious motivation behind the Aries tendency to make hasty or critical judgments about other people and to reject those who are not immediately responsive or who don't actively seek acquaintance or friendship. In other words, Aries are likely to reject others first before they are rejected. This is a definite and profound weakness in the Aries personality. There is a pronounced lack of effort to assess human nature and character because this requires patience and reflection rather than quick thinking. Therefore, Aries are not known for always developing their appreciable gifts of insight and often times because of their rash judgments, they make erroneous assessments of others-- either trusting those who flatter them too readily or disregarding altogether those more worthy of their appreciation.

The Aries ego is strong, vital, and robustly healthy in regard to its ability to strike balances through the use of logic, intellect, and reason. But when it is allowed to run freely, the Aries ego, uninhibited by restraint, may over-compensate for anxieties and fears of failure with egotistical convictions that only his or her ideas, concepts and methods have any worth or validity. There may even exist a distortion of the qualities of initiative, independence, and impatience to a degree that causes the individual to act and to react to irrational impulses and compulsions in an oppositional and forceful manner. And oppositional behavior can become a way of life for many Aries. Oppositional behavior can become a way of life for Aries.

The Aries vulnerability arises at several levels, even though they may feel wiser and superior to others. Being quick to reject people, they cannot tolerate rejection themselves and lack any comprehension of why they have been rejected. This conflict is resolved only with an emotional maturity which understands and appreciates the give and take that is necessary in human relations. Another deep-seated conflict occurs with the inability to reconcile their impulsiveness in romantic affairs and their idealistic concept of love and romance. Males born in the first and second decans manage to resolve this conflict by accepting themselves thus liberating them from anxieties over their behavior. Other Aries develop deep guilt feelings arising from their intense hatred of deceit and duplicity. In extreme cases, the burden of guilt may cause impotence in the male and hysterical frigidity in the female.

Many Aries have a tendency toward extreme jealousies stemming from unconscious fears of inadequacies. These jealousies may be exhibited in sudden, violent outbursts and even physical violence. Only emotional maturity and the development of a sense of security regarding personal adequacy can resolve this particular conflict. Otherwise, many Aries destroy their personal relationships with their extreme jealousies.

Aries' personalities, in many instances, lack a sense of proportion. They have a tendency to exaggerate, to be extravagant, to be over-optimistic, and to allow their enthusiasms to rule the day. Over-optimism, over-estimation, excessive enthusiasm and exaggeration can and do lead to invariably disappointing results in many of their endeavors. This causes painful moments and wounded feelings as Aries may not always be able to comprehend the cause of their problems. Quite obviously, there is a need to acquire a reasonable sense of proportion between exaggerated hopes and aspirations as opposed to reality and fact in order to prevent the possibility of eventual neurotic complications.

When badly aspected, the positive gift of leadership is warped and twisted into a domineering, even tyrannical nature. Dynamism is transformed into ruthless, demanding, slave-driving qualities. Aries should be ever aware of negative tendencies: the failure to follow through and see plans completed because of a lack of determination, perseverance and patience; nervous and emotional instability; arrogance; and a lack of consideration for the feelings of others.

While Aries is endowed with potential leadership abilities, they are often unable to discipline themselves because of their conceitful belief that they are right and consequently others are wrong and should concede and be grateful for the Aries presence. They demand that others, who often the Aries has aided or helped in some manner, should in turn be loyal and willing to unquestioningly follow their ideas and opinions. Aries demands that others contribute to and back their plans faithfully and with enthusiasm. Put simply, to question the plans of an Aries person is to appear disloyal and unfaithful--conduct which can result in the loss of the friendship or relationship or at the least in a healthy tongue lashing.

The otherwise healthy ego of the average Aries exhibit an innate ambition and a desire for achievement and recognition in ways that are constructively productive, aiming for goals that are real and tangible, that can be counted and gauged. The chances are that Aries has little interest in establishing his individuality within himself. His individuality has been established only when he has accomplished a measurable, proven goal, that is, when he has succeeded.

Aries most desire success. When they are defeated, it is many times because they defeat themselves. The seeds of Aries destruction lie within the personality. Their advantage is in the fact that they are capable of controlling their destinies to a far greater extent than most, providing they learn to exercise self-discipline. Remember, the personality of Aries is derived from its „Number One', first-sign position, and from the rulership of Mars. This is the sign of the overbearing dictator, the most political of the constellations, often full of energy and decision, generous but often unreliable, changing strides while vehemently insisting he was right all along.

Thus, Aries, you are not the type to sit quietly in a corner at a party. You prefer to talk and to move around, to work the crowd. Mobility is important to you. Your desire to stand out in the crowd leads you to move from one group to another, learning what others have to say. At the same time, you have difficulty relating to others. This detachment in your personal make-up is due partially to your feelings of superiority and partially to your self-protective defense mechanisms which protect you from rejection and disappointment in others and in yourself. You strive to be the leader in any group even with your friends, to be the best at every skill and competition. This drive to be superior, to be the best, leads to a contempt for familiarity. And you make every effort to illuminate any risk of bruising your ego.

Therefore, you limit your associates, your list of friends, to those you consider your entourage, followers, and confidants, and to those you view worthy of your time and friendship. In other words, people who impress you. These are the chosen people who you trust, judged through the narrow prism of your conscious attitude of superiority, to be worthy of your time. To these people, you are intensely loyal, although often this trust is misguided as you have a tendency to misjudge people.

Self-improvement strategies for any Aries who is interested would require (1) curbing the tendency to be outspoken and opinioned, (2) avoiding arrogance, and (3) forcing themselves to reserve judgments about others, allowing themselves the time to see past their initial first impression.

You are at your best when you are guiding, controlling, governing or commanding yourself and others. You have the ability to shape the outcome of the future and to develop and conceive great plans. You are in your element when you feel the strength and freedom of your independence and determination, the execution of your ideas, the drive of your energies at full force, and the admiration of others who follow and believe in your ideas and plans. You are not easily discouraged nor is your strong will power easily subdued. Those individuals who personify the pioneering spirit of the Aries sign incessantly pursue exercising their powers of decision-making and their independence which makes them self-determined people.

Aries Character

Ruling as it does over the brain, the Aries intellectual development can be exceptionally remarkable. This sign can produce the deepest thinkers with marked cognitive abilities who have the capacity to impart knowledge to others. They can be brilliant scholars and excellent conversationalists. It is through their brilliancy and exceptional wit that they charm and attract others to them. The Aries individual with his gifted and vivacious mind and excellent memory can readily converse on numerous subjects, appearing well-read and well-informed. They are never at a loss for words or for a variety of information on various subjects. The spiritually evolved Aries knows that his freedom and independence depend to a great degree on his intellectual and cognitive abilities. You love to be the provider of entertainment, information, assistance, and advice for your friends.

The sign of Aries is the first of the twelve signs of the Zodiac. It is also the Cardinal sign of the Fire Trinity. Mars gives you extraordinary character. You are highly regarded for your executive ability, assertiveness, speedy thoughts and actions, initiative, energy and determination. In these regards, you have no equals among the other signs. You are absolutely fearless when faced with opposition, and you may go through life feeling like you are forever relentlessly pushing through or riding over obstacles placed in your path as you attempt to accomplish your goals. Aries, you desire to be in the lead, feeling it your privilege and duty to command and rule over those around you.

You prefer public life to private life, group activities to individual companionship, and crowds to smaller, more intimate get togethers. While you are well known for being quick in thought and able to give impromptu little speeches, you may at times stammer in your impatience to get your thoughts out first, and may even have two or more ideas running consecutively through your mind. Being capable of appreciating and adapting to many points of view, while holding to your own, you may appear overly opportunistic. Aries, guard against this rash outpouring of words. Others may have difficulty keeping up with your overflowing rush of ideas.

The sign of Aries, influencing those born between March 21 and April 20, represents the Fire elements of energy and courage. It is a masculine sign with a tendency to come to attention. This person, who enjoys new endeavors, craves being exposed to a variety of prospects for enterprising and innovative ideas, schemes, or adventures. You obstinately hold to your personal impression of not only your self-worth but of the superiority of your ideas and plans. The sign of Aries marks the Spring solstice, the change of seasons. It is a Cardinal sign representing a strong determination, a courageous spirit, a power of command and execution, ambition, enterprising spirit, combativity, strong will, independence, activity and most of all the desire to rule. The intellect leads this sign; however, the person should be aware of his energies and take care not to expend them needlessly in too many directions.

Aries' greatest problem is impatience with others, especially those who don't always agree, which can lead to irrational and excessive fury. And while demanding total loyalty from others, fidelity is not a main attribute, thus allowing Aries to be easy going and capable of cheating--and capable of rationalizing such behavior afterward. Remember, Aries is always right. This person is a better friend than spouse, but a friendship before marriage may lead to a successful marriage. This person may have many problems with family members who ask for money but who at the same time are not loyal nor do they generally understand the strong characteristics of the Aries nature. While Aries is a caring person with a good character, they can be controlling to a fault.

Aries individuals possess great courage and an enterprising nature which is coupled with a tendency to change purposes frequently. They generally have many skills and stay busy in a variety of activities. They remain active even as they grow older. They love and appreciate music and can, if so inclined, become talented musicians. If they play an instrument, a powerful one is preferred with which to express the Aries vitality, energy, and passion. If in the military, the Aries person prefers leadership positions. Often a polished public speaker, Aries can gain success in politics or as a comedian.

The most remarkable types of Aries have become dictators. Others use this ability to control their families, and they most generally respect tradition. If someone attempts to change your routine, your life, or your ideas of traditions, you can become depressed. The Aries defect is that you are not a diplomat: if you do not like something, you leave--slamming the door or phone, first, before the other person has the opportunity to do so. And you never admit defeat. You are never wrong. Fault lies with the other person in all instances. Whatever has happened to you, whatever obstacles has held you back, it is someone else's fault. Your superior actions and ideas could not possibly be wrong. In a disagreement, you may become furious and use foul words, apologizing later and expecting all to forgive and forget, to move on. But no one should attempt to cheat or deceive you or even to disagree with you, for you find this unforgivable. The Aries person has a most difficult time trusting other people's advice.

If people are good and fair to you, you are very kind and generous. You are willing to help and to understand, and you go to great lengths to aid others. Aries, you are extroverted, outgoing, witty, and friendly, and you make an excellent companion and confidant. Your supportive, protective nature wants to take care of others, listening to their troubles and solving their problems. This is partially because of your need for praise and to be admired as a tower of strength and wisdom. Your conversation, Aries, is stimulating and amusing, and you radiate a vital energy that is appealing and magnetic. On occasion, you have a tendency to wear out your thought power, your cognitive ability and mental energies, because everything with which you come in contact must be scrutinized by your active mind and intellect. Watch that you don't fill your mind with various facts and opinions all at the same time.

You enjoy being surrounded by people and you stand out in a crowd. While you prefer to have many friends, you also like to think of yourself as a self-sufficient loner. You prefer to suffer alone. This is only another example of your method of compensation for your fear of rejection which causes you to hold people at a distance, secretly afraid that if you trust someone, that person will eventually reject you, or disagree with you, or do you in, or leave you. Learn to accept rejection from others as everyone has to come to terms with this, not just you.

You can be blatantly frank and up front with others when expressing your ideas and thoughts. This lack of subtlety or diplomacy, this preference for straight-forward, honest opinions, can be softened for better effect. And, Aries, is there any help for the person who has strong opinions that differ from yours? Despite your intellect, you have a tendency to use your temper, your natural aggression, to talk louder than your opponent, rather than using reason and patient persuasion to win your point.

The Aries propensity to make quick decisions results in a lack of intuition in judging other people. This can lead you to misjudge people and to place your trust in the wrong people. You base your judgments on superficial impressions that are often misguided. Hence, it is quite possible that you have rejected or chased off those who meant well, but who disagreed with you, while you chose to keep around those who know that if they flatter you, you will be pleased with them.

The artless, guileless Aries does not resort to the kind of strategies frequently used by those individuals of other signs. You have your own form of interpersonal gamesmanship. You steam roll over your opposition. Because you find it difficult to lie, you artfully use bluster, and sound and fury when cornered, hoping to avoid embarrassing, direct questions.

The shrewd Aries capitalizes on the ability to impress and gain points with a winning personality and mannerisms. By using the astute Aries mind, with astounding speed, you hit upon some gesture or point of persuasion that will gain you what you want while all the time appearing to be your usual super-charming, impulsive self. Those who would accuse Aries of fraud and deceit are misinterpreting the Aries ability to simply exploit an innate trait: and only when they are cornered or pressed is it used. This trait manifests itself naturally, effortlessly, and automatically. It hardly requires conscious thought. You use finesse in playing out the scenes in the drama of your own life sometimes to the point of resorting to artifice and stratagem which you manage to apply to your personal and public life. This constant exercise of cunning can build character into an abode where only tragedy can dwell, tragedy for yourself and for others caught up in the drama of your ideas and your life.

With maturity, Aries becomes capable of idealizing and universalizing his love of independence which is derived from his egocentricity. Your vitality and physical energy enhances this independence. You must be first in everything you do. You are a professional, competitive contestant in life. While your interest may appear to be material gain, your actual objective is to win. You never brag about being second. You are most concerned by the person who beats you at your own game. This Aries nature displays itself throughout your daily life. You walk one step ahead of your companions, entering through doorways first (sometimes even before ladies). You have the first word and often the last in any argument. You love a good argument, not so much in order to discover the truth as to demonstrate or prove that you are right. You often win by sheer volume and noise and vitality, forcing your opponent to submit to your ideas.

You are original and frequently novel in your effort to be first. But, consider the difference between novel and originality. When an Aries is original, he or she is a pioneer, an inventor, and a great thinker. When you are merely novel, you are putting forth your egotistical desire to be first, and often times neglecting sound ideas and practical methods. You thus can easily lose the benefit of your energy, genius and ambition. You must be aware of self-centeredness. This trait can make you arrogant, conceited, self-serving, overly aggressive, and in the face of opposition can lead to feelings of persecution and mild or acute self-delusions.

For you to forget the „self", and to become cognitively absorbed in intellectual pursuits, to insure that your original and novel ideas are well-grounded, and to be able to consider the other person's point of view, his or her needs, wishes, desires, just as seriously as your own, are the means by which you, Aries, may emphasize and benefit from your strong characteristics and insure that your desire to be first will actually result in you succeeding.

In spite of this natural desire of the Aries to rule and command, you are noble, charming and attractive as well as sympathetic, tender, loving, magnetic and progressive. You are known among your friends for your warm heart and remarkably passionate nature. Success is largely due to personal accomplishments or through a domestic relationship, social standing or influential friends. You have a strong appreciation for literature, science, study, philosophy, travel and all methods which you perceive will better your mind and your social abilities.

Being at your best in social situations and amidst elegant surroundings, you are drawn to luxurious, opulent settings, caring little if you appear ostentatious. You can be a show-off. You are generally considered wealthier than you are, perhaps because of your commanding, well-dressed appearance. You are often thought of as a progressive person who is ambitious and aspiring. At the same time, you can be candid, high-minded, ardent in your beliefs and arguments, and on other occasions, reasonable. You are usually well-respected, and this is important to you as you value the high opinions of your friends and associates.

You are more than willing to fight for your rights. You possess and exhibit strong and pronounced convictions as to what is right and what belongs to you. You would choose to destroy a possession rather than surrender it. In the courts, you will litigate and fight as long as there is anything to fight over. In many instances, it appears that the „fight' is more important than the end result to you. This may often lead you to engage in unnecessary disagreements. Other times, you may enter needlessly into conflicts, offending those who have the power to cause you harm or setbacks. There is a need to beware of depending on unrealistic hopes and to realize that common sense will suffice where luck may fail as wishful thinking may lead to extravagant planning. Difficulties may also arise in living up to promises made in those moments of impulsive generosity.

Aries are determined and set in their own ideas. At their best, they are willing to resort to any honest scheme to prove their point and to accomplish their goals. At their worst, there are those Aries who resort to dishonest means to accomplish their goals. Yet, you are rarely if ever unjust, seldom holding a grudge against even your strongest enemies. But, be careful. Once your confidence is lost, it is very difficult to reclaim it. You are willing to die fighting for a friend or a principle, standing by your friend or friends when it seems the whole world is against them; and while you are forgiving, you never forget transgressions or someone who you feel has done you wrong.

Aries are excellent advisers, often giving others better advice than they follow themselves. Many of your friends have faith in your judgment. You are most capable of sweeping away outmoded ideas from conservative minds and ushering in innovative, new ideas.

Aries Destiny

Optimistic and future-oriented in your thinking, you have a strong prophetic sense and may be inspired to act based on insights which come to you out of the blue. You desire most to be free and unrestrained, and you have the energy to perform that which your mind imagines. You, perhaps more so than any others, dare to go where others fear; dare to attempt what others fail to imagine; dare to strive for the impossible regardless of the obstacles; or of the possible adverse consequences to yourself or others. Often others follow out of sheer willingness to be led and because they are so impressed with your belief in your own plans and abilities. But when others fail to share your enthusiasm, or have the audacity to point out any pitfalls in your thinking, you are sincerely amazed--so strong is your belief in yourself.

Aries can expect a tumultuous life in which they pay for everything they achieve. Obstacles and troubles may appear in the first half of life. The social achievements obtained can be abruptly lost through violent incidents or bankruptcies, etc. Their life is active and athletic, but the end may be violent. Their personable qualities attract many friends who help in the most difficult situations, but they will create envy also. To summarize, a succession of great situations, unstable, never long-term ones, will find the Aries person in perpetual action. You are fond of traveling, of exciting adventures, and independent ventures. You no doubt will make every effort to carve out your own path, becoming the leader of whatever enterprise or endeavor you aspire to or in some way becoming prominent in your sphere of influence.

If well aspected, the Aries individual takes a leading role in the correction of human ills or conditions, or the reform of existing social institutions and there may be an incentive toward a public or political career. This person may feel strongly about mystical experiences and may have strong feelings about religious or spiritual matters. The well-aspected Aries, intensifies the feelings, emotions and senses, softening or elevating the disposition toward sympathy, benevolence, spiritual perception or inner strength and understanding. As Aries matures, there is a tendency to develop a viable philosophy of life.

If afflicted, there is some danger of drowning, trouble with the opposite sex, or changes of occupation and position. The afflicted may also suffer peculiar feelings, aversions, and premonitions in their thought processes. There may be an inclination toward addictive habits for pleasure and the gratification of the senses such as smoking, alcohol, drugs, or sex.

Aries, being at the head of the Zodiac, often initiate plans which aren't always finished or completed. Perhaps this is due to your remarkable quickness in grasping new ideas which leads you to abandon your previous pursuits. You are alert and longing to engage in new and great undertakings even when the results do not live up to your expectations. You become brilliant in everything that you do, especially where action is involved.

In describing any group of people, and endeavoring to describe their astrological paths, it is important to warn them of the inherent elements of discord and evil in their natures. The main defects or shortcomings in the Aries nature are impatience, anger, stubbornness, selfishness, foolish generosity, and fickleness of purpose. You are not revengeful and don't hold a grudge, but you are slow to forgive. Your egotism can lead you to talk too much and to brag about yourself, your possessions and your accomplishments. This can create envy and resentment on the part of your friends or associates. You have a defensive tendency to take everything personally, and you have definite leanings toward the selfish forces also. Jealousy in both Aries men and women often distracts from what would otherwise be a most charming personality.

By cultivating your higher nature and permitting it to dominate your lower nature in every circumstance, you can overcome any and all of your faults. You need to cultivate patience and the ability to wait out the workings of your plans, to see them through to conclusion. You need to become more patient with the weaknesses of others as well as with your own disappointments and shortcomings. This will prevent your fiery outbursts of anger and your intolerance of those who don't readily agree with you. Also, cultivating your spirit of true charity will enable you to do good for others more effectively and to improve your perseverance and patience. You must learn to apply concentration in all that you do. Concentrating your energy on one pursuit at a time will bring success.

While you love an argument, you can be sarcastic, critical and overbearing to a fault. You make enemies because of your forcefulness which you see as a strength of character. You are impulsive, irritable and quick-tempered. Yet, emerging from your passion when the storm has passed, you expect immediate forgiveness of your harsh and bitter words. You expect your opponent to forget your actions without the slightest admission on your part of poor or hasty judgment. You cannot tolerate to be contradicted, teased, or tormented, or told your faults. Your unwillingness to yield a single point in an argument marks you as impetuous, defeating your own best interest. You can be so headstrong and reckless that you plunge into a path or endeavor without any consideration of the obstacles or eventual outcomes. Aries people can never be coerced, driven or forced. You are obstinate and must be left to carry out your plans in your own way because if your plans are interfered with, you will abandon them. You have an innate desire, a compulsion, to direct the endeavors and even the lives of others.

You can never rise to any great height of accomplishment until you have acquired self-control. Do not expect God to grant power to those who have not mastered control of their personal appetites, desires, and passions. Remember, Aries, the physical body is influenced by the magnetic currents and solar forces which to a large degree effect the lower or animalistic nature thus slowing your progress. Aspire, Aries, to live a moral and chaste life and to cultivate the higher qualities of your sign. It is the cultivation of your intellect and the spiritual side of your life that will allow you to attain your highest goals, to amass great wealth, and to achieve high honor and distinction. Beware of your temptation to lead a hedonistic lifestyle or to live only for pleasure. Yes, you can rationalize your reason for doing this while satiating and satisfying your desires, but it slows and impedes personal growth. The argument that everyone else is doing it, does not justify you doing it. You delude yourself, and by so doing what you are actually accomplishing is a manner to distract yourself from your higher abilities. Intellectual pursuits and accomplishments of goals require self-control of the mind and body.

Aries, you should set aside a portion of each day to reflect in silent meditation on the important aspects of life. Search your soul. Make an earnest effort to focus your mind on the purity of your inner spirit which you possess. This effort will result in the ability and power to rise to the lofty height which is yours by right of birth. By cultivating these powers, you may obtain the greatest gains in life. Develop your mystical gifts which will give you a wonderful force and power enabling you to influence and control those with whom you come in contact.

When you strive to eliminate the faults in your nature, and to advance to a higher plane of life and conduct, you are assured of the most powerful assistance. Invoke this assistance by self-communion, by constant efforts to give your better nature dominion, and by contemplation of the great truths of science. If you will assimilate the truths of astrology, resolve to possess yourself of your heaven-sent heritage, and resolutely turn from the weaknesses and faults that threaten you, you can win success beyond measure including limitless honor, esteem, position, power, health and love. Search your own heart for the source of all evil and cast it out so that you can become powerful and magnetic.

If you were to accept advice, Aries, listen to this wisdom: cultivate your mentality and your intuition for with proper self-improvement and development, there is no limit to the greatness and heights you may achieve. Actually, it is next to impossible to conceal anything from the Aries who has recognized his or her power of intuition. Develop these, the natural gifts of the spirit, and then attain and grasp all of what is important in life and spirit. The intellect leads the sign of Aries, but they should always watch their energy level in that it might be used to their disadvantage and go beyond the rational limit. These are the words passed down to us for our knowledge from the great Sages and Seers of ancient times.

Found at his best, Aries implies a strong sense of self-reliance and self-assurance with a keenness for duty which compels the individual to persist indomitably, resolutely, through all vicissitudes. These individuals expect to carve their own niche in life succeeding through their own ability to exert themselves and their ideas and because they possess the courage of their convictions. They pay little attention to their conservative associates. Aries has a strong desire to broaden the scope of his experiences and generally will always have a distinctive philosophy of life, based not on an understanding of others, but on an urge to expand his own consciousness. The forcefulness of Mars found in Aries can produce boundless ambitions and can lead to the person seeking adventure. In fact, this person is often more refreshed by new sensations than by a period of rest. The main need is to slow down, pace yourself, and channel the vitality of Mars into worthwhile projects.

Aries Occupation

Resolute, determined, and ambitious for success, Aries aspire to be pioneers whether in the intellectual, business, civic, or military world. You have a love for independent thinking and action. You have an intense desire for freedom, positive forces, and impulses which increase your mental vitality. This not only produces but inspires activity, energy, resourcefulness, originality and inventive ability. You desire more than anything else to be recognized as an authority (on a wide range of topics) in order to be able to exercise your ability to organize and administer your affairs without taking orders or obtaining directions from others. You are eager to hold the reins of power in your hands, and with your capacity for sustained physical work, this often makes you the controlling element in complex situations.

Aries are not psychologically well equipped to be drones performing routine, dull, or monotonous tasks. You seldom enjoy coping with details, preferring a position where you can delegate these more tedious chores to others. Aries are known for originality and imagination, great mental and nervous energy, and for preferring work that requires these traits while providing an opportunity for advancement. You require endeavors that challenge your mind and your creative spirit. You become frustrated when working at a job requiring routine, repetitive tasks, even to the point of becoming rebellious and hostile. You perform best when working in a position that allows you to work on your own, directing others, and finding outlets for your talents and boundless energies. You have a strong aversion for all bonds, limitations or restrictions, preferring to be free to explore and pioneer into new areas of thought and activity. Seek these situations out. Don't settle for less than what you can achieve, or you will be unhappy in the long run. Aspire to success in all that you wish to accomplish. Only then can you realize your dreams.

Aries are excellent at communication and persuasion. Others love to listen to you talk, finding inspiration and insight in the energy of your convictions whether well-grounded or not. People believe in what you say, because you believe in yourself. You excel in all activities requiring quick thought, public speaking to groups, and impromptu speeches or conversations. Male or female, you perform well in occupations such as journalism, television and radio broadcasting, advertising, public relations, publishing, or promoting. Because of your strong drive for tangible goals, you excel as financiers and businessmen and in the arts and the entertainment fields as well.

Aries, influenced by Mars, is well-suited for military careers most particularly in the army rather than the navy or air force. But you prefer to be in command or at least in a leadership position. The Mars influence also produces skilled doctors, surgeons, nurses, and mining engineers, as well as persons skilled in refining and handling non-precious metals. Another well-aspected occupational field is law enforcement.

Many Aries are drawn to the field of literature becoming writers of fiction, poets, novelists and essayists. Persons of this sign make excellent lawyers and judges as their sense of justice and equality in many instances outweighs personal prejudices. And, of course, your arguments, being quick and to the point, carry much influence. Lovers of science, art and music, Aries are naturally gifted and may become talented architects and inventors. The self-assertive Aries, being an excellent conversationalist, make fine clerks, traveling salesmen, speculators, bankers, and brokers. You are very enthusiastic and exhibit great determination to win in whatever endeavor that holds your attention.

Real estate is another field in which Aries find successes. Aries consciously feel an advantage to acquiring and owning property. It was this restless search for new land that led many Aries pioneering West into new territories.

While Aries can be impulsive, you are serious about your business affairs and can be hard-headed and conservative in financial matters. You make successful financiers, being fast to grasp opportunities. You may spend money (preferably cash) for tangible assets which add to the value of what you all ready own. Being cunning and shrewd, you have a talent for making money, although, at least early in life, you may not have the talent of saving or spending wisely because you have a pronounced tendency to be rather extravagant and to spend freely. You are appreciative of physical pleasures and will spend money to stay in shape and to keep your body in good health in order to make the most of this adventure called life. The Aries individual has a pronounced fondness for travel, music, painting, sculpture, decorative art, singing, poetry, theater, entertainment, and you may well excel in sports.

You are generously endowed with natural gifts that aid you in your vocation. Learn to use these gifts. You have a keen intellect, initiative, intuition, inventiveness, energy, leadership ability, and enthusiasm. However, the Aries tendency toward impatience, not planning ahead, spending unwisely, and being bossy and domineering can easily offset your strong points. You must make every effort to develop self-constraint in order to succeed. Others will guide you, too, if you will learn to listen to their advice.

The Aries ego requires constant approval, compliments, praise, and attention. Without it, your efficiency and productivity declines. This need for positive reinforcement can be satisfied if you learn the value of intrinsic appreciation. In other words, your achievements become the rewards rather than the rewards being the words or praise from others. This reinforcement comes from within with a job well-done. Do this often enough, and your pride in your accomplishments will become real. And others will recognize and realize your abilities also.

The Aries inclination to boast and exhibit strong self-confidence, making claims to your ability to handle complex, unfamiliar tasks, rather than admitting a lack of knowledge or ability, can eventually result in a failure to produce results. Aries has the ability to convince and impress others with his strong self-confidence. You believe in yourself and what you say and you seldom admit defeat or faults. This is not a bluff or an out-and-out lie. Rather, it's the Aries trait that thrives on challenge; and remember, you are convinced that you can do anything. But sooner or later, you must follow through with your plans and aspirations.

This unconscious drive to compensate for your doubts about your abilities and your insecurities can hurt you in the long run. Strive to eliminate or at least control your penchant to attempt those tasks for which you are inadequately trained, or to bite off more than you can chew. You can do this by acquiring and developing an emotional balance of patience, self-discipline and the perseverance to stay at one task long enough to learn the requisite skills to allow yourself to excel and advance.

When well-positioned at the head of an undertaking, for example in the business world, you display creative drive and energy. Being adventuresome and ambitious, you should strive to associate with more conservative individuals who, while appreciating your strengths, would restrain your impulsive nature to make quick decisions. Benefit from the conservative nature of others. If nothing else, at least take into consideration what they have to say. You and they approach problems differently, but each of you can contribute to the outcome and eventual success of a project or an endeavor.

As a rule, you have an unusual executive ability, but, having great confidence and self-esteem, you tend to overestimate your powers and to become too enthusiastic and even reckless in your desire to succeed. Watch that you don't go down with your own ship. You have a strong dislike for all bonds, limitations and restrictions, preferring to be free to explore and pioneer into new ideas and activities. Your strong self-interest will inspire you to push forward in all your endeavors with very little outside encouragement or stimulus. You are self-motivated.

It is not unusual for Aries to change his pursuits during their lifetime and to have two very different occupations or careers. Aries, be confidant that you can expect prosperity through industry, diligence, hard work and perseverance. But remember also that you require an incentive. You must feel you have a goal you are working toward.

How to Find Your Soul-Mate, Stars, and Destiny

Aries Marriage

Aries men and women are extremely intense in their love relationships. This is due to Aries being at the head of the Fire sign, and ruled by Mars. They crave affection and sympathy and constant attention and praise. You may be more affectionate than passionate, but you have insatiable sexual desires. If you don't receive the requisite sexual pleasures and attention at home than you have no inhibitions about finding it elsewhere. This combined with your head-strong, impulsive nature provides the setting for the tempest in your many stormy relationships. Although you may be rash, you are most likely to sow your wild oats early in life and then to settle down with a person who you have carefully selected as your perfect mate. But you may find marriage similar to a balancing act, and you must mentally control your frankness and cultivate the art of give-and-take in order to maintain your balance.

Aries, usually so independent and cool, can be unexpectedly sentimental about their feelings for family and traditions. Being deeply rooted in your instincts, you long for a comfortable home and companion so that you can be coddled like a baby. This may be an idealized memory or fond thoughts saved from childhood that continue to plague your thoughts making you yearn to return from your travels and far-flung pursuits to the family hearth and to the warm, open arms of a loving, accepting companion.

The Aries nature infinitely requires great depth and dimension in love and marriage. Your strong opinions and idealism demand total loyalty and sexual fidelity from your partner or mate, even though the male doesn't hold himself to the same standards. You are likely to be extremely jealous, at the same time resenting jealously from the person who you love.

In order to make a total commitment, Aries, both male and female, have their respective criteria. Aries males demand a loyal woman who is submissive, dependent, and preferable one who appears helpless. In fact, a helpless woman attracts this man. And understand, that if he wants a particular woman he is attracted to, he will claim she is helpless. Then, because he is always right, he will go to great lengths to prove to her that, indeed, she is the helpless female in need of him. And he is there to save her. In order to feel successful in a domestic role, the male Aries must be the supportive-protective, dominant man who is in total control. This control must be in all areas of the family life, and most especially over every aspect of his partner's life. After all, this is the helpless female that he saved. She must relinquish all control to him in her appreciation of his attentions. Not only that, but he must receive total admiration, praise and flattery in order to remain the ideal lover or husband. And while he may stay with his wife, the slightest affront will give him the incentive he needs to head out the door looking for another woman to stroke his ego. Quite possibly, the Aries male with his self-doubts, insecurities and anxieties over his own masculinity demands this total submissive-female to soothe his strong ego or to reinforce and prop it up. Of course, to a lesser degree, males of other signs can also be beset by the same fears and negative qualities. In spite of his controlling nature, the Aries male, who strives to be a good provider, is likely to be an excellent, ideal husband in every sense except sexual fidelity. Expect him, generally speaking, to engage in numerous extramarital affairs.

However, don't expect these purely physical, casual affairs to be a threat to the marriage. The Aries male adheres to the double-standard: what is good for the gander is definitely not good for the goose. Intensely jealous, he tolerates no infidelities in sexual behavior from his wife.

However, you, the passionate female Aries, once a commitment is made, and you fall in love and marry, you make a total commitment including sexual fidelity. You too demand certain standards, requirements, and the necessary criteria from your chosen man before your love-life is complete. You are charming, physically attractive, sexy, and desirable, knowing how to use your charms and beauty to enhance your desires and get what you want from your many admirers and later from your husband. You know that you have much to offer a man, and, therefore, you pick and choose carefully, making an effort to find the right man; or unfortunately, all too often, who you think is the right man. (Remember, your tendency to misjudge people.)

The female Aries, with her strong personality, believes she can contribute and help the man she loves. Because of this, you are likely to select a man who is weaker than you, who you can dominate and who will allow you to be the boss. This can lead to domestic tragedy for you cannot be happy for long with a man who you do not respect. Once you realize that you are not merely guiding, but dominating your husband, you lose all respect for him. However, if you take the time to choose carefully rather than making a quick decision, if you marry a man who is right for you, you will make an exceptional wife. For you are a woman who considers marriage a never ending adventure, a complete partnership, in which you fully expect to carry your share of the responsibilities. You exert every effort and energy to work toward a successful marriage going so far as to place your husband's welfare and interests above your own. Your main requirements are to receive expressions of appreciation, love, and affection that make you feel wanted, admired and adored. You also demand to be sexually appreciated and satisfied.

Both Aries men and women may experience difficulties in marriage. You may discover yourself unhappily married because you rarely find partners who truly understand and appreciate your nature and your temperament. If you are not divorced in the first part of life, your marriage will survive throughout your life. Marriage is a precarious venture for Aries individuals. Although you make ideal companions, Aries people know little about domestic affection and tranquillity. The best choice of mates are those born under the sign of Libra and next Gemini. Ideally, such marriages generally produce more happiness. Marriage to another Aries can be good but may produce troublesome children.

The Aries Man

You, the Aries male, possess a very strong determination, a courageous spirit, a power of command and execution, ambition, enterprising spirit, combativity, a love of independence, and an overwhelming desire to be active and to lead. The brave, daring, and adventuresome Aries male is frank and outspoken to a fault, generously extravagant, and possesses a most stubborn, strong will to the point of becoming quarrelsome and petulant. You are well-informed, industrious, and ingenious, but rather limited in your knowledge of human character. You are opinionated in the areas of religion, politics, and social issues and would be the one most likely to rebel or crusade against existing institutions and limiting social constraints. In matters related to religion, you are broad-minded within the bounds of convention; however, you quite probably believe in believing rather than conforming.

In all matters, you may change your viewpoint and perspective, but you adamantly believe in your ideas and beliefs while you hold them. You are most remarkable for your quick thinking and your ability to act quickly. Although you may be somewhat bigoted, you are generally progressive in your thoughts and beliefs.

Aries wants to be first in all areas of his life. He transcends from ideas to action with hardly a backward glance. Your pioneering, adventurous spirit is rarely too discouraged to begin fresh or to start anew. Nor are you likely to outgrow your innate capacity to stake a claim and then move on, seeking ever greener pastures and loftier heights, and leaving the tedious chores of completion to others. As a result, you may find yourself missing out on the results of your own labor. Your reach greedily and avidly for your desires only to abandon them, leaving them by the wayside when unforeseen difficulties arise.

The Aries male remains absolutely confident in himself, his abilities and his present ideas and projects. You have no doubts about your ability to succeed at a plan. Even when shaken to the depths of despair by a crisis or personal setback, you remain self-assured. This attribute above all others, may be what attracts people to you and what gains you admiration from others. It is this confidence in yourself that influences others to believe in your ideas and to follow your lead.

It may appear that people, to you, are no different than things as you have a tendency to consider them in the context in which you deal with them. This makes you seem heartless at times, unless others understand your psychology. And this can be a difficult thought-pattern to follow for it seems that people are expendable; that it's acceptable to forfeit people in order to achieve the completion of the tasks or your success at an endeavor. In order to understand this psychology, consider that you are capable of combining the absolute extreme of freedom from superficial social conditioning. You resent all forms of criticism but you can respond to logic, reason and proof. That is unless you decide to overrule logic and proof believing that your ideas are right and others simply either don't know what they're talking about or are plotting against you.

You crave affection, attention and sympathy, but you may be unhappy in your domestic situation because of an inability to meet a woman who understands your nature. You seldom understand a woman very well and you continue to make mistakes in your dealings with women. Your sexual drive is strong and you prefer a very feminine, kind, soft, romantic, docile, generous and submissive female who is willing to forfeit all control to you. And you are more than willing to go to great lengths to find such a woman.

Your greatest desire is to be the leader, professionally, at home, and socially. Endowed with great mental energy, your greatest happiness seems to come from overcoming obstacles, succeeding at work, and leading others. There is no height to which you cannot succeed providing you keep your head about you. Success, though, in many instances can be your undoing. It can quite easily result in an over-inflated ego which prevents you from assessing your situation correctly. Study the facts and pay less attention to the flattery and praise from others. Remember, others are astute enough to know that flattery will get them everywhere with you. Tactless rejection of those who don't always agree with you, prevents you from attaining insights. Patience, my dear man, is a virtue.

The Aries Woman

The Aries woman, sensitive, caring, kind and independent, handles responsibilities well in various situations both personally and professionally. Whether at home or on the job, you are not timid about accepting new roles or assignments. You thirst for achievement and success, and are often praised for your enterprising nature. You have a strong desire to outshine others in your field.

You enjoy physical activity and may excel at sports. No sloucher, you are considered to be hardworking. You are both diligent and industrious, and you are known for you ability to organize. You are often wonderfully helpful to your friends and family, offering both advice, time, and lending a hand, even when you'd rather stay uninvolved. You prefer those around you to be active and busy. This is most especially true in your home and with your family. You love art and bright colors and enjoy searching for new and lovely items for your home. Modest and practical, you have few children, but you take excellent care of them, raising them in a loving, caring, and secure environment. If childless, you shower your attention on your nieces and nephews and the children of your friends. You love a good argument, but you never forget your well-polished manners which makes you better, in this respect, than the male Aries. All you really want in regards to your love life, is to find a man stronger than you, capable of dominating your strong, independent nature. As a wife, you are very dedicated, but be very careful in your marriage as you require not only appreciation but abundant affection to be happy.

There is one great obstacle that stands in the way of the Aries woman--that green-eyed creature called jealousy. This one pervasive fault has resulted in more unhappiness and heartache coming into the lives of the female Aries than any other they may possess. The Aries woman is extremely charming, possessing an entertaining and pleasing personality, except for this one negative trait. Jealousy can blind you from enjoying life; and if it were not for jealousy, you would otherwise have a beautiful temperament. You lose too much energy through anger, impatience, and a quick temper. These traits become an emotional drain on your other more remarkable abilities with which you are naturally gifted. To master these negative traits, you must diligently develop self-control or risk never attaining a true peace of mind. This will require a great deal of effort on your part because it won't come quickly or naturally; it goes against your grain not to respond quickly and often sharply. Stop sometimes and think. Practice schooling your mind to master and control your body and your impulses and compulsions. Possessing as you do a great will power, learn to use it to overcome your weaker tendencies by training your higher nature to rule and dominate. When this is accomplished, you will find joy, happiness and tranquillity, and abundant peace and prosperity.

Your intellect underscores your ability to speak effectively, but you have a inclination to recognize only your own viewpoint, your perspective. You may have a tendency to resort too quickly to argumentative or clever remarks thus offending the other person. With effort, you can control your stubbornness and your propensity to out talk others in a conversation. Learning to listen more and to talk a little less will benefit you by giving you insights into the interpersonal relationships with others who you must deal with on a daily basis. Learn to organize your ideas, concentrate your thoughts, and hold your tongue long enough to generate the power which comes from mental control and restraint.

The Aries woman does well in the professional areas of art, design, writing, sales, and management. Any position that requires a quick mind and a person who is unafraid of making decisions. You are highly capable of holding positions of authority, trust and responsibility. Remember, you are impatient and become irritable when criticized or limited by narrow, stifling rules and regulations. It is best that you have a thorough understanding of your undertaking, the task at hand, and then that you are left alone to carry out the task with your own methods.

Aries Love Life

The first-sign Aries natives, both male and female, are passionate, possessing a strong sex drive and a healthy appetite that demands variety. They have a strong libido and are headstrong and impetuous in love and romance. For you, sex is a pleasurable, transient pastime requiring only a brief commitment on the physical level rather than a strong emotional commitment. While romance includes sex, you also require an element of companionship and mutual respect, of liking the other person and of sharing an experience beyond the purely physical.

Love, on the other hand, is something entirely different. In your realm, for there to be real love in your life, you require full commitment and acceptance of emotional responsibility. Therefore, there are three distinct categories that fit within your love life. (1) You jump impulsively into an endless series of sexual adventures producing no emotional scars for either partner, or (2) you're less interested in casual romance, and (3) demand more than just passing pleasure or a sexual outlet. Unless Aries individuals learn self-control, numerous troubling situations, inconveniences, problems and annoyances are brought on by their involvement with the opposite sex, to whom they are strongly attracted physically, enjoying the sexual experience almost as much as success in other endeavors.

With the sign of self-expression in the house of pleasures, you gain personal satisfaction in the creation of spectacular effects which often produce dramatic results. You ardently desire praise and approbation, craving applause for what you consider one of your remarkable accomplishments. This urge to outshine, to stand first, may impel you to seek shortcuts perhaps through rash actions, speculation and gambling with chance. However, often these actions are designed for entertainment and, while others may question your actions, they do not jeopardize your basic sense of security. Your tendency to indulge in love affairs is often for the sake of ego-gratification and to gain even more praise and adulation.

The Aries desire is to share life with others. You crave seeing yourself reflected in someone else's affectionate and admiring gaze while at the same time you wish to have an influence over that person's thought process and behavior, right down to how the other person dresses. In your love life, you have a tendency to keep your deeper feelings well hidden and to repress the tender side of your nature. Generally speaking, you are more sensual than sentimental, and even though you have hidden depths of passion, you do not openly discuss your love life. You have the capacity to keep the different aspects of your life in distinct compartments, and you may be unaware of your own unconscious motives. Your active mind has so little time for introspection that you push your feelings into the background to prevent them from interfering with current projects. Then you are surprised, as is everyone else, that these suppressed elements break into the open in the form of sudden impulses and compulsive urges. Aries, attempt to restrain your libido, focusing your energies into socially acceptable channels of expression. You have the ability to renew yourself through sex and physical activity, but you should make an effort to reduce the number of incidental romantic affairs in your life.

The erotic overtones of your life are caused to a large extent by your enthusiasm, your spur of the moment inspirations, and the attraction to you of all things youthful. In love affairs, romance is sustained by this same charming impulsiveness, but often times it is too inconsistent for enduring affection. You not only enjoy but thrive on excitement, and you are known for starting new affairs before the last one is concluded. The excitement and joy you discover in your numerous amorous affairs may fill you with intense passions, but they rapidly lose their appeal. You may be in love with love, and you may find yourself searching throughout your life for new sensations, new romances, replenished love, until you finally come to the realization that continual gratification rarely guarantees real and lasting satisfaction. Aries, you must be careful not to become a slave to your own desires. You can never truly be the master of your own destiny, in control of your own fate, until you master controlling yourself, your whims, and your libido. That your list of accomplishments also includes your long list of sexual conquests only impresses you.

Aries Children

The Aries child can be difficult to manage unless there is an understanding of his nature which requires reason, love and kindness. They demand a reason and explanation for everything being stubborn and self-willed. Generally, they excel in school, perhaps because of their ambitions, retentive memories, and quick-thinking abilities. The Aries child is restless, inquisitive and prying. They are seldom content with one thing for any length of time. This child should be left to work out their tasks in their own way in order to develop individuality.

A calm and quiet talk at bedtime is the best method of correction for the Aries child. Physical punishment can be very harmful for them and should seldom if ever be used. An abundance of love and praise is the only influence that can gain control over these children. They should not be coerced, tormented, scolded, abused, or punished corporally. Kindness and gentleness accomplishes much more and they should be protected from excitement and unstable conditions. They do better in loving, secure environments offering a comforting routine which also provides an outlet for their inquisitive natures. Do not interfere with their endeavors or they will quickly lose interest and move on to another activity. Excessive constraint, may force them out of the secure home environment into the world before they are ready, causing them to enter into hasty marriages or in extreme cases to become involved in crime. Their stubbornness and determination results in them insisting upon carrying out their ideas regardless of the cost or consequences to themselves or others. Allow them some leeway, some freedom, in making their own mistakes and learning the hard way because they are not going to listen to a lot of verbal advice. Discover an interest, and encourage it, so that the active Aries mind can stay occupied. And while their interests may jump around from one activity to another, be patient and encourage these various interests. Verbal criticism is a waste of time. Patiently model correct behavior in a loving manner.

These chidden are happy and lively but can also be mischievous, requiring kindness and understanding more than strict authority from their parents. It may appear that they are more accident prone than the average child, and have more incidental, unexplainable accidents; and even little girls are somewhat more active and rebellious. The Aries child may find choosing a career difficult as their active minds jump from one idea to another. They possess an innate vitality and a love for nature and outdoor adventure. They love to discover mysterious places and seem to fear nothing (but watch out for those accidents). They exhibit an interest in animals and the natural environment, loving to learn all they can about not only these subjects but the universe beyond as well. While they may appear insensitive, they are easily hurt if they don't receive adequate attention, love and affection from their parents. The Aries child has the most sensitive nature of all the Zodiac signs.

Relationships with Other Signs

The ardent Aries nature is affectionate, demonstrative, generous in praise and affection, with a preference for love and admiration. You are warm-hearted, passionate and attracted to friends of the opposite sex as well as friendships and associations with the same sex. You excel at group situations, being entertaining and gregarious. You are a natural host, ever attentive to the needs of your guests. You love social functions, entertaining at home and in public, outdoor festivities, sports events, and any occasion or celebration providing the promise of a festive crowd. You have a keen sense of enjoyment, pleasures, fun and adventure.

You may have two types of friends: those with whom you associate in business; and others with whom you feel free to share your broader interests. You are attracted to people intellectually rather than sentimentally, and you may get along well with eccentrics, appreciating their talents and new ideas, and with others who share your strong opinions. Your personal insights and ideas often appear progressive, sometimes too much so to your social groups, and you need to watch that your liberal attitudes don't make you a disruptive element, allowing you to lead your many followers down the wrong path.

An afflicted Saturn in Aries may result in bringing about feelings of inadequacy which effects the personal area of friendship. These people may inadvertently react against strict limitations by becoming disciplinarians and by asserting themselves in aggressively authoritarian actions. And, a driving ambition may often work against harmony in interpersonal relationships. This person may be less sociable than other Aries, being overly dogmatic and exerting a certain aloofness in their desire to exercise control and command over others.

Aries does well with the moderating characteristics of the native Leo. And you can expect to establish positive relations with those born under the sign of Gemini and Aquarius.

Do not entertain high expectations for relations with persons born under the sign of Virgo who have a critical nature which, as has been mentioned, Aries can't tolerate. And relationships with Scorpio can lead to violent encounters while Libra attraction is primarily physical. Cancer and Capricorn relationships are infrequent in that they don't share your perception of life and the world. You may find Taurus and Pisces individuals easier to deal with professionally. Aries may be compatible with each other, but often these relations may become somewhat monotonous and, if romantic, may produce negative sexual attractions.

The many strong attributes of the Aries personality leads to popularity. You have many friends and associates. You may possibly have an early or hasty marriage or marriages and a long string of casual, sexual relationships.

You will find the most enduring and rewarding friendships with those born between July 21 and August 20-27; from November 21 to December 20-27; and also from September 21 to October 20-27. Aries have unusually strong will power and great obstinacy of purpose leading them to form strong and lasting friendships with certain individuals who are endowed with the abilities to admire their strengths while overlooking their strong dispositions.

Beware making enemies. It is not unusual for the arrogant Aries to be subject to exile in a foreign country or to be restrained in forced seclusion necessitating escape and flight from enemies. Enemies are found in the religious, legal and publishing fields, and are numerous but not formidable to the undauntable Aries. However, the most powerful enemies abound in foreign countries or are from foreign countries and will make every effort to harm or molest the Aries individual. It is quite possible that you will be the cause of your own death or downfall if you aspire to martyrdom or fight to boldly for what you perceive as worthy causes.

Aries Sexuality

That subject which interests us all: our own personal sexuality. Why does a person feel the way they do? Why does he or she like a certain person and not another? What arouses a person and why? On some level, these questions influences one and all. Like all aspects of our lives and lifestyles, the public attitude toward sex is ever changing and evolving. From the restrictive taboos of the Victorian Age, through the revitalization of the Industrial Age, to the make love not war of the 1960s to the commercialism of the 1980s and the 1990s, sex is always on our minds. Will the Age of Information or the Age of Aquarius bring new insights?

The American culture is not only influenced by popular trends and thought but by its unique cultural diversity as well. To the newcomer or newly arrived, American society can appear perplexing. What is difficult to understand is that in this freedom-based culture, the individual is literally free to be whoever he or she decides. And the gamut runs from the most traditional, reserved, cautious, and sexually repressed individuals to others who flaunt their sexuality, centering their lives around their sexual habits. Perhaps it is because of this very diversity that our culture makes some attempt not to be overly offensive to the sensitivities of some while giving a tolerant nod to the liberties of others. We are totally free, within the guidelines of laws, to seek divine enlightenment or to destroy ourselves with pleasures. Americans have the freedom to choose, individually, what importance their sexual behavior will play in their lives.

That being the case, sex is recognized by every serious discipline--from psychologists to scientists to astrologers--as being a central focus on individual lives. Freud saw sex as an influence on every aspect of the individual life. And from the sexist boys in the locker room to the most enlightened of intellectuals, sex remains a fundamental part of life that cannot be ignored. Get two friends together and the subject eventually turns to sex, romance, or marriage. One can blame it on the media, but sooner or later discussing the stock market gets boring, but sex never does.

There are those who hold to the theory that the primary function of sex is to have children and any other consideration is secondary. There are others for whom sex is an integral part of life, providing one of the greatest stress relievers ever invented. That all other living species procreate seasonally points to the reasoning of the second theory. But all pleasures (or temptations) in life also promote the possibilities of problems and health concerns unless a little logic is also applied.

Astrologically, the sexual nature has been examined from the Garden of Eden to the lives of contemporary celebrities. And what every serious astrologer will say is that how the individual relates to sexuality is not based on the Sun sign alone. The entire chart must be examined because each person is a unique combination of Sun, Moon, Ascendant, Planets, Houses and aspects. A comparison of two charts often sheds light on compatibility. Compatibility between two people is often found when the Sun sign is in the same sign as their lover's Ascendant, or vice versa. Opposite Sun signs or an opposite Sun sign and Ascendant may also blend well together.

In a woman's chart, the placement of Venus is indicative of her sexuality while the position of Mars and the Sun indicates what kind of man she is attracted to. In a man's chart, the position of Mars tells how he relates to women, and the position of Venus and the Moon indicates what type of woman arouses him. In comparing two charts, look for the aspects of conjunction, sextile, square, trine, and oppositions. Remember that oppositions can blend. The square brings differences but much energy while conjunctions can be beneficial. The sextile and trine bring harmony. When a person's Venus and their lover's Mars are in the same sign, there is a strong attraction even if differences of opinions occur. When Venus and the other person's Ascendant are in the same sign, it adds to the sexual compatibility. Venus in the lover's Sun sign brings a mutual interest while Mars in the lover's Moon sign is emotionally intense.

There is a vast variety of people found within each Sun sign, but basic characteristics and traits do exist. However, generalizations are just that and a fuller picture of the individual is reflected by the complete chart. The following section deals with Sun sign sexuality in a general manner. While the importance of sex remains the same in each Sun sign, the focus and attitudes vary.

Aries Sexuality - Man

Influenced by Mars, the Aries man has fiery emotions and is driven by strong physical desires. He is aggressive, pioneering and lustful for adventure. Sex is an integral part of life and rates high on the list of experiences and priorities to the Aries man. This man creates excitement and a casual nod or smile aimed at him will be perceived as holding sexual overtones. He can be selfishly ego-driven, thinking that every woman wants him and that every woman is there for his needs.

An Aries man can be brilliantly attentive, flattering, generous, and extremely difficult to resist especially once he sets his mind on a conquest. If he desires a woman sexually, he pursues her tirelessly until she relents. He believes in himself and will in all earnestness tell a woman he is a real man. He thrives on experiences, challenge and novelty, wanting to sample one and all. He wants to be the leader in any endeavor and in any relationship with a woman will think, talk, and expect sex. His sexual appetite is enormous and he is ready at a moments notice to participate.

However macho may be the mask he shows the world, beneath this exterior is found a man who yearns for the embodiment of the perfect female and true, romantic love. He seeks another who will devote her life to him in a selfless, generous manner. And if she fails him in any manner, that is an excuse to continue the hunt for the perfect female for him. This man must have a relationship in his life, however, and he will seek a new one before ending his present affair.

Aries is the infant of the Zodiac, and this man wants to be babied, attended to, and cared for. He can be demanding especially sexually because he must have his gratification, repeatedly and frequently. The very sexual act stimulates him to want more if not from one woman than from another. An if rejected by one woman, he may continue his pursuit of her while actively engaged with another. Sex is an all consuming part of life to this lustful and energetic man.

This is the man who will want to change and recreate the woman in his life into the picture of perfection he holds in his mind. He will want her to have style, class and the kind of looks that turns the heads of other men. But he is intensely emotional, possessive, and jealous, and his woman must be faithful and loyal even though he isn't. As he matures and gains financial security, he may feel as if he has to buy the attentions of women, but this is fine with him as long as he is in control. In fact, he can be so controlling and demanding that he leaves the woman in his life with little time for independent activities. And if he feels neglected in any manner, his behavior can turn childish, producing the temper tantrums for which Aries is infamous. This man can easily allow his passions and his desires to preoccupy his life.

Any woman can entice his interest, but if he finds independent and intelligent women too difficult to pursue, he will turn to one less well educated or a younger woman who is easier to control and dominate. He needs a woman who will allow herself to be molded and who will want to become what he wants in order to please him. Aries is impulsive and impetuous, and wants what he wants when he wants it.

The Aries male is susceptible to attention, praise, adoration, and flattery. He may overlook the more timid types for those who also like attention. And to get his attention, simply ask his opinion or his advice. He loves to talk endlessly and to offer advice and assistance. He also wants to be recognized and thanked for his generosity.

The sign of Aries rules the head and face, and any attention to this part of the body brings results. Gentle caresses, stroking the head or playing with his ears will get his attention. He also loves to have his face massaged as well as his scalp, and if you buy him any kind of facial treatment like a soothing mask, he will know you are in love. Don't forget, however, how important sex is to this man. He doesn't seek unfilled promises, he wants the real thing. And he likes for the center of his sexuality to be admired as well which means that his lover should praise his penis, giving it lots of attention. If he thinks she yearns for him and is addicted to his erection, he will desire her all the more. This man stays where he is made the center of attention and affection by a person who adores him and learns how to make him happy.

Aries Sexuality - Woman

The Aries woman can be aggressive and seeks what she wants, but she is also caring, kind and generous. She desires the perfect lover and mate to whom she can devote her loving attention. She is exciting and independent, and she loves sex and her sexuality. She wants to explore the compelling curiosity she possesses regarding her personal sexuality and preferences and will invest in all the literature, tapes, and paraphernalia required to satisfy her interest in this captivating subject. Men fascinate her, and she is drawn to explore as many as possible until she finally decides upon Mr. Right. Once her passions are aroused, this is not a timid or inhibited woman. Her Mars sign brings intense emotions, a fiery nature, and unlimited energy to her love making. One of her greatest challenges in life, in fact, may be finding a man who can keep up with her energetic drive.

She seeks and desires the perfect man to be her true love and soul mate and to fulfill her lust for life. Her lover must be attentive and demonstrative to make her happy. And an unhappy Aries woman can be a miserable person to be around when her frustrations turn to complaining. Her temper is just as fiery as her male counterpart, but remember, Aries soon forgives and forgets. This woman wants to be admired and made the center of attention whether it's in the privacy of her own home or in public. And the more daring a sexual adventure is, the more it will excite her. She seeks change, new experiences, and novelty as well as various forms of erotica. Like the male Aries, she may interpret the most innocent of attentions as being sexually oriented, believing that any and all men desire and want her. And since Aries is never wrong and never makes a mistake, no one could possible convince her otherwise. She can be restless, impatient, and impulsive to satisfy her sexual desires. Uninhibited, she may find it easy to reach a climax, but this woman may be dissatisfied with just one. And, being Aries, she may demand multiply orgasms on a regular basis. In fact, her sexual releases may be the one area of life where she is able to allow herself total freedom and lack of self-control. In other words, she isn't one to hold back. She wants the total experience. Even the most intellectual of Aries women will relent when their sexual nature is aroused.

Being an assertive female isn't the easiest of roles in any society (unfortunately), and this woman who seeks the perfect man to understand, cherish and adore her is often faced with disappointments in love. Men don't seem to understand her. In fact, she can destroy the macho and ego of any man and turn him into her slave. When she does find her mate, she will either negate his faults, praising him and forever offering illustrations of how perfect he is, or she will accept that no one is perfect and she must learn to live with his good points as well as his faults. Because of her outgoing and pleasant nature, she is accustomed to being made the center of attention by adoring male fans, and she will desire that this type of attention continue with her lover. She can devote herself totally to her lover, but she will want his admiration and total attention in return. But let's not forget that she must have sex, and if her lover in any way fails her in this department, she may have no choice but to seek it elsewhere. This is after all, a modern woman who wants all life has to offer.

Many an Aries female will crave to heighten the sexual adventure by seeking new experiences in unusual places. Whether this be the local bar or exotic places, the hint of daring excitement propels her to seek that new experience. She is a relentless explorer, and to experience a passing affair with a newly acquired acquaintance may entice her passions. The active Aries intellect rationalizes away perversity which is a word promoted by the more conventional thinkers. One can't think social mores and new experiences at the same time. And her lover must accept that she needs exploration and innovation in life and especially in sex. This woman is unafraid to take on a younger lover, and in fact a younger man may be able to keep up with her sexual drive and energy without attempting to put her in her place as older men are tempted to do. The Aries woman by nature knows her proper place, and she doesn't need to be told what it is. She quite easily makes that distinction for herself.

Aries stick to tradition, style, and convention as long as it serves their purposes and agrees with their lifestyles. Any inconveniences or obstacles are pushed to one side, as this formidable female sets about getting all she wants from life and lovers. The love of her life will always be held most dearest in her heart, however. And this career woman knows how to compartmentalize marriage, home, and family into manageable departments. She is a woman of her own making and much to be admired. She is forever the independent leader of new ideas, pioneering where other woman only dream of going.

Aries Health

Aries diligently adhere to a policy of hard work. You may abandon yourself freely to the pursuit of pleasure, but when the fun is over, you devote yourself to your labors and accomplishments. You have an intense interest in meal planning, loving to concoct gourmet delicacies for your friends and family. You seldom eat or drink excessively, however, due to your high regard for your body. It is a valuable instrument, a temple, to be as well cared for as an expensive piece of equipment, and to be ready to return to work. Illnesses for you are a major inconvenience, slowing your progress, restricting your freedom of motion, and preventing you from performing at your best in your endeavors. Your enterprising spirit leads you to cultivate a muscular, athletic physique ready for action.

Aries may require an abundance of sleep as compared to people of other signs. Plan large, well-ventilated sleeping areas that provide a constant supply of fresh air. A deep, natural sleep as opposed to a drug-induced sleep provides the most refreshing mental and physical rest. Attempt to plan a regular routine or sleep pattern, also scheduling the remainder of your day between work and recreation. Because of your active mind and body, you may have a propensity for headaches, eye problems, inflammations, and minor irritations or skin rashes. Make every effort to curb your appetites for luxurious surroundings and foods, social outings and an over active lifestyle. Plan to eat regular, well-planned meals providing nourishing foods. And curb your sweet tooth! Needless to say, you need to avoid alcohol and drugs as these will only acerbate your high energy level. You need to take care of your physical and emotional needs. A proper diet does much to forestall depressions or other general upsets. Be sure to avoid worry and anxiety and straining your brain which is sure to upset your general health.

Mars in Aries increases the vitality and energy level, but if afflicted can result in hasty temperamental displays and in a danger from fire and scalding, surgical operations, fevers, mental complaints, vertigo, and accidents. This can result in a mark or scar to the head or face. Becoming angry only deters from your general health. Be cautious of cuts and wounds or other accidents to the eyes, head, hands, and feet; of falls; and of danger from fire and explosions, firearms, and machines in general. Be careful of health disorders resulting from flatulence, digestive problems, and internal disorders of an inflammatory nature.

Aries rules over the head and is in sympathy with the stomach and kidneys. It is these parts of the body that are most susceptible to diseases. In particular, Aries are prone to colds, catarrh, high fevers, headaches, and problems with the eyes, ears, and teeth. You may frequently suffer from insomnia, convulsions, congestion, ruptures of blood vessels in the brain, dizziness and spasmodic pains in the head. There are possibly problems with trouble with eczema, ringworms, neuralgia, sunstroke, stomach, kidney and liver troubles, nervous prostration, paralysis and other ailments resulting from nervous conditions. Discords in the domestic situation, such as frequent squabbles, may result in sick headaches. Troubles resulting from worry, anger, jealousy, impatience, and lack of physical exercise can easily develop. Calmness, self-analysis, exerting self-control, meditation and some form of regular, physical exercise can overcome these tendencies. Fresh air, daily walks, or even a break in your routine such as short trips in the country, can be beneficial. Provided that physical mishaps and accidents are avoided, Aries possess enough vitality and energy to insure a long and most interesting life. When the end does come, it is usually sudden, since Mars in Aries refuses to put up with illness, disability, or slow decline. Herbs beneficial to this sign are mustard, eye-bright, bay and others of a pungent nature.

History of Aries

Early Babylonian zodiacs did not include the Ram. It did exist, however, in Egypt where it was considered exceptionally important. And the Ram in early Egyptian times apparently did represent the constellation that later came to be called Aries. The Ram was the sacred animal of the god Amun, after whom many pharaohs were named: Tutankh-Amun, Amun-hotep, Amun-em-het. Amun was originally the Hidden One or the Unknown Force, an expression which might mean either the life-force or the ‚most high god'. The concept of a universal, all knowing god was known in Egypt and India prior to the time that monotheism evolved and eventually ripped religions into warring sects.

Before the rulerships of the twelve signs were allotted to the planets, they were ruled by gods or spiritual powers. In Plato's time, Aries was ruled by Athena, the warlike goddess who sprang fully armed from the head of Zeus, so it follows that Aries rules the head. Athena was also goddess of wisdom and the inventor of weaving; she was not a single-minded entity such as Mars, the Roman god of war. The Greek name, Ares, has no connection with the Latin word, Aries which means ram. The Old Testament describes how, among the Jewish settlements, a lamb was sacrificed in every home at the time of the Passover. Its blood was sprinkled over the door in order that the Lord would "pass over" and not smite the house. The Bible describes the anger of Moses when he came down from the mountain top and discovered the people bowing before a golden calf. The shocking aspect of this sight was not the worship of the animal, but that the sacrifice of the he-lamb had been initiated among the children of Israel, and now they were regressing to the Egyptian cult of Apis, the bull, which, of course, was a belief that should have been abandoned after the Exodus from Egypt. However, even in Egypt, the worship of Apis was becoming the religion of Amen-Ra, the ram-headed god of the Hidden Sun. The bull and ram cults existed concurrently. It was the priests of Egypt, Chaldea and Greece who invested the signs, planets, houses, and aspects with their commonly accepted and applied significance and meaning.

How to Find Your Soul-Mate, Stars, and Destiny

Aries

March 21 - April 20

The Thebaic Calendar

Character, Personality, and Destiny

The Thebaic Calendar represents the daily notes that the ancient astrologers wrote on burnt stones or papyrus. This is an easy and fast way to find information pertaining to your birth date. The native will often find his characteristics and destiny around his date of birth.

Whether Aries is a person's Sun sign, the Ascendant, on the cusp, or found in a House, the characteristics of Aries are evident. Each sign of the Zodiac represents certain characteristics, and Aries is the sign in which the Sun is exalted, indicating that the Sun bestows upon Aries the principle of new beginnings. Aries, the first sign, occurs in the Spring and therefore is indicative of the beginning of a new cycle.

DUALITY: Masculine   **ELEMENT:** Fire   **QUALITY:** Cardinal   **RULER:** Mars

The characteristics of Aries are manifested through a powerful psychological drive for the individual to prove himself or herself through action. Aries is a Cardinal Fire sign resulting in an enthusiasm by the individual which manifests itself with a strong desire to impulsively rush into physical, mental, or emotional action. The sign of Aries represents not only enthusiasm but raw energy as if solar powered and an impulsiveness bordering on the militant which can be either seen as rash or courageous. Aries is not a timid sign, and it becomes evident that this raw energy must be in some manner focused and channeled in order for the individual to be productive. There is within the Aries individual an innate feeling or desire to be in authority--to be the leader--almost as if this person were born to rule through a natural superiority. While Aries can be most charming and charismatic, there is found a tendency to use aggressiveness and even force, if necessary, to get one's own way. In other words, the patient use of diplomacy and tact may be attributes the Aries individual must strive to cultivate. When an Aries fails to learn the art of persuasion in their desire to be in charge, they can appear pompous and foolish to others. None the less, the Aries-born remains undaunted. His strong will power and inability to admit defeat, let alone a fault, sees him through any difficulties and any resulting failures. Having been hopelessly shot down into the depths of despair, Aries will turn around and simply apply his or her energy to a new plan, endeavor, or enterprise--especially if such an activity hints at adventure. He is inspiringly unquenchable in his ability to renew himself and his energies. The highly competitive nature of Aries compels him to be recognized as the best and the first, or he is not in the least interested in being involved. On top of that, he wants the recognition that comes with being first--whatever is accomplished is due to Aries; whatever fails is the fault of the other person involved.

Being a Cardinal sign, Aries possesses a need for change and for new experiences both physical and mental which can either be seen as a positive trait or a negative one depending on how the individual focuses this desire. When this desire for new experiences or new plans is not focused, the individual may jump from one idea to another with a tendency not to see his or her plans through to completion. However, when this abundant energy and desire is focused and channeled into an orderly productivity, the individual's abilities to develop new plans and direct change are most beneficial. The pioneering and undaunting adventurous spirit of the Aries individual can be an invaluable personal trait and asset. Needless to say, the same thing can be said about the, at times, uncontrollable impulsiveness of Aries, which added to their apparent selfishness--they are of course the center of their own universe--deters them from the ability to fully appreciate one love at a time. It is almost as if Aries cannot slow down long enough to fully listen to or appreciate the needs or even the advice of another person. And when Aries finds him or herself in a situation that in any way limits or restricts him, he can become most restless, and that overpowering urge and need for change begin to stir within his very soul.

That is not to say that Aries cannot love. They love deeply and strongly, but their love is defined on their own terms. These are not individuals to be bound to a partnership in which they do not feel in charge of their personal situation. They must have a release for the immense energies, and they require a great deal of admiration from their romantic partners. Once that admiration so much as hints at fading, Aries loses interests, and before one relationship is ended will begin looking for another. This need to be admired and appreciated as well as loved both emotionally and physically underlies the most basic desires of an Aries individual. There may be that Aries that stays in an unhappy relationship, but they will no doubt be seeking not only pleasure but approbation somewhere else.

Aries seeks opportunities for action, and if one is not forthcoming, the Aries originates his or her own plans of activity. He loves to plan whether it is a new project, a day shopping, or a night out on the town. Dinner at home will find Aries planning the menu and adding the final flourishes to the festive entertainment. It is a rare Aries who needs or waits for someone else to come up with an idea. This person has no need for outside stimuli to prod him into action. Aries does, however, seek and desire knowledge and information to feed their restless minds. This is the self-starter whose only need in life is an entourage of happy and willing followers in order for them to feel fulfilled, energized, and ready to begin anew. As a positive masculine sign, Aries is by nature aggressive, active, and capable of initiating change--it is the completion of one project before beginning another that may be the biggest challenge for the Aries individual. The sign of Aries is manifested as the new cycle, the resourceful pioneer who can be fearless in taking on a new enterprise or reenergizing one that others have given up on.

Each of the twelve signs of the Zodiac are allotted thirty degrees, but it must be remembered that not all Aries, for example, share the same intensity of these characteristics. Each sign is further divided into Decans of ten degrees each, and each Decan has been shown to exhibit the characteristics of its sign in varying strengths.

The First Decan

Within Aries, the first decan is designated as 0 degrees to 10 degrees of Aries and includes those individuals born between March 21 and March 30. The primary characteristic of these individuals is a need and desire to feed their ego and their self-esteem through recognition, praise, and admiration by either their partners, associates, friends, or lovers. When they receive this approbation, they strive through all their energies, actions, and efforts to live up to it. Born in the First Decan of Aries, this individual has a basic need to feel good about himself or herself, and this self-respect is gauged by the amount of appreciation they receive from others. They apply all of their energies into winning the approval of others. When this is done in a positive fashion, it produces admirable results. But reckless and impulsive Aries can also go the extra mile and ruin everything by over-doing. Their physical, mental, and emotional need for action and their impulsiveness, impatience, and fiery temper can just as well serve as a detriment to receiving the very praise and admiration they so desire--but no doubt they will obtain more than their share of attention with such actions and antics.

The Second Decan

The second decan is designated as from 10 degrees to 20 degrees of Aries and includes those individuals born between March 31 and April 9. The Second Decan bestows upon the individual an electrifying energy, a pronounced courage, and a strong self-confidence and self-reliance that impresses others. At the same time, this individual can be self-centered, self-serving, and an authoritative demigod who rules with a firm hand. They possess a strong will power which in many circumstances can be unbendable. The Second Decan Aries may be more recognizable as the person who possesses a tendency to see their plans through to completion. They also have the ability to round up their followers, inspire others to action, and oversee their plans, all the while remaining the central focus and the center of attention of any group. This Aries thrives on the thrill of excitement and adventure and new experiences--which includes and defines their romantic lives as well. They most desire prestige, position, recognition and, of course, admiration from others. Their ego drives them to compete and gain for themselves that which they most desire.

The Third Decan

The third decan is designated as being from 20 degrees to 30 degrees of Aries and includes those individuals born between April 10 and April 19. The Third Decan Aries may be perceived as being more refined and cultured than those of the first two Decans. There is a tendency for these individuals to pursue education, philosophy or perhaps theology. Less self-centered than other Aries, this individual may strive to better the community or to become recognized for public service. They remain natural leaders who are enterprising and creatively adept at organizing new plans. They retain all the natural energies of Aries as well and may be forever on the go seeking new outlets for their physical and mental energies. Being Aries, it goes without saying that they hold firmly to their personal beliefs and at their worst they must guard against being bigoted or narrow-minded. And of course, being Aries they thrive on recognition and the prestige it brings.

First Decan of Aries:

March 21 - March 30 - First Ten Days

Character, Personality and Temperament:

The primary characteristic of these individuals is a need and desire to feed their ego and their self-esteem through recognition, praise, and admiration by either their partners, associates, friends, or lovers.

Cardinal Element:

Fire: Daring; aggressive; egotistical; pride; impulsive; brisk; passions rise to brutal force; risky actions; fiery, hot spirit and temperament.

How to Find Your Soul-Mate, Stars, and Destiny

Destiny:

Gains and losses leads to violent dizzy heights and abrupt falling; resourceful attitude and everlasting energy.

Star Date of Birth: March 21

Fighting temperament, stubborn character. Serious difficulties to cope with all life. You are a resourceful and energetic individual who works hard but who is not overly successful at any one thing. You can be cunning, shrewd and even mysterious with a marked exotic approach and attitude toward your sexual relationships.

Star Date of Birth: March 22

Calm determination, self-esteem. Stubbornness. Dangerous adversaries. Your greatest difficulty is putting your creative ideas into action no matter how great your self-confidence. You are sexually self-assured and your sexual experiences feed your ego. Your lovers often remain loyal to you for lengthy periods, and you possess the ability to comfort those who have been emotionally hurt or rejected by others.

Star Date of Birth: March 23

Determination to lead and control without warnings and punishments. Delicate situations in life. You find the greatest satisfaction in creative endeavors. You possess a tendency toward unusual and unorthodox sexual practices. Those who are financially secure but emotionally insecure are drawn to you for comfort. You meet others who could enlighten you, but you have difficulty listening and attending to their messages.

Star Date of Birth: March 24

Brutal temperament; completely against contradiction. Tumultuous lifelong expeditions. But you are a natural at entertaining a crowd and tempting the temptress. Your romantic encounters add to your feelings of prestige and your aim to please is high even though you may strive to please yourself first. You are for sure the soldier and the poet enduring side by side.

Star Date of Birth: March 25

Patient character, working spirit. Career with a lot of activity and good material result. You are content with your position in life and your lifestyle and don't exhibit the ambition to change yourself for the sake of change. But sexually you can be demanding, and you tend to put on a commanding performance. Those persons involved in frequent travel or who are visiting your locality are attracted to you.

Star Date of Birth: March 26

The person is courageous and hesitant at the same time; reflections and decisions are late. Many failures because of the insecure character. Your creative and ambitious ideas often lead you to make money. You have an active sexual life, but you have a tendency to remain intellectually involved rather than emotionally. You are sexually stimulated by those who can match your intellect or by others who have been involved in the military or intelligence.

Star Date of Birth: March 27

Exuberance, tendency to tell everything to everybody; this represents a mistake; the life can be ruined because of too much devotion for other people. However, your cunning and shrewdness prove financially rewarding. You are an expert at attracting and seducing others who are drawn to your persuasive style and while you like to have a partner in your life you are not always faithful to the loved one.

Star Date of Birth: March 28

Excessive courage. Crazy decisions. Bitter experience all through the life, but never fatal. You particularly enjoy the time you spend out of doors where you can appreciate natural surroundings. But you are also drawn to formal occasions and love to dress the part. Sexually, you have an experimental and expanding nature that desires new experiences.

Star Date of Birth: March 29

Fine, tempered activity according to necessities. Self-control. Chance in difficult situations. Your possessive tendencies are at play whether with family, friends, or associates. And in love you are a possessive and jealous lover even though you stray and are drawn to that which is forbidden. You are attracted to attention-getting types.

Star Date of Birth: March 30

Excessive spontaneity, trust, imprudence. If the native is a woman, other people take advantage. You possess a desire for real property, land, or possessions. Sexually, you are attracted to other arrogant, self-indulgent persons who are just as jealous and possessive as you and who share your tendency to stray.

Second Decan of Aries:

March 31 - April 9 - Second Ten Days

Character, Personality and Temperament:

An energy, a pronounced courage, and a strong self-confidence and self-reliance that impresses others. At the same time, this individual can be self-centered, self-serving, and an authoritative demigod who rules with a firm hand. They possess a strong will power which in many circumstances can be unbendable.

Cardinal Element:

Fire: Burning and blessed with enthusiasm; an energy and taste for creation and work; at times happy with a natural generosity; the native is a creator; innately creating a dominate enthusiasm around him; even after death the native influences his household; the native can unconsciously sacrifice slowly, slowly.

Destiny:

Difficult life; travel abroad; cheerful old age; more stable and patient; also more industrious and persevering.

Star Date of Birth: March 31

Clean soul, filled with ideals; strength and feeling of balance. Happy existence, divided between home and social activity. Enterprising, active spirit, getting everybody's appreciation. These characteristics are valid also for the ones born on the 1st of April.

Star Date of Birth: April 1

You are a strong-willed, ambitious, and creative thinker. Sexually, you experience dramatic encounters and never forget former lovers who seem to reappear in your life over the years. Your true love may well be experienced the second time around.

Star Date of Birth: April 2

Courage, determination, isolation, sorrow; the individual is not appreciated enough; his good acts are not recognized. Your favorite companion may be yourself or someone willing to listen to you talk about yourself which may lead to loneliness in later life. Sexually, you find yourself attempting not to make the same mistakes again, but you often do just that despite yourself.

Star Date of Birth: April 3

Naive enthusiasm, boredom. Your curiosity and your impressionable mind lead you to develop an interest in the paranormal or occult subjects. Through the years, you find yourself becoming more open to sexual experiences and encounters which allows you to gain the knowledge shared by others.

Star Date of Birth: April 4

Taste for everything big; strong organizations, vast enterprises. General success. Married or not, your strongest bonds, friendships, or relationships are formed with those of the same sex. The highlight of your sexual experiences may occur during the summer months when you have a tendency to focus your attentions more fully on your sexuality.

How to Find Your *Soul-Mate, Stars,* and *Destiny*

Star Date of Birth: April 5

Skill for scientific research, especially astronomy. Calm and clean life. However, you have a tendency to be impulsive and even reckless in your younger years which can lead to speculative or risky adventures. Sexually, your impulsiveness can turn to an urgent compulsion as you experiment with finding the perfect partner who you can idolize.

Star Date of Birth: April 6

Strong character; calm during disputes and skilled to solve things with a smile. Successful life because of this skill. You are in love with the idea of love and romance and seek sexual fulfillment in an ego driven, intellectually curious manner. This interest may lead you to study, research, write about, or, in some other manner, more fully develop your knowledge about this subject.

Star Date of Birth: April 7

Ambition and aggressiveness. Any failures may be due to this aggressive aspect; malicious ambition. Your passions and sexuality may dominate a great deal of your thought processes and your life. And those you desire seem to come your way as your sexual encounters continue to expand your experiences in love life.

Star Date of Birth: April 8

Irrational optimism in all aspects of life. Long voyages, adventure. Your changeable nature may make you moody with a tendency to be stubborn and obstinate in getting your own way. You possess a natural sexual allure that has nothing to do with fashion, fads, or the latest styles or trends.

Star Date of Birth: April 9

Justified optimism; self-esteem and the skill to get the best from everybody. Positive success in difficult situations. You desire a peaceful life which leads to contentment, but you pass up what could have been worthwhile opportunities. Your congenial nature lends itself to a warm and lasting sexual relationship, and you are drawn to those who uphold standards and traditions.

The Third Decan of Aries:

April 10 - April 20 - Third Ten Days

Character, Personality and Temperament:

More refined and cultured than those of the first two Decans. There is a tendency for these individuals to pursue education, philosophy or perhaps theology. Less self-centered than other Aries.

Cardinal Element:

Fire: Daring, enthusiasm, wish and willingness to act and to be active; focus on art and love. Native has a great passion and his existence will be felt by this. Massive expenses.

Destiny:

Creative with excellent, but expensive tastes; well brought up; learned and in charge of many things; native ends well.

Star Date of Birth: April 10

Laziness, sensuality, inactivity and a tendency toward a sentimental deception and complication. You are ingenious, flexible, and adaptable to new situations and new people. Your greatest challenge is in finding others who match your enthusiasm. Your secret loves may fan your flames more than other more conventional types.

Star Date of Birth: April 11

The individual loves partying; he has a lot of envious enemies; possible aggressions because of opposite sex. You see only your own ideas and opinions, many of which are developed at a young age, and you fail to recognize the importance of the ideas and insights. Always others must adapt to your wants and wishes making you inflexible and dogmatic. In your sexuality, you are always looking forward to the next conquest.

Star Date of Birth: April 12

Sensual excesses; problems with opposite sex. You can be inflexible in that you resist change and are reluctant to accept the advice of others. You are hard working but not particularly ambitious. You are knowingly perceptive of the sexual desires of others while your own desires are often heightened by formal social occasions when you are dressed for success and can appear dignified or glamorous.

Star Date of Birth: April 13

Dull attitude; jealous feeling; controlling temperament. Suffers because of lover's infidelity. Your tendency to follow your own lead can make you appear at times non-traditional and unconventional. You seek challenges and this is especially true in your rather dramatic sexual encounters. You keep tabs on former and present lovers while forever looking for the next one.

Star Date of Birth: April 14

The native would be proud to have a famous lover. Good luck with opposite sex. Your basic fear of being inadequate leads you to prove yourself over and over and this is especially true in your sexuality. You can be overly possessive and jealous in regards to your lover while at the same time you seek the next encounter with which to soothe your vanity.

Star Date of Birth: April 15

Mocking, distant character. Lucky in business for men and women. You are drawn to challenges, secrets, mysteries, and solving the unknown through your diligent efforts. But your changeability and impulsiveness to follow new ideas effects your relationships and your ability to transcend to deeper, more meaningful sexual encounters.

Star Date of Birth: April 16

Tendency towards romantic love. Help from the opposite sex; materialistic character. You have a strong need to be accepted and well liked by others and this need for approbation leads you to respond to those who express love and desire for you, but you are continuously seeking that new relationship which you believe will prove fulfilling. The exotic or those of foreign birth appeal to your insatiable curiosity in life.

Star Date of Birth: April 17

Lack of determination and balance in everything they do. Hard life; achievements later in life. Your spirituality leads you to seek time to yourself for personal reflection. But you also seek a great deal of privacy for your more intimate, sexual encounters and abhor those who kiss and tell. You attract ambitious and successful people to you.

Star Date of Birth: April 18

The native needs to be sheltered and protected by their partner. Insecure life, unstable situations. Your shrewd and cunning mind combined with your impulsive and rash nature can lead you into questionable activities resulting in failures, loss, fraud, and scandal. Your sexual experiences fuel your ego driven nature and enhance your feelings of importance and self worth.

How to Find Your Soul-Mate, Stars, and Destiny

Star Date of Birth: April 19

Self-control, decision, ability. Rough life, filled with serious difficulties which will be overcome. Healthy old age. Your success is assured when you develop your innate intelligence and talents. If a man, your masculinity is important to you; if a woman, your femininity; and you are drawn to sexual encounters with others who share and understand this need.

Star Date of Birth: April 20

Ambitions without result; out of luck. You are ambitious and strive to prove yourself through your success. However, you prefer that your romantic relationships provide you with an outlet for fun, distractions, lightheartedness, and generally a good time enjoyed by both you and the other person.

Colors:

The most favorable colors for the natives of Aries are all shades of red, rose, and pink.

Birthstones:

The birthstones for Aries are rubies, garnets, and diamonds.

Flowers:

Favorable flowers for Aries individuals are the rose, the geranium, and the red tulips.

Keyword: "I am"

POSITIVE TRAITS:

Pioneering; adventurous; trustworthy; steady; endurance; persistent; creative; self-reliant; persevering; enterprising; practical; courageous; fearless; kind; careful; humorous; energetic; freedom-loving; magnetic; direct; constructive; enthusiastic; imaginative; kind; careful; humorous; energetic; freedom-loving; magnetic; proud; direct; constructive; leader; optimistic; defender of the weak; seeker of new experiences; an idea person with initiative; intellectual; strongly sexed.

NEGATIVE TRAITS:

Selfish; self-centered; stubborn; unbending; blunt; domineering; hot temper; conceited; brisk; impatient; dogmatic; argumentative; covetous; amorous; lazy; lives in the present wanting everything now; jealous; possessive; impulsive; excitable; not domestic; hasty; sharp; overly competitive; resentful of restrictions; aggressive; irate; quarrelsome; rude; boisterous; foolhardy; brutal.

How to Find Your *Soul-Mate, Stars,* and *Destiny*

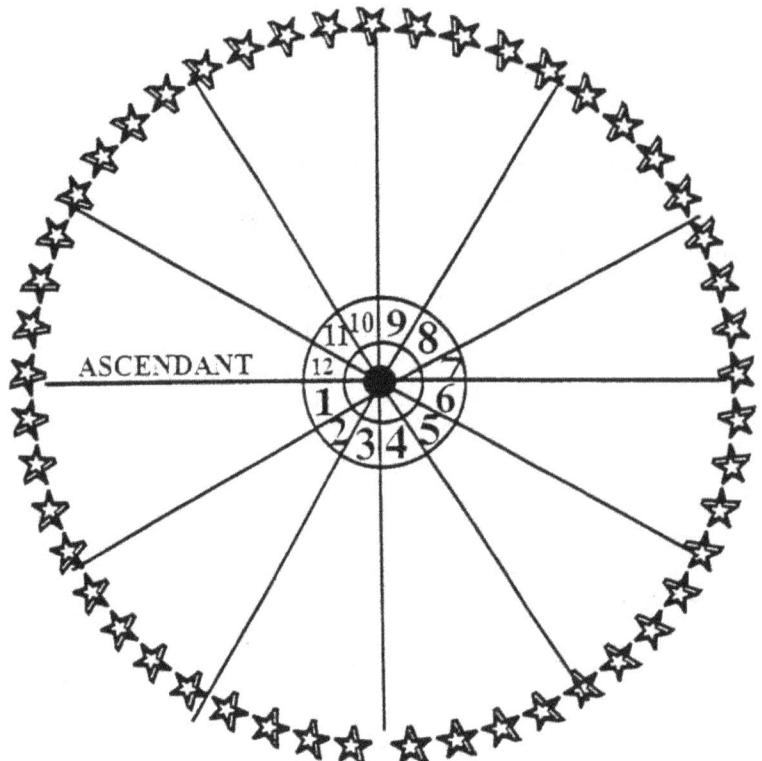

Aries

Personal Self-Expression and Mental Tendencies

1. Strong Wish, Demanding, Productive, Magnetism, Exploring, Gregarious
2. Proud, Hunter, Ideas to Create Change, Indomitable, Innovators, Pioneers,
3. Fighting, Courageous, Arrogant, Dexterous, Low self-sufficiency, Deceitful
4. Commander, Entrepreneur, Dangerous Situations, Energizing, Impusive, Positive
5. Good Will for Affirmation, Benevolence, Love and Travel, Selfish, Pugnacious
6. Spiritual-Force, Extremes, Attracted to Foreigners, Wanting Everything New
7. Efficiency, Follows, Instigates Power and Position, Rebellious, Being in control
8. Selfish, Prefers Not to be Questioned about Feelings, Self-effacing, Inconsiderate
9. Strong Stimulants, Holds Back in Intimacy, Selfish needs, Ruining Everything
10. Intellectually Guided, Restless Life, Balanced Soul, Short-Term Needs Important
11. World Constant Desire, Nice Soul Full of Ideals, Self-Focused Training, Satirist
12. Happy Life Divided between Home and Social Life, Noisy, Quick Tempered
13. Authoritative, Wishing to Impose Desire on Other People, Disrespect, Jealousy
14. Violent, Vicious, Unvanquished Will, Isolated, Disregard, Audacious, Vigorous
15. Belongs to Selfish Forces, Egotistic, Quarrelsome, Foolhardy, Self-Interest, Strong
16. Optimist, Enthusiastic, Drinking Vice, Violent Passion, Brutal, High-Minded
17. Instability, Activities Intense, Strong Personality, Imprudent, Insubordinate, Ardent
18. Impulsive, Fortunate, Harmonious, Industrious, Self-Assurance, Enthusiastic
19. Calm, Self-reliant, Feisty, Impetuous, Challenge, Inspiring, Forcefully, Impusive
20. Stubborn, Controlling, Blunt, Gambler, Talented, Mentally Alert, Violent, Bestial
21. Very Difficult, Defeatist, Impressionable, Have Many Roles in Life, Many Affairs
22. Adventuresome, Desires Affairs, Aries is Afire, Fighting, Impetuous, Easily Anger
23. Independent-Headstrong, Pioneering Leader, Big Ego, Easily Violent, Self-Value
24. Versatile, Demonstrative, Highly Motivated, Needs, Challenge, Arrogant, Outgoing
25. Manipulates Feelings, Half-moons Joined by Straight Line, Abrupt, Impulsive
26. Insensitive Toward Others, Inconsistent, Unrestricted, Blunt, Self-Secure, Religious
27. Self-satisfied, Everything Rotates Around Aries, Inconsistency, Defeated, Challenge
28. Multi-Faceted, Aries Looks Like the Horns of a Ram, Entrepreneur, Stimulated
29. Self-trusting, Dynamic, Impatient, Horny, Bitchy, Angry, Dynamo, Courage

30. Seldom Renouncing, Waiting to Fulfill Secret Sex in Public, Impressionable,
31. Impetuous, Self-conscious, Sexually Dominant, Impatient, Represssed, Unfaithful
32. Brisk, Susceptible, Sexuality in an Angry Relationship, Easily Angered, Controlling
33. Astronomic Studies, Poor Sexual Functioning, Stimulated, Social Climber,
34. Scientific Researcher, Orgasmic Impoverishment, Self-Centered, Adventurous
35. Extreme Jealousy by Partner in Home and Family, Impulsive, Dominating. Talented
36. Sexual and Emotional Exclusivity, Hesitations Agitate Life, High Self-Esteem
37. Ambitious Tough Pleasure, Boredom with Opposite Sex, Me First, Selfish
38. Creates New Things, Low Self-esteem with Repressed Anger, Easily Depressed
39. Manages Difficult Situations, Melodramatic Risky Affairs, Fights for Independence
40. Ascending and Descending, Sex Hunts, Multiple Affairs, Superior to Others
41. Combative Personal Relationship both Emotionally and Legally, Flamboyant
42. Self-impersonation, Independent Movement Controlled, Hypocritical Attitudes
43. Money-Making Schemes, Freedom Questioned, Free-Spirited, Foolish, Charming
44. Many Journeys, Sexually Dissatisfied, Never Stops Running, Wants Everything
45. Savage, Feels Unappreciated Without Control, Loves Sexual Experience, Powerful
46. Speculative, Risk-Taker, Mentally Stimulated, Challenged by Adversity, Expressive
47. Hasty Marriage, Divorce, Independent Direction, Falls in Love Easily, Obsessive
48. Powerful Personality, Self-Assertive, Emotional, Penetrating Mind, Magnetic
49. Nervous, Short-term Goals, Self-discovery, Falls in and out of Love Easily
50. Adaptable, Restless, Self-confident, Needs Experience, Easily Bored, Gregarious
51. Self-deceptive, Needs to Blow Off Steam, Penetrating, Convincing Liar
52. Separates from Family for Adventure to Find Love, Exaggerates, Idealistic
53. Follows Fashions, Involved in Business Enterprises, Opinionated, Exaggerates
54. Magnanimous, Vibrant Energy, Unfaithful, Audacious, Philosophical, Determined
55. Open-Hearted, Faces Change with Courage, Challenged by Fear, Impulsive, Clever,
56. Emotionally Stressed, Temporal, Ultra-Ambitious, Cultivates Soul and Mind
57. Lascivious, Penetrating, Speculates in Investments, Money Making Schemes
58. Indignant, Admirable, Intelligent, Responsible, Produces Success and Activity
59. Scientific, Philosophical in Male-Dominated World, Sinks to the Bottom, Elistist
60. Sharp, Progressive, Proud, Detached, Independent, Prone to Calamity, Charismatic
61. Determined, Expressive, Easily Angered, Vulnerable, Inspiring, Unhampered Spirit
62. Excitable Temperament, Fighting Spirit, Achieving, Leader, Outgoing, Fool-Hardy
63. Imposing, Interested, Self-righteous, Receptive, Passive, Low Self-Sufficiency
64. Vehement, Easily Shows Anger and Hurt, Enthusiastic, Foolhardy, Homocidal
65. Tribulations, Loss, scandals, High Spirits, Inexperienced, Likes Glamour, Foolhardy
66. Quick Recovery from Depressions, Judgements Made on First Impressions
67. High Self-esteem, Self-interest, Good Sense of Humor, Independent, Impatient

68. Susceptible to Accident, Emotionally Vulnerable, Cause Digestive Problems
69. Head Injuries, Face Inflammation, Optimistic, Watery Eyes Hands and Feet
70. Bold, Cunning, Fortune Hunting, Quite Self-confident, Extroverted, Melodramatic
71. Zealous, Critical, Cranky, Anxious, Suffers from Insecurity, Desires Knowledge
72. Pioneering, Commanding, Superior, Benevolent, Attempts What Others Fear to Try
73. Extravagant Love of Luxury Items, Resists Failure and Defeat, Problem Solver
74. Intellectually High-spirited, Manipulates Feelings-Love and People, Insomnia
75. Vain, Rash, Noisy, Pride is Double-edged, Reputable, Complex Personality
76. Reliable, Fearless, Noble, Generous, High Libido, Vulnerable to Rejection
77. Obstinate, Opinionated, Petulant, Quick-Spoken, Learns to Reject Others First
78. Resentful, Restless, Abrupt, Flattering Description, Dislikes Details, Risky Affairs
79. Vague, Tactless, Boisterous, Complex, Passionate, Cannot Keep Secretes
80. Sympathetic, Searching for Ideals, Surrounds Himself With Stimulating People
81. Self-controlled, Control-Dominate, Erotic, Survivor, Easily Wounded (Emotional)
82. Conquers Desires, Catalyst, Reluctant to Help Others, Demanding, Likes to Travel
83. Dislikes Details, Musically Inclined, Superficial, Hunters, High-Spirited, Inactivity
84. Intellect Relaxes Activity, Naturally Extroverted, Sensual, Sexually Romantic
85. Frustrates an Active Mind, Dislikes Secrets, Open Hearted to Himself Only
86. Always Planning Next Activity, Sweepingly Generous, Self-Centered, Worries,
87. Compartmentalizes Life and People for Own Needs, Fails Marriage, Fastidious
88. Possesses Leadership Powers, Responds to Compliments, Deceives Others
89. Seeks Satisfaction and Gratification, Demanding, Give of Gab, Irresistible
90. Gives a Lot to Win, Self-effacing, Inconsiderate, Falls Easily to Temptation
91. Win-Win Attitude, Highly Motivated, Prone to Gain Enemies, Unfaithful
92. Defies Social Convention, Luckey With Money, Appears to Be a Friend But Is Not
93. Flamboyant, Foolishly Charming, Hypocritical, Can Be Very Cunning, Impulsive
94. Multi-faceted, Powerful Aura, Demands Loyalty, Notorious, Very Fashionable
95. Sprightly, Mystical, Greatest Pleasure from Hunting, Brilliant Style, Antagonistic
96. Mysterious, Easily Bored, Convincing Liar, Gains Property and Money by Marriage
97. Obsessive, Wants Immediate Gratification, Feels Impelled, High-Spirited,
98. Desires Perfect Mate, Nosey, Enterprising, Kind, Sometimes Has Crazy Ideas
99. Easily Forgives and Forgets, Emotional Elitist, Susceptible to Headaches
100. Potent Chemistry, Attempts Things Others Fear to Try, Takes Chances, Vivacious

How to Find Your Soul-Mate, Stars, and Destiny

Celebrity Birthdays

March   Aries

21	Phyllis McGinley Timothy Dalton James Coco John D. Rockefeller III	Johann Sebastian Bach Cynthia Geary Shawnon Dunston Rosie O'Donnell	Patrick Lucey Ed Begley Rosie Stone Gary Oldman
22	Bob Costas William Shatner Stephen Sondheim Stephanie Mills	Werner Klemperer Karl Malden Lena Olin Wernher von Braun	Marcel Marceau Chico Marx Pat Robertson Orin Hatch
23	Lee May Chaka Khan Joan Crawford	Ric Ocasek Amanda Plummer Princess Eugenie	Marti Pellow Marty Allen Ron Jaworski
24	Robert Carradine Thomas Dewey William Goetz Lara Flynn Boyle	Steve McQueen Harry Houdini Dougie Thomson Donna Pescow	Norman Fell Lee Oskar David T. Suzuki Byron Janis
25	Bela Bartok Howard Cosell Simone Signoret Gloria Steinem	Frankie Carle Sarah Jessica Parker Arturo Toscanini Paul Michael Glaser	David Lean Elton John Bonnie Bedelia Aretha Franklin
26	Leonard Nimoy Tennessee Williams Sterling Hayden Al Jolson	Teddy Pendergrass James Caan Bob Woodward Leeza Gibbons	Diana Ross Erica Jong Alan Arkin Robert Frost
27	Maria Carey Wilhelm Roentgen Gloria Swanson David Janssen	Nathaniel Currier Sarah Vaughan Quentin Tarantino Talisa Soto	Michael York Cyrus Vance Judy Carne Tony Banks
28	Ralph Sanzio Reba McEntire Carolyn Jones August Busch	Ken Howard Pandro Berman Spyros Skouras Nelson Algren	Diane Wiest Irving Lazar Salt Dirk Bogarde

How to Find Your Soul-Mate, Stars, and Destiny

March　　　Aries

29	Jennifer Capriati	Ella McPherson	Eric Idle
	Pres. John Tyler	Warner Baxter	Pearl Bailey
	Walt Frazier	Eileen Heckart	Cy Young
	Denny McClain	Eugene McCarthy	Dirk Bogarde
30	Warren Beatty	Tracy Chapman	Turhan Bey
	Francisco Goya	Richard Helm	Eric Clapton
	Vincent Van Gogh	Frankie Laine	Celine Dion
	John Astin	Paul Reiser	
31	Rene Descartes	Rhea Perlman	Leo Buscaglia
	Cesar Chavez	Richard Chamberlain	Herb Alpert
	Liz Claiborne	Christopher Walken	Shirley Jones
	Arthur Godfrey	Franz Joseph Haydn	Red Norvo

April

1	Rachmaninoff	Jane Powell	Lon Chaney
	Ali MacGraw	William Manchester	Alan Blakey
	Debbie Reynolds	Emil Mosbacher	Gordon Jump
	Otto Von Bismarck	ToshiroMifune	Wallace Beery
2	Emmylou Harris	Linda Hunt	Dana Carvey
	Alec Guinness	Charlemagne	Emile Zola
	Max Ernst	Leon Russell	Casanova
	Buddy Ebsen	Gary Steven	Jack Webb
3	Arthur Murray	Eddie Murphy	Doris Day
	Marlon Brando	Wayne Newton	Jane Goodall
	Tony Orlando	David Hyde Pierce	Alec Baldwin
	Marsha Mason	Washington Irving	George Jessel
4	Nancy McKeon	John Cameron Swayze	Kitty Kelley
	France Langford	Elmer Bernstein	Gil Hodges
	Arthur Murray	Robert Downey, Jr.	Howard Koch
	Anthony Perkin	Maya Angelou	Nick Mars
5	Michael Moriarity	Agnetha Faltskog	Bette Davis
	Melvyn Douglas	Roger Corman	Gregory Peck
	Spencer Tracy	Chester Bowles	Colin Powell
	Joseph Lister	Herbert Von Karajan	Gale Storm

How to Find Your Soul-Mate, Stars, and Destiny

April   Aries

6	Harry Houdini	Billy Dee Williams	Raphael
	Lowell Thoma	Michelle Phillips	Merle Haggard
	John Ratzenberger	Stan Cullimore	Ari Meyers
	Walter Huston	Marilu Henner	Jaso Hervey
7	David Frost	Irene Castle	Jerry Brown
	Walter Winchell	Ravi Shankar	Billie Holiday
	Percy Faith	Jackie Chan	James Garner
	Francis Ford Coppola	Mick Abrahams	John Oates
8	Sonja Henie	Barbara Kingsolver	John Gavin
	Mary Pickford	Clementine Churchill	Robin Wright
	Connie Stevens	Patricia Arquette	Betty Ford
	Julian Lennon	Catfish Hunter	Warren Avis
9	Jean-Paul Belmondo	Tommy Manville	Hugh Hefner
	Paulina Porizkova	Charles Baudelaire	Dennis Quaid
	Paul Robeson	Michael Learned	Ward Bond
	William J. Fullbright	Abraham Ribicoff	Carl Perkins
10	Don Meredith	Clare Boothe Luce	Brian Setzer
	William Booth	John Madden	Omar Sharif
	Steven Seagal	Commodore Perry	Bobbie Smith
	David Halberstam	Chuck Connors	George Arliss
11	Ethel Kennedy	Dean Acheson	Joel Grey
	Stuart Adamson	Lisa Stansfield	Oleg Cassini
	Quentin Reynolds	Neville Staples	Bill Irwin
	Gov. Hugh Carey	Richie Sambora	Delroy Pearson
12	Andy Garcia	David Letterman	Lily Pons
	Claire Danes	Shannen Doherty	Ann Miller
	Alex Briley	Herbie Hancock	Tiny Tim
	David Cassidy	Vince Gill	Jane Withers
13	Thomas Jefferson	Rick Schroder	Don Adams
	Saundra Santiago	Butch Cassidy	Tony Dow
	F.W. Woolworth	Howard Keel	Ron Perlman
	Garry Kasparov	Lyle Waggoner	Alex Briley
14	Julie Christie	John Gielgud	Pete Rose
	Loretta Lynn	Sir James Clark	Rod Steiger
	Brad Diliman	Dennis Bryon	Jay Robinson
	Ritchie Blackmore	Larry Ferguson	John Shea

April — Aries

15	Emma Thompson Alfred Bloomingdale Leonardo Da Vinci Algernon Swinburne	Elizabeth Montgomery Samantha Fox Claudia Cardinale	Roy Clark Bessie Smith Graeme Clark
16	Henry Mancini Charlie Chaplin Wilbur Wright Kareem Abdul-Jabbar	Jimmy Osmond Gerry Rafferty Dusty Springfield Nikita Khrushchev	Ellen Barkin Jon Cryer Peter Ustinov Bobby Vinton
17	Gregor Piatigorsky William Holden Harry Reasoner Billie Holiday	Thornton Wilder James Garner Boomer Esiason Stephen Singleton	J. P. Morgan Anne Shirley Pete Shelley Liz Phair
18	Huntington Hartford Leopold Stokowski Hayley Mills Melissa Joan Hart	Conan O'Brien Philippe Junot Barbara Hale Les Pattison	Jane Leeves Rick Moranis Eric Roberts James Woods
19	Dudley Moore Jayne Mansfield Hugh O'Brian Kenneth Battelle	Paloma Picasso Frank Viola Mark Volman Larry Ramos, Jr.	Don Adams Tim Curry Alan Price
20	Don Mattingly Ryan O'Neal Joan Miro Harold Lloyd	George Takei Luther Vandross Adolf Hitler Harvey Firestone, Jr.	Nina Foch Bob Braun Jessica Lange Craig Frost

How to Find Your *Soul-Mate, Stars,* and *Destiny*

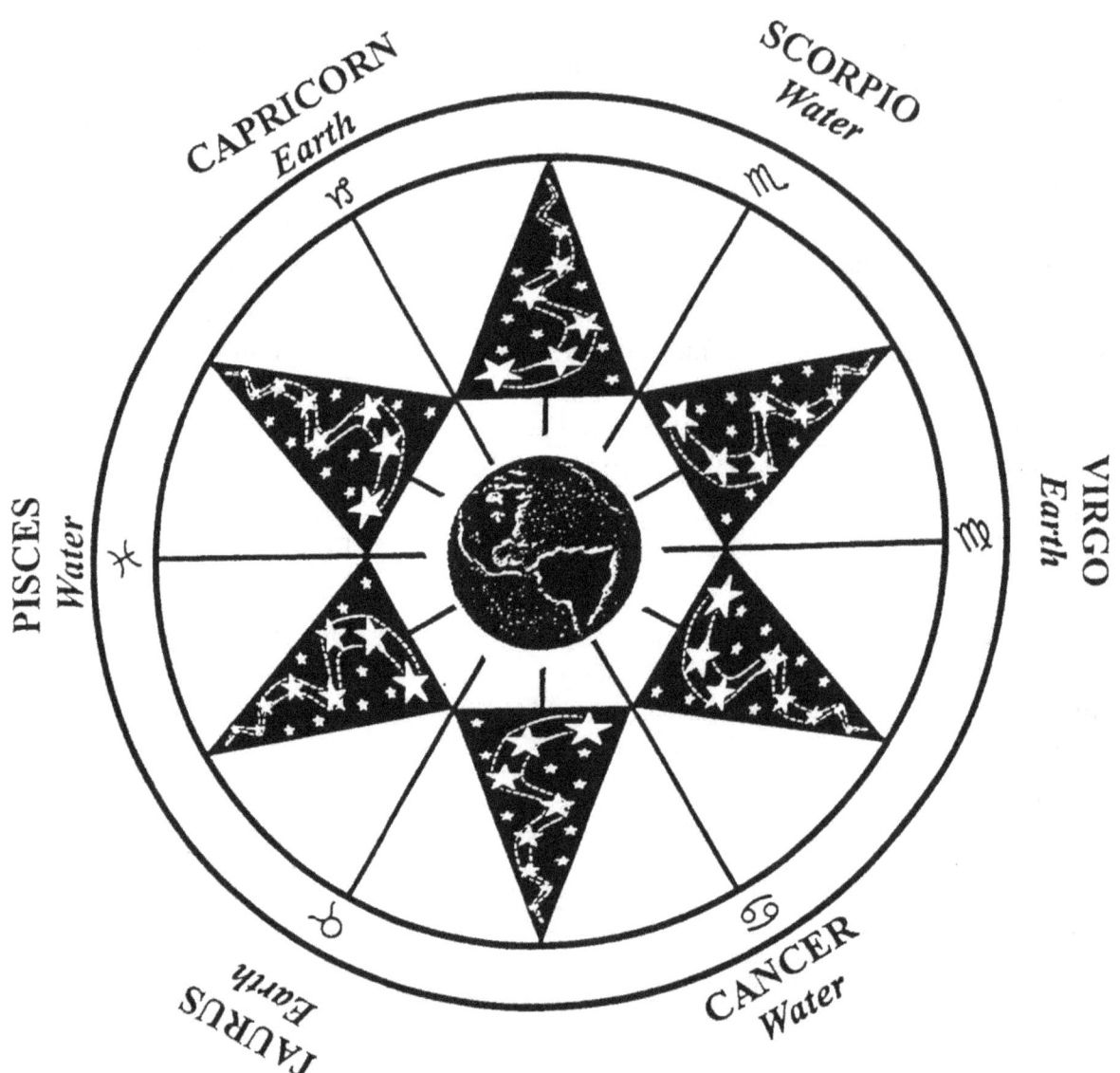

How to Find Your *Soul-Mate, Stars,* and *Destiny*

Date With Destiny

Share With Me Your Fantasy

How to Find Your *Soul-Mate, Stars,* and *Destiny*

Date With Destiny

Share With Me Your Fantasy

TAURUS

April 21 - May 20

Man - Woman - Child - Character - Relationships - Compatibilities - Love Signs

Taurus, the second Sun sign of the Zodiac, is symbolized by the Bull and takes its name from the Greek word for Bull. Taurus individuals are known for being as stubborn as a bull. This tenacity is applied to their diligent efforts and hard working efforts. This is the sign of possessions, and Taurus, while romantic and sensuous, is characterized by taking the ideas of Aries and producing results. Patient, productive, and dependable, they derive their basic sense of security from the acquisition of material possessions. They strive to control these material possessions and their resources in such a way as to provide security and leisure time for themselves and the others in their lives. Ruled by Venus, they are fond of beauty, refinement, and pleasures as well. They possess an appreciation for pleasant and beautiful surroundings, and, if it were not for their need of acquisitions, they would more than likely be content to laze around in a peaceful setting. They are patient and slow to anger, but they possess a clear stubbornness about what they want and how they want it. When pushed too far, many have the worst of tempers, and the come out charging like a Bull.

Taurus also has a deep love for natural settings, and with the right lover, this may be just the setting they select for the perfect sexual encounter. They are most generally loyal and domestic, much preferring a harmonious home setting, but there remains a deep love for luxury, comfort, and romance. Many a Taurus is not above seeking these things elsewhere when they are not found in abundance at home. This same love of luxury and possessions can lead Taurus to be selfish and self-serving, making it difficult for them to change, share, and five of themselves to others. Sentimental romantics they remain, forever seeking and searching for that perfect love to make their lives complete. On the other hand, they are more than likely creatures of habit and routine, much preferring a lifestyle geared to their ambitions and needs. Taurus doesn't care much for being inconvenienced. Taurus also possesses a great love for art and music, especially if these can be used to highlight and enhance their personal surroundings.

These characteristics of the Taurus Sun sign can be made stronger by the Moon sign, Ascendant, and placement of the Planets, or they can be made more subdued by specific influences. It is by ascertaining these different influences that one more fully understands the particular Taurus individual.

Venus is the ruling planet of the sign Taurus, the Bull. The sign of Taurus begins on April 20, but for seven days the second sign in the Zodiac is overlapped by the cusp of the previous sign, Aries. Taurus does not realize its full strength and power until about April 27th. Beginning on or about that date, the sign achieves its full potency until about May 20th, and then for seven days, it gradually loses its power because of the overlapping cusp of the incoming sign, Gemini. Venus predisposes its natives to follow the prompting of passion and earthy desires. This to some degree fits the nature of the stubborn, unyielding disposition of its symbol, the Bull.

In the Zodiac, Taurus has its back turned at the Aries and its front is facing the Gemini. The neck, chest and the right side of the nose and the right leg are in the Taurus constellation while the horns, forehead, eyes and left leg can be found in the Gemini constellation. Physically, Taurus rules the neck, cerebellum and the lymphatic system; and the throat, neck and ears are the most sensitive parts of the Taurus body. The mighty Taurus with its body of the Bull is covered by a cloud of stars. It is said that Jupiter kidnapped Europe, the daughter of the Fenician king while hidden by this cloud of stars; then he placed her on the back of Taurus who took her to the island of Crete.

The Earth element signifies hard work, patience, and practical feelings. The native Taurus is stubborn and conservative. The overriding tendency is toward possessing and this is achieved by the ability to engage in solid, inflexible hard work. This individual works for himself and his family, and others can depend on him to finish a task.

With Venus and the Moon controlling this sign, it is considered the mating season, and the natural attitude of Taurus is that of the lover. These individuals are gifted with beauty and kindness and with keenly alert senses which allows them to enjoy an extremely sensuous existence. Taurus is known for having the strongest appetites and passions of any of the twelve signs, but this is generally tempered by an unusually strong will power which allows them to subdue their natures. Without this overriding will power, passion can rob the Taurus natives of their better judgment. Therefore, there are actually two distinct types of Taurus: those who are hard-working and diligent, and those who are lazy and devote their lives to pleasure. These natives have a caring soul and peaceful character. While they hate violence, they have the ability to fight enthusiastically. The native-born Taurus is often gifted with psychic and clairvoyant powers, and may be guided by spiritual influences and intuition.

Taurus Personality

The Taurus individuals who have taken charge of their lives through strong will power are self-reliant and persevering. They are constant in their drive, conservative in their endeavors, and determined to accomplish their goals. At the same time, you are obstinate, proud and ambitious for possessions and power. People born in this sign delight in the indulgence of the pleasures. Your appreciation for good food and drink is not the only tie that binds you to pleasure. You are most fond of the opposite sex and like recreation, music, art and intellectual and cultural endeavors as well as ornaments and jewelry.

You can be sociable, affectionate and loving. You have a persistent nature and are capable of working diligently toward your goals and accomplishments. You can be quiet or noncommittal in your thoughts and opinions, and you may appear secretive, reserved or discreet about your business and personal affairs. You possess the energy and endurance of the Bull but are best known for having a pleasant and happy disposition. Your practical and determined mind reflects good reasoning abilities and sound judgment which is often displayed in a diplomatic manner. You can be dogmatic and opinionated in your strong likes and dislikes.

Usually patient, good-humored, and soft-hearted, you have a most companionable disposition. When you are unprovoked, you are gentle and loving. But when you are angered or opposed you have the ability to become stubborn and unyielding and as ,mad as a bull'. When angry, you insist obstinately on not being deterred from your own ways or your personal opinions. Straight-forward and determined, you, Taurus the Bull, destroy everything in your path when opposed. You plow through any and all opposition. Cornered, you may wait, showing patience and self-reserve, but when fed up, you will come out charging.

Taurus are most desirous of acquiring money, possessions and a well-established, stable income. This predisposition for accumulating possessions marks you. You may shop relentlessly, take your purchases home, and not bother removing the price tags. It is the acquisition, the acquiring, the accumulation of the material, tangible item that drives you.

You are careful, steady and capable of completing the projects you undertake. Practical, with strong organizational and managerial ability, you are usually sincere, reliable and trustworthy. Your capabilities include the competence to direct and provide you with excellent executive skills in order to carry through with your plans and ideas. Your prevalent tenacity leaves you undeterred by obstacles, and your determination and persistency gain you the desired end results. Through your strength of will and your capable mind, you attain a self-reliance that allows you patiently to wait out the fulfillment of your goals and desires. Persistence, thoroughness and your unchangeable single-mindedness endow you with excellent and efficient skills which quite often result in the accomplishment of your goals. You are detail-oriented at both the conscious and subconscious level to the point that some small, overlooked detail can actually prod you intuitively. You succeed at earning money for yourself and providing for your family.

Taurus are inspired by ambition. It appears easy for you to accumulate money, but you rarely hoard it. You have a generous nature and are quite capable of sharing your good fortune with others less fortunate. This generosity is more evident in your gifts or donations of money than in any empathetic consoling or expressions of sympathy.

You have a great love for justice and your nature is affectionate, generous, peaceful but firm. You love your home life and the security it provides. Travel may not be important to you except as it is necessary for a definite purpose such as health, business, learning, or then again your effort to seek a singular pleasure.

Planetary configurations, influenced by Venus, prevail over the sign of Taurus. Venus endows Taurus individuals with an enormous depth and intensity of emotion. Not only do you seek pleasures, you relish in them. You are not afraid of the pure, raw enjoyment of the senses. Allowing for the Sun-sign influence of this sign, the secretive Taurus may hide this more emotional attribute preferring to keep all true feelings concealed and private.

The typical Taurus makes every effort to adjust daily behavior in order to strive for stability and security. Your preferred tempo may be a slow, steady pace (like a bull) that allows you to patiently succeed in your efforts. The Taurus position represents the most direct manifestations of the self-preservation instinct which you satisfy intrinsically by material comfort and security.

Typically, you are a well-grounded person in your emotions with little predisposition toward being defensive in your nature. In other words, you don't suffer from or worry yourself with imagined slights and insults from others. This makes you an easy person to get along with as others can speak their mind around you without having to carefully choose their words in order not to give offense. You can be detached but gracious and entertaining.

When Taurus acquire material possessions, they feel the most secure and comfortable. You may develop a self-identification with work and possessions. In this situation, you can then appear too smug and self-assured. This self-satisfaction can easily become overconfidence which can, of course, be detrimental in your personal development. This can lead you to relax in your efforts, taking for granted your security, and to trust others who may not be quite as careful as you. If this results in a loss of your personal security, you will not rest or be at ease until you regain it. While you can be content and secure on little, in that you manage money well, there is a predominate need to be well-established.

Taurus have a strong self-image and a healthy self-esteem. You feel good about yourself and flatter yourself not because of any special quality but just because you like yourself. This isn't a case of being smug or conceited, but you might want to give more consideration to what others think of you. Being self-satisfied can at times lead to an almost lazy contentment with life in general. The lazy Taurus is the individual who hasn't developed a strong self-will, and with this person comes the desire to fulfill the more pleasurable pursuits and desires of life. Aligned with this problem is the natural inclination toward purely physical pleasures. Feeling good about yourself, eating, drinking and satisfying your sexual desires will, of course, deter you from any higher goals. You are frequently sociable, well-liked, and popular. At many times, you demand little of others or of yourself in your desire to simply enjoy the pleasures of good company, recreation or happy pursuits. The chances are that you aren't ardent in human relations. You prefer to take what comes. You assume that as long as you possess the good things in life, all else will take care of itself. Learn to energetically follow your Sun-nature so that you aren't caught up in relaxation and uselessness. You may have a joyful time at being pleased with life, but you need to consciously stimulate yourself. Find a catalyst, perhaps in an idea or in another person, that inspires you to act for at times you are not a self-starter.

The Taurus trait of being reserved can develop into retentive or even repressed personality patterns. It might also be perceived that the Taurus desire to acquire possessions and property is a self-defense measure, an effort to construct inner walls of security protecting one from deep-seated anxieties. Your fierce possessiveness may be compensation against a fear of rejection or a separation-anxiety. You also may have an innate fear of change. Remember, to a large degree, your feelings of security are based on your daily routine and well-established home.

Consider though, that whatever the emotional determination of the Taurus person, they will almost always find compensation for their temperament or their feelings in the form of material, tangible possessions. Your security is based on your financial security and your accumulation of possessions, the values of which are apparent and obvious to others. For example, while you unselfishly display your talents as a hospitable and generous host or hostess, these occasions may be only a manner of prestigiously exhibiting your possessions and, you feel, gaining the approval of your friends, associates or of the community.

Your inner personality, your true self may unconsciously never feel as emotionally secure as you present yourself to the outside world. In fact, your displays of possessions and your exhibitions may be only compensation for your more deep-seated inner anxieties. There is, or may be, an on going and subliminal struggle between the nature of the id and of the ego. However, it is your strong will power and sense of self that rescues you from submitting to these inner struggles. You are capable of conquering your deepest feelings of anxieties, your battle with the id, by complying with your self-imposed regulatory restrictions which prevail in your everyday life. Only when the unconscious is badly aspected and poorly developed does the Taurus individual submit to the temptations of self-indulgence and excesses in an id-obsessed life. This can result in pleasure-seeking addictions and eroticism.

These issues and an unrealistic fear of, or resistance to, change have brought many problems and failures into the lives of Taurus. Taurus must learn to accept that the world is a changing place. Customs, behaviors, traditions, people, all evolve and change. New ideas emerge incessantly to replace outmoded ones. Relax and accept this, and maybe loosen up a bit. As of yet, change has not brought the end of the world.

It could be suggested that Taurus individuals avoid occupations which require assimilating new procedures and techniques, or changing the way things are done. Remember, you accomplish your best results through persistence and will-power and not through hurried reasoning or impromptu action. Don't take this as a personal affront. Use this knowledge to improve your results. And, dear Taurus, learn to soften your nature just a little so that you'll be capable of accepting constructive criticism and learning from it.

If possible, give some consideration to the idea that there does exist values other than those related to acquiring possessions and money. There are other avenues for gaining the admiration of those around you. Discover those values and develop them. It is quite possible to even forego profit once in awhile in order to retain or gain the respect of others.

A poorly developed Taurus personality produces an individual who is capable of testing the loyalty of others in order to gain emotional reassurances. You want to know that others are devoted to you and that they will go to great lengths for you. While seeking this devotion, this acclimation from others, it may appear that you are using other people as you strive to accumulate more and more. This testing of the loyalties of others can become almost like a game for you, but, remember, games are not always appreciated by others. Often times, this is another incident or example of when you need to ‚lighten up'. Attempt to trust a little more and learn to appreciate others for themselves not for what you can gain from them.

In recreational pursuits, you steadfastly play by the rules as you do in all areas of your life. However, the afflicted second-sign native can also become a deadly opponent who is quite capable of discarding the rules in order to achieve personal gain. Whether it be material gain or prestige, or prominence and stature in the community, this native will go to great lengths to acquire it. This is the individual who will create causes or organize attacks against others. For example, this person might create charges against a public official demanding his dismissal. This type of Taurus will utilize all his powers of concentration, determination and organization to accomplish his goal and then will undoubtedly and loudly announce his success of having done something beneficial for his community. Quite fortunately, these vicious games are not played by the majority of well-meaning, conservative, and kind Taurus individuals.

Found in the baser types of this sign are people who are domineering, sharp-tongued and sarcastic. These people can be arbitrary, capricious, erratic, exacting and often insist on ruling or ruining. Needless to say, these individuals aren't as socially well-accepted, or as well-liked, as their better graced Taurus brothers and sisters.

There are also those second-sign Taurus persons who are capable of being aroused to violent outbursts of anger when faced with opposition or resistance. While Taurus aggressions are for the most part focused in a positive manner on succeeding or on constructive activities, when they are faced with what they consider sufficient provocation, they can become angry. Sufficient provocation might be perceived by the Taurus when they feel threatened by change, disapproval or loss of prestige, loss of possessions, or the disloyal actions of friends or loved ones. For this individual, there may be no conscious awareness that he feels threatened. It is just that the Taurus person is likely to be inflexible and intolerant. They may be convinced, that he is right, that his personal qualities are admirable and positive, above reproof, and that they are probably somewhat superior to others. Combine these personality traits with the Taurus self-restraint, control, and discipline, and the result can be suppressed aggressions. There is a definite tendency among some of these individuals to be passive-aggressive and under extreme pressures these pent up emotions can explode in aggressive hostilities and verbal or even physical assaults. These fits of passions can go so far as to make the person dangerous to live or associate with. They may rant and rave and wreck havoc with their angry outbursts. Completely unreasonable and unmanageable during these times, it is best that the individual is left alone to work out these emotional spells alone. Usually, deep regret will replace this uncontrolled display of passion if the individual is left to his own thoughts.

This propensity for aggressive behavior is less evident in the First Decan (April 21-April 30) and for those individuals on the cusp with Aries. It emerges more strongly during the Second Decan by April 28 and rises to its peak by May 2, but remains until the end of the Zodiac month. Those on the cusp with Gemini are also influenced by this tendency due to the duality of the Gemini sign and to Gemini's influence of its unpredictable, volatile planetary ruler, Mercury.

Astrology can be advantageous in describing our better natures, but it can also pinpoint our detriments, shortcomings, and faults. Taurus is urged to overcome these weaker, baser, more earthy tendencies of the personality. Numerous successful and famous people have had to master their personal failings and shortcomings in order to find not only success but an emotional security that allows individuals to truly feel positive and to enjoy everyday life. The otherwise attractive, magnetic, loving Taurus must develop self-control over any debasing habits and modes of life that would otherwise deter from finding long-lasting happiness. Taurus, the Bull, full of strength and vigor, can easily succumb to baser elements. Gain the full endowment of this natural, God-given strength by exercising your will towards what is powerful and good. Self-acknowledgment and self-control allows these individuals to discover the planetary influences which would generously bestow the more remarkable and lovable features of the native-born Taurus. Recognition and control of the earthly passions must become your main objective. You are more than capable of acquiring extraordinary psychic energy through these efforts. At the same time, you can easily become the perfect role model of dignity, courage, purity, loyalty and personal excellence to your family, friends, and community.

Taurus Character

Taurus are generally good, helpful, gentle and well-intentioned even though they have a tendency to be extremely, to the point of irrationally, stubborn and obstinate. There may be found in these persons the ability to dominate others without so much as a conscious effort. Taurus can be very unyielding in their determination, that is, except perhaps to the person they love. It is surprising that so many are hypersensitive, extremely vulnerable to change and adverse to accepting advice. It can be said that, you, Taurus, simply do not accept advice very well no matter how well intentioned or how constructive.

This produces a powerful resistance to any change rather it be in acquired customs, habits, ideas or lifestyle. You may appear to adapt to a situation if intensely pressured to do so, but at the first opportunity, you will revert to your more comfortable, old ways. Therefore, Taurus are sometimes known to ardently persist in their course of action even after it is not feasible to do so.

Your basic drives are powerful, readily recognizable and may be so easily definable as to be unmistakable. Your main goal in life is to possess or to accumulate material possessions. You appreciate having more than the necessary quantities of food, clothing, shelter, and companionship as well as the comforts of life and what you consider the better things in life. Although practical, hard-working people, Taurus maintain a strong attraction to material wealth and possessions. Your possessions represent security and stability, and you will work and strive all the harder to accumulate all that you deem necessary for yourself and for your family as well. The Taurus native also has a strong drive for prestige, status, and position in the community. You shine with self-respect when others recognize and admire you. You seek not only public honors and awards but public acclaim.

You are tenacious and methodical in achieving your goals and to do so you become probably the most industrious of all the signs. Taurus insist on setting and living by high standards. Reliability, as in a job well done, is one of the strictest standards that you set for yourself and for others. There is nothing shoddy about your work or your methods. Nor are you likely to be prone to making hasty or rash, impulsive decisions. You take your time in painstakingly making detailed plans which must be carried out with the same precision. To a large degree, your aggressions are focused and channeled into constructive and productive pursuits which are very often income-producing activities.

One of your chief guiding principles is conservatism, and this can be found in all of your endeavors. It is a procedure by which you attain and maintain a calmness of spirit and a serenity which allows you a greater ability to work unrestrained by other concerns. You are quite capable of resisting panic and the accompanying phobias of worry that is associated with less focused people. Taurus, the Bull, cannot be pushed or coerced into ill-advised decisions, practices, or actions. You are known for your customary, steady, regular, well-balanced pace in all that you attempt to accomplish.

The Taurus character is marked by a determination that can not be dissuaded. You strive with all your efforts to achieve stability and security by adjusting your behavior accordingly to a rather slow, tenacious tempo in all that you do. You patiently achieve your goals. You are capable of solving the most difficult problems and accomplishing the most complex tasks through perseverance and a will to complete or finish a project. In addition to that, you are known for handling other people in a diplomatic manner while at the same time carefully choosing the best methods for achieving your goals. In this you are patiently determined because you know that the end result will be according to your methods and efforts. The Taurus energy is focused on achieving your purposes and to that extent you appear calm, reflective and seldom emotional. You also can appear obstinate in that you won't quit a job until it is completed.

As a Taurus, you may be very attached to the land if that is your roots and inclination. If not, you form strong attachments to surroundings in which you feel secure both financially and emotionally. To this extent, you strive for a healthy income with which to provide the requisites of your securities.

Above all else, you know how to make a decision and aren't afraid to do so. You carefully decide a path to follow and with your abundance of natural energy, you follow that path. Once you have decided upon a course of action, you follow it in a most determined, routine, methodical method, completing the objective no matter what. Being detail oriented, you prefer to work slowly but surely. Your customs and habits are well determined and your ideas are well established. You do not like to change your focus until the job is completed.

At the same time, the Taurus individual is charming and well liked. You love all aspects of nature. And you have a strong appreciation for good food and for entertaining well. You never forget an excellent restaurant and may even be observed taking notes on frequented establishments.

Your friends know that you are dependable and that you never take unnecessary risks. You make wise judgments about situations and people through practice and because you are not naive. While not insensitive, you avoid people who are depressed by unfortunate circumstances. You prefer people who are willing to fight to overcome adversity. However, if your friends demonstrate this determination, you are more than willing to help them. And you are sought out for advice and counsel as you have the innate ability to soothe and comfort others.

Your love of nature leads you to look forward to long drives, walks, or hikes. Any activity that takes you into a more natural setting pleases you. And you like participating in a variety of recreational activities and sports. Later, in life, when you can no longer participate in sports, you may find yourself sponsoring a favorite team.

The singularity of purpose noted in Taurus individuals, that is, your loyalty to purpose, your strong will, and your enduring ability to work hard at completing tasks are all derived from your great need for security. Your drive for self-preservation is powerful, and you may have a tendency to withdraw within yourself when your security--emotional or material--is denied or threatened. You may be unaware of these drives for security as your powers of self-analysis may be weak. This is due to you having powerful and generally correct natural instincts that guide and direct you. And you have discovered that these instincts have quite often resulted in your desired results. Your sometimes unarticulated motives, while not selfish in the ordinary material way, insures that nothing interferes with the gratification of your instinctual urges, your self-preservation, and your immense need for self-fulfillment.

Taurus are confident that their pursuits are correct. You resent any implication that you need supervision or assistance in making your decisions or completing the tasks at hand. Your instinctual drive is to stay focused on your chosen objectives which you deem will provide the gains necessary to promote and insure your security. Nothing and no one can dissuade you from these decisions. You will cling tenaciously to your own ideas and once you have achieved your goal, whether it be a possession, a lover, money, a home, etc., it is yours forever.

Opportunity and security are one in your mind, but you do not jump at opportunities that require a risk. This limited daring may have resulted from a sheltered life that has always provided material necessities and security. On the other hand, if your life has been less sheltered, you still avoid gain by what you see as unnecessary risks because you manage to provide for yourself by using your own well-thought out methods. Having once inherited or achieved your security, you then seek out past times which will allow your natural energies to freely flow in personal and cultural activities which may provide for your main interests. Others may consider you the least materialistic person because once you have acquired possessions, you take them for granted and forget them, moving on with your life.

Taurus Destiny

Taurus is the Fixed sign in the Earth group. This second Sun sign is the most pronounced physical point of all in the Zodiac. It illustrates the pattern of distinctive, natural releasing of energies. Taurus are self-possessed to the point of being dogmatic at times, and they do not require or seek counsel nor do they accept any contradictions. It may be difficult to really get to know Taurus individuals as they practice a great deal of restraint. While slow to anger and equally difficult to pacify, this person may retain bitter feelings and resentments for a long time. In other words, while the person may be patient and kind-hearted, there is a tendency to seldom forgive an accuser and their retentive memories of wrong doings stay with them.

Taurus is affiliated with the Second House in its relation to money, finances, and material possessions of extrinsic value. Taurus are oriented toward the material aspects of life and will seek a tangible basis for a purpose in life. Travel or leaving home may not necessarily appeal to you as you are not always comfortable in new and unfamiliar environments.

You most naturally focus on matters related to security, and you are at your best only when these needs are assured. An incessant worry about money can throw you off balance. You have the desire to be able to take for granted the basic, essential comforts of a stable life. You may acquire, but you may also spend or lose your gains within your life time.

Being of the Earth, you are ardent and sexually active. You are generally stable in your love life and require sexual satisfaction. You desire satiation and satisfaction through the physical pleasures. In fact, the more ordinary Taurus, controlled by an ego-bound personality and transitory desires, may lazily waste away the days in the pursuit of sensual pleasures. You must become aware that in this as well as in your pursuit of money and other pleasures, you can easily enter the realm of excesses.

Being tenacious, you are set in your ways to the point of knowing how you want to do whatever task is at hand. You may not verbalize your point of view, you may not choose to argue over what you want, but you have a definite way of getting what you want. Your cheerful, winning attitude is, "let's just do it my way".

Taurus, generally speaking, lives a long and quiet life with an abundance of energy and drive for achieving your desires. While you may be stubborn to the point of being at times domineering and unyielding, you are considered trustworthy, steady, and persevering. There is no limit to your abilities to be enduring, persistent, and at the same time composed and diplomatic. Your self-reliant, constructive, and practical methods benefit not only you but your associates. Your friends know you for your humorous, kind, and sympathetic nature, and there is no limit to your magnetic forces. While you are careful, you can demonstrate fearlessness in the face of opposition. You appear to fear nothing. This is simply another display of your obstinacy, your inability to allow anything to stand in your path.

Having strong opinions about what is right, you also demand that justice prevail. This can make you overly curious and inquisitive. Your curiosity can develop often times to the point of being cunning and sly in your effort to learn what you perceive to be the truth.

If well-aspected, the spiritually oriented Taurus produces the tools needed for constructive living. It is this person who patterns material objects and cultivates the development of ideas that are scattered about like seeds by the restless Aries. The aspired Taurus individual forges onward as a potent force who produces materials and services for the good of mankind. Nothing diverts the gifted natives of this sign from their purposes. This person is compelled by the strongest urges to justify the existence through accomplishments. When this individual controls the urge to charge like a bull, and focuses fully on well-set goals, nothing can become a deterrence.

A certain degree of wealth may be obtained, but it must be protected against loss through legal disputes, unemployment, or divorce. Unforeseen inheritances or windfalls through legacy, partnerships or marriage may benefit Taurus. But, sorrows and grief may result from within the family sphere, especially with brothers and sisters. While the life may be calm and peaceful, unnecessary strife may occur due to the stubbornness, firmly held opinions, and obstinate resistance to obstacles and change of Taurus.

If well-aspected, Taurus can leash the vitality of Aries and become the bull which pulls the heavy load. In this, the verbosity of Aries encounters the material resistance of Taurus and is turned into practical methods and uses. Nature's whirlwind is slowed and contained. The compelling tumult of Aries develops into an intensity of feeling in Taurus. Aries expends its energies and resources while Taurus receives and conserves them. The rash fires of passion are contained to produce the warming glow of a steadier, more sustained satisfaction in the completion of ideas. The desire for sensation and new experiences is converted into the quiet capacity for enduring love.

The sign of Taurus represents the monetary values of possessions. In the Zodiac, each sign represents the values of the preceding sign. Selfhood emerges in Aries and the accumulation of possessions results in Taurus. Through careful conservation of resources, Taurus learns to appreciate the value and quality of material possessions.

The Taurus destiny involves strong inclinations for success, but in many cases uncertain and precarious misfortunes may prevail in the first part of life. Unless the Moon is in good aspect to Venus, there is a risk of loss of property, or of adversity, illnesses, divorce, and danger in travels during the 9th, 14th, 25th, and 32nd years; but if during these ages, Jupiter or Venus is in conjunction with Saturn, the threat of these disasters and misfortunes will either disappear or be greatly reduced. There may be sorrow or loss related to the family and unfortunate domestic experiences, but there is gain through thrift, economy and smart investments.

Those Taurus who aspire to a higher plane, are practical and dependable and worthy of honor and trust. They expect the freedom to do things in their own way, but they possess great courage and confidence to see things through to completion. People make way for the person who knows where he's going, and Taurus are rarely in doubt of their goals. These are the people who put into practice and carry through the ideas of others. The natives of this sign are endowed with capable, forceful minds. They make diligent students and succeed in superior intellectual accomplishments. These individuals have receptive minds and they assimilate not only information but the thoughts of others. The Taurus person may find it difficult to distinguish between his ideas and those which he has unconsciously absorbed from the minds of others.

Taurus Occupation

The main attribute of Taurus is personified in devotion, to a person, to an ideal, and most importantly to work. While Aries prefers to be the boss, Taurus is the worker. This individual wants to be on the job so much so that there is an impatience with the preliminary or planning stages of a project or undertaking. They are naturally gifted with great will power and make every effort to adapt to surroundings. This helps them to become successful in a variety of occupations.

Considering the inherent right of planetary endowment, the Taurean individual should be quite successful in any number of positions, professions or in the business world. You are determined, industrious, and reliable. You are honest, hard workers with a penchant for completing the job at hand. You have a natural ability for working with details or in work necessitating accuracy. Along with these talents, you are often known for your green thumb and love of plants and animals. These many talents combined with your infamous quality of methodical perseverance makes you successful in trade, industry, commerce, farming and ranching.

Taurus, with a pronounced predisposition toward the accumulation of material wealth, loves to count money. They derive a profound satisfaction from acquiring and increasing assets. For example, notice the bull that symbolizes a bull market in the world of finance. Taurus excel in financial pursuits, and their detail-oriented minds produce talented accountants. They are regarded as having unwavering fidelity which wins them esteem from their associates. Known for excellent judgment and steady persistency, they can make successful bankers and will also succeed in the world of higher finance. Endowed with self-reliance, Taurus have admirable courage and the ability to judge public opinion. They do well in the fields of politics and public relations, and they are excellent diplomats.

Taurus have the ability to take the plans of others and complete them. They do well as builders, contractors, and engineers. They may do well in any number of occupations which require mechanical ability or in the field of transportation as well. They are also excellent technicians in all fields.

Taurus have strong study habits and are gifted in mathematics, literature and music. They do well in the study of botany, chemistry, zoology and other sciences as well as in areas requiring a strong, retentive memory rather than creative originality. Taurus would do well in any field which requires a great deal of memorization of details and facts.

Blessed with a natural gift for learning, Taurus make successful philosophers, teachers, psychiatrists, therapists, social workers and counselors and find success in all fields requiring patience and a strong will power. With their love of nature, gardening, and plant and animal life, occupations in the fields of agriculture, horticulture, veterinarian science, and genetic research are favored. Taurus have a love for art and beauty and do well in fields encompassing these areas. In fact, the sign of Taurus has produced many talented and well known artists and writers. The Taurean love of tradition, appreciation of artistic beauty, memory for details, and inherent money-sense make them ideally suited for dealing in the arts and antiquities. Taurus are also talented in drawing, architecture, and sculpture. Then too, they do well as public servants, officials, and in government positions including the military. They also make talented and patient nurses, doctors, and technicians. Generally speaking, Taurus should avoid occupations which require instant, quick decision-making skills and actions. Exceptions to this advice include the scientific fields in which there are established criteria and procedural routines.

In the business world you are careful and make clear-headed decisions, and you have a tendency to simplify methods for practical application. You do not take unnecessary risks and, generally speaking, you handle business negotiations well. You make good administrators in fields which require a preponderance of utilizing and following rules and regulations.

As in most of your endeavors, your success depends a great deal on you. The extent of your success is directly related to your ability to utilize the strength of your self-will and to work hard at all of your endeavors while making a conscious effort to control your passions and pleasures.

Taurus Marriage

People born in this sign may be the easiest to live with. That is if you have the personal qualities that allow you to live with a Taurus without opposing their second-sign nature. One must understand that to live in harmony with Taurus translates to accepting the individual. Taurus don't consider cooperation the same as companionship or doing things together. At the same time, Taurus strive for a peaceful environment. They have a friendly nature, but they don't necessarily consider mutual pastimes as a requirement for happiness. This may annoy less self-sufficient people until they realize that Taurus inevitably comes home to roost especially when not coerced. Taurus, the Bull, will break down any barriers to doing things in his or her own way. There is noted among Taurus a resentment of any suggestion that they needs supervision of any kind.

Quite truthfully, the horoscope of the second-sign native is generally predisposed to two marriages. The first one may be a hasty marriage made early in life because of Taurus' strong passions and desire for the opposite sex and sexual gratification. Often, they are tempted into early marriages by flattery and attention, especially sexual attention. Unfortunately, these affairs of the heart often end disastrously with separation and, in extreme situations, even death. The Taurus person who realizes he or she has married the wrong person, will go to great lengths in their attempt to change the other person to their ways. Unfortunately, this rarely works. Neither the male or female of this second-sign should marry too young. The good news is that Taurus appear to learn from the mistakes of the first marriage, and the second marriage is much more likely to be harmonious and successful.

When you, Taurus, take the plunge and actually fall in love, your true and basic nature finally permits you to express your emotions, perhaps in your own way, and to satisfy your desires. Actually, as long as your Taurean physical needs are satisfied, you are extremely faithful and devoted to the person you love. Taurus prefer the security of home and fidelity and are sentimentally attuned to preserving the home situation. For the most part, you make ideal marriage partners.

Taurus males are tenderly considerate mates, being both protective and supportive while striving to be good providers for their families. Preferring not to be demonstrative, you may have a tendency not to verbalize your feelings; however, you are at the same time giving and caring through fidelity and devotion. You prefer a woman who you consider physically attractive and who maintains your interest in the love relationship. You stay faithful and kind if your wife doesn't argue with you about your likes and dislikes and if you are sexually satisfied; otherwise you may be prone to sexual escapades or at least flirting.

The Taurus tendency to be suspicious and jealous may cause them numerous problems. Your fear of publicity and of losing your self-esteem may inhibit you from seeking separations or divorces. You may even choose to ‚save face' by staying in a disastrous, unhappy marriage. In that case, you may prefer to engage in discreet arrangements outside the marriage. Then too, the Taurean character trait of being stubborn and obstinate may annoy their spouses. It must be accepted that Taurus are set in their ways, often times much preferring routine to change. This can, in a domestic situation, lead to boredom unless the spouse enjoys the same set patterns of behavior and daily living.

Taurus women make ideal lovers and wives. You love with a great degree of determination, devotion and single-mindedness, and, needless to say, passion. You are an ardent lover because you truly enjoy sex and sensuous pleasures. It is not a duty to you, but an activity you look forward to and to which you bring your own level of excitement. You, too, may find some difficulty in verbalizing your feelings or being overly sentimental. You are not a mushy, touchy-feely person. But, at the same time, there is an intense genuineness and sincerity in your love for you husband. And you strive to be supportive of your husband in every way. Your greatest requirement is to experience a feeling of security. Once that is achieved you are happy in your everyday life. There is, in addition, your great need for material possessions which may lead you to consider your marriage carefully with respect to the impending financial situation. The Taurus female is as possessive and jealous as her male counterpart in this sign. Any infidelity on the part of your spouse will cause you much emotional stress and a loss of your basic sense of security. Your instinctive drive is to retaliate, to get back at him, sometimes even in greater measure. You are less obstinate and intolerant than the male Taurus with a tendency to more lenient and permissive as long you don't feel your security is being threatened. The Taurus woman makes a very fine homemaker as she manages the home as well as she does her other endeavors in life. You prefer the best quality in furnishings, possessions, and food for your husband and family. You enjoy feeling like you have contributed to the success of the marriage through the procurement of material possessions.

In the home situation, Taurus natives love and enjoy entertaining. You have a preference for large, roomy homes that are well-furnished. You are totally devoted to your family and strive to provide more than adequate support. You help your children financially and enjoy giving them sound, helpful advice. At the same time, you have a need to feel appreciated for all your efforts. Your main ideals in life are to have financial security and health for your family.

The happiest marriage for the native-born, second sign Taurus may be with a Scorpio. Also consider the acceptability and compatibility of those born under the signs of Virgo or Libra.

THE TAURUS MAN

As Taurus is ruled by Venus, so is he ruled by his affections. His entire life can be altered by a casual remark from a friend or associate because when he does seek advice, he intends to follow it. However, in most instances this man prefers to handle his problems himself in a calm and dignified manner all the while maintaining his honor and position. He has a profound respect for money and almost every activity is connected with the possibility of acquiring it.

Taurus can be the most loyal of friends, but others must permit them to do things in their own way. The Taurus male is fond of the good things in life and loves to share his pleasure with his friends. He enjoys entertaining and providing the best of food and drink for his guests. He has a strong attraction for people with good imaginations as this stimulates him and focuses his initiatives into constructive endeavors. He chooses his friends based on who can be useful to him and who might be able to benefit him socially.

On the other hand, in some instances, this man can be dominating. And when the nature of the stubborn bull arises, others may find him too rigid and too intolerant of those who don't share his opinions. While Taurus makes the best of friends, they are the worst of enemies. Once he is angered, the Taurus

male rarely forgives or forgets. This is not a person to oppose without good reason. At the same time, he is by nature humble and seldom asks for anything for himself. He is generally more than willing to be inconvenienced in order to help others or to benefit a worthy cause. He appears to have resources for complicated, difficult situations. But for his good deeds and charitable attitude, he enjoys public acclaim and appreciation.

When selecting a gift for this man, choose one that is practical and useful. His clothes should be sensible, functional and of good quality. He loves fine jewelry.

These men are sensual and they know intuitively how to deal with the opposite sex. The young Taurus male has a strong predisposition toward promiscuity. Much of this has to do with his strong, erotic sexual drive, but, at the same time, this man apparently equates sexual conquest with the acquisition of possessions; he believes that he gains and hold status and prestige based on the number of his conquests. As he matures and discovers real love, however, his emotions are deeper and more long lasting, but all the same, he can be very sexually demanding.

THE TAURUS WOMAN

This woman is attractive and humorous, loving a good time. The influence of Venus, the planet of love and beauty, grants her a very special, appealing charm and personality. You possess a great potential for being an ideal lover and wife, and you love any and all pleasures, luxury, music, art and the good things in life. You have an appreciation for good conversation and the company of friends. You are graceful, seductive, and elegant with a fondness for stylish clothing and jewelry. You have had many admirers in your life, and later in life you'll find that the opposite sex continues to find you seductive. When young, you may seek reassurances of your desirability and attractiveness by being involved in a series of relationships and encounters. Your courteous and affable disposition, however, favors friendship, love and marriage. And once you fall in love, you love with the same degree of determination, devotion and single-mindedness that you show in all the other areas of your life.

You are lavish in your affections. Your warm-hearted, amiable nature wins you many friends and makes you dearly loved by all. And in this respect, you are sincere in your affections, feeling concern and empathy for your friends and family. Your charming personality is entertaining and others find you a delight to be around.

Family is an important part of your life. You have a great love for children, guiding them with your skill and wisdom, and your children are well provided for as you manage your resources well. You may marry young and give up your career for your family for, once married, you consider this the most important aspect of your life. You are unquestionable faithful, but you may enjoy flirting and the attention it brings. At the same time, you are known for being extremely jealous and possessive of the man in your life. However, you are a devoted and supportive wife, willing to endure any hardship or sacrifice for those you love and care about.

The poorly developed Taurus female, it must be mentioned, is more than a little prone to laziness, and it is this woman who desires more than anything to find a successful husband to support her. She is not above being cunning and manipulative to get what she wants. And when she does get the man she wants, she is not above cheating. Pleasure and gratification motivate her direction in life, and she shows little concern for who she hurts or who she uses. Unfortunately, those who suffer are most often her family members and friends.

Taurus woman are very private about their personal lives. You are not one to talk nonstop about your problems. In the face of problems, you prefer to remain calm and handle them as much as possible by yourself. You are typically conservative and may resist new concepts or change. You should remain on your guard against insincere flattery. Your kind and sympathetic nature at times makes you gullible and susceptible.

You may enjoy arts and crafts, drawing, and painting, but you should guard against your innate tendency to purchase more kits and supplies than you can ever finish or use. When you focus your energies and drives, you become skilled and talented in your pursuits.

In your professional life, you are determined and not easily distracted from your ambitions. Others note your dependable nature and your ability to work hard. You have a strong desire to excel in any and all of your efforts and pursuits. There is a tendency toward acquisition of friends, possessions, houses and lands. You are intuitive and as a rule display good judgment in matters related to financial security.

Taurus Love Life

Considering all that has been said, it becomes rather obvious that Taurus, the Bull, is of a highly sexed and sensual nature. Being ardent, passionate and impetuous, the nature of the second-sign native displays an attitude toward sex that is the most direct and uncomplicated of all the signs. This desire for all that is natural, earthy and pleasing leaves few inhibitions with this person. Uninhibited and free, seeking sensual pleasure at its fullest, there is no requirement for the niceties and subtleties of frills and pretenses. Glamour is not needed. This person knows what he or she wants, intuitively, and does not waste time questioning the motives behind these inner drives. The basic facts and desires need no explaining. In love, however, you have a natural inclination to be jealous and possessive.

This robust and physical response to emotionally sensual vibrations combines with the Taurus natives' great love of passion and affection. You are the individual who loves to romp naked in the fields and woods or on the beach with an attractive companion. Or perhaps being with your loved one in front of a blazing fireplace in the comfort of your home is more to your taste.

Ah, but Taurus, as has been mentioned, it is quite possible for your passions to get the best of you, to run away with you, to lead you astray. You are capable of being attracted to and seduced by practically any physically attractive person of the opposite sex. Your desires can easily lead you to a life of self-gratification. Because of this, you may come to experience both ecstasy and despair in your love life. Many of those individuals who become addicted to sex are second-sign natives. It is up to you to take charge of your life, preferable early on, and for you to gain control and command of your passions. At its highest level, the position of Venus in your sign allows you to elevate the physical, to transform the energies of your earthy desires and passions to a higher spiritual plane where you gain a glimpse of true joy and the beauty of true union.

While you love flirting and the admiration and attentions you can attain through your gracious efforts, you also have a more serious nature. The courteous and affable disposition of the better aspected Taurean leads the native to seek a love partner with whom to share both the physical and sensual aspects of a relationship and a life; but this individual also seeks an emotional commitment to establish a sound partnership in all aspects of life. Once you find the love of your life, you stick to this relationship with great tenacity. You love being in love. You may have a tendency to express your love wordlessly, but you are no less serious, ardent and affectionate in your feelings. In love, you are generous and will consider no sacrifice too great for the other person.

Taurus Children

Taurus children are sturdy and passionate with a care free and happy disposition which makes them enjoyable to be around. They love the attentions and affections of their parents and strive to attain it. Early on, they exhibit the ability to act like little adults, imitating and patterning themselves after their adult counterparts. They also show an early trait toward financial independence, and they love to purchase items for themselves to insure their security and to underscore being grown up and independent. With this basic nature comes a strident tendency to be determined, stubborn and high tempered. They have strong likes and dislikes. They may be predisposed to moodiness at times which can be upsetting to parents. They are most docile when surrounded by an abundance of affectionate attention.

Early on they display the ability to work hard and earn money with little jobs and chores. This adds to their need for independence and to feeling free of constraint from others and from authority that is too stringent. They prefer to set their own rules, but respond in a positive manner to a well established daily pattern and routine. They have a need for rules that make sense to them and that fit within their framework of how they view the world. They will not like rules which limit their ability to achieve independence and adult standing.

These children love nature, the out-of-doors, and both wildlife and domestic animals. Any opportunity for outdoor excursions that expose them to the beauty of natural surroundings are enjoyed and appreciated. Being affectionate they enjoy pets and shower their attentions on them.

When faced with unyielding opposition, this child may display a temper and fury that can be at times uncontrollable. This is their nature, and physical punishment only strengthens it. They require quiet, calm persuasion and even to be left alone to brood out their problems at times. While these children are headstrong, they are also susceptible to patient kindness and understanding. Don't attempt to drive this child against his will. Attempt at all times to use calm reasoning and to lead them to their better natures.

These children require strong role models. They are watching the adults in their lives in order to be more adult-like themselves. To develop to their fullest, they require that the strength of their natures be recognized, developed and channeled into positive attributes. These children will be a source of satisfaction to their parents and will show a natural inclination to be good students who achieve scholastically.

Relationships with Other Signs

Taurus are light-hearted, pleasant and joyful. Bright and witty, they have a congenial personality which others enjoy. They may be fond of music, dancing, poetry and art. You have a sympathetic and winning manner toward others. To a great degree, you are protective and gentle in your personal relationships. Being very magnetic and captivating you are a favorite at social occasions. You take much pleasure from being with others, and your friends and acquaintances are limited only by your need to occasionally have quiet times to yourself. You may have a tendency to try to hide your better nature, but your close friends find you out and to them you respond. You like the good things in life and are generous and willing to share your good fortune with your friends. A talented host or hostess, you love to entertain and are never happier than when you are providing well-prepared meals for your friends.

You make the most loyal friend or companion, and your dependability and obvious loyalty lead close friends to depend on you for advice and encouragement. As leaders, you can inspire love and devotion. But you must be permitted to have your own way, that is, to do things your way. You are also somewhat possessive in your relationships and can be unbending and relentlessly inflexible. Your stubbornness can be a liability. If angered, the intensity of your nature can destroy relationships and even make enemies. However, you respond to kindness and expressions of affection.

Taurus individuals discovery their most lasting friendships with people born between August 21-27, and September 20-27, December 21 and January 20-27. Your central affinities are found with people born October 21 to November 20-27. Your closest friends may be found in the signs of Virgo, Libra, Capricorn and Aquarius.

How to Find Your Soul-Mate, Stars, and Destiny

Taurus Sexuality

That subject which interests us all: our own personal sexuality. Why does a person feel the way they do? Why does he or she like a certain person and not another? What arouses a person and why? On some level, these questions influences one and all. Like all aspects of our lives and lifestyles, the public attitude toward sex is ever changing and evolving. From the restrictive taboos of the Victorian Age, through the revitalization of the Industrial Age, to the make love not war of the 1960s to the commercialism of the 1980s and the 1990s, sex is always on our minds. Will the Age of Information or the Age of Aquarius bring new insights?

The American culture is not only influenced by popular trends and thought but by its unique cultural diversity as well. To the newcomer or newly arrived, American society can appear perplexing. What is difficult to understand is that in this freedom-based culture, the individual is literally free to be whoever he or she decides. And the gamut runs from the most traditional, reserved, cautious, and sexually repressed individuals to others who flaunt their sexuality, centering their lives around their sexual habits. Perhaps it is because of this very diversity that our culture makes some attempt not to be overly offensive to the sensitivities of some while giving a tolerant nod to the liberties of others. We are totally free, within the guidelines of laws, to seek divine enlightenment or to destroy ourselves with pleasures. Americans have the freedom to choose, individually, what importance their sexual behavior will play in their lives.

That being the case, sex is recognized by every serious discipline--from psychologists to scientists to astrologers--as being a central focus on individual lives. Freud saw sex as an influence on every aspect of the individual life. And from the sexist boys in the locker room to the most enlightened of intellectuals, sex remains a fundamental part of life that cannot be ignored. Get two friends together and the subject eventually turns to sex, romance, or marriage. One can blame it on the media, but sooner or later discussing the stock market gets boring, but sex never does.

There are those who hold to the theory that the primary function of sex is to have children and any other consideration is secondary. There are others for whom sex is an integral part of life, providing one of the greatest stress relievers ever invented. That all other living species procreate seasonally points to the reasoning of the second theory. But all pleasures (or temptations) in life also promote the possibilities of problems and health concerns unless a little logic is also applied.

Astrologically, the sexual nature has been examined from the Garden of Eden to the lives of contemporary celebrities. And what every serious astrologer will say is that how the individual relates to sexuality is not based on the Sun sign alone. The entire chart must be examined because each person is a unique combination of Sun, Moon, Ascendant, planets, Houses and aspects. A comparison of two charts often sheds light on compatibility. Compatibility between two people is often found when the Sun sign is in the same sign as their lover's Ascendant, or vice versa. Opposite Sun signs or an opposite Sun sign and Ascendant may also blend well together.

In a woman's chart, the placement of Venus is indicative of her sexuality while the position of Mars and the Sun indicates what kind of man she is attracted to. In a man's chart, the position of Mars tells how he relates to women, and the position of Venus and the Moon indicates what type of woman arouses him. In comparing two charts, look for the aspects of conjunction, sextile, square, trine, and oppositions. Remember that oppositions can blend. The square brings differences but much energy while conjunctions can be beneficial. The sextile and trine bring harmony. When a person's Venus and their lover's Mars are in the same sign, there is a strong attraction even if differences of opinions occur. When Venus and the other person's Ascendant are in the same sign, it adds to the sexual compatibility. Venus in the lover's sun sign brings a mutual interest while Mars in the lover's Moon sign is emotionally intense.

There is a vast variety of people found within each Sun sign, but basic characteristics and traits do exist. However, generalizations are just that and a fuller picture of the individual is reflected by the complete chart. The following section deals with Sun sign sexuality in a general manner. While the importance of sex remains the same in each Sun sign, the focus and attitudes vary.

Taurus Sexuality - Man

Taurus is an Earth sign ruled by Venus, and this man takes his sexuality in stride. To Taurus sex is as natural as breathing, and he may wonder why other people talk about it so much when they should be enjoying it. Aries is the sign of innovative ideas, and Taurus is the sign of implementation. What Aries dreams up, Taurus builds no matter how much hard work it requires. The earthy passions of Taurus know few inhibitions. Taurus desires security and will set out in life to acquire material possessions. Home and family are important to this man, and therefore he takes his decisions seriously when it comes to love and marriage. But before he ties the knot and decides to settle down, he may feel it only natural to sample as much as possible, to broaden his experiences, and to know what is available. It must be noted that the Taurus male is considered one of the most attractive men in the Zodiac, and added to this is a unique magnetism that attracts sexual attention. Although, he is most aware of this, he isn't normally a vain man, like Aries. He takes it all in stride thinking that's just the way it is. Neither is he as impetuous as Aries, but then perhaps he doesn't have to be. Women seem to just flow to him. And even a woman who isn't interested in him, will recognize by that look in his eye that he is sexually secure.

This is a sensible, practical and cautious man who may frolic with the glamorous types for the fun of it but who much prefers the earthy types. He is most comfortable with a woman who is uninhibited and ready to enjoy the purest forms of sex. His sexuality is endowed with passion, ardor, and staying power. He may be slow and steady, but he never lacks for virility and endurance. Taurus greatly admires nature and appreciates natural beauty. His greatest appreciation may be for the form of the naked body, and he may most enjoy relaxing in the nude with his lover while admiring her. This man isn't prone to talking sex. He performs sex. And this is a man who, however serious he may be, enjoys the pleasures of life. He is drawn to comforts and conveniences but may enjoy sexual experiences in any and all locations. Natural settings especially arouse him.

How to Find Your *Soul-Mate, Stars,* and *Destiny*

An earthy nature compels this man to seek gratification and not to go without it for any length of time. Sexual gratification is, after all, a natural part of life. If his lover isn't totally satisfying his desires, he will seek additional outlets outside the relationship. If his partner accuses him of such activities, he can patiently wait out her accusations preferring not to be drawn in to any confrontations. Of course, if she manages to wear down his patience, his formidable Taurus temper will be aroused.

The Taurus patience and caution makes them men not to be rushed. They prefer to think about their actions first. In many instances, it is the woman who first approaches the Taurus man, and he is seldom at a lack for female attention. Once approached, if his interest is aroused, Taurus is not a man to disappoint a woman. He will go to a great amount of trouble to respond to her attentions, but he is a serious man and will expect serious action. In other words, this isn't a man to be teased. If a woman wants sex with him, she should let him know and he will respond either positively or negatively, but if he responds positively, it is definitely sex he wants, not companionship.

Eroticism and fun and games are all well and good, but what this man most desires is straight and direct sex. He doesn't need novelty to inspire his interest or his ardor. A roll in the hay may excite him as much as all the kinky deviations anyone can think up. He can be competitive though, and if a friend brags of four women in one night then Taurus will have to make it five.

Taurus responds best to positive attention, praise, and approbation. Compliments bring out the best in this man. However serious he may be at times, he likes for things to run smoothly and can be easy going and congenial. He can also be light-hearted, responding to fun, humor and laughter. A negative, overly critical or complaining person can drive him away or definitely turn him off.

The sign of Taurus rules the throat and neck, and this man responds to gentle neck messages and kisses to the neck and throat area. And most any form of oral gratification whether it be kissing or oral sex excites the Taurus man. The thought of his penis in his lover's mouth will always bring him back for more. Remember, he is earthy and sensual and the thought of giving oral gratification may entice him as well. This is as natural and earthy as sex can get, and Taurus responds in full measure.

Once this man finds the love of his life, Taurus is known for settling in comfortably and permanently. They are not prone to sudden changes for the sake of change. Taurus likes stability and security in love and life.

Taurus Sexuality - Woman

The Taurus woman is as feminine as the Taurus man is male. The sign of Taurus is feminine after all and it is brought to its fullest form in this Venus ruled female. She may strive for beauty in her efforts to bring her femininity into full play. She is the pleasing, easy going, domestic, and caring woman who stronger and more assertive women wonder about. That is not to say that this is a weak woman by any means. It is simply that being totally feminine doesn't offend her. This may be the woman who cooks, bakes, sews, and does home crafts to beautify her house. And her dress may tend toward a ruffle or two around the neck line and a flair for color. She is a woman drawn to home, security, possessions, and family with a tendency toward comfort, food and enjoyable pleasures. But even if she tends to gain weight with all that good living, she manages to always appear attractive, neat and well cared for. This is a woman who will expend much time, effort, and attention on her appearance.

Like the male Taurus, her sexuality comes naturally to her and she is most fulfilled when she has a man in her life. Sex is regarded as a most natural part of life, and this woman is happiest when sexually satisfied. It isn't that she likes to expose herself, but she finds the nude form compelling. This is a woman who is most at ease on a nude beach. Or running naked through the woods with her man seeking the perfect natural setting to do what comes most naturally--making love. Unsatisfied in an affair, this woman will be tempted to find additional sources of sex outside the relationship. At some time in her life, she may play at erotica just to see what all the fuss is about--after all, whatever is being done, it's only sex--but left to her own natural desires she much prefers direct and uncomplicated sex. She can become contemptuous and critical of a mate who loses interest in this vital aspect of life.

The Taurus quality of endurance is found in this feminine creature as well. She never seems to become exhausted by the physical exertion required in sex. In fact, she may yearn for just such exertion. This is not a woman who feigns headaches to get out of sex. She is most aroused by a man who can match her own ardor and emotions in lengthy sessions of love making. And she knows how to apply skill and technique in helping a man prolong his arousal. She may find oral sex a delightful way to make sex last and last and last, at least through a few orgasms, until she is ready to bring things to completion. And she may have filed away in her memory banks just how long it takes this particular man to recuperate and to be ready to go again.

At the heart of a Taurus woman will always be that idealistic dream of finding her true love and building a security based on home and family. And she makes the most perfect of mates, working hard to make the marriage successful. Unhappy, she can be critical, but when happy she is a delight. If disillusioned and disappointed in love, she may attempt to place other aspects of life above her yearnings, but sooner or later she is seeking love again. She is her most content with a man in her life. And that is especially true if that man is fulfilling her sexual desires as well.

Taurus Health

Taurus are extremely prone to the pleasures of life and have a great love for food, drink and entertainment. They love to indulge their appetites preferring rich, well-prepared food--often in excess. This natural inclination can, of course, lead to weight gain. And weight gain, needless to say, can lead to health problems. It is important for these individuals to consider a nourishing, well-balanced diet that is low in fat. It is also equally important to avoid an overindulgence in alcohol.

Preferring quiet, sedentary lifestyles of ease, Taurus would do well to plan a daily routine that included some form of physical exercise. This is beneficial to the mind, emotions, and the physical well being of the body as well as an excellent method by which to reduce stress. The more physically fit these individuals are, the better able they are to control their temperaments, their pleasure-seeking natures, and their tendencies toward angry outbursts. Remember, frequent anger quite often produces stress on the physical well-being of a body, and it is this stress which can develop into any number of nervous complaints and illnesses.

While it is true that the ruling planet, Venus, bestows much strength and vitality to the body, Taurus are susceptible to illnesses brought on by stress or that develop because of excesses in either work or pleasure. They may find themselves prone to depression, headaches, and stress-related illnesses. Generally, illnesses to be on guard against concern the throat and heart, and they may be susceptible to problems related to laryngitis, goiter, tonsillitis, sore throat, stiff neck, and diphtheria. Illnesses affecting the liver, spleen and kidneys are noted. Watch for problems with the skin, eyes, and vocal cords. The health is affected by maladies related to the spleen, liver and kidneys. Gaul stones and diabetes are frequent in this sign. Females should be aware of any developing problems with the ovaries. Rheumatism may develop in these individuals.

Of great benefit to Taurus would be the assimilation of practices of meditation and other stress-reducing activities. Meditation can actually improve self-control and strengthen will power while at the same time providing a certain peace of mind. By improving the state of mind, by offsetting worries, and by learning mental relaxation, these persons can actually improve their health, their temperament, and their general well being. Herbs beneficial to this sign are ground-ivy, deadly night-shade, and vervain.

History of Taurus

Taurus is symbolized by the Bull and this large animal is often considered dangerous, but that is not necessarily the case. The bull can be a very mild and docile animal especially when domesticated. To the Babylonians, the Bull was that area of the sky where the full Moon was found during the plowing season. In the original Babylonian Zodiac, which had eighteen signs rather than twelve, the Bull was divided among several constellations including the Tuft of Hair, the Old Man and the Charioteer. The Egyptian Zodiac contained thirty-six decans and all of these had ruling gods or spiritual powers which granted or bestowed characteristics on the signs or decans. Taurus symbolized resurrection to the ancient Egyptians. This sign was represented by the sacred Apis Bull which was thought of as a living representation of Taurus. The early European May Day festival with its pole and garlands may well have evolved from the ancient Egyptian festival celebrating the entrance of the Sun into Taurus.

In Assyrian religious rites, Taurus was the original Bull or Baal which was referred to as the "Sacred Bull" or the "Golden Calf". Four thousand years ago, Taurus marked the vernal equinox. Thus, when the ancient Persians designated the signs of the Zodiac by letters of the alphabet, the first letter represented Taurus. The ancient Jews also referred to Taurus as the first of the Zodiac signs.

The Old Testament refers to Haggai as a prophet and to Thaddeus, or St. Andrew, as an apostle of the sign of Taurus. It designates Asmodeus as being the angel of Taurus. In Hebraic mythology, the sign of Taurus is referred to as Ephraim who was Joseph's second son. Joseph also appears to be associated with this sign.

Another analogy includes the Bull, Apis, Reem, Aurochs, and the Unicorn which are described as being enraged and irresistible. In Greek mythology, Taurus the Bull carried Europa to Crete. Among other ancient civilizations the symbol of the bull was prevalent. In ancient China, Taurus was named the "Golden Ox" while in early civilizations of South America, this constellation was depicted as an ox.

Taurus is ruled by Venus and is the exaltation of the Moon (especially in the Third Decan) and the detriment of Mars who is uncomfortable in the home of Venus. The Pleiades, a cluster of seven stars, are located in Taurus. This "band of Orion" are known for their "sweet influences". In mythology, these seven stars were the seven daughters of Atlas, who held the heaven and the earth, and were known for their sympathy and affection. In other literary references, they were referred to as the seven virgins or the seven lamps.

In general, the ancient astrologers did not depict Taurus as being wild and fierce, especially considering that the ruling planet is Venus. Rather, these individuals were destined to be ruled by their affections. These natives, it was felt, wanted to stay on good terms with others and would go to great lengths to do so, but not by giving in to others as much as by being patient and calm and ignoring the problems or situations for as long as possible. This may be the reason that many consider them to have lazy attributes. The Taurus relation to the Earth, that is, being slow, methodical, and obstinate as a bull, may contribute to the association with laziness. That observation is in direct contrast with the general description of Taurus natives as being hard-working. But one must remember, each sign produces two distinct types of characteristics. So, it is felt that the ordinary, baser Taurean may laze away his days in the pursuit of sensual pleasures, while the more developed natives are steadfast and diligent with a determined will to matcrialize and embody the purposes of the Creator. As material people they like all that is physical and tangible.

Taurus is often associated with money, but originally the meaning was not the equivalent of money but of real wealth pertaining to the earthy forces of production. Modern astrologers frequently associate the influence of Venus with the earthy side of Taurus. But it can also be found that when Venus rules, the natives are fond of pleasure, music, art, and can be as generous as they are amorous.

This second-sign native is born to a heritage of strength and freedom, storm and stress. With their God-given capacity for great things, they have full powers to seek unlimited, unopposed development and fulfillment. It is an excellent birth sign, endowing its natives with positive attributes which can bring success and accomplishment.

Taurus

April 21 -- May 20

The Thebaic Calendar

Character, Personality, and Destiny

The old civilizations and calendars of the ancients once gave the destiny of individuals born on each day of the month. This is more tradition than scientific discovery. This is intended for an everyday use, when people want a quick reference to their destiny and the nature indicated by their horoscope. Each Zodiac sign is divided into three groups of ten degrees with each sign covering 30 degrees. This represents ten days of the respective Zodiac sign and gives the native a certain influence and destiny. These observations were completed for thousands of years by priests who recorded them in the Thebaic Calendars.

Whether Taurus is the person's Sun sign, the Ascendant, on the cusp, or in a House, the characteristics of this sign become evident. The Moon is exalted in Taurus, and in Taurus it is the most stable. This means that the usual impulsiveness and moodiness of the Moon becomes more balanced by persistence and determination, granting a hopeful and positive outlook on a native who is ambitious and reliable in action. Taurus is the first of the Earth signs, providing the substance for lunar forces to complete its work. But, it is to be noted that wherever Taurus is found in the Zodiac, it bestows practical results in work and projects.

DUALITY: Feminine   **ELEMENT:** Earth   **QUALITY:** Fixed   **RULER:** Venus

The Earth signs are most directed at tangible matters which the spirit must learn to harness and use in order to function. Taurus, as the Fixed Earth sign, is far and beyond the most stable and practical sign in the Zodiac. These individuals are down to Earth in there approach to life-- they know exactly what they want and that is what they pursue. Taurus is considered most concerned with the acquisition of possessions and security, especially financial security. The Taurus individual applies himself or herself to this task, either working diligently or concentrating dutifully on how to obtain the necessities of life: food, clothing, home, transportation, and the trappings of modern life. They are most concerned with the tangible proof of their possessions. These individuals are not necessarily selfish as compared to some of the other signs, but they are focused on obtaining what they deeply feel they need and want. And far be it for anyone to attempt to change the mind of the Taurus individual. These people set their hoofs firmly in the Earth and no force on Earth can change their minds. They are for the most part mild mannered and good natured, somewhat cautious but determined. That is, until someone attempts to change their minds or challenges their firmly held opinions. Now, there are instances when they can be persuaded and cajoled, but it is a waste of time to attempt to force the Taurus Bull. It is at that point that Taurus can exhibit the rage of the Bull to its fullest force. That is not to say that Taurus does not and can not aspire to great spiritual heights. Many Taurus individuals are serious about their religious and traditional beliefs. Also, many a Taurus illustrates the significance of this sign by becoming an administrator, builder, or in some manner a doer who seeks accomplishments in one form or another by managing material or financial resources.

Taurus may be the least concerned with self-analysis. They are adept at accepting themselves the way they are, and they generally feel quite secure in their perceptions of themselves and their beliefs. Even when they recognize the differences in others, they smoothly accept that material possessions are the basis for their security before continuing on in their quest to acquire more and better. In this way, they are quite lovable and endearing because it is not out of any contrivement or affectation that they proceed, but out of the purest form of their spirit and with the best intentions. Generally, Taurus makes little effort to interfere in the lives of others and they most appreciate the same in return. And they can make pleasant companions who are congenial and easy to live with--that is--as long as no one attempts to change them or to alter their routine or lifestyle. Prestige, appearances, and a respectable social standing are important which may make them at times a bit snobbish. But then again, they may also be somewhat shy and this slight air of snobbishness may simple be a cover for this timid individual. The greatest challenge in the life of Taurus is to watch for overindulgence in food and all the good things of life, or they may have a tendency to gain weight. But when all is said and done, Taurus remains remarkably persevering with strong powers of endurance.

The First Decan

The First Decan occurs from 0 degrees to 10 degrees of Taurus and applies to those individuals born between April 21 and April 30. With these individuals there is observed a relentless determination to satiate the desire for possessions, security, money, and status. These Taurus individuals are focused on achieving results. They may have a fondness for luxury and material comforts as well as good food and pleasure with Venus bestowing an appreciation of music or art. Not only are First Decan Taurus persons possessive, but they are highly jealous as well, especially of their loved ones or romantic partners. These are not people to take a risk or to gamble needlessly with their personal security. Rather, they are known to work hard and steadfastly toward their goals and objectives.

The Second Decan

The Second Decan is designated as from 10 degrees to 20 degrees of Taurus and applies to those individuals born from May 1 to May 10. These are individuals who perhaps most strongly exhibit all the characteristics of the sign of Taurus. It is also noted that the Second Decan individuals apply the use of a more detailed and analytical approach to problem solving, financial management, and acquisitions. They are practical, down to Earth, diligent, and, it must be noted, many possess a whimsical sense of humor that takes it all in, turns it around, and nails it soundly on the head. They remain, though, dedicated to their financial security, possessions, and home.

The Third Decan

The Third Decan is designated as from 20 degrees to 30 degrees of Taurus and includes those persons born between May 11 and May 20. While these individuals are approaching the cusp of Gemini, it should be mentioned, that it is probably Taurus who most influences any Gemini tendencies. But this may be the Taurus who is so gifted with the art of conversation and glib expressions. Third Decan Taurus individuals remain, as all good Taurus, centered on acquisitions of material possessions combined with the ability to luxuriate in comfortable settings. They are, of course, hard working, ambitious, well organized, and diligent in their continuing efforts to realize their goals and to achieve financial and personal security. That they are also graced with a bit of the magical Gemini personality is all to their benefit.

With that all said and done, refer to following specific birth dates within each Decan to learn more about your own personal information. Again, this is information gathered throughout the centuries from observations of Taurus individuals in order for the information to used on a comparison basis.

First Decan of Taurus:

April 21 - April 30 -
First Ten Days

Character, Personality, and Temperament:

The practical feeling is very developed; inventive, ingenious; good negotiator, skillful; all the time finds something to argue but avoids offending other people.

Fixed Element:

Earth: Stablizing and expressing stability of purpose; practical and industrious.

Destiny:

The best thing is to follow an independent career; help from the opposite sex is effective.

Star Date of Birth: April 21

Intuition, feeling of opportunity, interested love, conventional marriage. Your sense of self-protection leads you to be-critical of others. You are traditional and rather conservative but in regards to your sexuality you prove your stamina and endurance, remaining sexually active throughout life.

Star Date of Birth: April 22

Susceptible, sensitive, argumentative type; separations; love problems. You are creative and intelligent. In romantic relationships you respond well and return love when it is bestowed on you by your partner. You feel most gratified when sexually fulfilled, and you also feel that love brings you good luck in other areas of your life.

Star Date of Birth: April 23

You are warm-hearted and congenial with a good sense of humor. Your sexuality is expressed in a manner which brings you peacefulness and a desire to sexually fulfill your partner and to be generous. But you may find yourself drawn to cautious types who are miserly and skeptical of love.

Star Date of Birth: April 24

Quiet, calm character; good decisions. You easily become passionately dedicated to a good cause. Your sexuality is expressed in much the same way as your desire to give love knows few boundaries. You are attracted to others in uniform or those who represent worthwhile endeavors.

Star Date of Birth: April 25

Excellent memory; good at scientific career; fame and money. You are ambivalent in defining your goals, and all though you are not overly ambitious, you are drawn to speculative and risky endeavors. This tendency is also exhibited in your romantic encounters where you are extremely individualistic and original in your techniques.

Star Date of Birth: April 26

Charm, elegance; situation obtained through marriage. You are self-confident and strong willed. Your sexuality is enhanced by an ever awareness of opportunities for sexual encounters, and you respond accordingly; however, once involved, you can become cautious, involved, or shyly intimidated by the relationship.

How to Find Your *Soul-Mate, Stars,* and *Destiny*

Star Date of Birth: April 27

Inner beauty; loss of friends and affections; brief connections. You are drawn to the mysterious and darker aspects of the paranormal experience. But in regards to your sexuality, you can be rather self-protective, cautious, and conventional. Your experimental and curious stage develops into a more discriminating one as you mature.

Star Date of Birth: April 28

Happy character; wisdom and clear mind; modest and happy life. You are content with a peaceful and long-lasting relationship based on shared values. You have a tendency to adore and idolize your partner who in return attempts to live up to your expectations.

Star Date of Birth: April 29

Roughness and greed; success through hard labor. Your retained memories of happy experiences make you content and optimistic with an easy going manner. Your nature attracts the attentions of others, even those who are married or otherwise involved, and you are rarely at a loss for love or romance.

Star Date of Birth: April 30

Excessive sensual temperament; sentimental and emotional life, waste and complications. Your generous and caring nature does not detract from your ability to become financially successful. Your sexuality and allure is so powerfully attractive to others that many of your affairs are secretive encounters.

Second Decan of Taurus:

May 1 - May 10 -
Second Ten Days

Character, Personality, and Temperament:

Imaginative, diplomatic, skillful, fantasy, initiative, and reverence in the ways to get money. Possible compromise in business in order to gain easy success in life.

Fixed Element:

EARTH: Self-possessed, self-confident, self-reliant with a tendency to be resistant to changes.

Destiny:

Sparkling career but with an urge to change direction which from time to time brings unexpected events. You possess a receptive mind that easily assimilates thoughts. Great perseverance with an inflexible endurance.

Star Date of Birth: May 1

Romantic type; too ideal in order to achieve something; success in intellectual type of activities. Your good sense of humor gives way to a pessimistic and often negative attitude. Your sexuality is enhanced by feelings of deja vu during return trips to familiar locations. Introductions by family members or friends result in opportunities for romance.

Star Date of Birth: May 2

Practical feelings in art and love; desire for strong and lasting relations; open heart and hand; protective feelings; women are protective and severe. You apply yourself to dealing with what you perceive as your own negative attitude. Your sexuality is heightened by introductions to those in uniform, by endearing summer romances, and by those you meet on trips to different localities for either business or pleasure.

Star Date of Birth: May 3

Refined artistic feeling; artistic career; celebrity. You are a determined and diligent worker who applies yourself to attaining success in life. Romance for you weaves a pattern of the spiritual and physical, resulting in you desiring peace and contentment with your partner. You are uninhibited and devoted to giving when in love.

Star Date of Birth: May 4

Tendency for ideal and exaggeration; ignores reality. Your intuitive and perceptive nature leads you to develop your powers of observation. Romance teaches you the difficult lessons of life, and your sexuality finds fulfillment with the unique experience of meeting someone who leads you to follow a new path or direction of thought.

Star Date of Birth: May 5

Unlimited tendency towards sensual pleasures and adventures; easy love life. Your willingness to guide and teach others augments your accomplishments. Your sexuality is enhanced by natural settings where your love of beauty and nature allows you to dispel any inhibitions on your part. Love with a stranger excites your sensitivities.

Star Date of Birth: May 6

Refined and elegant taste; glorious and successful career. You can be overly indulgent and generous with those you love. Your sexuality is heightened by events involving music, musical settings, or people who musically talented. Your true love shares your interests resulting in a long-lasting relationship.

Star Date of Birth: May 7

Skillful to make money; material success in art; wealthy marriage. You can be restless, discontent, and yearning for new experiences and encounters when involved with a lover. Although you can be conservative and well meaning, you are also self-serving and self-protective with a tendency to over intellectualize and idealize the notion of romance.

Star Date of Birth: May 8

Easy-going character; career that depends on help from others. You have an alert mind and a natural instinct for business endeavors. This alertness becomes an awareness of opportunities in your sexual encounters as well. Your unique sexuality and outlook on life attracts others who are disenchanted with routine relationships.

Star Date of Birth: May 9

Dull character; restlessness; late success in life; ups and downs in achieving various activities. You have only to learn to put to use your alert intelligence and powers of concentration for success. You develop respect and adoration for your romantic partner, and if your family doesn't approve, you will come up with an endless list of excuses for any shortcomings.

Star Date of Birth: May 10

Contradicting character; hard to be understood; periods of activity and inactivity. You are capable of capsizing events with witty remarks, and others most enjoy and delight in your unique sense of humor. The unusual or unexpected brings you your most rewarding sexual encounters, some of which are with enchanting strangers who know how to tickle your fancy.

The Third Decan of Taurus:

May 11 - May 20 - Third Ten Days

Character, Personality, and Temperament:

The individual possesses a fundamental character with a mature and, at times, severe nature. At times, has a little difficulty in expressing himself. Intellectual concepts are more ripe and more profound.

Fixed Element:

Earth: Practical ability to accumulate and manage money and other material resources.

Destiny:

The success and contentment comes slowly and later in life after much dilifent effort.

Star Date of Birth: May 11

The native is serious; the situation is uncertain. There is no clear purpose about his personal situation. Your moodiness may distract you, at times, from your goals and ambitions. This leads you to be somewhat unpredictable in your sexuality, but that daring aspect of your nature leads you to encounter romance during travel, especially short trips, or during social occasions.

Star Date of Birth: May 12

Arguing attitude; jealous, aggressive and violent; numerous arguments in life. You are not accommodating nor open to new ideas or to meeting new people. But in your romantic life, you are self-confident and apply a wisdom that borders on shrewdness. Your sexual desires include immediate gratification and a need for a longer lasting fulfillment.

Star Date of Birth: May 13

Daring, tricky, cunning, intriguing character; nasty life filled with numerous experiences. You may question traditions and challenge conventional moral restrictions. Purely sexual encounters are not as fulfilling to you as those which include romance and love, but this romance must contain a promise of the imaginative, creative, unique, and memorable.

Star Date of Birth: May 14

Controlling character; success but without paying attention to noble actions and ideas. You possess an incredible memory for names, dates, facts, figures, and other details. But in romance you may be reticent to speak your mind about your true feelings and emotions leaving your desires and longings unspoken. You can easily be misunderstood by even caring partners.

Star Date of Birth: May 15

Indecisive character, careless; adventurous double life. Your need for possessions may make you appear self-centered, superficial, and shallow. But at heart, you are forever the romantic needing imaginative, daring, and fulfilling encounters and willing to offer the same to your lover in erotic play.

Star Date of Birth: May 16

Cold character; no attention to any artistic aspect; slow but sure of material success. You exhibit many good qualities, but you are too easily impressed with the deeds and the possessions of other people. You possess good intentions, however, and are strongly idealistic and outspoken about your values. But you remain more of a tempter and charmer than you are aware.

Star Date of Birth: May 17

Bright, positive spirit; poet or scientist; insecure career with many ups and downs. With your perceptiveness, you should learn to follow your intuitions. Sexually, you can be discriminating and unhesitating in dispelling unwanted sexual advances. You are aware of your unique preferences and willing to wait for another who shares your interests.

Star Date of Birth: May 18

Isolated character; problems with opposite sex. Versatile and adaptable, you are alert and quick to act, leading you to take advantage of new opportunities, and this is true of sexual opportunities as well. In this regard, as you mature you are not only lucky but also desirous of repeating those experience which adds to your sensations.

Star Date of Birth: May 19

Controlling, jealous and lonely life; no pleasures without new experiences. You are intellectual and versatile but seek the approval of others. Your sensitive nature makes you even more appealing as you always consider the needs of your partner. Your needs and desires augments and adds to your sexuality.

Star Date of Birth: May 20

Talent in leading people; administrative career. Your quick mind and mentality absorbs information and facts, and you are just as quick at putting this knowledge to good use. In romance, you are just as quick to act, not wanting to let any opportunities pass you by. You are entertaining and enthusiastic in your sexual encounters.

Colors:

The most favorable colors for the natives of Taurus are the shades of blue and mauve. Red is a compelling color, but it can prove to stimulating and exciting for Taurus individuals.

Birthstones:

The birthstones for Taurus are emeralds and turquoises.

Flowers:

Favorable flowers for Taurus individuals are the violet and the poppy as well as the apple blossom.

Keyword: "I Have"

Positive Traits:

Hard working; practical; reliable; endurance; patience; strong values; persistent; determined; strong willed; thorough; steadfact; conservative; warm and affectionate; trustworthy; dependable; appreciation for luxury, good food, and drink, and comfort.; gentle; loyal; domestic; proud; sensual and romantic; artistic; discriminating; self-reliant; sociable.

Negative Traits:

Possessive and jealous; lazy, self-indulgent in pleasures; dull or boring, opinionated; inflexible; greedy; selfish; obstinate; prone to routine; quick tempered; retentive; argumentative; stubborn; materialistic; dependent on others; parasitical; impractical and indecisive; weak-willed; careless; domineering; covetous; dogmatic; conceited; manipulative; hypocritical; money-hungry; lots of affairs.

Taurus

Personal Self-Expression and Mental Tendencies

1. Pleasure in Recreation, Likes Sociable Amusements
2. Congenial; Likes Music, Art, and Intellectual Activities
3. Practical, Determined, Concerned, Domineering
4. Tenacious, Good Judgment, Persevering, Obstinate, Discrete
5. Opinionated, Security Based on Having Possessions
6. Wants to Get Money the Easy Way, Wants Secure Income and House
7. Deep and Lasting Feelings, Loves Comfort and Relaxing
8. Does Not Want to Feel Insecure, Tenacious
9. Bull-Headed, Powerful, Carries Through Ideas to Completion
10. Love of Justice, Generous, Jealous, Possessive
11. Success Through Merit and Effort, Enterprising, Down to Earth
12. Patient and Enduring, When Angry Mad as a Bull With Rage
13. Strong Likes and Dislikes, Likes to Have Own Way, Stiff-Necked
14. Prefers Tried and True Methods, Traditional, Conventional
15. Inquisitive, Resentful but Easily Appeased, Prudent, Aspiring
16. Ambitious to Gain Possessions, Strong-Willed, Legal Profession
17. Difficult to Get Along With, Very Competitive, Reserved Feelings
18. Likes Lots of Companions Around Him/Her, Good-Humored
19. Needs Lots of Love, Sentimental, Discriminate, Scientific
20. Persistent, Gentle, Sometimes Trustworthy, Self-Composed
21. Exacting, Dogmatic, Conceited, Covetous
22. Highly Amorous, Affable, Courteous, Lots of Friendships
23. Energetic, Firm, Contented, Pleasant
24. Sometimes Lazy, Salt-of-the-Earth Attitude
25. Nice Spirited, Loving, Kind-Hearted, Affectionate
26. Desirous of Excelling, Bold, Languishing Nature
27. Victim of Miscalculation, Self-Deprecating, Shy, Placid
28. Dependable, Humble, Attractive, Magnetic, Self-Reliant
29. Self-Indulgent, Influential, Oblivious to Reality

30. Nervous Temperament, Self-Expression, Violent
31. Irritable, Confident, Likes Amusement, Loves Luxury,
32. Aplomb, Eyes Mesmerize, Earthly Delights Beyond Measure
33. Illusionist, Fantasizes About Love, Likes Luxurious Atmosphere
34. Rather Pompous, Self-Righteous Air, Conservative, Materialistic
35. Sensual and Slighty Bawdy, Desire to Control, Likes Sex
36. Complex Life; Likes Good Sex, Good Food, Good Company
37. Manipulates the World, Cannot Understand the Needs of Others
38. Romantic, Artistic, Self-Conscious, Habit-Bound, Runs in the Veins
39. Rich Imagination, Red-Blooded, Cries Softly, Good Actor
40. Molding, Artistic Feelings, Sense of Power, Knows the Art of Fine Living
41. Creature of Habit, Stubborn, Dogmatic, Self-Deprecation
42. Strong Self-Image, Self-Respect, Self-Worth
43. Strong Like Bulldog in Feelings, Has Knowledge of People
44. Caught Up in the Passions of Sex, Very Placid, Ownership is Everything
45. Woman is Unflappable, Unbelievable, Shy Around New People
46. Poor Self-Image, Lazy Self-Image, Endearing
47. Sensual in Sex - A Rich Dessert He/She Sees, Hears, Teels, and Taste
48. Gambles, Prefers Long Term Plans, Cautious, Stubborn Jealousy
49. Persistent and Dogged in Business Projects and Human Relationships
50. Small Scale, Cunning, Low Class, Seller, Money Maker, Greedy
51. Loves Excitement, Thrills, and Mystery; Yearns for Adventure
52. Possessive, Dogmatic Love Life, Emotional Superiority
53. Sensuous, Tolerant, Tactful
54. Methodical Builder, Organizational, Dependable Manager
55. Nature Loving, Selfish, Obstinacy
56. Beautiful, Resonant Voice, Has Many Material Resources
57. Likes Security and Leisure, Very Persistant
58. Loves Freely Given Money, Resourceful for Manipulating the World
59. Resourceful for Own Personal Use, Love Easy Money
60. Stubbornly Refuses to Acknowledges That Someone Else is Right
61. Cupboards, Drawers, Idealized Concept of Beauty
62. Health Suffers, Sensitive Shoulders, Weakened By Stress
63. Angry, Unflappable, Loves Money
64. Self-Depreciation in Poor Self-Image and Self-Worth
65. Dogmatic With Friends, Like to Gain Knowledge
66. Gentle, Lavishes Affection, Radiant
67. Bulldozer Feelings, Unyielding

68. Possess Self-Control, Never Tries to Hurry Their Possessive
69. Likes to Go First-Class, Sensuality of a Rich Dessert,
70. Gamble Preferring Long-Term
71. Impartial, High Professional Self-Esteem, Pragmatic
72. Negative Emotion, Loves Sensual Sex
73. Conceptualized Pattern, Seeks Materials Carefully
74. Architecture, Kind Humble Affection is Withdrawn, Embodies True
75. Seeks Recognition, Staying Power
76. Nature Loving, Productive, Angry
77. Tolerant, Energizing, Horseflesh
78. Use Sex and Intimacy to Gain Wealth
79. Love to Manage Money Functions and Love Affairs
80. Provides Excitement, Thrills, and Mystery
81. Protective, Philanthropic
82. Depression, Self-Hatred and Despair
83. Searching and Puzzled
84. Monogamy in Marriage, Self-Gratification, Tenacity
85. Fearful Tendencies, Excellent Candidate , Well Laid
86. Delights in Companionship
87. Fascination with Desire, Dominate in Love
88. Early Sexual experimentation
89. Radiates Exuberance and Charm, Well Adjusted, Hypocrite
90. Loves Self, Self-Preservation, Confident
91. Exchanges With Friends Conservative,
92. Precocious, Happy, Diplomatic
93. Uncanny ability, Experiments Clandestinely
94. Exterior Composed, Well Organized
95. Refined, Love of Achievements in the Arts
96. Determined, Friendly, Self-Centered
97. Good Reasoning, Discrete
98. Partnership or Marriage Sometimes Delayed
99. Nonplussed, Mystical, Aptitude for Difficult Mathematics or Legislation
100. Legal difficulties, Botany, Horticulture, Stock-Breeding

How to Find Your Soul-Mate, Stars, and Destiny

Celebrity Birthdays

April — Taurus

21	Catherine the Great Elaine May Anthony Quinn Rollo May	Charlotte Bronte Charles Grodin Queen Elizabeth II Hans Christian Andersen	Patti LuPone Shannen Doherty Tony Danza Iggy Pop
22	Yehudi Menuhin Immanuel Kant Glenn Campbell Eddie Albert	Queen Isabella I Vera Maxwell Aaron Spelling Joseph Bottoms	Jack Nicholson Peter Frampton John Waters
23	William Shakespeare Sergei Prokofiev Sergei Rachmaninoff Shirley Temple Black Valerie Bertinelli	Lee Majors Pres. Franklin Pierce Vladimir Nabokov Kate Smith	Sandra Dee David Birney Roy Orbison Halston
24	Shirley MacLaine Barbra Streisand Jill Ireland Anthony Trollope	William De Kooning Eric Bogosian Richard Sterban Glenn Cornick	Leslie Howard Doug Clifford Billy Gould Paul Ryder
25	Oliver Cromwell Guglielmo Marconi Ella Fitzgerald Al Pacino	Edward R. Murrow Melissa Hayden Meadowlark Lemon Andy Bell	King Edward II William Brennan Paul Mazursky Talia Shire
26	John J. Audubon Giancarlo Esposito Bernard Malamud Carol Burnett	Charles Richter Robert Plant J. P. Donleavy Emperor Marcus Aurelius	Duane Eddy Rudolph Hess Bobby Rydell
27	Pres. Ulysses S. Grant Mary Wollstonecraft Sandy Dennis Samuel F. B. Morse	Sheena Easton Anouk Aimee Kate Pierson Jack Klugman	Coretta S. King Pete Ham Judy Carne Anouk Aimee

How to Find Your Soul-Mate, Stars, and Destiny

April Taurus

28	Pres. James Monroe Eugene Delacroix Lionel Barrymore Ann-Margaret	Jay Leno Chris Young Marcia Strassman John Wolters	Carolyn Jones Bruno Kirby Saddam Hussein
29	Uma Thurman Rod McKuen Duke Ellington Zubin Mehta	Fred Zinnemann George Allen Carnie Wilson Jerry Seinfeld	Celeste Holm Emperor Hirohito Michelle Pfeiffer Andre Agassi
30	Jill Clayburgh Sheldon Harnick Don Schollander Perry King	Marlon Brando Cloris Leachman Gary Collins Conductor Robert Shaw	Willie Nelson Turbo B Ian Ziering Bobby Vee

May

1	Joseph Heller Bobcat Goldthwait Jack Paar Calamity Jane	Nick Fortune Scott Carpenter Duke of Wellington Steve Farris	Judy Collins Rita Coolidge Kate Smith Tim McGraw
2	Lou Gramm Bing Crosby Christine Baranski Jon Bon Jovi	Theodore Bikel Brian Aherne Engelbert Humperdinck Dr. Benjamin Spock	Bianca Jagger Larry Gatlin Lesley Gore Goldy McJohn
3	Niccolo Machiavelli Mary Astor Sugar Ray Robinson Wynonna Judd	Wynonna Judd Walter Siezak James Brown Pete Seeger	Mary Hopkin David Ball Christopher Cross Golda Meir
4	Randy Travis Vladimir Lenin Audrey Hepburn Roberta Peters	Francis Cardinal Spellman Luther Adler Ronnie Bond Pia Zadora	Moshe Dayan El Cordobes Ed Cassidy Jackie Jackson
5	Ian McCulloch Annette Bening Soren Kierkegaard Karl Marx	Michael Murphy Alice Faye Tammy Wynette Michael Palin	Tyrone Power Nelly Bly Gary Daly Kevin Mooney

How to Find Your *Soul-Mate, Stars,* and *Destiny*

May Taurus

6	George Clooney Lorie Singer Willie Mays Ayatollah Khomeini	Roma Downey Sigmund Freud Rudolph Valentino Mare Winningham	Orson Welles Robert Perry Stewart Granger Bob Seger
7	Rick West Michael Knight Anne Baxter Teresa Brewer	Darren McGavin Peter Ilyitch Tchaikovsky Gabby Hayes Robert Browning	Edwin Land Eva Per6n Johannes Brahms Gary Cooper
8	Keith Jarrett Don Rickles Sonny Liston Roberto Rossellini	Ricky Nelson Melissa Gilbert Pres. Harry S. Truman Peter Benchley	Toni Tennille Angel Cordero Alex Van Halen Gary Glitter
9	Mike Milward Albert Finney Glenda Jackson Mike Wallace	Pancho Gonzalez Candice Bergen J.M. Barrie Daniel Berrigan	Hank Snow Billy Joel Henry J. Kaiser Tom Petersson
10	Donovan Fred Astaire Max Steiner Sonny Bono	Graham Gouldman David O. Selznick Carl Albert Nancy Walker	John Wilkes Booth Ella Grasso Dave Mason Danny Rapp
11	Natasha Richardson Foster Brooks Doug McClure Phil Silvers	Martha Graham Irving Berlin Valentino Robert Jarvik	Eric Burdon Louis Farrakhan Faith Popcorn Les Chadwick
12	Emilio Estevez Burt Bacharach Howard K. Smith Philip Wylie	George Carlin Florence Nightingale Yogi Berra Katherine Hepburn	Steve Winwood David Walker Stephen Baldwin Billy Duffy
13	Harvey Keitel Joe Lewis Daphne du Maurier Peter Gabriel	Joseph Pulitzer, Jr. Empress Maria Theresa Bea Arthur Paul Thompson	Stevie Wonder Clive Barnes Walt Whitman Dennis Rodman
14	Meg Foster Bobby Darin Robert Zemeckis Ian Astbury	George Lucas Thomas Gainesborough Danny Wood Gene Cornish	Tony Perez Dante Fabrice Morvan David Byrne

How to Find Your Soul-Mate, Stars, and Destiny

May — Taurus

15	Jasper Johns Pierre Curie James Mason Lainie Kazan	Mike Oldfield Katherine Anne Porter Joseph Cotten Mayor Richard J. Daley	L. Frank Baum Graham Goble Eddy Arnold Brian Eno
16	Tori Spelling Janet Jackson Mare Winningham Pierce Brosnan	Henry Fonda Liberace Woody Herman Harry Carey Jr.	James Arness Tracey Gold Liberace Gabriela Sabatini
17	Archibald Cox Birgit Nilsson Stewart Alsop Bill Bruford	Debra Winger Maureen O'Sullivan Edward Jenner Taj Mahal	Dennis Hopper Bob Saget Pervis Jackson Trent Reznor
18	Reggie Jackson Robert Morse Renee Roca Joe Bonsall	Margot Fonteyn Pope John Paul II Bertrand Russell Frank Capra	Jacob Javits Ezio Pinza Perry Como Czar Nicholas II
19	Steven Ford Malcolm X Nora Ephron James Fox	Sarah Peale David Hartman Ho Chi Minh Grace Jones	Frank Lorenzo Pete Townshend Joey Ramone Dusty Hill
20	Cher Adela Rogers George Gobel Hal Newhouser	Joe Cocker James Stewart Dolly Madison Ronald Reagan Jr.	Honore De Balzac Joe Cocker Warren Cann Tom Cochrane

How to Find Your *Soul-Mate, Stars,* and *Destiny*

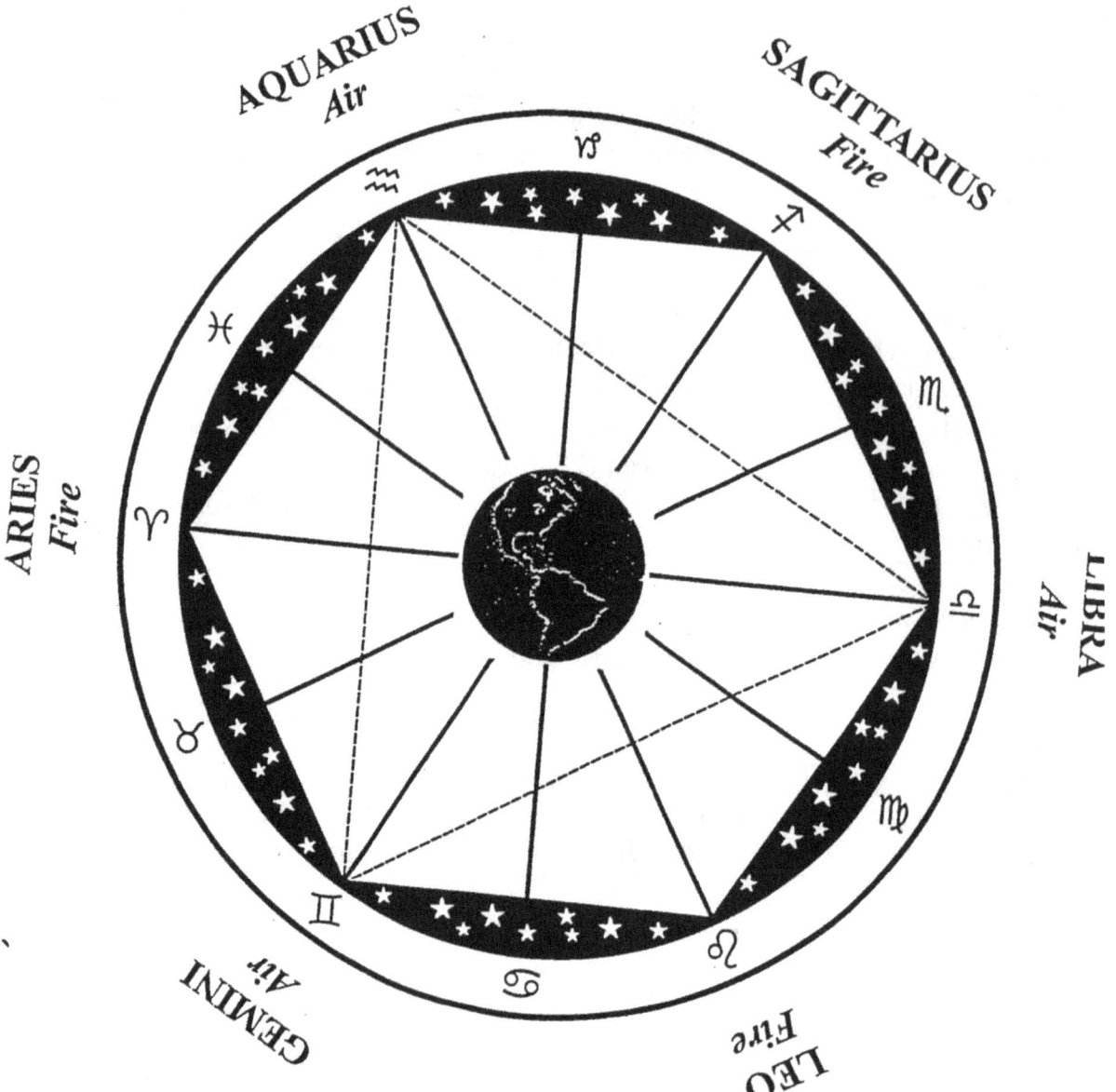

How to Find Your *Soul-Mate, Stars,* and *Destiny*

Date With Destiny

Share With Me Your Fantasy

How to Find Your *Soul-Mate, Stars,* and *Destiny*

Date With Destiny

Share With Me Your Fantasy

GEMINI

May 21 - June 21

Man - Woman - Child - Character - Relationships - Compatibilities - Love Signs

Gemini, the third Sun sign of the zodiac, takes its name from the Greek word for Twins, and it is this image of twins that best characterizes this enigma of the Zodiac. Gemini is best described as having a personality which the messenger of the gods, Gemini are adept at self-expression and communication. They are delightfully entertaining and sociable with a quick wit and an even quicker turn of words or expressions. They are versatile, lovable, and outgoing with an energetic, adventuresome streak which seldom leaves them sitting in one place for long. They like new experiences, meeting new people, and being exposed to new ideas and innovative methods. But then again, they are changeable, one minute headed in one direction in the best of moods, and the next moment confined to their beds in a state of self-pity, depression, or indecisiveness. They are best described as unpredictable, and no two Gemini individuals are alike. They develop various lifestyles to suit their particular fancy, and then may change for the sake of change. They are freedom loving, but one personality may be cautious while the other is daring. They are generally tolerant of others, inventive, creative, and just plain fun to be with. They are talkative, clever, and stimulating--that is, until their moods change.

Intelligent and intellectual in nature, they seldom allow emotional attachments to slow them down. They love sex and romance, but any encounter must also provide a provocative and stimulating mental experience. For Gemini individuals, sex may become an effective avenue for releasing the nervous tensions of their minds and bodies. Their minds are as active, alert, and inquisitive as their bodies are forever on the move. Routine, whether at work or at home, does not come easily for the Gemini native. A hint of adventure, or at least change, best suits the capricious individuals. Their friends and family have a tendency to stand by them through thick and thin because in spite of any faults, they are the most lovable of people.

These characteristics of the Gemini Sun sign can be made stronger by the Moon sign, Ascendant, and placement of the Planets, or they can be made more subdued by specific influences. It is by ascertaining these different influences that one more fully understands the particular Gemini individual.

The sign of Gemini, The Twins, belongs to those born between May 21 and June 21. It is overlapped for the first seven days by the cusp of the preceding sign, Taurus. Gemini comes into its full power on or about May 28th. It retains its full strength until about June 20th, and then for seven days loses its strength to the cusp of the incoming sign, Cancer. Persons born under this sign demonstrate the characteristics of Gemini, The Twins, and are dualistic in both character and mentality.

This sign is dominated by the planet Mercury, the planet of intellectual and spiritual activity that oversees trade and business. This is a Mutable Air sign indicating an intellectual and changing nature which is weightless and moving like air currents. It represents the intellectual light that creates a universal harmony and communication, and force and energy while achieving everything through innate intelligence.

As a Zodiac position, the Gemini touches the constellations of the Coachman and the Orion which are located between Taurus and Gemini. This constellation is shaped like two hugging children represented by the two stars Castor and Pollux. Castor is holding the lyre of Apollo, and Pollux is holding the bludgeon of Hercules. These two stars clarify the double nature of Gemini. As a duality, these natives may have an aerial nature making them isolated or withdrawn in their art, studies, or scientific or religious research while other natives appreciate the more material aspects of life along with commercial endeavors and an active social life.

Because of their dual character, the Twins appear to be continually pulling in opposite directions. They have an ever changing and contradictory character. While they may be gifted intellectually, there are times when they may appear to be lacking in purpose or direction. These may be the most difficult people to understand because they have the capability of being both cold and warm at the same time. One part of their nature is easy-going and loving while at the same time they can be critical or derogatory.

This sign is ruled by Mercury the planet of expression and this is noted in both oral and written expression. Mercury bestows on these individuals profound intelligence, and thus their ideas seem to spring forth into their daily conversations and writings. There is as well a strong indication of initiative or new ideas brought about by a compelling curiosity.

Gemini is a masculine sign that has control over the hands, arms and shoulders. The natives of this sign are considered the helpers of intelligent and intellectual pursuits. They are known not only for initiating but for executing ideas and plans. The phrase "to think" best illustrates the natural inclinations of the Gemini.

The process of fruitfulness in nature is observed at this time of year when the Sun is moving toward the Summer Solstice. Nature is alive with the blooms of plants and flowers and love is the air. Spring fever catches the Gemini native producing day dreamers with an easy-going nature. There is also a dominant element of curiosity which marks these individuals and which determines all positive and negative aspects of the personality.

Gemini Personality

The sign of Gemini, ruled by Mercury, endows its natives with innumerable abilities. It is this natural tendency toward being talented that is frustrating to anyone attempting to analyze those born under the sign of The Twins. These third-sign natives who are dualistic in nature are not only difficult to understand, but they may find it just as difficult to understand themselves. Why? Because there is no specific Gemini person.

In examining the nature of Gemini, it is best to always remember and be aware of this dual nature which can produce a multitude of conflicting traits all combined in one person. It is often noted that at the conscious level this sign produces people who are logical and mentally astute while having bubbly, extroverted, charming and magnetic personalities.

You, Gemini, have many positive qualities that benefit you in whatever you attempt to accomplish. You exhibit both flexibility and adaptability. You welcome new and unusual situations. You adapt and acclimate to new situations and new environments as well as to new viewpoints and attitudes with ease. Gemini have the natural ability to assimilate new ideas and facts and to investigate and ponder any mystery. Your precocious, alert minds are capable of rapidly analyzing the most complex problems.

Gemini make ideal companions. You have an extremely clever, entertaining personality and are known for your wit and enthusiasm. Being open for new experiences, you are always willing to embark on new adventures. You enjoy all contact with other people as well as attending and having parties with the fun-loving attitude that the more people the better. Often known as the life of the party, your lively demeanor gains you much attention. You appear to easily convince and inspire others, often to stimulate them, with your conviction that life is an adventure and new experiences are not only worth trying but will be pleasurable at the same time.

How to Find Your *Soul-Mate, Stars,* and *Destiny*

You are quite capable of succeeding in making a good impression, and you possess a remarkable and limitless capacity for having fun and seeking pleasure. Not only do you relish the opportunity for new experiences, but with your versatility and adaptability, you actually appear to flourish and thrive on variety and diversity. You have a natural inclination toward new and novel experiences because you want to experiment with your environment, and you do this at every available opportunity. At the same time, Gemini strive to attain and achieve and are known for their ambition and their drive for success. You can be cool and calculating which enables you to accomplish your desired results in spite of your restlessness and your strong desire for new experiences.

You are capable of displaying and exhibiting a nearly compulsive-obsessive desire to analyze. You find yourself forever examining and rationalizing your own thoughts, conversations, motives, conduct and responses as well as those of others. You want to discover the underlying influences, incentives, motives and dynamics behind all that you experience and encounter in life. This need is based on an underlying trait to discover and to understand the reasons why things happen or occur or exist. You are intuitively in search of the "why's" and "what for's" in any situation.

Often, Gemini acquire a vast amount of knowledge about a variety of subjects. Your curiosity and analyzing nature leads you to explore and to investigate, to learn and to retain at least a little information about a great many facets of life. Enough so that you appear to be capable of commenting on numerous topics and never being at a loss for words. With your cognitive abilities, you are able to assimilate a vast store of knowledge and insights based on this information-gathering trait and on your experiences which you retain and utilize when it is necessary.

On the other hand, the dual nature of Gemini arises and with it to a large degree comes unpredictability. While no one has the potential to be more charming and witty than Gemini, at the same time, no one can be more cynical, moody or irritable. Such a good conversationalist are you that you can play the advocate, arguing effectively either side of any subject. While this sign produces people who can be dazzling and irresistible, they are also inheritantly exasperating, inconsistent, and irrational. This duality is so transitory as to be elusive, and it is this quality that is most endowed by the influence of Mercury, the ruling planet of this sign. While the Gemini dual nature allows for charm and congeniality, there exists simultaneously the negative traits of impatience, restlessness, and a tendency toward being superficial. Without a variety of new experiences, you can easily become bored and apparently you want everyone around you aware of your feelings and moods. Nothing is inhibited or hidden. If you are miserable, you make sure those around you are miserable too. You are like the chameleon forever changing in your moods, direction, and desires. The inconsistency of your moods make you, at times, not only unpredictable but undependable.

However, at other times, you choose not to verbalize your misery during these frequent and unstable mood swings. One moment cheerful and happy, the next moment you are so depressed and on occasions so withdrawn that you might decide not to get out of bed. During these periods of depression, you may doggedly refuse to talk to anyone or to participate in any activities. Your mind remains active, though, and you continue your self-analysis during these withdrawn, morose periods in you life.

How to Find Your Soul-Mate, Stars, and Destiny

This duality of nature is a source of insecurity for the Gemini native. You may often feel threatened by the inconsistencies of your own personality. Your conflicting nature may also confuse you at times, leaving you even more frustrated and moody. This also leaves you susceptible to criticism which can make you feel hostile toward others and sometimes rejected by others. A bigger problem is your tendency to build hidden meanings or ulterior motives into the actions or remarks of others. This can easily develop into a pattern and increase your tendency to be in a good mood one moment, and then in the next moment, feel threatened and ill-tempered. The Gemini incorporates these feelings of hostility, whether justified or not. Your reaction is often a flight or fight response. And Gemini is capable of either response with the choice being absolutely unpredictable. The Gemini might respond to criticism with even more candid sarcasm or emotional responses aimed at hurting the other person. If the choice is to take flight, you find yourself retreating or withdrawing from the situation, becoming once again depressed and nonresponsive. The extreme of this personality trait produces individuals suffering from manic-depressive disorders or some forms of schizophrenic behavior. However, the unpredictability of the Gemini personality is generally considered within socially acceptable levels. Overly hostile and aggressive behaviors are rare. While at the same time, impulsiveness, hyperactivity in actions and speech, and perhaps sexually bizarre activities are noted.

Everyone has faults. When you recognize this and are honest about your own faults, the opportunity for personal growth exists. The undeveloped Gemini person can be suspicious, unreliable, untruthful and impatient with a tendency to complain and gripe. You are anxious and worrisome, many times easily irritated, and forever looking for the fast lane to success. Your drive for ever new and exciting experiences can leave you restless and impatient. The duality of your nature can give you inclinations toward uncertainty and discontent. You may have problems with decision making because your duality pulls you in different directions leaving you confused. While you desire social recognition and acclimation, the novelty of a situation may wear off leaving you feeling unsatisfied with your latest accomplishments and seeking some new diversion with equal enthusiasm. It is sometimes like you do not know your own desires other than you don't want what you have. Needless to say, you are a matter of great concern to both your friends and family who know you could succeed if ever you settled your mind down and stuck to one thing.

It is noted that in the cases of Gemini persons born with coarse hair and dark complexions, there is many times found a nature which exhibits combativeness and hostility, obscure notions and imaginings of evil, and a highly developed somewhat cynical and critical distrust of others.

The duality of Gemini in many instances produces unresolved conflicts. It has been mentioned that honestly accepting your faults can help. The next step is to accept yourself as your are. You are unique, thrilling and a constant challenge to others and to yourself. You add that element of excitement to life. Once you have accepted yourself as you are, strive to reach a compromise within yourself concerning your dual nature. Accept what is good while striving to cast out or weed out those components of your personality that are holding you back or are a detriment to your life. Through meditation and if necessary therapy, you can join the forces of your duality creating a more focused, accepting personality.

You are often considered a worldly, sophisticated, glamorous person who is generous, sympathetic, affectionate, and imaginative. Through careful cultivation of your higher nature, you have the potential to achieve remarkable distinction, power, and success in your endeavors.

Gemini Character

Gemini are pleasant, humorous and eager to be involved with ongoing activities. Both men and women are capable of being inventive, mentally alert and astute, and have delicate manners and refined tastes. They possess a natural affinity for beautiful objects often times with no consideration of the material worth. Sometimes naive, you can be gullible and susceptible and easily taken advantage of. You can play the diplomat and wittingly charm a crowd. You out do others with your quick thinking and your grasp of information. You are ambitious for social prestige and accomplishments. Accepted as you are, you are the most delightful of people, as long as no one attempts to limit your need for new activity.

In the case where this sign is rising or contains the Sun, Moon or a highly concentrated pattern of planets there is found the personification of air and its common characteristics. This is the ‚happy as a lark' person who loves the companionship of others and who is offended when not surrounded by a group of adoring people. There are those Gemini who are born the playboy or playgirl - out for a good and entertaining time without a care in the world. Then there are other Gemini who possess sentimental and adventuresome souls and who love to come to the rescue of others. Whichever the case may be, Gemini gain praise and acclaim by being closely associated with others and by winning others over with their personal appeal. They are rarely at a loss for a name and even more rarely does one find a Gemini without a long list of phone numbers. They are not so much interested in tangible, material objects as they are with people and their influences.

The well-developed Gemini is clever and resourceful with a unique sense of humor. Your intelligence is reflected in all you strive to achieve, but you can also be argumentative. You have a tendency to attempt to improve your destiny by yourself. You don't always take direction well, and, depending on your mood, you may disregard any and all advice.

One of your strongest character traits is your capacity to size-up others and to use your mentality and personable ways to make friends and influence people. While you may at times be too critical of others, you have a strong ability to understand human nature, and you seldom fail to use this information to your advantage. Left to your own pursuits, you are a crafty and cunning schemer, utilizing your ability to be shrewd, intuitive and well-spoken to advance yourself through life and through the uncertain and precarious world which you feel awaits you. You are forever the diplomat, meeting and charming others, pulling them to you, influencing them with your ideas and thoughts, while all the time attempting to accomplish a beneficial purpose, or to achieve an insight, or to gain an advantage.

The greatest distraction in your life is your active mind which is bent on scheming new plans and directions. This in part is due to your brilliant and active imagination, and your desire for your plans and ideas to outshine anything you've done before. You desire most a great accomplishment, an end to a means, and you are willing to take whatever short-cuts that you dream up in order to accomplish that purpose.

How to Find Your Soul-Mate, Stars, and Destiny

You crave knowledge and are a perpetual reader, viewer, or listener of topics covering a wide range of information. You are constantly seeking, learning, and exploring new thoughts and avenues of activity. The higher inspired Gemini individuals are great lovers of education, literature, science, art, and technical material and are capable of achieving accomplishments in these fields.

Gemini can also exhibit much courage and patriotic devotion. Faced with danger or uncertainty, you are quite apt to stand your ground in order to learn the outcome of the situation. This lack of fear combined with a compelling curiosity produces the most daring of adventurers who are forever seeking new thrills and exploits.

Then again, it is most difficult to attempt to describe any specific Gemini characteristic. You have a spirit of adaptation while at the same being uncertain. You have brilliant ideas, but there are times when you may not follow them through to any satisfactory conclusion. Your active mind and imagination often leaves you feeling nervous or irritable. And you have more than your share of moody periods of tension and pessimism. You deplore violence, but if highly irritated can resort to it. There are those Gemini who are superficial while others are very down to earth. Some may feel secure within themselves and with their abilities while the next Gemini that comes along harbors great feelings of insecurities. Gemini can be generous or stingy, willful or totally undecided, strong or weak.

Poorly developed Gemini are adept at cheating and lying. If not well-aspected, this person possesses no profound mental abilities. If a solution to a problem is noted, they may forget about it in their drive to move on to something new and better. They may change jobs or vocations as frequently as he changes moods or interests, and they don't handle responsibility well, preferring to leave it to others. These Gemini require a great deal of push from friends and family to simply accept the smallest amount of care and concern about their own life. Being nervous and weak, it is easy for poorly afflicted persons to find themselves in one problem after another. While these Gemini may believe they are truthful, honest and faithful, that is true for the moment, however, every moment may have a separate reality for this type of person. These baser types are unscrupulous in business and may make successful gamblers or individuals who succeed as promoters of get-rich-quick schemes. Nervously high strung and perpetually restless, your energy level predicts the events of the day. This type of person is quite capable of bringing much misery to the other people in their life.

In other words, the Gemini sign to a great extent influences two types of people who are very different from each other. One type may use the mind and intellect, learning, thinking and creating; while the other type finds their ideas through others, copying and imitating with ease. Both types are preoccupied to a large degree with thinking, contemplation, and self-analyses. There is a tendency to be extremists in either direction. They can achieve success and independence or nothing more than a lowly, unhappy existence.

Then too, the duality within each individual of the Gemini sign, is seen in contradictory inclinations and desires, in their moodiness and need to change, in uncertainty and discontentment. This person may seek advice from others than disregard it, preferring to rush off on his own path. And perhaps part of the problem is that these natives undertake too much at one time rather than focusing one endeavor at a time. As long as the enthusiasm for a project lasts, this individual can work diligently. But as soon as the focus changes, the current activity is abandoned. There is a tendency to dissipate their energies, to scatter their efforts in many directions, and to finally accomplish very little.

They may find it difficult to trust others. Skeptical by nature, they question all they hear and see and demand unrefutible proof. They distrust situations, institutions, and more importantly other people. Arguments and explanations are wasted on Gemini. They prefer to make their own decisions, in their own way, and in their own time.

Nothing is without hope, though. This sign promises much for those who choose to develop their powers of will and self-control over the mind and body. With careful introspection, Gemini overcome any and all faults and distractions. Patience and stillness must be sought out. A determined effort to serve the best interest in all that is attempted is required to realize the full potential of this sign.

Search for endeavors that utilize your gifts. Your combination of mental ability and your great imagination grants you the ability to achieve at an occupation while using your free time for other activities that might challenge your restless nature. This is merely a suggestion. You alone can make these decisions, discover your inner nature, and decide on a path that will lead you to happiness and fulfillment.

The well-aspected natives of the sign of Gemini are quite often kind, willing, flexible, and talented. They are humane individuals showing great sympathy and concern for others. The Gemini person is noted for being inventive, creative, vigilant, and a natural talker. This person has both a firm and strong will and a love of commanding, especially one's self, but never out of pride or tyranny.

Your many and great assets have already been listed, but worth mentioning again is your gift for inspiring others with your conviction that life is a great adventure well worth living. Life can be a fun and pleasurable experience if others simply allowed it to be, and there is nothing to fear in innovative changes, new attitudes and different experiences. This is true! And you are the gifted person who carries this message.

Gemini Destiny

Gemini's very existence is influenced by Mercury bestowing upon its natives a restless, impetuous nature. While excitement and change abound, success undoubtedly depends upon the individual. Many will not attain material success which might otherwise be well deserved. Some will fall to the deceptions of others by being too naive or because of too many changes in direction. Use your intelligence to seek quietness and calmness or else your life will know no rest from birth until death. Before anyone can judge a Gemini native, each individual must be considered separately. Some are bestowed with great and inspiring gifts while others possess weaker spirits.

If the Ascendant is Gemini, the person will find that life is difficult from the start, but they will always receive assistance from friends and family. This individual will be inspired by celestial secrets. There may be beneficial friendships with older men, however there is a propensity to lose money. If the Midheaven is in Pisces, this person may reside near water; or receive an inherited income from investments connected to transportation via water; or his livelihood will come from the property of others and his location and finances will be divided between two places. If the Descendant is in Sagittarius, he will cause much misery and grief to this family, and he will suffer from anxieties.

Many Gemini are extremely spiritual. Often their beliefs are not focused on a particular religion, though. There is a tendency to be tolerant of all higher thought and to have a respect for many philosophies, beliefs and forms of worship. If born under a positive influence, you may well inspire others with your goodness and faithfulness.

You, Gemini, are inspired by the powerfully mysterious and forceful magnetic and planetary influences surrounding you. Learn to gather these forces about you and to draw from them a personal strength of conviction. Pull from these forces insights into attaining a higher level of life. When this is accomplished, nothing worthwhile is beyond your grasp. You have strong inclinations for success through literature, travel, inventions, associations with large corporations or publishing. However, afflicted difficulties can arise through the same enterprises.

If Mercury is well-aspected, the Gemini native writes and speaks well and loves to travel. You are endowed with a mind that is mechanical, inventive and inspiringly ingenious. Your manner is practical, and you are a good decision maker. However, if afflicted, the native is often discourteous and forceful in his speech being overly critical and cynical of others. The mind is not only restless, but this person is also indecisive and making decisions becomes extremely difficult.

Mercurial pursuits may result in profit as well as pleasure from travel. Money may be gained from more than one endeavor indicating several jobs or occupations. The location of Venus has a strong tendency to influence this native to develop the finer attributes, to acquire refined skills, and to attain a good education in that the native is endowed with clear thinking, perception and inventiveness.

How to Find Your Soul-Mate, Stars, and Destiny

Nature has been generous to the natives of Gemini, granting them many gifts and talents. It is essential that these talents not be thrown to the winds to scatter as so many seeds upon the earth. It is mandatory that your dual nature be harnessed, controlled and channeled. Appreciate your God-given gifts, don't waste them or become too old to utilize and appreciate them.

Financial success may elude you as your tendencies toward new experiences can become expensive causing you to spend your money on your desires to see new places or to become involved in various activities. It may be mid-life before you acquire the ability to save money and to spend it more wisely. You may find you have the inclination to pursue two different avenues at the same time. Be cautious that as a wage-earner, you don't give away your money as fast as you make it. This tendency can be overcome by learning moderation in not only this but in all that you do. You can become thrifty and sensible which will give you a great feeling of security. Learning to handle your money well will provide you the ability to donate to charities, an activity that will enhance your natural desire to help the needy and the less fortunate.

Your great unrest may result in much unhappiness and deep regret until you learn to assume responsibilities for your own life and your own actions. Only then can you truly excel. It may require some great discomfort in your daily life or some struggle or serious problem before you fully accept your personal obligations and responsibilities. Your duality, in many instances, allows you to work best under enormous pressure. Then you produce your best results.

It is entirely up to the Gemini native through a process of evaluation and experimentation to discover his or her best nature. If necessary, make a list or an inventory of your strengths and weaknesses, your desires, and your experiences and then draw a map or a destination of where this particular combination of experiences and assets can take you. Learn your own nature best. And when you feel you have accumulated enough experiences, have gained enough knowledge and insight, have learned all there is to learn, then settle. When you reach this point, make a nest for yourself and create about you the harmony needed to realize, pursue, and achieve the dream you have chosen to pursue.

You may not fully appreciate traditions or sentiments nor do you tend to take life very seriously. That is your prerogative, but attempt to make every effort to learn to be tolerant of those who need these everyday institutions in their lives. Strive also in your personal and home life to associate with people who are calm and thoughtful and who have self-assured habits. These people can best influence you by comforting and quieting your turbulent nature. You require much love and protection from friends and family, and because of the basic goodness of your nature, others are more than willing to provide these elements of support to you. And you are well worth all the effort of others. You bring your own special charm and personal contribution to the lives of others.

It was once believed that Mercury chose to outwit conflict by cunning. He evaded the many battles of life by creating diversions on the flank of the conflict. Astrologers link this trait with the traditional "double nature" of Gemini which produces variations or the ability to change in midstream, so to speak. For example, if someone deceives a Gemini or takes advantage of this individual, they will vehemently hate the person today and forget all about it tomorrow. It takes the ability to focus on one thought to continue to hate. Or Gemini may abondon all thoughts of animosity if they see an advantage in being friendly.

The destiny of the Gemini native may include trouble and sorrow because of relatives and family disputes, unfortunate legal affairs, and false accusations, restraints or limitations from others. There may exist family secrets that result in strife. Then too, your fortunes may be subjected to many fluctuations and changes and most especially effected for both good and bad by the influence of the opposite sex. There will be secrets involved with clandestine affairs and amorous attachments and troubles occur through these love-affairs. Some of these individuals may marry twice or have two simultaneous relationships. Many problems can develop due to involvement with the opposite sex. Friends are numerous and may also be the cause of problems with some friendships leading to hostilities and animosities. While enemies may cause you harm, your spouse assists you throughout your married life. Though susceptible to accidents, you appear divinely protected. There may be an inheritance of land of houses. These individuals may experience both hardships and affluence during life, and it is quite possible that they are the cause of their own downfall or bad luck.

Gemini have few of the conventional inhibitions that repress others and which limit new experiences. You do not possess the traits of the more timid nor do you suppress your desires or repress your active mind or your impulses. Your many great influences and gifts allow you the ability to enjoy life at its fullest.

Gemini Occupation

Gemini are actually born for success, to achieve wealth and prosperity, and all else they desire. However, along with these possibilities come the influences of the Gemini dual nature. The negative aspects of impatience, restlessness, and your need for change effect your prospects as has been previously mentioned. Undeterred, these qualities can actually rob you of your potential for great success. Thus, you are either a hard-working individual who stays put at one job or a person who jumps from one position to another. While you can be quite industrious, your need for variation predisposes you against any position which requires you to engage in monotonous, daily routine.

Known for your energy, stamina, and drive, you possess a startling astuteness of intellect, the capacity to analyze and deduce, to grasp abstract theories, and to produce and realize specific results. Your versatile flexibility and adaptability, your creative imagination, and your ability to invent and initiate new ideas propel you into a world of achievement. What more could you want? You are already endowed with dexterity, coordination, a winning and gregarious personality, an independent nature and a talent for creating. Gemini have become famous in the fields of writing, art, and entertainment.

In the field of communication, many Gemini have become talented and effective journalists and radio and television announcers. Advertising and publicity are good fields of endeavor. You make excellent public speakers and lecturers. And of course with your insatiable wit and humor you could easily rise to great heights in the area of comedy. You do well in occupations such as interpreters, translators, or diplomats. Or consider a travel field, such as cruise ships, where hosting and entertaining are required.

Gemini make the best sales persons, excelling at both presentation and closing the deal. In business, you are the world's best at conceptualizing the precepts, inspiring enthusiasm in others, and then negotiating the final contract while keeping everyone involved pleased with the eventual prospects. Any position that combines travel with presentations and/or with sales affords you the opportunity for change that you so much desire. You would do well in fields which require a person who can influence others, and any vocation that requires meeting people, moving easily within a group situation, or bringing individuals or groups of people together to discuss, consider, or to mediate plans. You are the person to initiate and to put the deal together. Your natural interpersonal skills including perceptiveness, understanding, and adaptability are all traits put to good use in executive positions and in the area of trade and commerce. You also make excellent actors, attorneys and politicians as you exhibit a cleverness in your thinking and negotiations. You are most noted for being well-informed, subtle, flexible and businesslike in your professional dealings.

Gemini may frequently possess superior dexterity and are adept in jobs requiring the use of the hands. These individuals do well in any endeavor in which they can transform their ideas or the ideas of others into concrete results. You comprehend and grasp complex devices or patterns as well as the ideas, theories and even the thoughts of others. The areas of art, art design, graphics, and architecture are good for those so gifted as are numerous fields involving handiwork and precision. Other careers might include sculptors, highly skilled technicians in many fields, electricians, and computer software designers.

For you Gemini who love learning and research, the list of occupations in which you do well is endless. Persons, such gifted, may be at home in an academic setting where they feel they have a little world to themselves. Any activity requiring an active, seeking mind is suggested for your capabilities are limitless. Your mind is lofty and aspiring, and you have a strong potential for occult investigations and psychic talents.

Seek a career that affords new information, varying experiences either mental or physical, and an element of change to best take advantage of your natural abilities. You may have an aptitude for occupations in the fields of science, literature and mathematics and in investigative work. Because you are adaptable and resourceful, if you utilize your mind and your talents, you can succeed in any number of endeavors.

Gemini Marriage

In all matters involving love and marriage, Gemini are forever human puzzles. You can love passionately and at the next moment be thinking of something totally different. Only your extreme development of diplomacy and charm prevent you from making a general mess of your family life. Many Gemini wisely choose not to marry early in life. In youth, you crave the attentions of many.

When you do decide to marry, take time to choose a calm, gentle, self-possessed person who can offset your energies and drives. Suggestions for Gemini natives are to marry a person born to either the sign of Sagittarius, Leo, Aries or Libra. Then take time to develop a caring and loving relationship complete with patience and humor, giving and complementing, and sharing with each other.

There is some indication, based on the dual nature, for troublesome complications with the opposite sex. Two marriages may be frequent with people born under the sign of Gemini.

When the Gemini sign is at the Ascendant, Sagittarius is in the House of Marriage, and this will be a free union, but a second marriage is not excluded.

The Gemini Man

Gemini men, influenced by Mercury, can be as dualistic as describable. They can exhibit a great amount of affection and generosity or be hypercritical and selfish. No matter how personable he is, he may hold people at a distance allowing no one to discover both sides of his personality.

He is curious and seeking and at the same time rejecting the old for the newness of nonconforming pleasures, ideas, or people. Easily bored, he may gamble or change sexual partners often. He loves the company of people, but may always be seeking a different crowd with which to associate. He changes his friends and associates often, perhaps retaining old acquaintances, but always seeking to meet new ones.

While not a romantic, Gemini men love women, and he loves to change partners frequently. He is not noted for his fidelity in relationships, and he is set on enlarging his list of experiences and encounters. But believe it or not, you eventually fall in love, and you have to admit this to yourself. When in love, you become much more tender, caring and compassionate. And of course you are an artful lover. However, you love and enjoy your freedom also, maybe too much, for it can rate higher than your wife. Mr. Gemini, you aren't known for your fidelity even in the best of marriages. Your long list of excursions and affairs may well continue. The pace may slow after your marriage, but chances are, it will continue. Frequently, these affairs do not in any way threaten your marriage at the sexual level. Once in love, you prefer to remain with that partner on condition. You are supportive and show much concern over your mate as long as she holds your interest. For you, she needs to continues to stimulate you intellectually as well as sexually. If you ever become tired of her mind, her intellect, the chances are the marriage will not last nor hold your interest for long.

Another aspect of the male Gemini is that he is easily influenced by women for either good or bad. This inclination to be easily led astray can, needless to say, cause many problems both before and after marriage. Imagine the Gemini man who meets the girl of his dreams and her greatest desire is to immediately move to an island paradise.

This man can dream up more new and clever ideas than anyone else he knows. Many of these dreams concern making a lot of money fast and he isn't always adverse to using clever or cunning shortcuts. There is a strong inclination in the Gemini man to speculate on matters in either his business or personal life. He may thrive on living on the edge, taking a chance when no one else dares, and walking on precarious ground seeking excitement, pleasures, and the thrill of success. No one is more daring or adventuresome than this man. If he maintains the urge to be different, he will be a bad boy all his life, breaking rules and rebelling against authority and tradition.

This man may follow many paths in his desire to think and to do for himself. Self-discipline, education, and the desire to improve himself, under his own volition, is his salvation. If he can design a life which provides the opportunity for him to develop his higher nature while maintaining his independence and a strong feeling of being allowed to be himself, he can settle into a pattern of success. Ultimately, he strives to become the best that he can be at whatever it is that attracts his attention.

The Gemini Woman

The Gemini woman is remarkable in her capacity to be loving and generous. This woman is intuitive and enjoys her mind as much as others do. She is agreeable and optimistic and quite often well-educated. She is known for being congenial, warm-natured, and well-mannered. She is most happy in a domestic situation being a truly talented homemaker and enjoying making the home an attractive and pleasant environment for both her family and her friends. You make excellent wives and mothers as you are truly affectionate and caring. In return, though, you want affection and attention from your family.

Curious of others, and surrounded by people, she loves to learn the nature of her friends and associates. In the event that Mercury, her planet of influence, is positively endowed, the Gemini woman is both intelligent and successful. She may, however, have tendencies toward extravagances when she finds herself the least bit bored. The native-born Gemini female often will look young later in life.

Gemini women love to talk, to entertain their group of friends, and to gather and disperse information. Discretion is not always a strong characteristic as you sometimes talk before you think. You are capable of asking too many questions. At the same time, Gemini women are more than capable of being sympathetic and showing concerns for their friends and family. These women love to be loved, and are affectionate and demonstrative with their feelings expecting the same in return. Their feelings may easily be hurt as they are sensitive in their natures and prefer attention to being ignored, and affection to criticism. The Gemini female may seldom meet her true love early in life. She may discover she must seek and wait, look and be patient, and she may meet any number of men before she finds the most suitable man for her. In this she will do best if she chooses her intellectual equal because she can easily become bored.

When you do fall in love and marry, it is necessary for your husband to understand your independent nature. You require not only interests outside of the home, but intellectual and stimulating pursuits as well. At the same time, emotionally you may be dependent on your spouse to be very supportive and understanding and protective. The chances are that as a homemaker, you are a creative and talented cook and love to make beautiful things for your home. Your children appreciate your ability to be both a good parent and a pleasant companion.

Like her male counterpart, the Gemini female is dualistic in nature. While she may be generous when her income is limited, when she becomes more prosperous she watches her money carefully. She can either be unselfishly generous or the exact opposite. If aspects are afflicted, the Gemini woman is cold and greedy and would not hesitate to gain the advantage over others caught in bad situations. And while she may delight in driving a hard bargain, she is not always careful with her money. She changes her opinions as often as she changes her shoes. Often you may find yourself with too many irons in the fire, and you may find that many of your projects are either not finished or are postponed indefinitely. These women may lack the patience to establish a stable life pattern without a great deal of effort on their part to instill values and insight into their lives. Patience is necessary to develop these life skills.

Gemini females are endowed with both versatility and an indication for some eccentricities in both friendships and in expressions. Your natural gifts allow you to be original, intuitive and ingenious. You have both an observant and curious nature and a great interest in developing your mind with intellectual pursuits. You are both clever and quick of mind with the inventiveness and resourcefulness to be ever entertaining and delightful. Your friends consider you both good-humored and generous of nature. In your relations with others, you remain unbiased and seldom prejudiced. In your professional life, you are perceptive and shrewd, well-spoken and well-informed. You may be very fond of travel, reading, science and primarily the acquisition of knowledge.

Gemini Love Life

Gemini love to live life in a constant whirl of excitement, flitting from one place to another, from one group of friends to another, and from one attraction to another. Fortunately, you have a great need for others to like you, and they do. The Air sign of Gemini indicates a nature that loves to communicate, idealize and intellectualize. Their charming talent for expressing themselves eloquently and their alluring presence acts like a magnet attracting the opposite sex to them. Mentally astute, they love to apply reasoning to all of their pursuits and encounters, but at the same time they are the people who add that ingredient of fun, light-hearted enjoyment, and that special touch of magic to all that they do. Be prepared for a pleasurable encounter full of surprises for this sign predisposes its natives to be changeable and versatile with a knack for responding to the mood of the moment. Gemini particularly find enjoyment in spending money freely, sometimes to the point of extravagance, on entertainment and entertaining, adding to their care-free nature.

Gemini desire to sample all there is in life forever seeking the fresh thrill of new encounters, knowing that each relationship will add its own special spark to the moment and to their accumulation of insights and experiences. These people love to flirt and to admire and to allow their energies to flow naturally into affairs of the heart. In all matters of affection, you remain an enigma, a happy puzzle, who at one moment is in the throes of passionate love and then the next moment you are intellectualizing and pondering other matters that draw your attention. People of this sign are forever astonishing and surprising others with their perplexing paradoxes.

Gemini is a double-bodied sign which means that Mercury can at times bring about troublesome complications with the opposite sex. And as has been noted, prone to fun and flirting, Gemini can also easily be led astray by the opposite sex. You are a bit of a sensualist and purely enjoy the physical aspects of love and romance. And while variety is the spice of your life, you do prefer quality to quantity. You want an experience that traps you in the moment, that catches your mind and engages your curiosity, an experience so sensual as to be memorable. If the affair doesn't offer a hint of a thrill, a chance at discovery, or some other aspect of adventure, while captivating your mind and intellect at the same time, you soon lose interest.

Anyone who falls in love with a Gemini must accept their need for change and variety. You may actually see absolutely nothing amiss with your frequent little infidelities. Most particularly, the Gemini male is compulsively drawn to affairs both before and after marriage. You may find yourself involved in two or more love affairs at the same time. You are more than capable of being intensely involved with another person and then suddenly ending the affair and forgetting all about it. It appears to others that your feelings are shallow and selfish and that you are cool and calculating in your relationships. Your relationships may be based on self-gratification and personal pleasure rather than on any need to give or to satisfy the other person. But then you are ever inclined to experiment and can be somewhat lacking in conventional moral restraints. Only you truly understand your mind, Gemini. But this may be something others find difficult to understand. That is, that you have a compulsive need to seek the thrill, the erotic, and to taste life now while you can. To you, that is what life is all about. And with your charm and warm affectionate appeal, you find that all is usually forgiven anyway. It takes a certain maturity to recognize that being true to another will build a lasting and more permanent relationship. But then, only you can make those decisions for yourself as, after all, it is your life.

To be attracted to another, you require that the person stimulates you mentally and intellectually as well as physically. Anyone attempting to gain your attention, should simple ask your opinion on a subject and then prepare to sit back, listen, and allow you to engage in one of your favorite past times, talking.

Gemini have a need to be aware of the negative aspects of the sexual urge which is envy, jealousy, and even hatred. These strong emotions can greatly frustrate you. If allowed to take hold, these emotions produce hostilities and aggressive behavior. Maintain your general cool and impersonal manner in dealing with these strong emotions.

Gemini Children

Gemini, The Twins, are frequently illustrated as children because they have the capacity for being childishly fun-loving and carefree. As children, they are often intelligent, eager for what each new day may bring, and restless to discover some new secret of life. In their daily lives, they are often very busy and seeking something to do, something to get into, or some new place to explore. They are constantly busy, intensely restless, and seldom content to be idle. Their level of activity, while within normal standards, can be tiring for their adult counterparts. This is not the content, passive child who sits in one spot occupying his mind with one toy or play thing or activity. This is the seemingly restless, inquisitive child who is forever exploring, forever charming and entertaining, and the delight of others who have the time and energy to keep up with this level of activity.

These Gemini children have lively imaginations and enjoy being entertained with books of pure childish fantasy, adventure movies, and excursions to places like museums and other centers which have well-designed activities and educational exhibitions for the young. Not only do they like children's stories, but with their active imaginations they can spin creative tales of their own and love to do so. They require activities and outlets for these strong creative natures. Their natural curiosity and delight in the world and in all that is new and unknown make them a pure pleasure to be with for the parent who wants to spend time instructing, guiding and entertaining them.

These children respond best to loving affection and guiding attention. They crave attention from their family, teachers and young friends. It is best for parents and teachers to use methods of patience, understanding, and acceptance while guiding and instructing these children. They have a strong need to have their minds occupied, to be exposed to a variety of activities, and to be offered the opportunity to be engaged with other children in group play and activities. In school, they may be the class clown or entertainer always quick with a cute remark or especially funny antic. They have a great love for wit and chatter and love to entertain the other kids and to receive the attention of the group. Without them, school would be a total bore for everyone, teachers included. While learning to be responsible for his or her behavior is important, strong opposition or restraint, or a negative unaccepting attitude of what appears to be restless behavior, will result in these children being compelled to over activity and exaggerations and even to becoming tricky, evasive and deceitful. If kept at one task for too long, this child may become fidgety, high-strung and nervous. Therefore, breaks in routine are necessary, but of course it is also necessary that the child learn to finish and complete tasks. Like so many children, they love to play outside and appear to need a great deal of physical activity. If confined indoors for a prolonged period, this child easily loses interest in what is being said or done, and the busy little hands and feet get in trouble. This is not the child to listen to a long set of instructions or to remain satisfied with paper and pencil tasks and other busy work. This child demands that his or her intellect be challenged with new activities and information.

Gemini children may have a tendency to be dissatisfied with their accomplishments. Their curious and sometimes restless natures want to move on to something else. They may be easily distracted by another activity or something happening on the other side of the room. It may require a great deal of positive reinforcement and a more than adequate amount of praise for completed tasks and for jobs well done before this child interprets the intrinsic value of succeeding at a job well done. Stress the positive aspects of what these children do and accomplish. Don't dwell on the negative. Look for ways to highlight their strengths and many natural abilities.

These children are quite capable. They are versatile and adaptable and inquisitive while at the same time they may appear restless, nervous and overly curious. In an emergency, this may be the child who rises to the situation by thinking, responding and acting quickly. This precocious child demands and deserves an understanding of the complexity of his or her nature. Patience and understanding are the key words in dealing with them.

Relationships with Other Signs

With your natural wit and charming personality, you are forever loved and appreciated. You are surrounded by loyal friends and companions who truly appreciate what you have to offer. Many of these friendships endure a lifetime as you definitely have something to add or to give to others. It is your enthusiasm and pure joy in living that attracts the attentions of other people. You can often be found either with your friends or on the phone with one person or another. So contagious is your love for life, that friends will often overlook any and all of your faults just to be in your company.

On the other hand, you also attract casual friends like a magnet, winning, charming and then discarding them one or all with the same ease. These casual relationships can be superficial with little or no emotional commitment from you. You have a distinct tendency to find so many people temporarily amusing. They satisfy your curiosity for the moment, but then you tire of them and move on.

It may be found that the native Gemini with their many countering characteristics is best attuned with Aries and Taurus most especially in spirituality and sensuality. Then too, you are companionable with Leo professionally or socially. Leo and Aries, however, may perceive your changing nature as a threat to their own security. Point in case, Aries may often lack the intuitive powers to understand your complexities although at the same time these people are drawn by your charm. But you are in good standing with Cancer who is also curious and seeks changes. Any companionship with Virgo is not predictable. However, a relation with a Libra is probably the most perfect in that the attraction is strongly physical and offers mutual tastes and interests. For some reason, Gemini and Libra appear to understand each other on another level, even if they don't always agree. Scorpio and Sagittarius offer Gemini only a sentimental or strictly professional association. Capricorn offer an undecided connection, and Pisces, while they may make good neighbors, rarely make positive connections with Gemini. Two Gemini are completely at odds with each other. They may share spiritually and intellectually, but the chances are they will become overly critical of one another. You are perhaps most favorably regarded by Cancer and most dearly loved and appreciated by Libra.

Take some care, Gemini, not to cause too much harm or needless worry to your friends, family and casual acquaintances because of your dual nature. Otherwise, you will find yourself forever harboring a bit of guilt and chagrin in regards to your friendships and with your closest loved ones. Learn to accept the responsibility of love that is so generously offered to you by your dearest friends and family.

Gemini Sexuality

That subject which interests us all: our own personal sexuality. Why does a person feel the way they do? Why does he or she like a certain person and not another? What arouses a person and why? On some level, these questions influences one and all. Like all aspects of our lives and lifestyles, the public attitude toward sex is ever changing and evolving. From the restrictive taboos of the Victorian Age, through the revitalization of the Industrial Age, to the make love not war of the 1960s to the commercialism of the 1980s and the 1990s, sex is always on our minds. Will the Age of Information or the Age of Aquarius bring new insights?

The American culture is not only influenced by popular trends and thought but by its unique cultural diversity as well. To the newcomer or newly arrived, American society can appear perplexing. What is difficult to understand is that in this freedom-based culture, the individual is literally free to be whoever he or she decides. And the gamut runs from the most traditional, reserved, cautious, and sexually repressed individuals to others who flaunt their sexuality, centering their lives around their sexual habits. Perhaps it is because of this very diversity that our culture makes some attempt not to be overly offensive to the sensitivities of some while giving a tolerant nod to the liberties of others. We are totally free, within the guidelines of laws, to seek divine enlightenment or to destroy ourselves with pleasures. Americans have the freedom to choose, individually, what importance their sexual behavior will play in their lives.

That being the case, sex is recognized by every serious discipline--from psychologists to scientists to astrologers--as being a central focus on individual lives. Freud saw sex as an influence on every aspect of the individual life. And from the sexist boys in the locker room to the most enlightened of intellectuals, sex remains a fundamental part of life that cannot be ignored. Get two friends together and the subject eventually turns to sex, romance, or marriage. One can blame it on the media, but sooner or later discussing the stock market gets boring, but sex never does.

There are those who hold to the theory that the primary function of sex is to have children and any other consideration is secondary. There are others for whom sex is an integral part of life, providing one of the greatest stress relievers ever invented. That all other living species procreate seasonally points to the reasoning of the second theory. But all pleasures (or temptations) in life also promote the possibilities of problems and health concerns unless a little logic is also applied.

Astrologically, the sexual nature has been examined from the Garden of Eden to the lives of contemporary celebrities. And what every serious astrologer will say is that how the individual relates to sexuality is not based on the Sun sign alone. The entire chart must be examined because each person is a unique combination of Sun, Moon, Ascendant, planets, Houses and aspects. A comparison of two charts often sheds light on compatibility. Compatibility between two people is often found when the Sun sign is in the same sign as their lover's Ascendant, or vice versa. Opposite Sun signs or an opposite Sun sign and Ascendant may also blend well together.

In a woman's chart, the placement of Venus is indicative of her sexuality while the position of Mars and the Sun indicates what kind of man she is attracted to. In a man's chart, the position of Mars tells how he relates to women, and the position of Venus and the Moon indicates what type of woman arouses him. In comparing two charts, look for the aspects of conjunction, sextile, square, trine, and oppositions. Remember that oppositions can blend. The square brings differences but much energy while conjunctions can be beneficial. The sextile and trine bring harmony. When a person's Venus and their lover's Mars are in the same sign, there is a strong attraction even if differences of opinions occur. When Venus and the other person's Ascendant are in the same sign, it adds to the sexual compatibility. Venus in the lover's sun sign brings a mutual interest while Mars in the lover's Moon sign is emotionally intense.

There is a vast variety of people found within each Sun sign, but basic characteristics and traits do exist. However, generalizations are just that and a fuller picture of the individual is reflected by the complete chart. The following section deals with Sun sign sexuality in a general manner. While the importance of sex remains the same in each Sun sign, the focus and attitudes vary.

Gemini Sexuality - Man

This versatile, witty and charming man is sexually appealing, but a lover may become perplexed if she attempts to understand him. Gemini, sign of the Twins, has a dual nature and is more than a little perplexing and confusing to one and all. Just when his lover thinks she knows him well, his changeability produces an entirely different personality and she must begin a new trying to get to know him well. Gemini is ruled by his intellect not his emotions. He is a thinking man whose curiosity is attracted to the possibility of new experiences. Gemini is one of the most difficult signs to make generalizations about. This man more than likely prefers to appear well dressed and conservative, but there is every possibility that his thinking and many of his actions are anything but conventional. He is impulsive and may start his sexual experimentation early in life and may on impulse even marry young. Then again, he may dance around romance and marriage and decide not to marry at all.

A smooth talker, women are attracted to him, and he may find himself involved with more than one at a time with very little effort. He can be subtle and persuasive and a woman who is enjoying his friendship or a working relationship, may find herself in his bed and enjoying herself whether or not she ever intended on a sexual relationship. The Gemini man can be selective, preferring an intellectual attraction and a woman who appeals to his discerning nature. But then his duality kicks in, and he is also impulsively drawn to an attractive woman who not only appeals to him intellectually but who also offers the thrill of a new or daring episode to add to his list of mental conquests. Gemini can be open minded in this regard, and he may be attracted to older or younger woman alike. Age can easily be rationalized away by this thinking man. What is important is the new experience. If asked why he is in a particular relationship, this man may reply, "I thought I might learn something new."

He can be entertaining and energetically alive, but don't expect a lot of gushy emotionalism. At the most, he may be a bit sensitive at times, but generally, he is too busy collecting experiences and meeting new people to focus his attentions on one aspect of his life and this is especially true of his emotions. He may appear to love them and leave them, but what he is actually doing is moving on to the next experience. And remember, it is the thrill of the unconventional that may appeal to him most. An adventurous Gemini man may have on his list of experiences phone booths, parking garages, beaches, a ski resort, the path between two different lovers' homes, an airplane, train, or the living room of his girlfriend when she isn't home. He can even find himself in a tangled web of involvement with two female friends one of whom is blackmailing him for more sex. Don't expect this man to be demonstrative or affectionate, but do expect a sensual approach at the most unlikely of times whether in public or private. If he travels, Gemini is the man with a woman in every port or city whichever the case may be. The physical act of sex can serve as a great stress reliever to this active and thinking man. It eases his tensions and allows him to balance his dual nature and to think more clearly and effectively. Sexual deviations may not appeal to him, but he likes a partner who is willing and able whenever the mood strikes him. And he likes an experience he can cherish and add to his memories and one which will forever satisfy both sides of his dual nature.

When it comes to marriage, Gemini again does a switch and becomes discerning and somewhat conventional. He prefers a sensible partner who is socially adept and attractive with a conventional style. Marriage works best when his mate is also his intellectual equal or a person whose intellect and interests he admires. He may most want a person who is moderate in all areas of life including emotionally. This isn't a man who appreciates temperamental or emotional displays or loud or annoying scenes. To live with a Gemini means pleasing both sides of his duality. He can be impulsive, rash and changeable, and he appears to sense that he needs someone down-to-earth and reliable as his life's partner. Will he be faithful and devoted? In love, he will be devoted. Faithful is difficult to predict. But his very versatility means that he will never be boring. Apply to his intellect and not his emotions. A demanding, clinging or overly emotional woman may drive him away. But a woman who holds and gently caresses his hand may delight both his mind and sensitivities arousing him to a quick and eventful passion.

Whatever his predisposition, this is a man who needs sex in his life. The difference in appearance of a Gemini man is remarkably apparent when he is actively engaged in a sexual relationship. It adds to his vitality, his youthful appearance and his energy level. Sex provides for this man a physical outlet for his mental tensions.

Gemini Sexuality - Woman

The Gemini woman may know her mind or then again, she may not. How can she ever make a reasonable decision unless she meets enough people and collects a variety of experiences from which to choose? She is versatile and adaptable and can turn on an alluring charm that is appealing and attracts the attention of any number of men. Since she is at this point only collecting experiences, she can be casual and easily turned off by a man who is too doting and overly gushy and mushy. She much prefers a bit of a challenge, especially intellectually, and that alluring hint of a new sexual adventure. She likes them young, she likes them old, and she likes them bold and daring. If she has a domestic nature, she may have a thing for kitchen countertops, closets or that new plush carpet in front of the fire place. If she is a career woman, she may have a thing for elevators, conference tables, under a desk, or that plush executive chair. A thinking woman who has collected and analyzed her experiences, she knows how to excite a man and to move him to new heights of pleasure.

She may appear casual or conservative, and she likes to be socially acceptable whatever her circumstance may be. But beneath that cool exterior beats the heart of her duality which propels her to seek the off beat. She knows she must eventually settle for a sensible man, home and family, but he must be intellectually stimulating, sexually active and experimental. Boring and routine does not appeal to this woman. An attentive suitor may besiege her with well-meaning attention, but there is every possibility that she will meet her mate through friends, work, or a casual outing. That he talks about something besides sex appeals to her because she recognizes that enticing twinkle in his eye that promises the kind of true adventure that doesn't require speech. When they are alone, this daring man reaches for her hand, applying gentle kisses to her fingertips while building her anticipation of what is to come. He then guides her hands over his body, again adding to her pleasure through the sensitivities of her Gemini hands. From there, they explore each other in a quick frenzy or an enduring bout of love making--whichever the mood may call for. And she likes both types of love making. An inhibited person need not approach this Gemini female.

Give her a role, and this woman may love to play out her lover's sexual fantasy. But her favorite role may be the femme fatale. In love, she may turn possessive and jealous, but if this love fails, she isn't one to cry for very long. She pulls out her list of phone numbers and moves on to the next relationship. In casual affairs, she may be more than willing to share with one and all as long as there is an element of fun and pleasure. A need for variety may lead her to keep a string of lovers who are willing and ready to satisfy her ever changing nature. If she makes enemies it is with insecure and clinging females who don't understand that when she flirts with their men, she means no harm. She is only collecting more experiences, and if their men are of the dull and routine type, they need not fear her anyway because she has little interest in such types.

There is, of course, that conservative Gemini woman who may sublimate her sexual nature for reasons of propriety or because she was never exposed to the more adventurous types capable of arousing her passions and compelling her to forego her restrained lifestyle. This woman may exchange her sexual energies for intellectual pursuits and a career. If married, she may read romance novels, watch day time dramas or the talk shows that exploit other people's lives.

If happily married or involved in an ongoing sexually satisfying relationship, the Gemini woman glows with energy and delights in life. Her sexuality may quell her restless nature allowing her to focus her energies on positive pursuits. While not intensely emotional, she is intensely sexual which is to her benefit.

Gemini Health

The sign of the Gemini rules over the shoulders, arms, hands and lungs. You may find that you more prone to accidents, and you should be extremely careful and cautious of accidents to these areas of the body. These natives must also be ever watchful of bronchial and pulmonary illnesses, asthma, hay fever, inflammation and congestion of the lungs, pneumonia and pleurisy. The chest and lung area should be well protected against cold temperatures and bad weather.

Many Gemini are restlessly nervous, easily annoyed or irritated, and become over anxious with worry and anxiety. Some may try to exist on their nervous energy and one result may be frequent headaches. It is important for them to be ever watchful for signs of depression. Many of these individuals have propensities for disorders with the nervous system which can develop into facial twitches, skin complaints, or blood disorders. These nervous problems can also develop, in both men and women, into illnesses of the digestive system with indigestion, stomach problems, or in kidney problems and poor circulation. There is noted in addition some problems related to glandular disorders which must be watched for. Your personal planetary influences may also predispose you to little-known or rare ailments. Gemini may find that they have a sensitivity to prescription drugs, and this can cause many of them to ignore the advice of doctors and seek self cures or natural cures.

As with all of us, the best advice for Gemini is to strive for peace and harmony in his or her everyday life. In your busy life, remember to take care of your body. A body that is physically strong, will resist the above mentioned problems and illnesses. Your body also requires a good diet and both your body and your mental well being requires plenty of rest. While you love the good life and good food, learn to slow down a little and to give thought and time to taking care of yourself. Rest and relaxation and the development of an inner tranquillity will only better prepare you for your busy life. You can maintain your usual good health by cultivating a good physical regime. Breathing exercises are of a great benefit as the person must take time out from a busy schedule for them. Along with that, a cultivation of a calm, peaceful and positive attitude, at least for a part of your day, will produce great results in your mental abilities and in your ability to feel good about yourself.

History of Gemini

In modern times, The Twins are ruled by Mercury, the planet of writing, education, trade, commerce and exchange. It is accepted that these attributes are the natural inclinations of the Gemini natives. However, long before the rulerships were taken from the gods and given to the planets, the sign of Gemini was ruled by Diana, goddess of the crescent moon and twin sister to Apollo, the sun-god who ruled, at that time, Sagittarius.

In Greece, the original Twins were two stars of equal brightness close together. In Babylon they were referred to as the Great Twins to identify them from the Little Twins, and the ancients of Egypt referred to them as the Two Stars. In the Hebrew Zodiac, this sign indicates the tribe of Benjamin while in early Christianity, it was used as a mystical symbol for Christ.

As the story goes, Zeus descended from Olympus in the form of a swan to the bed of Leda, wife of Tyndareus, the king of Sparta. From this union of Zeus and Leda came two eggs. From one egg came Clytemnestra and Helen, later known as Helen of Troy; from the other egg came Castor and Polydeuces (or Pollux). Now, Castor and Clytemnestra were actually the children of Tyndareus so he was appeased. In time, Castor and Pollux (boys), as well as their non-twin sisters, represented the mortal and immortal aspects of life. Castor tamed horses, and Pollux taught boxing. In other words, one was peaceful while the other was aggressive. When Castor was killed, Zeus appeased the grief of Pollux by reuniting the twin boys in the stars as the constellation of Gemini.

The twin stars best represent the duality of the nature of the persons born under the sign of Gemini. Mercury, the messenger of the gods, quite naturally bestows upon these individuals a vivacious temperament, a quick wit, and an ever lasting versatility. Gemini natives are within the realm of the intellect and intellectual pursuits. They are regarded by many modern astrologers as remaining in balance between the sentimentally inclined and the overly worldly.

How to Find Your Soul-Mate, Stars, and Destiny

Gemini

May 21 -- June 21
The Thebaic Calendar
Character, Personality, and Destiny

Astrology is the ancient and noble study and science that has occupied the minds of intelligent people of both old and modern times including kings, Popes, scholars, philosophers, presidents, and heads of state. The more that is known, the more individuals seem to become caught up in its mysteries. Many times, those persons with certain inclinations and mystical abilities and skills become interested in it and want to know more. The following individual days of the sign of Gemini were first noted by the ancients in this field of study and from their observations the Thebaic Calendar was born.

Whether it is the Sun sign, the Ascendant, on the cusp, or in a House, the characteristics of Gemini are exhibited. Gemini is the first Air sign, and as such is an intellectual sign of conscious reasoning. When you determine which House Gemini is in your personal chart, you will discover that area of life where you reason and communicate your interactions with others and the situations regarding that particular environment. Gemini concerns intellectualizing and communicating those thoughts with others whether they be lessons learned, questionings, observations, or simply clever witticisms that compel others to listen. The Sun sign of Gemini bestows a responsiveness to intellectual reasonings and impressions, and it necessitates the collection of experiences from which to gather the information needed for further consideration. The Gemini mind is forever active and busy storing information, whether it be tidbits of facts or in other instances simply impressions or interesting reactions regarding their surroundings. Gemini is busy collecting and categorizing impressions and is happiest when called upon to relate and communicate these impressions to others.

DUALITY: Masculine   **ELEMENT:** Air   **QUALITY:** Mutable   **RULER:** Mercury

The influence of Gemini bestows upon the individual the ability and power to reason, intellectualize, and experiment in order that they might discover the ability to interact with others. This is best accomplished through the development of the mind but also through the development of the oratory abilities. As the famous messenger, Mercury, allows and influences, Gemini talks and communicates and carries the messages of the Universe. If this communication requires cooperating with others, then this is the lesson Gemini is challenged to learn and assimilate. If all knowledge all ready exists in the Universe, it would require a Gemini to gather this information and to disseminate it to others: this is the calling of the Gemini. And if it were possible to formulate a new idea from all these ideas floating around, it quite possibly would be a gifted Gemini who would do so, so astute are they at pondering ideas. What Gemini is best at is not only producing the thought or the process of formulating the thought, but of communicating this first germ of thought to others. And it is the frustrated and moody Gemini who is in the process of formulating a new thought, but who hasn't quite decided how best to express the idea to others. It is as if this kernel of a thought floats around in the Gemini intellect as mere air waves, waiting for the mood of the contemplating Gemini to change so that this person can grasp and conceptualize it. But that is not enough for Gemini. The mood doesn't lift or change entirely until Gemini has formulated not only the thought but the best words for expressing the thought. And it is the personable, likable, sociable Gemini who arises from their dismal mood to once again gad about from group to group spreading their latest thoughts and proving to one and all that pleasantries combine quite well with intellectualizing.

Wherever Gemini is found in a personal chart whether it be the Sun sign, Ascendant, cusp, or House, it is this area where a person is challenged to apply the skills of positive interactions and communication with others. And this process requires a conscious or overt, intellectualizing effort on the part of the individual. Whatever area of life a person chooses to excel at requires conscious effort, and this is just as true in the area of interacting with others. Would you apply negative efforts to bettering your occupational skills? By the same reasoning, the improvement of relationships requires a positive effort. And how one improves relationships depends to a great degree on how well one learns the art of communicating positive thoughts through an intellectual effort which promises to improve one's personal interactions on all levels. Those bestowed with the communication abilities of the gifts granted by the Sun sign Gemini come by this art and capability most naturally of all of the signs, but they may not be born with the knowledge of how to use it. Thus, the moods of the Gemini who is forever attempting to put each thought in its proper order. Mutable Gemini graced by adaptability doesn't bother with confronting obstacles head-on like the Ram. They are much more prone to dance around the problem, talking their way out of or around any such difficulties. And this capability adds to the endearing charm with which Gemini faces life and his or her interactions with others. Their very intellectualizing abilities and gift of conversation and glib chatter may make them appear somewhat detached and impersonal to those who want to get to the heart of personal feelings, but Gemini loves with the art of the charmer and gathers friends and lovers just as easily. Whatever the faults of the Gemini individual, others more than likely choose to over look them and to stand by this delightful person. Their ability to perform a balancing act of diverse interests while dancing in and out of social groups and family and friends gains the attentions of one and all.

The First Decan

The First Decan is from 0 degrees to 10 degrees of Gemini and applies to those born between May 21 and May 31. This Decan bestows unusual communication and intellectual ability to a person born on the cusp of Taurus which no doubt applies the balancing attributes of productivity and of being well grounded to the Earth. As a Gemini, these individuals are not only adaptable but are known for an impressionable intelligence that grasps the details and facts necessary for comprehension. Their quick perceptions and curiosity allows them to gather to them for assimilation those external stimuli from the environment which filter through to their eager consciousness. If unable to filter external stimuli effectively, this person may appear nervous and indecisive, with somewhat scattered and diffuse thoughts.

The Second Decan

The Second Decan occurs from 10 degrees to 20 degrees of Gemini and applies to those born between June 1 and June 10. This is that graceful and charming Gemini bestowed with the ability to verbally persuade others to their point of view. They grace any social circle of their choosing, delighting one and all with their quick wit and ability to turn a quick and entertaining phrase. All of the characteristics of Gemini apply most strongly to this Second Decan born. They are endowed with all of the strong and positive characteristics of this Sun sign as well as all the changeable, impulsive, and moody traits that in some instances may deter, distract, and diffuse the thought processes of this most lovable character. Their curiosity about all aspects of life are heightened and this spans from the thoughts and actions of those people with whom they come in contact to the sexual possibilities and propensities available to them. They want to experiment, gather new and different experiences, and they conclude with wrapping it all up nicely in a well phrased prologue or epilogue.

The Third Decan

The Third Decan occurs from 20 degrees to 30 degrees of Gemini and includes those persons born from June 11 to June 21. Falling on the cusp of Cancer, the Third Decan born retain all the traits of Gemini but are influenced as well by the insecurities and self-centeredness of Cancer. This is an intellectualizing but questioning person who gathers truisms and doubts equally well. The creativity and dream-like quality of Cancer adds to the originality of the Third born Decan. Then too, this is perhaps the most romantic of those born to the sign of Gemini. Their ideas may be easily impressed by the influence of others, but they retain their ability to rationalize and to communicate to one and all.

First Decan of Gemini:

May 21 - May 30 -

First Ten Days

Character, Personality, and Temperament:

Gentle, kind; notoriety; weaknesses brought on by being gullible and possessing questionable credibility; poor judgement concerning friends and family; easy going nature. These individuals may well lack the inner energy and drive that is needed to achieve goals and purposes. It is quite common for them to waste themselves in needless pursuits.

Mutable Element:

Air: Versatile ability that is given to adapting ideas in order to more easily communicate thoughts.

Destiny:

Energies diffused through following various pursuits of an intellectual nature.

Star Date of Birth: May 21

An abundance of sincerity, love, admiration, friendship and protection which compensates for the lack of energy. You are quick to take advantage of any given opportunity and just as quick to spot the humor in those aspects of life that others take too seriously. You have a realistic approach to sex, seeing it as a part of life that offers fulfillment and enjoyment.

Star Date of Birth: May 22

You develop your intellect, but your unpredictable nature may lead you either to success or to acquiring new and unrelated experiences. Your sexuality is enhanced by your imaginative, romantic, and desirable allure which often attracts the glamorous types.

Star Date of Birth: May 23

A wandering character who has intellectual abilities and is intelligent but often unproductive. The stars have bestowed upon you many good attributes, but you may feel unchallenged which can lead to laziness. Sexually, there are times when you are not sure what you want, making you a demanding and surprising lover, but this doesn't dispel the desire others have for you.

Star Date of Birth: May 24

A very open individual who is in a decent and honorable situation. You admire and are drawn to the artistic, musical, and written work of others. Sexually, others are attracted to you because of your magnetism and allure which promises what you fulfill which is the energy and stamina to physically please yourself and your partner.

Star Date of Birth: May 25

Changing, surprising situations; possesses different skills for different jobs; may enjoy changing occupations or jobs. You are restless and may change jobs or activities in an effort to satisfy your mind. others are impressed with your optimistic and congenial nature and your willingness to please and entertain the group. Sexually, you are attracted to those with a good body, but you are also capable of spotting those who tend to hide their best attributes.

Star Date of Birth: May 26

A calm, smart, balanced life; medical or technical skills; research ability. You are creative and talented with an artistic inclination. Your sexuality is expressed in your daring and unorthodox manner, and you pursue those who you feel can best stimulate your imagination and satisfy your curiosity. And you prefer to wait for just this type.

Star Date of Birth: May 27

A very friendly and enthusiastic person; life's obstacles and problems are going to be resolved. You thrive on intellectual and sophisticated experiences which stimulate your own creativity. Your sexuality is enhanced by love and kindness that is shared with your partner. The physical aspects of love must stimulate your intellect as well as your physical needs.

Star Date of Birth: May 28

Great spiritual and religious feelings. A desire to attract and draw attention; a great deal of luck in destiny. However, intellectual you are, you are open, flexible, and accepting of other people and their lifestyles. There is nothing stuffy about you. Your sexual encounters expose you to fresh experiences and new feelings and emotions which furthers your ideas and perceptions of life.

Star Date of Birth: May 29

Skills for judicial or political studies; diplomatic; a well oriented life toward studies. Your moodiness can lead you to become disenchanted with life and when this happens you often hurt the feelings of others and may end up hurting yourself as well. When your mood changes, you are the type who gives more than you receive and experiences more emotional levels than most.

Star Date of Birth: May 30

A pronounced, sharp sensitivity and a nervousness; many unexplained failures; ups and downs in love life. Many of your difficulties in life are brought about by a tendency to be overly quick to act and to be careless in your decision making. Your sexuality is enhanced by the atmosphere of new, exciting, or exotic places, thus satisfying your need for experiences.

Second Decan of Gemini:

May 31 - June 9 -

Second Ten Days

Character, Personality, and Temperament:

An inclination for argument which spoils the spiritual qualities. Ingenious and seductive ideas which will be presented either boldly or violently or without any interest. Irritability will affect the entire character.

Mutable Element:

Air: Intellectual and mental abilities combined with the ability to communicate and adapt ideas to changing circumstances.

Destiny:

The individual will be controlled by too much susceptibility. Good situations will be lost because of the tenacious character.

How to Find Your *Soul-Mate, Stars,* and *Destiny*

Star Date of Birth: May 31

Curiosity for the past and for antiquities; an active life which may lead to exhaustion. Friendly and extroverted, you seek new experiences and are drawn to large group activities and the opportunity to meet new people. Your insatiable curiosity and need for adventure and new experiences leads you to meet others who are sexually attracted to you because of these traits.

Star Date of Birth: June 1

Adventurous, courageous spirit; troubles with friends' death. Music enhances your own creativity and dispels your moodiness. Your sexual attitudes are progressive, and you are drawn to those willing to test the limits of their imaginations. You are bold and adventurous with a need for new experiences.

Star Date of Birth: June 2

Intense curiosity for religious or for mysterious, occult, and magic things. Short but enthusiastic friendships. You are by nature charming and friendly, requiring little effort on your part to be well accepted and well liked by others. Your ambitions are motivated by your romantic relationship while your sexuality is enhanced by your inventive and creative nature.

Star Date of Birth: June 3

A light sadism; the chance or opportunities are wrongly used. You are a creative dreamer who ambitiously makes every attempt to turn your ideas and visions into reality. Sexually, you learn the lessons life has to offer and apply these to new encounters, further fulfilling and satisfying your desires and curious nature.

Star Date of Birth: June 4

A light-minded, fun loving attitude; superficial friendships; lovers can lead you astray. You are sensitive and perceptive, responding most to tactile stimulus, creating and imagining with your hands that which your mind envisions. Your sexuality is highly related to your ability to turn your dreams into reality with those who share or appreciate your abilities.

How to Find Your *Soul-Mate, Stars, and Destiny*

Star Date of Birth: June 5

Unhealthy tendency towards discussion, arguments and conflicts; stupid and mean friends if you are not careful. Your open and accepting nature leads you to be overly trusting which others may take advantage and which may result in your feelings being hurt or your emotions played with. Your best bet is to stick to meeting people through friends or family and this is also true in your romantic relationships and sexual encounters.

Star Date of Birth: June 6

A pronounced lack of judgment; a continuous modest situation. You may have difficulty getting a handle on your cash flow as it seems to flow out as fast as you make it which can seem distressing. You meet lovers during your travels, and your lasting love may be encountered when you visit a new and distant location.

Star Date of Birth: June 7

A nice, quiet spirit and uneventful life; a lack of purpose or acceptance of your present situation. But, you seem to know instinctively what you want and how to get it whether it concerns business, finance, or your personal life and family. You can be assertive in your romantic affairs but possessive of lovers as well, and others may find you more of a seducer than a lover.

Star Date of Birth: June 8

In some people a malicious, tricky spirit; the purpose in life is often changed or may never be reached. You are prone to seek the pleasures of life and over indulgence tempts you. You can be clever, cunning, and shrewd when it comes to taking advantage of romantic opportunities. You tend to be always on the go, preferably to those busy places where people gather to meet and socialize.

Star Date of Birth: June 9

A stubborn, complicated mind and character. You desire a peaceful and contented life, but may avoid situations which you feel may lead to difficulties in obtaining what you want making you discontented regarding missed opportunities. You can be overly idealistic about sex and romance wanting your relationships to add glamour and fulfillment to your life.

The Third Decan of Gemini:

June 10 - June 21 -
Third Ten Days

Character, Personality, and Temperament:

A brilliant intelligence with talents in the fields of literature, science and art. Continuous activities that mingle with each other.

Mutable Element:

AIR: Flexibility in adapting ideas in order to communicate them to other people.

Destiny:

Medium financial situation; not all activities are prosperous; restless and adventuresome but risky life; long voyages.

Star Date of Birth: June 10

A lazy existence with little motivation; little self-discipline; much wasted time to dreaming, but you are motivated by success which can lead you to work diligently to renew this feeling. You attempt to practice restraint in your sexual life, but your compulsiveness may lead you to be tempted again and again by love and romance until you find the person you feel is the perfect partner.

Star Date of Birth: June 11

A great spiritual and religious depth and originality; a serious and independent career. Your optimism may lead you to overlook any problems until it is too late to deal with them effectively. Your innocence and naiveté in romantic relationships leads you to link your sexual experiences with your feelings of fulfillment.

Star Date of Birth: June 12

Artistic skills; a quiet family life; sensitive and well-liked. Restless and impulsive, your moodiness can lead to periods of dreamy self-delusion and at other times to despondency. Your sexuality relationships is enhanced by relationships with persons introduced to you by friends and family. A commanding personality attracts your attention.

Star Date of Birth: June 13

Indifference for future; troubles; danger to become isolated in hospital or jail; risk to lose money or situation. But your optimism and trust in the future underscores your successes. You have a yearning to express yourself through your sexuality which leads you to seek new experiences; your most fulfilling relationship is with a renewed love perhaps with a person from your youth.

Star Date of Birth: June 14

Happy, friendly and charming character; success through friends or inheritance. You build on your successes or those accomplishments of your family members. Your personal security may be tied to your financial position, but you seek more fulfillment from your romantic relationships wanting a lasting bond between you and your partner.

Star Date of Birth: June 15-16

A desire to study or complete research; lucky situations; success in endeavors. Your shrewd cleverness leads you to set others against each other which allows you to succeed. In your sexual relationships, you feel at ease and uninhibited wanting both fun and frivolity to prevail. You seem to want it all: money, success, fun, and games.

Star Date of Birth: June 17

Instability and hesitation; many interrupted relationships; many changes in situation. Your personal success is based on your ability to focus your energies on your creative endeavors otherwise you become nervous and worrisome. sexually, you are adept at adapting to new people and any situation, wanting to please your romantic partner and in so doing please yourself.

Star Date of Birth: June 18

A tendency for life in the country; quiet, simple life; existence based on hard work. You may appear more financially well off than you actually are because you know how to make the most of what you have. You are drawn to people who share your interest in property and possessions. Your sexuality acts as a rejuvenating force in your life.

Star Date of Birth: June 19

Ever changing character; love for luxury; in search of an ever-lasting happiness and success. You can be pleasing but less than productive until you find your chosen direction then you apply yourself to putting your ideas into action. Your confidence and self-assured attitude spills over into your sexuality, attracting the attentions of your chosen romantic partners.

How to Find Your Soul-Mate, Stars, and Destiny

Star Date of Birth: June 20

Many different skills; highly adaptable in various activities; productive, creative life. You wish to please and be of service to others but may find yourself pitted into the role of the martyr. In your romantic relationships, you become devoted, loyal, and self-sacrificing. You are especially drawn to those in the entertainment field.

Star Date of Birth: June 21

A polite and generous nature; life supported by women. Your moodiness may lead to unstable habits and questionable actions and activities. In your sexual relationships, you may have a tendency to cling to the memories of your past encounters even while pursuing new ones.

Colors:

The most favorable colors for the native of Gemini are the bright colors of yellow, gold, and violet.

Birthstones:

The birthstones for Gemini natives are the agate.

Flowers:

Favorable flowers for natives of Gemini are lavender and lilies.

Keyword: "I Think"

Positive Traits:

Adaptable; intellectual; versatile; expressive; eloquent; witty; idealistic; logical; active; energetic; curious; studious; inquiring; amusing; flair for languages and writing; companionable; sociable; congenial; sympathetic; liberal; broad minded; resourceful; generous; responsive, tolerant; youthful appearance; humane; dexterous; courageous.

Negative Traits:

Changeable; restless; cunning and shrewd; verbose; tricky; overly curious and inquisitive; inconsistent; gossipy; critical; nervous; superficial; shifty; diffusive; vindictive; lazy; impulsive; exaggerates; braggart; wayward; common; violent; scatter brained; stingy ; selfish; delusional; deceptive; cheat; manipulative; envious and jealous.

Gemini

Personal Self-Expression and Mental Tendencies

1. Full-Fledged, Suffers Disapproval, Overly Criticized, Ever Elusive
2. Sex and Love Synonymous, Head-Over Heals, Erogenous, Mind
3. Sharing Sex to Actualize a Fantasy, Acknowledging the Experience
4. Aggressor for Sexual Needs; Performs Fellatio, Kinky Sex; Likes to Travel
5. Restless and Curious Mind, Seeks More Satisfaction from Sex
6. Inconsistent, Witty, Clever, Communicative, Youthful, Impractical
7. Footloose, Inquisitive, Broad-Minded, Inventive, Freedom-Loving
8. Adventuresome, Outgoing, Neurotic Sex Drive, Multifaceted, Dramatic
9. Versatile, Spendthrift, Ambidextrous, Devoted, Opportunist
10. Noncommittal, Unpredictable, High-Strung, Nervous, Capricious
11. Short Attention Span, Stimulating, Entertaining, Scattered
12. Quick, Mercurial, Fantastic Imagination, Exhilarating Charm
13. Personality is Hard to Pin Down. Moods and Roles Confined
14. Deals With Messages of Intellect, The Gods Fleet-Footed
15. Facilitates All Communication - Writing, Reporting, Newscasting Gossiping
16. Intense Mental Activity, Totally Immersed in Other People
17. Unable to Change the Mind, Disinterested in Projects and Experiences
18. Compulsion to Talk About What is Seen, Heard, or Felt
19. Feelings of Fragmentation, Seeks to Find Wholeness, Nervous Energy
20. Scattered Emotions About Self, Multiple Personalities, Responsibilities
21. Experiences Sex Vicariously, Complex Relationships in Love Life
22. Complex Personality, Pursues Physical Sexual Unions, Energetic Mind
23. Hyperactive, Powerful Mind, Manipulative, Intelligent, Witty
24. High-Strung, Racehorse, Battle-Ready Warrior, Nervous Tension,
25. Self-Controled, Calm, Entertaining, Exudes, Gyrations
26. Nonstop, No-Turning Back Lifestyle, Stimulates and Stretches Mind
27. Excess Nervous Energy, Pushing, Prodding, Nagging, Ambidextrous
28. Free-Flowing Conversation, Divulges Secrets, Analytical Mind
29. Good Propagandist, Half-Truths, Outstanding Talent for Self-Expression

30. Irresistible, Great Diplomacy, Witty, Charming, Instant Appearance
31. Rearranges Filing Systems, Excels in Multiple Jobs Simultaneously
32. Races, Bicycling, Exploring, Excitement, Wishes to Be Free
33. Eager for Adventure, Rushes Helter-Skelter, Exotic, Inventive
34. No-Strings Attached, Independent, seeks Quality Relationships
35. Loves Gadgets; Cerebral of Two Minds; Many Positive Traits
36. Restless Mental State Leads to Insecurity, Insomnia, Confusion, Errors
37. Exhaustion, Explodes Emotionally, Duality Manifestations
38. Idea of Security, Ephemeral Nature of Existence, Love, and Marriage
39. Loves Routine, Obligations, and Permanence of Possessions; Skittish
40. Dramatic Self-Expression, Game Player, Verbose, Lacks Concentration
41. Intellectually Interested, Believes That Sex is Important Part of Life
42. Idealized Self-Image, Position and Security. Good Samaritan Nature
43. Explosive Sex, Mainstay in Many Games and Plays, Self-Directed Games
44. Demands Consistency and Responsibility, Exaggerates Own Accomplishments
45. Wit, Self-Imposed Demands, Tells a Lie Often Enough to Believe It
46. Downfall, Truth Comes to Haunt, Makes Friends Easily
47. Very Shrewd in Getting Commitment, Grabs Opportunity
48. Circumstances Fit Principles, Rationalizations to Fit Peccadillo
49. Infatuations, Capitalizes on Opportunities, Perceptive, Quixotic Traits
50. Ambidextrous, Spendtrift, Physical Reality, Love Power
51. Money and Possessions Slip Through Fingers
52. Empathizes, Tolerant, Institutions, True Compassion
53. Talkative, Outwardly Broad-Minded, Openness, Glamour
54. Learns to Display Multifaceted Knowledge, Well-Rounded Personality
55. Fickleness is Legendary, Love is Most Important Comfort
56. Luxury of Vulnerability, Searches for Soul-Mate or Other Half
57. Has Good Understanding of Own Emotions, Instability, Calm
58. Loves Renewing Old Friendships, Old Flames, Sexual-Priorities
59. Ages Very Slowly, Retains Youthful Air
60. Crabes Intimacy, Inward, Doesn't Expect Heaviness
61. Usually Skilled in Conducting Several Different People and Relationships
62. True Love Affairs, Commitment to Ideal is Very Real and Strong
63. Idealizes or Idolizes Nature, Develops Follow-Up Failures
64. Frighteningly Believable When Embellishing Facts
65. Extremes in Sexual Experimentation, Self-Assured, Fascinating Mind
66. High Self-Respect and Self-Esteem, Defense Mechanisms, Fears Intimacy
67. Deep-Seated Feelings of Loneliness, Tendency to Idealize Others
68. Fantasies are Disappointed, Polishes Personal Style, Mental Stimulation

69. Traditional Meanings, Pronunciations, and Origins Important
70. Physical Stimulation, Unsavory Behavior, Good Permanent Friends
71. Needs Stimulation From Many Different Directions
72. Fear of Losing Both the Lover and the Freedom, Humanitarian
73. Very Vulnerable in Love Situations, Stress, Nervous System Can Suffer
74. Has Qualifications for Lovers, Sexual Quickies, Loves Himself
75. Conventional Lifestyle, Works Hard to Find Excitement
76. Double-Feature Old-Time Movie, Sexually Unique
77. Uniquely Mysteriously, Infinite Manifestations, Courageous
78. Understandins Complexity, Caprices of Fortune, Sagacious Mind
79. Downfall in Great Distress, Public Disturbances, Wisdom, Eloquence
80. Malefic Danger,Captivity Following Accusation of Forgery
81. Elevation for Priests, Commerce - Wines, Perfumes, Nocturnal
82. Few Lucky Chances, Diurnal Homicidal Instinct, Little Prudence
83. Enthusiasims, Mental Aptitude for Art, Amorous, Pursues Very Young Lovers
84. Necessity to Flee, Dangerous Accusations, Many Misfortunes, Quick, Scattered
85. High-Strung, Changeable, Helpful, Promiscuous, Stable, Giggling
86. Acquisition of Literature, Several Occupations, Accomplished Speaker
87. Feel for Music, Clear Ideas, Intuitive, Inventive Ability, Good Humor
88. Friendly, Sociable, Likes to flirt, Many Love Affairs, Mystical Nature
89. Perceptive; Acute, Keen Intellect; Combative; Plain Spoken; Forceful
90. Often Disagreeable, Satirical, Fault Finding, Critical, Benevolent
91. Courteous, Truthful, Trustworthy, Lofty Prophecy, Adaptable,, Resourceful
92. Prophetic, Masculine, Violent, Enemy of Liars, Sacrificing, Barren, Sanquine
93. Mentally Sensitive, Sympathetic, Sorrow Through Relatives, Linguistic
94. Symbolic Dreams, Abstract Sciences, Prone to Anxiety, Carelessness
95. Prone to Destruction by Striving Against the Difficulties of Life
96. Neglect of Own Interests, Empty Headedness, Vain, Quick at Learning
97. Good Disposition, Humane, Sometimes Shy and Retiring, Eloquent
98. Capable of Acquiring a Good Education, Quick Witted, Expressive
99. Tenderness, Progressive, Ingenious, Seldom Prejudiced, Studious, Inquiring
100. Discrete, Ambitious, Shrewd, Dexterous, Cunning, Vindictive

How to Find Your *Soul-Mate, Stars,* and *Destiny*

Celebrity Birthdays

May   Gemini

21	Leo Sayer Judge Reinhold Peggy Cass Mike Barson	Dennis Day Robert Montgomery Harold Robbins Ronald Isley	Mr. T Albrecht Durer Raymond Burr Fats Waller
22	Naomi Campbell Richard Benjamin Laurence Olivier Judith Crist	Charles Aznavour Sir Arthur Conan Doyle Susan Strasberg Paul Winfield	Peter Nero Bernie Taupin Arthur Conan Doyle Richard Wagner
23	Scatman Crothers John Newcombe Drew Carey Betty Garrett	Rosemary Clooney Joan Collins Douglas Fairbanks Sr. Bill Hunt	Jewell Barbara Ward Anatoly Karpov
24	Gary Burghoff Queen Victoria Siobhan McKenna Priscilla Presley	Tommy Chong Roseanne Cash Fatty Arbuckle Wilbur Mills	George Washington Lilli Palmer Bob Dylan Patti LaBelle
25	Robert Ludlum Leslie Uggams Hal David Lindsey Nelson	Gene Tunney Mary Wells Lawrence Ralph Waldo Emerson Frank Oz	Miles Davis Dixie Carter Kitty Kallen Beverly Sills
26	Artie Shaw John Wayne Aldo Gucci James Arness	Peggy Lee Laurance Rockefeller Alec McGowen Helena Bonham-Carter	Genie Francis Norma Talmadge Sally Ride Stevie Nicks
27	Isadora Duncan Henry Kissinger Vincent Price Lee Meriwether	Rachel Carson Hubert Humphrey Siouxsie Sioux John Cheever	Christopher Lee Herman Wouk Cilla Black Louis Gossett Jr.
28	John Fogarty Stephen Birmingham John Fogerty Roland Gift	Kirk Gibson Dietrich Fisher-Dieskau Gladys Knight Kylie Minogue	Sondra Locke Jim Thorpe Carroll Baker Barry Commoner

How to Find Your Soul-Mate, Stars, and Destiny

May   Gemini

29	King Charles II Patrick Henry Annette Bening Melissa Etheridge	Bob Hope Helmut Berger Pres. John F. Kennedy Clifton James	Beatrice Lillie Eric Davis Lisa Whelchel Anthony Geary
30	Clint Walker Billy Baldwin Benny Goodman Cornelia Skinner	Gale Sayers Christine Jorgenson James Farley Nicky Headon	Mel Blanc Lisa Kudrow Ted McGinley Michael J. Pollard
31	Sharon Gless Clint Eastwood Joe Namath Lea Thompson	Norman Vincent Peale Don Ameche Brooke Shields Augie Meyers	Johnny Paycheck Fred Allen Tom Berenger Peter Yarrow

June

1	Lisa Hartman Pat Boone Brigham Young Ron Wood	Marilyn Monroe Jonathan Pryce Powers Booth Rene Auberjonois	David Rockefeller Joan Caulfield Andy Griffith David Berkowitz
2	Noah Wyle Hedda Hopper Stacy Keach Marvin Hamlisch	Marquis de Sade Chuck Barris Martha Washington Jerry Mathers	Johnny Weissmuller Sally Kellerman Michael Steele Milo O'Shea
3	Suzi Quatro Josephine Baker Jefferson Davis Colleen Dewhurst	Tony Curtis Scott Valentine Allen Ginsberg Deniece Williams	Billy Powell Paulette Goddard King George V Marion Davies
4	Noah Wyle Robert Merrill Michelle Phillips Rosalind Russell	King George III Dr. Ruth Westheimer Parker Stevenson Roger Ball	Bruce Dern El DeBarge Charlie Whitney Scott Wolf
5	Pancho Villa Bill Moyers Kenny G Karen Sillas	Laurie Anderson Richard Butler Bill „Hopalong Cassidy' Boyd	Marky Mark Don Reid Freddie Stone Bill Hayes

How to Find Your Soul-Mate, Stars, and Destiny

June   Gemini

6	Robert Englund Roy Innis Nathan Hale Amanda Pays	Bjorn Borg Empress Alexandra of Russia Sandra Bernhard	Achmed Sukarno Gary Bonds Tomy Ryan Pushkin
7	Rocky Graziano Jessica Tandy James Ivory Tom Jones	Liam Neeson Thurman Munson Paul Gauguin Prince	Fred Waring Beau Brummel
8	Bonnie Tyler Alexis Smith Griffin Dunne Kathy Baker	Mick Box Barbara Bush Frank Lloyd Wright Mick „Red' Hucknall	Nancy Sinatra, Jr. James Darren Robert Schumann Joan Rivers
9	Johnny Depp Robert McNamara Peter the Great Fred Waring	Cole Porter Jackie Mason Trevor Bolder Michael J. Fox	Jackie Mason Jon Lord Happy Rockefeller Billy Hatton
10	Maurice Sendak Human Beatbox Prince Philip Rene Novotny	Elisabeth Shue F. Lee Bailey Hattie McDaniel Frederick Loewe	Saul Bellow Judy Garland Robert Cummings Elizabeth Hurley
11	Joe Montana Richard Strauss Chad Everett Gene Wilder	Paul Mellon William Styron Rise Stevens Jacques Cousteau	Vince Lombardi Bonnie Pointer Joey Dee George Willig
12	Chick Corea Anne Frank David Rockefeller Reg Presley	Vic Damone Jim Nabors George Bush Sherry Stringfield	Ivan Tors Irwin Allen Brad Delp Timothy Busfield
13	Tim Allen Don Budge Prince Aly Kahn Luis Alvarez	Richard Thomas Basil Rathbone The Olsen twins Ally Sheedy	Paul Lynde Red Grange Christo Howard Leese
14	Steffi Graf Rod Argent Marla Gibbs	Gene Barry Jimmy Lea Donald Trump	Eric Heiden Muff Winwood Pierre Salinger

How to Find Your Soul-Mate, Stars, and Destiny

June   Gemini

15	Ice Cube Erroll Garner June Lockhart Terri Gibbs	Courteney Cox June Lockhart Edvard Grieg Russell Hitchcock	Jim Belushi Morris Udall Malcolm MacDowell Helen Hunt
16	Laurie Metcalf Erich Segal Helen Traubel Joyce Carol Oates	Katharine Graham Stan Laurel Joan Van Ark Gino Vannelli	Derrick Sanderson Jack Alberts6n Eddie Levert Ian Matthews
17	Barry John Hersey Peter Lupus Igor Stravinsky	Jason Patrick Dean Martin Elroy „Crazylegs' Hirsch Dave Concepcion	Phylicia Rashad John Wesley Red Foley Ralph Bellamy
18	Paul McCartney E. G. Marshall Alison Moyet Lou Brock	Sammy Cahn Jeanette MacDonald Isabella Rossellini John D. Rockefeller IV	Carol Kane Anastasia Kay Kyser James Brolin
19	Tommy DeVito Gena Rowlands Guy Lombardo	Salman Rushdie Charles Coburn Louis Jourdan	Icing James I Lou Gehrig Phylicia Rashad
20	Kathleen Turner Nicole Kidman Lionel Richie Lillian Hellman Chet Atkins	Dame May Whitty Cyndi Laupe Audie Murphy Danny Aiello Brian Wilson	Ann Wilson John Goodman Anne Murray Dave Thomas Errol Flynn
21	Juliette Lewis Maureen Stapleton Judy Holliday Prince William	Mary McCarthy Lalo Schifrin Ernest Hemingway Meredith Baxter-Birney	Derrick Coleman Francoise Sagan Jean-Paul Sartre Mariette Hartley

How to Find Your *Soul-Mate, Stars,* and *Destiny*

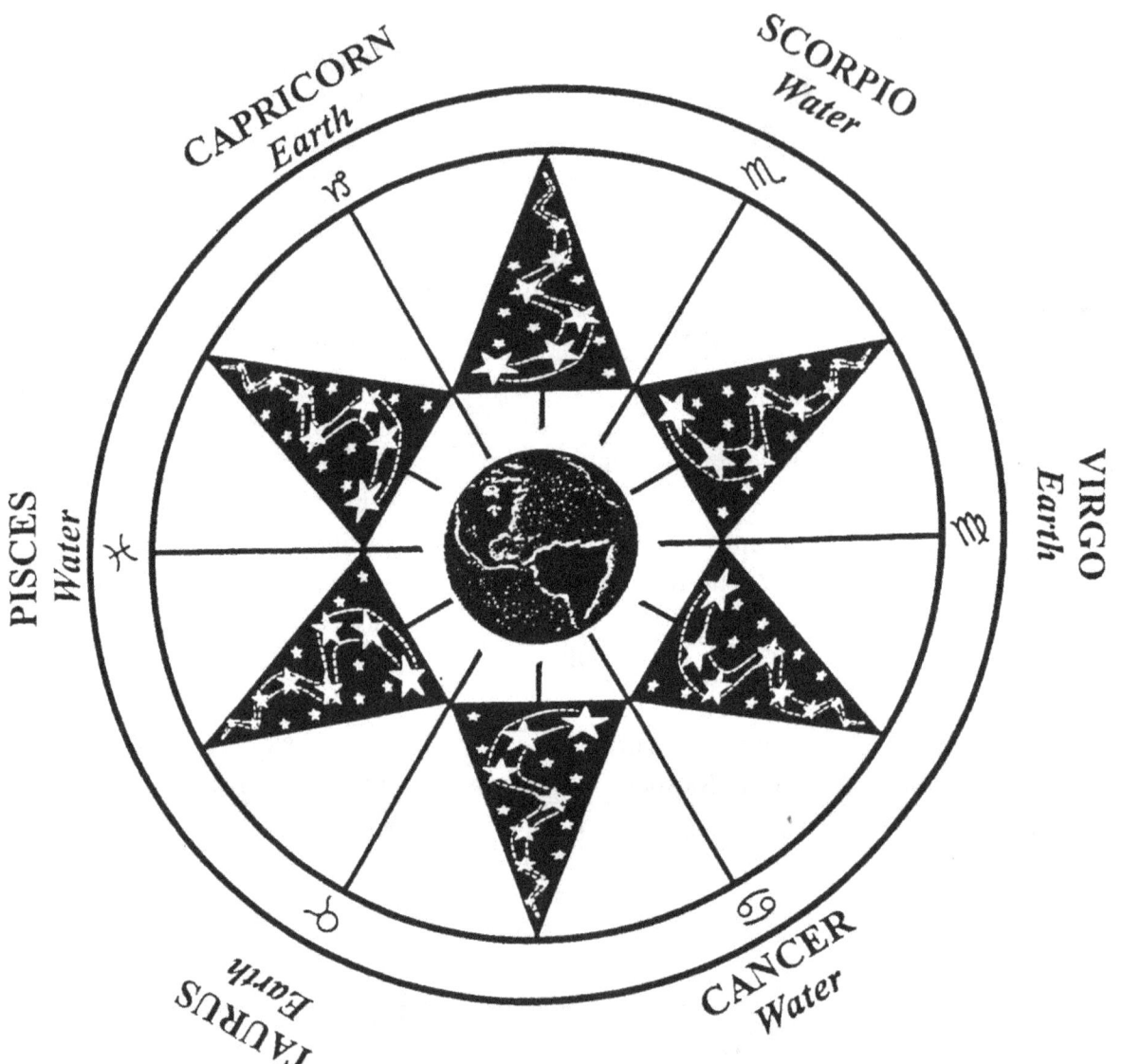

How to Find Your *Soul-Mate*, *Stars*, and *Destiny*

Date With Destiny

Share With Me Your Fantasy

How to Find Your *Soul-Mate*, *Stars*, and *Destiny*

Date With Destiny

Share With Me Your Fantasy

CANCER

June 22 - July 23
Man - Woman - Child - Character - Relationships - Compatibilities - Love Signs

Cancer, the fourth sign of the Zodiac, is symbolized by the Crab, and takes its name from the Greek word for Crab. Like the Crab, it carries its defenses and protectiveness on its back. Ruled by the Moon, Cancer is moody and changeable, waxing and waning with the phases of the Moon. Like the Moon, Cancer individuals can be reflective and easily influenced by their surroundings and the people around them. They are known for being attached to their home and quite often their lives are greatly influenced by their mothers. They do enjoy travel, sightseeing, and being exposed to new places and people. This is an emotional sign, and when moody or offended, the sensitive Cancer native will retreat behind the protection of their shells. Home, family, friends, and food provides them with their greatest source of security. They are highly introspective, intuitive, imaginative, creative and resourceful with the ability to withdraw into a dream world of their own making. This is a domestic sign, and the Cancer native is protective of home, money, and possessions. Quite often this tendency can be manifested in the form of selfishness in a person with a self-centered nature who shrewdly plans how to manipulate or turn a situation into his or her best advantage. But then again, they possess not only a dramatic flair but a great sense of humor and a creative way with words. Many are talented musicians, actors, or artists.

They are the sentimental romantics of the Zodiac who be come devoted companions to their lovers. Will they cheat? Only if it suits their fancy. Remember, Cancer is retentive, materialistic, self-centered, and security conscious. They will do what is best for them. At the same time, they make the best of parents and provide a protective and loving environment for their families. Cancer natives establish strong friendships which they nurture and from which they receive nurturing. Cancer requires admiration, adoration, love and respect. Cancer take in their surroundings, reflecting what they want others to see, and retaining what they want to keep.

These characteristics of the Gemini Sun sign can be made stronger by the Moon sign, Ascendant, and placement of the Planets, or they can be made more subdued by specific influences. It is by ascertaining these different influences that one more fully understands the particular Gemini individual.

The sign of Cancer, the Crab, belongs to those born between June 22 and July 23. Cancer is influenced by the Sun while it is under the rulership of the Moon. It is during this time of the year that the Sun has completed its long journey and appears to stop in the Sky which is referred to as the Sol Stat. From this is derived the word solstice. In other words, the Sun attains its highest point in the northern sky, remaining (or standing still) for about three days before it slowly begins moving backward (crab like) towards its southern location. The Sun is looking backwards like the Cancer. That is, the ancients perceived the Sun at this time of the year as appearing to advance and retreat in the sky similar or very much like the movements of a crab. The sign of Cancer marks the Summer Solstice, a period it was said in olden times that was similar to a cloud of vapors which any change in temperature transformed into rain. The days are long and the warm nights are the shortest of the year.

While the sign of Cancer begins on June 22, for seven days it is overlapped by the previous sign, Gemini. It attains its full strength on or about June 28 and retains its powers until July 20. Then for seven days it gradually loses it strength becoming overlapped or on the cusp of the incoming sign, Leo.

It is accepted that the Moon provides a pull on the tides of the Earth's waters and that it can influence not only atmospheric conditions but people also. The Moon influences natives of Cancer by controlling the natural instincts, regulating the sentimental life, and stimulating the desire for change or travel. It offers a great degree of sensitivity to these individuals and favors their intuitive abilities. It is possible for the Moon to predetermine a passive nature. And it is felt that the Moon has a strong influence on a woman's fertility and births. With a negative influence, the Moon influences Cancer natives to be nervous, extravagant and over active.

Beginning around June 22, the Moon climbs higher in the night Sky and the Moon's influence increases. The influence of the Moon is thought of as inconsistent. The Moon's influence in Cancer produces an individual who waxes and wanes (like the Moon) in attitudes, with their moods rising and falling much the same as the tides of the oceans. This can make individuals nervous or over active while changing their attitudes or going to the extent of producing dreams and fantasies. The individuals so influenced can become sad or happy, optimistic or pessimistic. In other words, Cancer natives are more sensitive to these atmospheric conditions than are persons of the other signs. If the sky darkens so does the mood of the Cancer individual. If it is a sunny day, expect an exceptionally similar sunny disposition in this person.

The Crab which carries its house on its back, represents possessions and retention. The symbol of Cancer, the Crab, is depicted with folded claws representing a nurturing and retentive spirit. This sign is also said to represent the female breasts. It is both assimilating and reflecting the surrounding conditions. If these individuals are not physically active, they are actively preoccupied with observing (many times taking mental notes or clicking away like a camera) their surroundings and the activity going on around them. They observe and sense emotions at the same time. Persons born under the sign of Cancer are known to respond to life more with emotions than with intellect even when the intellect is highly developed. These are lovely and sincere people who desire most in life to receive the adoration and attention of their friends and loved ones. Cancer belongs to the Water element predisposing its natives to be inspirational and at times impressionable.

Cancer Personality

Cancer are perhaps best known for having sensitive and imaginative personalities. They are both tenacious and at times emotional. The positive traits of Cancer include the ability to be hard working, reliable and dependable. They are known for being thrifty, conservative and for having a preference for domestic surroundings. While loving and sympathetic, Cancer are not necessarily outgoing or extroverted. Many born under the sign of Cancer are passive, shy and timid with a tendency to be overly reserved, discreet or restrained. While affectionate in your nature, you are not overly demonstrative toward others. However, you can be dependent on others for affection, attention, devotion and praise. Persons born under the sign of Cancer are also known for desiring material possessions and security. They are sometimes possessive to a fault, guarding and protecting his or her possessions as if they were treasures.

Many times these individuals, being reserved, cover up an intelligent, introspective, and reflective nature capable of strong cognitive reasoning ability and insights into the world around them. Behind what could be considered a rather protective wall, this insular person is compassionate and well-meaning although at times they may appear overly passive.

How to Find Your Soul-Mate, Stars, and Destiny

Basically, Cancer are above all else emotional and sentimental with a strong tendency to be romantic. They are more than a little inclined to have powerful and creative imaginations and fantasies. And it is through these mental pictures, story lines or fantasies that they develop their ideals of life. That is, their thoughts and the story line of their day dreams reflect their ideals and fantasies.

Cancer then too can be somewhat moody, one moment happy and content and then changing becoming discontent. Cancer thrive on and desire attention and affection. They love to be the center of attention, to be generously and, if their wishes were to come true, constantly praised for their accomplishments. There is a tendency for some of these individuals to behave like spoiled children who want to be constantly pampered and praised. But this is what the Cancer ego requires to flourish or so it seems.

Cancer have a preference for discretion and can withdraw from a situation that becomes in any way uncomfortable or threatening to their emotional natures. At other times, they don't keep their hurt feelings to themselves, but are seen moping about as if some comment or insult has injured their pride beyond repair. And any real or imagined slight or perhaps a critical remark no matter how constructive can be taken right to heart, producing in the female Cancer even tears of despair. Taken to task too seriously, Cancer will complain of being picked on and misunderstood. This is not a person to admit a fault or a wrong doing.

One of the problems faced by many Cancer natives is a sense of emotional insecurity resulting in a certain vulnerability. It produces an overly sensitive, overly protective individual who reacts to words, actions and perhaps even the gestures and expressions of others. This individual is innately inhibited and passive, restricted by his or her emotions, guarded against criticism or, taken to the next step, persecution by others. And being tenacious and stubborn, this individual closes the claws of the Crab, closely guarding these inhibitions and insecurities just as well as his or her possessions are guarded. Don't expect this person to change any time soon. Knowing that he or she is constantly picked on by others, the next step is for this person to feel victimized. And of course, the next easy step after victim is martyr. Along with martyrdom comes a certain degree of self-satisfaction and self-gratification. After all, history provides a long list of real and famous martyrs of good cause with whom to identify. Taken to extreme cases, these personality traits can result in the person withdrawing to a highly imaginative and entertaining fantasy world, all played out in the head, where they are the heroes of their own dramas.

These personality traits appear out of step with the more positive attributes of Cancer. It may be assumed that there is a great deal of differing opinions about natives of this sign. There are those people who love and adore the Cancer natives and their personalities finding them fine people deserving of devotion. Other people consider the natives of this sign as being among the most greedy, closed-mouthed, and shrewish of all the signs. Needless to say, every sign has a propensity for two types of individuals and no doubt that is what is being discovered in the Cancer sign as well.

No matter how intelligent the Cancer individual, life is dealt with through the emotions rather than on an intellectual level. In other words, you may find yourself considering your feelings about a situation first before using your intellect to interpret what is happening at the moment. You feel first, then you think. When you do begin to think about a particular situation, you may then use your intelligence to rationalize that your feelings and your point of view, opinions and behavior are correct. This pattern is also carried over into how you make your plans or establish your goals. Many aspects of your life are based on your emotions. The primary problem with this technique is that, at the same time, you must remember that you are susceptible to changing your mind as often as your moods or feelings change. Responding to emotions rather than gaining some degree of control over them may result in a person who lives in conflict with his or her inner nature. Overcome by emotional responses, a person may feel predestined or predisposed to accept what comes in life or even to failure in life. This person is forever the victim of the up's and down's in everyday life that we may all experience to some varying degree.

It is only when people come to grips with or understand their emotional nature that they begin to find fulfillment and then strive to attain a degree of success in life. Many Cancer individuals attain this position by conquering or learning to live with their emotional conflicts. That may not be as difficult to achieve as it might sound. Learn to set easily obtainable objectives first. Then accomplish each objective one at a time. Use your intellect and your intelligence to do this. As you successfully meet each objective, you will then feel more emotionally secure and better about yourself. Remember, you have no more obstacles to fear in life than anybody else. It is a turbulent life full of up's and down's, good and bad, cynicism and criticism. But everyone else has to face these aspects of life the same as you do. If for some reason you continue to feel overwhelmed or overpowered by life, the best alternative for you, and anyone else in this situation, is to seek counseling or therapy.

In the long run, what may save the Cancer individual so afflicted is the strong desire for collecting material possessions and personal security. This strong drive appears to balance the emotionally charged individual producing a person who also strives to succeed. And it is the achievement of success and security that often appears to bring about a drastic change in the Cancer native. Once some degree of security is attained, the Cancer individual's personality alters from the passive and dependent to being more assertive. Once the Cancer native decides to come out from behind their protective walls, they are then even more capable of attaining additional achievements or of maintaining a positive position in life. It is most desirable for these individuals to attain this independence in their lives. No matter how much a person might decide to remain withdrawn from others, the planetary influences necessitate the companionship of others in order to attain personal fulfillment. Remember, you crave the attention, praise and even devotion of others and you are drawn to seek such attention.

As with all the Zodiac signs, Cancer individuals are either one of two distinct personality types. (1) You are introverted, timid, and dependent, emotionally justifying your personal preferences by staying close to home and insulating yourself from the world. (2) You strive to overcome your emotional nature by assertively going out into the world to prove yourself.

Cancer remains a most powerful and extremely complicated position. The well developed Cancer individual is conscientious, devoted, versatile, adaptable, imaginative, and sociable.

Cancer Character

The Moon bestows upon these natives of Cancer the capacity for kindness, politeness, emotions, and a love for family and country. And like the Sun that is moving backwards in the Sky, the Cancer individual has a tendency to look for everything that happened in the past, like old songs and stories, old memories and old friends and family members. Their character is noble and proud. They dream, fantasize, and contemplate. The native is endowed with ambition and an enterprising nature. If well-aspected this person is a competent and hard worker. They are humane, charitable and sympathetic to others while striving to make society better. Cancers are curiously seeking to understand and gain knowledge of the world around them in order to improve their base of knowledge. They have an appreciation for the arts and cultural events and a great love of travel. There is also indicated an appreciation of position, wealth and honors. The location of the sign of Cancer predisposes the natives with a love of home, with strong domestic inclinations, and with a strong love for the mother.

The Cancer natives are known for being good-natured, diplomatic and tactfully mindful of others. They may be somewhat reserved in their personal and social life, but they are faithful and loyal to close friends and associates. They greatly desire friendships and can be very sociable and congenial, but they may at times prefer the solitude of their own homes. Cancers are readily adaptable to surroundings and other people, but they are known to change their minds easily almost as if with the wind. The restless Cancer mind requires numerous sources of stimulation and diversions in the form of entertainment or intellectual information to occupy the mind and to provide it with material for reflection and contemplation.

Persons born in the sign of Cancer begin in childhood to desire a stable economic position. Cancer are well connected to their homes and customs. They have a great need for a secure shelter where they can live safely and take care of their personal possessions. They are sensitive, emotional and domestic with a great love for home and family. This person may have an interest in ancestors and may have studied the family genealogy and traced the family tree. Cancer can possess a strong patriotic nature and an interest in historical events. They are interested in national affairs and in the public welfare as well as other social issues. The well developed Cancer native is capable of assisting in important national affairs or in the development of local social institutions and other community matters. The Cancer native remains active in many endeavors throughout life.

Cancer have a strong emotional need for a person who loves them and who showers them with attention, affection, and encouragement. With that person, Cancer become devoted, loving and capable of sacrifices. If, on the other hand, the Cancer native feels misunderstood or unappreciated by this special person, they can give up and feel depressed, moody or despondent.

Cancer derive a great deal of satisfaction from their generosity. They love to help others. This may be the person who volunteers for charity work, or who becomes involved in community affairs, or who takes an interest in national affairs related to society. Cancer often achieve recognition and honors from these endeavors, and it may appear that it is this recognition and praise that often inspires them to join in community affairs.

At the same time, Cancer prefer to lead rather than to be led and can be quite obstinate in this. When others attempt to lead you or even give you instruction or ask you to do something, you feel like you are being dictated to. And this you resent. This tendency at times makes you difficult to work with and to live with. However, when treated with confidence, you can be faithful and devoted.

Cancer have a quiet, reserved nature, and they prefer discretion. They may at times be impatient, but generally if a Cancer native becomes angry, it is only for a short period of time. This person often keeps anger hidden because of the fear that others would laugh at him or her. Attempts to draw this person out, to ask one of them to explain their feelings, or any attempt at even constructive criticism can result in a defensive response of, "Why is everyone always picking on me?" or "I didn't do it".

These individuals love to be the center of attention, and they crave any and all publicity. They may easily become overly self aware. They frequently suffer because they feel that other people are not paying enough attention to them or that others want to hurt their feelings. They retain a large degree of hubris-inspired pride and a great vanity. Being noble and proud, at times, can even lead to an excessive vanity. Born under a negative planetary influence, this excessive vanity can develop into impulsiveness or an extremely selfish nature. Their pride often times leads them to be autocratic and somewhat austere. Gifted with imagination and the powers of fantasy, the overly defensive Cancer often imagines themselves set upon by others. At the worst, a morbid vanity develops and they play the role, as in fantasy, of the hero or martyr. Being dramatically gifted, they can do this ever so effectively often to the point of attracting the attention and sympathy from others that they so much desire.

Cancer is a Cardinal Water sign and as a rule is an original thinker who is sensitive but enterprising. At the same time, the Moon often makes them unstable. The nature, in other words, is sensitive but ever changing. If not well developed, the individual may be either too easy going or uncertain of where he or she wants to go. There are strong indications for these negative or uncertain inclinations. The feelings and emotions being overly sensitive can result many times in a cranky and restless disposition and at its worst produces an eccentric individual. This type of person may be drawn toward self-gratification which can easily be manifested in over eating, drinking or seeking other pleasures.

The Cancer gift for drama and the desire and flair to be the center of attention can be original and creatively novel and entertaining, exposing a quick wit and a talent for amusing others. On the other hand, if the Cancer native is too insecure or lazy, this flair for drama is used to copy others or even to plagiarize. This is sometimes done not just in their little dramatic scenes, but also in everyday life. In other words, the Cancer native may have a little trouble deciding who he or she wants to be that day, and so decides to copy someone else. This ability to assimilate the traits of others requires a great deal of skill, but often is not fully appreciated by those who don't understand the needs and drives of the Cancer individual.

The Cancer nature to a large degree depends on the circumstances. Cancers can be courageous or at other times timid. There may be over exaggerated fears of the dangers in life, but at the same time the person may be brave in mental and moral attitudes. Cancers can be at times distrustful and at other times cautious or prudent, but then may suddenly reverse and desire fun, gayness, and cheerfulness or perhaps even a little romance.

Most generally, Cancers are indicative of a conservative sign loving all that has past (which may signify walking backwards like the Crab). They many times exhibit a strong interest in history and historical events, and/or in their personal histories and in the lives and progenies of their ancestors. This person may be known for collecting historical records or memorabilia, old records or books, or stamps and souvenirs, and no doubt numerous photo albums of their life and of their family. Generally speaking, they have a strong patriotic sense of duty and a love for their homes and community and nation.

There is a great depth to the Cancer native and this can be observed both in their emotions and in their intellectual abilities. This person, when well aspected can achieve much in life.

Cancer Destiny

Cancer individuals are dominated by a defensive, protective nature. They strive to achieve material possessions, security and a domestic situation. They are capable of either a great self-sufficiency or of being overly dependent on others to the point of being clinging and possessive (male or female). The Cancer destiny is determined in some measure by their positions or standing. If, on one hand, independence augments their security, they will be independent. However, if this individual's security depends on another person, the Cancer will become excessively dependent, clinging to the other person. In another instance, if security depends on taking a chance, Cancer will choose to take a chance, particularly if it is with someone else's finances. Thankfully, in this case, Cancer are as responsible with other people's possessions as they with their own. Cancer are patriotic, loves traveling and has an interest in civic or legislative activities. This sign indicates much originality in ideas, imagination and in expressive creativity.

The natives of Cancer, influenced by the ever changing Moon, have a destiny made most remarkable by changes that occur. They will experience numerous ups and downs and fluctuations in their financial situations. In many cases, there will be noted an attainment of notoriety, fame or power with much publicity. There may be difficulty in attaining wealth and frequently it is seen that inheritances are lost by influences of relatives, speculations, children, or through romantic affairs. But your thriftiness may well produce economic security.

This location signifies a great love of home and domestic situations with a strong affection for the mother. There may be a parent fixation. The nature is predominately sympathetic, loving, and emotionally responsive. There may be several love affairs, a number of secret affairs, and a marriage to a mystically inclined person or to an older person. If left alone, you are generally a happy and sociable person. Others need to be diplomatic and kind to you and appreciate you. You do not like to be forced to do anything. No one should take anything from you without first asking. You can be superstitious and you believe in good days and bad days. You dream a lot and pay too much attention to things that aren't important to others. You are overly sensitive to other people's opinions about you. You have a great love for your country and for traditions.

While Cancer have a great love for home and family, there can be domestic problems or estrangement. This sign can be opposed to marriage, and many of these natives do not find a great deal of happiness in their home lives. There may be loss or great difficulties brought on by houses, land or other property. If Venus is in Cancer, there may be unforeseen difficulties and obstacles in marriage either because of parents, finances or occupation. There may be friendships with afflicted people who cause the Cancer problems.

Cancer are shown to have contradictions in life. There is a strong love for the domestic situation, but then their mood may change, and they will long for travel or some other change. They are seen as always acquiring a home and then for some unforeseen reason, losing it. For some reason there are more than the usual amounts of problems in the home. Eventually, they succeed in establishing both home and domestic life.

How to Find Your Soul-Mate, Stars, and Destiny

Cancer are anxious about money and possessions. They make a great effort to make money and then guard it protectively. In their early life there may be more than the usual number of up's and down's, and in order to succeed they must work very hard. Once they finally become successful, they manage to stay that way. You enjoy helping others and are known for your kind words and deeds. This will bring you much satisfaction in life and make you feel good about yourself.

There are those Cancer who, while trying to acquire money quickly, develop strong inclinations toward speculation. There is a tendency for the Cancer to lose when gambling in this manner. They will experience many gains and losses unless this speculative nature is controlled early in life. However, Cancer can experience success in business otherwise and if wealth does come to them, it can be beyond their imaginations.

Many Cancer natives are known dreamers who design big plans for themselves or for others. When met with any opposition or criticism, they suffer greatly, and often silently, while at the same they can be cynical and poke fun at others.

Cancers may indeed inherit money and property, perhaps through marriage, but not without many difficulties. There is noted the possibility of premature death of a brother or sister; and troubles with relatives with whom the Cancer native disagrees. In many cases, there is a second family who the native lives with or is adopted by during some period of his or her life. There will be frequent traveling, with some long trips, which are successful and some bring publicity. The sign indicates strife, but the native will succeed through his or her own efforts. The eventual position in life becomes determined after the age of thirty-five. Much support is provided by female friends; but it is a female friend who will cause a reversal in position. Watch for injuries from falls.

If Mars is afflicted there is an inclination for the early death of the mother or strong disagreements with her. There may be domestic problems or problems with an unhappy spouse. There will be many worries, irritating situations, sorrows and changes of residences. Other problems exist with damage to properties through natural disasters or theft. Gain is seen through real estate or parents or in businesses related to water. There is a great love for family, customs and traditions.

When Cancer is at the Ascendant, the Capricorn sign is in the House of Marriage. This will indicate for the Cancer woman a marriage with an older person which will be socially positive. For the Cancer man it represents a moment of balance, of obstacles, or of a late marriage with an older person.

Cancer are not noted for being lucky or for being overly fortunate in their endeavors. But they are known for being hard working and industrious. Change seems to dominate their lives, and both good and evil can influence and have an effect on their lives.

Among the sensitive Cancer, there is noted an ability in metaphysical matters. Many acquire a love for the mystical. If so gifted, you become talented and well regarded in this area.

Cancer, strive to direct your emotions and your energies and not allow them to direct you. To some extent, you must control your energies and your active imagination. You at times have a tendency to be too obstinate in your efforts rather than using your intuition and imagination for the best results. You often endanger your own security. Many of your fears are unjustified. Rather than exaggerating them and focusing on them, master them. You take yourself and your fears too seriously. Redirect and focus your energies on your successes in the world.

Cancer Occupation

Ever so like the Crab, Cancer natives progress and then retreat both professionally and in their ideas. These individuals may carefully make career decisions, attain desired positions, and then change their minds, deciding on a new direction. And they are quite capable of achieving success in whatever direction they elect to take.

Their remarkable and creative imaginations make them naturals in the fields of art, writing, music and composing. Not only do they have marked artistic and performing ability, but many possess a strong mechanical ability as well which can be useful in many technical fields.

Cancer do well in any field of endeavor related to the home. Whether it be decorating, remodeling, designing or construction, Cancer excels. There is a natural affinity for any career associated with property, real estate, homes, homemaking or home improvement. Others prefer methods of improving the domestic situation with arts and crafts or projects designed for one's entertainment at home. Many Cancer find that they do well in any area of the food industry whether it be distribution, processing or food service. Many feel you make the best chefs, cooks and caterers.

The Cancer inclination toward leading and helpfulness can make these individuals very successful. Often they develop strong business skills and find remarkable successes in private businesses or in many positions in the corporate world. You are hard working, loyal and trustworthy, and with your interest in money, any area of finance and banking may best suit your skills. With your deep regard and concern for others and for the community, you would do well in careers in medicine, nursing, teaching, and public relations. And of course, the love of history and of collecting augments any career along the lines of antiquities and collectibles either in buying, selling, or trading. This interest in history would, of course, predispose one toward the fields of historian, teacher, or writer. Other fields include archeology, anthropology, and the list continues. Combine a love of history with your strong imagination, and you could easily become an historical romance novelist. Or consider simply using your imagination to become an inventor like Henry Ford, a Cancer native. Other native Cancer have found successes in the fields of diplomacy and politics. The middle of the Sky of the Cancer sign favors a profession related to publicity, or as a social manifestation of the native, or shipping and trading, sailor or merchant marine.

You are noted for being gifted with talent. You are known for being tenacious, conscientious, and thrifty as well as patient, persistent, and a diligent worker. When you decide on your direction in life, you will no doubt find many successes.

Cancer Marriage

Cancer, the fourth sign of the Zodiac is a Cardinal sign and the first Water sign. Ruled by the Moon, Cancer natives are the most domestic and home-loving of all the signs. When you love, it is strong, and you are not inclined to break up your marriage or your home and family frivolously. You most desire in life security for yourself and your family.

Fourth-sign males make excellent husbands even though they can be emotionally vulnerable. To remain content and happy with their home life, they require compliments, affection, support, and reassurances from their wives. They thrive on attention. Their natures may be somewhat passive, but they are also protective and come to depend to a large degree on their spouse and their home life. A woman who fully understood this loving and, by nature, domestically-seeking, peaceful-loving man would be adored by the Cancer male. He is ardently faithful and strives to provide well. His main interests and endeavors center on his family.

Preferring to be faithful, and not to bring any harm to his family, the Cancer man seldom strays. If he does so it is usually in an effort to find the affection and attention he most desires in life. There is an inclination for the Cancer man to be possessive and to prefer a wife who also wants to center her life around the home and family. He also wants to be the head of the family and to lead in all matters of importance. If his sometimes reticent manner is misunderstood and the female attempts to be bossy or dominating, he will become unhappy.

Female Cancers are very well suited for marriage. She is capable of finding complete emotional fulfillment through her domestic life, and she has strong maternal instincts and loves to be surrounded by children. Cancer women are faithful, loyal and devoted wives and mothers. Your strongest desire is to give love and affection and your greatest need is for it to be returned to you by those you hold most dear. If you are vulnerable, it is in this area. If your need for affection and admiration isn't forthcoming, you become disappointed in your situation. You can become withdrawn even to the point of being depressed. Or you may choose to change your tactics and attempt to gain attention by complaining--anything, you feel, is acceptable in order to receive what you most desire from your mate and family. And what you most desire is an abundance of love and attention.

Advice to Cancers would be not to marry young. An early marriage might be tempting to you with your strong urge to have family and security, but do not be too hasty. Many times an early marriage does not turn out well. You will find your nature and your likes and dislikes changing as you mature, and it is best to wait until you are sure you know your mind. It is also best to take time to really get to know the other person. Does this person understand as well as love you? Will the marriage be harmonious? You love harmony and peaceful settings and you do best in such surroundings, so give a little thought to your marriage prospects.

Suggestions for harmonious marriages would be Pisces (February 19-March 20) who are unselfish; Capricorn (December 21-January 19) who are constant, but be sure of mutual likes and dislikes; and Libra (September 23-October 22). If you consider a Scorpio (October 23-November

21) be sure you are compatible. Some astrologers feel that Leo (July 23-August 22) individuals also make good mates for Cancer.

It is through family, home, spouse and children that many Cancer individuals find their true natures. In the home, you seem to lose many of your inhibitions about life in general. You no longer feel the need for your strong emotional defenses. The walls can come down, and you can be yourself and express yourself. And most importantly, you feel more free to express your needs. You shower your spouse and children with love and attention. Your greatest desire is to be with them, provide for them, and protect them.

In this regard, you earn the greatest degree of admiration from friends and family alike. It is your natural character of loving the home and family that others most admire and aspire to. In many ways, this sets the standard for what many consider the most desirable situation for society. This, combined with your conservative nature, makes you the picture of perfection to many of your friends and associates.

The Cancer Man

Often considered appealing and handsome, the Cancer male looks calm but has much inner energy. He both desires and expects an abundance of affection and understanding from the significant other in his life. He is not overly materialistic, and he prefers to take care of this area of his life himself. His home may well be decorated with collections and memorabilia. This man is very proud and does not appreciate criticism in only form no matter how justified. To get along well with a Cancer male requires diplomacy and good manners. While he may enjoy his wife's successes, he often prefers that she depends on him in some manner.

The Cancer male has emotional responses related to a rather direct goal: his need for security and home. Your love is loyal and devoted, but you can be overly possessive. Even with this great need for home and family, though, you are often fearful that you may fail in this aspect of your life. If this fear becomes too great, you may decide to remain a bachelor rather than taking the chance on love and marriage.

Like the Crab, the Cancer male may at times seem rather crusty and reserved. This natural reservation may be a defense mechanism for your vulnerable personality which you strive to protect. Your emotions are actually very close to the surface. You are easily hurt or offended. When this happens you may find it easiest to withdraw into your shell even more. Because you are ruled by the Moon, you are much more susceptible and affected by it. You are restless, changeable, emotional and romantic. And when you accomplish or achieve success, you suddenly drop your shell because your ego has been so greatly boosted. While you need friends and companions and love socializing, you often prefer to spend time by yourself.

You are well known for your generous character, and your love, concern and effort to help others. You can be happy and talkative, while maintaining at the same time a certain degree of distance, reservation, or discretion--much preferring to maintain your privacy and your private thoughts. You enjoy a variety of amusements and good entertainment, and you crave knowledge and love to read and to be well informed.

You have a profound interest in current affairs, both locally, nationally, and internationally. This interest regards not only politics, but social affairs and social institutions as well. At the same time, your love for the past finds you reading many historical novels and chasing down information on your favorite topics and interests.

You develop many diverse interests throughout life. These may be intellectual, educational or in the form of hobbies and pastimes. Your intellect demands that you develop as many of these interests as possible. You are seldom superficial in your interests. Besides a creative imagination, you possess an excellent memory for details and concepts.

If well-aspect, the Cancer male is a paragon of truthfulness and loyalty. If not well-developed, however, their claims at truthfulness are only artful lies. This person is inclined to fabrication, slyness, and simply avoiding the truth in many instances. This man desires material possessions above all else and will use any and all artifices to acquire it. Even if they don't go so far as to lie, the poorly afflicted Cancer male is extremely egotistical seeing all of life only as it relates to him. This man is responsive to any and all advances of the opposite sex. He can be promiscuous and driven by his sexual urges. Many times he experiences much emotional trauma through their affairs of the heart. This man, while he strives for success, often times never finds it, or when he does succeed, it is only to lose it again. He suffers from the instabilities in his life.

In many instances, outside the family, Cancer men are sought as a friend and confidant. This points back to your loyal nature. As with your family, you must avoid being overly protective of your friends. You can't assume full responsibility for their happiness.

Your restlessness, your mood swings, and your changeability are the biggest challenges to others in your life. Others may not accept or understand these characteristics of your nature. Finding and developing interests that hold your attention will offset these tendencies. Not only that, but these types of endeavors and aspirations will make you all the more interesting to your companions and friends.

When you are young, you may find that your search for the right job leads you from one to another in your pursuit to find the perfect one that stimulates you and holds your attention. As you mature, your restless nature will be more abated, your interests more focused, and it may become easier for you to decide on one selected goal, career or major interest in life. You, Cancer, can be counted on to continue to strive and to seek until you discover that which will best suit your talents and abilities.

Your many talents and sensitive, imaginative nature serves you well. You are generally well liked and well accepted by your family, friends, and business associates.

The Cancer Woman

Cancer is considered the most feminine of the twelve signs possessing all the strengths found in the heart of a maternal, good mother. The Cancer woman is best known for her qualities of being maternal, passionate, good-hearted and generous. She has a flair for fashion, preferring to appear well-dressed and elegant. Her major attachment is to her home, and after she settles, she becomes devoted to her family.

You love change, and without enough diversions in your life, you may find yourself rearranging furniture or moving other articles around your home in an effort to still your restless nature. Of course, you may also go through any number of changes in your hair style and fashion. You love to change clothes frequently, always pausing to see how good you look in each new outfit. Known for your moodiness, you find yourself becoming depressed on gray, cloudy days and exuberant on sunny days. This is only natural with the Moon's influence. Your moods are going to change, and you need to accept this and learn to deal with it. Guard against making significant decisions or listening to your desires or emotions during these times of emotional changes.

You love both children and animals and find yourself surrounded by both, and if it were up to you these would be your main preoccupations in life. You also have a sincere concern for others and your community. You make every effort to help in some way such as by becoming involved in charitable organizations where you feel your time and effort can do the most good for your community.

Cancer women are inclined to marry once. You are the most devoted of wives. And when you find the fulfillment you most desire, you remain happy. It is when you don't receive the admiration, love and attention of your family that you feel most remorseful. In those situations, you are not always at your best and can be insensitive toward others. The other people in your life need to realize this great need you have to feel appreciated.

Guard against being overly sensitive, jealous and possessive. This is when your tongue can get the better of your mind, and you say things that you later regret. Remember, your mind has a tendency to be over active and can imagine much of what you perceive as real. Strive always to improve your deportment and to feel good about yourself in all that you do. When you feel good about yourself, this shows in your everyday life.

You are known for your lively, happy disposition and your talents. You are a good conversationalist and enjoy the companionship of your friends. While you can be passionate in your feelings and opinions, you often keep your most private thoughts to yourself preferring to be discreet and reserved. You must feel a great deal of trust in the other person before you actually open up and talk on a personal level.

You are as possessive as your male counterpart, and have a strong inclination toward acquiring material possessions and security. However, when well-aspected, you remain generous, caring and kind in all that you do. You show a great concern not only for others but for society in general.

The poorly-afflicted Cancer woman can be overly protective of her material possessions to the point of hoarding. She becomes extremely selfish in nature, but has a tendency not to admit her faults to herself. Her need to feel or to gain security is so strong that she becomes tenacious in acquiring and not letting go, of not spending or losing her possessions. This can develop to the point of actually being an obsession. This woman may even guard against sharing her affections needlessly, and she can take being defensive to a new level.

Quite fortunately, the better aspected Cancer female makes up for these negative traits often moving in the opposite direction to be overly generous and caring for her friends and family. Watch that you don't take on more than you can handle, and learn to allow your children to learn from their own mistakes or small accidents. You can not be everything to everyone or you will lose much of your energy.

If you decide on a career in your life, you will pull all of your energies and creative abilities together to focus on that goal and to succeed. You are blessed with talents, skills, and abilities and can easily achieve at whatever you decide to pursue. Your life will be active, your interests varied, and your destiny rests in your hands. When you develop your better nature, you will find that other people are not only attracted to you but appreciate and admire you for both your empathetic, maternal nature and your quick, creative imagination. When you are in the mood, you are the most entertaining person in the group. You are not only entertaining, but you also have the ability to show concern and devotion to your friends and family. Drop your defenses and let others know how much they mean to you. Then you will find that they return your affections just as strongly.

Cancer Love Life

In its best developed state, the Cancer ability to be protective transforms itself into an all encompassing love which is warm and comforting and that fills the world of all those lucky enough to exist within it sphere of influence. But it is very lucky individuals, indeed, who discover and find that kind of emotional strength and love. And Cancer may have to work through many emotional diversions and inhibitions before attaining this capacity to share their feelings.

Cancer can be the most romantic of all the signs. Imagine the extent of this sensitive nature to explore and dream of romantic interludes. And Cancer are best known for dreams and fantasy. These individuals are also known for having sensitive and responsive emotional natures, for feeling rather than thinking about the needs of others. It is easy to imagine and speculate that the uninhibited passionate Cancer must, therefore, make among the best of lovers. Add to that, that this individual wants most in life to find the perfect mate and home and security. What more could anyone ask for than to meet such an person?

As with many people, life never seems to be that easy. Any number of Cancer hides behind fears and inhibitions, building walls of defensive protection. In many of these people, there is found a reservation, a restraint that prevents them from fully developing emotionally to their best potential. Sensitive people can also be shy and somewhat fearful of involvement or of being too open with others. The Cancer native who chooses to hide behind these walls of protection can live in a world of seclusion, safe from the world and all pain and hurt. Then too, Cancer individuals in some cases are retentive and prefer to keep their feelings closely guarded rather than sharing them with others. In other instances, there are found those Cancer individuals who remain unattached because their protective instincts have developed into fear or even selfishness. This person protects himself from disappointments, rejections and pain by withdrawing within himself and making his security alone. Unfortunately, many of these people will never experience the joy, the fun, and the sharing that love brings into life. After all, love can be the greatest adventure of all, and with a little mutual daydreaming it can develop into the most pleasant of experiences.

The best advice for Cancer in regards to their love life is simply to be yourself with others. Let others get to know you and to judge you on your own merits. You might be surprised how successful you can be because you have many positive qualities. Come out from within your shell and learn to share your feelings with others. And when you meet that special person allow him or her to experience your tenderness and warmth. Yes, you will meet with the same number of rejections and disappointments in life as does everyone else. But this is the only way to meet others and to develop relationships. And relationships require time and work. Work as hard at your relationships as you do at your job and your hobbies, and you will find the results pleasingly surprising.

Many Cancer have learned to shower others with affection and attention, but at the same time they are generally practical and independent. You, Cancer, can be obstinate. You strongly and stubbornly desire to have your own way. To relate well to others, you must learn the art of give and take. Others want their own way too. And when others express this to you, don't take it as a personal criticism. Your defensive wall doesn't need to reinforce itself. Other people simply prefer to express themselves and their emotions. There is no reason to be or to feel threatened by this. It is only natural. No real harm to you is intended. Grow in your interpersonal skills. Become as curious about the nature and feelings of others as you are about so many other aspects of life and the world. And every once in awhile, dear Cancer, allow yourself to be led a little, to bend a little. Then you will discover the great opportunities existing in relationships with others.

This discussion would not be complete, of course, without mentioning the Cancer natives who forgo meaningful relationships in favor of casual ones. It is possible for people who hide behind walls of defenses to prefer unchallenging, casual relationships. No commitment is necessary. Not a lot of effort is necessary. No sharing or sincere expressions of emotions are necessary. This person can be free to keep his or her most inner sensitivities and thoughts to himself or herself while enjoying the pleasure of the company of others. And perhaps, most importantly, in casual affairs this person can retain that feeling of being in control of his or her life. Who is to judge the decisions of others? It is your life. You make your own decisions.

When that special person does come along, Cancer, you are considered the best of mates. Your caring and loving nature, you attentiveness and genuine concern, and your protectiveness are now showered on someone else. In love, you are romantic, devoted, tender and sensuous. Most Cancer individuals have a sincere desire to establish a lasting relationship based on love, to make a home, and to become a parent. And when you achieve contentment at home, you have the ability to attain great successes in life. It can be the best of all possible worlds for you.

CANCER CHILDREN

Cancer children are intelligent, lively, curious and imaginative. They function best in a loving, secure home surrounded by their possessions and toys. They enjoy having friends and playmates and many excursions, activities, and adventures, but quite often they may prefer the solitude of their own room where they can go to think, play and entertain themselves by allowing their imaginations to run wild.

And this is an imaginative child. This is the child who entertains the adults with an abundance of little skits and self-produced plays. The Cancer child pulls old clothes from the closets, trinkets and glittery things from the jewelry boxes, gathers paints and make-up and old shoes, and transforms all of these treasures into bizarre costumes for every member of the latest skit. This child's imagination seems to have no limits. Often, a quick wit develops early in life and then every member of the family becomes a volunteer from which the child gathers material to turn into comedy routines. The Cancer child craves being the center of attention. And the more laughter and praise they garnish from the skits and comedy routines, the more they desire.

This child flourishes on praise and compliments. But then when the active imagination is transformed into little devilment's, and the child is suddenly in hot water and requires discipline, problems arise. This child does not respond well to any form of criticism. At times, it seems the Cancer child would prefer not having any restraints, but would rather be allowed to roam free and at will. Of course, every child needs restraint, and it is the gifted parent who manages the Cancer child well.

Cancer children, being active and creative, require an adequate number of outlets for these characteristics. Provide plenty of play time both indoors and outdoors with enough room to run wild for some period during the day. Then plan quiet times to bring the active nature back into acceptable limits. These children love books, children's movies, and all forms of arts, crafts, and creative projects. There is also a strong love for animals, and this child possesses a nurturing nature which showers the family pets with attention and love and devotion.

Attempt to channel the Cancer child's energies and creativity into positive endeavors while keeping the mind busily engaged in one project or activity or another. Search and find the best method of disciplining the child without being harsh or too critical. Much praise and positive remarks should be focused on the Cancer child. And if possible, strive to teach this child to share both possessions and the lime light with other children. In one way or another, attempt to draw the child out of his room and his solitude. Of course, this to a certain degree is normal. All children enjoy playing alone at one time or another. But taken to the extreme like Cancer children can often do, it removes them from the greater learning experiences of life and the opportunity to learn and develop interpersonal skills. It is as children that many of these skills are acquired and then later refined as adults. Do this in a gentle manner, not as a discipline. Draw the child out. Teach this child to express the emotions and thoughts and dreams that are running wild in his or her overly creative imagination. Make every endeavor to produce harmony in the home and provide a loving, trusting, and secure environment where the Cancer child can flourish and lay aside any and all fears.

Relationships with Other Signs

Cancer most impresses others with their generous character. You receive much satisfaction in being able to help others, and you love the companionship of friends, associates and relatives. There is often times a warmth and gentleness about you that attracts others to you. And when your reserved, conservative mantle drops, you are one of the most entertaining and witty of people. It is often times the drama of life that you most appreciate even more so than close interpersonal relationships. Cancer, a Cardinal sign of the Zodiac, implies an outgoing nature even though it retains a passive and sympathetic side. Your friends will come to learn that you prefer a harmonious life and that at the first sign of conflict, you will retreat into your shell of protection. Your friends also need to accept your changing and at times moody tendencies which to some degree are beyond your control. While at times charming, witty and entertaining, you can in a matter of minutes become shy and retiring, excusing yourself from congenial activities to seek the comfort of your secure home.

You have a strong intelligence which others admire, but you first serve your emotions. Your reactions to situations often spring from your feelings at the moment. And for some reason, you fear these same emotions. You many times find yourself fearing rejection and even fearing ridicule for being yourself. These are the traits you must learn to control. Let others get to know you, learn interpersonal skills, and grow emotionally. It would be great if we could always be accepted just the way we are, but life is seldom like that. Life appears to expect us to grow and change, to leave off childish behaviors and to mature. A challenging life demands that we learn to adapt, to be somewhat flexible, and to be tolerant of others. We can't all be the same. It's the variety of personalities that predisposes the world to be interesting, challenging and perplexing all at the same time. You fit right into this mix with your own personal combination of traits, desires, and quirks. People will accept you as you are; people will criticize you at the same time; people will love you, reject you, accept you and hurt you. That's life, baby. Learn to live with it not against it.

You, Cancer, may find that your closest friendships and relationships are made with other Cancer individuals. Perhaps they will best accept and share your likes and dislikes. Other strong friendships can be made with Libra and Scorpio persons. Libra can be very accepting of others and always looking for the best in the individual. Scorpio may occasionally give you a bad time, but this will only make you a stronger person in the long run. Pisces is another sign where you may find strong friendships as they share your same strong creative spirit. Stay on your guard not to take advantage of your Pisces friends though as they have a strong desire to share and are not at all retentive. Within limits, you will get along well with Taurus natives, however, they too want to be in charge. The Aries personality may be too strong for you to handle well. And while you may become friends with Gemini, your conservative nature may not ever understand their duality.

How to Find Your Soul-Mate, Stars, and Destiny

Remember, that your intellect and your restless but energetic nature craves stimulation. Find others with similar interests to yours, and expand your mind by meeting people outside of your usual routines. No one becomes more excited than the Cancer native who discovers a new and exciting friendship or relationship. It's meeting and getting to know this new person which stimulates your mind and leaves you feeling good about yourself. The sign of Cancer provides for a strong spirit of assimilation and an inclination towards not only tradition but for dreaming. Your other strong traits include a love for family, a conservative nature, and the ability to love and be loved. You have a persistent, tenacious and economical character. These are all positive and strong traits which bring admiration to you from those with whom you associate.

Many Cancer natives may find they have a small circle of what they consider close friends with whom they prefer to associate. Within this circle of friendships are people who would do anything for you. They are charmed by your abilities and talents and are devoted to their friendship with you. Strong friendships and an abundance of admiration is important to you. Maintain these friendships carefully, nurturing them and caring for them. It is this type of friendship that most attracts and pulls you from your shell. Feeling secure within this supportive circle of friends, you will open up and learn to share your most inner thoughts and dreams. Even if people laugh at you, they often find your thoughts and dreams particularly unique and daring.

You need not fear friendship nor be defensive about it. If anything, you should consider guarding against your tendency to be impressionable. You have a strong character and like to lead. But you can also easily assimilate the characteristics or personality traits of others in your effort to mimic or copy them. This is all right if these individuals are admirable. But be careful of copying the less desirable behavioral traits of the people you meet. Taken to the extreme, this can be even be dangerous.

In your relationships with others you can be most diplomatic and tactful. When you are in the mood, you can mix and meet at social gatherings easily and with little effort. But watch your emotional nature. You sense the moods of others. Don't allow the moods of other people to affect your own or to have a detrimental effect on you. In other words, don't let someone else's bad mood turn your good mood sour.

It may be that your conservative nature and the manner in which you steer clear of exuberant expressions of emotion, saves you from many of the real dramas of life. While your list of true, close friends may be limited, these friendships are strong and based on devotion. Both your family and friends regard you as dependable and trustworthy. It is your inner compass that when expressed well will win you the most friends and companions. You are a person of many talents, many beneficial and positive traits, and a will to succeed at life. Let any and all insecurities fall by the wayside as you strive to ever be a better person. In your life you will meet many other people who will be accepting and deserving of your friendship. Take the time to get to know these people, to appreciate their strengths and personalities, and to accept others into your life.

Cancer Sexuality

That subject which interests us all: our own personal sexuality. Why does a person feel the way they do? Why does he or she like a certain person and not another? What arouses a person and why? On some level, these questions influences one and all. Like all aspects of our lives and lifestyles, the public attitude toward sex is ever changing and evolving. From the restrictive taboos of the Victorian Age, through the revitalization of the Industrial Age, to the make love not war of the 1960s to the commercialism of the 1980s and the 1990s, sex is always on our minds. Will the Age of Information or the Age of Aquarius bring new insights?

The American culture is not only influenced by popular trends and thought but by its unique cultural diversity as well. To the newcomer or newly arrived, American society can appear perplexing. What is difficult to understand is that in this freedom-based culture, the individual is literally free to be whoever he or she decides. And the gamut runs from the most traditional, reserved, cautious, and sexually repressed individuals to others who flaunt their sexuality, centering their lives around their sexual habits. Perhaps it is because of this very diversity that our culture makes some attempt not to be overly offensive to the sensitivities of some while giving a tolerant nod to the liberties of others. We are totally free, within the guidelines of laws, to seek divine enlightenment or to destroy ourselves with pleasures. Americans have the freedom to choose, individually, what importance their sexual behavior will play in their lives.

That being the case, sex is recognized by every serious discipline--from psychologists to scientists to astrologers--as being a central focus on individual lives. Freud saw sex as an influence on every aspect of the individual life. And from the sexist boys in the locker room to the most enlightened of intellectuals, sex remains a fundamental part of life that cannot be ignored. Get two friends together and the subject eventually turns to sex, romance, or marriage. One can blame it on the media, but sooner or later discussing the stock market gets boring, but sex never does.

There are those who hold to the theory that the primary function of sex is to have children and any other consideration is secondary. There are others for whom sex is an integral part of life, providing one of the greatest stress relievers ever invented. That all other living species procreate seasonally points to the reasoning of the second theory. But all pleasures (or temptations) in life also promote the possibilities of problems and health concerns unless a little logic is also applied.

Astrologically, the sexual nature has been examined from the Garden of Eden to the lives of contemporary celebrities. And what every serious astrologer will say is that how the individual relates to sexuality is not based on the Sun sign alone. The entire chart must be examined because each person is a unique combination of Sun, Moon, Ascendant, planets, Houses and aspects. A comparison of two charts often sheds light on compatibility. Compatibility between two people is often found when the Sun sign is in the same sign as their lover's Ascendant, or vice versa. Opposite Sun signs or an opposite Sun sign and Ascendant may also blend well together.

In a woman's chart, the placement of Venus is indicative of her sexuality while the position of Mars and the Sun indicates what kind of man she is attracted to. In a man's chart, the position of Mars tells how he relates to women, and the position of Venus and the Moon indicates what type of woman arouses him. In comparing two charts, look for the aspects of conjunction, sextile, square, trine, and oppositions. Remember that oppositions can blend. The square brings differences but much energy while conjunctions can be beneficial. The sextile and trine bring harmony. When a person's Venus and their lover's Mars are in the same sign, there is a strong attraction even if differences of opinions occur. When Venus and the other person's Ascendant are in the same sign, it adds to the sexual compatibility. Venus in the lover's sun sign brings a mutual interest while Mars in the lover's Moon sign is emotionally intense.

There is a vast variety of people found within each Sun sign, but basic characteristics and traits do exist. However, generalizations are just that and a fuller picture of the individual is reflected by the complete chart. The following section deals with Sun sign sexuality in a general manner. While the importance of sex remains the same in each Sun sign, the focus and attitudes vary.

Cancer Sexuality - Man

Secretive Cancer may sneak up on a woman before she realizes he's even interested in her. This is not a direct and forceful man, but one who approaches in a round about manner--but approach he does. Romanticism seethes beneath his surface, and recognizing this, many a woman will approach him, enticing him into any number of illicit affairs. The Cancer man is generally attracted to a particular age group, usually younger. And while he may mature, the age group of his lovers remains the same. This is a very sensitive man whose feelings are very easily wounded. His fear of rejection or being misunderstood, may explain his round about approach, or in many instances he may wait for the advances of the woman--which quite often are forthcoming. Cancer readily recognizes the importance of sex and is open to any opportunity which presents itself.

Charmingly self-centered, this man may judge his sexual relationships based on how attentive his lover is and how much she does for him. That is simply his nature and should be overlooked because it can't be helped. The nature of Cancer is emotional, sensitive and focused on his own needs. But he is extremely romantic and attentive to the women in his life. In order to attain sexual fulfillment, this man must feel that his lover wants him, is attracted to him, and desires to fulfill his every need. This is not a man to be aloof or cool with. Any hint of rejection or lack of physical pleasure or excitement can cause him to lose his erection. And the chances are he has little interest in intellectual compatibility in bed. In fact, he probably prefers a woman who is less intellectual and who will look up to him and admire him. This is a man looking for an admirer not a challenge. A true romantic, his masculinity may be based on the number of women on his long list of admiring lovers. He may hold a memory of his true love in his mind and even use that experience as an excuse to jump from one female to another. But in his heart, he must know that he is a sexually driven man. Sex excites him. Romance excites him. Affection, flattery, and the encouraging attentions of females excite his imagination.

He may not be direct and assertive, but he responds to the attention from a woman. And he especially responds to spur of the moment opportunities. His graphic imagination can run wild with talk of sex resulting in an immediate erection. He also responds to a woman who runs her hands over his chest and sighs imploringly. And his imagination becomes explosive when his penis is in his lover's mouth. He is a possessive man who will want to know that his lover is always available and always responsive to his needs. He can be sensual and lusty. He is also highly secretive and may carry on any number of passing affairs at the same time. Cancer is ruled by the Moon, and his changing and fluctuating nature can produce a sexual need that must be fulfilled. And his life can be so charmed that this is the man who drives home from work to find a young, beautiful damsel in distress waiting in his driveway. What can he do but invite her in and soothe away her problems?

In love, this is the man who expects total adulation and faithfulness whether or not he is faithful. If he discovers his lover is unfaithful, he will be totally dismayed. How can she love him and want another? If he isn't the center of her attentions, the relationship is over. In marriage, he will also want to be the center of attention and to have his needs catered to. He may at some time in his life decide upon a monogamous relationship, or he may not. There is that Cancer man who attains a spiritual enlightenment and develop an interest in home and family. And never doubt that security and home are of the utmost importance to this man. But it will always be important for his needs to be met and fulfilled. And Cancer is too defensive to ever talk openly about his emotions, his sexuality or his actions. In fact, any such talk can drive him into seclusion or into the arms of the first available other woman. This is a man to be pampered, attended to, loved and cared for, and who needs his imagination played with. He comes alive when made the center of adoring attention. One thing for sure, this man's sexuality is alive and well, and he will always know the importance it plays in his life.

Cancer Sexuality - Woman

A Cancer woman can be the lusty prostitute working the local street corner or the devoted and loyal wife who centers her life on her home and family. Much of her life depends upon how she views her childhood. She is prone to imaginary slights and feelings of rejection. If she feels she didn't receive enough attention as a child, she can become rebellious at an early age and turn to sexual promiscuity or inappropriate affairs. She must have adoration and adulation. She must be the center of someone's attention. If this desire isn't fulfilled, she will turn herself into whatever it takes to accomplish this purpose. She may seek this necessary attention through a string of affairs. Or she may use her lively imagination and create an entertaining and elusive persona on the stage of life. She is susceptible to being led into questionable activities by anyone who recognizes her needs.

This woman has a deep-seated need for security and possessions. She is comfortable with older people, and she may feel most secure with the protection offered by an older man, especially if he is financially secure. In this instance, there is every possibility that her sexuality and needs will even be sublimated by her greater need for financial security and a feeling of well being. If she isn't overly wrapped up in her active imagination, she may seek the companionship of a lover or two--but they will always be discardable.

That's not to say that the Cancer female has any trouble attracting men. She is a friendly person who has an alluring quality and often a come-hither look that accentuates her sexuality. She knows how to walk, how to talk suggestively and how to apply makeup like a show girl. She has a tendency to pick and choose rules that best apply to her life and her wants and this applies to the men in her life. They must be attentive, they must pick up the bill, and they must make her feel like a princess. She likes fun, pleasure and frivolity, and is more than a little prone to over indulging. And once she samples the joy of sex, it may take her some time to become fully satiated. She likes to play out fantasies, loves costumes, and is excited at the thought of erotic play. Cancer rules the breasts, and this woman loves to have her breasts fondled, kissed and messaged which will excite her most passionate and ardent sexual desires. Many a Cancer woman also has an anal fixation and desires attention paid to that part of her anatomy as well. She may be a social whirlwind and caught up in any number of activities, but this woman will always find time for sex and the pleasures it provides. Intelligent discussions are fine, once she has satisfied her sexual hunger. She may play the huntress or the hunted, but play she does, and when she plays she focuses all the creativity and imagination of her fun-loving mind.

Arguments, disagreements, or any type of emotional upset can move this emotional woman to immediate tears and moodiness. A break-up in a relationship or a divorce is disastrous and all those old feelings of resentment for never being truly loved or appreciated may reappear in her life. This is not a woman to be kept down for long, though. Her mood changes and her self-driven concern for security and protection propel her out the door to find yet another admirer who hopefully is also a provider and protector. She is happiest when in a relationship, or if promiscuous, several relationships. She is generous and giving if it makes her feel good, but for the most part she wants to receive first and if she does give she wants tons of admiration in return. An unhappy Cancer woman turns almost invariably crabby, critical and complaining.

That brings this section to that luckiest of Cancer females who survived childhood, has a happy relationship with her parents, especially her mother, and found true happiness with a loving, protective, and caring husband. With a strong and loving man in her life, she directs her creative energies into being a supportive partner who dotes on home and family. Her sexuality remains alive and well, and if her husband finds her to be sexually exciting and fulfilling then this is indeed a happy woman. The Cancer sexuality provides a creative outlet for the flights of fantasy and the delightfully fun imagination of this female.

Cancer Health

Cancer, influenced by the rulership of the Moon, rules the breast (lungs and chest) and stomach, left eye of the male and right eye of a female. Cancer is referred to as being receptive, transforming, metamorphic, nurturing and fruitful. However, Cancer may be lacking in vitality. The stomach, it is felt, is the most sensitive area for health problems, and particular care of the stomach should be taken when the Moon is moving through Cancer. The Cancer natives should also watch for colds or chills. And as there is the distinct and probable problem of mood swings with these individuals, care should be taken not to become overly nervous, anxious or distraught. Problems of depression develop in many of these individuals and should be guarded against. Being imaginative, many Cancer convince themselves they are suffering from one disease or another. Cancer are susceptible to stomach pains, gastric problems, diarrhea, and a sensitivity to some types of food. Be cautious against illness including inflammatory diseases, rheumatism, tumors, varicose veins, and problems with the legs and feet and circulation.

A well-balanced diet is the best defense against stomach and digestive problems. You may find that your system is overly sensitive to some foods, and you should probably choose to avoid any foods that don't agree with you. Many people prefer a healthy but somewhat bland diet that avoids spicy foods. Others love the spice but choose to limit spicy foods for the benefit of their sensitive tummies. Add plenty of fiber to your diet and a daily supply of fruits and vegetables.

Some Cancer individuals may find that they are sensitive to their environments. In the modern world this is rapidly becoming a major concern of many people. In such cases, you may want to avoid harmful chemicals. Even everyday chemicals can produce reactions to sensitive tissues. If this is a problem with you, look for products that are unscented. And don't let advertisers dictate what products you use in your home. Learn to select those products which do not have an ill effect on your well-being. You can best do this by simple observation of what agrees with you and what doesn't.

As with most people, the best advice for Cancer is a well-balanced diet, a good exercise program, and plenty of fresh, clean air. Developing a healthy attitude as well will take care of many of the nervous disorders associated with worry and anxiety. Take charge of your life, scheduling your day to include a balanced diet, an exercise regime, and a focus on not only your health but on positive thoughts as well.

History of Cancer

As the Crab doesn't originate in any of the other ancient civilizations, it is assumed that it was first used by the Babylonians to imply or symbolize coming from the water. The Egyptians used the Scarabeus to represent or symbolize the sign of Cancer because it lived beneath the Earth and when it emerged, it spread its wings and flew through the air. This represented the soul's changing, incarnating, and releasing the experiences of old. To the Egyptians this figure of the Zodiac symbolized the progress from darkness to light, from restraint to freedom and to the secure possession of eternity. The Moon in ancient times was referred to as Isis, Esses, Luna, Eleusis and the Virgin Mere. It was the Moon that maintained dominion over the ebb and flow of the tides bringing change to the weather and to the seasons.

The Greeks represented this sign with a tortoise whose ruling god was Hermes. Hermes, after his birth, slayed a tortoise and used its shell as a lyre to play his music. Therefore, the tortoise became a symbol for music. Within Greek mythology, however, Hermes didn't retain rulership over Cancer as it was passed on to the Moon. Perhaps the Moon received rulership of this sign when Greek traders discovered that on the Syrian coast it was a crab ruled by the Moon. These planetary rulerships were most probably developed after the Babylonian, Egyptian and Greek thoughts became blended together soon after Alexander the Great conquered the then known world some time around 300 BC.

In ancient times, the Moon and the Water represented travel and trade, and at that time it was felt that this required a strong, persevering individual. It wasn't the crab's sensitive nature and protecting shell that was emphasized at that time. The Moon, it was felt, represented the face that an individual exposed to the world. Cancer became the Ascendant of the world because the ancient Egyptian year began with the rising of the star Sirius during the Summer Solstice that occurred during this sign. Aries later became the first sign and Cancer the fourth sign.

Cancer is the exaltation of Jupiter, the detriment of Saturn and the home of the Moon. The Moon in ancient times was maternal and related to pure, virginal, undefiled water which was used in early religious rites. The constellation Cancer is very faint and the least noticeable in the night Sky. It has been referred to as the dark sign.

How to Find Your *Soul-Mate, Stars,* and *Destiny*

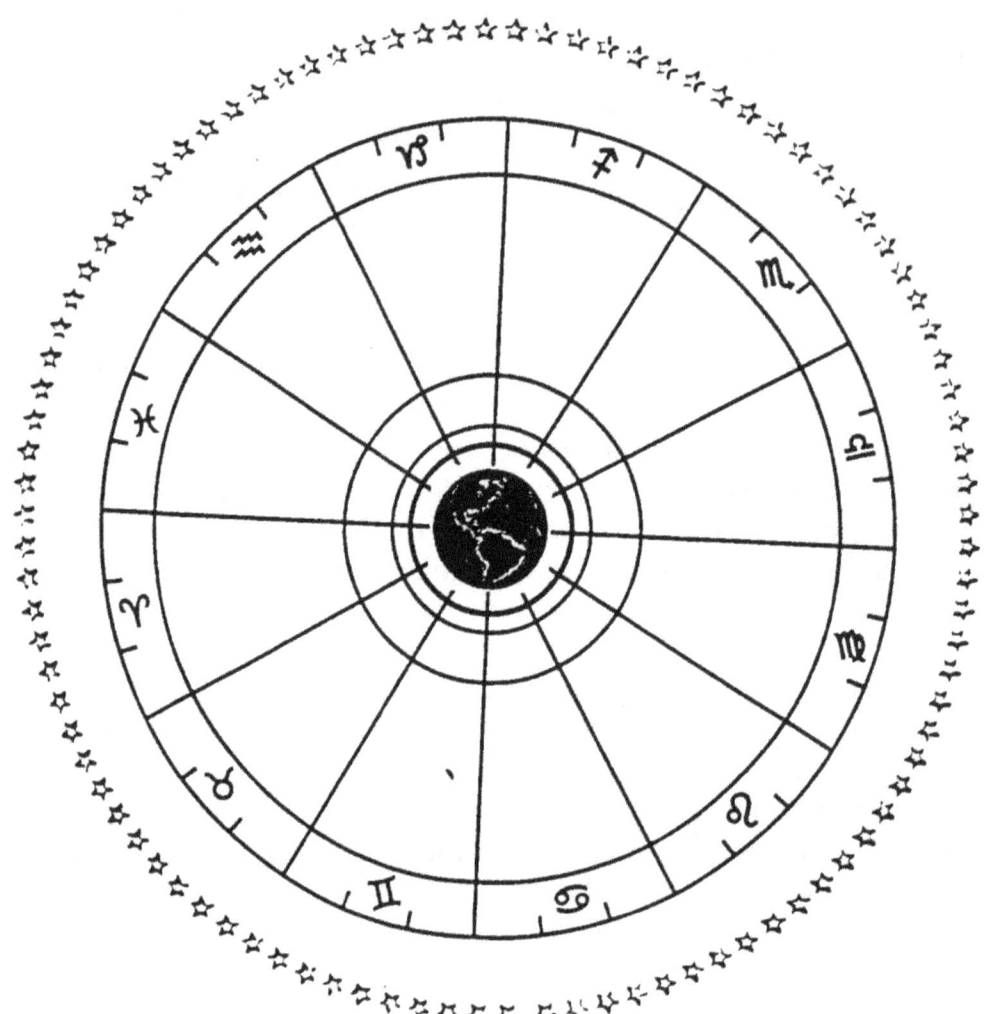

Cancer

June 22 – July 22
The Thebaic Calendar
Character, Personality, and Destiny

The Moon, which rules Cancer, exerts an immense influence over the daily affairs of the lives of these individuals. The Moon makes a complete transit of the Zodiac, or a complete revolution through the horoscope of every person during the month of the sign. As it passes through the different Houses and influences the various aspects of the planets at the time of birth, it also influences conditions, events, feelings and states of mind or health. The Moon's monthly revolution produces all manner of varying conditions. The following calendar provides an indication of individual conditions by days of birth. It was compiled by ancient Astrologers and carried forth to this day.

In Cancer, the Sun reaches its highest point of northern declination and retreats, crab like, backward toward the ecliptic. The sign of Cancer denotes containment, possessions, and retention. Whether Cancer is the Sun sign, the Ascendant, on the cusp, or in a House, these characteristics are noted as it pertains to that aspect of the personal chart. Cancer is ruled by the Moon, and as a Water sign it is emotional and intuitive. As a Feminine sign it is receptive. That part of the chart where Cancer is found is where the person will sustain strong feelings for home and family. A Cardinal sign usually implies action and decisiveness, but in Cancer these feelings are generated toward protecting possessions, home, and family. Cancer most likely takes action when motivated by outside stimuli. Therefore, there is a tendency for Cancer to attract what it needs and wants rather than actively seeking and pursuing it, and afterwards the necessary actions take place.

DUALITY: Feminine   **ELEMENT:** Water   **QUALITY:** Cardinal   **RULER:** Moon

Sensitive and emotional Cancer uses its protective shell to defend itself against any perceived threats and this protectiveness applies to criticisms as well. Cancer natives may present a hardened exterior to the world, but more than likely they maintain a strong stand silent defense against what they perceive in the world which might take advantage of them or harm them in any way. All in all, their softer, more vulnerable and tender feelings are protected by this shell from other people. Cancer natives can be cautious, prudent, and protective of their resources, saving what they need for that eventual rainy day. In their possessiveness, they can be shrewd, defensive, dependent, and clinging. But once they truly trust another, they become most considerate and generous.

How to Find Your Soul-Mate, Stars, and Destiny

The entire being of Cancer is propelled by feelings and emotions and there tender intuitions which they rely on to interpret their environment and their interactions with others. Retreating from the world at large, the dreams and fantasies of the Cancer native can seem more real and enjoyable than anything they encounter in their day-to-day lives. Seeing the world through the vision of the emotions, they have a tendency to cling possessively and to hold on retentively with a claw-like tenacity to all that they hold dear to them. Cancer natives, to feel most secure and at ease in their environment, require peaceful and comfortable surroundings, and the companionship of those they love and trust. They have an especially intense need for security, protection, and a home where they feel at ease and at peace with the world. And within this home environment of security, Cancer excels at loving, caring, and protecting its closest friends or family members through a strong maternal instinct. There is an innate need among Cancer natives for a sanctuary, a private place where they can allow themselves to be at peace, or to dream, or to create their fantasies, music, or poetry.

Jupiter is exalted in Cancer, and it may well be the expansive nature of Jupiter that augments the wonderously creative imagination and dream-induced fantasies of the Cancer mind. But at the same time, Cancer natives appear to be challenged to learn the lessons associated with home, family, mother, children, and property. Cancer is the most domestic of the signs, the natural home maker attuned to nurturing and caring for their family members. Among those natives who are denied or who deny themselves this nurturing instinct, it is observed that they become all the more self-protective, selfish, self-centered, and greedy. Found among Cancer natives, are the well-developed, emotionally strong as well as the emotionally weak, clinging and dependent. And whether emotionally strong or weak, Cancer will insist tenaciously on doing things their own way. They are not prone to following the advice of others even if they do learn to patiently listen to such advice. That is, there is that Cancer who will listen, nod his or her head, then do as they please. That is, if they don't become offended in the first place that someone has the audacity to offer advice. The Moon directly affects the ever changing moods and emotions of the Cancer natives, allowing them to reflect either the pleasantness of being cheerful, sweet, funny and entertaining, or to become as dark and gloomy as any particular day.

Each of the twelve signs of the Zodiac are allotted thirty degrees, and each sign is further divided into decans of ten degrees each. And each Decan has been shown to exhibit the characteristics of its sign in varying strengths.

The First Decan

Within Cancer, the First Decan is designated as from 0 degrees to 10 degrees of Cancer and applies to those individuals born between June 22 and July 1. Being on the cusp of Gemini, these individuals are no doubt especially changeable and impulsive with an over active imagination that allows them to dream away their days if they so choose. They are romantic, sentimental, and attached to their possessions. They have a strong tendency to take on the moods of those in their environment or even to absorb and reflect the personality of those people around them. They can be extremely defensive and may over react to criticism or even image slights and insults.

The Second Decan

The Second Decan is designated as from 10 degrees to 20 degrees of Cancer and includes those persons born between July 2 and July 11. These Cancer natives most strongly reflect the characteristics of this Sun sign. They are also more than likely the most obstinate type of Cancer exhibiting a willful and stubborn manner which in some instances does work to their advantage. They are intensely emotional, sensitive, jealous and possessive, but they go to great lengths to protect this sensitivity from becoming known. That is they may show one personable face to the public, but keep their inner feelings and reflections to themselves. They are creative and witty or cunning and shrewd. They attend to their own affairs and are most content when at home with family and friends where they feel the most comfortable and can relax and be themselves. They are resourceful and at times ingenious. They are also intuitive and perceptively sensitive which may produce within them an interest in the metaphysical or the occult.

The Third Decan

The Third Decan is designated as from 20 degrees to 30 degrees of Cancer and includes those individuals born between July 12 and July 22. The Third Decan approaches the cusp of Leo and finds its natives exhibiting many of the stronger emotional traits of that sign. It also augments the Cancer natives need to be the center of attention and to receive an ample amount of attention and praise from friends and family. The home remains an important aspect to this Cancer native Cancer finds a native who may develop an interest and higher c, and they strive to protect all that they hold dear to their hearts. The Third Decan alling to the spiritual plane. They are also dutiful individuals who become involved in community affairs and social work. They are sociable as well as creatively entertaining.

First Decan of Cancer:

June 22 - July 1 -

First Ten Days

Character, Personality, and Temperament:

The taste for sensual pleasures is intensified. This person is moody and changeable and may be unstable and unfaithful in romantic relationships due to a lack of belief in true love.

Cardinal Element:

Water: An enterprising and outgoing utilization of emotions and intuitions.

Destiny:

These natives have a destiny that is positively influenced by the opposite sex.

Star Date of Birth: June 22

A person whose character is polite but careless. This person finds an easy job. He means well, but there are times when he lacks the will power to carry through on opportunities. There is a chance of success in life. He is a sensitive and kind person who sexually strives to indulge his partner in an effort to show his appreciation for their being with him.

Star Date of Birth: June 23

How to Find Your *Soul-Mate, Stars, and Destiny*

The person is interested in many things; very thoughtful and absent minded. This person has luck and success. Your charm serves you well in your youth, but it is through developing your mind and your skills that you achieve success in later life. Your spontaneity is reflected in your sexuality as you much prefer spur of the moment encounters especially with those who must abandon their inhibitions to fully enjoy the experience.

Star Date of Birth: June 24

This person prefers a soft life but is easily bored; always in love. Good but short and tumultuous connections. Your resourcefulness sees you through difficulties that others would succumb to. You are sexually most fulfilled with another person who shares your need to communicate feelings and emotions. You prefer there not be any secrets in the bedroom.

Star Date of Birth: June 25

An exaggerated and sensual temperament; there may exist many painful separations. You are self-reliant and care little about the conventions of society, preferring to harbor your own thoughts and imaginary visions during your private moments. Sexually, you excel at giving pleasure and in return you receive your greatest moments of gratification.

Star Date of Birth: June 26

This person may experience a wandering life. There is an indication of weaknesses in women. Yours is a life of extremes from great successes to subsequent losses with the climb back to the top depending upon your own ambition and drive. Your sex life is often intertwined with your career goals, but you derive the greatest sexual pleasure when sex is combined with love.

Star Date of Birth: June 27

There is an indication of unbalance and instability. The person's life depends on somebody else. Reserved and dignified, you find that others may take advantage of your acts of kindness. Your imaginative use of intrigue and secretive mystique in the bedroom transforms you into a skillful lover who both gives and receives pleasure. You bloom when in love.

How to Find Your *Soul-Mate, Stars,* and *Destiny*

Star Date of Birth: June 28

A careless, easy life. There is a tendency toward laziness but the latter life is successful. Your spirituality is important, either leading you to follow a religious order or blending harmoniously with the other aspects of your life. Your sexuality is enhanced by your ability to use imagination to dramatically set the scene for romance.

Star Date of Birth: June 29

Excessive susceptibility. Life is taking place on an inferior level which may cause the person's decline in success. You are greatly depended upon the other people in your life, often affecting their traits rather than exposing your true self. Sexually, you are drawn to successful and powerful people from who you can tap vitality.

Star Date of Birth: June 30

The person shows much hesitation and deception and experiences different losses. You are alert and aware of your intuitive perceptions and sensitivities. Your sexuality is enhanced by spontaneous experiences while traveling or with those involved with music. You are also drawn to ethnic types who feel exploited by the system.

Star Date of Birth: July 1

This person lives life one day at a time. There is an indication for day dreaming and an opaque existence. You desire fame and recognition and if it is not forthcoming, you imagine it in your fantasy world. Your creativity and imagination combined with your intuitive abilities enhance your sexuality making you more desirous to your partner.

Second Decan of Cancer:

July 2 - July 11 -

Second Ten Days

Character, Personality, and Temperament:

The general characteristic of this Cancer native is colored by ingenious abilities. Individual can be congenial or courageous depending upon what is necessary. He influences everyone through subtle sentimentality.

Cardinal Element:

WATER: Emotions and intuitions guide the compassions.

Destiny:

Life will oscillate between great joys and great deceptions.

Star Date of Birth: July 2

A very active life; the characteristics are noted as strong, positive, and successful. Your ambitions dominate your lifestyle, subordinating your qualities of kindness, caring, and generosity, making you appear selfish and self-centered. Your sexuality may also be suppressed at times, but you respond to sexual encounters while traveling and to sex that can benefit you in your career or socially.

Star Date of Birth: July 3

There is great pleasure in long voyages, adventures and risks; active existence. You are able to rationalize even immoral acts if they result in you obtaining what you want. Your sexuality is often an avenue of escapism and distraction from the world, and you much prefer natural settings away from the city and other people where you know there will be no competition for the attention you seek.

Star Date of Birth: July 4

This person has a cruel indifference toward other people's suffering; accidents may lead to short life. You set high standards and are most loyal to your friends, but you expect others to appreciate and repay you in attention and acclamation. Sexually, your intuition, sensitivities, and awareness works to your benefit when you meet those who are attracted to you.

Star Date of Birth: July 5

A serious, hard-working and active life. There may be success in a scientific activity. You wear the mask of congeniality, but your cunning and conniving mind is shrewdly aware of what it takes to place you at the advantage. Sexually, you are capable of transforming yourself into what you intuitively perceive your partner wants you to be.

Star Date of Birth: July 6

You take great self-pride in your achievements which leads you to be ambitious of more success. Sexually, you are drawn to strong, independent types who express themselves through cheerfulness but who are equally as ambitious, persistent, and persevering as you.

Star Date of Birth: July 7

A distant, careless, superior character. Success will come through isolation far from the public. You make every effort to maintain and increase what you already possess. Your self-confidence and self-reliance are reflected in your conventional, conservative, and reserved manner. Your sexuality and sensitivities are best appreciated by a newcomer to your community.

Star Date of Birth: July 8

A reserved, dignified individual; success against enemies. Romance registers high on your list of priorities even though you appear cautious, reserved, and extremely careful in your affiliations. When you meet a potential lover, however, you turn on the charm and become as assertive as you deem necessary to obtain what you want.

Star Date of Birth: July 9

An indifferent, negligent character; undeserved success. You appease your great vanity by constantly verbalizing your achievements. Praising yourself and your romantic accomplishments makes you an even greater lover in your mind, but in this area of your life you are kinder and possess a softer heart which draws the attentions of love.

Star Date of Birth: July 10

This person shows an easy discouragement, but finds luck and positive chance. Your tendency to follow those who allow you to consider yourself a close friend can lead you to losses unless you learn to discriminate between friend and foe. Sexually, with the right partner, you become an intimate helpmate who understands the needs of the other person.

Star Date of Birth: July 11

Strong inclinations toward love affairs, chance, and games. Unlucky in gambling but successful in other activities. You are perceptive and sensuous although self-indulgent in the pleasures of life. Your ease in communicating well with others and adapting to new situations lends itself to you meeting romantic partners who are charmed by your pleasantries.

Star Date of Birth: July 12

This person has strong indications toward combativity, stinginess, humiliations, and deceptions. You never miss an opportunity to improve your status or finances and can even be ruthless when necessary regardless of the plight of others. Sexually, you are drawn to lovers involved with writing, publishing, journalism, or public relations who impress you with their wordy compliments.

The Third Decan of Cancer:

July 13 - July 22 -
Third Ten Days

Character, Personality, and Temperament:

Hypersensitivity and impressionable; psychological exaggerations.

Cardinal Element:

WATER: Sensitive and sympathetic but changeable and easily influenced.

Destiny:

Much in life including success depends upon associates, friends, and family.

Star Date of Birth: July 13

A happy person; perseverance. Life filled with connections. You have difficulty letting go of the past and greatly depend upon the lessons you learned in childhood. Sexually, you can be the aggressor, but you know how to camouflage this tendency effectively. You find sex most gratifying when enjoyed in natural settings.

Star Date of Birth: July 14

Naive, superficial life; not very active, but tumultuous life. Because your rich fantasy life is so rewarding, you may have a tendency to drift along in life with little ambition. But your creativity is highly reflected in your sexuality where you are a proven pioneer and a sensual lover who strives to gratify your partners desires.

Star Date of Birth: July 15

An extremely unstable, unreliable person; everything is as God's will. You recognize your desire for fame and success in early life and strive to prepare for that purpose. Your sexuality is enhanced by impromptu meetings, unexpected travel, and reunions that bring together old friends--all of which sparks your imagination.

Star Date of Birth: July 16

Receptive to all kinds of influences; distinguished existence. Your motivations are often secreted beneath the face you show the world, and your moody nature makes it difficult for others to truly understand you. But sexually, you are drawn to those who exhibit a tendency toward nostalgia or an interest in the secrets of history.

Star Date of Birth: July 17

A very stingy person; frequent but short-term successes in life. You maintain close ties to your family and home town, but life leads you away from your roots. Sexually, you have the knack for making others feel better about themselves and more secure with their lives while for you, sex inspires feelings of youth and vitality.

Star Date of Birth: July 18

Independent, exaggerated, daring spirit; adventures and travels in life; some success. You are personable, charming, and perceptively intelligent with the ability to achieve what you want. Sexually, you want to experience life to the fullest, realizing all your potential and the potential of your partner. You are put off by those who hold back.

How to Find Your *Soul-Mate, Stars,* and *Destiny*

Star Date of Birth: July 19

A person who is looking or waiting for something unusual to happen in his or her life. You exhibit an originally creative streak, but you are hesitant to pursue your ideas or to allow others to. Sexually, you are inspired by artistic or creative types, and find the greatest gratification in making the other person feel better with themselves or life in general.

Star Date of Birth: July 20

Great malleability. The person listens to everybody and agrees with everything. Not very successful because of the indecisive character. Your success is associated with international connections. Sexually, you desire that romance be entertaining, pleasurable, and fun for both you and your partner, and you make every effort to please and be pleased.

Star Date of Birth: July 21

Very careless; head in the clouds; dangerous life. You pride yourself on your memory for facts and details relating to history and family. Sexually, you at times respond when you sense that the other person hasn't initially responded to you, resulting in you both being pleasantly surprised by the love making that follows.

Star Date of Birth: July 22

Thoughtful spirit; always relies on someone else's effort. Adventure calls to you, and the thought of it excites you to the point of feeling self-important. Your sexuality is enhanced by your vitality and the essence of mystery and secrecy that you bring to your sexual encounters. Glamorous and permissive types attract your attention.

Colors:

The most favorable colors for Cancer natives are all shades of green, beige, silver, aqua, and white.

BIRTHSTONES:

The most favorable birthstones for the natives of Cancer are pearls, emeralds, diamonds, opals, crystals, cat-eyes, and moonstones.

METAL:

The metal associated with the sign of Cancer is silver.

KEYWORD: "I Feel"

POSITIVE TRAITS:

Kind; patient; sensitive; maternal or paternal; caring; devoted; warm-hearted; tenacious; adaptable; economical; thrifty; sympathetic; imaginative; protective; cautious; sociable; domestic; loyal; patriotic; creative; personable; entertaining; active; good memory; talented.

NEGATIVE TRAITS:

Overly sensitive and emotional; defensive; paranoid; temperamental; timid; changeability; moody; vain; fanciful; untruthful; grasping; clinging; dependent; proud; resentful; jealous; possessive; untidy; insecure; unstable; easily flattered; lazy; stingy; selfish; self-centered; shrewd; pleasure seeking.

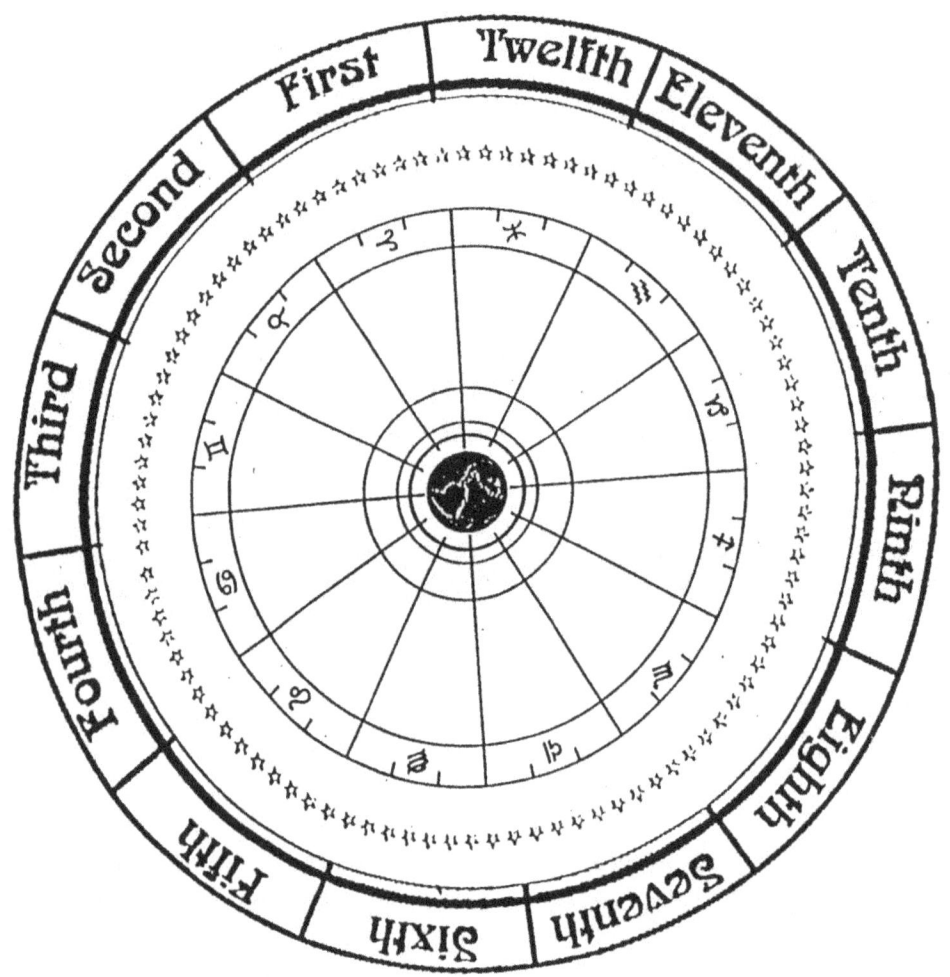

CANCER

PERSONAL SELF-EXPRESSION AND MENTAL TENDENCIES

1. Fascinating, Changeable, Moon Children, Intense Emotionalism
2. Physical, Face Resembles Full-Moon, Physical Plane, Control-Life
3. Mentally Logical, Impulsive, Likes Challenge, Ceaseless, Changeability
4. Dynamic, Unpredictable, Full-Fledged Human, Self-Expression
5. World Beyond the Home, Emotional, Impressionable, Self-Idulgent
6. Absorptive, Imaginative, Psychic, Resistance to Change, Materialistic
7. Subjective, Dramatic Self-Knowledge, Self-Revelation, Subtle
8. Indulgent, Storyteller, Humorist, Domestic, Tenacious, Intuitive
9. Subjective, Sensitive Ego, Self-Centered, Selfish, Patient
10. Mediocre Self-Esteem, Possessive, Moody, Imaginative, Dreamy
11. Introspcctivc, Sccurity-Consicious, Absorbs Information Quickly
12. Petentive, Fearful, Thin-Skinned, Vengeful, High Sex Drive
13. Overprotective, Nostalgic, Sentimental, Enjoys Good Quality of Life
14. Manipulative, Magnetic, Great Sense of Humor, Fertile Imagination
15. Feminine, Love and Marriage, Sympathetic, Internal Adventures
16. Courage, Eyes Sparkle, Inhibitions, Exotic Love Games, Sensitive
17. Illusion Opens Sexuality, Loses Control in Orgasm, Social Nature
18. Reserved, Retiring, Sensitive Disposition, Versatile, Love of Gain
19. Ups and Downs, Occupation, Gains Feeling of Accomplishment
20. Possesses a Fertile Imagination and Drama, Manipulatively Angry
21. Loves Nature, Adventure, Strange Experiences, Fantasize and Fantasy
22. Influenced by Surroundings, Creates a Harmonious Ambience
23. Industrious, Prudent, Frugal, Conscientious, Desire for Sympathy
24. Retentive Memory, Love Approbation, Kind, Tending to be Spiteful
25. Fears Ridicule, Fruitful, Reproductive, Patriotic, Irrational Maneuvers
26. Attached to Home and Family, Copes Constructively With Angry Tantrums
27. Economical, Likes Historical Events, Likelihood of Acquiring Wealth
28. Anxious, Fear of Criticism, Dangerously Strong, Strong Emotions
29. Conventional, Easily Encouraged by Kindess, Flucuating Nature
30. Delights in Beauty, Scenery, and Romance, Vital Temperment

How to Find Your Soul-Mate, Stars, and Destiny

31. Very Conscientious, Expresses It Dramatically, Appreciates Himself
32. Receptive to New Ideas, Adapts Easily to Environment, Prudent
33. Caters to Public Needs and Desires Compassionate Artist of Living
34. Vital Temperament, Least Resistance, Friendly, Sociable, Gossip
35. The Planetary Significator is the Moon. Forces Himself on Others
36. Feeling and Emotion are Active - Usually for Good. Receptive
37. Words Sense, Physical Condition, Residence Near to Water
38. Conscious or Unconscious, Attracted to His Mother, Protected
39. Imposition Without Act; Good, Sensitive, Superior Nature
40. Struggles Hard, Great Obstacles, Voyages, Loves Traveling
41. Deals With Public, Liquids, Chemistry, Catering, Shipping
42. Antiques and Curious Things, Provides Comfort for Loved Ones
43. Ability for Acting and the Thoughts and Emotions of Others
44. Faithful, Tactful, Descreet, Encouraged by Kindness
45. Good Natured, Intellect, Retentive Powers, Discreet
46. Opinionated, Sociable Disposition, Very Impressionable
47. Pleasures, Picnics, Family Reunions, Public Entertainment
48. Restless Mind, Psychic Investigation, Patient Listener
49. Domestic, Attracts Others, Kind-Hearted, Loving Receptive
50. Several Love Affairs, Secret Attractions, Loved, Memory
51. Considerable Difference in Age With Mates, Internal
52. Not Wholly Fortunate in Marriage, Obstacles, Dramatic,
53. Money and Occupation: Unforeseen Difficulties, Irritable Tendencies
54. Mediumistic Gifts, Fearless, Ambitious, Sudden Outbursts of Temper
55. Fond of Luxury , Somewhat Sensouous, Excellent Educator
56. Original, Independent, Rebels Against Authority, Mediumistic
57. Mystucakm Psychical, Metaphysical Subjects, Mystique
58. Separation, Disagreement, or Discontent With Marriage Partner
59. Many Worries, Annoyances, Sorrows, Vivacious, Stoutness
60. Changes of Residence, Land, Property, and Inheritance
61. Charitable, Benevolent, Humanitarian Tendencies, Occult
62. Courteour, Truthful, Trustworthy, fond of Novelty, Bold
63. Intellectual Development, Mind is Lofty and Aspiring, Ideas,
64. Restless Feelings of Uncertainty or Changeability, Tenacious Memory
65. Differences or Separation From Relatives and Loved Ones
66. Dissatisfied Feelings Causing Many Changes of Residence and Pursuits
67. Changeable Moods, Somewhat Fretful, Discontented or Jealous
68. Domestic Troubles, Anxieties, and Sorrows With Parents, Home, and/or Children
69. Eccentric, Cranky, Impatient, Peculiar, Radical, Position

How to Find Your *Soul-Mate*, *Stars*, and *Destiny*

70. Estrangement, Loss, and Difficulty With Land or Property
71. Expression, discontent, Strong Desire, Sexuall Omnipotent Fantasies
72. Delicacy, Refinement, Idealism, Spiritual Faculties
73. Peculiar or Mysterious Experience, Mediumistic Faculty
74. Passive or Negative States, Nervousnes, Extremely Nervous
75. Domestiv Affairs, Appreciation, Recognition, Admiration
76. Movable, Watery, Fruitful, Maternal, Many Changes
77. Tropical, Solsitial, Mute, Cold, Moist, Phlegmatic
78. Cardinal, Possession, Retention, Whores, Artists, Saints, Wives
79. Symbolical of Progress from Darkness to Light - From Bondage to Freedom
80. Vicissitudes to Secure Possession of Treasures for Eternity
81. Emblematic of the Soul's Incarnation Experiences
82. Holding, Possessiong, Anger in Day Dreaming, Emotions
83. Avoid worrying about Finances or Diseases, Grabby
84. Metamorphic, Nurturing, Fructifying, Lacking in Vitality
85. Patient, Tenacious, Conscientious, Retiring, Communicative
86. Devotional, Versatile, Adaptable, Sexually Refreshed Regularly
87. Timorous, Variable, Vain, Fanciful, Dramatize the Anger
88. Untruthful, Changeable, Touchy, Grasping, Talkative
89. Proud, Unadaptable, Disorderly, Resentful, Indolent
90. Inconstant as the Moon, Success Late in Life, Fretful,
91. Desires Success, Fraud or Deception, Disappointment
92. Mystery or Complications Concerning Home Affairs and/or Property
93. Mental Distress, Suicide or Liability to Sudden End by Accident
94. Stomach and Digestive Organs - Cramps or Ulcers, Breast, Migraine Headaches
95. Romantic Interludes, Making Love in Water, Petty
96. Skill and Confidence, Building Exercises, Exclusive Relationships
97. Disliking, Fulfill Needs, Self-Confident, Maneuver, Diplomatic,
98. Sexual Aggression, Heights, Theatrical Displays, Physically Sick
99. Extremely Destructive, Crying From Anger, Suffers Frm Physical Equilibrium
100. Paints a Picture of Helplessness and Irrationality, Capriciousness

Celebrity Birthdays

June Cancer

22	Michael Lerner Gower Champion Clyde Drexler Lindsay Wagner	Billy Wilder Kris Kristofferson Anne Morrow Lindberg Joseph Papp	Meryl Streep John Dillinger Freddie Prinze Mike Todd
23	June Carter Cash Dr. Alfred Kinsey Eric La Salle Richard Bach	Bryan Brown Francis McDormand Will Rogers Empress Josephine	George Abbott King Edward VIII Karin Gustafson Adam Faith
24	Mick Fleetwood Phil Harris Norman Cousins Peter Weller	Nancy Allen Henry Ward Beecher Jack Dempsey Andy McCluskey	Michele Lee Jeff Beck John Illsley Jeff Cease
25	Carly Simon Eddie Floyd Sidney Lumet George Abbott	George Michael Allen Lanier Marusia Timm Finn	Clint Warwick Ian McDonald June Lockhart Willis Reed
26	Peter Lorre Anna Moffo Pearl Buck Chris Isaak	Eleanor Parker Stuart Symington John Tunney Mick Jones	Billy Davis Jr. Greg LeMond Larry Taylor Jeanne Eagles
27	Isabelle Adjani Henry Ross Perot Emma Goldman	Lorrie Morgan William G. Armstrong Helen Keller	Julia Duffy Bob „Captain Kangaroo' Keeshan
28	Kathy Bates Richard Rodgers Ashley Montagu Mel Brooks	Noriyuki „Pat' Morita Jean-Jacques Rousseau Mary S. Masterson King Henry VIII	Lester Flatt Rachel Perry John Cusack Alice Krige
29	Richard Lewis Gary Busey Nelson Eddy Little Eva	Nancy Allen Sharon Lawrence Ian Pace Slim Pickens	Fred Grandy William Mayo Ruth Warrick Peter Paul Rubens

How to Find Your *Soul-Mate, Stars,* and *Destiny*

June   Cancer

30	Lena Horne	Robert Ballard	Andy Scott
	Susan Hayward	Martin Landau	June Valli
	Buddy Rich	William Zeckendorf	Glenn Shorrock
	Hal Lindes	David Alan Grier	Adrian Wright

July

1	Princess Diana	Estee Lauder	Charles Laughton
	Jamie Farr	Karen Black	George Sand
	Leslie Caron	Alanis Morissette	Genevieve Bujold
	Pamela Lee	Olivia De Havilland	Dan Akroyd
2	Ron Silver	Johnny Colla	Imelda Marcos
	Paul Williams	Thurgood Marshall	Dan Rowan
	David Webb	Arthur Treacher	Cheryl Ladd
	Hermann Hesse	Brock Peters	Joe Puerta
3	Tom Cruise	Montel Williams	Pete Fountain
	Neil Clark	Earl Butz	Johnny Lee
	Paul Anka	Laura Branigan	Michael Cole
	George Sanders	George M. Cohan	
4	Ann Landers	Louis Armstrong	Gina Lollobrigida
	Neil Simon	Abigail „Dear Abby'	John Waite
	Bill Withers	Van Buren	Louis B. Mayer
	Tokyo Rose	George Steinbrenner	Geraldo Rivera
5	Huey Lewis	Julie Nixon Eisenhower	Mack David
	P. T. Barnum	Henry Cabot Lodge	Cecil Rhodes
	Katherine Helmond	Robbie Robertson	Shirley Knight
	Babe Paley	Michael Monarch	Jean Cocteau
6	Susan Ford Vance	Emperor Maximilian	Gene Chandler
	Merv Griffin	John Paul Jones	Sylvester Stallone
	Rik Elswit	Nancy Reagan	Andrei Gromyko
	Janet Leigh	Ned Beatty	Bill Haley
7	Shelley Duvall	Pierre Cardin	Ringo Starr
	Gian-Carlo Menotti	Marc Chagall	Leroy 'Satchel' Paige
	Michelle Kwan	George Cukor	Joe Spano
	Doc Severinson	Jessica Hahn	Gustav Mahler

How to Find Your *Soul-Mate, Stars,* and *Destiny*

July   Cancer

8	Vivien Leigh George Romney Walter Kerr Faye Emerson	Anjelica Huston Steve Lawrence Billy Eckstine Kevin Bacon	Kim Darby John D. Rockefeller Raffi Andy Fletcher
9	Tom Hanks Kelly McGillis O. J. Simpson Ed Ames	Barbara Cartland Elias Howe Brian Dennehy Marc Almond	Bon Scott Lee Hazelwood Fred Savage Debbie Sledge
10	David Brinkley Saul Bellow John Calvin Marcel Proust	Virginia Wade James Whistler Ron Glass Max Von Sydow	Arlo Guthrie Fred Gwynne Sue Lyon Eunice Kennedy Shriver
11	Peter Murphy Yul Brynner Sela Ward Bonnie Pointer	Richie Sambora E. B. White Pres. John Quincy Adams	Leon Spinks Tab Hunter Giorgi Armani
12	Bill Cosby Milton Berle Mel Harris Van Cliburn	Kristi Yamaguchi Oscar Hammerstein Andrew Wyeth Richard Simmons	Cheryl Ladd Josiah Wedgewood George Eastman Julius Caesar
13	Harrison Ford Dave Garroway Cheech Marin Jack Kemp	Louise Mandrel Sudie Bond Lawrence Donegan Patrick Stewart	Spud Webb Stephen Jo Bladd Robert Forster
14	Terry-Thomas Polly Bergen Matthew Fox Pete Rose	John Chancellor Ingmar Bergman Harry Dean Stanton Pres. Gerald Ford	Rosey Grier Chris Cross Woodie Guthrie Irving Stone
15	Linda Ronstadt Dorothy Fields Brigitte Nielsen Willie Aames	Forest Whitaker Alex Karras Jan-Michael Vincent Brian Austin Green	Patrick Wayne Barry Goldwater, Jr. Mother Cabrini Harding Lawrence
16	Ruben Blades Sir Joshua Reynolds Ginger Rogers Mary Baker Eddy	Barbara Stanwyc Margaret Smith Court Phoebe Cates Desmond Dekker	Mickey Rourke Sonny Tufts Ronald Amundson Corey Feldman

How to Find Your Soul-Mate, Stars, and Destiny

July   Cancer

17	Donald Sutherland Diahann Carroll James Cagney Lou Boudreau	Art Linkletter Eleanor Steber Erle Stanley Gardner Lucie Arnaz	Geezer Butler David Hasselhoff Spencer Davis Phyllis Diller
18	Red Skelton John Glenn Hume Cronyn Nick Faldo	Elizabeth McGovern Chill Wills Harriet Hilliard Nelson Ricky Skaggs	Nelson Mandela Dione DiMucci Martha Reeves James Brolin
19	Anthony Edwards George McGovern A.J. Cronin Ilie Nastase	Allen Collins Edgar Degas Duchess of Windsor Charles Horace Mayo	Brian May Vikki Carr Samuel Colt Bernie Leadon
20	Chris Cornell Diana Rigg Natalie Wood Elliott Richardson	Tony Oliva Sir Edmund Hillary Kim Carnes Carlos Santana	Dino Esposito Paul Cook Mike McNeil Donna Dixon
21	Robin Williams Ernest Hemingway Janet Reno Isaac Stern	Edward Herrmann Don Knotts Henry Priestman Francis Parkinson Keyes	Kay Starr Cat Stevens C. Aubrey Smith Jon Lovitz
22	Jason Robards, Jr. Danny Glover Amy Vanderbilt Rose Kennedy	Oscar De La Renta Willem Dafoe Alex Trebek Orson Bean	Sparky Lyle Louise Fletcher Raymond Chandler Don Henley

How to Find Your *Soul-Mate, Stars,* and *Destiny*

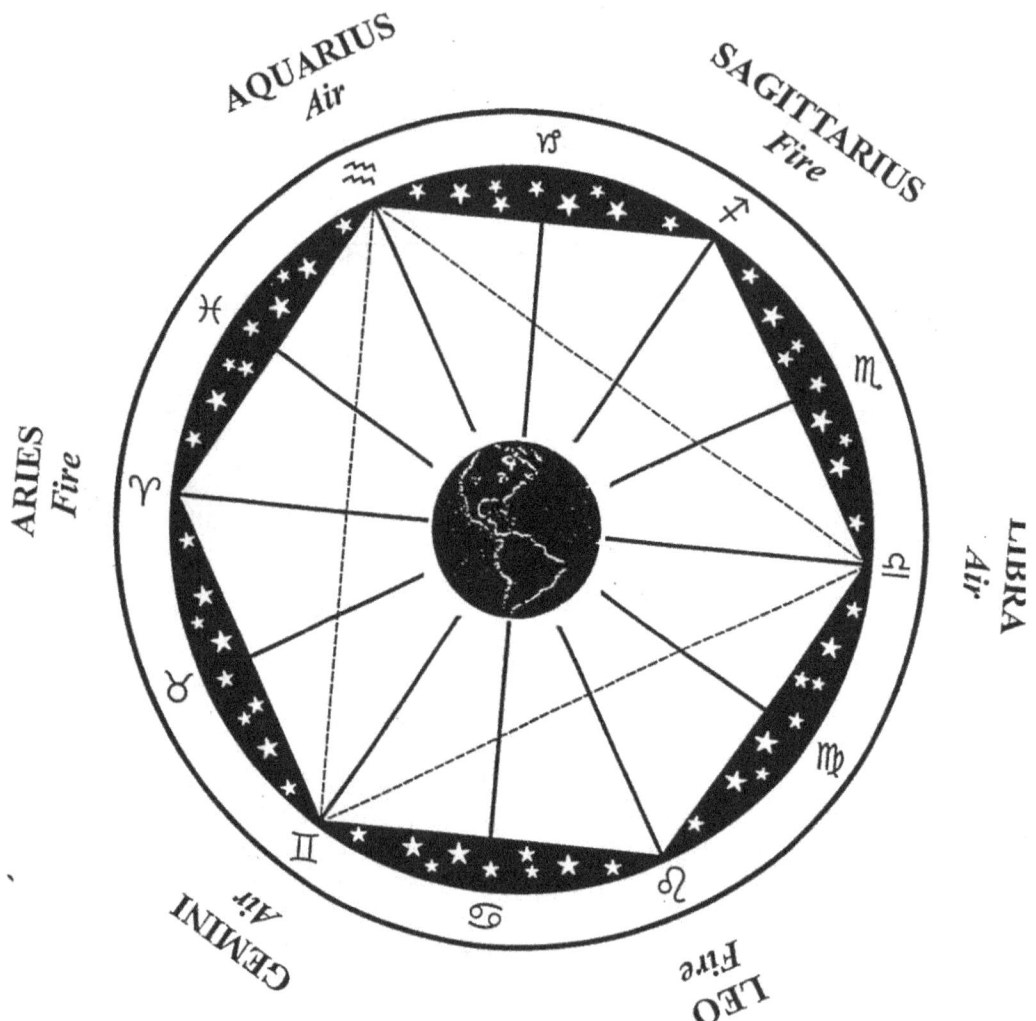

How to Find Your *Soul-Mate, Stars,* and *Destiny*

Date With Destiny

Share With Me Your Fantasy

How to Find Your *Soul-Mate, Stars,* and *Destiny*

Date With Destiny

Share With Me Your Fantasy

Leo

July 23 -- August 22
Man - Woman - Child - Character - Relationships - Compatibilities - Love Signs

Leo, the fifth Sun sign of the Zodiac, is symbolized by the Lion and takes its name from the Latin word for lion. Like the lions and kings of fables, this sign is associated with the bearing of royalty, and an individual with a strong Leo personality may well exhibit the demeanor and ego-driven characteristics of one born to rule. Leo natives may possess the best and the worst of human traits. They can be brave, noble, and generous or cold, brutal, and vicious. These are magnanimous but egocentric persons who are particularly sensitive to the response others have toward them. They appear to need a following or even a fan club to feel complete. From this following, they receive admiration and affirmation that they seek in order to feel fulfilled and good about themselves. Leo natives struts like the Lion and with a magnetic, charismatic appeal turn a flair for the dramatic into attention getting maneuvers. They have a graceful, dignified allure which attracts attention wherever they go, and they strive to be the center of attention. They take for granted their right to this attention and their birth-given right to be superior and to rule over others. This self-confident, self-reliant nature when embodied in a person who has worked hard to gain the necessary skills, education, and accomplishment, produces natural and authoritarian leaders. In others, it produces a person who is dogmatic, demanding, and difficult to please. Leo natives can either be inspiring and impressive or opinionated and vain. They also possess a heightened sense of fun and adventure and an intense need for romantic involvement. These individuals may know few boundaries in their yearning to taste and sample the best of life. As well, they may possess dynamic, creative impulses which demand to be expressed. On the highest level, a well developed Leo personality represents the opportunity to aspire to spiritual expression or the need to better humanity.

These characteristics of the Leo Sun sign can be made stronger by the Moon sign, Ascendant, and the placement of the Planets, or they can be made more subdued by specific influences. It is by ascertaining these various influences that one can more fully understand the Leo individual being studied, or more importantly, one can more fully understand one's self.

The sign of Leo, represented by the Lion, is ruled by the Sun which is the center of our solar system. In the constellation, the Lion is looking towards the Cancer and the legs are in the next sign, Virgo. The Sun is in the constellation of Leo at this time of year, and it rules ultimately and supremely at this time of the year. The ancient astrologers considered the Sun at its greatest power and glory when it attained its peak in the arch or vault of the Sky at this time of the year. Leo represents that season when summer is coming to an end. Leo, the Lion, therefore, symbolizes the incandescent heat of July and August when the Sun pours forth its greatest strength and intensity onto the Earth. It denotes the extraterrestrial vastness of the Universe where the Sun radiates, focusing, at this season, its oblique, cone-like, luminous brilliance of magnificence and abundance. Leo best represents all that is dignified, valiant and brilliant.

While the Zodiac sign of Leo begins on July 23, for the first seven days it is overlapped by the cusp of the previous sign, Cancer. It attains its full strength and power on or about July 28 to July 30, and retains its power until about August 20. Around that date, Leo begins to lose its strength as it enters the cusp with the incoming sign, Virgo.

Leo is the Fixed sign in the Fire group. Ruled by the Sun, Leo, the Lion, endows its natives to radiate with a luminous nature and a vigorous mind. The energy of these Leo born natives is vivacious and bold yet noble and determined with a kindly generosity. Leo, the sign of Fire, is most generally impulsive and spontaneously courageous. It symbolizes the ruling, ambitious and steadfast spirit. It is considered a masculine, dignified sign of the Zodiac. Individuals born under this sign are predisposed to be pleasant, warm, and sincere. They have a love for honors, uniforms, authority, and high rank. Their ideals are majestic and noble and without malice. Leo natives would resemble the Aries, but Leo has a higher natural feeling of values and honor and prefers persuasion to artifice. Leo has historically represented the imperial or government powers. The people born under this sign have a virile capacity, a noble and patriotic character, and a spirit for justice. This noble spirit elevates the native Leo to loftier heights above all the small and tedious daily aspects of life.

Ruled by the Sun, the sign of Fire, Leo is the strongest of all the Zodiac signs. The Sun gives these people the so-called "God's light". The native-born Leo is best known his strong will. He is generally successful in work and in life. He has a very special generosity marked by his noble, proud and lofty spirit. Sun-like, Leo thinks on a grand scale and aspires to grandeur.

While Cancer may often be observed succeeding by charm and wit and playing up to the situation, Leo succeeds by imposing himself on the situation. While a Leo may possess talent, often the success of these individuals is due more to the sheer force of his or her personality. Leo is most capable of making a grand entrance, of flourishing in the lime light and attention of others, and of holding that attention. Their entire stature and bearing demands and commands the attention of other people. With the full strength of all the power of the Sun, Leo struts with the innate embodiment of regal force, almost as if commanding the attention of anyone and everyone. That attention is given to the Leo native too while others strive to understand and comprehend this bearing and presence. This innate ability to so impress others simply with bearing and pride and noble-like grace produces a complex and curious person who others want to know and understand. And Leo is well worth knowing. For only Leo aspires to shine as the Sun and command and direct as forcefully as the light from the Sun commands our interests and directs our everyday lives.

The emotional natures of the natives of Leo are suggestive of the fiery white heat of the glowing Sun. Their warmth seems to glow and encompass those around them. They are endowed by the rulership of the Sun with the vigor and vitality of great personal strength as well as a powerful and discerning righteousness. They love what is fair and just. Leo individuals make natural leaders and are capable of attaining great heights and immense successes in life.

How to Find Your Soul-Mate, Stars, and Destiny

Leo Personality

The Sun, the planetary ruler of Leo, bestows upon the natives of this sign a seemingly energetic and vital force which radiates as a powerful aura, enhancing the lives and prospects of these people. Leo individuals exude optimism, making a strong and lasting impression on others. And they are all too self-aware of this attribute as well. The well-aspected Leo native is in full command of any and all situations, directing and steering others toward an accomplishment whether it be for pleasure or for financial successes. There is an almost regal air of authority about this person. They even walk with pride. Others sense this as well as the Leo's natural ability to lead, to make instant decisions, and to follow up with aggressive actions. Leo is also capable of being impulsive and of following hunches. Leo seems to be born with a strong luck and very often succeeds at what others, especially those more timid, might have failed at or surely would never have dared to attempt in the first place.

With their strong, outgoing personalities and characteristics, the Leo native is quite capable of being dramatically outspoken. For many this can develop into a fiery temperament if it serves their purpose. These people are ambitious and aggressive. They lead to the forefront with direct, dynamic and energetic action and are never fearful of being authoritative or reluctant to be commanding.

But then all of the signs of the Zodiac produce two very different types of persons, and this is true of the individuals born under the sign of Leo as well. If not well-developed, or well-aspected, the Leo individual can be domineering to the point of being tyrannical. This individual's pride grows into a calculating arrogance. This is the person who uses pure aggression to attain leadership or to reach the top of a group, using whatever means are deemed necessary. And they show no fear or doubts about pushing the group in whatever direction they feel is best suited for their personal purposes. The natural Leo pride turns into an overbearing boldness. The mannerisms of this person can be patronizingly haughty and disdainful of others. Many of these people display an insolence that turns ambition into pretensions. There is found in many of these individuals the same desire for recognition, but they want it now not after attaining any great skill or achieving any accomplishments. These persons possess the same burning desire for fame, power and leadership, and will not stop at anything to obtain what they feel they all ready deserve.

Most Leo's fall short of that description, and are found to be both loyal and trustworthy. Generosity is also top on the list of Leo attributes. But Leo natives, if not cautious, have been known to be generous to a fault. Like Aries, they aren't always the best at judging others, and because they love being the center of attention and gathering praise, their pride can be their downfall. These individuals are very susceptible to flattery and adoration. Gregarious and often fun loving, Leo's warm up to the group, and often the group consists of people who are naturals at compliments and flattery and of taking advantage of the Leo nature.

Leos aren't above reproach. Many of these individuals will play favorites among friends or business associates, making promises that are impossible to keep. Some use their sense of self-worth and pride as sources of snobbery, and they take the royal treatment just a little too far.

Be cautious of disagreeing with the mighty Leo. This is almost against his ability to comprehend. And then too, once Leo determines a person has been guilty of insincere or excessive flattery or praise, that person will encounter the infamous Leo fury which is capable of swift, forceful and unrelenting action. Once the Leo anger is dispelled, these natives tend to push it from their minds. Their active lives and busy minds are far too busy on other pursuits to hold grudges or even waste time thinking about past transgressions. They want to move on. Leo natives are capable of erasing people and events from their minds if it is inconvenient to dwell on the subject.

The very nature of Leo compels him to strive to achieve, to reach the top, to better the competition, to succeed at all endeavors in life. From a psychological perspective, this person must out reach or better their own beginnings. They must prove to their own fathers and mothers that they can achieve even more, do even better, acquire even more. The Leo son of a brilliant and successful father is a very frustrated individual. Leo is born self-aware of his strong powers, but to sustain these qualities, this person must also prove his or her worthiness. Leo natives possess a drive to utilize their aggressiveness to produce effective results for themselves and for others. This is necessary in order to win the praise they so much crave and need for their self-acclimation. Their very generosity develops from this nature to reward those who have enabled them to lead and to provide. Leo's motives are consciously positive and well intended. They want what's best. And they want to decide what is best. This is necessary to underscore their own sense of accomplishment.

Leos are driven for accomplishment and to lead; and to attain this requires knowledge and experience. A well-aspected Leo individual has not only acquired those traits, but they also possess some degree of wisdom and a strong desire to provide support and protection to others. This person uses fair and constructive authority and sound judgment to make decisions. They have a maturity and understanding that comes from empathy, kindness and a capacity for loving others. Leos understand that they must earn the admiration and adulation of others by achieving and succeeding at their goals. Secondly, this aspiration can also bestow upon these individuals their inclination toward a generous nature. Leo natives most realize and appreciate the full strength of their leadership abilities when it results in success for their goals and their aspirations for themselves and for others. It is necessary that this success also result in praise for the Leo who brought about the accomplishment in the first place.

Leo natives are known for having a magnanimous personality. They are extroverted and charming, and overly capable of functioning well with other people and in a crowd. They are spontaneous in speech, mannerisms and wit. The Leo natives appear to possess a natural magnetism, and at the same time are generally well meaning. They are direct and open, and have a tendency to frankly state their opinions. At times, however, they can be too direct and blunt, and they don't always consider what response others will have to their opinions and to their commanding natures.

As with all the Zodiac signs, there are some Leo natives who are not particularly industrious. In fact, there are those Leos who are considered lazy. This develops through the same innate tendencies possessed by other Leo individuals. These people have the same inherent pride and sense of self as other Leo natives. But, naturally gifted with a radiant personality, they don't develop any other aspect of their lives. That is, there is a lack of substance to their personality. The lazy Leo predetermines that his or her way is best, and then simply chooses to delegate any and all tasks to others. Perhaps, the lazy nature is best exposed in some Leo students who attempt to pass through school on the power of their personalities rather than scholastic achievements. The attitude might best be explained as a feeling that life is so good and so easy, why work at it. Many of these individuals, to their chagrin, often have rude awakenings when they realize that much of life is dependent on skills, a developed intellect and hard work.

What is to be made of the claim that many Leos have a quick temper? That may quite often be the case. Then again other Leo natives channel this type of energy toward tenacity and determination. Their strong wills and determination may lead them just as they lead others. Known for loyalty and for their leadership abilities, Leo is most offended by betrayal, insincerity, or deceit. This can offend Leo to the point of making him vulnerable, disappointed, and disillusioned. It is at this point that his anger may be exposed in harsh and violent words.

It is the Leo, possessed by a strong drive and a desire for success, who can easily develop into a workahlolic. It seems that he very naturally becomes dedicated his career, and he strives to attain his goals and the eventual success that this hard work will bring. Some Leo individuals become perfectionists in their drive to be the best at what they do. The Leo self-respect is most directly related to a job well done, and you have a tendency to expect the same of others. This tenacity provides you with the desire to excel no matter how initially tedious the task at hand may become. You understand that it is by these minor accomplishments that one day you may well be the person in charge, the leader.

Others appear to be drawn to the powerfulness of the Leo personality. This may partially be due to Leo's confident and vigorous nature. Leo individuals aspire to success and at the same time, success, honors and awards follow this dynamic and hard working individual. Your magnetic personality results in others wanting to know you, and this is only natural. To do well, the Leo native must adopt the sensitivities necessary to deal with the interpersonal relationships in both his or her private and professional life. Adulation will carry one only so far. After that, people want to get to know the real person behind this strong, outgoing nature. True success in life can only be realized after a person develops the inner strengths necessary for sharing himself with others. And any real sharing of any depth comes with possessing the ability to listen to and to learn from others. What are the dreams and desires of others? What are their inner thoughts? By becoming aware of the needs and desires of others, Leo individuals attain an even higher position in life. One that is granted by a true and accepting nature of others while at the same time acquiring all the successes and honors that are needed to make you feel that true power of attainment.

How to Find Your *Soul-Mate, Stars, and Destiny*

Leo Character

Leo, the Lion, proud and arrogant, grants the natives of this sign a confident and persistent nature. Born of the Sun sign, these individuals appear to exude warmth, and there seems about them an aura of dynamism and strength. With their lofty and ambitious natures, comes a natural bearing of dignity and distinction. The intuitive intellect of these individuals aspires to noble causes, success, and important and grand ideas. The native Leo is persevering and loves above all else to be a leader among men and women. These people are also loyal and trustworthy and make every attempt to avoid unfair treatment of others. They much prefer to be honorable in all aspects of their lives. Magnanimous and warm-hearted, they possess a liveliness of imagination and inspiration. They are known for their penetrating, determined minds and strong organizational abilities.

Leo natives love being surrounded by people. If necessary, this individual will draw an admiring crowd. This is true in both the personal, social and business life of the Leo native. You love being surrounded by your friends, family or associates. Not one to sit at home alone, you seek out social or community activities in which you can become involved. You also enjoy cultural events whether it be music, art or other performances. Any activity involving other people or crowds attracts your attention. You also find yourself drawn to sports and athletic events.

Leo natives have an almost urgent desire to dominate and control their situation. Not timid, you express your opinions eloquently and strongly, and you are seldom at a loss for words. You may be impulsive and controlling, but generally you are kind and gentle at the same time. You know and realize your power and your ability and most of the time you don't feel that harsh words are necessary to obtain what you want. You would much prefer to be persuasive and simply have others agree with you without any argument. When others do disagree with you, this comes as somewhat of a surprise to you and you find yourself having to stop and think, to re-judge the situation, and then to firmly restate your opinions. You are not one to give in easily or to be easily persuaded against your personal ideas or ideals. This is especially true when it comes to your values which you feel strongly about. You feel you are right, and, therefore, there is no reason for any discussion. This also may be partially due to your strong inclination toward not wasting your energy unnecessarily. You much prefer to reserve your energy for more important activities rather than using or wasting it on needless discussions or arguments. Leo natives feel so strongly about their personal opinions that they sometimes have problems identifying with or relating to the ideas and feelings of other people. This, at times, causes you problems and on more than one occasion, your interpersonal skills appear to lack in development.

Your radiant vitality actually seems to burn brightest when you are showered with praise and compliments. And in return you are generous in your admiration for others too. Your passion for acquiring immense power and position doesn't prevent you from being generous, especially if you are admired for it. In fact, you have been known on numerous occasions to be overly generous. But then, for the most part, you handle your finances well and your generous nature doesn't appear to become a problem in your life.

How to Find Your Soul-Mate, Stars, and Destiny

Your confidence in yourself, your self-awareness and self-reliance draws others to you and enhances your leadership abilities. Others seek you out to lead or to take charge because you seem to be able to direct energetically but at the same time effortlessly. Leo natives are themselves drawn to people of position, power, influence and affluence. And these people are as easily impressed by and drawn to the magnanimous aura of Leo natives as are other people. The Leo native is appreciated and admired by many because this person has a strong desire not only to lead but to succeed as well. The great love in your life is success more so than even money. Financial success is a secondary goal proceeding naturally from the primary goal of attaining a worthwhile and praise worthy position in life.

At the same time, Leo doesn't reject others based on their lack of attainment. Leo natives are known to be accepting and tolerant of almost everyone including the less fortunate. Again, in this respect, the Leo native is quite capable of displaying his or her generous and giving nature. You appear to enjoy offering your assistance and guidance to another person then sending the other person on his way. This copious giving of your resources and of your time and energy provides you with a feeling of fulfillment, a sense of power and achievement.

Leo natives are inspired most with clear, spontaneous and enlightening ideals and values. These are most usually based on down-to-earth principles not on abstract theory. You appear to know inherently what is right and what is wrong. While not judgmental, you have a strong sense of what is just and you can become indignantly opposed to unfairness. You combine most naturally idealism with realism. This Leo objectivity is exhibited not only in your everyday life, but in the manner in which you set your goals, your values in life, and how you establish your overall outlook or perception of life.

In so many areas of the Leo native's life there appears to be no middle ground. With your strong opinions and your strong natures, you take a firm stand and hold your ground against any and all opposition. You have a strong dislike for any injustices, and you have no appreciation for the middle ground. There is no gray area as far as your are concerned. Something is either right or wrong, good or bad, the right decision or the wrong decision. You make a decision and you hold your ground in all matters. And in difficult matters, you are capable of reacting instantaneously.

Leo natives have a strong temperament. You understand what needs to be done and how to do it. The Leo native is compelled to think big and can refuse to accept limitations on his or her ideas or actions. You know and understand your purpose. Opposed, you are capable of a quick and spontaneous temperamental outburst even to the point of becoming furious at times, but this anger is quickly dispelled. At the same time, for the most part you are not mean spirited or hateful. You resent all forms of complications and personal criticism as you don't feel this is necessary or the correct method for handling difficult situations. You have no interest in the many little intrigues of interpersonal relationships that seem to distract others from their purpose. You are direct and strong and straight to the point, and you don't waste any of your efforts or energies on thoughts or actions involving revenge. You don't feel that expending your energies in the pursuit of revenge would further your own personal ambitions.

By nature, you show a preference for stability and calmness in your life. The Leo individual can be extremely patient and long suffering. However, you can also be intense and impetuous and, once aroused, you know no fear, you neither accept nor acknowledge a defeat, nor do you readily admit to a fault. Like the Lion, Leo persons, with their quick and fiery temper, can be pushed to that point of reacting to a situation. Then with your inherent directness and frankness of speech, which is quite often delivered eloquently, you at times alienate people. And unfortunately, as you go through life, you will probably make more than one enemy.

Leo natives have a preference for establishing and building their existence based on their own work and accomplishments. It goes without saying that you love being your own boss. As in all other areas of your life, you love your freedom. It is also important to you to be actively engaged in some pursuit to further your goals. You prefer to be working and you focus a great deal of your energies both mental and physical toward your career. If some circumstance forces you out of your career, job or business, you can become despondent and depressed.

Loyal to your friends, a Leo native will defend a friend, stand up for a principle, and go to battle for a cause. You are known for being truthful and honest, and because of this you are susceptible to the lies and deceitful actions of others. Once so deceived, you can become bitter and severely over-critical of others. Your great pride is your greatest source of strength, and at other times, the greatest cause of your defeat.

Leo demonstrates a great tenacity to follow his purpose or his ideas and goals. He is determined and have a strong will power to succeed at all his endeavors. Then too there are those Leos who will choose to attempt daring, adventuresome or difficult, and bold endeavors. The Leo character, in these instances, are rash and impulsive, and seems not to know nor to accept any boundaries.

The Leo natives strive to succeed, to lead, to rise above the ordinary, to boldly attempt whatever actions will bring success and acclimation into their lives. You have that quality about you that inspires others, and you are the most naturally born leader. Many Leo natives have a love for attainment whether it be power, leadership, fame, success or financial riches. Your aspiring and ardent desire for recognition and accomplishment lead you just as you choose to lead others. You exhibit a firmness and resolution to be steadfast and reliable and to set a determined direction for yourself and for those who you are involved with. Your vivacious and proud spirit abides in you and in all that you do.

According to the ancient astrologers, you, Leo, were born to know great successes in life. This will, of course, depend to a large degree on how well you utilize the abundant gifts that the rulership of the Sun granted to those born of this sign.

How to Find Your *Soul-Mate, Stars,* and *Destiny*

Leo Destiny

Leo appears to be born for success. These individuals set high goals and seek to rise above the masses, to reach the top. At the same time, they are drawn to other people with strong personalities who exhibit purpose, individuality, and strong egos. Leo is considered a sign of abundance, generosity and eventual success. The Leo natives attain positions of authority, power and prestige through their own hard work and tenacity. Their honors and awards are well earned. The location of the Moon has an uplifting affect on the native emotionally and socially, predisposing the individual to responsibility and to respect or to positions of leadership and management.

It is considered that there will be gains through others including superiors and those of position and social standing. It may well be that a wealthy patron will see in you that special quality that deserves a chance at leadership and attainment. There is some indication that the native will receive financial resources through investments. Or these may come through speculation. In some cases, these resources will be realized from an inheritance, and in other cases it will be associated with occupations connected with entertainment.

If Mars is afflicted, it threatens disappointment and sorrow in love, the death of a loved one, or an emotional separation. There may be problems with both supervisors and with subordinates in your career life. There is a strong indication of loss through speculative ventures. Also, there may be difficulties through accidents, injuries, and/or fires.

The Leo native has an inner drive to be industrious and aspiring, but this person may also be inclined toward moderation. The individual can become strong willed, ardent, determined and even appears at times to be eccentric in wanting his or her own way. With an occasional inclination to disregard traditions and conventions, this person can display a strong, independent and at times rebellious nature. This may be because Leo's don't handle being ordered about by others very well, and have a strong dislike for having their own opinions and orders contradicted. These natives possess an emotional attachment for being free of constrictions and limitations in order to experience the adventures in life, and they have a pronounced inclination toward impulsive, daring and exciting experiences. There may be what appears to others as unusual and strong preferences, particular likes and dislikes, and forceful opinions pertaining to almost all areas of life. From time to time, the Leo native may be involved in unusual experiences developing from relationships with the opposite sex that may include danger, unhappiness, separation, and estrangement. Leo natives may experience difficulties in youth brought on by their overly energetic and willful natures and in some instances through their father.

If well-aspected, there is an indication that the Leo native is not only ambitious but dignified, benevolent and kind with a generous and sympathetic nature and some intuitive ability. The emotions are well developed adding to the intuitive ability and allowing the native to be understanding and perceptive of the need of others. This person is highly developed spiritually.

There is also a strong indication for a love of sports, entertainment, recreation and the fine arts including literature, music and the visual arts. There may be an intense love of poetry, drama, and public office. Tthis individual also experiences unusual drives, inclinations, and feelings.

Frequently relationships with the opposite sex can develop into unusual situations, and with some individuals these will result in great disappoints and emotional turmoil.

If afflicted, the Leo native is overly aware of the pleasures in life and spends an excessive amount of time on pleasure and self-gratification. This person will most probably allow the emotions and senses too lead rather than using sound reasoning ability. The afflicted individual expends his or her energy reserves rapidly and often times uselessly in unproductive pursuits. This person may be more impulsive and thoughtlessly generous expending his sympathies on unworthy causes or friends who use flattery to sway the thoughts and feelings of Leo, who is all too susceptible to praise.

If Uranus is well aspected, there is an indication for metaphysical insights and intuitions or an aptitude for electrical and engineering mechanics, or a distinctive public or professional position. This person becomes spiritually inclined and aware.

Leo strives to do well at whatever he or she attempts. These individuals are very thorough in their work and will go to great lengths or even risks to complete what was started. Often honors or acclaim are awarded without the individual seeking them. Success often is found through personal endeavors and hard work, but can also come through relations or influential people. There is an indication for gain through associations with friends and/or by commodities trading. The father is important to the success of the Leo native, and these individuals may experience disagreements with the father at times. But if the father dies before the individual is an adult, it can result in unforeseen difficulties. In some instances, Leos suffer the death of the first born child. These natives may also experience accidents through travel, but no serious injuries. There are numerous journeys, but most of these involve travel by land which is often associated with business which produce good results. The Leo native may be aided by a wealthy or well-placed person of the opposite sex. Financial gains may be experienced through associates or friends even though the Leo temperament may cause arguments at the same time. Unknown enemies of the opposite sex are indicated but are not a cause for distress. There is some indication for friendships with artists and writers.

Whatever the natural inclination that predisposes these Leo born natives, the Fire sign of the Sun is known for being graced with successes in life. Again, it is for the most part up to the individual to develop the skills and attitudes necessary for success and to exploit these natural gifts to their fullest.

How to Find Your Soul-Mate, Stars, and Destiny
Leo Occupation

Leo natives appear to have been born to lead. The diligent individual who acquires the experience, education or training, and knowledge is endowed with the qualities necessary for positions of authority, responsibility and leadership. You appreciate it when your accomplishments and leadership abilities are recognized by others. You strive not only for recognition but also for the opportunity for advancement. You appear to prefer mental to physical endeavors. And being extroverted and congenial, you possess the talent to inspire others and to be a leader among your friends and business associates. The natives of this Sun-sign are bestowed with a luminous quality. They love to be center stage. You are ardent in your presentations and command the attention of others. You are quite often literally the center of attention. You possess an innate sense of power, and on more than one occasion you have been accused of throwing your weight around. You are not one to work quietly out of the lime light. You have a great desire to be in the public eye and you love publicity and public acclaim. You are greatly attracted to all the glitter that is associated with fame, position and success. You feel born to a position of greatness.

With your fondness for recognition and accomplishment, you aspire to positions of responsibility. Leo natives have been known to make successful attorneys, judges, bankers, financiers, brokers and CEOs. You have a tendency to make aggressive but conservative and responsible decisions. Leo natives find that they have a love for uniforms and rank, and you may find that you excel in military careers where you can be promoted based on the merit of your accomplishments and skills. At the same time, other occupations that offer the opportunity to show off your regal bearing while wearing a uniform might appeal to you also.

With the ability to deduce and assimilate information, Leo natives are strongly inclined toward all scientific fields of endeavor. They possess the ability to perceive the essence of facts and theories, to test the possibilities of theories, and to focus their energies on explaining and providing this information to others. Leo individuals are profound at realizing the importance of current information and utilizing it to produce new and more interesting ideas. The kindness of the Leo character and their strong verbal abilities allow them to explain to others what they have discerned in their studies.

Other Leos have utilized their talents to become well known ministers and public speakers. Leo naturally does well in any field which requires a magnanimous person who can lead, inspire and persuade others while all the time being both entertaining and uplifting. He has the ability to intuitively read his audience and to respond to it. This ability rests with his charismatic and genial manner. Again, he is the natural leader and this is best seen when he is in front of a crowd. This flair for the dramatic also produces talented actors and entertainers. With the natural flair of the Leo, it is recognized that both men and women born under the influences of this sign are remarkable cooks and chefs.

In the financial or business world, the Leo native is known for his or her ability to take that necessary risk to achieve success. In this way, you excel where others might not be as daring or as imaginative as you. And as always, you strive to be the leader in the situation, showing others how best to complete the job at hand while at the same time striving for your own personal success. Leo natives have been known to be successful in the fields of advertising, publicity, publishing, television and radio, the film making industry, stage productions, and even in manufacturing and sales.

Leo, guard against being overly persevering and agressive in your business life. Watch your tendency to be bossy or impatient with others. Unfortunately, you may have to climb that ladder of success rather than pushing your way to the top. But whatever field you decide to enter, be aware that you possess all the qualities necessary to attain your goals and desires. By best understanding yourself and by taking a personal look at your strengths and weakness, you can determine for yourself which field of endeavor you are most likely to succeed in.

Leo Marriage

Taking into consideration the very nature of Leo natives, it is imperative that they exercise great care and judgment in choosing a mate. Leo individuals, to be successful in marriage, have a great need for a spouse who is understanding and emotionally supportive. Leos will not find a great deal of enjoyment with companions who play the adversary or with spouses who want to be in the right, all-knowing, and to have their own way in the marital arrangement. The spouse of the Leo native needs to be diplomatic in deportment as well as caring and compassionate and possessing a talent for being complimentary. On the other hand, an individual who is too meek, reserved or less than passionate will not hold the heart of the Leo individual either. Leos require a person who displays a mixture of loving concern and an active mind and energetic nature. This doesn't mean that you won't do well with an independent mate. Quite the opposite. The chances are that you choose to go your own way quite a bit, and the other person in your marital relationship needs to be capable of having a life of his or her own as well.

Leo natives as young adults may be virile, impulsive, and at times rash. They may be convinced that they know their own mind and that their decisions are correct. Rebelling against all restraints, parental influences, or societal conventions, Leo natives at this age may decide to jump into an early marriage which they are convinced was destined to be. However, Leos should restrain from marrying too young or too hastily as this step can lead to unhappiness, heartache and even to sorrow and disastrous situations. It is important for Leo individuals to take their time to meet the right person and to develop a strong and lasting relationship based on shared values, interests, and a devotion to each other. To do this successfully requires some degree of emotional growth. The person must know his or her own nature as well as the nature of the other person. That type of knowledge comes with a maturity derived from life experiences. And life experiences require a bit of time to acquire and to learn from. Leo natives do best when they wait until they have settled somewhat into their positions and their lifestyles. Then it is a much less complicated task to find another person who fits best in that life with you.

For some reason, Leos appear not to have the best of luck in marriage. This is especially true for those born in the first and second decans of this sign. This is often attributed to the Leos lack of ability to judge the character of others. Then again, the fault may rest more with the Leo individuals who project themselves through their magnetic personalities rather than allowing others to really get to know them. In other words, there may be Leo natives who charmingly put forth their best foot while disguising or hiding any faults in order to impress the other person. And remember, there are those Leo natives who only develop their personalities, and who find that they do just as well in life. However, when a mate realizes that there's little substance behind this glorious personality, it can be a major disappointment.

Some people will work hard to save a relationship, and others will get out of an unpleasant situation as fast as possible. Leos when faced with a troublesome relationship, will often choose to end it and move on, regardless of the emotional consequences to the other person. And chances are the Leo native wastes little time moving straight on to another relationship. Leo women are often found to be more successful at marriage, and this may be due to their sincere and caring natures.

If Leo is at the Ascendant, the Aquarius is in the House of Marriage, and marriage will come later in life and will be very rational. Marriage with an Aquarius (January 20-February 18) who has a compatible nature is a suggestion. It is the opposite sign of the Zodiac, but offers fewer inharmonious characteristics than persons born of other signs. You might also consider marriage with an Aries (March 21-April 20) native if both of you exhibit mature and understanding characteristics. Remember that Aries individuals can be strong-willed and impulsive also, and to do well with a Leo native these inclinations must be well controlled. The Leo native might also consider marriage to a Libra (September 23-October 22) when both parties are well-developed emotionally. A relationship between poorly developed Leo and Libra individuals could easily lead to a life of pleasures rather than accomplishments. There are many cases of Leo and Virgo (August 23-September 22) being strongly physically attracted to each other and making good marriages.

It is of greatest importance to Leo natives to find a mate who shares the same degree of development socially, culturally and educationally. Someone who shares your likes and dislikes, and who has similar interests, values and sentiments will be the most compatible and will enable you to find fulfillment and happiness in your home life. Take the time to develop your emotional capabilities in order to be able to share life fully with the person who you choose.

How to Find Your Soul-Mate, Stars, and Destiny

The Leo Man

Leo, ruled by the Sun, is bestowed with an intense and forceful personality. You are dynamic and possess a great personal charm. You have a flair for drama and love to entertain your group of friends, family or associates. Your strong extroverted characteristics are displayed in your ardent and often times fiery nature. You are capable of being either eloquent or flamboyant, which ever the situation calls for. And you can be either conservative and conventional or the greatest risk taker of your day. The risk or thrill of adventure calls to you and you seek some avenue for a release of these impulses. You never fear being overlooked in the crowd as you know you will stand out and be noticed, will draw attention even when you don't strive to do so. You are quite capable of possessing outstanding illustrious qualities and the regal bearing, like the Lion, of a natural leader of others. You appear remarkably bright and marked with a brilliance of expression. You are ardent in your zeal and your personal opinions. And with your noble nature you appear to soar above the crowd like a lofty hawk.

Above all else, the Leo man appears to grasp and fully understand the importance of being himself. You have a strong self-awareness of your strengths of character and of your abilities. You know within yourself that you were born to lead. You are charismatic and draw others to you. You inspire others to believe in what you have to say (even in the instances where your manner is stronger than your content). You are discerning and knowledgeable and firmly believe in your opinions.

As with persons of other signs, there are Leo natives who are poorly developed also. These persons have a tendency to use their natural gifts to get by in life rather than to develop or utilize these gifts to the fullest. This person has a tendency to use his charm to his advantage rather than to more fully develop his intellect. In other words, once the verbiage is dropped there isn't much to be found behind the personality. This person is overly concerned with winning praise and applause rather than achieving any real accomplishment. Or perhaps it is this craving for personal glory which drives the person who wants more than anything to have others constantly feeding his ego with praise and flattery. Other Leos are overly arrogant, intimidating and condescending especially toward those in a subordinate position. And still others are conceited, pushy, and ruthless people who will stop at nothing to gain the top position or to reach their goals whatever they may be. These individuals would benefit from analyzing their personal motives and then striving to overcome these lesser abilities and traits.

As has been mentioned, the Leo native is best known for his concern for his fellow man and for his generosity. He must be careful not to become too generous and also to examine his motives in this area. Charity, to be genuine must come from the heart not from a desire for praise and recognition.

In his relationships, the Leo man, while being personable and shining in a crowd, can actually be somewhat withdrawn or aloof in more personal relationships. He has a tendency to hold back and to not open up. He doesn't share his inner self freely with the world or those around him. He can be both virile and passionate in a romantic involvement, but not always sharing. In other words, he loves sex, but not necessarily emotional intimacy. In fact, some Leo's are known for being great sexual partners, but emotionally cold and aloof. If he is unfaithful it is because of his great vanity, and his need to be admired. In marriage, the Leo male while being possessive may give his wife complete autonomy because he is preoccupied with his own personal, social and professional affairs. This man is generally well-dressed and neat. You possess an admirable affinity for many aspects of life including work, love, and entertainment. While you are a good husband and father, you must guard against being too preoccupied with other aspects of life to fully enjoy family life. There is also some complaint that Leo men can be possessive, overbearing, and even tyrannical. Rather than argument, this may turn his way with words into insults and verbal abuse in his effort to break down his opponent and to win.

Of course, no discussion of the Leo male is complete without mentioning his courage. This is the man who more than any others is ardently aspiring in his desire for rank, fame and power. As determined as a force of nature, this man may trip on his journey through life, but he will find few obstacles that he can't overcome. And they proceed dynamically with daring and courage in all that they undertake. It has been said that the men born of this sign are as courageous as the Lion. When it comes time to do battle, it is the Leo-born man who one wants on his side. Many of the greatest warriors and leaders in history were born to this sign including Napoleon Bonaparte. The Leo man personifies and exemplifies the strong heart and will power necessary to attain all that he is capable of dreaming. His aspirations in many instances become his realities.

The Leo Women

Leo women are greatly gifted with the same qualities as the men of this sign. Strong, independent and inspiring, they too possess the glowing, luminous personality bestowed by the rulership of the Sun. You are crystal clear in your wants and aspirations. Leo women are known for being as extroverted as the men of this sign. They too possess a certain prowess, a certain majesty that is shown in their bearing and presentation. You are at home in a crowd and love the opportunity to mingle with others and to express yourself. Your sympathetic, generous and warm-hearted affections gain you the admiration of others. Generally speaking, you are self-assured, and you take a great deal of pride in yourself, your home, and your career. You possess a winning attitude in whatever you aspire to accomplish whether it be social or professional. However, you aren't recognized as one who is open to compromise. More than anything else, you know your mind. Neither are you known for being overly modest, humble or demure. You have never been accused of being the shrinking, timid or dull female. In fact, you may rarely ever admit that you make a mistake. You are known for your enthusiastic outlook on life which when necessary is courageous. You face life bravely putting forth your best face daily. You do not shirk from responsibility or avoid situations requiring a strong will and hard work. If anything, you must guard against focusing your great courage of life into smaller conflicts of interest where your enthusiasm and strength become revengeful or develop into animosity toward those who disagree with you or who have tried in some way to hurt you. However, your greatest weakness is being too nice to people, especially men, who pay you compliments. Attempt to develop your judgment in these matters.

How to Find Your Soul-Mate, Stars, and Destiny

If your preferences were known, you would choose a loving and lasting relationship over a series of less serious love affairs. You are loving, kind, affectionate, and faithful when you find the love of your life. It is necessary for you to select a mate who is as strong emotionally as you are. A weak man will not be able to sustain your interest, and you will find yourself walking over him and propping him up at the same time. When that does happen, you are not fully opposed to playing the field in an effort to find someone who challenges your spirit. You will also find that you need to find that special someone who is your equal socially, culturally and intellectually and who is equally passionate in order to remain interested in the relationship.

While you are not the most sentimental of people, in love you become devoted and faithful. You are sincere in your caring and in your affections for your loved ones. You are a good, kind and loving wife and mother. As a mother, you are gentle and compassionate but also highly protective. And, like the Leo man, you may be a talented cook if you decide to develop this skill.

Above all else, you desire some element of adventure or challenge in your life. The mundane or monotonous daily routine is not for you. Your career should be a challenging one that offers you the necessary outlets for your personality and abilities as you too possess the talents necessary for being a successful and powerful leader. In this area, you may find that you prefer your own business rather than working in a subordinate position for another company. You have the personal strength to do well on your own in your own business, and you prefer to focus your abilities on your personal successes. You are proud and independent, generous and gregarious, and endowed with an imaginative mind capable of assimilating facts and details. Combine that with the willingness to work hard, and it sounds like the ingredients for success in whatever endeavor you choose.

Many Leo women may find that they are natural actors with a flair for the dramatic. With their astute, capable minds, this appears to be a natural field for a career choice. Added to this is the Leo grace and command of presence. You always enter a room as if it were a stage, and you were the main character in the play of life. Being a romantic adds to this flair for drama and your natural love for entertainment.

The Leo woman must guard against being over generous, seeking flattery that can be insincere, and also failing to develop her natural gifts. Beware the power of pleasures over the mind and body. You are ardent in all that you do, and if your mind turns to the pursuits of pleasures only, you will find yourself bankrupting yourself emotionally and time and again financially.

Use all your natural talents and gifts to inspire others, to lead, and to find your well-deserved successes in life. Use the natural warmth and glow of your personality to enhance not only your life, but the life of others fortunate enough to know you. Share your passion for life with your friends, business associates and most importantly with your family. You are destined to achieve all that you aspire to and to find much success and happiness in life when all your talents are developed.

How to Find Your Soul-Mate, Stars, and Destiny

Leo Love Life

Both native men and women Leos are loving, warm, and passionate as well as intensely exciting people. They can be both loyal and protective of their lovers or mates. They are generous sometimes to a fault, and at times there appears to be few boundaries to their sentimentality and romantic expression. They are capable of loving deeply, but at the same time they expect that their admiration be returned in the same measure. With your zest for life, you are passionate and warm hearted. You have never been accused of being a dull companion, and you shun all that would hint of being boring. You are forever seeking some colorful new hint of daring excitement or adventure. New places, travel, and meeting new people appeal to you.

As a young adult, the Leo native may love a variety of experiences and pursue a number of affairs. He loves to be admired, and this seems to drive him to find new and even more admiring persons with whome to surround himself. He also loves the thrill of pursuit, the adventure of new experiences, and most of all meeting and getting to know new people.

You are not inhibited in your passions or your desires. While others may be critical of too many affairs of the heart, the Leo native derives a certain satisfaction in getting to know as many people as possible. Whether a passing fancy, a strong platonic relationship, or a sizzling rendezvous, you are receptive. Your nature is sympathetic, passionate, and fiery. You are both sincere and decisive. You know what you want, and you don't hesitate to pursue a relationship, or to guide the relationship once it is yours. Your inner feeling of regal exaltation draws others to you who want to experience this same excitement and zest for life.

Then too, Leo, when your rash and impulsive nature takes over you are more than capable of being susceptible to flattery and compliments. You may easily find yourself falling in love and losing your heart too rapidly. Especially in early adulthood, you have a tendency to follow your emotions and not your intellect. You may be completely blind to any shortcomings or incompatibilities of your partner. When you finally become aware that you made a mistake, when you finally admit it to yourself, you may well suffer great emotional trauma. However, you will rarely admit that the fault was yours. The chances are that you bounce back quickly, and soothe your wounds by finding someone else to fill your mind.

Many people play games at love, but this doesn't appear to be the nature of Leo. These individuals are emphatically direct and to the point. Having possessed a grand and illustrious personality all their lives, there was never a need to develop any forms of artifice or subtleties or to engage in attempts to charm. These people charm by nature. So the little nuances and game play of everyday life may go right over their heads. The Leo individual is much more inclined to use a lofty nature or a commanding presence to gain the upper hand in relationships and to bring the other person back under his or her command. And if that doesn't work, the Leo native is not above turning on that natural charm, barraging the other person with compliments or even flattery, or finding an outlet for his or her generous nature in what some might term bribery. But it isn't bribery to you. It is merely what you see as a sincere means of regaining a balance and harmony in the present situation so that you can get back to your life and your endeavors. Learning to use understanding and tolerance and to accept the ideas of others might add more validity to your relationships.

How to Find Your Soul-Mate, Stars, and Destiny

If you were born under the sign of Leo, you are a romantic and sincere lover who greatly appreciates that special person who shows a willingness to accept you and to admire you and above all else to allow you to lead and to dominate the situation. Above all else this person must allow you to retain your dignity. Leo natives, like all people, desire to be loved and wanted. When you find that very special person, you become not only loyal and devoted but also protective and supporting. Matched with the right partners, you Leo natives make especially devoted, admiring and protective companions. The love of Napoleon for Josephine is one of the great love stories of history.

Leo Children

Children born under the sign of Leo and the rulership of the Sun possess warm, fun-loving, and outgoing personalities. They have a vitality for life that allows them to develop numerous and diverse interests. They have a joyful quality about them, and they display this by entertaining their friends and the adults in their lives with their animated chatter and antics. They are generally talented, self-assured, strong willed and have the ability to imitate or assimilate the qualities of others. While they require strong role models, excessive demands and restrictions can prohibit them from developing their inner qualities and can even make them rebellious and contrary to adult influences. They do require discipline though and this is best supplied by providing the expectations that come from a well-established daily routine. The child also needs to learn responsibilities and self-control, but this must be accomplished in a loving and affectionate manner. The Leo child responds best to praise, compliments and positive reinforcement. Being compelled to live up to the standards others set for him, may be disagreeable to this child. Leo children have a strong sense of their own being and their own likes and dislikes. They do best when the adults in their life recognize and respect their natures.

Blessed with strong mental abilities, many of these children may learn quickly, but at the same time they may not like to study. Encouraging these children to develop study habits will benefit them by providing them with the knowledge necessary to sustain them in life. It is all too easy and too tempting for these children to run joyfully through life on the strength of their wills and on their boundless personalities. By offering the best in education, this child also learns to develop all of his or her other natural gifts.

These children do not respond well to criticism. They may simply just not agree with the adult who is criticizing or punishing them. Adults need to take the time to explain the situations that arise and to talk to these children offering them explanations and illustrations. Teach cause and effect. Teach consequences but guard against doing this in a harsh or punitive manner.

These may well be the children who perceive at an early age that they are meant to pursue a particular field or to accomplish a worthwhile deed. Encourage their aspirations, their dreams and their role-playing. This is after all training for the adult years of their lives. Encourage the natural creativity in these children, their love of life, and their abundance of charm and warmth. Their energy level will appear to subside if it is well channeled into positive and challenging activities. Make every attempt to guide this child into healthy and productive pursuits such as sports or other recreational activities. These types of activities prove beneficial in providing outlets to be with other children in the same age group. And it is group activities that will teach them to interact with others in a positive manner. After all this planning of activities what is next? At home, these children would benefit from having a well scheduled day that included plenty of rest and a time for relaxation in a quiet, peaceful setting. They are already excited enough. They don't need their environment to further excite their natures.

Above all else offer a family setting that provides for emotional security and that offers an environment of acceptance, love, and appreciation. These children love to be needed. Let them know that they are both needed and wanted.

How to Find Your *Soul-Mate*, *Stars*, and *Destiny*

Relationships with Other Signs

Leo natives make warm and lasting friendships many of which last for a life time. They are devoted to their friends and will inconvenience themselves to help out a friend with a problem. You are the person who appears to need being needed. Your friends know that they can depend on you to be there. This is, of course, great for your ego, but if the truth were known you are sincere in your regards toward your friends and your companions. You have a tendency to take the lead, to initiate plans, and to set the pace for your group of friends. Generally, you are most gregarious and love to entertain your friends or to plan social gatherings or outings.

Then too these natives, forever blessed by the Sun, are warm and fun-loving. There is often some excitement in the air when they are around. This draws friends and attention to them. Once they make a friend, Leo natives are quite capable of remaining devoted and loyal for life. In no other sign does one find an individual who is more benevolent to his enemies or a friend more loyal. Leo natives are masters of their own feelings. They are unbendable, determined and secure within themselves and of their means for achieving their purposes. They are as determined as a force of nature.

In friendships, you may find that you get along well with Aries natives as this sign is also known for being forceful. You may find that you and Aries have similar likes and dislikes. In comparison, you may discover that Taurus individuals are too reserved and conservative for your nature, and the Taurus natives may not appreciate your extroverted manner. With time and effort, you get along well with Gemini natives who are also sunny and outgoing. You may find similar interests with natives of Cancer who share your flair for drama and who prefer lasting, devoted friendships. Other Leo natives may be compatible with you in that they naturally share your love and zest for life. While Libra may share your idealism toward life, Scorpio natives, while interesting and stimulating, may have very different interests and perspectives than you. In some regards, Leo individuals may find that they most prefer Sagittarius natives. Virgo individuals can prove to be similarly brave and loyal in their friendships.

Your friends need to remember that for a strong and lasting relationship, you require their admiration and loyalty. You are capable of being kind and gentle when others treat you well. You are most sincere in your efforts towards your friends, and in this area of your life you will never be at a loss. Your life will never be dull or lonely. That is, not if you have anything to say about it. As all who know you soon learn, your greatest attribute is your kindness, and your main weakness is found in your spirit of absolute domination. You don't appreciate your authority being questioned, not by your friends, spouse or subordinates. Many will find this fault forgivable if you lead well. But of course, many others upon getting to know you well, will prefer if you learn the art of compromise and of giving of yourself. And it would be nice if you learned to admit to a fault or to a mistake once in awhile. Then again, taking into consideration the desires, likes, and dislikes of what others want is a trait worth acquiring.

Leo natives will find their strongest friendships with other Leo's and with people born around March 20 to April 17-23; January 19 to February 16-26; and November 19 to December 18-25. Those persons who are born on the 2, 8, 20, or 26 of each month as these are seen as compatible with the sign of Leo.

The source of your great strength, ardent passions and endearing charm seems to be the compliments and adulation you receive from others. You are aware of yourself and of the impact you make on others. While you aren't introspective or discerning of your own faults, you are perceptive to the effect you are having on others. You are the master at standing out in a crowd. And quite fortunately for your friends and associates, you have no malice towards others. You would much prefer to be a friend to all, to gain as much attention as possible, and to forever shine as fiercely and with as much fiery luminance as possible. That is your inner nature, and who of us can criticize you for it?

Leo Sexuality

That subject which interests us all: our own personal sexuality. Why does a person feel the way they do? Why does he or she like a certain person and not another? What arouses a person and why? On some level, these questions influences one and all. Like all aspects of our lives and lifestyles, the public attitude toward sex is ever changing and evolving. From the restrictive taboos of the Victorian Age, through the revitalization of the Industrial Age, to the make love not war of the 1960s to the commercialism of the 1980s and the 1990s, sex is always on our minds. Will the Age of Information or the Age of Aquarius bring new insights?

The American culture is not only influenced by popular trends and thought but by its unique cultural diversity as well. To the newcomer or newly arrived, American society can appear perplexing. What is difficult to understand is that in this freedom-based culture, the individual is literally free to be whoever he or she decides. And the gamut runs from the most traditional, reserved, cautious, and sexually repressed individuals to others who flaunt their sexuality, centering their lives around their sexual habits. Perhaps it is because of this very diversity that our culture makes some attempt not to be overly offensive to the sensitivities of some while giving a tolerant nod to the liberties of others. We are totally free, within the guidelines of laws, to seek divine enlightenment or to destroy ourselves with pleasures. Americans have the freedom to choose, individually, what importance their sexual behavior will play in their lives.

That being the case, sex is recognized by every serious discipline--from psychologists to scientists to astrologers--as being a central focus on individual lives. Freud saw sex as an influence on every aspect of the individual life. And from the sexist boys in the locker room to the most enlightened of intellectuals, sex remains a fundamental part of life that cannot be ignored. Get two friends together and the subject eventually turns to sex, romance, or marriage. One can blame it on the media, but sooner or later discussing the stock market gets boring, but sex never does.

There are those who hold to the theory that the primary function of sex is to have children and any other consideration is secondary. There are others for whom sex is an integral part of life, providing one of the greatest stress relievers ever invented. That all other living species procreate seasonally points to the reasoning of the second theory. But all pleasures (or temptations) in life also promote the possibilities of problems and health concerns unless a little logic is also applied.

Astrologically, the sexual nature has been examined from the Garden of Eden to the lives of contemporary celebrities. And what every serious astrologer will say is that how the individual relates to sexuality is not based on the Sun sign alone. The entire chart must be examined because each person is a unique combination of Sun, Moon, Ascendant, planets, Houses and aspects. A comparison of two charts often sheds light on compatibility. Compatibility between two people is often found when the Sun sign is in the same sign as their lover's Ascendant, or vice versa. Opposite Sun signs or an opposite Sun sign and Ascendant may also blend well together.

In a woman's chart, the placement of Venus is indicative of her sexuality while the position of Mars and the Sun indicates what kind of man she is attracted to. In a man's chart, the position of Mars tells how he relates to women, and the position of Venus and the Moon indicates what type of woman arouses him. In comparing two charts, look for the aspects of conjunction, sextile, square, trine, and oppositions. Remember that oppositions can blend. The square brings differences but much energy while conjunctions can be beneficial. The sextile and trine bring harmony. When a person's Venus and their lover's Mars are in the same sign, there is a strong attraction even if differences of opinions occur. When Venus and the other person's Ascendant are in the same sign, it adds to the sexual compatibility. Venus in the lover's sun sign brings a mutual interest while Mars in the lover's Moon sign is emotionally intense.

There is a vast variety of people found within each Sun sign, but basic characteristics and traits do exist. However, generalizations are just that and a fuller picture of the individual is reflected by the complete chart. The following section deals with Sun sign sexuality in a general manner. While the importance of sex remains the same in each Sun sign, the focus and attitudes vary.

How to Find Your Soul-Mate, Stars, and Destiny

Leo Sexuality - Man

Leo the Lion struts through his kingdom forever the king of the jungle. Always the star of his own show, wherever he goes, he bestows his most winning smile on his subjects and fans alike. Energized by the Sun, Leo knows he was born to win, and his self-confidence and magnetism illuminates that attitude. And his approach works on so many women, he loves them and leaves them, falling in and out of love and moving on to his next conquest. His companionship and his bed are a royal favor he grants to his most admiring fan. Leo thrives on admiration, recognition, and attention, and responds to flattery. Leo doesn't necessarily need to be told he's good in bed, however, because he knows he is good in bed. And with all that Sun-filled energy, sex is a requirement of life for this man.

A Leo man who finds himself in a situation where he loses his erection, is a man whose regal sensitivities have been offended in some manner. He is a natural leader, and in sex, he must dominate as well. This is a man who most prefers being on top, and who is always loyal to the most important person in his life--himself. If he becomes involved with a woman who wants to take center stage or to lead, he may as well move on to his next lovely admirer because he'll never be completely happy in such a situation. This is the stud of the jungle as well as the king, and any woman who doesn't know how to enjoy his prowess is missing out on a memorable experience. That's not to say that in modern life there isn't a Leo man who has been brow-beaten into losing his regal and erect bearing. But if that be the case, that man needs to find a Scorpio to reinstall his faith in himself and his manhood. A relationship with a Scorpio may or may not last long, but the sex will be a dynamo of exploded energy.

A debauched or perverted Leo is a man responding to something other than his Sun sign influence. The average Leo (although average hardly describes him) is a person who while he wants to lead also wants his subjects to respect his good judgment and fair-minded ways. Remember, this is a man who thrives on respect. The Sun is considered a positive influence, and that royal smile comes naturally straight from this radiant source. This is a man who wants to be trusted, who doesn't lie, and when he says he'll do something that's what he means. If he decides to be unfaithful, he isn't going to dream up a string of lies to cover his activities. He rules his own life, and he doesn't have to explain his where abouts. He goes where he wants and does what he wants. And in his own mind, he has a very good reason for being unfaithful. Either he is in a bad relationship, or his current partner isn't giving him enough adulation or proper respect or satisfying his needs. There are any number of women who will swear that this doesn't describe their wonderful Leo man. But those are the same women who are bragging and endlessly praising their Leo partner which in return makes him a man deserving of such adulation. He is a man's man who must sow his wild oats when he is young and who can't be alone. To find fulfillment, he must have admirers in his life. And he wants to rule the one he loves.

What excites Leo in bed? Energy. However demanding his daily routine, Leo always has the energy for sex. He has a preference for a very feminine partner who is sexually alluring. Fragrances and make up should be subtle and refined--nothing over powering and nothing to distract from his royal performance. Night wear should be feminine and sexy but nothing that would draw attention from the star of the show. Leo has a mental picture of his perfect lover who conforms to his standards and who he may cherish and respond to with enthusiasm. It takes little to get a response from Leo because he usually leads in this department.

To please a Leo man pay attention to his back with long, loving embraces and gently strokes up and down his spine. Back massages, kisses and trailing the tongue along the length of his back guarantees his appreciation. Leo requires little in the way of imaginative fore play or novelties in sex. Generally, the conventional methods best suit his purposes and his needs. Sexually, Leo must expend his abundance of energy and, in so doing, he replenishes his own supply. Fortunate is the woman with a happy Leo in her life. Once he settles on his true love, he has a strong preference for staying and for building a home and family.

Leo Sexuality - Woman

A sexual dynamo all wrapped up in her finery, jewels, and adornments and energetically adding to her list of available admirers. There is every possibility that this woman rules over a fiefdom of doting subjects ready and willing to do her bidding in order to win her favor. If she isn't the star of her own show, she will make a show to star in. Sun-energy driven, she is happy when being admired. And to be admired one must be admirable, which she is. The Sun influence makes the Leo man more masculine and the Leo woman more alluringly and magnetically feminine. Her very bearing draws attention to this lovely woman. She puts her emotions in their proper prospective and focuses on her needs--and being human she has sexual needs. Long ago in some faraway land, her Leo sisters more than likely decided that what was good for royalty was also good for them, and they commenced to begin the sexual liberation movement ages before it ever become popular with the public.

That's not to say that the Leo woman is any more promiscuous than women of the other signs. But this woman possesses a deep-seated need to be wanted, attended to, and openly admired. It is also important to be socially accepted and respected, and she is capable of using a great degree of calculation to remain socially acceptable and to satisfy her desires as well. But this woman can add so much energy to conventional practices that men willingly oblige her. This is a woman who has a mental picture of her perfect suitor and she may go through a long list of others before she finds her perfect match. If she settles for less than her model of perfection, she may become discontent in some manner. Does she grow old looking for her King? Some Leo women do--but not alone. Generally, though, this dynamic woman meets a man worthy of her attention and time and makes a most devoted mate. And if it doesn't work out, she always has a list of admirers to turn to. Leo are strong and daring people, but they are not loners. They cannot be alone. A Leo isn't satisfied unless receiving adulation and attention. This is a trait Leo is born too and which each Leo handles with aplomb. In other words, it simply isn't a difficult task for Leo to be surrounded by an attentive audience. Leo's drive, ambition, and dramatic flair propel her into activity, and other's can't help but be impressed with her strong self-confidence and winning air. Then there is that regal bearing and pride. This is by all means an impressive woman. And the other strong signs of the Zodiac most generally do admire her.

This isn't the tearful little lady who needs the protection of some big strong man. This is a woman who seeks a strong, powerful man who can match her own energies and who isn't frightened off by an exuberant display of lustful hunger. She may engage in unconventional sexual practices, but in her own mind she doesn't really find it necessary. She puts enough drive into the most conventional of sexual practices to make it the most memorable of experiences. She is not a woman who by nature represses her sexuality. To her sex is natural, beautiful and necessary. It is an energy which must be expressed. And with this healthy attitude, she is easily a woman who out distances her more timid female counterparts. While other women are wondering how to find a man, any man, the Leo woman is qualifying and disqualifying and adding to her list. She is comfortable and at ease with men and knows how to move in, around and through them. If this doesn't describe your Leo female, check her Moon and Ascendant.

How does a man win a Leo woman? Begin with praise and even flattery both of which she responds to. Remember, this is a competition so forget criticism and control-tactics which won't impress her in the least. She is impressed with impressive men and men strong enough to allow her to be herself. She wants plenty of attention, but this is an active woman who also needs time for her many other activities. And she needs a man strong enough to allow her to be center stage. He can also impress her with his drive and ambition. She wants a man who is going some place.

The Leo woman doesn't need to be told about her sexuality. She may have written the original book on the subject and starred in its production. She has her own personal ideas which she puts into action. She is not deterred or distracted by her sexuality which she uses quite well to her advantage. She is a sexual being, and she knows it. Her sexuality serves her well.

Leo Health

It was felt by astrologers of olden times that the Leo child, that person ruled by the Sun, was born charged with solar electromagnetic radiation. It is generally felt that the natives of Leo possess a strength and vitality that produces strong recuperative abilities. This sign rules over the heart and any problems with health may well stem from this association. Health problems to watch for include heart disease such as palpitations or irregular heart beats, high blood pressure, strokes, and heart attacks. Other illnesses indicated may include fevers, meningitis and spinal cord difficulties, angina, inflammations, problems with skin disorders, pleurisy, gout, jaundice, and other illnesses associated with poor circulation.

The Leo native's great resources of energy can produce a nervous temperament, and other health problems may be attributed to this highly charged nervousness. You may also find that you are affected by the weather, and that the sun has a great influence on your temperament. Then too, Leo natives are prone to health problems associated with the constant excitability of their natures and to overexertion. You have a tendency to be always on the go or in the middle of some activity. If proper precautions are not taken, the physical well being of the body can become run down and weak leading to a susceptibility to headaches, common colds, viruses, the flu, and kidney and bladder infections. Accidents may occur because of the active and busy lifestyle which may well result in some injuries to the legs or feet.

The best remedy for many of these illnesses is for the individual to take control of his or her life. It should be well ordered and allow for calmness and quietness. And you should schedule in plenty of time for rest and for sleep. Above all else it is recommended that these people stay away from an overindulgence in alcohol and/or drugs. Any tendency to relieve the everyday pressures of life with these substances can be harmful. Then too an overindulgence in the pleasures of life including these and other activities will eventually catch up with the person. You may find that your moods and your busy and demanding lifestyle have an adverse effect on your weight gain, and it is especially important that you watch your diet. Everyone loves to eat, but the Leo native, like other people, has to avoid eating too much of his or her favorite foods, a habit which can lead to only self-gratification until those pounds start to add up.

Leo needs to find positive channels for expending the forceful energy that is a part of his or her nature. This can be done quite effectively through an exercise program. Physical exercise also drains off all excess nervous energy, builds the muscle of the heart making it stronger, and improves circulation. A healthy diet is also important. Many authorities recommend that these people avoid stimulating foods and beverages. Regular check-ups and a healthy regime will aid the Leo natives in living better more effective and successful lives. Taking time from your busy day to relax and to find time for reflection, both meditative and spiritual, will improve your emotional well being as well as your thought processes. In this one area of your life, Leo, you need to acquire the skill of listening to the advice of others who care about you.

The Leo-born is most likely to be the individual who hates to be sick and prefers not to stay in bed or to take time off for illnesses. Leo individuals are not inclined to take the time to run to the doctor with every minor complaint, and you may find yourself also avoiding visits to the doctor for more serious illnesses also. You should know better, and you must come to realize that your health is dependent upon how well you take care of it and on your personal merit in this case. In other words, the time and effort you spend on your health will be repaid to you in a longer more healthy life. And you will find yourself even more productive and successful in your endeavors if you take the time to prevent illnesses by taking care of your body now. Taking time and care with your emotional well being is equally as important. All of this requires a little time from your busy day, but it is well worth the effort. You must learn to protect your health as well as you protect your loved ones.

This can be done easily when you focus the same compelling energy on your health and well being as you do on all the other areas of your life. Whatever nervousness you experience in your daily life can just as easily become focused into a more positive light and more influential style. Your over abundance of vitality and strength can be harnessed to produce even better results. With increased health and physical strength, you will find that renewed intensity needed to face all that life offers. And new experiences will be even more enjoyable if you are in top shape. Therefore, Leo, take the initiative. Plan for your future and for your future health as well.

History of Leo

Ancient scholars associated Leo, the Lion, with the Nemean Lion which leaped from the sky and was killed by Hercules. The Sun is in the constellation of Leo at that time of the year when it has always been considered to rule the universe. It was referred to in ancient civilizations as, the "mansion of power and glory."

The principal star of the constellation has been referred to as the fortunate star, the royal star, the kingly star, and the ruler of the affairs of heaven. In the times of the early Christians, the Lion was said to symbolize or represent St. Thomas. In Jewish mythology, the Lion was the symbol of the ancient tribe of Judah, and throughout these ancient writings there are references to the lion. This sign is noted as being both masculine and fortunate. It represents the heart of humanity just as the Sun represents the center of the universe. The Lion which symbolizes Leo was considered to represent great courage and a luminous, fiery nature. The sign of Leo is bestowed with the principle capacities of masculine virility, ambitions, noble aspirations, a strong patriotism, and a spirit of knowing what is just. In ancient times, the Zodiac sign of Leo represented the crystal clear, incandescent fire which was as hot as melted metal.

Many famous and great individuals were born to the sign of Leo. There is also a spiritual side to the nature of these fifth-sign natives. If the Sun-inspired natives choose to live a wholesome life, it is more than possible for them to attain a highly developed spiritual nature and to develop a strong intellect. With these attributes, these individuals are capable of molding and casting and setting forth the ideals and the social standards of the world while becoming great in their own manner. These individuals overcome any and all obstacles to achieve their personal goals whether spiritual or material.

How to Find Your *Soul-Mate, Stars,* and *Destiny*

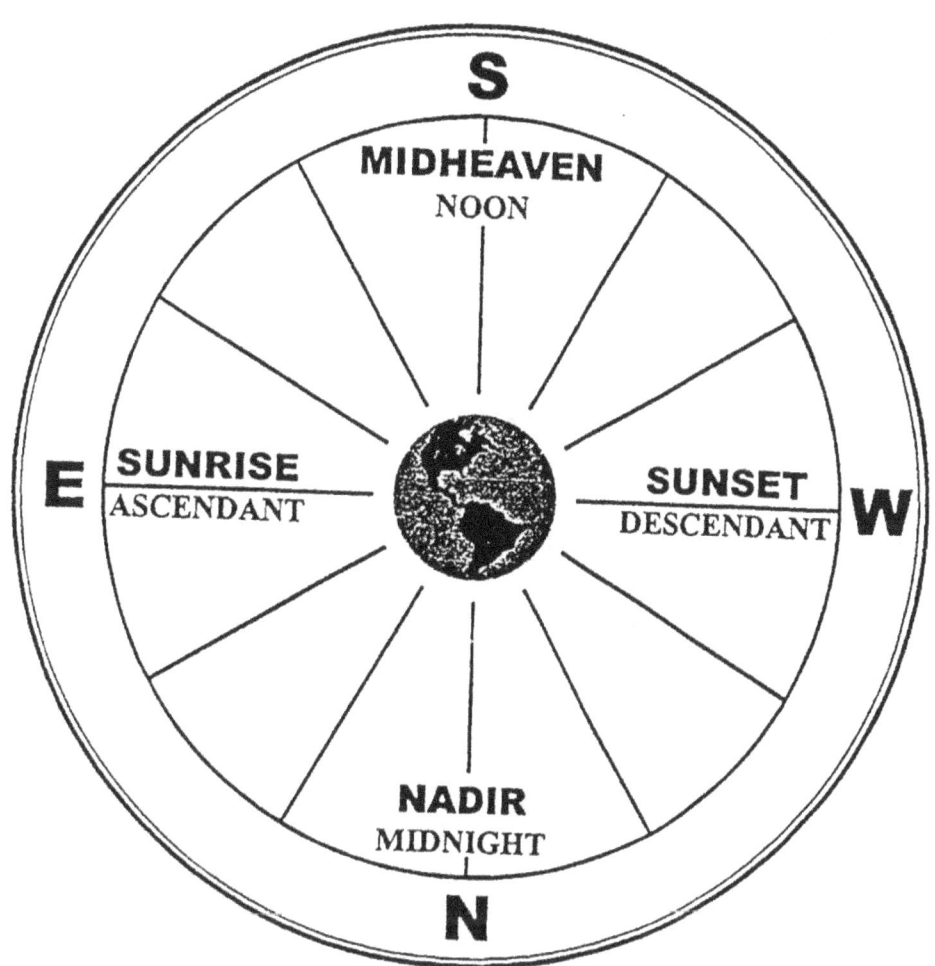

Leo

July 23 -- August 22
The Thebaic Calendar
Character, Personality, and Destiny

The ancient astrologers studied the heavens and at the same time compared the lives of individual persons on Earth. The following is the accumulation of the personalities of individuals based on observations of people during the ages. It reflects a daily guide to the characteristics and destiny of a given birth date.

Whether Leo is the person's Sun sign, the Ascendant, on the cusp, or in a House, the characteristics of this sign become evident. This masculine Sun sign is ruled by the Sun, from which it is bestowed electrifying, radiant, and magnetic qualities. There is a warm radiance that permeates and influences the natives of Leo, granting them the noble forbearance of royalty. A powerful strength and will power makes these individuals impressive and natural leaders. Neptune is exalted in the sign of Leo and when it falls in this sign it bestows upon the natives its qualities of idealism, imagination, spiritualism, and creativity. But it is no doubt the Sun which grants these magnanimous individuals their flair for being the central dramatic persona that draws the attentions of one and all, making them a central focus and force.

DUALITY: Masculine   **ELEMENT:** Fire   **QUALITY:** Fixed   **RULER:** Sun

A masculine sign is direct while the Fire signs are enthusiastic, and the Fixed signs are firm and resistant to change. The sign of Leo grants its natives a radiance and vitality and an innate faith in themselves which others admire. Leo is of an elevated nature and strong will with an open, frank, and noble spirit. The natives are ambitious, persevering, and honest with a tendency to see things through. However self-possessed and masterful, they can also be presumptuous, overly proud and egotistical. There is a quick temper when provoked, but these temperamental outbursts seldom last long. These individuals admire loyalty, faithfulness, and devotion-- especially when they are the recipients of such. In love and romance, they must be made to feel like royalty, admired and appreciated for simply being, or no doubt their attentions will turn to other admirers. This is a patient, hard working person who exhibits great endurance, but Leo is also drawn to public acclamation and covets being the center of attention. And for this, these natives possess a natural and distinct flair for the dramatic. It is said that their bearing alone draws the attentions of others, and when they walk in a room, all heads turn. Even the shyest of Leos will prefer to be the king of the walk at home. This is a person of fixed and firm opinions and strong passions and emotions. They effortlessly gather an entourage of admirers and followers wherever they go. As a Fire sign, Leo encompasses activity, power, and drive. But where in Aries, the Fire sign, the natives rush out toward plans and people, in the Fire sign of Leo, the natives draw everything to them as to a center or focal point. And these individuals are self-propelling as if energized for perpetual motion. Leo are active and interested in sports, recreation, exercise, entertaining, and adventure. Add to that a creative flair in either acting, writing, poetry, art, or comedy. Leo thrives on turning an original, quick expression or humorous witticism in his or her efforts to please the crowd. Leave it to creative and ingenious Leo to so impress others with their enthusiasm, inspiration, or spirituality. Whatever is required, Leo loves the spot light. So inspired are they by this attention from being in the spot light, that they will work earnestly to justify the confidence that has been placed in them.

Leos can be so impressed with themselves and their opinions, that they may well reason they have the answers and the solutions to solving the world's problems and will strive to prove themselves. Their spirituality and personal belief in what is right and wrong augments and justifies their positions on any and all issues. They know they are right. They are Leo after all-- the most powerful, the most just, and without question the best at leadership, showmanship, and just plain gutsy show-off-ness. But let us tread gently here. Leo does after all expect acclimation and acclaim mixed with plenty of praise and out and out flattery does no harm either. This is, after all, a self-aware person. They may actually study the effects they have on others, analyzing and perfecting their entrances, their self-display, and their royal diplomatic skills. In fact, their creative abilities may be best exhibited in their self-creations. At their worst, they are superficial, but it should be remembered that they do mean well in most instances.

THE FIRST DECAN

The First Decan of this sign occurs from 0 degrees to 10 degrees of Leo and applies to those born between July 23 and August 2. This position of the First Decan arrives on the cusp of Cancer, granting these Leo born more creativity and imagination combined with an ample amount of self-confidence, authority, determination, and endurance. They are capable of giving form and substance to their creative ideas whether they are actors, artists, inventors, or craftsmen. They can also exhibit the tendencies to be stubborn, prideful, egotistical, self-centered, and overly concerned with being the center of attention. They are at their best when receiving recognition for a job well done. And in all that they do, they strive to do their best in order to receive the personal attention and acclaim which they desire.

The Second Decan

The Second Decan of this sign occurs from 10 degrees to 20 degrees of Leo and applies to those born between August 3 and August 12. These natives exhibit all of the characteristics inherent in the sign of Leo, but they may also exhibit an interest in either educational, cultural, or spiritual pursuits. They possess leadership abilities and an interest in social events. If a well developed individual, these Leo take an interest in contributing to community affairs by becoming involved in one manner or another. Many times they are either influential or persuasive in their approach to problem solving, and they have a strong inner sense of direction. Being outgoing, they may also love to entertain or are in some manner socially active. Their energy seems to know no boundaries. They strive to perform well in all that they do, being capable of rationalizing their decisions.

The Third Decan

The Third Decan of this sign occurs from 20 degrees to 30 degrees of Leo and applies to those born between August 13 and August 22. These Leo's possess all the magnetism and vitality inherent in this sign. They are approaching the cusp of Virgo which can add a serious outlook toward their productive ambitions. They are authoritarian, self-confident, assured, and self-assertive, but the influence of Virgo may make them more cautious and analytical. They possess a strong egotistical nature and a belief in their own abilities to either make decisions or to lead. They are generally intelligent with a self-assured persuasive ability that they put to good use. Whether in love or business, they strive to lead and to be an authority who earns respect for all that they do.

First Decan of Leo:

July 23 - August 2 -

First Ten Days

Character, Personality, and Temperament:

The quality of Leo is a compromise of the general contradictions. Sometimes they feel like they will suffocate which destroys their qualities and abilities. One part of the life of Leo is difficult. Enthusiasm and intelligence are manifested, but obstacles make some area of life difficult. There is an obsession with diverse and creative thoughts, like an imagination taht is running wild. Successes but at times with suffering from making the wrong decisions.

Fixed Element:

FIRE: Stable energy to be creativity and to see plans through. Fixed and firm opinions on how to proceed.

Destiny:

Wherever this person is situated in life, the position is going to be stable. The destiny is less shiny but is solid and strong. This person may not become wealthy, but whatever they decide to do, they remain stubbornly and obstinately with it. They like jewelry and everything that sparkles.

Star Date of Birth: July 23

A person with a determined character; all difficulties are overcome. Ambitious, diligent, and hard working. If you achieve success, fame, or financial security, you find yourself more interested in the accomplishment and the acclaim than the success itself. In your sexual encounters, you desire the same measure of success and acclaim and strive to be a good lover giving as much pleasure as you derive.

Star Date of Birth: July 24

This individual is tricky and courageous. This person enjoys both an athletic and successful life. You are a nature lover who is most comfortable with other people who share your need to find contentment with a simpler lifestyle. Your sexuality is defined by a strong need to feel in control, and you maintain a strong balance in your sex life between your desires and your fulfillment.

Star Date of Birth: July 25

This Leo native possesses spontaneous energy. There are characteristic events that can be good or bad for this person. You strive to be in control of your own life but there are times when you are easily influenced by other people and tempted by your desires for pleasure. You like to be fashionable and current and your lifestyle, values, and sexuality may be based on what is popularly accepted.

Star Date of Birth: July 26

This person possesses a balance between the desire to work and to seek pleasure or relaxing times. The destiny includes family funerals and renunciations. Others naturally respond to your tranquil, easy going nature, and it is with little challenge that you please them as well as yourself. Sexier than most, your sexuality is enhanced by your willingness to become involved with those who find you attractive and who admire you.

Star Date of Birth: July 27

The person is active, careful and patient with the ability and talent to temper difficult situations. Success is noted. Your active mind combined with your energy level leads you to restlessly take the lead and seek the next challenge whether in business or your personal and social life. You are open to discussing your sexual preferences and those of your partner which adds to your pleasures and relationships.

Star Date of Birth: July 28

There is a good balance and diplomacy in life. This person's life is surrounded by caring and interested friends. Both popular and well liked, you strive to contribute constructively to whatever it is you are involved in. You are at home in a group but are also drawn to smaller gatherings where you can express yourself openly. Strangers and new acquaintances find you attractive and sexy.

Star Date of Birth: July 29

Surrounded by friends. Always wanting to do your best and be at your best, you accept responsibilities willingly. You are at your best when your abundant sexual appetite is satisfied with a partner who shares your needs and desires and with whom you feel free to respond openly.

Star Date of Birth: July 30

This person has a quick character and at times a violent nature; always ready to fight. There are many successes which are compromised before they are achieved. You mean well by others, but you do best when life is centered around you otherwise you can become discontented and irritable. You perform best sexually when you feel your partner is totally devoted to you and admires your good qualities and abilities.

Star Date of Birth: July 31

This native possesses a great determination but rigid ideas. Success is indicated. You plan for the future and are interested not only in what is going on today but how it will effect the future. You are drawn to large group activities whether sports, music, or social events, and this may be the arena where you meet new acquaintances who become lovers.

Star Date of Birth: August 1

Much generous activity is noted with a respect for the needy and weaker people. A famous situation and success is noted in the life of this individual. Your sociable nature makes you well liked and admired. And although you prefer to be in control of your own life, your touch of impulsiveness and spontaneity may find you throwing your plans to the wind as you respond to your sexuality and the opportunities that come your way.

Star Date of Birth: August 2

This individual has much ambition and drive, but short-term fame is indicated. A likable person, but your periods of indecisiveness may result in losses unless you learn to include others in your plans. You are easily the center of attention, but in more intimate relationships, no matter how good the sex, you may have difficulty expressing your emotions.

Second Decan of Leo:

August 3 - August 12 -

Second Ten Days

Character, Personality, and Temperament:

All qualities become clearer, more compassionate, more authoritative, and humanitarian. The feeling of justice moderates the tendency towards too much pride. There is often a great common sense that tempers the bursting character of this individual.

Fixed Element:

Fire: Energy and enthusiasm centered on decisions and opinions.

Destiny:

The life of individuals born during the Second Decan is happy. The native can be considered a humanitarian healer or benefactor of others.

Star Date of Birth: August 3

This person possesses a kind and strong character. There is an indication for an easy life. Your tenacity leads you to continue your efforts until you succeed. In your sexual relationships, you are just as successful, but you must determine for yourself the difference between lust and love and what it is you most desire in order to find contentment and happiness.

Star Date of Birth: August 4

There is a tendency for parties and feasts and an indulgence in pleasures. Your active mind leads you to be productive and to enjoy that which you seek. Your sexuality reflects your basic instinct to satisfy your own desires and in this way you can be self-centered. You are attracted to pretentious persons whose dramatic, center-stage attitude matches your own.

Star Date of Birth: August 5

These natives strive to bring happiness to their children. A comfortable marriage and home situation are indicated. You take pride in your efficiency and achievements and apply yourself to carefully thinking through your actions. Sexually, you are self-protective and determined to make the right decisions even though you are tempted by those who travel in the fast lane.

Star Date of Birth: August 6

An indication for a firm, stubborn character. Achievement for this individual takes a long time. But you know how to make the most of your personable attitude, electrifying presence and physical attractiveness. You are effective at putting others at ease, and this is true as well in your sexual relationships where you effortlessly draw out those more inhibited than yourself.

Star Date of Birth: August 7

There is seen a lack of initiative for this Leo person and an unstable situation. You strive for a positive attitude, rarely faulting others even when personal relationships don't develop as you anticipated. Your steady, sunny disposition leads you to radiate enthusiasm, an even temperament, good manners, and diplomatic abilities often with good results in matters related to sex and romantic relationships.

Star Date of Birth: August 8

This individual is an authoritarian with a determined temperament. A happy life surrounded by many friends is indicated. You are self-confident, self-reliant, and especially self-sufficient which draws others to you. This attitude leads you to win over uncertainty in your romantic partners who respond to your winning mannerisms resulting in you being a well admired lover.

Star Date of Birth: August 9

This person enjoys a calm, modest life, but there may be some instances of weak health. In your youth, winning came easy for you which may have left you unprepared for the more challenging obstacles you face as an adult. You are drawn to that which is elegant, but in your sexuality you may find that your partners somewhat resent that you derive more pleasure than they.

Star Date of Birth: August 10

The Leo native is known for perseverance and tenacity. There is an indication of missions in far away places. Your magnetic appeal makes you well liked and popular which adds to your self-confident nature. Sexually, though, you prefer to magnetize in private and to turn your thoughts totally to your sexual partners who are impressed with your genuine efforts.

Star Date of Birth: August 11

The person has a passionate desire for education and educational pursuits. Success is seen. You adapt well and instinctively know how to make an entrance and to attract the attention of others. Sexually, you strive to counter any impulsive thoughts by appearing in control of the situation, but you are drawn to sex like a bee to honey.

Star Date of Birth: August 12

A somewhat isolated and quiet character who is kind and sensitive. A wealthy situation and a happy marriage are indicated. Your calm attitude exudes a reliable, self-contented nature that impresses others and which leads you to strive to find contentment in all that you do. Your sexuality, though, reflects an inner experimental nature that makes you want to experience it all.

The Third Decan of Leo: August 13 - August 22 -

Third Ten Days

Character, Personality, and Temperament:

There is a strong indication for big plans for the future but life is wrought with obstacles and hardships. There is a tendency toward excesses, exaggeration and exuberance.

Fixed Element:

FIRE: Fiery enthusiasm and combativity, compassion.

Destiny:

The life is shiny but with a high price in struggling.

Star Date of Birth: August 13

There is a tendency to be fast and impulsive. In difficult situations, this person receives a lot of help from friends. You are respectful and well mannered with a pleasing nature that impresses others. You often meet your sexual partners through organizations, clubs, and social activities. Beneath your pleasantries is an electrifying presence best expressed through sexual encounters.

How to Find Your *Soul-Mate, Stars,* and *Destiny*

Star Date of Birth: August 14

The individual enjoys an enthusiasm for artistic activities. A modest situation next to wealthy people is seen. You escape your need for excitement and adventure through sedentary past times and even occupations that offer a quieter setting. But you explode with magnetism and electricity in your sexual relationships when you prove that you know the basic requirements of pleasing another.

Star Date of Birth: August 15

The individual possesses an authoritarian spirit with leadership and aggressive qualities. There is an indication for a bright public life but a private life that is tormented. You would be happier if you received the acclaim and credit you feel you rightly deserve, but you keep these thoughts to yourself and rarely express your inner feelings. It may be a Pisces who draws you out, sexually teaching you to get in touch with your truer feelings.

Star Date of Birth: August 16

An admirable intellect with strong deductive reasoning abilities is seen. This individual's situation is always inferior to what is deserved. You exhibit a flair for drawing others together and leading others in worthwhile causes. Your ego is soothed and expanded at the same time through your sexual encounters which prove to you just how successful you can be in that arena because of the praise you receive.

Star Date of Birth: August 17

An intense character who is self-assured with a cleverness and self-confidence. This person's life is happy with no great worries. You are thoughtful and make diligent efforts to be decisive and effective in your presentations. You counter any impulsiveness by trying hard not to speculate on business or pleasure. In this way, you are also very much in control in your sexual relationships.

How to Find Your *Soul-Mate, Stars,* and *Destiny*

Star Date of Birth: August 18

This person as an authoritarian character and is unwilling to compromise with others. A hard, difficult life is indicated. You reap the benefits of being trustworthy, dependable and reliable in business, social, and personal relationships. Your serious outlook doesn't prevent you from being friendly and fun-loving, and in your sexual relationships you enjoy the ability to excite your partner.

Star Date of Birth: August 19

A predisposition for unvanquished stubbornness. This individual has a life filled with struggles. You are alert, energetic, and physically active with a robust constitution and larger than life presence. You are at ease in a crowd, and you like to fit in well, but in your sexual relationships, you are often drawn to those with a unique lifestyle and individualistic approach.

Star Date of Birth: August 20

Quiet, serious life with strong contact with people, and if this does not bring the individual complete satisfaction, it will provide protection against loss of status. You know how to divide and conquer being unafraid of challenges and preferring to win in all that you do. Your aggressive nature plays well in your sexual relationships as well where you are uninhibited about making the first advance or in carrying through to ecstatic pleasure.

Star Date of Birth: August 21

Happy, good person always smiling and helpful; and surrounded by children, grandchildren, and great-grandchildren. A life around family. Your ambitions serve you well as you work hard to plan and attain a successful and financially secure position. In your sexual relationships, you maintain a well thought out balance between your desires, your emotions, your physical needs and what is best for all concerned.

Star Date of Birth: August 22

Lots of friends but little money. This individual has an enterprising character, but is often hostile or indifferent. You are sensually aware of all that life has to offer, but you apply a cautious approach to all encounters, knowing best how to limit desires within the framework of tradition.

Colors:

The most beneficial colors for the natives of Leo are all shades of yellow and orange, pale green and white.

Birthstones:

The birthstones for the sign of Leo are topazes, amber, rubies, and diamonds.

Metal:

The metal associated with the sign of Leo is the luminous gold.

Flowers:

Favorable flowers for Leo natives are the sunflower, marigold, and rosemary.

KEYWORD: "I WILL"

POSITIVE TRAITS:

Loyal; generous; kind; creative; magnanimous; outspoken; sincere; honest; ardent; tolerant; expansive; good organizer; inspiring; magnetic; industrious; aspiring; fearless; flair for showmanship and drama; chivalrous; hopeful; ambitious; aspiring; idealistic; hospitable; congenial; confident dignified; love of children.

NEGATIVE TRAITS:

Snobbish; arrogant; dogmatic; overbearing; bullying; condescending; pompous; domineering; impetuous; promiscuous; intolerant; self-centered; lazy; fussy; opinionated; hot-tempered; patronizing; power hungry; sensitive; conceited; pleasure seeking; greedy; impulsive; extravagant; braggart; showoff; big talker; sarcastic.

How to Find Your *Soul-Mate, Stars,* and *Destiny*

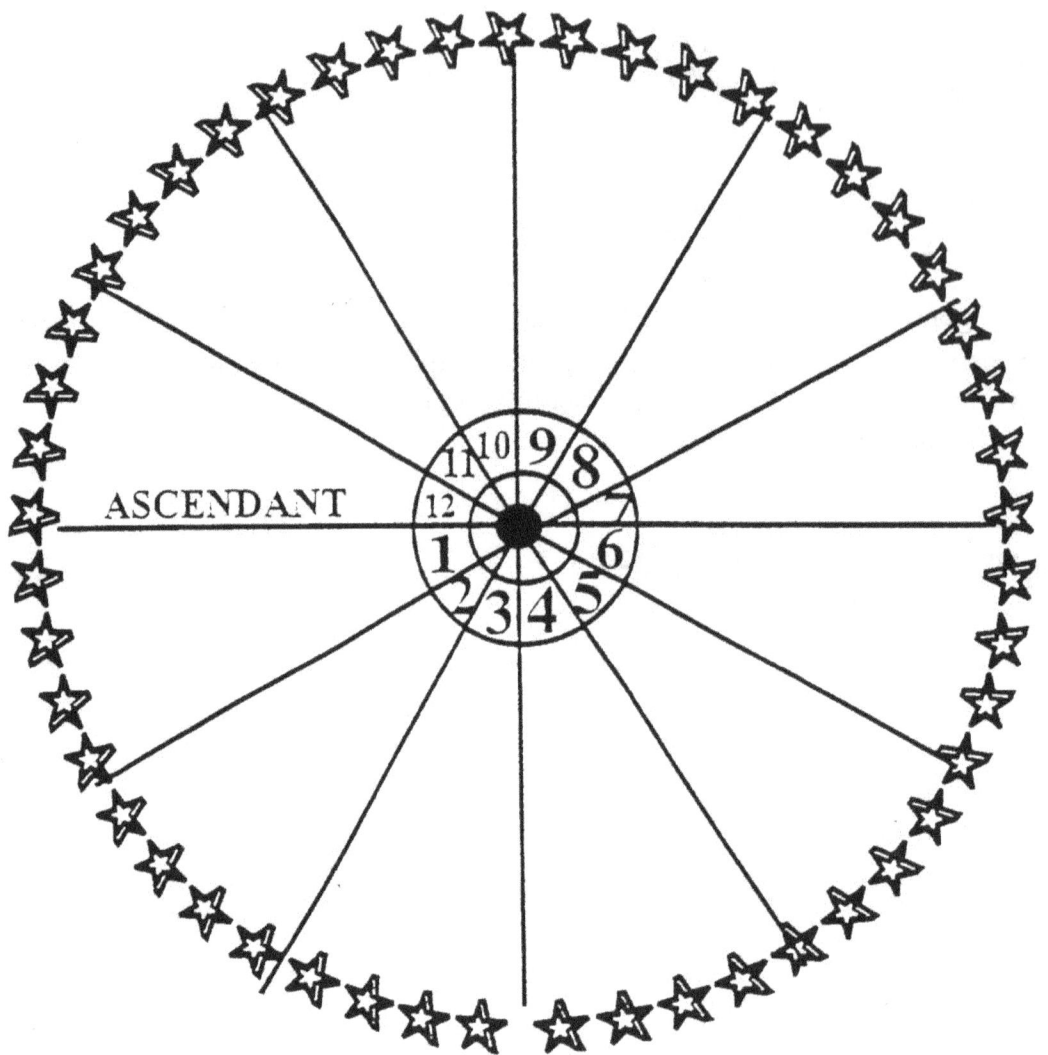

LEO

PERSONAL SELF-EXPRESSION AND MENTAL TENDENCIES

1. Active Minded, Good Natured
2. Generous, Many Friends, Natural Leader
3. Ambitious, Independent, Determined, Persistent
4. Honest, Very Conscientious, Philosopical
5. Philanthropic, Quickly Angered, Appeased
6. Sunny Disposition, Frank, Outspoken, Candid
7. Greatly Appreciates Affection, Sincere, Magnetic
8. Intuitive, Inventive, Fond of Children, Sports
9. Drama, Honors, High Office, Unrestrained
10. Kind-Hearted, Noble Disposition, Impulsive
11. Forceful, Demonstrative Manner
12. Electric Nature, Inspiring, Has Great Hope
13. Faith, Fortitude, Energetic, Lavish
14. Vital, Aspiring, Executive Departments
15. Sympathetic, Loyal, High-Strung
16. Ardent, Passionate, Charitable, Free
17. Adaptable, Popular, Forceful, Industrious
18. Imperious, Fond of Power and Command
19. Very Forgiving, Does Not Hold a Grudge for Long
20. High Ideals, Receives and Grants Favors
21. Usually Fortunate in the Long Run, Temerament
22. Succeeds Best Where They Have Authority
23. Love, Responsible, Position, Manager
24. Honorable, Warm-Hearted
25. Self-Confident, Fearless, Impulsive
26. Persevering, Distinction
27. Cheerful, Optimistic
28. Self-Reliant, Money Matters
29. High Minded, Magnanimous

How to Find Your Soul-Mate, Stars, and Destiny

30. Lively, Penetrating Mind, Organizing Ability
31. Popular With the Opposite Sex, Sincere Love
32. Home and Honor, Intuition Genius, Gives a Free Heart
33. Love of Pleasure, Music, Singing, Drama, Fine Arts
34. Tendency to Uplift, Mentally Strong, Social, Trust
35. Place Him in Positions of Trust, Respect, Fiery
36. Management of Enterprises, Confident, Persistent
37. Dignified, Aspiring Intellect; High, Noble Ideals
38. Will Seldom Stoop to Low Actions, Mentally Positive
39. Governing, Controlling, Strong Will-Power
40. Expansive Development, Concentration
41. Children, Pets, Government Affairs
42. Self-Indulgent, Attracted to the Opposite Sex
43. Amusements of All Sorts, High Rank
44. Judicious Investments, Speculation, Inheritance
45. Occupations Connected With Pleasure
46. Success and Good Fortune, Industrial Concerns
47. Public appointments, Gain by Speculative Investment
48. Judgement in Stock-Exchange Matters, Insurance
49. Aren't in Affection, Love, or Pleasure; Often Hasty
50. Emotions of Passion, Big Ego, Impulsive
51. Positive, Militant, Agressive, Defiant, Sympathetic
52. Strong in Arguments, Reasonable, Progressive
53. Enthusiastic, Broad-Minded, Liberal, Possessing
54. Adventure, Risky Enterprises, Hazardous Occupations
55. Occult Phenomena, Psychic Conditions
56. Financial Gain Later Life, Threatened by Disappointment
57. Sorrow in Love, Death of Loved One, Separation
58. Superiors and Also Subordinates, Idealistic, Noble
59. Amorous, Bold, Contemptuous of Danger
60. Hazardous, Strenuous Pursuits; Compassionate
61. Benevolent, Prudent, Strengths, Strong Constitution
62. Endowed With Wisdom, Enjoys Prestige
63. Diplomatic, Philosophical, Religious
64. Goverment Employee, Positions of Prominence
65. Long Journeys With Sports, Education, or Diplomatic Affairs
66. Bold in Spirit, Strong-Willed, Secret Enmity
67. Consciously or Unconsciously Affect Their Health
68. Sorrows Through Love Affairs and Children

69. Extremely Industrious Mentally, High Aspirations
70. Physically Disposed to Great Moderation
71. Head-Strong, Eccentric, Rebellious Disposition
72. Freedom, Exciting, Strange Aversions and/or Attractions
73. Experiences, Connects Affections in Love Affairs
74. Amateur Therapist, Childlike Fun, Dramatize
75. Gullible, Stylish, Regal, Good Executive
76. Formal, Hates Details, Shirks Routine, Vain
77. Warm, Anxious, Gossipy, Big Spender
78. Political, Authoritative, Showy, Has High Self-Esteem
79. Opinionated, Actor, Creative, Often Gifted
80. Brash, Self-Conscious, Immature, Insensitive
81. Self-Promoting, Complacent, Needs a Fan, Extremely Proud
82. Hearty, Outgoing, Vindictive, Money-Lending

How to Find Your *Soul-Mate, Stars,* and *Destiny*

Celebrity Birthdays

July — Leo

23	Woody Harrelson Haile Selassie Dino Danelli Don Drysdale	Marlon Wayans Stephanie Seymour Terrence Stamp Pee Wee Reese	Michael Wilding Harry Cohn Alison Krause David Essex
24	Robert Hays Bella Abzug Amelia Earhart Ruth Buzzi	Michael Richards Alexandre Dumas Laura Leighton Simon Bolivar	Heinz Burt Alex Cohen Lynda Carter Chris Sarandon
25	Estelle Getty Frank Church Thomas Eakins Walter Brennan	Matt LeBlanc Erick Hoffer Stanley Dancer Joseph Kennedy, Jr.	Iman Ray Billingsley Barbara Harris Jim McCarty
26	Mick Jagger Gracie Allen Stanley Kubrick Duncan Mackay	Kevin Spacey Carl Jung Dorothy Hamill George Bernard Shaw	Sandra Bullock Aldous Huxley Blake Edwards Jason Robards
27	Joshua Reynolds Leo Durocher Keenan Wynn Betty Thomas	Maureen McGovern Peggy Fleming Bobbie Gentry Jerry Van Dyke	John Pleshette Norman Lear Al Ramsey
28	Jim Davis Sally Struthers Rudy Vallee Joe E. Brown	Rick Wright Jacqueline Kennedy Onassis George Cummings	Vida Blue Bill Bradley Harry Bridges
29	Patti Scialfa Marilyn Quayle Dag Hammarskjold Benito Mussolini	Peter Jennings Martina McBride Rasputin William Powell	Alexandra Paul Neal Doughty Booth Tarkington Sigmund Romberg
30	Delta Burke Casey Stengel Henri Moore Larry Fishburne	Peter Bogdanovich Henry Ford Kate Bush Arnold Schwarzenegger	Emily Bronte Paul Anka Buddy Guy Lisa Kudrow

How to Find Your Soul-Mate, Stars, and Destiny

July   Leo

31	Sherry Lansing	Wesley Snipes	Dean Cain
	Milton Friedman	Jean Dubuffet	Geraldine Chaplin
	Evonne Goolagong	Norman Cook	Don Murray
	John West	Curt Gowdy	Gary Lewis

August

1	Francis Scott Key	Rick Anderson	Robert J. Waller
	Yves Saint Laurent	Herman Melville	Tempestt Bledsoe
	Jack Kramer	Dom DeLuise	Robert Cray
	Giancarlo Giannini	Robert Todd Lincoln	Ricky Coonce
2	Edward Furlong	Cynthia Stevenson	Joanna Cassidy
	Jack Warner	Peter O'Toole	Linda Fratianne
	James Baldwin	Westbrook Pegier	Carroll O'Connor
	Myrna Loy	James Baldwin	Edward Patten
3	B.B. Dickerson	James Hetfield	John Landis
	Leon Uris	Martin Sheen	John Eisenhower
	Dolores Del Rio	Martha Stewart	Jay North
	Tony Bennett	Ted Ashley	Rod Beck
4	Richard Belzer	Frankie Ford	Isaac Babbitt
	Percy B. Shelley	Mary Decker Slaney	Cleon Jones
	Queen Mother Elizabeth	Billy Bob Thornton	David Carr
5	Patrick Ewing	Jonathan Silverman	Rick Huxley
	John Huston	Roman Gabriel	Loni Anderson
	Neil Armstrong	Robert Taylor	Guy de Maupassant
	Geraldine Stutz	Rick Derringer	
6	Stefanie Kramer	Paul Bartel	Dorian Harewood
	Lucille Ball	Alfred, Lord Tennyson	Franz Allers
	Robert Mitchum	William B. Williams	Abbey Lincoln
	Clara Bow	Catherine Hicks	Pat McDonald
7	James Randi	Evgeny Platov	Bruce Dickinson
	Billie Burke	Andy Fraser	B.J. Thomas
	Lana Cantrell	Dr. Louis Leakey	David Rasche
	Mata Hari	Stan Freberg	Ralph Bunche

How to Find Your Soul-Mate, Stars, and Destiny

August   Leo

8	Peter Weir Chris Foreman Harry Crosby Andy Warhol	Donny Most Dustin Hoffman Sylvia Sidney Esther Williams	Connie Stevens Keith Carradine Larry Wilcox Mel Tillis
9	Melanie Griffith Gillian Anderson Billy Henderson.0 Robert Shaw	Whitney Houston Kurtis Blow Ken Norton Benjamin Orr	Amanda Bearse Sam Elliott David Steinberg Isaac Walton
10	John Starks Jimmy Dean Herbert Hoover Michael Bivins	Rosanna Arquette Antonio Banderas Jon Farriss Eddie Fisher	Ian Anderson Rhonda Fleming Bobby Hatfield Lorraine Pearson
11	John Conlee Buddy Hackett Mike Douglas Alex Haley	Elizabeth Holtzman Lyle Stuart Claus Von Bulow Hulk Hogan	Denis Payton Chuck Connors Arlene Dahl Lloyd Nolan
12	Pete Sampras George Hamilton Jane Wyatt Michael Kidd	Suzanne Vega Parnelli Jones Cecil B. DeMille Wilt Chamberlain	John Derek Diamond Jim Brady Pat Metheny Buck Owens
13	Danny Bonaduce Alfred Hitchcock Feargal Sharkey Alfred Krupp	Dan Fogelbert Bert Lahr Menachem Begin Neville Brand	Annie Oakley Fidel Castro Kathleen Battle Don Ho
14	John Galsworthy David Crosby Magic Johnson Susan Saint James	Danielle Steel Bricktop Buddy Greco John Ringling North	Halle Berry Steve Martin Robyn Smith Russell Baker
15	Linda Ellerbee Sir Walter Scott Pete York Signe Hasso	Tess Harper Ethel Barrymore Jill Haworth Edna Ferber	Julia Child Robert Bolt Jimmy Webb Napoleon Bonaparte
16	Angela Bassett Fess Parker Eydie Gorme Robert Culp	Frank Gifford Kathie Lee Gifford James Taylor Ann Blyth	Belinda Carlisle George Meany Timothy Hutton Madonna

How to Find Your Soul-Mate, Stars, and Destiny

August — Leo

17	Donnie Wahlberg Orville Wright Mae West Boog Powell	Kevin Rowland Larry Rivers Robert De Niro Davy Crockett	Sean Penn Gary Talley Maureen O'Hara Colin Moulding
18	Roman Polanski Patrick Swayze Robert Redford Roslyn Carter	Shelley Winters Gus Edwards Caspar Weinberger Antonio Salieri	Madeleine Stowe Dennis Elliott Caspar Weinberger Emperor Franz Joseph
19	Malcolm Forbes Jill St. John Billy J. Kramer Willie Shoemaker	Christian Slater Coco Chanel John Stamos Peter Gallagher	Matthew Perry Bill Clinton Orville Wright Alfred Lunt
20	Paul Tillich Isaac Hayes Connie Chung Theresa Saldana	Joan Allen Graig Nettles James Pankow Pres. Benjamin Harrison	Robert Plant Rudy Gatlin Phil Lynott Doug Fieger
21	Kim Cattrall Carl Giammarese William ‚Count' Basie Princess Margaret	Archie Griffin Kim Sledge Melvin Van Peebles Carrie Fisher	Wilt Chamberlain Joe Strummer Kenny Rogers Clarence Williams III
22	John Lee Hooker Claude Debussy Roland Orzabal Theonis V. Aldredge	Valerie Harper Jacques Lipchitz William Bradbury Norman Schwarzkopf	Tori Amos Ray Bradbury Cindy Williams Honor Blackman

How to Find Your *Soul-Mate*, *Stars*, and *Destiny*

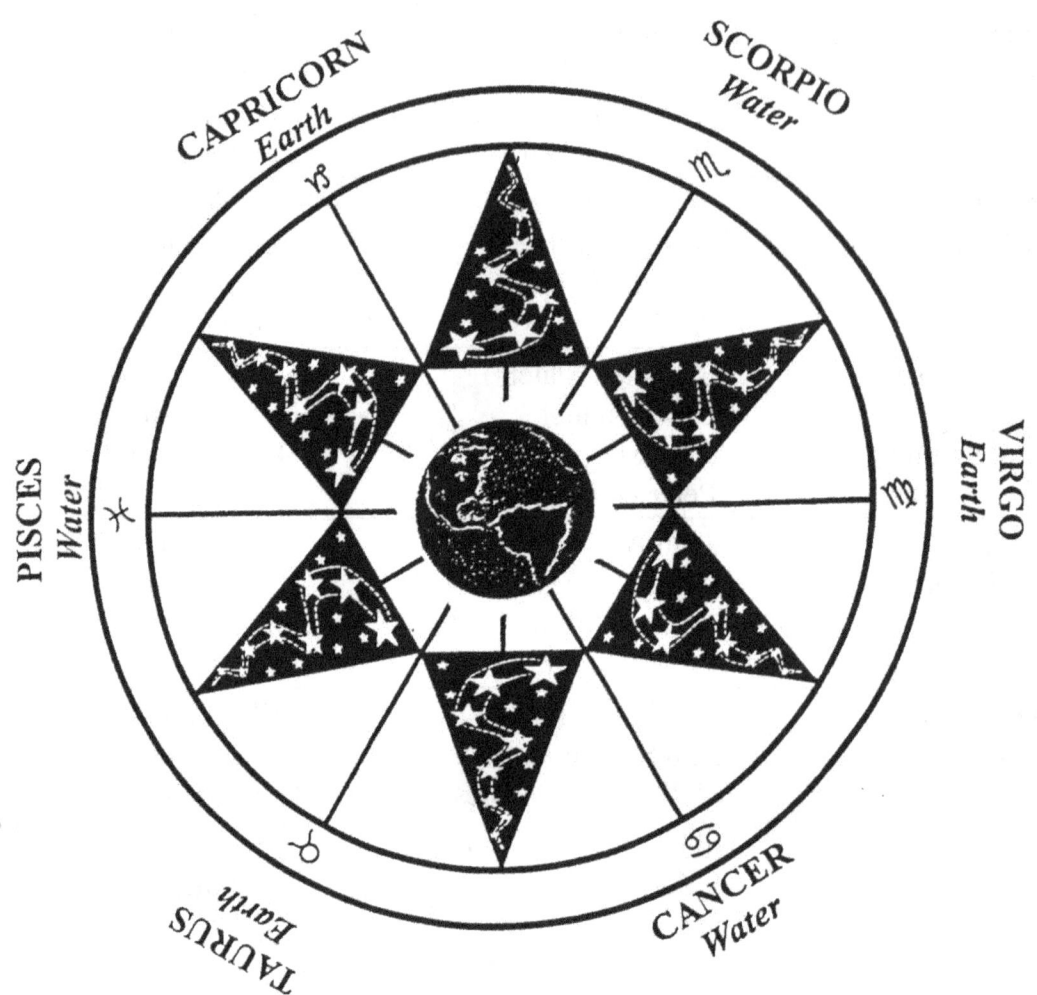

How to Find Your *Soul-Mate*, *Stars*, and *Destiny*

Date With Destiny

Share With Me Your Fantasy

How to Find Your *Soul-Mate,* Stars, and *Destiny*

Date With Destiny

Share With Me Your Fantasy

Virgo

August 23 -- September 22
Man - Woman - Child - Character - Relationships - Compatibilities - Love Signs

The sixth Sun sign of the Zodiac, Virgo is symbolized by the Virgin, and takes its name from the Latin word for Virgin. The sign of Virgo best represents the harvest which results from the labor of one's efforts and hard work. Thus, it is felt in Astrology that the successes the Virgo natives attain in life is based not so much on good luck as on their diligent, patient, and self-sustaining efforts. Less ego-driven than other Sun signs, the Virgin has also been represented by the Serving Maid, and Virgo is the sign of service to others or service to mankind. The Virgo natives are most content when they feel like they have provided good service to others and this trait combined with other positive traits makes them the best friends or family members. They are efficient, practical, well organized, and responsible individuals who put their gifts of memory, analytical skill, and a mind for details to good use. Their worst faults are a tendency to worry too much, to become anxious, and to get bogged down under the consideration of all the details in any situation. This makes them extremely cautious, and their critical and even self-critical nature can influence every aspect of their lives. They are highly curious but with a compulsive nature that leads them to repress many of their feelings and urges. Being particular and self-demanding leads them to also be demanding and expectant of others. They are not above judging others by the high standards they set for themselves to the point of being self-righteous. This highly selective and discriminating person may hold off on marriage and romance until someone who meets all of their criteria is found. This is an Earth sign which grants these natives a particularly earthy outlook on love making. Virgo is also noted as the sign which focuses all of these traits toward the subject of health, diet, and fitness, and the Virgo native will more than likely take an active interest in planning a fitness regime. That this same person may have a propensity toward weight gain only signifies their interest in the better things in life.

These characteristics of the Virgo Sun sign can be made stronger by the Moon sign, Ascendant, and the placement of the Planets, or they can be made more subdued by specific influences. It is by ascertaining these various influences that one can more fully understand the Virgo individual being studied, or more importantly, one can more fully understand one's self.

The Zodiac sign of Virgo influences those born between August 23 and September 23. The constellation of Virgo is symbolized by a young girl holding a sheath of grain. This symbol of the Virgin is an allusion or represents Spica, the star located in this constellation. The Sun at this time of year is in transit to the Autumn Solstice. The days are shorter at the end of summer and the natural bountifulness of the Earth is now at rest. This is the sign of Mother Earth who gathers her child to her breast. It is the last sign of summer, a time for harvest and for gathering the fruits of one's efforts in a practical, orderly and methodical fashion.

The sign of Virgo begins on August 23, but initially it is overlapped by the cusp of the previous sign, Leo. Virgo realizes its full strength on or about August 30. Then for seven days it slowly begins to lose its strength as Virgo approaches the cusp of the incoming sign of Libra.

Virgo is a feminine Earth sign dominated by Mercury, the ruling planet of intellectual, spiritual, trading and business activities. Gemini is also dominated by Mercury, but Gemini is an Air sign. Being an Earth sign, Virgo is logical, practical and analytical. The sign of Virgo is considered the sign of order, clarity and purity. The native of Virgo is known for thought and reflection rather than impulsiveness. This person is hard working and economical and recognizes life's limitations.

While Taurus, another Earth sign, represents substance, material possessions and money, in and of itself, Virgo represents the link between matter and the task of becoming fruitful or productive. Virgo individuals are more disposed to take action in the form of sustained mental or physical effort rather than being concerned with theories or idealism. The strength and virtue of the Virgo natives are found in their ability to labor toward their potentials. They pursue service and duty rather than speculations or abstractions. The natives of this sign are endowed with prudent and sensible judgment.

Being a feminine sign, Virgo natives prefer to solve conflicts amiably rather than continuing to argue. Virgo persons do not run head first into conflicts or obstacles as do many Aries and Leo natives. The sign of Virgo symbolizes a peaceful nature that strives for harmony and serenity in all things. The natives of this sign are most easily concerned and pained by all matters pertaining to strife and conflicts. The main desire is to avoid the battle and to seek peace. This person would rather size up the situation, avoid conflicts, and progress past them in a logical manner. As nature has reached the end of its growing season and is preparing to rest, Virgo reflects less quick action and more sustained effort.

These are people of great discerning powers and abilities. They possess the ability to observe and then to separate and distinguish the component parts of a situation or problem and to discover its true nature or inner relationship. They appear to know intuitively what is of importance and what is not. This is the person who can express a reasoned opinion on a matter especially if it involves a judgment of its values, truth, righteousness, beauty or technique. They are known to be ingenious, and in this they exhibit intelligence and an aptitude for discovering, inventing or contriving. They are forever marked by originality, resourcefulness and cleverness in all that they strive to accomplish. These individuals are known for being reserved and thoughtful. The Virgo native is also known for being tactful and discrete.

Virgo individuals can be very energetic, but they rarely act in a rash manner. As an Earth sign, Virgo natives possess the spirit of realism and are characterized by the term, "to analyze". Virgo seeks a moral purity best expressed in their desire for perfection in all that they do in life.

Virgo Personality

Virgo, ruled by Mercury, is influenced by this planet to be intelligent and creative while possessing a great analytical ability which allows them to gather and assimilate information quickly and precisely. Mercury's otherwise volatile qualities are transformed in this particular sign to energy, diligence, and self-sufficiency. There appears a rather fundamental stability and balance to the personalities of these individuals. Rather than falling prey to their own weaknesses, insecurities, or fears, the Virgo native attempts to simply avoid them. Virgo individuals, as has been said, do not like complications. They are pragmatic and impersonally logical in their outlook on life. Rather than dominate, this person may well choose to serve others becoming devoted at home and at work to other people and the tasks at hand.

Virgo natives have a reserved and confident bearing and are inclined to be discerning in their relationships with others. While you are conservative by nature, you are known for being charming and cheerful but modest, witty and then again sensitive. You are often considered thoughtful, serious, intuitive and perceptive. You are not known for going to extremes, preferring to remain calmly on middle ground. You have a great love for order and harmony in both your personal and professional life, and you greatly appreciate all expressions of respect and dignity.

The Virgo drive for perfection gains you much respect and esteem in your career. You have the ability to get your ideas across to others, to explain and then to delegate responsibilities to others. And generally speaking, Virgo natives are very helpful people. You derive a great deal of satisfaction from getting the job done and from being of service to others.

In your personal life, Virgo natives are known for being involved and productive members of their communities. You are a person who can be trusted to be dependable and responsible. Your civic duties rank high with you, and you take them as seriously as you do all other aspects of your life. In this regard, you gain a degree of satisfaction in knowing that in some way, either small or large, you have benefited your community by doing your civic duty.

Then again, everyone has faults and this is true of many of the Virgo natives as well. The afflicted Virgo native displays as many faults as do people of other signs. Many of these individuals may have tendencies toward self-gratification and pleasures. This baser nature focuses on sexual pleasures and the many distractions in life that are available to satiate these particular tastes. Also, the poorly developed Virgo individuals are capable of exhibiting a great deal of pride and egotism. This can produce a person who is jealous and unhappy. These types of Virgo natives may have problems getting along with other family members. The overly sensitive Virgo, when faced with difficulties, can become bitterly sarcastic and moody. Their curious natures can at times lead them to be overly nosy. And this same inquisitiveness can lead to a habit of gossiping about others. Your discerning nature quite easily develops into being overly critical of other people, and you are not above making derogatory comments about others. Then too, the poorly developed Virgo individual, however well detail-oriented, is not above dishonesty or lying. Others have tendencies toward exaggeration and are persistently selfish and self-absorbed. Still others are at times treacherous, cold and impersonal.

The poorly aspected Virgo personality can produce a person who is discontented and who makes others just as unhappy. These people are narrow-minded and even retentive. The tendency to be overly critical can be destructive to the person who is otherwise striving for some sense of perfection. Being overly demanding of himself can also make a person overly demanding of others rather than understanding and perceptive of others' abilities.

Then there are other Virgo natives who dwell on details to the point of being meticulously precise rather than systematic or methodical. These people inadvertently waste time by focusing their attentions on too many unnecessary details. They appear to be searching or scrutinizing facts which are actually useless to their endeavors. This trait may easily prevent the person from being as productive as he or she would like to be.

Faced with opposition, conflicts or hostilities, Virgo natives are prone to simply leave rather than face the obstacles and problems of life. And being at times overly sensitive can lead to frustration and a vulnerability in their everyday lives. Virgo natives may choose to withdraw silently and to pout while suffering in silence. At its worse, this situation can lead to a highly paranoid person who feels others are picking on him or her.

There are those Virgos who go to great extremes to meet and associate with people who they consider important or influential. These natives aren't above the habit of name-dropping in their effort to appear more important and to gain access to more influential people.

Not to dwell on the negative, but there are those Virgos who do not develop their intellectual potential. These people base their strong egos on a feeling of natural superiority and take every opportunity to be outspoken and blunt in their drive to be better than others. This, of course, results in more harm than good, but this individual rarely realizes the mistakes being made in life.

In many of these afflicted Virgo natives there may also be found that person in whom the meticulous nature of this sign has been focused on health. This is the overly discerning individual who feels every ache and pain is a sure sign of serious illness. Either the over active mind is at work in these cases, or the person is striving to gain more attention from others. In either case, it is a negative personality trait that can cause a great deal of inconvenience not only for this person but for the other people in his life.

There are those Virgo natives who become too self-absorbed with themselves and their own ideas to the point of developing into a rather self-centered or selfish person. Others are capable of being eccentric and of going to extremes rather it be for good or bad. If these individuals possess a love for money, for example, they will pursue it with all their will becoming cunning and crafty while using other people in pursuit of their wants and desires. These particular individuals can be the most difficult for others to understand.

It is quite necessary for Virgo natives to overcome these negative tendencies and to develop their more positive attributes. All instances of discontent, impatience, unrest, inquisitiveness, cunning, deceit, and the constant pursuit of pleasure must be dealt with before these natives can attain their true power and influence. The well developed Virgo is known for being energetic, bright, industrious and ingenious. Those are traits well worth striving for in order to attain happiness and insight into life. True success in life is found only when one finds happiness and acceptance within himself.

Generally, however, being well-balanced, Virgo natives find much satisfaction in doing for others. These individuals prefer to help others rather than to dominate a situation. This is the person who is forever ready and willing to offer one favor or another to a friend or an associate. They are obliging in their everyday lives, and want to feel appreciated, useful and needed. They appear to find the greatest comfort in being able to serve others both in their personal and professional lives.

The well-aspected Virgo native is more than well prepared for a life in the modern world. Being pragmatic, analytical, and creatively discerning gifts you with the ability to succeed in a highly structured, detail-oriented life. Many feel this is the type of person who will be necessary to carry our culture and society forward in the world. Empirical thinkers are those who can handle the abundant amount of information that is encompassing our daily lives and forcing us to realize the impact of the Information Age. Others realize that when there is a task or an endeavor to be undertaken, it is the Virgo native who can best analyze the situation, deduce which aspects of the project to retain and which to eliminate, and then finish the project. You are not marked by intense emotion, activity or instability, but with a steady, well-balanced and practical nature.

How to Find Your Soul-Mate, Stars, and Destiny

Virgo Character

The Virgo natives are most inclined to be decisive and resolved. They analyze a situation, problem, or task then arrive at a solution in order to end any uncertainty or dispute. They then work diligently to complete the task at hand. There is a strong desire within these individuals to serve mankind, to better society, and to be dutiful and persevering in all that they do. The strongest word to describe the character of Virgo natives is devotion. These people are devoted in their efforts to serve and to aid others.

They are distinctive and reserved and are known for a disposition that is inclined toward moderation. This person is neither overly animated nor overly sedate. The vitality of these individuals is seen in a calmer more controlled strength and effort. Virgo is the individual who is thinking the situation out while others are rashly barging ahead in a frenzy of activity.

You, Virgo, love organization and this is reflected in your everyday life. You strive to establish a sensible daily routine that allows you to complete all the work at hand. You are not overly receptive to unnecessary changes, interruptions or surprises. And you can find unexpected events, conflicts or disruptions upsetting. You are reserved and discreet in your personal and business affairs, and at times you feel that the introduction of new people into your life is somewhat bothersome. Of course, you are flexible enough to accept compromises but only after much thought and deliberation. The uncertainties in life are most appalling to you, and you have no time nor appreciation for exaggerations or imprecise information. Neither is there time in your life for disorder or situations leading to confusion. Life, for you, should be exact and to the point. Our very reason for being, you feel, is to be productive and anything that distracts you from that pursuit is an annoyance.

The sign of Virgo influences its natives to be serious, competent, and responsible. Duty and responsibilities are important to you, and you devote yourself to working diligently, methodically, and industriously. Virgo natives are known for being detail oriented and systematic. You actually enjoy the procedural aspect of the task at hand. You discern the necessary techniques and from these fashion an effective method for proceeding. These skills carry you far in life because they are becoming more and more important in the modern world with our fast paced lifestyles and technologies.

Virgo natives enjoy seeing the results of their labor, and, needless to say, you genuinely appreciate being sincerely praised and admired for your conscientious hard work. Virgo individuals are known for being the most devoted and dependable of people. Other people realize that in all matters, Virgo can be depended on for results. But you don't waste your energies on grand ideas, speculations, or schemes. And you may reject what you feel is impractical or too visionary. You much prefer to deal with what you feel pertains to reality. You know yourself well. You realize what it is you are pursuing, what you are working toward, and how best to achieve those goals. You analyze not only others but yourself, and you set reasonable expectations as well as limitations on yourself. You have little patience with others who do not live up to the standards that you set for yourself.

Virgo natives, the same as others, strive for security and for attaining material possessions. At the same time, you are an individual recognized for being economical. You don't squander your money aimlessly buying unnecessary things or foolishly spending for pleasure. But, at the same time, you are not accused of being selfish or stingy. Because you conserve your abundant energies and resources, you are always able to give when it is necessary. And because you are a devoted person, you will at times make sacrifices if it will benefit others. You have a great need to be needed by others and to have others appreciate you. Above all else, you desire in your life other people to whom you can be a devoted companion, friend, or associate.

Wanting above all else to be a worthy person, Virgo individuals set high standards for themselves. You are a virtuous person who, after careful and discerning consideration, establishes a code of personal conduct which enhances an habitual practice of orderliness and regularity. This rational orderliness carries over to all aspects of your life. In addition to that, the chances are that you have a great respect for customs and traditions or at least your personal preference in such matters. Having established your individual preferences, you then not only hold yourself to these standards but others as well. You want for all things in life to make sense and to fit into rational categories that can be inspected, observed and analyzed. And from these observations, you draw conclusions pertaining to life and to yourself and to people in general. You are conservative and cautious in this regard, wanting what is best for all concerned.

Your high standards lead you to be a person striving for self-improvement also. Virgo natives with their well organized and methodical minds easily deduce that there are means by which people can better all areas of life. Be this intellectually, spiritually, or physically, you perceive that by making every effort to improve yourself, you will in the long run be a better person. You energetically seek means by which you can develop your potentials into the best possible person you can be. In this pursuit of self-improvement you deploy the same depth of detail and care as in all other areas of your life.

The Virgo native relies most heavily on a well-developed and strong intellect and on reasoning ability. You have strong deductive reasoning abilities which you utilize to the utmost. In this regard, you can be a critical thinker. And this purely innate characteristic also leads you to be discriminating and tasteful in the other areas of your life. While you may possess a creative nature, you take great care to shy away from being the center of attention. You are much more likely to stand away from the group and to use your observational skill to draw conclusions pertaining to the surrounding activities. You love to observe, to take notes, and to size up the situation and other people, and in this you can be quite astute. You are aware of the interplay of other people, but you prefer to remain reserved and to draw your own conclusions.

This well developed sense of observation combined with a creative and natural wit produces a person who can size up a situation and offer categorical comments at will. You possess the ability to be concise and to make your point with a certain brevity of expression. You are not one to waste time or energy on elaboration. You can be brief, to the point and at times terse. Observing as you do all that is going on, you can at times be not only critical by what others might think as being a bit caustic in your comments. You would prefer that others lived up to your standards, but that is not always the case. Some Virgo natives have been known to be aloof, cold and harsh in their treatment of other people. This for the most part is only the natural Virgo ability to observe and critique the situation or persons at hand. Being direct and to the point, you may become impatient with others who don't possess this ability.

There are some Virgo individuals who are known for taking excessive time to deliberate before making a decision. This person is prone to procrastination rather than taking the chance on speedy or hasty actions. Faced with a difficult situation, this person may lose his energy and become physically and mentally exhausted. There are many Virgo natives who pay too much attention to detail and who spend too much time in deliberation while overlooking the bigger picture. This makes it difficult, at times, to take decisive action.

The Virgo native is best known for being well balanced in their personal and professional lives. They love to work and to be productive. They are both skillful and methodical. Many of these individuals possess the talents to become successful in their pursuits and to find fulfillment and happiness in life.

How to Find Your Soul-Mate, Stars, and Destiny

Virgo Destiny

Endowed with the many natural gifts of the sign of Virgo, these natives can well expect successes in life. With your keen intellect and sensible natures you possess your own perspective on the world around you. You strive and endeavor to accomplish whatever you set out to do. You are discriminating and exhibit sound judgment in your daily life and in your professional life. Generally speaking, you are not easily taken advantage of or deceived in life. You accomplish your goals, and your successes are realized through your hard work and natural capacities. You may well expect to attain your goals and realize your wishes in life with high expectations of a calm and peaceful retirement.

There is an indication for the Virgo natives to have a life that is exposed to some dangerous situations, accidents, or illnesses. Also, there is a tendency toward material losses. It is seen that the life of Virgo individuals knows both loss and gain, and the person realizes a progressive gain with the life becoming even better and more secure with time. The person ends up in a better situation than where he or she began.

Gains will be realized through hard work and diligence. In young adulthood, material gain may not be great, but while there may be some losses, the person becomes more fortunate. There is some inclination for gains through inheritance and perhaps the accumulation of property through a spouse or business partner. Gain is shown through the professional life and at times through marriage. Some natives will acquire financial success through travel, most particularly to foreign countries. While Virgo natives may find that they are successful in business enterprises, this same luck does not generally hold in speculative matters. In many cases, relatives and neighbors do not bring luck or success in business.

If well aspected, the Virgo native is inclined toward financial gains through public occupations or associations with government agencies and civil endeavors. Virgo is favored toward realizing profits from trading, commodities, sound investments, and import and export businesses. Success is also seen in scientific endeavors and with others in farming or ranching.

If afflicted, there is every indication for numerous difficulties and disappointments. There may be difficulties associated with employees or through the place of employment. The afflicted individual suffers from limitations and restrictions found in the work place or in the career. This person may also suffer from sudden illnesses. The afflicted can also suffer from a selfish, deceitful nature which is inclined toward the use of drugs and alcohol which may cause illnesses.

The location of Mars may place obstacles in the path of Virgo natives causing many struggles in life. These obstacles may produce reversals in gains, annoyances or oppositions to the Virgo natives' ambitions and desires. When Mars is afflicted, the native may well become irritable, rash, stubborn, egotistical, withdrawn and revengeful. These people may suffer from loss of friends and associates through quarrels, misunderstandings, or harsh words. Excessive work may cause accidents or illnesses.

Venus in Virgo places an inclination for these individuals to experience some delay and disappointment in love affairs. There may well be secret love affairs and perhaps more than one affair at the same time. Also, there is seen the possibility of a relationship with a person who is either an employer or an employee. Be careful of making an enemy through a love affair.

After many difficulties, Virgo natives generally realize success in life, but numerous difficulties and strife result in inconveniences to those born of this sign. There may be numerous changes in locations and residences. At or after retirement, the Virgo native may have more than one residence.

Changing associations and friends is indicated. The changes in life bring about relationships with different groups of friends or associates. There is also an indication of friendships or partnerships that are made through travel. Persons of a speculative nature will not appreciate the Virgo native's restraint. This person may cause you problems. Then too, there are those native Virgos who pay too much attention to the moral attitude of other people. These natives can easily become too critical and stubborn, and in their effort to remain pure, they become inhibited. Because of this, their natural intelligence and talents are not utilized to the fullest.

Native Virgos are for the most part very serious thinkers, and duty and responsibility are important to them. The people of this sign gravitate toward moderation in all aspects of life. This person is well organized and detail-minded and is seldom caught unaware by unexpected events resulting from a lack of foresight or poor planning.

Overall, the destiny of Virgo natives is to achieve successes through their efforts. Taking advantage of their natural strengths will gain for them much accomplishment and fulfillment in life.

Virgo Occupation

Many Virgos are overly endowed with gifts and abilities which endlessly enhance their professional lives. There are any number of career choices available to these industrious people. The most difficult problem must be choosing which field of endeavor or which career field is most suitable for you. Chances are that after careful consideration, thought, and planning, which ever decision you make, you will excel and find success.

For example, many Virgos find success in the medical professions as either doctors, nurses or diagnosticians. Other Virgos develop their skills to become noted philosophers and analytical thinkers. Still others are talented and naturally able teachers. Then too, the analytical skills and inclinations of Virgo individuals provide them with natural abilities to achieve in scientific fields. This is also the person best suited for technological fields which require precision and a detail-oriented mind.

It is quite obvious that being systematic and methodical, these individuals are well suited for a career in business or accounting becoming talented CPAs or statisticians. Virgo natives with their sense of structure and organization make capable and responsible administrators, managers, and department heads. These people attain prominence in the fields of education and in corporate law. Success has also been realized in the literary fields as writers and editors and in areas requiring technical writing and production. These are the people who excel at preparing textbooks, manuals, guidelines, and instructions for others. Another area of interest is computer programming and hardware design.

The Virgo mind readily grasps the concepts involved in trading whether it be in commodities, stocks and bonds, or in commercial enterprises. You may well find success in any area of the import or export business which requires an astute mind. At the same time, many Virgo natives are drawn to military careers or to government employment as civil servants, diplomats, and technicians. These individuals are talented not only in technical but also in mechanical fields.

Other Virgo natives develop their talents for analyzing and for detail and combine these with a sense of color and form to make outstanding artists, graphic designers, and skilled draft persons. Others prefer to develop their musical talents and become notable entertainers. Any field of endeavor requiring the acquisition of these skills will be suitable for the concise Virgo mind. Actors born to the sign of Virgo are creative people who apply themselves to their art, but they may find that they have a need to overcome their reserved nature in public.

Mercury, the ruling planet of this sign, endows its natives with naturally quick wits and a sense of humor and also with an ingenious mind. Virgo natives are quite capable of applying this charm in all that they do. They are also quite capable of losing themselves in their work and what they see as their duty. This is the person who isn't afraid of self-sacrifice, restraint, or self-denial to realize the fruits of his or her efforts. They love to devote themselves to the task at hand and to serve well their current endeavors. Virgos quite easily become dedicated to their careers and make outstanding professionals. The combination of their many strong and worthwhile attributes often leads to a successful life for the persons born to the sign of Virgo. In this respect, it is seen that hard work and diligence are most beneficial traits.

Virgo Marriage

When Virgos find harmony, congeniality and companionship in marriage they also realize a great deal of security in life. Marriage can be an enriching experience providing for these individuals a source of contentment and happiness. Virgo's are for the most part marriage prone. Marriage is seen as representing a secure environment offering a safe harbor. A home after all can provide a peaceful routine, and the affections, comfort, and tranquillity a loved one can provide. Virgo natives are gentle, protective and supportive of their spouses. It is important in the area of marriage for Virgos to seek spouses who share their inclinations and interests in life. This must be a person who also seeks the comforts of routine and a peaceful setting. The discerning native may well decide to take his or her time in selecting a mate before making that final decision to settle down.

A Virgo may discover that the most suitable person for marriage is another Virgo because they may most appreciate each other's traits and personalities. In this case, it is very important that these two share the same outlook and perspectives on lifestyles, values, interests and standards.

Other compatible partners may be found in the sign of Pisces (February 19 to March 20) who are also sensitive in nature. Then too, you may find that an Aries (March 21 to April 20) best appreciates your devotion. Taurus natives (April 21 to May 20) share your inclination toward hard work, diligence, efforts, and home.

The Virgo native is most outstanding in his or her ability to remain faithful in marriage. However, if the person feels that a mistake has been made in a marriage, this may not hold true. There is some indication for a second marriage in the lives of many Virgo individuals.

Virgos prefer a peaceful setting, and if instead they find themselves in a situation that offers uncertainties, complaints, and disruptions, they will become unhappy and discontent. The Virgo above all else must feel needed and appreciated, and in marriage, these people have a desire to feel loved and wanted. If, for one reason or another, this person becomes dissatisffied in the domestic situation, he or she can become over demanding, critical, moody, and discontented with life in general.

It may well be that Virgo natives choose to marry later in life after they have established their careers and lifestyles. Many Virgos prefer to take their time in selecting a mate. This is not just being picky in this area of life, there is certainly no reason to rush or to make hurried decisions. Virgo individuals are discerning, and marriage to them is a very important decision, as well it should be. When this person does decide to marry, he or she becomes devoted, loving, and tender. Virgos tend to work as hard at their relationship as they do at all other aspects in their lives. Being astute, the Virgo native realizes that relationships and love grow and mature with time.

While many Virgos are not overly demonstrative, they are affectionate and passionate. These natives enjoy the physical and sexual relationship of marriage, and this is an area where compatibility is most important. If Virgo finds a mate who makes that him feel most needed in this area of life, then there is rarely any straying. Chances are that this sharing and affection will carry over into other areas of their lives.

When the Virgo sign is at the Ascendant, the sign of Pisces is in the House of Marriage. In many instances, this indicates arguments, divorces and other marriages. These marriages are not well-balanced. However, as has been stated, otherwise Pisces and Virgo can also make a good match. The importance of getting to know and appreciate the other person is noted.

If at all possible, Virgo natives prefer to keep their marriages intact and will make every attempt to do so. Of course, this requires effort and determination on the part of both of the individuals involved. Virgo must guard against harassing his spouse with critical or sharp remarks. Often the damage done in these instances is not easily repaired. In order to receive love and affection, turn on that famous charm and remember to be loving and affectionate yourself.

The Virgo Man

Virgo men are pleasant and attentive, and if he has a reserved nature, it doesn't prevent him from being cheerful and charming. These men are also contemplative and provident. Of all the signs, this man may be the most productive. A hard worker, he also has a love for the domestic situation and makes a good provider who is supportive of the other person in his life. Virgos are generally neat and well organized in both their person and their surroundings. This man is particularly fond of and proud of his powers of observation. Virgos are problem solvers, and no problem is too small nor too large for this man to undertake and contemplate. In fact, he may well be known for his shrewdness in solving everyday problems. He loves to analyze and to pick apart the details in a complex situation. He is curious in nature and has a great desire to acquire knowledge and information. He has many interests and energetically pursues them all.

In appearance, he is generally reserved and carries himself in a dignified manner. He can even be quite elegant at times. Because of his reserved manner, he may appear more serious than happy, but he is most content when his mind is busily engaged. It may be that his many intellectual interests preoccupy his mind to the point that he doesn't appear to be a romantic, but don't let that fool you. He may be reticent in his approach toward the opposite sex, but once aroused he is most ardent in his love affairs. And as is true in other areas of his life, he takes his romantic relationship quite seriously.

If the Virgo man has a critical nature it is simply a reflection of how his mind works more than an attempt to hurt the other person. More than likely, he is as critical of himself as he is of others. He strives for self-improvement and is most particular in this regard. He sets high values and standards for himself, and to be happy and content, he desires to find another person who shares these same feelings as well as a sense or need for practicalities in life. He has an appreciation for order and neatness and he appreciates these attributes in others.

This man is settled within himself. He is both self-confident and self-assured. He is very rarely rattled, but inconsistencies or the impulsive actions of others may upset him. He attempts in all things to be logical and to apply sound reasoning ability to all aspects of his life. Others are attracted to him for this reason. Many will seek him out for help or assistance in solving problems. Virgo men make the most devoted and dutiful partners in all relationships.

The Virgo Woman

Virgo women can be sensitive and shy or flirtatious and buoyant. They have strong minds and intellects, and are just as hard working as their male counterparts. With a high regard for standards, these women aspire to set high aspirations and to hold themselves to them. Many times this comes across as a certain purity in their nature, for they strive to do well in all that they attermpt to accomplish. Being critical thinkers, they have a keen appreciation for purity of thought. A well-formed idea or thought is valued by this woman.

The Virgo woman is both loving and affectionate. But her greatest virtue, she believes, is found in her desire to devote herself to the other people in her life. She discovers within herself a self-appreciation and a self-reward when she is allowed to express this great need. She would very much like to see others happy and content because, according to her higher reasoning ability, this is what life is all about. It only makes sense for life to be a pleasing experience, and to this end she strives to give, to aid, and to help others find this inner peace.

The Virgo female is particular in her dress, fashion, home, and career. She is detail-oriented and all the little details of life should fall into place neatly and in an orderly manner. There is no time for anything less to her astute mind. To a large degree, she may be absolutely correct. Of course, others may fall short of this expectation ofperfection and then the trouble can begin. Like the male Virgo native, this woman has developed being critical into a fine art. And it is this which she must most strive to control. But perhaps the world could use a good critic, and who better than a Virgo woman.

Virgo women have a strong maternal instinct and make excellent and devoted mothers and wives. In a domestic situation, finally surrounded by others who need her and depend her, the Virgo woman finds bliss. To seduce a Virgo woman, be neat, punctual and display characteristics of genuine concern and honesty.

In her professional life, the Virgo female deploys her greatest skills and practical mind toward becoming devoted to others in the work place and to succeeding at any and all endeavors. This is a highly capable and perceptive women who is not afraid of making every diligent effort to succeed.

The women of Virgo are for the most part known for an enduring charm and for a sensitive and loving nature. And it goes without saying that they are as passionate as they are loving. They love with a great depth of emotion which displays the purity of their hearts. These charming and devoted women, born under the sign of Virgo, display many of the talents and skills necessary to acquire satisfaction, fulfillment, and successes in life.

Virgo Love Life

You, Virgo, are the most discerning of people and this trait carries over into your love life and romantic relationships. You are not a person to leave your love life to chance, but rather you take every opportunity to analyze your relationships--which is only natural with the rulership of Mercury. You can make love and even sex more complicated than it is for others. You set high standards for yourself and for others. There will be those more emotional persons who consider you cold and aloof, but you must remember that not all people in life are as particular as you. No one need tell you that this is a higher quality in life than accepting anyone and everyone who comes along. But, all that aside, you have another, rather contrasting characteristic in your relationships. This is found in your most basic need, and this is your innately profound nature which desires to be loved and appreciated for all of your good qualities and diligent efforts to succeed. At the same time, you are both passionate and desirable, and you desire and seek the same qualities in your romantic partners. While you most enjoy being devoted to another person, you greatly appreciate it when these sentiments are returned in equal measure. And who would desire anything less? You are attracted to others who are dignified and intellectual, and you prefer being treated with a high degree of regard and respect. For the most part, you don't possess an inclination to be experimental with love. You know what you want, and that's what you are seeking in a relationship - the fulfillment of your wishes, dreams, and aspirations.

There are those Virgo natives who appear somewhat reticent and even fearful or shy when it comes to matters of the heart. These individuals are reluctant to become involved and are hesitant to commit to any long term emotional involvement. This can be taken too far, in some instances, and can result in disillusionment and disappointments because it may be difficult to find a balance in emotional ties and relationships. At the same time, Virgos desire a strong, loving relationship with another person with whom to share their innermost thoughts and even their emotions.

In matters of the heart, when you do find that special someone and fall in love, you not only become devoted but you are willing to forsake all else for that person. When it is a good choice, you and your loved one discover many of the joys of life, sharing and exploring the world. You do best with a person who excites your mind with his or her equally well developed intellect, curiosity and keen nature. And you also love to be told repeatedly that you are loved and wanted.

The only advice necessary for these discerning Virgo individuals is to watch against being susceptible. Many people project the qualities they most want into another person rather than seeing the real person as he or she is. And this pattern can continue for years while the individual attempts to persuade the other person to live up to some vague projected image. These situations don't work out well for either party. When the Virgo individual finally realizes and admits that this isn't the right person for him or her, it is a disappointment. But Virgo natives may attempt to hold on to this love by carrying it in their heart for a long time.

How to Find Your *Soul-Mate, Stars,* and *Destiny*

That caution aside, Virgo, you have a healthy and robust libido. You are strongly attracted to the opposite sex, and you enjoying flirting and socializing with those who intrigue you. At times you become a bit of a tease while you observe and attempt to make up your own mind. And then too, you may simply love the attentions of others and the fun that can be found when you are surrounded by interesting people. You find that your attraction to another person is heightened and your curiosity captured when there is more than just a physical enticement. You have a strong desire to explore the other person's mind, personality and intellect. When you find an individual who fully attracts you, and who proves to your discerning mind to be worthy of your attentions, you shed all inhibitions and shower the other person with caring, tenderness, and your own very special responsiveness. You are ardent in your attentions, and it is important to you that there is a mutual sharing that is satisfying and gratifying.

You may discover strong physical attractions to Leo (July 23-August 22), but be sure that you allow this person to lead and to be right in any discussions. Also, there may be intense physical attractions between Virgo and Sagittarius (November 22-December 20) although you two may have different perspectives on life. You will also find attractions between yourself and either Capricorn (December 21-January 19), or Pisces (February 1- March 20) natives or then again consider Aquarius (January 20 - February 18) individuals.

With your busy and demanding days, this is an area of life when you find yourself having to make time. You are a person with a great variety of interests and pursuits, and at the same time you require for yourself a peaceful and calm setting in order to function to your fullest, most productive ability. Therefore, your social life and your love life in particular require an added degree of attention. If you want to expand this area of your life, you will need to cognitively make the time to investigate and explore the social avenues available to you. This isn't as difficult as it sounds, and it won't require as much time and effort as many of your more serious contemplations, but it will require a definite effort on your part. This isn't an area of life to be safely placed on a shelf while you wait for the time to attend to it. Find the time, devote your creative resources to it, and fully pursue relationships with others which will in return provide you with an additional outlet for your energies. Others will discover that your personal traits make you a most desirable person with whom to become acquainted.

Virgo Children

Virgo children have been observed to mature at an early age. They possess serious and curious minds. They find enjoyment in achieving in scholastics, and, if not it is because they have focused their keen minds and observational skills in another direction. Be assured they are studying something. If they are quiet, it is because their busy minds are actively pursuing some subject matter which is important to them.

This child becomes discerning and particular early in life. At times, it may seem that the child is picky and bossy at home. Actually, this child has a pronounced perception of how she or he would like to have things done. They have strong opinions, and, feeling secure at home, they aren't bashful in speaking their minds.

A highly curious mind can be quite beneficial, but it can also get a child into trouble. As with all children, the Virgo child requires supervision and guidance. Satisfy the mind of this child, and no doubt, he or she will prefer to steer clear of any real problems. A secure family environment which provides a peaceful, calm routine will best benefit this child. Make every effort to provide an abundance of materials for creative play, investigation and problem-solving. These children want to know how things work, so don't become upset if different things around the house show up in pieces, taken apart and then not put back together. You will not be able to change this natural inclination, so be prepared to accept it. Both you and the child will be happier in the long run. This is a child who wants to be happy and loved, and to express the same in return.

Express yourself to the Virgo child and help these children to express themselves. This is a worthy learning experience for both adults and children and draws them closer together. And close relationships can benefit both children and adults. Draw the Virgo child out through conversations and activities, and teach them to describe what it is they are thinking about. Also, help this child to express his or her emotions and feelings. Discuss and set limits and standards with these children, and they will respond much more readily to your suggestions. Don't forget to let this child know that you are devoted to him or to her, that you love them, and that they are important.

Relationships with Other Signs

The Virgo native being self-confident and reserved, in most instances doesn't feel the need to impress others and to stand out in the crowd. This is the friendly and charming person who may prefer to stand apart from the group, and it may be necessary for others to seek him or her out. This has nothing to do with being friendly or unfriendly, it's just that Virgo individuals are self-composed. They don't require the constant attentions of others to make them feel good about themselves or to reassure their egos. It isn't necessary for this person to be in the lime light or to be the center of attention. In fact, they may just shy away from such overt attentions. Virgo natives are sincere and trusting people. With a group of close friends or associates, their natural humor and quick wit emerges and they are engaging and interesting conversationalists.

You are as discerning in your public relationships as in all other areas of your life. You have so much going on in your life already, that you prefer to make friends with people who share a similar serious attitude and outlook on life. You appreciate other people who are hard working and talented and who can carry on an intelligent, well-informed conversation. At the same time, you are accepting of others and generally speaking are not accused of being a snob or discriminating against those who have different interests than you. Rather, you find that such a person has much to offer in the way of new information and new insights into the world around you. You are forever curious about other people and love to observe the crowd. Given the time, you would enjoy nothing better than the opportunity to observe and analyze the behavior patterns of others. Possessing a strong interest in the well-being of society, you would love to apply your observations and patterns to the betterment of society at large. You would also like to know what makes it all tick, why is it happening, and where is it all going. You may find that you don't fully appreciate being around people with strong, forceful personalities.

This is the person that others turn to with personal concerns because Virgo natives are adept at problem solving. Add to that a sincere and caring nature, and it only stands to reason that others will seek you out. Others discover that they can trust your opinion in important matters. In many Virgos this fulfills for them their need to be of service to others and to help people however and whenever they can. If you make a Virgo friend, you will soon discover and realize that it is a relationship with one of the most devoted and genuine of people. Yes, it is true that this same person can be critical and demanding, but this comes naturally combined with witticism and flair rather than an intent to harm. Virgos' friends learn to appreciate this discerning and critical nature and are rewarded with a glimpse at new insights of the world at large.

The hard working and tenacious natives of Virgo and Taurus (April 21-May 20) may find that they share tendencies to be truthful and faithful, and they may well establish strong friendships. Virgos may share cultural and spiritual inclinations with Gemini (May 21-June 21), but Gemini's pursuit of change will leave Virgo's more serious nature feeling slightly unbalanced. While Virgos will be attracted to friendships with Geminis (May 21-June 21) because of their introspective natures, Virgo is often the more rational person and Gemini may be too sensitive to any Virgo criticisms. While you may find the robust energy of Leo (July 23-August 22) physically attractive, it is important to develop mutual interests and respect with this native, and you may discover that to engage in meaningful conversation means to agree with Leo. Libra (September 23-October 22) natives develop a great deal of respect and regard for the natural inclinations of Virgo, and they find your ability to critique all situations charming rather than offensive. You may find that you lack an appreciation for Scorpio (October 23-November 21) who love a good and lively argument while you prefer that everything be settled peacefully. Pisces (February 19 - March 20) who are loving and have an imaginative personality which you find inspiring. It may be found that you discover your most enduring friendships with others born to the sign of Virgo and with persons born: on the cusp of Aries and Taurus, the cusp of Taurus and Gemini, the cusp of Capricorn and Aquarius, and the cusp of Pisces and Aries.

While not the most extroverted person in a group, the self-confidence of the Virgo native predisposes this person to be surrounded by close friends and associates who appreciate their ingenious, serious, responsible, and sincere characteristics. You are a good and faithful friend. Seek out those who appreciate you the way you are because you have much to offer to other people. Become aware of the more sensitive natures of those individuals who can't handle your sharp wit and critical perspectives on life.

Virgo Sexuality

That subject which interests us all: our own personal sexuality. Why does a person feel the way they do? Why does he or she like a certain person and not another? What arouses a person and why? On some level, these questions influences one and all. Like all aspects of our lives and lifestyles, the public attitude toward sex is ever changing and evolving. From the restrictive taboos of the Victorian Age, through the revitalization of the Industrial Age, to the make love not war of the 1960s to the commercialism of the 1980s and the 1990s, sex is always on our minds. Will the Age of Information or the Age of Aquarius bring new insights?

The American culture is not only influenced by popular trends and thought but by its unique cultural diversity as well. To the newcomer or newly arrived, American society can appear perplexing. What is difficult to understand is that in this freedom-based culture, the individual is literally free to be whoever he or she decides. And the gamut runs from the most traditional, reserved, cautious, and sexually repressed individuals to others who flaunt their sexuality, centering their lives around their sexual habits. Perhaps it is because of this very diversity that our culture makes some attempt not to be overly offensive to the sensitivities of some while giving a tolerant nod to the liberties of others. We are totally free, within the guidelines of laws, to seek divine enlightenment or to destroy ourselves with pleasures. Americans have the freedom to choose, individually, what importance their sexual behavior will play in their lives.

That being the case, sex is recognized by every serious discipline--from psychologists to scientists to astrologers--as being a central focus on individual lives. Freud saw sex as an influence on every aspect of the individual life. And from the sexist boys in the locker room to the most enlightened of intellectuals, sex remains a fundamental part of life that cannot be ignored. Get two friends together and the subject eventually turns to sex, romance, or marriage. One can blame it on the media, but sooner or later discussing the stock market gets boring, but sex never does.

There are those who hold to the theory that the primary function of sex is to have children and any other consideration is secondary. There are others for whom sex is an integral part of life, providing one of the greatest stress relievers ever invented. That all other living species procreate seasonally points to the reasoning of the second theory. But all pleasures (or temptations) in life also promote the possibilities of problems and health concerns unless a little logic is also applied.

Astrologically, the sexual nature has been examined from the Garden of Eden to the lives of contemporary celebrities. And what every serious astrologer will say is that how the individual relates to sexuality is not based on the Sun sign alone. The entire chart must be examined because each person is a unique combination of Sun, Moon, Ascendant, planets, Houses and aspects. A comparison of two charts often sheds light on compatibility. Compatibility between two people is often found when the Sun sign is in the same sign as their lover's Ascendant, or vice versa. Opposite Sun signs or an opposite Sun sign and Ascendant may also blend well together.

In a woman's chart, the placement of Venus is indicative of her sexuality while the position of Mars and the Sun indicates what kind of man she is attracted to. In a man's chart, the position of Mars tells how he relates to women, and the position of Venus and the Moon indicates what type of woman arouses him. In comparing two charts, look for the aspects of conjunction, sextile, square, trine, and oppositions. Remember that oppositions can blend. The square brings differences but much energy while conjunctions can be beneficial. The sextile and trine bring harmony. When a person's Venus and their lover's Mars are in the same sign, there is a strong attraction even if differences of opinions occur. When Venus and the other person's Ascendant are in the same sign, it adds to the sexual compatibility. Venus in the lover's sun sign brings a mutual interest while Mars in the lover's Moon sign is emotionally intense.

There is a vast variety of people found within each Sun sign, but basic characteristics and traits do exist. However, generalizations are just that and a fuller picture of the individual is reflected by the complete chart. The following section deals with Sun sign sexuality in a general manner. While the importance of sex remains the same in each Sun sign, the focus and attitudes vary.

Virgo Sexuality - Man

After applying his analytical thinking, critical skills, and observations in history, human behavior, or sexuality, it may have been a Virgo man who first noted that convention and societal mores change, vary, and evolve with time and culture. And that homosexuality existed with the ancients (for example the Greeks), with other societies, and with native peoples of the earth all of whom accepted this aspect of sexuality with tolerance. Having arrived at that conclusion, the Virgo man will decide upon his own sexuality but may out of caution remain an observer rather than an active participant. There is so much to think about regarding any subject related to sex and romance. And think he will while enumerating in great details the disadvantages verses the advantages of becoming involved in a sexual relationship. This isn't a man to follow his desires or to make rash and impulsive decisions. Many of his female acquaintances while enjoying his companionship, will remain friends only while he further thinks about it. He may relent and enter into a number of relationships but always with some fear that it might lead to an unwanted pregnancy or a relationship he will have difficulty getting out of if he decides it isn't the one for him. And with the prevalence of sexually transmitted diseases, even that age-old standby of the prostitute may be viewed as definitely questionable. As he matures and becomes financially secure, he then has to worry about finding a woman who isn't after his money. He is salt-of-the-earth and hard working and expends his diligent efforts and energies on succeeding at his endeavors. His stress level summits at extremely high levels while he continues to think about his situation.

Virgo is the virgin of the Zodiac, and even those with a sexually active life retain some form of the virginal attitude in their encounters. Given a few planetary aspects or an adventuresome Moon or Ascendant, he may experiment with sexual diversions, but in his mind these are always explainable and he remains the virgin in thought. The Virgo man may find that throughout life he is attracted to younger females or women who retain a virginal look. But that in itself presents a problem because this is a very conventional man. His actions must appear within the guidelines of appropriate social behavior.

This is not a macho man driven to prove his masculinity. This is a rational, thinking man who knows intellectually that there is absolutely no need to prove what he already knows. He is a man. Virgo can take this analogy to the extreme and use his mind to maintain control over the sexual demands of his body. He sets high standards for himself and for the others in his life, and this relates to his sexuality as much as any other area of his life. This is the "nice guy" of the Zodiac, and he attracts his fair share of attractive females who realize what a gem of a person he actually is. He is a wonderful companion who is fun to be with, talkative, companionable, and sincere. He doesn't lead a woman on just to get sexual favors--that would be beneath his standards.

He is a warmly lovable man and what finally captivates his attention is finding a woman he can trust and who fits within his safe and sure guidelines, precautions and standards. Then he becomes more than willing to participate in an active and fun sex life. Yes, for all his seriousness,

Virgo does like the spice of fun in his relationships. These two may have so many activities in their life from careers to gardening to planning a proper diet and health regime that sex is relegated to its more than proper perspective.

Is this attitude unhealthy? This attitude works for Virgo, and he knows that. He knows exactly what works and what doesn't work in his life because he has thought about it and deduced the proper prospective for all areas of his life. What can catch him unawares is if some scheming female sneaks up on the back side of his caution and takes advantage of his pent up sexuality knowing that once she has him in bed he'll be a push over. But Virgo is well aware of that possibility and stays alert just to prevent such an occurrence. It is the lucky Virgo man who finds that perfect and true woman of his plans - one who can fulfill his earthly passions in bed and be a lady in public.

Virgo Sexuality - Woman

Using the same Virgo logic as the man, the Virgo woman arrives at an entirely different conclusion. If life's perfect order is for a woman to marry and start a family, then she must marry. She may think about it for some time, and like the Virgo male, put it off a little longer than other people--but her biological clock is ticking granting her only so much time to think. Action is called for in this event. What saves the day is that this is a demure, soft spoken and feminine woman who without much effort knows how to make a man feel like a man. All she has to do is admire Leo and let him lead, make Aries think he is the greatest, or appreciate hard working Taurus, etc. Is she happy then? Let's hope she is happy because if she isn't, this modern version of the virgin can come out with a string of expletives that would put a sailor to shame. This is a sharp women with a quick mind. If Aries isn't producing new ideas, if Leo isn't leading in a positive direction, or if Taurus is loaning money to his Gemini brother again, this isn't a woman content to sit quietly by. Her observations can become critical and what men call nagging.

Moving on to the happy Virgo female, she is talkative and involved in a number of activities. If she is a career woman, then she is good at what she does. She knows how to put her sexuality in the proper perspective, and she does this effectively. If in a relationship with a capable, well meaning, and loving man who shares her interests and values, then her sexuality becomes a natural part of life.

The Virgo female is as intelligent as her male counterpart in the Zodiac and knows it. After she has thought about it and decided what she wants in life, she goes after it. Many a Virgo female, after giving it careful consideration, will decide that if her sexuality can serve her in her purposes then she should use it. She is an astute observer of history herself and realizes that women have been using their sexuality for centuries either because they had to or because that is the one area where men are weakest and most vulnerable. And men are vulnerable to her charms. She could be criticized herself for that attitude, but then if life were a fair and equal playing field, her attitude wouldn't be necessary. Many a Virgo female is looking for a rich man to support her. Because she can keep her own sexuality under control, she is capable of analyzing what a man needs and wants, and not easily shocked, she can use whatever technique, toy or manner of erotic persuasion that best excites him. Passions and emotions may be left to the other signs while this woman concentrates on technique.

Virgo is by nature distrustful of emotions--that world of unknown or unpredictable conclusions. She is much more comfortable relying on her mind and evolved thought processes. She is self-possessed and uses her energies to control her emotions. She can be discriminating and discerning and will take the time she needs to decide upon a man or a relationship. And she takes her time in falling in love. This lack of spontaneity hides a deep, earthy passion which can be unlocked when the right person comes along and proves to be not only trustworthy but worthy of her affections. Then her sexuality blooms and blossoms, slowly unfolding all of her natural instincts for creativity and affection. She can be warm and responsive and on other occasions light hearted and fun. Within each Virgo woman is held the true persona of the loving female who wants to devote herself fully to her mate. But winning this woman requires a person willing to strive and to make the effort to please her and to fulfill her. In return, she is a person who gives in full measure.

Try a little play time in the bath or shower to arouse the Virgo lover. And in bed pay special attention to stroking and kissing the length of her body from her neck and breasts over her abdomen and back up again. Virgo likes efficiency, and once she is aroused, oral sex or a vibrator will heighten her pleasures bringing alive her desire for more of her lover and her sexual energies will come into full play. Then be prepared for an energetic race to the finish line with this winsome woman. Virgo develops her own sexuality depending upon her rationale and thought processes. This is a thinking woman and hopefully a sexually fulfilled one as well.

Virgo Health

Virgos are often knowledgeable about health and nutrition, and this is the person who will tell others all about the benefits of a low fat diet. The sign of Virgo rules over the digestive system, and Virgos are found to be as particular about their diets and food preparation as they are about other areas of their life. These people appreciate meals that are well-prepared, and table settings that are pleasing. In other words, their food should not only taste good and be good for them, but also look appealing. This is one area of life where presentation ranks high. Many of these people realize the importance of the relationship between diet and health. Mars in Virgo provides these natives with the ability to resist disease by utilizing proper hygiene and by taking the necessary dietary precautions. At the same time, if health problems do occur they may well be associated with complaints related to the digestive tract.

Virgos may find themselves sensitive to their environments and surroundings. Any disturbance of the natural setting may well leave these individuals feeling nervous or upset. This nervousness can lead to related health complaints such as headaches, nervous stomachs, and in some instances even despondency or depression. In some instances the Virgo discovers discomforts associated with the lungs such as colds and viruses. Also there is some inclination for problems with pain and discomfort in the arms and shoulders. It is important for these natives to use moderation in their alcohol consumption. And an overactive mind may lead many Virgos to have problems obtaining sufficient rest and sleep. This too will add to any nervous problems which these people may already be suffering from. Virgos are susceptible to problems associated with the throat and eyes, bowel disorders, colic, dysentery, diarrhea, uterine infections, constipation, and associated blood disorders.

There may be times when the native feels mentally and physically tired or exhausted. Then at other times this person may have periods of being overly active which in turn leads to periods of mental and physical overexertion. This may well be related to an overactive thyroid which the native must become aware of. This condition is treatable with medication.

There are those Virgos who easily develop into hypochondriacs, imagining a great many more illnesses and complaints than actually exists. These are the people whose very thoughts can turn imaginary illnesses into real ones.

Virgos have a need to leave their comfortable surroundings and to seek activities out of doors. An exercise program which preferable includes outdoor activities is beneficial and enjoyable. The Virgo, once he sets his or her mind to it, develops a great appreciation for these types of activities. Pushing one's self physically results in a stronger more vigorous nature which reduces problems with being overly nervous or concerned. Worries may fall by the way side because the individual actually feels like he or she can handle anything that comes along. Virgos are already prone toward self-improvement and when this trait is focused on diet, health and exercise, the person naturally responds to the challenge.

Physical health also adds to the mental abilities of the Virgos. Many Virgo individuals are strongly influenced toward spiritual and meditative powers, and a healthy mind and body adds to the receptiveness of the person to fully appreciate and to develop his or her inner strengths. The fully developed Virgo personality is possessed with the ability to realize the energies of the Universe and to do this in a manner that promotes a peaceful and tranquil state of mind. Seeking the calm and peaceful setting that you most enjoy will enhance your stamina which in many instances is fueled by nervous energy, and nervous energy can lead to stress. Develop your keen and observational mind, but also learn the powers of relaxation and meditation to discover the available and abundant amount of mental and physical energy to carry you through your day. Your great amount of reserved energies will improve when you learn to realign your emotional well being. Rely less on your nervous energy and more on the natural physical and mental energies available to you.

History of Virgo

The Greek's considered the constellation of Virgo to be Parthenos the Maid which was ruled by Demeter, the Earth Mother. In Babylon, the sign of Virgo was called the Furrow and was represented with a corn-goddess. But the rulership of Virgo was eventually transferred to Mercury. The association of the Virgin with Virgo may well have more to do with purity of thought and a love of what is just and appropriate behavior. The Greeks and Romans associated Virgo with Astraea, a goddess of justice. Astraea lived during the Golden Age when all was at peace in the heavens and on Earth. When war and corruption came to the Earth, Astraea chose to live in the heavens where she became a star in this constellation.

There are those who consider that the Egyptian Sphinx was a combination of Leo and Virgo, that is, half woman and half lion. This would symbolize the joining of spirit and matter, of the Sun (ruler of Leo) and the Earth element (and Virgo is a Mutable Earth sign). In mythology, Virgo is sometimes associated with Joseph and Mary, Adam and Eve, and the fruitful tree in the Garden of Eden. The prominent fixed stars in the constellation of Virgo are Caphir, the submissive one," and Spica, "Arista" or "Alpha Virginis" which means seed.

The concept of the sign of Virgo representing virginity may be slightly misunderstood. Virgo is an Earth sign, and it represents the Earth at the end of the growing season. This is the season of harvest. The season for gathering the fruits of one's efforts. The Earth at this time of the year might be perceived as beginning it's period of rest. The part of the year falling under Leo and the Sun was intensely hot, fiery and vital. The part of the year found in Virgo expresses less vitality and more restraint. This is a period of renewal, of beginning the preparation of the Earth to allow it to rest. It is a cyclical experience for the Earth, the Seasons and for all the people living upon the Earth. And Virgo is a feminine sign. It represents the Earth itself which in the process of a year transits through the complete cycle of feminine life. One of the primary purposes of the Earth is to be fruitful, to produce crops, but this can not be accomplished without fertilization and without the heat from the Sun and the moisture from the rain. This is a calming time for the Earth, and a time to become pure by reserving its great resources and renewing its strengths and energies.

How to Find Your *Soul-Mate, Stars,* and *Destiny*

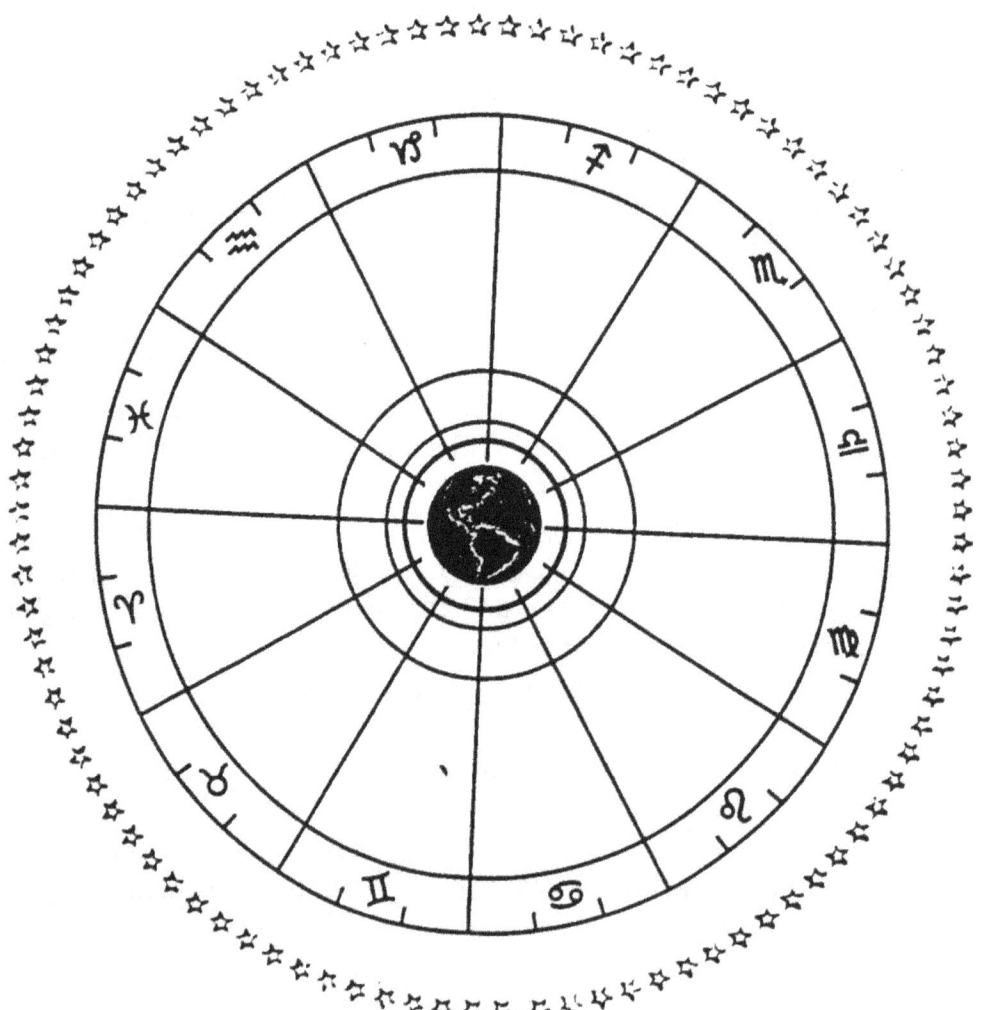

Virgo

August 23 -- September 22
The Thebaic Calendar
Character, Personality, and Destiny

The Thebaic Calendar represents the daily notes that the ancient astrologers wrote on burnt stones or papyrus. It provides information on the characteristics and destiny of the natives for specific birth dates. This is an easy and fast way to find information pertaining to your birth date. The native will often find his characteristics and destiny around his date of birth.

Whether Virgo is the Sun sign, the Ascendant, on the cusp, or in a House, the characteristics of this sign are exhibited. Virgo is a Mutable sign meaning that these natives adapt resources to improve upon the conditions and situations presented to them. Virgo deals most generally with memory, the past, and the assimilation of the details and resources to use information. A Virgo native may take the ideas presented to them and then analyze them and categorize them into workable components. This Earth sign deals with facts, opinions, and ideas in a down-to-earth, practical manner. And Virgo natives are called to be of service to others, perfecting their skills and abilities and working diligently toward their plans while being mindful of the needs of others in their lives, especially their families.

DUALITY: Feminine   **ELEMENT:** Earth   **QUALITY:** Mutable   **RULER:** Mercury

The ruling planet Mercury bestows upon Virgos intelligence and reasoning ability, but with perhaps a high-strung temperament. And where Mercury influences Gemini to communicate, this planet influences Virgo to assimilate ideas. The challenge presented to all Virgos, therefore, is to be able to discriminate and to perfect service through diligent efforts and hard work. Virgos strive not only to serve, but to do so with as much precision and perfection as possible. Their plans and efforts are thought out in great detail to which they apply all their great analytical skills and thought processes. No idea or thought is too small or unimportant to capture the Virgo mind in their efforts to get it all right. They ponder and analyze and become gifted critics. They can be their own worst enemies when they turn this ability inward and begin analyzing and criticizing themselves, making them self-effacing. The Earth sign of Virgo, blessed with practical abilities, is concerned most with concrete and tangible results. And these abilities are applied to all areas of their lives whether it be business, family, personal, or social. Then too, Virgo, so prone to worry, anxieties, and nervous habits from seeking perfection, must turn their attention to health, diet, and food preparation in order to prevent stomach disorders, health problems, and a tendency to gain weight.

Wherever Virgo is found in the horoscope may well be where that person seeks to apply mind over matter. All processes in this area of the life are thought out, information is sought, and the maneuvering of the physical world to meet the present needs are generated. It might also be that area of life where a person is most cautious because Virgo, with all this analytical ability, can easily become overwhelmed with information, and prefers to apply an abundance of caution to any decision making. That does not mean that they are indecisive. They simply decide to go the cautious route, and in this manner it is the Virgo native who quite often misses out or turns down good opportunities rather than taking a chance or a risk. Dependable, calculating Virgo is not one to take any unnecessary chances on life, home, or possessions. That they are endearing friends who go to great lengths to help one and all makes them lovable. That they stand by their friends and family in good times and bad, makes them dependable, reliable, and admirable. Which brings us to another quality. Strive as they do to do their best, they respond best to admiration for all their good qualities, and this is not so much stated as felt in all sincerity. Virgos strive to do thei best for all concerned.

The First Decan

The First Decan occurs from 0 degrees to 10 degrees of Virgo and applies to those persons born between August 23 and September 2. These Virgo natives handle their responsibilities in a practical and efficient manner. They are mentally proficient, collecting, handling, and assimilating details with ease, which makes them capable of working with facts and figures. They have remarkably good memories and retentive abilities and often make good students and proficient workers. Others are manually dexterous as well and enjoy work that keeps their hands busily engaged and occupied, whether it be gardening, mechanics, or home projects. These Virgos take an active interest in health, proper hygiene, and a well balanced diet, and they generally enjoy cooking and preparing nutritious and tasty meals. They have a strong preference for dressing nicely and are particular about their personal fashions. They love to talk, preferably on an intellectual level, with friends and family, but by the same token they can be somewhat reserved and even shy around strangers. Those on the cusp with Leo find a strengthened avenue of pursuing their plans and ideas.

The Second Decan

The Second Decan occurs from 10 degrees to 20 degrees of Virgo and applies to those natives born between September 3 and September 12. These Second Decan natives most strongly exhibit all the characteristics of Virgo. They make excellent administrators who can observe, take into account, and utilize all the necessary details for planning and carrying through a project or plan. They apply their strong powers of observation, analyzing, and critiquing to all that they do. They take an interest in community, national, and international events and issues, applying this same analytical methodology to whatever attracts the attention of their intellect. They are active people, both socially and in community affairs. And they maintain strong family ties, remaining responsible family members with others' best interest in mind. These are patient, careful, cautious decision-makers who others turn to for the best advice. They are hard working and diligent, and they have the highest respect for others who exhibit similar qualities. They make the best of friends in that being of service to others makes them feel good about themselves. Occasionally they can become temperamental and it is best to allow them to take a cooling off period.

The Third Decan

The Third Decan occurs from 20 degrees to 30 degrees of Virgo and applies to those natives born between September 13 and September 22. Those Virgo natives born in this Decan are approaching the cusp of Libra which bestows upon them more of diplomatic approach in their dealings with others. They may be more outgoing and sociable then their other Virgo sisters and brothers, preferring to turn on the charm and entertain others with their mental abilities and witty humor. They have a good business sense, however, and make applicable decisions based on their comprehensive data collecting abilities while they seem to sense the correct market forecast. These Virgo natives may exhibit more of a tendency to enjoy the pleasures of life with a strong preference for tasting and sampling the fruits of their labors.

First Decan of Virgo:

August 23 - September 2 -

First Ten Days

Character, Personality, and Temperament:

The quality of the sign is large and bright and goes straight to the art of life, wanting to use their minds and hands for surviving.

Mutable Element:

Earth: These individuals have a need for other people, using their memories of the past and the resources of their environment to improve on their situation to make them stronger and more successful.

Destiny:

These natives are in strong contact with other people. This brings the individual satisfaction and fulfillment and will grant the person protection from losing status.

Star Date of Birth: August 23

The native has an enterprising character but is sometimes indifferent toward companions. You find relocating from your home town for work is appealing. And you may have a tendency to relieve your sexual tension when far from home as well. Whatever your sexual tensions, you do not express any problems to your romantic partner but turn your energies to other matters.

How to Find Your *Soul-Mate, Stars,* and *Destiny*

Star Date of Birth: August 24

This person is attracted to luxuries and perhaps to overeating. A happy life is seen with material successes obtained. There is a zest for life. You are cautious in relationships to the point that you may either decide to marry late in life or not at all. Sexually, you are attracted to those either much younger than you or in an older age bracket. You recognize when romance beckons, but you may procrastinate and miss out.

Star Date of Birth: August 25

The individual is wise and easy to satisfy and possesses a calm temperament. A life without heartaches and troubles is indicated. You are outspoken and at times aggressive enough to qualify as a mercenary. In matters related to sex, yours is the strong shoulder for quieter persons whose shyness attracts your attentions and to whom you feel protective and ready to serve.

Star Date of Birth: August 26

There is a hard working nature. The person is talented and active. There will be seen rewards for the successes which required hard work and effort. You are a pleasant, sociable person, but one who most desires a relaxed and happy home environment. But sexually, you are creative and ready for experimentation, knowing how to expertly lead the inexperienced into the playground of romance and love.

Star Date of Birth: August 27

This person is a good listener with a reserved and less colorful nature. There is indicated successes through real estate, farming and agriculture. Your analytical ability often leads you to be outspoken and critical. But in romance, you most desire permanency, feeling that all there is to offer in love only grows and gets better and better. Your sexuality is enhanced with a partner who is reawakened to the joys of loving.

Star Date of Birth: August 28

Reserved nature, good listener, attentive and likes to serve others. Success through property and products of the land. You thrive in the home environment surrounded by family and children. You find your sexual relationship as natural as breathing, and your sexuality is enhanced by a warm and loving partner who admires and appreciates you.

Star Date of Birth: August 29

The individual has a daring and bold temperament, observing and taking notes on everything until such information is needed, then makes rapid decisions for fast success. Your spirituality becomes one of the highlights of your life. In love and romance, you desire to express yourself fully with a partner who equally shares your joy in the relationship and matches your enthusiasm sexually.

Star Date of Birth: August 30

This person has an affectionate, demonstrative nature; enterprising. There is seen good fortune through the opposite sex and a marriage that will increase social status. If not held in check, your analytical and critical nature can lead to periods of moodiness and despondency even depression. You are most comfortable in a sexual relationship that began as a friendship and grew into love.

Star Date of Birth: August 31

An indifference and lack of interest in frivolous pursuits is seen for this individual. Some degree of success is seen and a calm, peaceful, and sedentary lifestyle. You are involved both in business and socially, but you are drawn to spending time at home as well. Your sexual encounters are enhanced by outdoor activities and sporting events where you are prone to meeting others who share your interests.

Star Date of Birth: September 1

A strong conscience, honesty and integrity is seen. This person will be inclined to worries and cares especially for the family. You can outline the details and debate either side of most any issue, especially those relating to history and current events. In romance, you are a responsible and reliable partner whose sexuality is enhanced by a predictable relationship based on shared desires.

Star Date of Birth: September 2

Inclination toward apathy and an avoidance of too much effort. There may be some degree of egotism, self-centeredness or selfishness. There is seen some discord in the marriage, however, this person will be lucky in affairs outside of the home. Your spirituality is an important aspect of your life, and you devote a great deal of thought to exploring the truth in the human experience. But love brings a sense of fulfillment as well, and you enjoy the sensual side of romance and togetherness.

Second Decan of Virgo:

September 3 - September 12 - Second Ten Days

Character, Personality, and Temperament:

The individual will follow a sure and personal plan, continuing on his or her path with confidence. Continues to improve, work and ascend along this course.

Mutable Element:

Earth: Past memories remain important as native observes, retains and analyzes details, applying practical and stable tendencies while adapting and changing to meet their goals.

Destiny:

Exalted successes through quality and hard work. Acquires honor and position on merits of diligent effort.

Star Date of Birth: September 3

The individual will be inclined toward comfort and the easy things in life. A life with no big difficulties is seen. Cautious and not as self-assured as you feel you should be, you look at situations through the perspective of your own needs and weaknesses, failing to see the importance of others. You prefer tantalizing romance that is guarded by secrecy, but when you awaken to truer feelings you are less inhibited.

Star Date of Birth: September 4

This person will have an active nature and be enterprising and cunning. A brilliant position in life is seen, at least in appearance. You strive to do your best but find you must be content with your position in life. But your good nature and enthusiasm wins you rewards in romance where you can climb to amazing heights of fulfillment and intense feelings of oneness with your partner.

Star Date of Birth: September 5

There is seen an impetuous, quarrelsome nature. Solid friendships will sustain this person through life's struggles. You have a tendency to live a bit vicariously, collecting details and information on the lives of others and criticizing what you don't feel is acceptable. You are curious about romance and especially sex which you enjoy when you allow yourself that pleasure.

Star Date of Birth: September 6

An easy going, relaxed and laid-back nature is seen with the tendency to be exploited. There is seen the possibility of becoming wealthy, but you may achieve a limited success because you choose not to take unnecessary chances or risk what you already have gained. At the same time, you communicate well and yearn for that true friend and soul mate with whom to express yourself sexually.

Star Date of Birth: September 7

A somewhat submissive personality is seen, however, the person is a good conciliator and mediator. The person will struggle with plans and goals.
You apply caution to all your decisions, but in matters related to the heart this leaves you vulnerable to those who know that once they have you in bed you are easily influenced and persuaded. Sexually, you are versatile and anxious to please your partner as well as yourself.

Star Date of Birth: September 8

This person has a devoted but somewhat fearful nature. There is a hesitancy to take advantage of several good opportunities in life, causing you to lose out. You are sensitive to the emotional losses you may have experienced at an early age. You are slow to give your trust in romance, but once you have established a trusting relationship you are a sensual, giving and loving partner.

Star Date of Birth: September 9

This person may be too harsh and have a love for money. Success is seen through involvement with others. You can be combative and aggressive, but you are also most generally fair in your deliberations and decision making, preferring to consider the needs of others and yourself. Your sexuality allows you to explore a need for experiencing the wide range of emotions romance provides.

Star Date of Birth: September 10

An indecisive nature is noted with a distrust and strong doubts about making decisions. A calm destiny is indicated without any unforeseen events.

You seem almost against your will cast into situations of intrigue and drama which may result in restrictions and even periods of isolation. Your sexuality allows you another avenue of finding fulfillment or relaxation from the trials of life.

Star Date of Birth: September 11

The person has an obliging nature full of goodwill. An humanitarian life that is advantageous to society is seen, but there is a lack of appreciation by those close to the person. You may have experienced obstacles in your youth, but you enjoy greater rewards as you mature. This is especially true in your sexuality where you find romance and sexual encounters which provide an outlet for your emotions.

Star Date of Birth: September 12

The individual possesses a dynamic personality. The life is eventful. There is seen a scattered existence. You feel life would be easy if others allowed it to be, and this can either make you lighthearted or worrisome. Your sexuality is based on an earthiness and endurance that fulfills your needs and is pleasantly surprising to your partners.

The Third Decan of Virgo:

September 13 - September 22 -

Third Ten Days

Character, Personality, and Temperament:

The qualities of Virgo are strong and become sweeter and sweeter with adventure and a love for their enterprises. Tendency to seek love, art, and elegant fashions and to establish close relationships with friends and family. In maturity, wants an intimate family life while they keep active socially.

Mutable Element:

Earth: There is a mental ability to guide work and to carefully consider resources while making plans for the future.

Destiny:

The qualities of the sign of Virgo are exalted and emphasized. The native may have many things in hand at one time, but eventually the destiny increasingly becomes precise and follows well-planned ideas.

Star Date of Birth: September 13

There is a 'take charge' personality. The person is able and loyal but does not display humility. There will be some grief and worry in life because of a lack of appreciation from others. Great struggles are seen. The failure of early romances may leave you hesitant to give your heart again, but others continue to seek you out, sensing your hidden sexuality and your desire to experience your sensual nature to the fullest. Thus, in love, you find that which can fulfill the heart and your sensuality.

Star Date of Birth: September 14

The person possesses a business sense and a flair for negotiating. Successes are seen later in life, but they are of significant importance. Prone to doing what is best for yourself, you are not always the most sincere in relationships. This leaves you vulnerable to continuing romantic relationships based solely on sexual needs and desires rather than developing a more well rounded relationship.

Star Date of Birth: September 15

There is seen some lack of common sense as the rationality is dominated by over sensitivity. There are many ups and downs in life, but these will decrease with age. You may seek affirmation and respond to the admiration and flattery of others. You seek to be well organized and to establish a routine, but your response to your sexuality may see you throwing all to the wind for pure enjoyment and the delights of love and romance.

Star Date of Birth: September 16

There is seen a love of travel and a variety of occupations. There is a risk of losing big money. At some point in your life, you seek adventure and the challenge of finding your measure by facing the forces of nature. Your sexuality is enhanced by your experimental nature and your willingness to explore the heights of sensuality and emotions.

Star Date of Birth: September 17

The individual may well be naive and susceptible and have some lack of good judgment. This person falls an easy victim to sly and cunning people.
You possess an analytical mind that thrives on details, facts, and figures. Your sexuality is enhanced with a partner who is more lighthearted and fun loving and who leads you to relax through romance and sexual encounters which you find you enjoy.

Star Date of Birth: September 18

The individual possesses a spiritual nobility, but an awkward sincerity or can be brutally honest. There are seen numerous enemies. You are a productive worker, but you enjoy an active social life as well. You prefer to remain in control of yourself, but this is easily abandoned through sexual encounters with partners who add a special thrill and excitement to your life.

How to Find Your *Soul-Mate, Stars,* and *Destiny*

Star Date of Birth: September 19

There is a curiosity and indiscretion based frequently on service to others. A lack of luck is seen with moderate material successes. You strive to make your friends and family proud of you by working hard and doing the right things to achieve your goals. You possess an old-fashioned sex appeal that speedily develops into a sensually creative approach to romance and love.

Star Date of Birth: September 20

The person has a shy, hesitating character and is reluctant to make decisions or to take actions. Numerous problems with the opposite sex are noted. You are an emotional person with a love of either drama, singing, or a religious lifestyle. In romance, you find your greatest degree of sensuality and fulfillment often with persons who respond to your hidden compulsive nature and desire to experience a thrill.

Star Date of Birth: September 21

Spiritual qualities are noted for the individual. There is a habit of talking too much. Material success is noted. You strive to be practical and sensible but are tempted by what you perceive as good opportunities. In romance, your otherwise conventionality is susceptible to those who challenge traditions and social standards--and by doing so you experience the thrill that sex has to offer.

Star Date of Birth: September 22

A clever, inventive mind is indicated. The person encounters a tranquil life without struggles. You find a great deal of satisfaction from investigating the past and exploring history. You romanticize your relationships, wanting to imagine your romance as one of the greatest loves of all time. Thus, you devote yourself fully to exploring the sensuality of love.

COLORS:

The natives of the sign of Virgo may find that the best colors for them are all the pale shades, light brown and gray-blue, and silvery colors with a sheen.

BIRTHSTONES:

The birthstones for this sign are emeralds, diamonds, sapphires, pearls and glittering jewels.

POWER STONES:

The power stones for Virgo natives include amazonite, peridot, and rhodochrosite.

METAL:

The metal associated with the sign of Virgo is gold.

KEYWORD: "I Analyze"

FLOWERS:

Favorable flowers for Virgo natives include small, brightly colored blooms such as the morning glory and the pansy.

POSITIVE TRAITS:

Thoughtful; discriminating; meticulous; active; serious; modest; tidy; reserved; concise; analytical; discrete; sensitive; efficient; cautious; intellectual; contemplative; observant; domestic; prudent; industrious; thrifty; methodical; warm; kind; responsible; loyal; faithful; deatil-oriented; good reasoning; perceptive; clever; seeks knowledge; practical; thoughtful; active; humane; dexterous.

NEGATIVE TRAITS:

Calculating; selfish; anxious; worrisome; fussy; gossipy; irritable; cold; indifferent; finicky; apprehensive; discontent; secretive; hypercritical; overly conventional; fussy; fastidious; skeptical; nonresponsive; indecisive; timid; insecure; quick tempered; disceitful; unfaithful; liar; self-critical; overly cautious; inconsistent; hypocritical; sarcastic; selfish; self-centered; cynical; lacking purpose; slick; argumentative; mental stagnation; two-faced; deceitful; high strung; scheming; cunning.

Virgo

Personal Self-Expression and Mental Tendencies

1. Modest, Thoughtful, Industrious with Desire
2. Contemplative, Refine the Mind, Acquire Knowledge
3. Learns Quickly, Good Reasoning, Enjoys Materials Comforts
4. Good Command of Language, Good Endurance, Rserve, Force
5. Quick Recuperation, Does Not Show Their Age, Quick Tempered
6. Prefers Arbitration; Loves Order, Beauty, Art, and Literature
7. Not Easily discouraged or Kept Down, Idealistic Yet Careful
8. Frugal Yet Speculative, Ingenious, Dynamic Interrelationships
9. Cautious, Endowed With Good Forethought, Rarely Misses a Trick
10. Very Active, Seldom Contented, Desires Easy Wealth, Gloom
11. Conservative, Mentally Motivated, Tenacious Worker, Ingenious
12. Over Anxious, Sensitive to Surroundings and to Conditions of Others
13. Quite Discriminative and Careful of Details, Cautious, Practical
14. Diplomatic, Tactful, Prudent, Economical, Messenger of the Gods
15. Practical, Acts With Forethought, Careful Supervision, Clairvoyant
16. Commercial, Business Affairs, Fond of Learning, Active Minded
17. Good Mental Abilities, Critical, Thoughtful, Methodical
18. Undecided, Nervous, Lacking Self-Confidence, Perceptive
19. Sometimes Intuitive, Good Memory, Can Be Messy and Confused
20. Intellectual Pursuit, Psychometric, Capable of Extreme Self-Denial
21. Intuitive Faculty, Unostentatious, Unpretentious, Shrewd
22. Fertile Imagination, Fondness for Change, Traveler, Investigator
23. Reserved, Has Many Friends - Especially of the Opposite Sex
24. Secret, Sorrows Through Marriage, Sadness, Successful,
25. Good Trustworthy Servant, Comprehensive, Pets
26. Discriminative, Versatile, Inventive, Exacting
27. Possesses Ability, Studies by Memorizing, Philosophical,
28. Power of Persuasion, Innate Love, Mystery of Occult
29. Skeptical, Affairs, Risks, Adventures, Introverted

30. Understands Thoroughly Before Being Convinced
31. Mathematics, Literature, Undertakings, Endowment
32. Disappointment in Love Secrets or Dual Attachments
33. Servants or Subordinates Positions, Analytical, Wisdom
34. Bold and Scientific Enterprises, Matter-of-Fact
35. Many Struggles of a Peculiar Nature, Good Worker
36. Ambitions and Desires for Power and Fame, Difficulties
37. Downfall, Obstacles, Annoyance or Opposition, Favors Profit
38. Mentally Very Active, Quick-Witted, Inquisitive
39. Discrimitive Possessions, Reserve Force and Energy
40. Nervous System, Suffer From Complaints, Misunderstanding
41. Irritable, Hasty, Proud, Obstinate, Ambitious,
42. Secretive, Revengeful, Practical Scientific Knowledge
43. Suffer From Loss, Friends, Co-Workers
44. Accidents an dSickness From Overwork, Quietude
45. Mental Inclination, Directions, Intellectual, Materialistic
46. Method and Concentration, Serious, Employ
47. Worried, Doubtful, Mistrustful, Very Gloomy
48. Depressed Easily, Discouraged, Mysterious, Scientific
49. Difficulties, Struggles, Sorrows in First Half of Life
50. Mind is Subtle, Independent, and Original
51. Eccentric, Stubborn, Fond of Curiosities, Great Success
52. Disappointed, Restricted, Connected With - Occupation
53. Spiritual Faculties, Psychical Phenomena, Seclusion
54. Mediumistic Tendency, Gentleness, Constant Patience
55. Neutral, Sexless and Convertible, Absorbs Characters
56. Good for Commissions, Business and Responsible Positions
57. Adaptable, Fertile, Quick Comprehension
58. Studious, Logical, Sharp, Persuasive, Expressive
59. Restless, Quick in Speech and Action, Clever and Progressive
60. Successful Travels, Mental Development, Accomplishments
61. Sarcastic, Untruthful, Hasty Tempered, Fine Mind
62. Marriage is Generally Result of Writings or Traveling
63. Strifes, Worries, Vexations, Disorders, Speech
64. Traveling is More Through Mind Senses or Emotions
65. Contracts, Traveling, Legal Affairs, Disposition
66. Trouble, Quarrels, Difficulties, Partners Regarding Money
67. Worry in Connection with Financial Affairs, Dissension,

68. Busy, Danger of Legal, Knowledge of Distant Places
69. Public Service, Restless Nature, Subtle, Impulsive Speech
70. Untruthfulness, Able, Penetrating, Deceptive,
71. Resourceful in Business, Love of Mystery, Petty Worries
72. Annoyances, Small Enmities, Power or Opportunities to Manifest
73. Humanitarianism, Happy and Prosperous, Benefit the Native
74. Furnishes the Mental Force Necessary, Nervous
75. Argumentative, Imaginative, Fond of Novelty
76. Mentally Powerful or Intelligent, Mind Influences Rest of Body
77. Diagnosticians, Watchmakers, Repairmen, Sedentary
78. Methodical, Approaches Any Problem, Extremely Conscientious
79. Haphazard, Guesswork, Desires Perfection, Tendency to Repeat
80. Procedure is Already Satisfactory, , Everything in Order,
81. Scientific Accomplishment, Courteous, Modest
82. Well-Mannered, Natural Bearing, Demeanor Will Impress Others
83. Honest, Trustworthy, Reliable, Shirks Responsibility
84. Imagination for Constructive, Practical Purposes
85. Enjoyment from Reading or Attending Lectures
86. Fertile Brain, Retentive Memory, Don't Display Knowledge
87. Interesting Conversationalist, Superior Powers of Observation
88. Excellent Profreader and Literary Critic, Impulsive Action
89. Analyzes Judgement Before Acting, Business or Social Contacts
90. Estrangement, Sensitive, Opposites Attract, Wary
91. Does Not Show Real Feelings Especially in Affairs of the Heart
92. Sometimes are Not Emotional, Physical Relationships, Joy in Destruction
93. Tendency to Accept Marriage as Matter-of-Fact, Unmindful, Weakness
94. Mental Rather Than Physical Abilities, Aptitude for Scientific Research
95. Prefers Good Quality, Financial Condition Largely Up to Themselves
96. Hypercritical, Mental and Physical Fears of Illness, Non-Productive
97. Excellent Housekeeper, Spotless and Hygienically Clean
98. Practical and Restrained, Timid, Aptitude for Mechanical Pursuits
99. Would Probably be Happiest if Predominately Responsible in His Marriage
100. Closely Associated with Mental Activity, Undue Concern Over Health Issue

How to Find Your Soul-Mate, Stars, and Destiny

Celebrity Birthdays

August   Virgo

23	Rick Springfield Louis XVI Gene Kelly Richard Adler	Nicole Bobek Vera Miles Richard Sanders Barbara Eden	Shelley Long Bob Crosby Dorothy Parker Shaun Ryder
24	Steve Guttenberg Jorge Luis Borges Richard Cardinal Cushing	Marlee Matlin Monty Hall Preston Foster Cal Ripken Jr.	Claudia Schiffer Mason Williams Jeffrey Daniel Ken Hensley
25	Claudia Schiffer Elvis Costello Mel Ferrer George C. Wallace	Anne Archer Sean Connery Billy Ray Cyrus Regis Philbin	Sean Connery Monty Hall Walt Kelly Ivan The Terrible
26	Chris Burke Branford Marsalis Jay Pritzker Jet Black	Macaulay Culkin Christopher Isherwood Prince Albert Chris Curtis	Geraldine Ferraro Vic Dana Jan Clayton John O'Neill
27	Mother Teresa Martha Raye Samuel Goldwyn Frank Leahy	Pee Wee Herman Daryl Dragon Georg Hegel Harry Reems	Barbara Bach Tommy Sands Tuesday Weld Tim Bogert
28	Emma Samms Wayne Osmond Bruno Bettelheim Charles Boyer	Todd Eldredge Scott Hamilton Donald O'Connor Lou Piniella	Ben Gazzara Elizabeth Seal Ron Guidry Goethe
29	Richard Gere Ingrid Bergman Elliott Gould Robin Leach	Sir Richard Attenborough Barry Sullivan Dinah Washington Michael Jackson	Rebecca DeMornay Oliver Wendell Holmes William Friedkin Isabel Sanford
30	Fred MacMurray Geoffrey Beene John Phillips Shirley Booth	Micky Moody Tug McGraw Timothy Bottoms Regina Resnick	Jean Claude Killy Elizabeth Ashley Huey Long Kitty Wells

How to Find Your Soul-Mate, Stars, and Destiny

August   Virgo

31	Marcia Clark	Debbie Gibson	Glenn Tilbrook
	William Saroyan	Alan Jay Lerner	Richard Basehart
	Frank Robinson	Arthur Godfrey	Van Morrison
	Maria Montessori	Buddy Hackett	James Coburn

September

1	Alan Dershowitz	Ann Richards	Dave White
	Lily Tomlin	Walter Reuther	Barry Gibb
	Gloria Estefan	Edgar Rice Burroughs	Conway Twitty
	Yvonne De Carlo	Rocky Marciano	Bruce Foxton
2	Christa McAuliffe	Keanu Reeves	Mark Harmon
	Jimmy Connors	Joan Kennedy	Marge Champion
	Jean Dalrymple	Rosalind Ashford	Martha Mitchell
	Cleveland Amory	Sam Gooden	Marty Grebb
3	Charlie Sheen	Eileen Brennan	Donald Brewer
	Kitty Carlisle Hart	Eddie Stanky	Mort Walker
	Alan Ladd Sr.	Al Jardine	Tompall Glaser
	Valerie Perrine	Steve Jones	Gary Leeds
4	Richard Wright	Sen. Thomas Eagleton	Ione Sky
	Judith Ivey	Martin Chambers	Gary Duncan
	Henry Ford II	Ken Harrelson	Merald Knight
	Mitzi Gaynor	Greg Elmore	Ronald LaPread
5	Raquel Welch	Bob Newhart	Dweezil Zappa
	Darryl F. Zanuck	Carol Lawrence	Jesse James
	Frank Yerby	John Mitchell	Jack Valenti
	King Louis XIV	Arthur Nielsen	William Devane
6	Jo Anne Worley	Jeff Foxworthy	Swoosie Kurtz
	Billy Rose	Richard Barr	Mel McDaniel
	Jane Curtin	Marquis De Lafayette	Dave Bargeron
	Mike McCoy	Joseph P. Kennedy	Clayde Smith
7	Taylor Caldwell	Michael Feinstein	Chrissie Hynde
	Julie Kavner	Richard Roundtree	Buddy Holly
	Queen Elizabeth I	Peter Lawford	Grandma Moses
	Elia Kazan	Susan Blakely	Benmont Tench

How to Find Your Soul-Mate, Stars, and Destiny

September   Virgo

8	Patsy Cline Sid Caesar Anton Dvorak Peter Sellers	Henry Thomas King Richard I Frankie Avalon Jonathan Taylor Thomas	Ann Beattie Michael Lardie Penny Singleton David Steele
9	Hugh Grant Michael Keaton Pepa Sylvia Miles	Cliff Robertson Colonel Sanders Joseph E. Levine Leo Tolstoy	Adam Sandler Roger Waters Alf Landon Doug Ingle
10	Bob Lanier Fay Wray Arnold Palmer Roger Maris	Amy Irving Tommy Overstreet Jose Feliciano Jerome Bradshaw	Charles Kuralt Joe Perry Don Powell Siobahn Fahey
11	Rita Rudner D. H. Lawrence Mick Talbot Earl Holliman	Harry Connick Jr. Tom Landry Virginia Madsen Lola Falana	Amy Madigan O'Henry Dennis Tufano Kristy McNichol
12	Ben Shahn Alfred A. Knopf Terry Bradshaw Brian Robertson	Barry White Barry Andrews Cannonball Adderly Maurice Chevalier	Linda Gray Tony Bellamy Jesse Owens H.L. Mencken
13	Peter Cetera Jacqueline Bisset Claudette Colbert Richard Kiel	Mel Torme Dr. Walter Reed Leland Hayward Herbert Berghof	Randy Jones Joni Sledge Barbara Bain
14	Zoe Caldwell Pete Agnew Margaret Sanger Barry Cowsill	Clayton Moore Nicol Williamson Ivan Pavlov Morten Harket	Mary Crosby Joey Heatherton Walter Koenig Faith Ford
15	Tommy Lee Jones Agatha Christie Les Braid Jackie Cooper	Oliver Stone Bobby Short Robert Benchley William Howard Taft	Prince Henry Gaylord Perry Roy Acuff
16	David Copperfield Lauren Bacall Peter Falk Bernie Calvert	Susan Ruttan J.C. Penney Allen Funt Ed Begley Jr.	Richard Marx B.B.King Janis Paige Kenny Jones

How to Find Your Soul-Mate, Stars, and Destiny

September Virgo

17	Jeff MacNelly Roddy McDowall Anne Bancroft Fee Waybill	Elvira Hank Williams Sr. Lamonte McLemore	Warren Burger Ben Turpin John Ritter
18	Samuel Johnson Greta Garbo Rossano Brazzi Jack Warden	Jimmy Rodgers Frankie Avalon Eddie „Rochester' Anderson	Robert Blake Ricky Bell Joanne Catherall Dee Dee Ramone
19	Trisha Yearwood Twiggy John Coghlan Joseph Pasternak	Jeremy Irons David McCallum Brook Benton Bill Medley	Adam West Jim Abbott Joan Lunden Nile Rodgers
20	Upton Sinclair James Galanos Sophia Loren Crispin Glover	Anne Meara Rachel Roberts Chuck Panozzo Alexander The Great	Allanah Currie Pia Lindstrom
21	Stephen King Henry Gibson Larry Hagman H.G. Wells	Cecil Fiedler Rob Morrow Hamilton Jordan Trugoy the Dove	Ricki Lake Bill Murray Dickie Lee Leonard Cohen
22	Bonnie Hunt John Houseman Martha Scott Paul LeMat	Michael Faraday Shari Belafonte Tom Lasorda Debby Boone	Joan Jett Scott Baio Ingemar Johansson David Coverdale

How to Find Your *Soul-Mate*, *Stars*, and *Destiny*

Date With Destiny

Share With Me Your Fantasy

How to Find Your *Soul-Mate*, *Stars*, and *Destiny*

Date With Destiny

Share With Me Your Fantasy

LIBRA

September 23 - October 22
Man - Woman - Child - Character - Relationships - Compatibilities - Love Signs

The seventh Sun sign of the Sun sign of the Zodiac, Libra is represented by the Scales and takes its name from the Latin word for pound weight or scales. There is an association with the sign of Libra and the qualities of balance, equilibrium and justice. Libras seek this balance by taking into consideration both sides of any argument and to this end they can appear at times indecisive in their efforts to make the right decision. Also associated with Libra are the characteristics of attractiveness, sophistication, elegance, refinement, artistic appreciation, sentiment, and a tendency to be sociable, diplomatic, adaptable, and pleasing. At their best, Libras take an intense interest in all aspects of human relationships becoming involved in either the arts, law, diplomacy, humanities, music, beautification projects, decorating, restoration, or remodeling. At their worst, they are self-serving with an over active dependent on others. For the most part, Libras seek approval, order, and harmony in all relationships. This need for the best of everything in the best of all possible worlds leads Libra individuals to be argumentative for the perfect harmony, their sense of balance or their personal set of scales can easily become off-balanced, tilting to one side or the other, and any such situation can upset and even depress these sensitive Libras. They are also known for being energetic and socially active, but periodically they must take time to rest and recuperate, especially from the stress of constantly being well balanced and in tune with all of life. One cannot begin to discuss Libra without mentioning that they are the infamous romantics of the Zodiac. Romance and sex, to the Libra, only adds to the beauty and joy of living and loving. Above all else, Libra strives throughout life to arrive at an inner feeling of peace, harmony, and balance. Their ability to see the world in their mind and to apply this imagery to life itself may be the reason for the pleasant smile and winning popularity that highlights the Libra existence. That they will use manipulation if necessary to attain this perfect balance in an imperfect world goes without saying.

These characteristics of the Libra Sun sign can be made stronger by the Moon sign, Ascendant, and the placement of the Planets, or they can be made more subdued by specific influences. It is by ascertaining these various influences that one can more fully understand the Libra individual being studied, or, more importantly, one can more fully understand one's self.

The sign of Libra, the Balance, occurs during that time of year when the Sun has reached that time of year referred to as the Autumn Solstice. The days are shorter and are becoming of equal length with the nights. This is the sign of equilibrium within nature, and it is the sign of the same equilibrium within people born at this time of the year. The Sun is in transit to the Southern Hemisphere, and as it approaches the equator, the light received in the Northern Hemisphere is lessened. The Sun's rays were considered by ancient scholars to be waves of vital fluids. The nature of the Earth becomes tired and ready for winter slumber. The Earth at this time of the year is under the influence of Venus, the ruler of this sign. Saturn is in exaltation, that is in favorable vibration with this sign. Both Venus and Saturn, while planets of very different natures, add to the synthesis of the concept of equilibrium and justice in the world. The word Libra is actually the Latin word for balance, or scales, which is the symbol for this sign.

The constellation of Libra extends to the front legs of the Scorpio which follows this sign. Within the constellation are found three beautiful and favorable stars, Arcturus, Centaurul, and Vacarul.

The sign of Libra begins on September 23, but for seven days it is on the cusp of the previous sign, Virgo. It attains its full strength, and then for seven days at the end of the month, gradually loses its power to the incoming sign of Scorpio. Thus, we say that some people are born on the cusp and may have influences from both signs.

Like Gemini and Aquarius, Libra is an Air sign and is consequently changeable, intelligent, intellectual and sociable. It is the Cardinal sign of Air representing the Autumn solstice, and because of this, it assimilates easily with the constantly changing air whether it is a cool breeze or a strong, violent wind. This depends upon the influence of either Venus or Saturn. Libra is a masculine sign and this inclines the natives to be able to adapt to and to live in their perspective environments whatever and wherever that might be, but they may have difficulty submitting to it.

In that Libra maintains the balance between day and night, it represents the Sun rising and disappearing at the horizon. Venus influences the natives to be well balanced and neat with a feeling of measure. These individuals strive to diplomatically defend justice. Venus influences these natives to the principle of work and this is done through peaceful and quiet methods. The natives of this sign strive to arrive at their goals while at the same time seeking to strike a balance between people, rules and regulations. They seek harmony, even in opposed forces, and attempt any means to achieve reconciliation where needed. The verb for the sign of Libra is "to balance", but this stability requires a great deal of effort on the part of these natives because, needless to say, there is no end to the amount of opposition or to the number of people who prefer havoc to balance. Saturn intervenes for these natives providing them with the natural instinct of self-preservation against violence which is used when it is absolutely necessary.

Venus impels the natives of Libra toward art, kindness and happiness. These individuals possess the natural talent for executing their personal plans without making an excessive show of their true intentions. They appear to achieve their goals almost effortlessly, but this is only an appearance which is affected by these natives who are in reality working diligently. These natives are pleasant and sensible. They are both delicate and refined, and they exhibit a love for justice, peace and tranquillity. They are known for being amiable, generous, and courteous, but their nature is always changing. Others can find this changeability unpleasant in that often these natives will change their minds frequently and will even break promises or commitments over theoretical disagreements and arguments pertaining to justice.

Libra Personality

The seventh-sign natives desire more than anything to live in peace and harmony and for all of life to contain an emotional feeling of balance and well being. Accepting and tolerant of others, they are natural conciliators and mediators who prefer, for the most part, to adhere to the middle of the road in their actions and in their daily lives. Dissension, disagreements, strong and forceful actions, and obstacles are aspects of life to be avoided at all costs. These people are great compromisers and are willing to go to great lengths to either regain or maintain serenity, and a calmness and a pleasing, pleasant environment. Life, to these individuals, was intended to be enjoyed, not wasted in discord and discontent.

In this regard, the Libra native may shy away from a firm stand or from taking extreme measures. There is a reluctance to do anything that will enhance or heighten an atmosphere of contention. Being extremely sensitive to their own feelings as well as the emotions and well being of others, Libra individuals feel pain profoundly and are often disturbed by the harsher realities of everyday life. Within the Libra nature is the ability to wait out problems. They are patient and may feel that time will solve many problems.

If Libra natives were to realize their deepest desires it would be to live in an environment where charm, friendliness and tenderness were mutually expressed. Possessing these qualities, the natives use their natural charm and wit to make friends and to be liked by others. The native Libra goes to great pains to suppress any feelings of hostilities toward others in an effort to be pleasing and positive. Angry words are avoided as are overly aggressive or assertive behaviors. It might well appear that these natives just do not feel that such behaviors are worth their time or energy.

The native Libra is not the initiator of serious arguments or of violent words. And while they will go to great lengths to avoid conflicts, faced with stubbornness or strong opposition, the Libra native is not a coward. These individuals, when nothing else works, will stand up to and face any and all opposition, exhibiting an anger bordering on fury.

Gracious and generous, the Libra natives are outgoing and extroverted in a group. They enjoy entertaining friends and being entertained by others. Outwardly, they are almost always warm and affectionate toward others. At other times, these individuals, with their changing natures, prefer the solitude of their own companionship.

Being prone to change, the personalities of these people can fluctuate from the positive, cheerful and hopeful to the depths of melancholy and depression. These extreme mood changes or swings often happen quickly and unexpectedly. Gloomy surroundings, contentions, disagreeable people, or problems can quickly make them despondent. At times, these mood swings are brought about by being out of balance or harmony with their environment or surroundings.

As with people found in any of the Zodiac signs, Libra natives have faults. For one, being so perceptive to the minds and personalities of other people, a Libra individual can readily adapt and adopt the mannerisms and opinions of others, and just as readily drop these affectations as it suits their mood. Other Libras are too impatient and too prone to being overly impulsive. This person will act too hastily or will rashly come to a decision or take an action which in some instances can cause them unforeseen problems. Then too, Libra's love praise and attention, and any negative comments can cause this person distress. And while they go to great lengths to help others or to be of service to others, they often feel their efforts are not fully appreciated or recognized by those same people. The Libra tempr is infamous. When faced with stubborn opposition, or forced to explain or justify their actions, they can become impatient and angry. And while they seldom display their anger, when they do so it is with sharp, cutting remarks which leaves little to the imagination. When they become impatient, it results in a loss of energy and their entire nature appears to lag. In these instances, these individuals can become confused and even more inclined to procrastination.

There are those Libras who become materialistic and develop a love for luxury and a life of ease. And these particular people have no hesitancy in flaunting their possessions. These individuals measure their self-worth based on their personal accumulation of possessions as compared to others. This passion for elegance can lead to financial problems caused by over spending. The ego of this type of person must be always reassured, bolstered and praised. This person's need for friends leaves them attempting forever to please others in an effort to receive more praise and flattery. And like the poorly developed natives of other signs, these individuals pursue the worldly gratification of pleasures, fun and sensationalism. Under a negative influence, Libras are inclined to be lazy, too sensual and too passionate. They can easily become a person who uses friends, family and lovers for their own benefit and satisfaction. The Libra native should strive not to be lazy as this can lead to carelessness and inactivity. If the Libra is disloyal it is because this person wishes to avoid problems and prefers to find the easiest way to solve them.

Like the Cancer native, Libra when threatened by the harsh realities of life, may withdraw into an elaborate fantasy world of his or her own making. Being intelligent and creative, the wish not to accept or to see what is bad, this person may take great efforts to distort or to create illusions in order to make everything good again. These people become professional dreamers who live in a fantasy world where nothing distasteful can touch or effect them. Faced with oppositional forces in life for which there are no resolutions, Libra will enter a fantasy world of the mind more real and pleasing to themselves than anything in real life.

The changeability of the Libra nature can lead to a person who sets a goal and diligently pursues it wishing only for goodness and harmony, but then becomes distracted, realizes a new direction, and pursues it with as much diligence and commitment as before. Rather than creating harmony, these actions produce only confusion for themselves and others.

It is most important for Libras to work for and to strive toward stability of nature. The very tolerance and generosity of their spirits must be harnessed in order not to waste and flounder their strengths, energies and gifts. In order to help others, this person must discover his or her own balance first. They must come to realize that to acquire a balance, one must seek this equilibrium in all of life and must accept and face what can not be changed. The Libra, graced with remarkable abilities and potentials, must come to terms with their own natures.

Well-developed Libras achieve this balance in life and acquire an emotional maturity that allows them to be productive and to realize many of their goals and desires. These individuals develop avenues of self-expression which allows them to impart their ideas and precepts of harmony, peace and tranquillity to others. This provides them with an outlet for their emotions which otherwise could become so pent up as to cause innumerable problems. All Libras should strive to develop their higher, more noble characteristics.

The best advice for the Libra native is to realize that once you develop your emotional and psychological balance, you can then set your personal lives in order by adjusting your ambitions and aspirations to reasonable and acceptable goals. Once a person acquires the emotional strength to accept the harsher, more unattractive realities of life, a strong positive force will take over to guide his or her life. Unfortunately, it will appear that while you are on this path, every imaginable toil and turmoil will be sent your way if for no other reason than for your educational experience and to taunt your sensitivities. Your intelligence, your ability to work hard, your charm and your extroverted nature are more than adequate gifts to sustain you on this path. But, like others, you may find that your unique sense of humor and your true love for others carries you through life and any and all difficult times. With maturity you will discover that you possess a true and genuine understanding and acceptance of others, and that balance is at times relative.

Libra Character

The symbol for the Zodiac sign of Libra is a set of scales which represents balance and justice. Libra natives possess the inclination to weigh up life, sizing up the situation by insightfully and intuitively judging and at the same time balancing and comparing. This inclination for justice grants them a fairness in their opinions and judgments, but at the same time these natives strive to perceive the mental processes of other people. Often the Libra native is persuaded or influenced by the feelings, thoughts or opinions of others. This is because they can visualize, rationalize, or understand both sides of a situation or of an argument. Being tolerant, the Libra natives realize and accept the inclinations of others. Another person has a thought or a persuasion, and the Libra native recognizes it and accepts it.

Justice and liberty are the strengths of the native Libra, and the true character never attempts to misuse these strengths or powers. A Libra native will assist someone else in all that the person wants to accomplish right up to the point that the native realizes the other person is up to no good. Then Libra backs up, reassesses the situation, and may do an about face, changing his or her mind and abandoning the project. The goals and actions of the natives of Libra must meet certain standards which pertain to a clear understanding of justice.

The Libra individual can quite literally feel what is right and what is wrong. At times, they actually feel the truth or lack of truth, or the good or bad in a situation. These people possess a highly developed discerning nature and at times even feel with a foresight, a vision, and at other times sense the emotions and desires of others becoming influenced as much by the thoughts as by the actions and words of another person. At the same time, they can be quick in speech and actions. Often their first impressions or feelings are correct, if they listen to them. Being a person destined to always judge and balance, Libra takes this responsibility seriously, and rather than heeding his or her first impression, this person may well procrastinate before making a decision. At other times this individual may be impulsive and appear hasty or rash, but actually these first impressions and decisions generally work out well if they are based on the intuitive ability of the native and not on the influence of others. Libras need to learn to listen to themselves.

Family members and friends of Libras may find it difficult to understand them because they often appear to be intent on a purpose of their own making, but no one else may know what it is or fully understand it. The highly developed person of this sign is not given to accepting unwarranted advice, direction or persuasion from other well meaning people who have no idea what the Libra native is up to. They are persuaded by their own intuition and ideas of liberty and freedom. At times, they don't express these ideas to other people, not out of secrecy, but more so because, perhaps, they feel others not only won't agree with their decisions (which are often based on intuition rather than on facts) but will also not understand their purposes. They are in many instances rather original in their thinking and planning, and their personal ideas are at times too out of the ordinary or too advanced to allow these natives to remain content in carrying out the plans of others or to remain in subordinate positions. These individuals prefer to be in the planning stages of ideas rather than to simply carry out the plans of others. In subordinate positions they can become somewhat frustrated and impatient. They work well when they are allowed to work within their own methods, to have a certain autonomy in their work habits. Traditions, rules, regulations, and customs are often felt or perceived as constraints to accomplishing better and faster results.

Libra natives prefer to focus on the big picture, the overall goal. Long, tedious discussions of what appears to be minute details are too time consuming for the Libra mind which much prefers action and getting down to the business of completing the task at hand. One can't finish a task until it is started, and Libra wants to start and finish in order to move on to something else. At the same time, these people are persistent, hard working, and diligent in their efforts and in completing work conscientiously and carefully.

Libras easily recognize the imperfections and limitations of others, and while they accept these flaws, they impulsively offer suggestions for improvements and will go to great lengths to help others either improve their methods, complete their tasks, or facilitate their thinking. Libras will also concern themselves with helping other people to attain an emotional balance, to feel better about their lives and life in general. The Libras are the natural ‚balances' of incomplete, imperfect, or unfinished work. They love the feeling of completion, of a job well done, as this augments their need for balance and equilibrium in life. So often, it appears to these individuals that others lack a clear vision for finding a pattern or system for completing even the simplest of tasks. Libras are forever looking for harmony and balance in whatever needs to be done, and this compels them to look for the easiest, most efficient manner of working things out. The stubbornness of others in these matters often leaves the Libra feeling distraught.

Libras are both generous and approachable. They possess a love and acceptance of others because they are capable of perceiving the good (as well as the negative) aspects of other people. These individuals appear always available to help others. Libras listen and judge impartially the plights of others, and then attempt to judiciously assist them in doing right or in righting wrongs.

Individuals of this sign are known for a tenderness of heart. They become distressed over injustice in any form, especially in inhuman or harmful treatment of others. Because of their tenderness, empathy and sympathy, they possess a great love for humanity in general and abhor all forms of suffering and pain. They are deservingly compassionate towards the unfortunate, the distressed, and the afflicted, wishing to help and to serve in whatever means possible.

It must be stated that the natives of Libra also possess a great love for excitement and adventure. No impulse is too rash to attempt. No endeavor is too remotely removed to venture towards. In their tenderness, social awareness, and love for humanity, it goes without saying that Libras love people and gravitate to groups and to busy activities. Then too, remember that the Libra nature is inclined toward change. This, combined with a love for excitement, can lead many of these individuals to readily agree to a new course of action, plan or cause. Being tolerant and sympathetically understanding of others and susceptible to the thoughts and desires of others, Libras can easily respond to the ideas and inclinations of others. If these ideas offer the possibility of change or of a novel or exciting opportunity, Libra may well leap at the opportunity. The Libra individual can be so responsive to others as to become susceptible and vulnerable. There is a tendency to see what he or she wants to see rather than what is really there. Because of their empathy and understanding of the other person, Libra can be easily persuaded to overlook his or her own judgments and to follow the dynamism of another person--up to a point. One might always be asking the Libra native, "How did you ever get involved in that situation in the first place?"

In these situations, the Libra individual loses the natural balance of his or her nature as the scale tips to one side or the other. This person may become somewhat confused and become a procrastinator. Also the person may seek out the counsel of others, and then attempt impatiently to decide upon following that advice or listening to his or her personal intuition. And after all, very few people in this concrete, material world of ours give much weight to intuition. So, it is easy to understand the confusing state that Libras discover themselves at this point. When fear is cast aside and the intuition trusted, then the native regains his or her feeling of balance. It is imperative that the natives of Libra maintain their sense of balance and equilibrium in order to discover their natural perspective. The influences of others must not be allowed to tip this scale, this natural order, out of balance.

Influenced by Venus, the natives of Libra also possess a love of harmony and beauty in their surroundings. They love nature and the out of doors where beauty can be found in its purest and most natural settings. And there is a strong desire to see and to experience the grandeur of God's natural creations.

Libra Destiny

Libra bestows upon its natives a gentle nature that is flexible and sensitive, but which is at times influenced from being hopeful and happy to becoming melancholy, depending on the prevailing situations. The natives of Libra are courteous, honest, and possess a keen sense of justice which prevails over their basic natures. There is a tendency for them to be kind, compassionate, and affectionate while at the same time being frank and outspoken. There is some inclination for extremes in moods and temperaments, and the individual may become angry but can be easily pacified and persuaded otherwise.

In life, for many of these individuals there is found a degree of uncertainty and indecisiveness. These persons can be patient to a fault while waiting to see what the outcome of a situation will be. A strong will power and endurance is indicated in many while others may not be willing to prevail over or to endure all that comes their way. The native is quick and perceptive, has a flair for assimilating and learning new information and for handling business affairs well.

There is some indication for disputes and losses realized through a connection with affairs associated with water or fluids such as transportation or trading. In other instances this loss may be associated with or caused by the death of or disagreement with a business partner. Every Libra native should be on guard and should scrutinize all contracts as there is an immanent danger of loss through these legal arrangements.

Large families are indicated either before or after marriage, and in many instances there are seen numerous disputes and discords among relatives which influence the happiness and well being of the individual. In some cases there is seen some hindrance associated with the father causing trouble or loss. The native may have few children, but the children will bring much joy and satisfaction. In many instances, the extended family will be large through previous marriages of either the individual or the spouse.

There is some indication of problems in regards to married life with an indication for violence, sterility or threats of problems through the marriage with separation, divorce, or death of the spouse. In some cases, there is an inclination to marry a person who is financially secure or wealthy. The subject may gain through unanticipated inheritance from the opposite sex. There may well be numerous and extended travels and journeys, some to foreign countries, and some difficulties and even dangers are experienced with these travels. The native will experience many connections with less fortunate individuals, and many of these experiences will be involved with travel. There may well be an occupation which involves relocation and changes. The middle of life may bring a change of circumstances for the native of Libra with the mother perhaps being the cause of the change.

The family may be of assistance in the acquisition of public awards, but because of the instability indicated, awards and acclaims may be of a short duration. The native may discover friends and support groups among artists and professionals and may develop a close friendship with one of these people. There is some indication that the native may inadvertently distress this person. There will be help from friends in some instances of difficult problems. The native acquires during his or her life enemies who remain secretive, and these enemies may be among family members. Family affairs will cause much discord and unpleasantness.

Libras readily and easily acquire information and knowledge and effortlessly adapt to a number of endeavors or occupations. In many instances, however, the marriage is not well balanced. Financial loss or other problems may occur through listening to or being influenced by the wishes, advice and wants of friends, family or associates. Libra individuals need most to develop their own lives and to listen to their intuition in these cases. The poorly aspected Libra will incur problems developing this gift of insight because of the pursuit of pleasures and passions.

Venus favors positive activities and financial success. There are strong indications for success in life, for friendships, and for security as the native becomes older. Success is noted in the home town or country of the native. The children are often the strongest friend and supporter of the native in old age. The native of Libra may in some manner be the cause of his or her own death.

Mars in Libra may well influence the native to be passionate and impulsive. The attraction of the opposite sex is a distraction and influences the well being of the native. There is an inclination to become entangled with the opposite sex causing the native and others to suffer numerous problems. If Mars is afflicted, there may be found many separations and broken relationships among friends, relatives and associates.

It may well be found that many of these natives are psychic and experience premonitions through their strong intuitive abilities. A number of these individuals concentrate too strongly on finding the proof and the underlying causes and reasons to a situation, thus negating the strength of these psychic abilities. However, Libra natives are rarely deceived if they trust their personal intuition and judgment. This requires much patience to learn to accept and trust their own intuitive minds. If these native born Libras learn to develop their gifts, perceptiveness of mind, and abilities, they will live on a higher plane of life and will not want for friends |or success. These individuals are surrounded by a strong and wonderful magnetic force which grants them vigor and vitality, and they are phenomenally gifted with the ability to acquire spiritual enlightenment. A life time of experiences and education leads the native to develop good judgment.

Endowed by Venus, your planetary ruler, you are more than well aware of your strengths and inner values and your great need to facilitate them. Your conversations, your actions, even your surroundings reflect your inner sensibilities and artistic inclinations. Your personal desire to seek out the companionship of others leads you to meet many unusual, interesting, and gifted characters, some of whom are even a little bizarre. Take caution against judging yourself by the measure or wishes of other people as this can lead to confusion and undermine your stability. Also take caution against losing your energy by being overwhelmed with the needs of others. Take the time to focus on your own needs and well being as well.

Libra Occupation

As an Air sign, Libra is a talented communicator. In this regards also, Libra is naturally inclined toward diplomacy and entertaining. These individuals seek knowledge and make serious students who continue learning throughout their lives. Among so many of these natives there is a highly developed nature which is concerned with the well being and welfare of others. Then too the highly developed intuition adds a natural ability to be successful in many occupations.

With the strong desire to seek and to serve justice, Libras are well suited to be attorneys, judges, mediators, diplomats, and politicians. Libras appear to be drawn to the law, and it is not just a coincidence that the symbol of the scale of balance adorns many courthouses. Many of these natives excel in these occupational fields, discovering a love for what is just and fair and a true concern for establishing worthwhile benefits for society in general.

Possessing a strong desire for knowledge, many Libra seek a life of study and research usually in regards to a particular subject matter in an effort to learn all there is to know about this field and to weigh or add to that information. These individuals excel as scientists and researchers, and others enter the field of medicine where many become specialists. This interest in study, research, and literature leads other Libra individuals to become academicians as professors, teachers, or librarians.

Venus, the planet of love, art and beauty, rules over the sign of Libra. Then too there is the congeniality and personable charm of the Libra native. Many express this innate charm through acting or modeling or other fields requiring grace and presence. There are those drawn to positions involving art, creative endeavors, music, writing, design and to the beauty and fashion industry.

The desire to listen to the concerns of others and to help others leads many of these natives to careers as counselors or therapists. Others pursue positions with charitable organizations and associations where the primary interest is working towards benefiting others and the community. Worthy causes appeal to these kind-hearted natives, and they are capable of making sacrifices and of dedicating themselves to these professions.

Libras possess the ability to make astute business decisions and can excel as managers, sales persons, retailers, personnel managers, and in the fields of advertising and consulting. Others become successful as buyers or traders. These individuals appear to have a feeling for what is going to be popular in the upcoming season. Many have an appreciation for luxury items. They sense the trends before they happen and are capable of judging upcoming events. Also, many excel at sensing the moods and taste of others, knowing almost before the other person realizes it himself what his wishes or decisions will be. Other Libra natives excel as stockbrokers, accountants, bookkeepers, and CPAs while still others display a natural talent for acquiring languages and working as interpreters, journalists, and in other business concerns. You can find success in positions in galleries, museums, or at resorts. These individuals often make successful speculators, appearing to sense the outcome of a project even before it is off the ground. The

Libra makes a trustable, dependable and dynamic partner in business dealings. They much prefer to be honest and hard working, and they shy away from unfavorable situations. Many develop a love of real estate which reflects their love of nature and the land in general.

Libras most prefer work that they enjoy and which is located in a pleasant environment with other people who are companionable. Dismal and depressing work environments and working with negative or hostile people are counter productive to the Libra nature as are situations where conflicts arise or where resolutions to problems are not readily forthcoming. Many Libra individuals dislike any and all confrontation, and yet these same people appear to act like a magnet, attracting just such attention. In fact, there are numerous famous military figures and sports personalities found within this sign.

There is also a natural inclination to know how things work and when this is combined with a highly developed skill, these people become talented mechanics, mathematicians, inventors, jewelers and crafts persons. Many exhibit an unusual skill in working with metals and natural resources.

An exceptional skill is exhibited in any field requiring a discerning nature and insight into human nature. These people will carefully make and execute plans and objectives and then work diligently to see them through, often making every attempt to ignore the seemingly irrelevant suggestions of others. At the same time, this person is more than willing to accept responsibility for any mistakes or failures incurred in such endeavors.

Libras realize success in their occupational fields when they have most developed their skills, talents and natural gifts. And for these natives that appears to be an easy enough task which they accomplish seemingly effortlessly. Libras walk through life with an ambiance of elegant grace, and your charm and graciousness draw other people to you. When situations call for diplomacy, mediation, counsel, or a courteous resolution, you are the person others look toward for advice and help. As the Balance in the Zodiac, you seek to establish and to maintain an equilibrium that is advantageous for all involved. You are both an energetic and a hard-working individual who doesn't shy away from challenging endeavors especially if these allow you to express yourself. Venus endows you with the ability to add a flair of class or individuality to any and all situations and endeavors.

Libra Marriage

When the sign of Libra is at the Ascendant, life is a drama, and perhaps this is especially true in the married life of Libra natives. It hasn't gone without notice that a disproportionate number of inharmonious, unhappy and even disastrous marriages have occurred to natives of the seventh-sign. There are a number of reasons for this.

First, there is the Libra inclination to see in others what he or she wants to see. Add to this the propensity to be tolerant and accepting of others and to see or find the good in other people. These individuals have a tendency to marry people who are less developed. While being accepting of others is a great attribute, Libra when faced with another person on a daily basis may lose patience with the real person he or she has married. Libra will make every effort to attempt to help the other person in changing for the better, but they may discover that his or her spouse has no wish to make any changes at all. Remember, Libras are easily influenced by the wishes of other people. With absolutely no desire to get married, Libra may discover that he or she is aggressively pursued and persuaded in this aspect of life. Then there is the Libra inclination to be a romantic when in love, and you have a tendency to endure all for the sake of love.

In other instances, the Libra native may marry a person who is practical, sensible and who prefers a quiet, routine life where decisions are based on sound judgment and facts. Asked to explain his or her Libra intuitive-decision making process, Libra individuals will easily become confused, finding it impossible to explain their thoughts. This leads to impatience and, in some cases, to discontentment, anger and disagreements. Many Libra natives are independent and when they find themselves in marriages with a dominating, overly controlling person, this can also result in disastrous situations. Then again, if these natives find themselves in a marriage arrangement where both individuals prefer the party life and the pursuits of pleasures, this can result in unfavorable circumstances.

The Libra has a love for independence and freedom as well as for happy, light hearted, and undemanding circumstances. Many of these individuals simply may not enjoy the constraints and daily routine of married life. They need to seek out extremely companionable and understanding spouces who are capable of allowing the other person his or her own space and freedom to think, live and enjoy life. Both the men and women of this sign prefer harmony and can not easily tolerate dissension. Libras require mates who are willing to work toward establishing a meaningful, peaceful, pleasant, and harmonious relationship which is filled with compatibility, love, affection, passion and a strong respect, desire, and devotion for each other.

Favorable marriage partners are found with those born in the sign of Aries (March 21-April 20). The Aries individual must be highly developed though because otherwise persons of this sign can be controlling and domineering. Libra will never find Aries boring though. Sagittarius (November 22-December 20) is a favorable sign for marriage as is Aquarius (January 20-February 18). Aquarius is another Air sign, however, and care must be taken that this combination doesn't produce a poorly balanced life filled with instability. Pisces are strongly inclined to marry Libra individuals, but it is often noticed that these two signs are incompatible in marriage. Pisces may dwell on the motives for actions and deeds, and this trait upsets Libra. Also, if the Pisces becomes depressed this makes the Libra person tired and exhausted. Libras are peaceful and quiet and prefer someone who can be relied on not someone who needs permanent moral support.

Often Libras marry young and unexpectedly. While the love may be strong, there is some indication for divorce or separation in marriages entered into too early in life. You prefer your commitment to marriage to be one for life, and if it doesn't work out you find yourself carrying this love with you for life. It might be a wiser choice to wait for marriage until you are mature and your restless nature has somewhat diminished.

Libras desire a mate with whom they can share their thoughts, dreams and inspirations. These individuals possess the ability to enjoy life fully, and when they become interested in marriage, more than anything they would love to find a compatible person to love. Their love is strong and enduring. Libras also have a strong desire for passion and mutally compatible sexual relationships. Then, too, it is important for your marital relationship to reinforce your spiritual perspective on life.

Being a born romantic and a person who thrives on the companionship of others, once you have settled into your own life and developed your personal lifestyle, interests and skills, it will be an easy accomplishment to find the perfect person to share this life with you. Your patience and forbearance will see you through in these matters. Simply remember to think you decisions through and to marry a deserving person who is willing and worthy of accepting your love and devotion.

The Libra Man

The Libra man is kind and amiable and a natural romantic. He is subtle, well-informed, and understanding with a strong preference fpr not being unpleasant to others. Life for this man is focused on emotional and physical feelings and wants. He is a thinker and enjoys studying, philosophizing and meditating on subjects of interest. For the most part, he is not argumentative, and he would rather leave than become involved in long drawn out explanations and heated discussions. This man is gracious and tactful and admires similar qualities in others. He loves socializing and all aspects of entertaining and being entertained. He is an aesthetic and loves the opportunity for finding and appreciating the beauty in others. He also has an appreciation for elegance and luxury. There is a tendency for this man to ascend to the top position in relation to his career.

The Libra man appreciates being admired and praised. Being a sociable person, receiving this attention isn't very difficult. At the same time, this is a sensitive person who doesn't appreciate disparaging remarks. This man isn't fond of being inconvenienced either. Life should run fairly and smoothly in order for him to attain happiness and to be content. Never openly attack this man because he does have a temper, however much he would like to think otherwise.

How to Find Your Soul-Mate, Stars, and Destiny

This isn't a person to coerce with strong opinions. Use concise, informed persuasion and appeal to his better nature for understanding your differing viewpoint. He loves to please others, and when the best approach is undertaken, he is the easiest person in the world to deal with.

This is a person who possesses a keen sense of observation and is considered an astute judge of the characters of others. He reads meaning into the slightest facial expressions or gestures, and more often than not, he is correct in his assumptions and conclusions. He prefers fairness in all his dealings, but expects the same in return. The Libra man can be direct, outspoken and frank with a tendency to speak his mind, but he is seldom bold or ungracious.

It may be found that the Libra man is not overly materialistic. He may seek possessions more out of a wish for comfort than anything else. Also, he loves to acquire those things in life that add to his base of knowledge. He has a preference for books, for information from different media, and for training and the acquisition of skills. He may also enjoy gadgets, electronics, boats, cars, etc., with which to occupy his mind and time. It is important, however, that these items are not in any way an inconvenience.

It is important to this man that his wife or companion be understanding, caring, appreciative, and above all else passionate. He loves change, and if he strays, it is for this reason. This is a man whose mind must be captivated by the other person in his life. Some men born to the sign of Libra allow their wives to seemingly dominate the relationship. This may be due to the fact that their minds are actively engaged elsewhere, and it's easier and more convenient to have a marriage partner who handles all the day to day affairs.

The Libra man is tender and compassionate, but he can also be strongly independent. He has some problems expressing and explaining himself to others as he keeps his more personal thoughts to himself. He has a strong desire to be on the other side of the world just to discover what is going on there. In other words, "What would life be like somewhere else? It must be entirely different. There must be different lifestyles." Etc. If these thoughts become too pronounced, this man may satisfy his curiosity by picking up and relocating to that far away place. This is not the most steady or trustworthy type of Libra man. He can lie, cheat, and con to get what he wants. He can be a great manipulator, actor, and story teller. What you see may not be what you get with this particular type of Libra man who can never be trusted in love or business or life or friendship.

There is of course a love for justice, neatness and order, peace and harmony. If he is angered, he is generally easily appeased. The Libra man is found of nature, art, music, and literature. He may well be gifted in either or several of these interests. Many also possess a love for sports. He appreciates cultured pleasures and amusements and has a strong desire for the companionship of others who are happy, joyful and humorous people who also possess an energetic drive for life. At the same time, he appreciates modesty and refinement. He possesses the ability to be adaptable, constructive and inspirational. The Libra man is also a natural romantic and flirt.

The Libra Woman

The women of Libra are kind-hearted, refined, and tasteful. They have a love for happy and responsive companions, and can be amiable and undemanding. She appreciates entertaining and congenial people and situations. Many of these woman are either artistic, or they possess a strong appreciation for beauty and natural settings. They also have a refined taste for clothing and fashion. They prefer that their home environments reflect their good taste.

As with the men of this sign, Libra women are extremely courteous and sociable. She too loves to be surrounded by friends and families. And she loves the companionship of well-spoken and well-informed individuals. In fact, while she preserves her privacy, she gravitates toward group activities and pleasant activities.

The Libra woman possesses a personal grace and an individual style. And she has an apparently insatiable curiosity about people. Libra women are adept at holding the attention of numerous admirers while making no one jealous. She does not promote jealousy, but rather admiration, praise and harmony. Others appreciate her harmonious nature. This is an attractive, feminine woman with expressive eyes and gestures, and she is an incurable flirt.

Women of this sign become devoted to their husbands and children, and no sacrifice is too great for their families. You are affectionate as well as understanding wives and mothers. You strive to make every attempt to remain cheerful under difficult circumstances and to endure discomforts with great patience. You are most interested and concerned (sometimes showing the capacity to worry too much) over the welfare of your family. You also have a tendency to set high ideals for your family.

There is an indication for Libra women to be happier on the social level rather than on the more intimate, familiar level. There are risks of misunderstandings and quarrels with the family: husband, wife, brothers, sisters, children, nieces and nephews, and grandchildren. There can be implications for court cases involving relatives which may have deplorable results.

Fortunately, you, Libra, are strongly inclined toward the development of your faculties of perception and observation. You sense with all your being, from a very early age, your strong intuitions and perceptions of life and of other people. You possess a strong desire for happiness in your life and in the lives of others. In fact, if we lived in the best of all possible worlds for you, everyone would be happy and the problems of the world would be set aside. You have a strong love and acceptance of others. Your fondness for people in general leads you to become involved in helping others. This may be in the form of listening to the problems of friends or in volunteer work through community charities. Your grace, charm and sincere concern for others attract many people to you.

There are those Libra women who have been accused of being overly vain and of wanting far too much admiration and adulation. The women of this sign love the idea of love. They are passionate and sensual and possess a strong appreciation for the opposite sex. In some circumstances, men can exercise much control and influence over Libra women.

Of course, to be truly happy in a relationship or in marriage, the Libra woman does need appreciation and a companion who is willing to be understanding and supportive. This is a dynamic and independent woman. She has her own ideas, and her strong intuitive abilities occupy her mind with the many possibilities in life.

Developing and realizing your inner strengths and needs allow you to discover your natural affinities. This enables you to produce better results in your life and to be a positive influence. Guard against continually placing the needs of others above your own welfare. Also, learn to trust your own judgment and to listen to yourself. No one else can better understand you or your needs than you can. When you become strong and develop your intuitive powers, it will be much less likely for others to take advantage of your kind and generous nature. And it will be much less likely for others to lead you astray or away from your personal objectives and goals in life. Recognizing the good in others is a remarkable attribute, but learn also to recognize and accept the unfavorable traits of others. In all that you do, hold on to your humor and your ability to enjoy life to its fullest. Like a last strong ray of Autumn sunshine, you are capable of radiating your peaceful, loving energy to one and all.

Libra Love Life

Libra, your love affairs must provide a spark, an intensity, a thrill of adventure. A romantic, you are inclined to be most drawn to another person when your eyes meet and there is an instant connection, a desire, an attraction. While you are out collecting friends and while you flirt with one and all, you are somewhat more selective in your love life for you seek a partner who can join you on a subliminal journey. Love making becomes an art form that enhances the wildest imaginations of your mind. Life is a grand adventure, and you collect stories of experiences as well as tales of heart break and of victories because when you love, you love with all your heart and emotions. On the road of life, you have no doubts that many a member of the opposite sex continues to think about and to remember that exquisite and remarkable experience with you. You much prefer to be sought after than to be aggressive yourself. And you radiate a magnetism when you perceive the attentions and adulation of someone who is particularly interesting and stimulating.

You discover a special attraction to other members of the Air signs--Gemini, Aquarius, and Libra--who share your ability to experience relationships emotionally and mentally, almost as if on another dimension. Leo, Aries, and Scorpio natives capture your imagination with their energy, strong wills, and love for adventure, but unless this person also shares your views of justice and harmony, you may continually feel unsettled or unbalanced as if some unanswered question is floating about in your mind always just out of reach. With Taurus you share an aesthetic appreciation for life, but there may be something in the Taurus nature which leaves you feeling less than excited as this person may not know how to act as a catalyst for your creative spirit. Cancer's devotion is appealing if somewhat sporadic. You find yourself admiring Virgo's keen mind and powers of observation, but the thrill of risk-taking may at times be absent. Sagittarius, on the other hand, may well share your love of adventure. Capricorn while being a little controlling is powerfully attractive. And while it may seem that Pisces offers the perfect romantic involvement, this emotional person may distract from your sense of calmness and peace.

Libra natives can drive their admirers crazy by not making up their minds, sitting perplexed on the fence attempting with all their mental energies to come to a decision. Or, they can impulsively jump into a love affair that lasts for years. While it has been said that the Libra native is at times easy to lead, what actually persuades this individual is that special element of charm, excitement and an energetic strong will. But once persuaded into a relationship, don't expect the Libra native to stick around forever or to be content if there is the smallest hint of the affair being one-sided. It's not that Libra's need to dominate (as you have been repeatedly accused), but you desire what is fair. Never forget, your overriding insistence on balance in life. This desire for fairness in a relationship will most often lead Leo, Aries and Scorpio to insist that you are controlling and dominating which is only a reflection of their own personal desires to do just that.

Libra individuals love to give and receive affection. You are caring and generous people. And it is only natural that in your desire for fairness, you would much prefer that these attributes be shared by your loved one. Do not be surprised, however, if others make every maneuver to take advantage of your good nature. And when you withdraw, don't be surprised if it is you who is accused of being selfish. Your selfishness is a necessary self-defense mechanism in many instances and may be all that you have to protect you from the harsher realities of life. It may seem that others criticize you while they themselves are striving to better their own positions. Take all criticism into consideration, and use your abilities to examine both sides of the issues at hand. Then for the truth in these issues, listen to your own counsel, your own self-advice, and your personal intuition. When it comes to yourself, you are your own best judge. Your intuition will provide you with a list of your weaknesses which you must work on in your own way.

Never become overly worried about your love life. With your love of travel and adventure and your openness to others, you will find that you meet any number of members of the opposite sex. Your biggest problem will be picking and choosing. Whatever your life brings you, you will maintain your faith in romance and will forever be in love with love.

Libra Children

The child born under the sign of Libra is often found to be a quiet, peaceful child who loves to facilitate the lives of the adults in the family by being pleasant and helpful. These children are enthusiastic and positive and actually enjoy the company of adults. Like the adult natives they can be sensitive, preferring harmony in the family, and dissension or harsh comments can be upsetting to them. These are extremely lovable and affectionate children, and they seem to glow when surrounded by a loving, demonstrative family.

These children are generally not persistent in wanting his or her own way. They much prefer to seek what would make everyone happy and by doing so hope to enhance the overall serenity and happiness of the entire family. It may appear that these children have few intense desires, but actually the most important wish they possess is for the well being of their loved ones. Rather than longing for a particular toy, this child longs for the adult to think about them and then to present him or her with a surprise or a toy which symbolizes the love and concern of the adult. If the parents of this child are happy, then the child is happy.

These children are graced with a curious, seeking nature. They develop an interest in learning and appreciate books or instructional material. They benefit from activities which allow them to express themselves creatively such as drawing or painting. While they can be quiet, they are also energetic and love the outdoors. These children are imaginative and creative and love play acting. Also, there is a strong affinity and love for water, nature and animals. They often develop an interest in sports which offers an avenue of learning and the companionship and camaraderie of others in their age group. They prefer games that also require some patience and thought. And often the Libra child exhibits an outstanding inventive ability or an originality of ideas.

These children appreciate a secure home which provides guidance and security. They also appreciate a certain degree of order, cleanliness and organization which augments their cognitive abilities by not distracting their minds from their thoughts or pursuits. These children require supervision and guidance as they can be easily led. However, they also possess a strong sense of justice and while they experiment with their environment as all children do, they prefer that eventually all matters fall within a certain, acceptable framework. This child prefers guidance to strict or harsh discipline and will readily respond to sensibly discussions of appropriate conduct and responsibilities.

Relationships with Other Signs

There is no exaggerating the magnetic appeal of the positive characteristics of the seventh-sign natives. It is almost, at times, as if other people persistently want to adopt you. You are pleasant and charming, reasonable with a touch of eccentricity, restless and fond of travel, and you possess a powerful imagination as well as a tasteful appreciation for the finer things in life. You are fond of pleasure and fun, social occasions and amusements while being good-natured, agreeable, and tactfully courteous. You are both passionate and compassionate in your relationships with others. Charm comes so easily for you that you can turn it on at will, and at other times it simply requires walking into a room full of people for your radiance to shine. Loving peaceful settings, without people around you, you become calm, quiet and introspective and your own best friend.

The well-developed Libra native is sought out by others to conciliate, arbitrate and settle differences or in other instances just to calm the fears or anxieties of the other person. While others fuss and argue over details and how to proceed, you calmly discern the easiest most productive path and would love to send others on their way. It can become frustrating to the Libra native to discover that other people appear to adhere to confusion rather than to action. But friendship is very important to you, and you patiently hold to the belief that time will solve most problems. You have the ability to perceive both sides of a problem as well as both sides of a person's character and to see clearly the obstacles other people face. (However, you are not always so astute about your personal decisions.) At any rate, other people turn to you for impartial judgments and decisions, and while you abhor the endless effort, you are ready for any sacrifice to attain a balanced situation.

Libra natives discover harmonious relations with Gemini (May 21-June 21), Sagittarius (November 22-December 20), Aquarius (January 20-February 18), and Leo (July 23-August 22). You may find disagreements with Capricorn (December 21-January 19), Cancer (June 22-July 22), and Aries (March 21-April 20). However, while you may be able to develop a conducive professional relationship with Aries, Capricorn may well display differing precepts of life and Cancer may be a bit too possessive. In Taurus you will appreciate the caring nature, and Gemini adds a dimension of excitement and fun to any social occasion. Scorpio loves a good argument and this can become tiresome. You may find that you get along well with other Libras in professional settings. And Pisces always make good friends. Aquarius may also well share your spiritual inclinations to the point that you may on occasion submit to this person's controlling nature.

Seek your most enduring friendships with persons born between January 19-22, February 16-29, May 18-22, and June 18-29. Also, look to those born in your own sign or to those people born between March 18-21 and April 16-28.

How to Find Your *Soul-Mate, Stars,* and *Destiny*

While you, the Libra native, are most prone to weighing and balancing, in your never ending curiosity to seek out and understand others, you may fall in with characters whose activities you would otherwise find somewhat vulgar. This experimentation with vulgarity, whether it be actions or words, does not augment any aspect of your better qualities. So, Libra, once you have satisfied your curiosity in this regards, feel free to move on.

Libra individuals make good and loyal friends, and the fundamental extroversion of your personality is an asset in all of your endeavors. You are not a critical person, which people appreciate, but remember that others may shy away from accepting your advice. It appears to be a construct of life, that people must learn from their own mistakes, and it also appears that any number of people are slow learners in this regard. In order to mature well, refrain from offering advice unless it is sought and then offer it only tentatively and patiently, and don't be alarmed if others don't follow your advice. Be very careful of persons who seek advice, follow it in some form, then blame you if they don't like the results. There are many people in life who more than anything need someone to blame for their own shortcomings. Take some precautionary measure not to fall into this trap. One other small word of advice, don't take personal criticism too much to heart. Don't be overly sensitive. You will learn that many people project their faults onto others, and to be sensitive in these particular situations is really a waste of time. There are also those who use criticism as a means of breaking down your spirit, weakening your will, and making you submissive. Learn to brush off these attempts by others to overcome your gentle, balancing, happy nature.

You will find that making friends is as easy as walking out your front door. Libra natives are known for making friends and associates in every sphere of activity, and your greatest asset is found in your graceful ability to interact easily with any number of people from varying walks of life. Others enjoy your companionship and will not hesitate to include you in activities. You no doubt will realize many productive and enjoyable relationships and experiences in life.

Libra Sexuality

That subject which interests us all: our own personal sexuality. Why does a person feel the way they do? Why does he or she like a certain person and not another? What arouses a person and why? On some level, these questions influences one and all. Like all aspects of our lives and lifestyles, the public attitude toward sex is ever changing and evolving. From the restrictive taboos of the Victorian Age, through the revitalization of the Industrial Age, to the make love not war of the 1960s to the commercialism of the 1980s and the 1990s, sex is always on our minds. Will the Age of Information or the Age of Aquarius bring new insights?

The American culture is not only influenced by popular trends and thought but by its unique cultural diversity as well. To the newcomer or newly arrived, American society can appear perplexing. What is difficult to understand is that in this freedom-based culture, the individual is literally free to be whoever he or she decides. And the gamut runs from the most traditional, reserved, cautious, and sexually repressed individuals to others who flaunt their sexuality, centering their lives around their sexual habits. Perhaps it is because of this very diversity that our culture makes some attempt not to be overly offensive to the sensitivities of some while giving a tolerant nod to the liberties of others. We are totally free, within the guidelines of laws, to seek divine enlightenment or to destroy ourselves with pleasures. Americans have the freedom to choose, individually, what importance their sexual behavior will play in their lives.

That being the case, sex is recognized by every serious discipline--from psychologists to scientists to astrologers--as being a central focus on individual lives. Freud saw sex as an influence on every aspect of the individual life. And from the sexist boys in the locker room to the most enlightened of intellectuals, sex remains a fundamental part of life that cannot be ignored. Get two friends together and the subject eventually turns to sex, romance, or marriage. One can blame it on the media, but sooner or later discussing the stock market gets boring, but sex never does.

There are those who hold to the theory that the primary function of sex is to have children and any other consideration is secondary. There are others for whom sex is an integral part of life, providing one of the greatest stress relievers ever invented. That all other living species procreate seasonally points to the reasoning of the second theory. But all pleasures (or temptations) in life also promote the possibilities of problems and health concerns unless a little logic is also applied.

Astrologically, the sexual nature has been examined from the Garden of Eden to the lives of contemporary celebrities. And what every serious astrologer will say is that how the individual relates to sexuality is not based on the Sun sign alone. The entire chart must be examined because each person is a unique combination of Sun, Moon, Ascendant, planets, Houses and aspects. A comparison of two charts often sheds light on compatibility. Compatibility between two people is often found when the Sun sign is in the same sign as their lover's Ascendant, or vice versa. Opposite Sun signs or an opposite Sun sign and Ascendant may also blend well together.

In a woman's chart, the placement of Venus is indicative of her sexuality while the position of Mars and the Sun indicates what kind of man she is attracted to. In a man's chart, the position of Mars tells how he relates to women, and the position of Venus and the Moon indicates what type of woman arouses him. In comparing two charts, look for the aspects of conjunction, sextile, square, trine, and oppositions. Remember that oppositions can blend. The square brings differences but much energy while conjunctions can be beneficial. The sextile and trine bring harmony. When a person's Venus and their lover's Mars are in the same sign, there is a strong attraction even if differences of opinions occur. When Venus and the other person's Ascendant are in the same sign, it adds to the sexual compatibility. Venus in the lover's sun sign brings a mutual interest while Mars in the lover's Moon sign is emotionally intense.

There is a vast variety of people found within each Sun sign, but basic characteristics and traits do exist. However, generalizations are just that and a fuller picture of the individual is reflected by the complete chart. The following section deals with Sun sign sexuality in a general manner. While the importance of sex remains the same in each Sun sign, the focus and attitudes vary.

Libra Sexuality - Man

Libra, the romantic of the Zodiac, is in love with sex, romance and love and all subjects which fall into that realm. Like Virgo, Libra is a thinker and will have thought long and hard about his sexuality. Unlike Virgo, Libra will want to collect a substantial amount of evidence and proof to back up his conclusions and theories. Libra brings the judicious balancing act into play, and it may have been a Libra (man or woman) who was the first to recognize and acknowledge that there is nothing perverse about any sexual act between two consenting adults. In fact, much of what is considered perverse by the more inhibited types is considered quite pleasurable by Libra, especially when the partner is trustable and both are seeking an avenue of fun and eroticism. After all, Libra argues, sex is listed among the pleasures and therefore is fun, enjoyable, an excellent stress reliever, and an even more excellent form of physical exercise. Given all that profound logic, Libra may then add his own ingredient of refinement and tastefulness, and golden showers and other acts will be definitely ruled out. Libra doesn't like to get unnecessarily dirty--he wants to have fun, thrills, excitement and a jolly good time. This man is also a connoisseur of affections, attentions, and pleasing the ladies. He harbors no fears of rejection in this department mainly because his experiences have proven otherwise. He is a man's man who knows instinctively how to be a ladies' man. (Homosexual brothers can change the appropriate words to make the sentence read correctly.) He loves beauty and is highly appreciative of the beauty found in the human form--the naked human form with all of its lines of perfection perfectly molded into a graceful creation. And he is drawn to experience and view as much of this beauty as he can in one life time.

Libra knows how to make the most of his youthful good looks and attractiveness and adds to that a personable diplomacy and tact. He is accepting of others and especially tolerant and accepting of the sexuality of others realizing that each and every person is interestingly different with various preferences and attitudes. Seeking peace and harmony, he is a person who likes to make other people happy and finds his own happiness in so doing. He is a great conversationalist and can discuss or debate most any subject that comes up.

Inherent in the sexuality of the Libra man is his need for love and affection. Sex without love, while entertaining, is somewhat of an empty experience which lacks the deeper feelings one person can have for another. He prefers quality over quantity and while men of other signs are compiling a list of sexual conquests, the Libra man is adding to his memories of loving and romantic encounters. This isn't a hasty man who wants to jump in and out of bed and then move on to the next activity. Neither is he inclined to have sex and then roll over and go to sleep. Each and every one of his romances have brought a different experience, but he has strong preferences for romantic settings, conversations laced with innuendoes, and long and loving glances that promise a perfect completion. For Libra, love making is an art form that builds upon and heightens the sensuality of the experience. He is an artist of foreplay leading to an exquisite sexual encounter and ending with loving embraces. He knows instinctively that sex is experienced through all the senses and he is aware of the sights, sounds, and smells involved as well as the importance of the sense of touch. Sex is an aphrodisiac in itself which mingles and meshes and combines the mental, emotional and physical experience into one. If sexual play leads to the fun of bondage, the Libra man will suggest tying his partner to the bed with a long string of pearls.

With this healthy sexual attitude, Libra the deliberator is more than a little confounded by more inhibited types or by people who turn sex into something dirty. Until he discovers otherwise, he may think that everyone is enjoying sex as much as he. A picture of two beautifully formed bodies is not viewed as dirty by Libra, but as a form of artistic expression. He may be just as equally confounded by society's over interest and exploitation of sex. And he may deliberate some more and balance this out by thinking that if more people were enjoying good sex fewer people would be talking about it. A Libra man doesn't need a section of a book to explain his sexuality. He knows he is a sexual being.

Libra Sexuality - Woman

The Libra woman contends with the giggling of the other signs over what they call her naive sexual attitude which she shares with the Libra male. But then like the Libra man, she may feel that those who giggle do so because they aren't experiencing enough romance and sex in their lives. But is she naive? Not to over generalize, but a Libra woman in her love for the sensual and with her ability to overlook the bad in others and to see only the good, can be naive in that she is easy to take advantage of. She will stay in a bad relationship too long while attempting to understand and to be tolerant of the other person, and she will even tolerate abuse while she strives to turn the relationship into one of perfection. But even in her worst of relationships, the sex will be good. If the sex and romance fades from a relationship, there is every probability that the Libra woman will bid her fair adieu. She is an idealist who at times loses her ability to be pragmatic. She too loves beauty and appreciates the human form, and this may lead her to forever enjoy relationships with young, physically fit men. And young men seem to enjoy her special kind of attention and adulation as well. But then she is also a logical person whose reasoning abilities delight in good conversation, and younger men may not possess that intellectual capability that comes with observing and having been there. A partner who captures her mind or her imagination is interesting as is that man who tends to carry a little weight but who is jolly and fun because he knows how to enjoy the pleasures of life. She likes a strong ego, a daring character, or a hint of the eccentric. In fact, she may work her way through the entire Zodiac before she finds the perfect partner.

Libra is ruled by Venus, that wonderful goddess of love, and Libra is all female. She wants the man to be assertive and to allow her to be the feminine mystique that responds to his advances. Like the Libra man, she wants her sexual encounters to include an alluring romance, affection and love. Add to that an imaginative partner with stamina and virility who is willing to experiment with eroticism and she is a happy female. Sex becomes an art form in which nothing is perverse as long as the two people involved are enjoying themselves. And having applied a logical and analyzed approach to the sexuality of the men she meets, she knows that men each seek something different from their sexual experiences. And whether it be that man who prefers sex slow and steady and tenderly loving or that man who wants to release his pent up adrenaline in pure madness and force, Libra anticipates his needs. Some men hold themselves in check with demure females, but this isn't necessary with Libra. She wants to know and experience what drives them wild. An inhibited partner who can't express himself sexually is of little interest to this precocious female. She wants each lover and each romance to be thrillingly unique and different. The ho-hum sameness of the routine sex act holds little interest for her. There must be a hint of intrigue, and it must be an electrically charged event that makes it memorable. And she can pass by any number of men while waiting patiently for that one in particular who can look at her and send charges through her body and who responds to her in the same way.

The sign of Libra rules the lumbar region including the lower spine and back, and a Libra woman will respond to a sensual back rub (especially with fragrant oil) and any attention given to her buttocks. From there she likes her other erogenous zones explored and excited while she enticingly discovers her partners own most sensitive areas.

The sign of Libra influences a person to seek balance, harmony and equality, and the Libra female applies this to love and romance in her on going efforts to discover the perfect love relationship. Those who giggle about sex can keep on giggling because Libra is busy enjoying it.

Libra Health

The seventh-sign natives are generally speaking healthy and optimistic. The sign of Libra rules over the kidneys and adrenal glands. The symbol of the Balance, the scale, is said to represent the spinal cord and the above mentioned organs. Therefore, natives of this sign may develop difficulties with nerves, back pain, problems with the kidneys, and headaches. Kidney problems may include cystitis, kidney stones, infections or inflammations. Other natives may suffer from skin disorders. There is some indication for health problems associated with the liver, intestinal complications, and problems associated with the feet. With many Libra natives accidents take preference over illnesses. Be cautious of injuries to the head, shoulders and/or back. Others are susceptible to throat and lung infections or to colds, flu, viruses and staph infections. There is some propensity for diabetes and for Bright's Disease.

Suggestions to prevent kidney problems include consuming an adequate amount of fluids in order to keep the system properly regulated. Also, it is suggested that sweets be limited and that the consumption of meat be moderate.

It is also important to take precautions against back injuries. Methods of prevention include strengthening the back and stomach muscles to develop a muscular system to support the back. Learn methods of working and lifting which will prevent placing undue stress on the back.

As with all people, it is highly recommended that Libra natives pay careful attention to their health and diet. You require foods that sustain your energy level. Take care that you aren't relying on caffeine to get you through your busy day. A well-balanced diet with an adequate amount of fresh fruit and vegetables as well as a plentiful supply of fiber will help you maintain that graceful body. And it goes without saying that your physical body requires physical exercise. A combination of a healthy diet and a work-out routine will add to your energy level, make you even more physically attractive, and improve your health while adding years to your life.

History of Libra

The Balance, the symbol for the sign of Libra, is most closely associated with Astrea and Athene of Greek and Roman mythology. Astrea or Athene were thought of as the patron goddesses of righteousness, justice, and order. The symbol of the scales remains today closely associated with court houses and with courts of law where it is often displayed. This legal association with Libra is traced back to the Babylonians. Saturn is in exaltation in Libra, and to the Babylonians, Saturn was the planet of righteousness. The Babylonian name for Libra was Zibanitu which, in some manner, is related to the star of Spica. In Hebrew mythology, Libra is associated with the Biblical tribe of Asher, one of the original twelve tribes of Israel.

In the Zodiac, Libra is the seventh-sign. Ancient scholars perceived an importance and significance in the number seven because of the recurrence of this number in nature. These scholars regarded this sign as the harmonic one of the twelve Zodiac signs. The number seven represented perfection and quality while the number twelve represented completion. Seven, as observed in nature, is seen in the seven colors of the rainbow, seven days in a week, seven notes in a musical scale, or seven sacred candlesticks. The ancient scholars felt that all of life runs in cycles of seven.

The sign of Libra in relation to the Sun, marks the place where the Sun attains the ecliptic and crosses the Equator during the Autumn equinox. At this time, the days and nights attain an equal length, or balance.

The Scales might be seen as balancing day and night and making them equal. The Scale is the sign which leads men to righteousness, safety, and redemption. The Babylonians placed the Judgment of Souls during Autumn, and the fates for the upcoming year were realized in the Spring.

This inclination for Libra to provide a balance is realized as precarious and might better be perceived as maintaining balancing or equilibrium while riding a roller coaster. In the constellation, the Balance contains leveling influences such as Bootes with its bright star, Arcturus, the Northern Crown (Corona Borealis), and the Serpent's Head. The other scale contains the Wolf, the Centaur's Spear, Circinus, and even the tail of Hydra, the Snake. It is supposed that the inanimate symbol of the Scale is actually being held by the goddess Astraea, although there is some contention as to whether these two symbols are one in the same.

Thus it falls to the natives of the sign of Libra to seek and to establish a balance from the precarious routines and influences of life. These natives attempt to accomplish this by realizing the middle road or the middle ground in their search for harmony, enlightenment, and fulfillment

How to Find Your Soul-Mate, Stars, and Destiny

Libra

September 23 -- October 22
The Thebaic Calendar
Character, Personality, and Destiny

In the past, calendars depicted the destiny of individuals on each day of the month. This calendar is intended for an everyday use when people want a quick reference to their destiny and to their nature as indicated by the horoscope. The Thebaic Calendar represents the daily notes that the ancient astrologers wrote on burnt stones or papyrus. This is an easy and fast way to find information pertaining to your birth date. The native will often find his characteristics and destiny around his date of birth.

DUALITY: Masculine   **ELEMENT:** Air   **QUALITY:** Cardinal   **RULER:** Venus

Whether Libra is the person's Sun sign, the Ascendant, on the cusp, or in a House, the characteristics of this sign become evident. The sign of Libra is the Cardinal Air sign which allows Libra to use ideas to make judgments. As a positive and masculine sign, Libra achieves these judgments and results by taking action. Venus, the ruler of Libra, bestows upon this sign the ability to attract new energies, and Libra is called upon to interact with these energies in a disciplined, harmonious, and well-balanced manner. Libra is the sign in which interpersonal relationships are based on cooperation with the individual learning to manage within the group and to maintain harmony within the group. Libras are thought of as the diplomats of the Zodiac. They not only want to communicate ideas, as the Gemini Air sign does, but they want the ideas well thought out and balanced. They strive to make judicious decisions by collecting information from all sides in a dispute, for example, and then acting accordingly. This is not always easy for the Libra individual who has the ability to see both sides of any argument, and who can argue either side equally as well. This necessity that Libra always make correct decisions can leave the Libra native deliberating, pondering, procrastinating, and anxiously indecisive until they come to the firm agreement within their own minds that the proper decision has been arrived at. This mental process involving the intellect can drain energetic Libra of his or her energy resulting in a much needed rest in order to revitalize their strength and mental preparedness. Once well rested, however, Libra is back in the fray, going to great extents to see that everyone is happy, contented, and at ease with the situation. Libras are at their best when cooperating, planning on an intellectual level, and operating within a framework of ideals and purpose. While Aries, the polar opposite of Libra, sets out with self-made ideas to better himself, Libra takes the ideas and applies principles to them which work for all concerned. Libras are sociable, well meaning, companionable, pleasant to be around, and simply seem to know intuitively how to deal with other people. They strive to put others at ease and make remarkable hosts or hostesses. This balance and justice in their dealings with others require a conscious effort to be selfless--to think of the well being and feelings of others--and to have the courage to do what they feel is right.

However, along comes Libra's difficulty in making decisions combined with their ability to see the good in all. In the wrong situations, Libra is left a bit defenseless against those who make a strong impression, persuade in the wrong direction, and lead one astray. Then too, Libra isn't totally against experiencing a little excitement and adventure, or displaying bold and daring moves which either adds spice to life or leads Libra into questionable situations. But with Libra it's live and learn, and certainly it does require experiences in order to gather the information necessary for making all those decisions properly. And how else does one learn to move easily in and around other people without an abundance of such experience?

The planet Saturn is exalted in Libra, and when it is found in this sign it brings an outward expression of Libra's best qualities making the native kind, pleasant, and likable. Saturn can add patience, spirituality, and a reasonable outlook to the Libra intellect. Judgment and impartiality are strengthened, and even with Libra's flexibility, this in itself can help in making the native more decisive. But Saturn may also suppress Libra's need for a partner which can result in a more independent but a lonelier individual.

To do well, Libra natives require a peaceful environment and pleasant surroundings in which to think and ponder. But they also do best with a partner, and may well spend a great deal of their time seeking the perfect partner with whom to share their aspirations and dreams. With the wrong partner or surrounded by others who drain their energy, Libra can become despondent to the point that the usually happy disposition becomes dry and bland. Also, that simmering Libra temper waits patiently beneath the surface of all well meaning Libra natives, but once it decides to surface, all who are near become aware of this fury and strong-headed temperament. And nothing makes Libra more frustrated or angry than poor decisions or actions which do not stand to reason. Libra doesn't like to be ordered around, but prefers that requests are well presented with reasoning. And once the request is understood, Libras are most generally more than willing to comply, that is, if Libra decides after careful thought that the request is reasonable.

The First Decan

The First Decan occurs from 0 degrees to 10 degrees of Libra and applies to those individuals born between September 23 and October 2. With these individuals, especially those born on the cusp of Virgo, there is found the tendency toward intellectual activity and activity which is of service to others. Hence, these natives are drawn to the study of psychology, sociology, political science, or theology. They possess practical skills but with a need to apply these skills to dealing with people or groups. They may see themselves as drawn to a higher purpose with a wish to design or find a certain utopia within society. And to this ideal they aim with all their thinking abilities. Not as cautious as Virgo, they can try any number of ideas or paths before finding the one for which they are best suited. Togetherness in the form of partnerships, friendships, and romantic relationships become a matter of importance to these individuals. They may be socially and artistically inclined, or they may develop an interest in literature and writing.

The Second Decan

The Second Decan occurs from 0 degrees to 20 degrees of Libra and applies to those individuals born between October 3 and October 13. The characteristics of the sign of Libra are strongest with this Second Decan making the natives more persevering and enduring. With all of the Libra qualities highlighted, they make excellent attorneys and judges, capable of arguing either side of any issue. These natives are more material minded in their goals and objectives and exhibit more of an optimistic outlook in their dealings with others. These Libra must learn the lessons of life through experiencing difficulties first hand. They achieve their goals gradually, step by step, through their efforts to achieve. They possess all of the diplomatic and people traits inherent in this sign, and they know intuitively how to perfect these skills and use them to their best advantage. Adaptable and flexible, they enjoy friendships with others of various ages and lifestyles, promising unusual experiences. These natives find success and happiness although for many it comes with maturity.

The Third Decan

The Third Decan occurs from 20 degrees to 30 degrees of Libra and applies to those individuals born between October 13 and October 22. Those Libra natives approaching the cusp of Scorpio find that they possess the same inherent qualities of their Sun sign of good will and generosity toward others, but it is combined with an authoritarian spirit. In other words, they want what is best for all, and they may even insist upon it. Stronger by nature than the other two Decans, they endure any amount of hardships in order to persevere and find their way within the world. Success can seem illusive to these natives, but they are never without the basics or necessities of life. The intuitive abilities and sensitivities are heightened as well as the ability to read other people. And while they continue to see the best in others, they recognize and find themselves have to peering over other's faults before gaining a clear sight of any positive attributes. But Libra continues to accept others at face value and reserves judgment for careful deliberations. The Third Decan natives like variety, new experiences and a taste of adventure. They are capable of adapting to various types of people, different lifestyles, and all most any social situation.

First Decan of Libra:

September 23 - October 2 -

First Ten Days

Character, Personality, and Temperament:

The character of the natives born at this time is inclined toward utopia, and novel and seductive pursuits which are fanciful. The consciousness touches everything, but does not focus on anything. The natives of this Zodiac sign spend much energy between the clouds, looking and touching all which they come in contact with, but never seeming to find where to stop. They run as if after two rabbits at the same time.

Cardinal Element:

Air: Enterprising use of ideas and ideals to make balanced judgments regarding relationships with others.

Destiny:

Life gets better and better by chances and with new opportunities, and new things come for the natives of this Decan.

Star Date of Birth: September 23

There is an inclination for this native to be gullible and to experience confusion and frivolity. There is indicated separations and a loss of material possessions. You like to have all the facts before making a decision. In romance, you do best in a relationship when you feel loved, needed, and appreciated. You are open hearted and positive with the ability to respond to spur of the moment romance and sex.

Star Date of Birth: September 24

There is seen a susceptibility and an irascibility in the character. An agitated life is indicated with complications through adulterous adventures and arguments. Able to see the good in others, you are not always as discerning as you should be as to who is trustable and who makes a good friend. This makes you gullible in love and romance as well, and however sensual and loving you are, you are easily taken advantage of.

Star Date of Birth: September 25

There is a scientific curiosity and a great ability to assimilate. A very visible career and fame is indicated. Charming and sociable, you are well liked because of your diplomatic manner and ability to put others at ease. Romantically, you know how to turn on the charm as well and are a born flirt. You are especially thrilled when you entice another away from a busy schedule to be with you.

Star Date of Birth: September 26

There is an inclination for apathy, softness, and resignation. An unsteady, unsure life is indicated and unrealized dreams. You seek justice and readily defend what you perceive as a just and right cause. You enjoy romance for the sake of romance and your numerous encounters lead you to gather experiences which augment your more serious relationships when you are ready to settle down with that special person.

How to Find Your *Soul-Mate, Stars,* and *Destiny*

Star Date of Birth: September 27

The individual possesses good taste in social gatherings but there is some lack of common sense. The career will border on a genuine vocation. You are a lover of nature and beauty who strives to find balance and peacefulness in life and love. Sexually, you are able to perceive when others are attracted to you almost telepathically. This reaffirms your feelings of the importance of love and romance.

Star Date of Birth: September 28

A combative, aggressive personality is noted. There is indicated a life filled with arguments and dangerous situations. You are hard working but recognize the importance of finding the right partner in business and love to further and fulfill your efforts and abilities. Love and romance makes you feel young, energetic and alive. Your sexuality is enhanced by your open-minded outlook.

Star Date of Birth: September 29

There is seen an excessive naiveté and the person is too trusting of others. This person's life will be exploited by others close by. Without a loving partner you can feel unambitious and even depressed. In romance, you are giving and know how to make the other person feel needed and wanted which in return rewards you and makes you feel even sexier and more devoted to pleasing your partner. You can teach love.

Star Date of Birth: September 30

There is a tendency to overlook reality, and the spirit is somewhat pessimistic. There is seen an unstable life that is prey to all kinds of events and circumstances. Able to seek and find a balance between emotions and reality, you can lose patience with those who are overly emotional. You are attracted to romantic partners who have lost out on love in the past and who you wish to console and pamper with your sensual nature.

Star Date of Birth: October 1

Sensibility is noted for this individual. In life, a dependency on others is indicated, and you will find yourself towed by other people. Believing in what you feel is right, you can be outspoken in your beliefs, offending those who are more traditional. Even so, you feel the need to guard your reputation as your youthful appearance results in romances with those outside your age group.

Star Date of Birth: October 2

There is indicated a lack of self-confidence. The destiny is filled with worry and anxiety which makes you feel discouraged and tortured. Hard working and productive, in your social and romantic life you let your hair down to a good time and the thrills of adventure and new experiences. Avoid friendships with those who gossip because your private life may produce scandals among loose tongues.

Second Decan of Libra:

October 3 - October 13 -

Second Ten Days

Character, Personality, and Temperament:

The effect of this Decan is completely opposite from the First Decan. The qualities of the sign are more concentrated and gravitate toward more material and more optimistic and positive goals.

Cardinal Element:

Air: Enterprising and outgoing with an intellectual outlook and a tendency toward communicative skills.

Destiny:

The destiny of these individuals will be realized in a difficult way. It will be realized slowly but surely. The mature years will be happy.

Star Date of Birth: October 3

The person is inclined toward a reticent, brooding personality. A life of suffering without many joys is noted. Love and romance are an essential ingredient to life for you. You live for the thrill of new experiences, but are also drawn to establishing a fulfilling relationship with a special person who you feel will reciprocate your truer desires and wishes. Love and sex seem to improve with each year.

Star Date of Birth: October 4

This individual has a mocking personality and can at times be cruel. An easy life with moderate accomplishments is noted. You love to act out your feelings and emotions. In romantic relationships, you go the limit in being kind hearted and considerate always considering the needs of the other person, but it is important to you to feel loved and needed in return.

Star Date of Birth: October 5

Pessimism is noted for this individual. Either a literally or figuratively speaking solitary life is seen. You are energetic but have problems focusing this energy in any one direction which brings on periods of restlessness and a need to then rest up for the next go around. You are a lady or gentleman and know how to be elegantly sensual and sexual in the bedroom.

Star Date of Birth: October 6

This person is too suspicious of others. The material life will be satisfying, but the happiness will be clouded by the suspicious nature. Wanting to do what is best for all concerned makes it difficult for you at times to make decisions. Your sexuality is enhanced by your ability to appear as though you were born to please others. You are drawn to strong willed people who know their minds.

Star Date of Birth: October 7

You can be discerning in your approach, and you appear reserved, refined, elegant, and quietly dignified but this is all forgotten in the bedroom where you respond to the thrill of togetherness and delight in outstanding performances of sexuality. Not being one to kiss and tell, your eyes are the only hint to your truer nature.

Star Date of Birth: October 8

This individual possesses a temperament which can not tolerate any constraints. The life will be well managed and there will be your share of happiness with no major headaches. You are open minded and capable of exploring the lifestyles of others. You are optimistic in romance, believing that the ending of one relationship is the opportunity to discover a better one in the future, and you respond to this attitude in others.

Star Date of Birth: October 9

An artistic temperament which is talented and imitative. A cheerful, playful, and happy life is indicated. The experiences of your childhood make you self-sacrificing and forgiving of the faults of others, but that doesn't prevent you from responding to your own needs or from being tempted to explore the possibilities in love and romance. You often desire the most life has to offer in romance, love and sex.

Star Date of Birth: October 10

There is an inclination for well thought-out ideas and perseverance. Travels, missions, and explorations are noted. You set high standards for yourself and others, but you are especially loving and understanding with your loved ones. You are particularly devoted to your romantic partner, but you desire the same in return. Persons who require this degree of devotion are drawn to you romantically and sexually.

Star Date of Birth: October 11

This individual possesses the soul of a critic; there is a tendency to overlook the experiences of others. Many deceptions are noted in the life of the individual. Indecisive and prone to procrastination, you may become easily confused in love and romance and are easily led astray by those in whom you place your trust. You can become disappointed when others do not return your devotion and love. Sex and love attracts your attention.

Star Date of Birth: October 12

This person possesses a personality that is both adaptable and which can be accommodating; this person is thankful and optimistic. A happy life is indicated without any a lot turbulence. Your quick smile adds to your resourcefulness often winning you the edge in any argument. You feel lucky in love, romance, and sex which serves to boost your good feelings about yourself. You hold your own in ego contests, appreciating the ego-driven nature of others while appeasing your own feelings at the same time.

The Third Decan of Libra:

October 13 - October 22 -

Third Ten Days

Character, Personality, and Temperament:

The characteristics of these individuals indicate a lot of goodness and generosity with at times an authoritarian spirit but one which is of good will. There is indicated a strong concentration and contemplation of how to arrive at one's goals and dreams.

Cardinal Element:

Air: Strong, enterprising nature that utilizes ideas to communicate and accomplish what is worthwhile in life.

Destiny:

A pleasant fate is noted with abundant material goods. In the worst case scenario, there will be found all the basic necessities.

Star Date of Birth: October 13

An authoritarian character is noted which is unable to tolerate and who suffers from contradictions. There is career success, but there are unpleasant situations in the family life. You are capable of applying logic to your intuitive guesses at forthcoming trends. Sexually, you prove yourself an ideal partner wanting the most romance has to offer in thrills and ecstasy and wanting to give the same in return. Your partners never complain about your sexual abilities.

Star Date of Birth: October 14

The temperament indicated is that of a leader, but this person will listen to advice and suggestions of others. Success is indicated, but never as much as anticipated. Your powers of observation give you a keen understanding of others which makes you likable and popular. Sexually, you desire to please as well as be pleased and this ability continues to develop as you mature. But you are also discerning, wanting the best rather than the most.

Star Date of Birth: October 15

An overconfident individual who is inclined toward daring actions is seen. The success of this person is hindered by hazardous enterprises. Your easy going nature grants you the time to lose yourself in dreams, romance, sex, and fantasies. Your tendency to think too much about what is right and wrong may lead you to be somewhat inhibited in your approach to sex, but chance encounters lead you to drop all inhibitions.

How to Find Your *Soul-Mate*, *Stars*, and *Destiny*

Star Date of Birth: October 16

The person is overly detail oriented. Success is found in the sciences where the attention to minute details is considered a virtue. You are generous and self-sacrificing, but you like to be appreciated for your efforts. Sexually, you are drawn to those who you feel need you or who you feel need to be saved from their own faults. You experience romantic and sexual encounters with those who have different values or political opinions.

Star Date of Birth: October 17

This individual is inclined to be prudent and skillful and at times cunning and overly confident. Victory is noted but at the price of battles with treachery. The thrill of adventure leads you to associate with those willing to take a risk. You secretly fantasize about the perfect soul mate or sexual partner who understands and appreciates you and who shares your desire for fulfilling sex.

Star Date of Birth: October 18

This native possesses the gift to enchant people and is a little overshadowed by vanity. Success is noted through this persons personal qualities in love and in business affairs. Knowing what you want leads you to lose interest in those who don't share your feelings. When you find that perfect partner, you are loving, kind, and giving, wanting to experience the most and best in love, romance, and sex, and you are unafraid of devoting yourself to that purpose.

Star Date of Birth: October 19

This person is ambitious but lacks appropriate measures in these undertakings. Success is seen after much agitation; at times success is prevented by obstacles. Even your enemies admire your ability to be graceful and resourceful under fire. You know what you want from others and how to diplomatically place all in the right position for the most promising outcome. Sexually, you are open to new experiences, but again you are happiest with the best there is to offer.

Star Date of Birth: October 20

There is a strong indication of generosity and devotion. A life without great wealth is noted but it is happy. You know how to keep all your ducks in a row, but you are at times tempted by the taste of adventure. Sexually, you respond to the thrill of new experiences and the ecstasy of desire, but you maintain an intellectual self-control and know when to step out of any given situation.

Star Date of Birth: October 21

This person is inclined toward both perseverance and stubbornness. Accomplishments are noted after a great deal of effort which will also bring security. You are strongly independent and your need for a partner is offset by your desire to find the right partner. Knowing what you like and what you want, you are rarely bored with sex and romance, always knowing how to add that spark of fun and sexual delight.

Star Date of Birth: October 22

This person begins projects with difficulty; a shyness or lack of will power is noted. A life of laziness, habitual idleness and sluggish is indicated. This person tolerates all experiences, not being able to react against them. Always willing to give the benefit of the doubt, you are at times led astray by less than well meaning people who take advantage of your better nature. Sexually, you desire to explore the possibilities of love and romance, wanting to experience as much as possible before settling down.

Colors:

The natives of the sign of Libra may discover their most favorable colors are all shades of blue, violet, purple, and pink.

Birthstones:

The birthstones for Libra include the opal, pearl, sapphire, or diamond.

Power Stones:

The power stones for Libra include tourmaline, kunzite, and blue lace agate.

Flowers:

The most favorable flowers for Libra natives are plants and vines with blue blooms, the violet, the rose, or the gardenia.

Keyword: "I Balance"

Positive Traits:

Thoughtful; charming; harmonious; pleasant; cheerful; sociable; easy going; impartial; adaptable; flexible; tolerant; judicious; gracious; modest; refined; romantic; diplomatic; idealistic; forgiving; generous; tactful; artistic; appreciative of beauty; sympathetic; persuasive; affectionate; well balanced; impartial; intellectual.

Negative Traits:

Indecisive; vague; susceptible; uncertain; resentful; frivolous; reckless; hesitating; procrastinating; discontent; pleasure-seeking; impressionable; vain; aloof; careless; vacillating; flirt; misrepresentation of truths; exaggeration to prove a point; self-centered; disloyal and unfaithful; temperamental; lazy; weak-willed; excessively romantic; melancholy; manipulative; user.

How to Find Your *Soul-Mate, Stars,* and *Destiny*

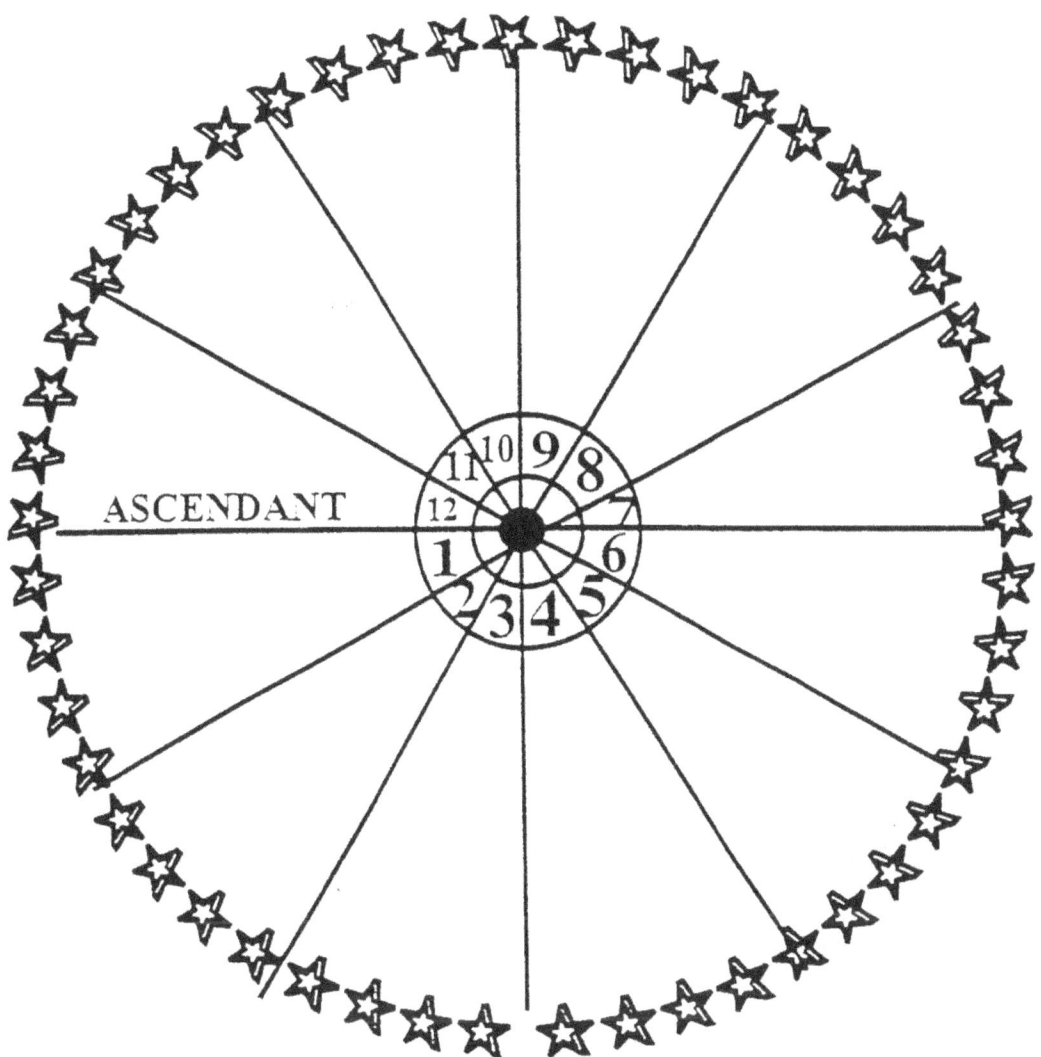

LIBRA

PERSONAL SELF-EXPRESSION AND MENTAL TENDENCIES

1. Love of Justice, Peace, Harmony; Very Courteous; Pleasant
2. Agreeable, Even Tempered, Affectionate, Sympathetic, Sensitive
3. Surroundings and Conditions of Friends, Peacemaker, Just, Vigor
4. Kind, Amiable, Generous, Modest, Neat, Orderly, Particular
5. Refined, Pleasure and Amusements, Artistic, Unclean Work
6. Intuitive, Objective Foresight, Vitality, Virile, Vivifying
7. Quick to Anger, Easily Appeased, Analytical, Fussy, Hypercritical
8. Happy, Sunny, Mirthful, Compassionate, Idealistic
9. Adaptable, Constructive, Impressionable, Abnormally Conventional
10. Admire Modesty, Ambitious, Discord, Finicky, Inhibitions
11. Professionist, Good Taste, Mentally-Vital, Changeable, Flirtatious
12. Well-Formed Body, Good Complexion, Good Mental Abilities
13. Good Comparison, Imaginative, Good-Natured, Hopeful, Warmth
14. Cheerful, Genial, Loving But Changeful, Weak Against Strong
15. Fond of Pleasure and Society, Favors or Inclines to Unions
16. Partnerships, General Popularity, Amorous, Clothes, Jewelry
17. Warm-Hearted, Affable, Inclined to Love and Marriage
18. Kind in Manner, Makes Friends Easily, Adornment, Luxury
19. Approbations, Refined and Harmonious Influences, Inspirational
20. Prefers to Work in Association With Another, Wasteful
21. A Refined, Good, and Broad Mind; Quiet; Tender, Tidy
22. Judgement and Reason, Taste for Mental Pursuit, Throne
23. Mathematical Work or Inventions, Intellectual Development
24. Contributes to Kindness, Marriage and Partnership, Literature
25. Pure and Refined Affections, Rich Love of Nature, Gullible
26. Marriage Conducive, Friendships, Sociability, Walnut
27. Fruitful Union, Spring of Talent, Philosophical
28. Good Social Standing, Affection for Cousins and Other Relatives

29. Lives With Several Partners, Follow Traditional Sex Roles
30. Promotes Development of the Faculties of Perception and Observation
31. Clear Vision, Refined Tastes, Idealistic Temperament
32. Business or Professional Career, Competitors But Survives Enemies
33. Meets With Rivalry, Opposition, Enmity and Criticism, Secret
34. Ardent, Rash, Impulsive or Passionate Love, Opposite Sex
35. Entangled Through Affections Causing Much Suffering, Grief, and/or Trouble
36. Other Testimonies Concurring, Peaceful Life, No Ambitions or Desire for Wealth
37. Disappointment in Love Delays Marriage, Mainly Sensual
38. Endowed With Superior Intellect, Intense, Procrastinating
39. Separations, and Difficulties Between Partner, Friends, Associates, and Relatives
40. Seductive, Compliant, Forceful, Controlled, Sensual, Adaptive
41. Cool, Attractive, Self-Protective, Team Worker, Yellow
42. Self-Indulgent, Subtle, Multiple, Paradoxical
43. Sophisticated, Strong, Narcissistic, Sociable
44. Aggressive, Ugly-Duckling, Melancholic, Cooperative
45. Diplomatic, Sensitive, Argumentative, Dedicated of Causes
46. Manipulative, Indecisive, Loves Art, Contradictory
47. Rational, Polite, Ambivalent, Detached, Self-Doubting
48. Self-Righteous, Lazy, Frivolous, Overly Fastidious
49. Direct Tactics, Uncomfortable, Paradoxical, Midnight Sun
50. Avoid Emotional Scenes or Confrontations
51. Demeanor, Charm, Softness, Low-Key Approach
52. Staggeringly Agressive, Full of Contradictions
53. Superficial, Substantial, Decorative, Managerial
54. Subtle or Blunt, Beauty and Pleasure, Frequent Pleaser
55. Poor Self-Image, Service of Humanity
56. Exaggerated Wish to Please and Belong
57. Mediator in Family Dispute, Master of Survial Tactics
58. Indirect Suggestion, Sublimation, Anticipation
59. Evasion, Naturally Elegant and Charismatic
60. Mentally Active, Movements, Sensualists, Undulating Grace
61. Spanning Generations and Geographical Distances
62. Sophisticated Taste, Supportive Friend, Admirable Lover
63. Communions, Openings, Morbid Sensitivity, Passive
64. Depressed, Slightly Paranoid, Self-Nourishment
65. Self-Esteem, Self-Confidence, Effectiveness, Sex Appeal
66. Gem-Studded Goals, Perpetually Tipping, Hostility
67. Curvaceous, Art of Seduction, Sensuous, Lazy, Feminine

68. Charm, Self-Denial, Torrid, Associations
69. Decisions With Competence, Involves Emotional Risk
70. Expresses Disagreement, Secret Love Affairs,
71. Assertive, Effective, Dedicated, Caring
72. Artistic Gifts, Sensual Potential, Mysterious, Mischievous
73. Submissive and Fragile, Love With Skepticism, Possessive
74. Draw People and Opportunities, Marries Several Times
75. Good Conversation, Everything in Balance
76. Sexually Insecure, Negative Body Image, Sexual Fears
77. Voyeurism, Exhibitionist, Feel Loving, Greedy, Lusty, Jealous, Sad
78. Selfish, Depressed, Hostile, Guilty, Worried, Withdrawn
79. Demanding, Accommodating, Romantic
80. Sense, Discretion, Excesses in Eating and Drinking
81. Energetic, Enthusiastic Worker, Excessive Acts of Indiscretion
82. Carelessness, Extravagance, Accidents
83. Change and Travel, Discord, Discontent, Hasty, Enmities, Assaults
84. Unexpected Enmities or Attacks, Matrimonial or Business Worries
85. Unsettled Mrried Life, Many Inharmonies, Sarcastic, Untruthful
86. Hasty Temper, Shrewd, Active, Clever, Progressive
87. Social Success and Popularity, Hopes and Wishes
88. Love the Mysterious, Difficulties With disreputable
89. Many Oppressors, Witty, Illusive, Taken alone,
90. Money, Property and Possessions, Marriage, Friendships
91. Cardinal Movable, Equinoctial, Airy, Hot, Moist, Semi-Fruitful
92. Humane, Scientific, Masculine, Sanguine, Estates of Immortality
93. Defaults, Defects, and Accusations; Impartial; Unprejudiced
94. Conciliatory, Justice, Judical, Gracious, Meticulous
95. Decorous, Persuasive, Forgiving, Tactful, Well Balanced
96. Uncertain, Extreme, Reckless, Temporizing, Hesitating
97. Susceptible, Impressionable, Pedantic, Vain, Aloof
98. Over Puncitious, Shirking, Careless, Vascillating
99. Astarte, Accord, Appease, Approve, Aphrodite, Artistic
100. Admirable, Adolescent, Adorn, Adulterous, Affiance

How to Find Your Soul-Mate, Stars, and Destiny

Celebrity Birthdays

September — Libra

23	Bruce Springsteen Walter Lippman Ronald Bushy Jason Alexander	Mickey Rooney Walter Pidgeon Ray Charles Romy Schneider	Mary Kay Place Julio Iglesias Augustus Caesar Lita Ford
24	Phil Hartman F. Scott Fitzgerald Anthony Newley Cheryl Crawford	Jim Henson 'Mean' Joe Green Linda McCartney	Gerry Marsden Jim McKay Eric Soderholm
25	Heather Locklear Barbara Walters Sheila MacRae Cheryl Tiegs	Dmitri Shostakovic William Faulkner Cesare Borgia Mark Hamill	Christopher Reeve Michael Douglas Juliet Prowse Will Smith
26	Bryan Ferry Pope Paul VI George Gershwin T. S. Eliot	Mary Beth Hurt George Raft Linda Hamilton Olivia Newton-John	Joe Bauer Donna Douglas Marty Robbins Georgie Fame
27	Meat Loaf Sam Ervin Greg Ham Wilford Brimley	Randy Bachman Vincent Youmans Sada Thompson Greg Morris	Sarah Chalke Jayne Meadows Shaun Cassidy William Conrad
28	Confucius Al Capp William S. Paley Brigitte Bardot	Moon Unit Zappa William Windom Ed Sullivan Janeane Garofalo	Jeffrey Jones Ben E. King Tom Harmon John Sayles
29	Ken Norton Jr. Stanley Kramer Gene Autry Jerry Lee Lewis	Emily Lloyd Greer Garson Trevor Howard Anita Ekberg	Bryant Gumbel Larry Linville Madeline Kahn Patricia Hodge
30	Marc Bolan Dewey Martin Angie Dickinson Marilyn McCoo	Fran Drescher Truman Capote Johnny Mathis Victoria Tennant	Deborah Kerr Jody Powell Barry Williams Crystal Bernard

How to Find Your Soul-Mate, Stars, and Destiny

October — Libra

1	Richard Harris Pres. Jimmy Carter Faith Baldwin Julie Andrews	Walter Matthau George Peppard James Whitmore Randy Quaid	Tom Bosley Howard Hewett Mark McGwire Stella Stevens
2	Annie Leibovitz Mahatma Gandhi Graham Greene Rex Reed	Freddie Jackson Groucho Marx Don McLean Mike Rutherford	Sting Maury Wills Bud Abbott Donna Karan
3	Fred Couples Jack Wagner Chubby Checker Gertrude Berg	Gore Vidal Thomas Wolfe Pamela Hensley James Darren	Dave Winfield Emily Post Warner Oland Damon Runyon
4	Susan Sarandon Jim Fielder Charlton Heston Sam Huff	Anne Rice Chris Lowe Jan Murray Buster Keaton	Armand Assante Pancho Villa LeRoy Van Dyke Felicia Farr
5	Steve Miller Barry Switzer Karen Allen Clive Barker	Leo Barnes Josie Bissett Eddie Clarke Jeff Conaway	Jeff Conaway Brian Connolly Bob Geldof Kate Winslet
6	Britt Ekland Thor Heyerdahl Shana Alexander Kevin Cronin	Bobby Farrell Thomas McClary Matthew Sweet Bob Weir	Jenny Lind Jack Sharkey Carole Lombard
7	Helen MacInnes June Allyson Yo-Yo Ma Henry Wallace	John Mellencamp Kevin Godley Oliver North Andy Devine	R.D. Laing Dave Hope Martha Stewart Alfred Drake
8	Sigourney Weaver Rona Barrett Johnny Ramone Sarah Purcell	Chevy Chase George Bellamy Stephanie Zimbalist Michael Dudikoff	Jesse Jackson R.L. Stine Paul Hogan Hamish Stuart
9	John Lennon Scott Bakula Camille Saint-Saens Michael Pare	Sean Ono Lennon Robert Wuhl Walter O'Malley Aimee Semple McPherson	John Entwistle Jackson Browne Freddie Patek

How to Find Your Soul-Mate, Stars, and Destiny

OCTOBER   LIBRA

10	James Clavell	Charles Dance	Jessica Harper
	Giuseppi Verdi	Helen Hayes	Johnny Green
	Harold Pinter	Vernon Duke	Ben Vereen
	Tanya Tucker	Martina Navratilova.	David Lee Roth
11	Luke Perry	Joan Cusack	David Morse
	Joseph Alsop	Eleanor Roosevelt	Daryl Hall
	Jerome Robbins	Charles Revson	Dottie West
	Ron Leibman	Icing Richard III	Grant Shaud
12	Chris Wallace	Susan Anton	Kirk Cameron
	Sam Moore	Joe Cronin	Brian Hyland
	Perle Mesta	Luciano Pavarotti	Dick Gregory
	Tony Kubek	Dave Vanian	Adam Rich
13	Nancy Kerrigan	Demond Wilson	Paul Simon
	Karen Akers	Margaret Thatcher	Lenny Bruce
	Lillie Langtry	Nipsey Russell	Tisha Campbell
	Shirley Ceasar	Marie Osmond	Anita Kerr
14	William Penn	Dwight D. Eisenhower	Anne Rice
	Roger Moore	Allan Jones	Bernie Siegel
	Ralph Lauren	Greg Evigan	Cliff Richard
	Lillian Gish	John Dean	Roger Moore
15	Penny Marshall	Sarah Ferguson	Lee Iacocca
	Mario Puzo	Arthur Schlesinger Jr.	Chris De Burgh
	P. G. Wodehouse	Linda Lavin	Richard Carpenter
	Friedrich Nietzsche	John Kenneth Galbraith	Jean Peters
16	Kellie Martin	Eugene O'Neill	Wendy Wilson
	Tim Robbins	Linda Darnell	Suzanne Somers
	Oscar Wilde	Tony Carey	Noah Webster
	Angela Lansbury	Robert Ardrey	Bert Kaempfert
17	Arthur Miller	Jean Arthur	Irene Ryan
	Evel Knievel	Spring Byington	Margot Kidder
	Montgomery Clift	Pope Paul I	Jim Seals
	Vince Van Patten	Jimmy Breslin	Rita Hayworth
	Tom Poston		
18	Pierre Trudeau	George C. Scott	Martina Navratilova
	Lotte Lenya	Hilly Elkins	James Gaffney
	Melina Mercouri	Laura Nyro	

October   Libra

19	Jack Anderson Amy Carter	Jeannie C. Riley Lyn Dickey	George McCrae
20	Dr. Joyce Brothers Art Buchwald Stuart Hamblen	Herschel Bernardi Arlene Francis Mickey Mantle	Jerry Orbach Bela Lugosi Christopher Wren
21	Georg Solti Dizzy Gillespie Christopher Columbus Whitey Ford	Carrie Fisher Jade Jagger Bill Russell	Michael Landon Samuel Taylor Coleridge Manfred Mann
22	Timothy Leary Franz Liszt Constance Bennett	Catherine Deneuve Joan Fontaine Sarah Bernhardt	Teresa Wright Annette Funicello Dore Previn

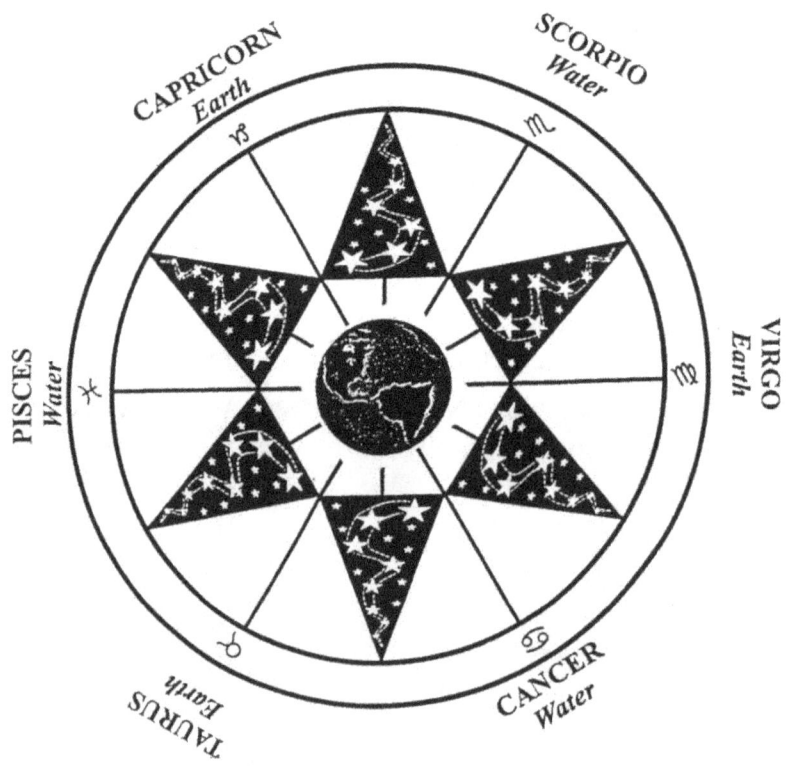

How to Find Your *Soul-Mate*, *Stars*, and *Destiny*

Date With Destiny

Share With Me Your Fantasy

How to Find Your *Soul-Mate, Stars,* and *Destiny*

Date With Destiny

Share With Me Your Fantasy

SCORPIO

October 23 - November 21
Man - Woman - Child - Character - Relationships - Compatibilities - Love Signs

Scorpio, the eighth, Sun sign of the Zodiac, is symbolized by the Scorpion and takes its name from the Latin word for scorpion. Scorpio is associated with sex, reproduction, regeneration, birth, death, and the underworld. In fact, in ancient Mesopotamian mythology, it was scorpion men who guarded the gates of the underworld. Where does all this leave Scorpio natives? They are considered intense, passionate, strong willed, and provocative and precocious.

How to Find Your *Soul-Mate, Stars,* and *Destiny*

The sign of Scorpio is often associated with an eagle as well, representing the evolved soul soaring above earthy concerns, and this relates directly with the Scorpio tendency to develop an interest in spirituality on a higher level of expression. Many a Scorpio possesses an inner sense of this spirituality and spends a life time coming to terms with it, exploring it, and making an attempt to find the right words to express their insights. Many never feel that they can fully explain these feelings or insights and thus select to keep their thoughts to themselves in a rather secretive way. At the same time, Scorpios may sense that others would not fully understand these complex an mystical sensitivities. The perceptiveness of Scorpio allow them to size up the strengths and weaknesses of other people, knowing in a short time whether the other person is as strong a person as they or whether others are weak-willed, insecure, and fearful. For the sign of Scorpio predisposes an individual to be somewhat fearless, courageous, bold, adventuresome, impulsive, and seeking. They seek experience, seeing new experiences as not only exciting but as providing an avenue for learning more of life's lessons. Scorpios appear to be born with a thirst for power or the freedom that comes with power, and this is manifested in an urge to control their personal situation. They are born to experience all of life, its successes and its losses, and in this manner sorrow or pain may force the Scorpio to also experience a rebirth or regeneration of the spirit which goes so far as to alter their lifestyle or change their mind set. Their sexuality is all encompassing and remains a central focus in their lives. A Scorpio is capable of using sex, in fact, to gain control or power. Their intensity brings with it a jealous and possessive nature which they must learn to deal with in personal relationships. They must also come to terms with a vindictive nature. A sign of endurance, perseverance, and patience, Scorpios can wait for the opportune moment to seek revenge on an enemy.

However, they are also highly protective of their loved ones, generous to friends and family, self-confident and capable, and willing to endure the worst of times as well as the best of times.

These characteristics of the Scorpio Sun sign can be made stronger by the Moon sign, Ascendant, and the placement of the Planets, or they can be made more subdued by specific influences. It is by ascertaining these various influences that one can more fully understand the Scorpio individual being studied, or, more importantly, one can more fully understand one's self.

The Zodiac sign of Scorpio occurs during that period of time which precedes winter. During this time of the year, nature sheds her greenery, the leaves turn reddish brown and cover the ground of the forest with a coppery, rustling carpet. Beneath this ground cover, small creatures scurry and forage, hidden from the light while they hide for winter. There is an interlude from the Sun while nature, under the apparition of nonbearing, is completing the transformation of matter. New essence is metamorphosing and transforming under this cloak of decaying matter. Scorpio is one of the most important signs of the Zodiac in that it represents that moment in nature when everything is changing, preparing for a long winter in the bosom of nature from which will crop possibilities for new existence. The people born during this time will lead a life of struggle and continuous transformation in the sphere of existence.

The constellation of Scorpio is one of the vastest because part of it is a neighbor with the plates of Libra while another part is in Sagittarius. The stellar symbol of Scorpio, as compared to the other signs, most clearly represents that for which it was named, the scorpion. This constellation contains some beautiful stars as well as the Corona Boreal.

HOW TO FIND YOUR *SOUL-MATE, STARS,* AND *DESTINY*

In ancient Egypt, Osiris was god of the dead. However, the scorpion was deified in the form of Selket, the scorpion-goddess, who was the protectress of the dead. In astrology, the sign of Scorpio governs the influence of the Eighth House, the House of Death and Regeneration. One of the mystical houses, it is associated with spiritual transformation and rules the life forces surrounding sex, birth, death, and the afterlife. This is also the House of psychic powers and of occult studies and knowledge. The verb characterizing the sign of Scorpio is, "to desire."

The scorpion appears to have attained some respect in ancient times, unlike the descriptions associated with it by modern, city-bound astrologers. This is a small, compact creature whose presence mystifies. Come within sight of this little being, and it immediately magnetizes your complete attention. The scorpion doesn't go out of its way to assertively cause harm, but this is not a creature that you want to step on. It's sting is painful. It is a being which demands attention and respect.

The sign of Scorpio is ruled by Pluto (although at one time Mars was associated with this sign). Pluto rules regenerative forces associated with the beginnings and ends of stages in life. Its keyword is elimination, and it is said to wipe out the old and to begin the new. It influences originality, artistic and business activities. Pluto represents the highest and lowest of which man is capable of attaining.

Scorpio is the fixed Water sign, representing still water that is stationary and motionless. In nature, it is as turbulent as the agent of heat in boiling water. Scorpio, as a fixed sign, will persist without rest until an obstacle is conquered. Scorpios will patiently wait for the most favorable moment of action to pursue their purpose. As a feminine sign, Scorpio is receptive and meditative. The resources of this sign are immense and the ideas are abundant, governed or mastered by an energy kept in reserve to be used at the most opportune moment. The greatest quality attributed to Scorpio people is ingeniousness, and the greatest defect is envy.

Scorpios are energetic, dynamic and always ready to be of help to others. They can be contradictory in nature, holding to their own opinions against all obstacles and willing to oppose others with tenacity. They are known for being somewhat secretive, for hiding their inner tendencies, while they pursue their objectives. Many can be a bit mysterious with a tendency toward jealousy. When offended, the Scorpio will attack and sting like the creature representing this sign. Scorpios can become very good friends who are both sincere and generous. They are hard working and dutiful and being energetic never seem to rest. The native Scorpio is a fighter who struggles for future happiness or prosperity rather than waiting for what the future may bring. And these natives do this with patience while at times life seems to be a merry-go-round, going round and round before arriving at its destination. Scorpio natives can be a better judge for others than for themselves. They will easily forgive weaknesses in other people, but they seldom forget mistakes and prefer that everyone does their best. Anything is possible for the person born to the sign of Scorpio.

Scorpio Personality

Scorpio can be an enigmatic sign to discuss in that it portrays a seemingly natural combination of materialism and spiritualism. It is said that this sign includes the best and worst of humanity, and therein lies the mystery. There appears an incessant search for the meaning of life, for the answer to the puzzle. In everyday life, the Scorpio individual may seek the meaning behind the words and actions of others. On a higher plane, many of these individuals seek the meaning of life itself. And this drive can either become enlightened or can turn to darker more stormy inclinations.

With the natural magnetism of the Scorpio native comes a person who never produces a mild impression on others. Other people will immediately like or dislike this individual. It is often said that the sign of Scorpio never produces a dull or shallow person. A remarkably powerful pride, intensity and determination is present in these individuals. These eighth-sign natives prefer to dominate in their purpose and forcefulness, sometimes to the point of being ruthless in their attempt to obtain their desired results. There is a tendency to be doggedly ambitious with inclinations toward secretiveness, jealousies, and combativeness with a distinct vindictiveness when opposed.

Scorpios appear capable of any achievement they set their minds to, and fortunately these goals are generally constructive. Their will power and resourcefulness can at times produce results which are astounding. Scorpios are self-sufficient individualists who exhibit no fear, hesitations or inhibitions in achieving their goals. They are unhesitatingly assertive. They face life head on, come what may. These individuals are generously well endowed with strong leadership qualities, and they are unafraid to take on leadership roles.

Scorpios are self-discerning in that they adapt to moral codes and to moral responsibilities but within the framework of their own perceptions. These persons reserve for themselves the decision of what are and are not appropriate mores, attitudes, and behaviors. Many socially acceptable behaviors may be viewed by these natives as being arbitrary and even hypocritical. These individuals are perceptive enough to realize that social standards, practices and inhibitions evolve and change with time.

It is generally recognized that there are two distinct types of Scorpio natives. The first type are those individuals who appear to have attained great heights in their development. These people almost appear to be surrounded by the aura of the invisible Sun. This person, like the phoenix or eagle, views life from a loftier plane, and with a sharp eye discerns and investigates, views and judges all that is going on below on the earthly plane. This person has a clear, detached vision of all of life. These individuals are virtuous and just exhibiting a subtle, dignified grace and a clear conscience.

The second type of Scorpio native lives in a more restricted world and can be compared to a creature more closely associated with living close to the earth such as the snake or crocodile. They possess rather mean and low instincts and openly exhibit the envious, jealous nature, listening only to revenge and vindictiveness. These individuals don't hesitate to insult others, but will not suffer any insults themselves. They lack tact in everything they do, and proceed selfishly through life with no regard for others. They are drawn to all that is rotten and morally corrupt in life and become totally objectionable type people. If the natives of this sign are thus afflicted there can be found much malevolence and even viciousness in their nature. Then too, these people are well known for having volcanic tempers, for being domineering, and for ruling through fear and tyranny.

Therein lies the enigma residing in the sign of Scorpio. It goes without saying that with all these traits, a great deal of self-development is required to achieve a well balanced and productive life. The average persons of this sign may find themselves fighting a battle of wills from within their own natures. Choosing to become well-balanced individuals may mean for these people a constant pull or inner struggle to overcome more baser elements inherent in their nature. Of course, these goals can be achieved, and as with all people, it is only after much effort has been expended and devoted to self-improvement. It is this very struggle with one's own nature which may hold the key to Scorpio's more secretive tendencies. How could anyone be expected to explain an ongoing and searching nature bound to inner struggles of envy and vindictiveness? The road to learning forgiveness, to abandoning vengeance, and to mellowing one's own temper can be a long, tedious and up hill climb.

Perhaps it is this ongoing inner struggle that makes Scorpios appear to be striving to achieve self-fulfillment. It is the attainment of just this balance, or inner fulfillment, that allows so many of these natives to acquire phenomenal successes in life. The Scorpio native can live with or without the praise and adulation of others. This sign is self-propagating. This person must feel good and accept himself or herself. What others may think can seem inconsequential and unimportant as compared to what Scorpios think of themselves.

This is the individual who is at home with himself or herself. This person is never particularly lonely. At the same time, they can be as sociable and charming as persons born to any of the other signs. They are totally likable and lovable people who will go to great lengths for friends, family and associates.

Many astrologers recognize those born under the sign of Scorpio as being the most highly sexed of all people. These are highly motivated and sexually oriented people. While not all may indulge in erotic excesses, this remains an important aspect of their lives. It is found that the Scorpio native makes no effort to repress the libido. These are uninhibited individuals who find a care free expression, almost an art form, in their sexuality. In other words, these natives are best known for being relentless in their sexual drives and desires.

Scorpio natives have active minds and keen perceptions. They may possess a dignified and at times silent bearing, but they possess a strong will power which enables them to effectively influence the thinking and the actions of others. They are persuasive, clear and concise in their words and conversations and are impressive speakers capable of inspiring confidence in others. This strong and dignified bearing coupled with an inherent calmness and determination may be the source of the accusation that Scorpio natives can be cold or unfeeling. Actually, as any good counselor would advice, this is a healthy attitude which benefits many professionals. One wouldn't want a nervous, high strung, emotionally distraught person as a surgeon or in any other field requiring skill, precision and sound thought processes. That is to say, that of course Scorpio natives are capable of being and feeling emotions deeply. It is their display of emotions that differs from others. This is the individual who chooses to remain level headed and to keep the ship on course during the storm. In many individuals this self-control is admirable.

The minds of these Scorpio natives are consciously and exceedingly progressive. They are forever contemplating new and more efficient ideas and methods. Found in this type of people are the social engineers who are drawn into everyday conversations if not major think tanks for the betterment of society. Scorpio natives are capable of being critics, political agitators, political consultants, reformers, or social planners. They appear to know what should be done and how to accomplish it.

Scorpios may appear to exist on two planes. One is very sociable, strong and outgoing. The other is personal, private and alone with inner thoughts. These individuals are not easily coerced or frightened by slights, assertiveness, or even natural disasters. Outdoor sports appeal to these energetic people, and many of them excel in any and all sports activities. The ocean and bodies of water has a special attraction to Scorpio natives, and they are entranced with the power and beauty of these natural settings.

For self-improvement, the Scorpio native is advised to guard against self-defeating thinking and actions. Focus your energies and power of observation on your inner weaknesses which you are more than capable of discerning. Your intuitive nature will point out your own faults for you if you allow it to. Listen to this intuition and begin a determined plan to improve your nature. Some natives, for example, will be impulsively selfish, using other people while at the same time being overly critical and harsh toward others. You are strong, magnetic and energetic. You have unlimited abilities and potentials. Discover your inner strengths, your gifts, and your limitless abilities and take control of your life. Teach yourself the strength of controlling all feelings of envy, fault-finding, and vindictiveness. And make every effort to gain power and control over your impulsive temper and that quick, stinging scorpion tail. Not only are there two types of Scorpio's, but there are found individuals of every degree of development which is only natural and to be expected.

Scorpios are also known for being direct and for possessing strong and intense inclinations, desires and ideas. Their feelings are black and white, and these people spend little time vacillating in the gray areas of indecision. These natives know their minds. There exists a compulsive urge to achieve and to fulfill their potentials. This inner drive takes many Scorpio natives far in life.

These natives possess a strong inclination for vigorous activity, an enterprising will, determination and practical ability. They are firm and self-confident with an innate drive to succeed in any and all pursuits. While they can be impulsive and abrupt, they have a tendency to take care of and to protect their own. The sign of Scorpio endows its natives with a fondness for pleasure, comforts and a satisfying life. These people are energetic and forceful while being independent and masterful. They can be courageous and positive while at the same time being aggressive. Sometimes quick tempered, this individual does not tolerate imposition or inconveniences and does not appreciate any obstacles. They will also exhibit an ability to make sacrifices, and they possess an appreciation for all acts of kindness.

Scorpio Character

The Scorpio native is the personification of the Water and Fixed characteristics. This person writes his or her own destiny, or prefers to, right down to the smallest detail of everyday life. They are the most self-intent of the twelve types. Scorpio individuals possess idealistic and a seemingly unlimited supply of motivation and judgment. Less introspective people can appear superficial and inadequate to them. They are generous and cooperative when other people work as hard and energetically as they are prone to do. Scorpios are also obstinately determined in their course of action even to the point of being cruel when forced to change their plans or methods. They strictly deal fairly with others, but it is by their own standards.

The Scorpio has a sense of inner completeness, and at times doesn't recognize that other people are less independent or less psychologically secure. This person will seize the moment, holding to his or her opinion without enmity, and expect others to be understanding and unquestioning. In other words, this person expects others to be as equally strong and capable of understanding the purpose at hand.

The sign of Scorpio usually influences its natives to possess strong and powerful characteristics. They possess a keen judgment and are shrewdly critical and skeptical as well as tenacious with an enterprising and energetic nature. The natives are not easily fooled or offended, but are found to be self-confident, brave and most of all, daring and fearless. The sign of Scorpio grants its natives a strength of mind and a strong will. These natives exhibit a great determination and persistence coupled with a strong power of concentration and an indomitable spirit that cannot be broken by resistance, obstacles, or difficulties. These individuals can be both bold and stubborn, at times acutely sharp spoken and blunt, but then again at other times reserved and exhibiting great restraint. There is a secretiveness while at the same time an aggressive, forceful and even rebellious and tyrannical nature. They are frequently at odds with other people, authority figures, or with common and accepted opinions.

The lives of the Scorpio natives are quite often divided between contradictory aspirations. On one hand, these individuals are spiritually and religiously inclined, but, conversely, many of the natives are drawn to the earthly desires for ambition, sexuality, financial successes, a determination to dominate, and to power and authority. The individual's nature is influenced by both of these determinations, but if there is a strong enough character, a balance will be discovered at some time during the person's life. If, however, there is a weak character, this individual will face a life of being a slave to his or her feelings and desires and may even choose a life of crime to obtain their personal wants. Others will become melancholic or pessimistic. Whether well-balanced or not, these natives possess a mystical nature that at times appears mysterious and secretive. It is, for example, as if the native is controlled by a subliminal or stronger, guiding force. If there is an artistic talent present, the native appears exceptionally gifted. At any rate, the native does not appear to trust others well enough to let anyone else in on their more private, inner thoughts, drives and nature.

How to Find Your Soul-Mate, Stars, and Destiny

A Scorpio native is most generally found to be an idealistic person whose actions cannot be persuaded or stopped against his or her wishes. They place their objectives above everything and are willing to expel a great deal of energy to obtain or to complete them. They defend not only their actions but their work against any and all oppositions choosing to face aggressiveness head on and to conquer it. This person is protective of friends and family. And this is not the person to attempt to cheat. These natives attack without mercy even becoming brutal in certain situations.

There is found an intuitive nature as well. Scorpio individuals appear to be able to perceive other people's weaknesses and defenses. And these natives are not timid about using that information to their own advantage. With this intuition comes the power of observation, and these natives will study and observe others in a situation before deciding upon a course of action. There is a need to determine the point of view of other people, of where that person stands in regard to the situation or to the native. Scorpio wants to know the other person's perspective and what that person really wants or what the person is after. This may simply be an effort to discern the nature of the other person in order for Scorpio to be able to out maneuver or out talk the other person in any subsequent discussions. Scorpios like to win, and they don't waste much time on the opinions of others in important matters. In other words, these individuals are not known for being diplomatic in their affairs. Scorpio natives have been called the born dictator.

Scorpios can possess an excellent character and will face anything to defend, help, or protect a friend or to shelter the weak. They are also noted for being generous in times of need. At the same time, these natives are pragmatic to the point of appearing cold and unfeeling. These are individuals who have never been referred to as „faint of heart'. The very strength of their nature forbids any unrational sensitivities to interfere with their lives. There is found an innate ability to disassociate with the more emotional, traumatic feelings and occurrences which might distract others from the task at hand. In many fields of endeavor, this is an admirable trait leaving the individual with the ability to persevere and to continue in the face of adversity.

Among Scorpios are found those who are capable of exhibiting the attributes of a violent, authoritarian, revengeful and ambitious nature. This person, while not being sensitive, is easily offended. These individuals never forget and will patiently wait years for the opportunity to seek revenge. It is perhaps these individuals more than any other who have underlined and brought to notice the stinging nature of the sign of Scorpio. And even the most well developed Scorpio native will be forced to deal with this tendency and to attempt to control it as well as themselves.

Scorpios regard opportunity in relation to their own more personal needs. They are most generally successful due to the fact that there isn't found a conflict between their inner nature and what society perceives as important. These natives forever strive to eliminate all that would produce unhappiness or inharmonious situations and adhere instinctively to that which is satisfying and rewarding.

This is apparently a good sign for being successful in life. This may be because these individuals seem to be able to produce a magical effect on others and will appear to be the right person for the job. You then attack the job at hand with all your energy exhibiting a large degree of efficiency in your work methods. When you are in a position you like, you work effortlessly and with authority, gaining the respect of others. Opportunity appears to flow to you, and you appear to possess an inherent ability to select the right position. You are more than capable of being successful in whatever endeavor you decide upon.

Scorpios possess a powerful magnetism. In its most advantageous forms, it produces a deep personal security and the vital forces serve well, drawing and holding the attention of others, while producing the ability to obtain great benefits from the world both materially and spiritually. If not well developed, this same magnetism and energy when turned inward, produces in some natives a profound fear that their hopes and desires will not be realized. This native may seek avenues of escape from these persistent fears, becoming reticent, procrastinating, quarrelsome, self-indulgent and exhibiting other weaknesses of character. These feelings of insecurity can of course produce feelings of jealousy, possessiveness and suspicion.

Scorpio possesses a quick, alert mind and communicates well. He can build up others or just as effectively tear them to shreds with just a few, well-chosen and effective words. His instincts are so powerful, that his very gestures, actions and the tone of his voice is as effective and powerful as his words. In fact, he can almost be as powerful in silence as he is with words.

The sign of Scorpio grants its natives a powerful will, an indomitable strength, an energetic disposition, and an ambitious enthusiasm for life. These natives are self-confident, resolute, and analytical. He is subtle but proud, lofty and aggressive. His nature is both fruitful and productive, and he can be most generous. His emotions are deep, passionate, and tightly held and your ardor for life is unsuppressed and at times unrestrained. He pursues love and good fortune with the same profound degree of endurance, strength, and persevering effort. Little can or does stand in the way of the Scorpio once he sets his mind to a goal or plan. A Scorpio is as adept as Aries at making plans and as talented as Virgo in outlining the details necessary for carrying through these plans.

Action may best describe the mode of operandi of these natives. Little is left to the imagination when Scorpio decides upon his plan of actions. Fortunately, Scorpios are, for the most part, well meaning and possess the best of intentions in their dealings with others. This is not a person to take for granted or to misuse in any manner. The Scorpio memory is formidable, and while they may choose to wait patiently for life to take its course, they will push in one direction or the other to achieve their desires.

How to Find Your Soul-Mate, Stars, and Destiny

Scorpio Destiny

Scorpios with their great magnetism and power are generally courteous and affable while at the same time exhibiting an intense determination. These are exceptionally efficient people with a clearly defined course of action in their minds. Once they take on a pursuit or an endeavor, they become tenacious and persistent. Scorpio natives may most often be predisposed to experience many achievements and reversals in life. They may endure many hardships and have to overcome numerous obstacles on their road to success and accomplishment. A rather stern sense of justice prevails in these natives allowing them to develop an interest in the concerns of the oppressed, of the afflicted, and of others who are less well off. There is a spirit of generosity for deserving persons.

The destiny of these individuals is as diverse as the natives themselves. There is seen for some an association with governmental officials or some connection with the government. There is found camaraderie among powerful associates or with influential people in society. There is a hint of professional secrets or intrigue and the gaining of information which effects the lives of others. Many of these natives are drawn to friendships of a questionable nature or to those with peculiar or mysterious interests and personalities. There is some indication for intrigues with employers or with superiors. Unusual adventures and strange experiences through travel or journeys are noted, especially associated with water and voyages. Many of these natives may experience sorrow through love affairs, secret alliances, romantic encounters, and other intrigues or through domestic difficulties. There is seen friendship with people with artistic inclinations and with others involved in occult practices.

If well aspected, there is seen profitable gain through the careers of these natives perhaps in the areas of litigation, arbitration, inheritance, legacy and public investments. If afflicted, there may well be seen difficulties and strange occurrences involving jealousies and powerful enemies, and loss through questionable or unsound investments and speculations. There is also seen misfortune or death through water and voyages and danger through social or political connections. Also for the afflicted, there are seen difficulties with quarrels and litigation with those involved in law, science, religion or medicine.

The location of this sign has some significance for attachments or attractions in which difficulties arise with the opposite sex. Some natives will experience problems and an inharmonious situation in their marriage. There are secrets in the lives of the Scorpio natives and many of these involve love affairs. A love affair may well advance or reverse the position of the native. There is a strong indication that the natives will marry more than once. The location of Venus adds to the passions and intensity of emotions and provides the Scorpio natives with a love and a desire for sensation and pleasure. These individuals are ardent in love, many times unable to control their compulsive passions. Attractions to the opposite sex may develop into compromising situations, disappointments, or delays in marriage.

For many of these natives the second half of life is prosperous and there is indication for financial success related to business in foreign lands. Generally, there are two distinct sources of income for these natives. There is strong indication that the sign of Scorpio produces eventual wealth and prosperity for its natives. A series of difficulties and obstacles in early life will eventually lead to a good position and success. The family and relatives of the native are positive and supportive. If enemies are found, they are among close associates or lovers. The native will be protected by providence from danger of covert violence in foreign lands.

    The natives of Scorpio are known for being generous and even lavish in expenditures. It is often found that financial success can be realized in some association regarding water or career pursuits related to water. If other influences are positive, there will be gains through gifts, partnership or marriage, but obstacles in connection with these may make them less attractive. Overall, this is a sign for successful completion of pursuits, for pleasure, and for financial success. And it is no doubt the careful planning of the Scorpio native combined with their tenacity, passionate desires, and strong drives which propel them forward in the world and up the ladder of success. That so many Scorpio natives endure so much and struggle so diligently against any and all odds adds to their eventual positive outcome. These are individuals who face adversity bravely and who learn from any and all experiences, whether positive or negative. Then they skillfully apply this knowledge to their future endeavors, gaining that which they most desire.

Scorpio Occupation

The resources of the natives of Scorpio are immense. They have abundant ideas and a reserve of natural energy to carry them through all endeavors. With their strong magnetic personalities, these individuals are enthusiastic and persuasive speakers. They possess many talents but their discerning natures and their power of keen observation, skill and calmness predestine them to successful careers in numerous fields.

Scorpios do well in business enterprises and in leadership positions as they adapt to long term plans knowing instinctively how to program their goals. Many of these individuals will assume leading positions in their professions, and they organize the necessary tasks to be accomplished according to their plans and principles. They expect their associates to be serious and productive workers also as the Scorpio natives strive for few mistakes and better, more productive results.

Many of these natives are especially well endowed to fulfill government or military positions and supervisory positions. These individuals are talented managers and leaders and do well in any decision making position and in positions requiring leadership abilities. They are especially gifted in getting the job done and in getting the best and most work out of others. Many excel in any and all positions related to the political or social forum. Other natives do well in all branches of trade and enterprises requiring an acute business mind. Merchandising appears to be a natural field as these natives are extremely shrewd and perceptive in this area. Also, many do well in all areas of sales in that they are energetic, persistent and they speak effectively. There is a strong inclination for success in the fields of insurance or securities. Others do well in the field of advertising or in consulting work. Many make fine attorneys and judges and others enter that area of the legal field which deals with wills, estates and business or corporate law.

Persons born under the influence of this sign are known to have strong powers of concentration and this combined with their forceful personality allows them to become excellent writers or to excel in careers requiring new and resourceful ideas such as directors, producers or performers. This excellent creative ability combined with an intensely dramatic flair and descriptive abilities allows many to find expression in music or art or in the fields of decorating and design.

There is a strong indication for success for Scorpio natives in fields requiring patience, perseverance and strong powers of concentration. The ability to be emotionally in control of the situation and to make decisions in a calm manner leads many to become successful surgeons or to achieve in other areas in the fields of medicine and science.

Keen observational abilities and a drive to uncover the truth in matters may lead the Scorpio native to positions such as researcher, philosopher, detective, or secret service operative. And to others, the area of occult investigations is appealing. Then too success may well be found in areas associated with water or with tools. The fields of engineering, mechanics, transportation and manufacturing favors many of these individuals, and others seek positions in banking or finance. Other natives are drawn to aviation or occupations requiring some risk such as sports car racing or other sports.

Scorpios are well endowed to become great humanitarians or social scientists with the desire to help society. Many gain a reputation as peace makers and go to great lengths to settle the problems of others. As social reformers and political advisers, they become compelled to seek the truth and to find avenues of dealing with the many problems of society and the world at large.

The sign of Scorpio endows its natives to success in any number of occupations. In fact, there are very few fields in which the Scorpio native would not be able to excel as long as the position allows for the expression of these many positive traits. Scorpio endows its natives with strong characteristics and perceptive judgment. These individuals are shrewd and critical decision makers. They are skeptical and keen observers while being tenacious, enterprising and energetic. Generally, they are not easily fooled, but remain positive, self-confident and determined while at the same time being brave and daring. This is the person to depend on in times of crisis when calm decisions and directions are needed.

Confident in your abilities, once you decide your direction in life, you will no doubt harness all your energies and pursue your goals creatively and productively. The sign of Scorpio endows you with all the gifts necessary for success regardless of the effort required.

Scorpio Marriage

It is most probably the immense resources of energy, determination and intensity that allow Scorpio natives to develop strong marital and family ties while at the same time continuing to balance a very busy professional life. You of this sign have strong passions and desires and when you find that special someone, you devote your energies and drives into creating a lasting relationship. You are capable of loving deeply and loyally, and you exhibit the same intensity in your love life that you do in the other areas of your life. This same intensity may at times lead to frustration and anger, and your marital partner is best someone who understands your nature. You are not the best person to live with a combative or insecure person. You crave and desire another person who exhibits strength of character and fortitude, and who has the ability to be independent, but who at the same time can love passionately and deeply.

A harmonious relationship may be found with the Pisces (February 19-March 20) native who is capable of devotion and is also passionate and imaginative which sparks your creative nature. You will appreciate the mind and personality of the Virgo (August 23-September 22) native who is also loyal. You will find a Cancer (June 22-July 22) native accepting of your leadership, strength and protectiveness but guard against this person becoming too dependent on your strengths. You may find that with Taurus (April 21-May 20) you share an earthy and uninhibited ability to express yourself. Scorpio and Capricorn (December 21-January 19) may discover mutual interests as they are both ambitious, determined, serious and responsible. A relationship between a Scorpio and Scorpio depends entirely upon the two individuals involved.

It would be an uncommon occurrence to find a Scorpio man or woman who is dominated by the marriage partner. These are strongly independent people who flourish when allowed to follow their own natural inclinations. A person who is seeking a mate to change or to mold into their personal picture of perfection should pass on by the Scorpio native. You, Scorpio, possess no desire to be changed or to alter your personal patterns for the whims of another. You accept yourself, and you expect your spouse to do the same. When dealing with either the male or female Scorpio, do not expect negligence or infidelity to be taken lightly. Scorpio is fiercely possessive and jealous when in love. This is not the person to taunt with flighty flirtations in order to gain attention.

Scorpios handle marriage with as much devotion and diligence as the other areas of their lives. This person is a natural manager and doer and expects the other person in his or her life to be just as intense. Persons born to this sign are good providers for their families. They are for the most part faithful, devoted, and practical. These individuals require a mate who shares their uninhibited sexual drive and need for excitement in this area of life. Scorpio may well experience two marriages. These individuals are well experienced in affairs of the heart, and if the first marriage fails, undoubtedly another will follow.

The Scorpio Man

The Scorpio man is passionately intense about all areas of his life, and there is no getting around the strength and power of his personality. At the same time, he may appear calm and in total control. This exterior of calmness only underlies his magnetic presence. The sign of Scorpio is the sign of extremes in nature. And this man may be either the best or worst of human beings. While he at times may appear impassive and unapproachable, he is the embodiment of ardent emotions. Many of these men are daring risk takers. There are some with a pronounced mocking nature that offends the overly sensitive or insecure.

You are charming and witty with friends and associates, and you find that you are either well liked or strongly disliked by others. You are robust and possess nerves of steel, and you like to be in control of whatever situation you find yourself dealing with. You may not want to dominate, per se, but you do want to know that everything is running smoothly according to your perceptions and preferences. You have little patience with the mistakes or incompetence of others. At the same time, you can be dogmatic, controlling, and demanding in relationships expecting your desires to be met.

You appear to possess a magnetic influence over members of the opposite sex who go to great lengths to win your heart. You can be both passionate and sentimental and with women you are convincing and sincere. You strive to be the absolute man, the embodiment of strength and power. You are also adaptable to new and even more challenging situations, always feeling that you can handle whatever may come.

The woman in your life should both admire and respect you. And she should know how to encourage you to take the lead, allowing you to think that everything is your idea. Because with your own ideas at the forefront of your thoughts, you excel, pursuing all that is imaginable. An admiring and understanding female who shares your imaginative and passionate cares will best suit your inner nature.

You are sensual in nature and enjoy the finer things in life finding pleasure in a comfortable, well planned surrounding and home. Everything must fit together well in your life for you to find contentment. You are big on organization and of taking care of the details in life so that the bigger picture becomes more evident and easier to strive towards.

You are already aware of your possessive and jealous nature, but the chances are that this self-awareness leads you to attempt to control these traits. Then too, when confronted or offended there is that irascible Scorpio temper to deal with. Many Scorpio men will discover that one method to overcome this impulsive temper is to exert a control over who enters their life. You know there are certain people and certain personality types you need to steer clear of. This stinging temperament may mellow with age, and you will either miss the energy of it or be greatly relieved to find that you can finally relax. Developing the right friendships and associates augments this. Also, learning to brush off the offenses of manipulative people rather than taking their slights and insinuations seriously will help. Yes, there are any number of people who will purposely needle you just to see the resultant fireworks.

Your relationships may often appear to be complicated and entangled as if nothing is ever going to come easily for you. Considering that an understanding of moderation may not come easily to you may explain these predicaments. Then too, it could just be your destiny to feel like you are forever going up against insurmountable difficulties. And it isn't in your nature to quit. Your life will be filled with innumerable experiences and adventures just as your love life will be varied and filled with captivating and interesting encounters. You demand a lot from life and life pays you back in full measure, exacting from you all that you have to give.

You are known for being both kind and generous with all who know you. And you develop many long and lasting friendships that see you through life and through all of your endeavors in life. At the same time, you appear to be a law onto yourself, and you don't go out of your way to impress others with anything but your natural and enduring personality. You are the real thing, and everyone who meets you will instantly recognize that. Either people will accept you or they won't. You express yourself through your thoughts and actions, and at times your forceful nature puts others off. You can be outspoken and to the point, not always taking into consideration the feelings of others as you assume others are as capable as you of dealing pragmatically with words and facts.

You will find that when you learn to focus your energies and your drives on the pursuit of success and happiness, you will eventually realize your goals. Yes, life is a struggle, but you have the ability to make that struggle worthwhile. Scorpio, it has been stated, is the sign of success.

How to Find Your Soul-Mate, Stars, and Destiny

The Scorpio Woman

However quiet and demure this lady may appear, this is no shrinking violet. This is an insightful and intuitive woman who reads the nature and perceives the inclinations of others. Your main strength is your loyalty in all matters. You are a highly magnetic person who possesses an inner force which appears to draw other people to you. In you, other people find a person who is direct, well meaning, and sincere. You can size up a situation or a person with a few well-chosen words, and while others admire you for this remarkable ability, there will be some who feel daunted by your presence.

You are often considered efficient, well organized and particularly capable of handling large or small affairs with ease. In this, people draw you out to be in charge or to handle tasks by taking on the direction or the planning aspect of the endeavor at hand. You can also be demanding in your attempt to extract the most and the best from other individuals who are more hesitant to act.

You are an innately intense person, at times driven to accomplish your goals or to possess that which you most desire. Your thoughts can compel you to actions, but your mind is also busily planning the next step to your accomplishments. You at times exhibit a well controlled, determined and tenacious exterior, and you wish that other more flighty people could learn to do the same.

You may be the person who is working on plan one while your mind is engaged in outlining plan two. And you are creatively original in your plans. You aren't one to follow or to copy the plans of others or even to follow in the path of others. You want to make it on the strength of your own desires, plans and endeavors. Marrying for gain appears to you to be the easy way out, and you have seldom in your life taken the easy road. You are more likely the woman who meets up with other adventurers and sets out to find that lost gold mine in the desert or the sunken treasure in the ocean. If it suggests adventure, you are tempted. If you fail, you see the experience as a lesson in life, but you are well experienced in successes also.

It is not that you cannot be dominated, it is simply that there is no reason for you to be dominated. You are a strong, independent woman with imagination and ideas of your own. You are not one of the less secure women who needs a man to protect and lead her. And if that is what a man is looking for, he may as well keep on looking. You are the embodiment of strength, the woman best suited for wanting and accomplishing it all. For a man to meet your needs, he too must be independent enough not to need subordinates to prop him up. And the man in your life must share your passions. You recognize and acknowledge that you are a sexual being and in this area you most desire to be satisfied, physically and emotionally. You no doubt will have many admirers in your life who are drawn to your energy and your enigmatic nature.

In marriage, you make a good partner and a competent parent. You are devoted and loyal. And you devote all your skills in making your home life successful. You are loving and kind to your children, and you enjoy the time you spend with them. You enjoy sharing and making a home that reflects your good tastes but one which is comfortable and relaxing. You are known for your sacrifices and for the time you devote to your family. Yes, you can be possessive and jealous, and you recognize that as well. The well-developed Scorpio female makes every attempt to control these traits, but even if they lie dormant for awhile, the feelings remain. This requires a lot of work on your part to increase the harmony in your life.

Your friends and business associates consider you reliable and hard working. You apply yourself to all endeavors wanting most to realize the successful accomplishments of the goals at hand. Your friends find you a good listener, kind and generous in your affections. You are known for being a good friend who makes a sincere effort to be there for others.

You are a constructive person with purpose of mind. When you decide to apply yourself and your skills to an endeavor, you will no doubt realize success and fulfillment. Others respect and admire you with good reason.

Scorpio Love Life

Less energetic people probably should forego love affairs with Scorpio natives. These individuals have reached mythical proportion in what the world reports about their love lives. Sex and love, for all apparent appearances, are important to the lives of Scorpio individuals in that it seems to enhance and to fortify their energy resources. Rather than exhausting their energy, time spent with a lover seems to intensify their mental and physical inspiration and drive in other areas of their lives.

You desire to be close to another person and to share your love and affection freely, and your passionate sensuality appeals to others. So it is that you seem to have many offers from the opposite sex all of whom want to win your heart. And to put it bluntly, you are said to be the most highly sexed of all the signs. Some form of individuality must enter in here, and certainly no statistics are available to support this supposition. But that is the report of the word-of-mouth calculations of people who take note of such things.

Perhaps this is best understood by remembering that Scorpio natives are seldom repressed or suppressed. They are uninhibited and know their minds. They know what they want, and what they like, and they aren't timid about pursuing it.

There is some suggestion that other Water signs might be fortuitous for the Scorpio natives. Those would be Cancer, Pisces and other Scorpio individuals. Pisces no doubt would stimulate your romantic nature. And another Scorpio may well be able to match your physical stamina, but for you mutual well being, don't get into any arguments. And remember that Cancer doesn't appreciate criticism in any form. Aries will catch and hold your attention with their amorous natures right up until your first serious discussion. Taurus natives share your love for pleasures and sensual desires. But while Gemini is electrically stimulating, witty and entertaining, you will never feel in control with these natives. Leo also shares your passions but the dominating nature can wear thin eventually. Virgo is neither flighty or superficial, and Libra is tolerant of your strong nature. Sagittarius and Aquarius may be attractive but too determined in their own pursuits. You may discover that Capricorn may be the best choice of all for compatibility.

To your benefit, it is noted that many Scorpio natives prefer to develop a lasting and strong relationship rather than to play the field indefinitely. Needless to say, your partner must fill your needs, attract your attention, support you in all your endeavors, and be there when you come home. And no doubt, you don't feel that's too much to expect. You, Scorpio, are the delight of many, and even with your jealous temper, you are truly be a remarkable person to know and love.

Scorpio Children

The children born to the sign of Scorpio are precocious and lovable. That is if they ever slow down long enough to be loved. They are the embodiment of free flowing energy. These children possess a love for adventure and nothing appears to be too risky for them to attempt at least once. They seem to know no fears, or at any rate aren't as fearful as other children.

They also possess a love for the mysterious, and will pursue with intent little investigations into the nature of their surroundings. The Scorpio child seems to possess a love for intrigue, and will arrange secret excursions to forbidden places. Their hearts race at the thought of a new adventure or experience which they pursue with all their energy. They require lots of open spaces and the freedom to explore their environments. Their favorite movies and books will be about adventure and far away places. This is the child who excels at sports and physical activities.

This child can be demanding and exacting. He or she will ask endless questions regarding how, why, when or where, for the natural curiosity is highly developed. Focusing this curiosity and abundant energy, both mental and physical, can require a lot of imagination on the part of parents and educators. This child does not seek immediate and easy answers. They want to know precisely and exactly the answers to their questions. And there may be found a tendency not to listen to the guidance and advice of adults for these children may possess a strong inclination to learn about life the hard way, that is, by direct experience.

These busy minds and inexhaustible bodies require an abundance of activities and past times. Don't leave this child with nothing to occupy his or her mind. This is the child who will dream up some little escapade of his own design.

A well established routine and well established expectations of behavior are necessary. But these must allow for the energetic nature of these children. Plan excursions that are exciting and educational and that fill their minds with wonder. Surround this child with educational materials that enhance his or her curiosity. And build into the daily routine just enough structure to limit the wandering spirit.

These children require acceptance from the adults in their lives. They can at times easily be a bit dominating or controlling. They can come out with little remarks that offend. The adult dealing with this child needs to recognize this and to work with the child and not against the child. This inherent nature cannot be changed, but it can be molded into socially acceptable patterns of behavior. Praise the good, and to a point ignore the negative. Whatever you do, don't dwell on the negative with these children. Offer them abundant and plentiful outlets for creative expression and positive outlets for their ability to scrutinize their environments.

These are after all remarkable and gifted little individuals who need your love and support. There will never be a dull moment with a Scorpio child in your life. Pay close attention to the needs and development of this child, and strive to provide a healthy, nurturing and secure environment where his or her spirit can develop to its fullest potential. This is a child who you may need to work with through their strengths rather than weaknesses. Encourage all of their endeavors while realizing that their intensity is natural and not something that can be controlled. This intensity can be, however, channeled into positive, creative, and productive past times. Learn to enjoy the active mind of this child, and to find delight in their antics and quick wit. The precocious child is often the most entertaining to be around, but as the adult in this child's life, it is up to you to provide the necessary guidance and support for positive interactions. This will require time and devotion on your part, but you will find this time well spent and rewarding.

Relationships with Other Signs

If you are lucky enough to have a friend who is a Scorpio native, you may feel secure in asking this person to solve the most difficult and impossible problems because he or she will do just that. One of the major characteristics of Scorpio born natives is patience. These are personable people who love and respect their friends, family and associates. Most noted are their kind qualities of caring and generosity.

Native Scorpio's will find their most lasting friendships and unions with people born to the signs of Capricorn, Virgo, Pisces and Cancer. While you may respect the ideas and find Aries interesting, you may also notice an inclination to stay on bad terms with them. Friendships with Taurus natives may be either good or bad, depending on the person. You may find Geminis inspiring, but there is in their nature the inclination toward duplicity which you have problems dealing with. Leo, on the other hand, can be blunt and straight-forward, and you will tire of their need to dominate.

Professionally, you will find successful relationships with Libra natives who seem to enjoy the strength of your nature. Aquarius requires some understanding on your part. You may find that you enjoy friendships with other Scorpio natives, but both of you must keep your possessive, jealous natures and your tempers under control. Capricorn natives are calm and loyal while Pisces and Scorpio often discover an affinity and deep regard for each other. Look for friendships and affiliations with persons born under the sign of Scorpio as well as with those born between June 18-22 and July 16-24. Other indications are for relationships with those born from February 10 to March 15. There is some indication that your closest friends may be members of the opposite sex.

Many eighth-sign natives are extremely selective in making friends. But at the same time, you don't restrict your friendships to any particular group of people. You enjoy meeting and getting to know all kinds of people who are involved with differing interests and pursuits. The greater the variety of people you meet, the more personal energy you feel, as meeting others inspires your thoughts and your creativity and somewhat satisfies your curiosity. That is not to say that you trust anyone and everyone, though. You can be suspicious and doubting of other people's motives and desires. This is a self-defense mechanism that might serve you as well as the sting serves the scorpion. Just remember that once you get to know others well, you can relax and enjoy their companionship without constantly being on your guard.

Your friendships and associations provide for you not only the companionship you desire, but an outlet for your need to help others. This is a strong inner drive, and one that is self-rewarding. It makes you feel good about yourself, and really there is nothing wrong with that. You are a good and deserving friend who is forever loyal and devoted. You make many strong and lasting friendships. As like anybody else, you have strengths and weaknesses, good points and otherwise, which you must continue to work on in order to become an even better and more positive person. You will find that your close friendships will augment these desires and drives. Your inner sense of fulfillment is found through your associations with others.

Scorpio Sexuality

That subject which interests us all: our own personal sexuality. Why does a person feel the way they do? Why does he or she like a certain person and not another? What arouses a person and why? On some level, these questions influences one and all. Like all aspects of our lives and lifestyles, the public attitude toward sex is ever changing and evolving. From the restrictive taboos of the Victorian Age, through the revitalization of the Industrial Age, to the make love not war of the 1960s to the commercialism of the 1980s and the 1990s, sex is always on our minds. Will the Age of Information or the Age of Aquarius bring new insights?

The American culture is not only influenced by popular trends and thought but by its unique cultural diversity as well. To the newcomer or newly arrived, American society can appear perplexing. What is difficult to understand is that in this freedom-based culture, the individual is literally free to be whoever he or she decides. And the gamut runs from the most traditional, reserved, cautious, and sexually repressed individuals to others who flaunt their sexuality, centering their lives around their sexual habits. Perhaps it is because of this very diversity that our culture makes some attempt not to be overly offensive to the sensitivities of some while giving a tolerant nod to the liberties of others. We are totally free, within the guidelines of laws, to seek divine enlightenment or to destroy ourselves with pleasures. Americans have the freedom to choose, individually, what importance their sexual behavior will play in their lives.

That being the case, sex is recognized by every serious discipline--from psychologists to scientists to astrologers--as being a central focus on individual lives. Freud saw sex as an influence on every aspect of the individual life. And from the sexist boys in the locker room to the most enlightened of intellectuals, sex remains a fundamental part of life that cannot be ignored. Get two friends together and the subject eventually turns to sex, romance, or marriage. One can blame it on the media, but sooner or later discussing the stock market gets boring, but sex never does.

There are those who hold to the theory that the primary function of sex is to have children and any other consideration is secondary. There are others for whom sex is an integral part of life, providing one of the greatest stress relievers ever invented. That all other living species procreate seasonally points to the reasoning of the second theory. But all pleasures (or temptations) in life also promote the possibilities of problems and health concerns unless a little logic is also applied.

Astrologically, the sexual nature has been examined from the Garden of Eden to the lives of contemporary celebrities. And what every serious astrologer will say is that how the individual relates to sexuality is not based on the Sun sign alone. The entire chart must be examined because each person is a unique combination of Sun, Moon, Ascendant, planets, Houses and aspects. A comparison of two charts often sheds light on compatibility. Compatibility between two people is often found when the Sun sign is in the same sign as their lover's Ascendant, or vice versa. Opposite Sun signs or an opposite Sun sign and Ascendant may also blend well together.

In a woman's chart, the placement of Venus is indicative of her sexuality while the position of Mars and the Sun indicates what kind of man she is attracted to. In a man's chart, the position of Mars tells how he relates to women, and the position of Venus and the Moon indicates what type of woman arouses him. In comparing two charts, look for the aspects of conjunction, sextile, square, trine, and oppositions. Remember that oppositions can blend. The square brings differences but much energy while conjunctions can be beneficial. The sextile and trine bring harmony. When a person's Venus and their lover's Mars are in the same sign, there is a strong attraction even if differences of opinions occur. When Venus and the other person's Ascendant are in the same sign, it adds to the sexual compatibility. Venus in the lover's sun sign brings a mutual interest while Mars in the lover's Moon sign is emotionally intense.

There is a vast variety of people found within each Sun sign, but basic characteristics and traits do exist. However, generalizations are just that and a fuller picture of the individual is reflected by the complete chart. The following section deals with Sun sign sexuality in a general manner. While the importance of sex remains the same in each Sun sign, the focus and attitudes vary.

Scorpio Sexuality - Man

The sign of Scorpio rules sex, and the Scorpio man is not about to fail to live up to that responsibility or the reputation of this sign. He may begin his sexual experimentation early in life, even before puberty in some cases, and doesn't spend a lot of time considering what is wrong and what is right. Sex is accepted as an important part of life to this man, and he is drawn to acquiring as many experiences as possible. In fact, he may take it as his duty to act out the conclusions arrived at by Virgo and Libra. While Aries is compiling his list of lovelies and jumping from one to another in fifteen second spurts, Scorpio is the three-hour man and however many women he has on the string, he prefers exclusive rights with at least one of them. He is an emotionally passionate man who is always interested in the delights of sex and is more often than not successful in getting what he wants. Quite often, it isn't necessary for him to go on the prowl because women come to him, and he finds something to love in each woman. He is a determined man--determined to make all women happy. This is a man who wants to teach a woman to abandon her inhibitions and allow herself to fully enjoy the sexual act and the sexual release of climaxing. And once her inhibitions are forgotten, he will patiently train her how to satisfy him, again, and again, and again. The Scorpio man may play around with sex toys just for the fun of it and the experience, but he really doesn't need any extra help. This man is a sexual instrument himself, varying his technique, maneuvers, skill and rhythm to incite his partner to the purest heights of ecstasy. He is in love with the human body. He instinctively knows where all the erogenous zones are located, and he explores and tantalizes each and every one with devoted attention. But it is his intense staying power and endurance that attracts women of all ages, and he is never satisfied with just one orgasm for himself or his partner. He takes it as his responsibility to entice, excite and to fully satisfy the other person.

Does that mean he's still there in the morning? That depends upon the individual situation and the relationship. While he is intensely emotional, Scorpio doesn't confuse sex with the other areas of his life. He exhibits a great deal of self-control in this department and doesn't necessarily allow sentiment or romantic overtones to confuse his purposes. The most important thing for the Scorpio man to guard against is overindulgence. Although, he appears to revitalize his energy level with sex. While sex drains some people leaving them ready for sleep and recuperation, sex in itself may regenerate the Scorpio reserve of energy. It also drains him of any excess nervous energy, relieving his stress level, and making him even more confident and self-assured and ready to face the world. In other words, sex makes him feel good about himself perhaps because he is so good at it.

He seems to possess some unconscious natural force that makes an unforgettable impression on the women in his life. Having experienced a relationship with a Scorpio man, a woman may forever use that experience as a basis for comparison with other men. And two Scorpios together have a relationship that each recognizes is a once in a lifetime experience. Whatever is good or bad in his relationships, the sex will always be good.

It would almost be a shame to ask such a man to be faithful. His gifts should be shared with as many people as possible. Everyone needs unforgettable experiences to help them get through the routine of everyday life, and Scorpio takes it upon himself to fulfill that purpose. But can he be faithful? This is a generalization and not applicable to each and every individual, meaning no doubt there is that Scorpio man who may choose to be faithful to one person throughout life. But such a person may be more the exception than the rule. A good percentage of the women calling psychics for love advice are asking about a Scorpio man. If a woman is in love with a Scorpio man perhaps the best advice is to let him go about his business and trust that he will return. When in love, this man is intensely possessive and not a man to give up his true love for a passing fancy. Nor is he a man who easily turns loose of his true love. And there is little use in attempting to use guilt, shame or arguments to control his actions. This man has no shame, little guilt, and his own secretive, hidden agenda which he follows. It is more likely that a woman will leave him because of his infidelities, his possessive and controlling nature, his jealousy, or in other cases, his over indulgence in pleasures. But, no doubt, he will always be the love of her life. Relationships come and go, but there is no forgetting a relationship with Scorpio man.

Scorpio Sexuality - Woman

A Scorpio woman is faced with quite a challenge in life. She must find a man who can handle her passions and her needs. This is not an easy task. She is a sensual and sexual person, and if she is a career woman, her sexuality is a feature of her nature which she must subdue, and thankfully, she possesses a great reserve of self-control. But what she may have the most trouble controlling are those Scorpio eyes--and this may be true to some extent for both Scorpio men and women. Early in her life, she will learn that there is something about her eyes that actually frightens timid, inhibited, insecure people. But that same something draws adventurous, daring and less inhibited people to her. Until she learns to control her direct, intense gaze, she may even advert her glance, preferring not to look at too many people directly. (Thus, she is called reserved and shy.) There is something hypnotic about this glance, and until she can get it under control, men who she has little to no interest in are drawn to her like magnets. Even after she has learned the necessary self-control to look at people directly, she will find herself, no matter her age, walking across a crowded room and a man will look up and catch her gaze and immediately react. And this is how she gauges courage in a person, either looking at a person and seeing fear or strength in that first glance. She learns that men are easier to come by then they are to be rid of, and she becomes somewhat discerning. She doesn't want just sex. A Scorpio woman wants good sex with an uninhibited man to whom sex is as equally important as it is to her. She turns down more opportunities than she accepts, seeking that special someone to whom sex is a lively adventurous experience filled with thrills, eroticism, and excitement. In her embrace, a man soon forgets himself and becomes a highly charged, electrified sexual instrument. She brings out in a man his most intense desires and passions. And it is not unusual for a man to stop himself in the middle of this frenzy, remember he is with the weaker sex, and ask her if he's hurting her before loosing himself once again in all out passion and unsupervised energy.

Some Scorpio women will go so far as to lie about what sign they are in order not to be cast as that mysterious and feared woman of the Zodiac. That, of course, relates to the infamous sting of the Scorpio. And it goes without saying that Scorpio are people to whom it is not wise to lie, cheat, steal, or mistreat. When offended, she can turn cool and cut the other person out of her life as if he never existed. And Scorpio never forgets a wrong doing. But the average Scorpio woman is kind, compassionate, and caring and goes out of her way to treat other people as well as they treat her. In love, she becomes possessive and jealousy until a great deal of trust is developed. And in love she will want a total commitment to which she can devote herself completely. But in her more casual relationships, like the male Scorpio, she maintains a balance and self-control over her emotions. That she enjoys sex with a man doesn't necessarily mean she wants to take him home to meet her family. She is capable of having an ongoing relationship that lasts for years even when she knows it isn't going to lead to a commitment. She may love all her lovers, but she doesn't confuse this with the rest of her life. Like the male Scorpio, she is always ready for sex, but how much she allows this indulgence to influence her life may depend upon the individual woman. A self-assured, strong and confident woman, she may wait patiently in between lovers for the next remarkable person to come along. She holds in disdain, somewhat, the sexual attitudes of other women who are so loved-starved and sex-craved that they fall into the arms of any and every man that comes along. Anybody can have sex, but she wants sex that is compelling from that first glance right up to the last good-bye nod.

The sign of Scorpio rules the genital area of the body, and to heighten the arousal of a Scorpio, either man or woman, pay attention to this area of the body. A Scorpio woman welcomes a hand on her knee as a promise for further exploration of the more sensitive areas of her body. Oral stimulation is especially gratifying to this woman as it is also to the Scorpio man.

This is a woman who wastes little time over shame or guilt about her sexual inclination. Sex is perceived, for her, as a wonderful aspect of life to be enjoyed to its fullest with a partner of a like mind who shares her preferences and passions. With the right partner, a Scorpio woman gives her heart totally and with it her devotion, wanting only to please and be pleased.

Scorpio Health

The sign of Scorpio rules the reproductive system, in particular, the sexual organs, the bladder, the urethra, the uterus, the groin, the prostate gland, the rectum, the colon, the gall-bladder, and a portion of the kidney functions. This is the area of the body which rules over reproduction and the life-producing force. Scorpio is the sign of eliminating the old and beginning the new.

Natives of this sign may find that they are prone to problems and infections of the sexual organs. Other problems include gall-stones, kidney stones, ruptures, hernias, and a susceptibility to skin irritations of this area of the body and venereal diseases. Other health problems may include skin disorders, asthma and various types of allergies.

Scorpio natives must take care in the excesses of life or in indulging their pleasures. Those who are inclined to over eating will find that weight gain and its associated problems will effect their health. It is also very important that Scorpio natives watch the amount of their alcohol consumption. Many of these individuals don't exhibit the ability to stop with one drink. Alcohol and its related illnesses may well effect many of these individuals unless self-control is manifested.

While other Zodiac signs must deal with problems of nervousness, the Scorpio individual more than likely will not suffer from nervous disorders as much so as problems associated with the intensity of their natures. Your blood seems to boil with such intensity that at times others feel like they can actually see your blood pressure rising. Any individual with blood pressure problems or its associative problems needs to seek the advice of a physician. However, it goes without saying that watching your diet and a healthy exercise program will help in this regard.

This same intensity and the energetic drive inherent in the Scorpio nature may produce individuals who are prone to exhaustion. It appears that the Scorpio native requires an abundant amount of sleep and relaxation. A good sleep pattern should be established that provides for sufficient rest to restore the individual and to prepare the body for the next day.

In afflicted individuals there is noted a propensity for psychological disorders of varying severity. Some individuals appear to be in touch with or have experiences from another plane of consciousness as if almost from another dimension. They are sensitive to and hear, see and feel disturbances from outside their own being. If any evidence of emotional problems exist, the native should seek the counsel of professionals trained in this area.

Scorpio natives with their highly charged natures and desires to fulfill their pleasures, must above all else take charge of their lives in order to establish self-control. This self-control must be over their minds, their bodies, their diet, their daily routine and their overall health. These people more than others may need to develop an effective exercise program. This will restore your natural energy while allowing your body and your mind a diversion from everyday problems and pursuits. And exercise is a healthy pursuit. And remember, Scorpio, sexual activities, while healthy, are only one form of physical exercise. Take the time to develop others. Your diet should include foods which also restore your energy and which aid in the elimination process. Include an abundance of fruits, vegetables and grains. And watch your intake of rich foods and desserts. Yes, these are delicious and stimulating, but everyone has to exert some pressure on one's self to be responsible in this area of life. For self-fulfillment, relaxation, and enjoyment, include in your life the companionship of entertaining and calm people who appreciate you and your natural gifts. Avoid the company of people who you know will upset you and your daily routine. Focus your drives on the success of your life, and take care of your health and your body in the process.

History of Scorpio

The sign of Scorpio is the source of many legends and myths. Among the mythology concerning the constellation of Scorpio, which straddles the heavens, is the story of the scorpion, a servant of the god Apollo, created to destroy the lusty, glorious hunter Orion, the ravisher of maidens and beasts. In another version of the story, Diana, the moon-goddess, was jealous that Eos, goddess of the dawn, fell in love with Orion, and Diana created the scorpion to kill Orion. After Orion's death, some of the stories say Apollo, some say Jupiter, placed both Orion and Scorpio among the stars as constellations. Another version has Juno commanding the scorpion to rise from the earth to attack Orion. At any rate, Scorpio continues to this day to chase Orion from the sky. There is also the myth that it was the scorpion who caused the horses of the Sun to bolt when driven for a day by the boy Phaethon, after which it was chastised with a thunderbolt.

Ancient weather forecasters used the constellation of Scorpio to predict storms and rain. And among students of the metaphysical arts, Scorpio was perceived as the best sign during which to attempt to change metal into gold. Hebrew mythology associates Scorpio with the tribe of Dan, one of the original twelve tribes of Israel. Early Christians associated the constellation with the emblem representing St. Bartholomew.

The constellation of Scorpio and that of Gemini, the Twins, are the only two names in the Zodiac that are attributed to their shapes among the stars. The names of the other signs are for the most part seasonal, and the remaining are mythical.

How to Find Your Soul-Mate, Stars, and Destiny

Scorpio

October 23 -- November 21
The Thebaic Calendar
Character, Personality, and Destiny

The Thebaic Calendar was designed by ancient scholars to denote the horoscope and destiny of individuals. It represents the daily notes that the ancient astrologers wrote on burnt stones or papyrus. This is an easy and fast way to find information pertaining to your birth date. The native will often find his characteristics and destiny around his date of birth. It can be used as a quick reference to find the characteristics for the day of birth.

Whether Scorpio is the person's Sun sign, the Ascendant, on the cusp, or in a House, the characteristics of this sign become evident. Scorpio as the Fixed Water sign influences the emotional and intuitive powers of the person with a tendency to be resistant to outside controls. The planet Uranus is exalted in Scorpio and when found there bestows an energetic and sudden release of power to be humanitarian, friendly and kind, or, if afflicted, eccentric, cranky, and rebellious. The tendencies of the sign of Scorpio are manifested through powerful feelings and emotions with an emphasis on the depth of the passions, especially those pertaining to sexual matters. The sign of Scorpio rules sexual relations, and this the Scorpio individual accepts as his or her domain of dominion. And as in this area of life, in all other aspects of life, the Scorpio natives remain just as passionate, energetic, and driven to be active and involved. As a Fixed sign, these natives are determined and reliable. And if unpredictable, they are predictably unpredictable. But trust a Scorpio to know his or her own mind, even if these deeper emotions remain somewhat hidden and secretive while this native remains as expressive otherwise as anyone else.

DUALITY: Feminine **ELEMENT:** Water **QUALITY:** Fixed **RULER:** Pluto

As a feminine sign, Scorpio is considered receptive and magnetic and possessing a power and strength derived at through inner resources. The element of Water signifies not only intense emotions but a creative and stirring imagination, a pronounced sensitivity, and a spirituality that leads and guides the natives. And the Fixed quality pronounces a persistence and single mindedness. Scorpio has been compared to still and deep waters that are as firm and strong as a steady and permanent iceberg. Scorpio, it has been said, have the necessary ability and power to attract the people and circumstances needed to succeed and to survive. They do succeed even against great odds and seemingly insurmountable obstacles. That is, they either succeed and arrive at a special spirituality that guides them and leads them, or they succumb utterly to their predictaments and situations with the propensity to become depressed and despondent. The sign of Scorpio rules the underworld and, as such, touches grace and fall from grace. The secrets of the Universe they carry in the mystical glance and expression in their eyes. They see all and know all as the Eagle soaring high. Of course, no discussion of the Scorpio is complete without mentioning that infamous stinging tail. Scorpio carries its revenge with him or her, waiting patiently for the most opportune time to inflict that deserved punishment and to intuitively get the better of any enemy or wrong doer. Perhaps it is the knowledge of this defense mechanism that grants the Scorpio native such verve, courage, and fearfulness in the face of opposition. Their vitality, energy, force, and spirit appears to know few limits.

Native Scorpios are found to be reserved and dignified, hiding their passions behind the twinkle in their eyes; or they can be as outgoing and witty as one would wish--with the same mischievous twinkle giving away their true natures. In either case, no one can claim to know the mind of these men and women who challenge with a glance and promise an irresistible and, of course, unforgettable experience. They are driven by their desires.

The First Decan

The First Decan occurs from 0 degrees to 10 degrees of Scorpio and applies to those individuals born between October 23 and November 2. Those natives who are on the cusp with Libra are gifted with the additional charm of diplomacy and congeniality. The First Decan Scorpio's are resourceful and enterprising. They exhibit much energy that is directed and focused toward their purposes and goals. They can be tenacious, enduring, and persevering with a headstrong urge to complete what they have started no matter the odds or the obstacles. Being driven by their desires, they can be somewhat intolerant of those who stand in their way or slow them down, becoming especially impatient with others who are lazy or hesitant. But then these native Scorpios are fun loving and pleasure seeking with the same amount of energy as is dispelled toward their more serious objectives. And their secretiveness and efforts to be discreet overshadow all that they do.

The Second Decan

The Second Decan occurs from 10 degrees to 20 degrees of Scorpio and applies to those individuals born between November 2 and November 11. These are individuals who most strongly exhibit all the characteristics of the sign of Scorpio. They can be kind, sympathetic, and generous with a desire to help those in need, but after this help they expect the other person to be on their way under their own steam. If this doesn't happen, Scorpio can become indifferent and suspicious. The Second Decan also includes those natives who are predisposed toward a great vanity and an underlying mean streak bordering on cruelty. These natives can be impulsive and reckless, plunging through life with a total disregard for the effect their actions have on others.

The Third Decan

The Third Decan occurs from 20 degrees to 30 degrees of Scorpio and applies to those individuals born between November 12 and November 21. Those individuals born during this Decan who are approaching the cusp of Sagittarius are more inclined to be philosophical but retain all the sensuality of the Scorpio native. They are sensitive, intuitive, and perceptive with a tendency to be more resistant to restraints or any limitations to their freedoms. They can be fun loving and happy go lucky individuals but they also possess the tendency to turn moody and to have dark moods. Generally, however, they are sociable with a tendency to like groups and interactions with others. While striving to maintain control of their lives, they often feel as if they are submitted to experiences which fate throws their way, and it requires a great deal of their energy to regain their way while dealing with these unexpected occurrences. Their emotions and passions are deep and heart felt, but they have difficulty expressing the depth of their feelings. But at the same time, there is a tendency for these natives to be direct and outspoken in their dealings with others.

First Decan of Scorpio:

October 23 - November 2 -

First Ten Days

Character, Personality, and Temperament:

The character of the individuals born under the First Decan of the sign of Scorpio is strong and powerful without special nuances or artifices. The natives exhibit the ability to develop self-discipline and can apply patience and perseverance to facing problems.

Fixed Element:

WATER: The Fixed quality grants an enduring stability and strength to the emotions, intuition, and passions.

Destiny:

The native takes pride in his or her steadfastness and dependability, but this person will stay and endure a questionable situation long after others would have given up and moved on.

Star Date of Birth: October 23

An enterprising personality and temperament are found for those born on this date, but the person may be easily frightened. Partial success is noted in all undertakings. Enjoy life while you are young because in your maturity while you earn a good living, it is rarely enough to cover those expenses brought on by difficulties. Indecisiveness gives way to boldness in love and romance. Protective of your lover, you are secretive in affairs of the heart.

How to Find Your Soul-Mate, Stars, and Destiny

Star Date of Birth: October 24

This person exhibits characteristics of boldness, decisiveness, and direct action. There is seen the possibilities of causing someone else accidents or wounds or injuries. You adapt readily to situations but are capable of leaving one set of circumstances behind and moving on to another. You are self-assured sexually and passionately drawn to ego-driven, strong willed individuals like yourself.

Star Date of Birth: October 25

This individual exhibits moderation in all things and possesses a precise sense of when to take action. Success and victories are noted. Your docile mannerisms nicely cover your bolder needs in love and romance, and sexually you sizzle, getting your way and easily attracting others. Those who have been denied sexual gratification in the past find you most stimulating and rewarding.

Star Date of Birth: October 26

This person has a tendency to procrastinate by leaving what can be done today until tomorrow. There is an indecisive nature. A great deal of success is not seen and in life this person will almost be defeated. Your adventurous life is based on being fearless of taking risks which you most likely endure with fortitude. Having found and experienced the best in sex, you are left wondering if it will come your way again. You avoid the faint hearted and less than secure individual.

Star Date of Birth: October 27

This native possesses a reckless boldness which seems to overcome any measures. There is seen artificial and temporary success. With your strong will power, you know how to put your charm and charisma to good use in getting what you want. You strive to subdue your sexuality which without effort attracts and persuades even the most reluctant lover. And interested or not, you make others feel desirable and sexy.

Star Date of Birth: October 28

An enterprising spirit that is both patient and persevering is noted. There may well be a passion for the occult. Success comes slowly but surely for these natives. Your life is a cycle of good fortune and misfortune which attunes your mind to being creatively cunning; but whatever you achieve, you know that new obstacles are forthcoming. You find not only passion and satisfaction, but relief and relaxation in your active sexual life.

Star Date of Birth: October 29

This person shows good taste and refinement in all aspects of the life. Brilliant and substantial success is seen. Research and ferreting out information comes naturally with your unusual perceptions, intuitions, and insights which also spill over into your sexuality. You may keep your thoughts secretive, but you sense the needs and desires of your romantic partners and apply your energies to doing your best to please.

Star Date of Birth: October 30

This individual has an agitated nature and is always scheming something. Material success is noted. Your mystique, personal charm and charisma serves you well, most especially in your romantic relationships. Others are attracted by your allure and tempted to uncover your secrets in order to know you better, and your greatest secret is knowing how to enhance this mysterious image.

Star Date of Birth: October 31

The natives born on this date are inclined toward inertia and apathy and are incapable of work. This life may be full of failures unless the native takes some action. Your persuasive charm barely hides your aggressive nature which wins you both friends and enemies. Your sexual adventures are overshadowed by your memories of former lovers, and your most endearing moments are with these lovers from your past.

Star Date of Birth: November 1

This person is extremely honest, sometimes brutally outspoken. It is indicated that this person will handle business affairs well even though tact may be compromised. Whatever life dishes up, you learn to be a survivor, giving as well as you take. You are sexually perceptive and aware of chance opportunities related to travel and isolated locations. Secretiveness and mystery enhances your romantic moments making the encounters exciting and thrilling.

Second Decan of Scorpio:

November 2 - November 11 - Second Ten Days

Character, Personality, and Temperament:

The individuals born during the Second Decan of Scorpio have inclinations toward kindness, sympathy, and generosity or toward vanity and an irresponsible cruelty. They exhibit the characteristics of benevolence or of someone who goes blindly and recklessly through life without realizing that they can hurt others.

Fixed Element:

Water: Strongly resistant to outside influences and trusting until the native has the chance to make up his or her own mind.

Destiny:

The destiny indicates that the native becomes more kind and beautiful through his or her career gaining prestige and a good reputation.

Star Date of Birth: November 2

The individual possesses a nasty, quarrelsome character. A difficult life which can make the person bitter is indicated unless drastic steps are taken. Your bravery and courage overcomes any need for caution in your encounters with others. The strong willed, adventurous type and the loner feels at ease in your presence and you may find yourself enjoying sexual encounters that were totally unexpected.

Star Date of Birth: November 3

There is seen an invincible will power to succeed. An endangered life with hidden threats and merciless enemies is indicated. Strong of heart and mind, you are benevolent and most humane especially with those who are weaker. Persons appear and reenter your life unexpectedly, bringing with them the opportunity for sexual fulfillment and the ecstasy that comes from sharing secretive moments together.

Star Date of Birth: November 4

This person has a nervous personality and is always obsessed by the worst that can happen. This native will have a life not established on a solid foundation. You accept your losses and mistakes knowing they are often brought on by your willingness to take a risk, especially if adventure is offered. You are most comfortable with a sexual relationship that is well developed and based on understanding and shared desires.

Star Date of Birth: November 5

A fiery temperament is indicated for this native. Success is seen through defeat of adversaries. You are capable of bearing the greatest of inconveniences and suffering without complaining. You are adept at reading other people, knowing their strengths, weaknesses, and sexual preferences--all of which you use to your advantage.

Star Date of Birth: November 6

There is a strong inclination toward profit even if this person has to steal. A life with an ugly ending is noted if the native cannot conquer these tendencies. You are a resourceful individual who knows how to turn a situation to your advantage. You accept sex as a natural part of life which puts you ahead of the game. You avoid inhibited people who are not prepared for your boldness.

Star Date of Birth: November 7

A fatalistic personality is noted, and this native has difficulties with accomplishing pursuits. There is indicated a sentimental happiness and a mediocre material success. You strive to establish a contented life, especially in your romantic relationship. This is enhanced by your insights and awareness and your intuition of what is to unfold in the future. Your friendly and self-assured ways puts you at ease in your sexual relationships.

Star Date of Birth: November 8

A spiritual nobility is seen for this individual with a lack of interest in material pursuits. An honest life is seen which is filled with depth and meaning. You accept and adapt to changes easily both in your professional and personal life. This is enhanced by your ability to relate well and to come to a quick understanding of others. Sexually, you are perceptive at knowing not only the desires but the inhibitions of others.

Star Date of Birth: November 9

There is an indication that this person will have an unchangeable, stubborn personality. This life may be shadowed by an atmosphere of hidden enemies. Your enthusiasm and energy underlies all that you do, and you aptly apply this same enthusiasms to your romantic relationships. You are aware of sexual opportunities and the attraction that others feel for you through a highly developed perceptiveness.

Star Date of Birth: November 10

This person finds fault with everything and attempts to find motives for quarrels with others. An insignificant life is indicated with unhappy love affairs. You apply your resourcefulness to facing challenges and obstacles. Sexually, you are most at ease with another who is willing to take the lead and initiate even more thrilling experiences to add to your growing list of passionate accomplishments.

Star Date of Birth: November 11

This individual has an inclination toward an irascible nature. There is an indication for struggles and heartaches, but life is lived without any lack of necessities and at times abundant material possessions, pleasures and lots of love. It seems as though others deliberately stand in the way of your ambitions, but you face these challenges tenaciously and are often successful in overcoming them. Sexually, your self-confidence and self-assurance is rewarded by those who are attracted to you and find you irresistible.

The Third Decan of Scorpio:

November 12 - November 21 -

Third Ten Days

Character, Personality, and Temperament:

The spirit of Scorpio natives born at this time is more tamed and prone to philosophical tendencies. The temperament associated with this sign is directed toward sensuality and a free spirit.

How to Find Your *Soul-Mate, Stars,* and *Destiny*

Fixed Element:

Water: The native has a strong sense of their own ideas, values, and direction with a tendency to build on trust slowly.

Destiny:

The destiny of these individuals is tumultuous and can be turbulent. At times success is credited to certain endeavors that are risky and daring and perhaps not highly recommended.

Star Date of Birth: November 12

This individual has an inclination not to trust anyone and is rather sullen about life. There is seen material success through hard efforts that will lead to slow profits. Your sensuality highlights most every aspect of your life making you readily willing to engage in sexual activities and the pleasures of life. You make every effort to please your lovers, pleasing yourself in return.

Star Date of Birth: November 13

A decisive temperament without scruples is indicated. The individual encounters distant travels and adventurous expeditions. You hold strong opinions some of which are based on the learned prejudices of childhood. Sexually, you like to make others feel good, and this leads you to want to make as many people as possible happy--thus satiating your own ego by your ability to live up to the task.

Star Date of Birth: November 14

This individual is inclined toward a subtle personality and a penetrating intellect. Success is noted with an interest in the occult. You delve into the secrets of life wanting to uncover the reason for why the world goes round. This adds to your sexual mystique which is further enhanced by your ability to turn a situation into fun and games. Thus light-hearted and mysterious at the same time, you further intrigue others.

Star Date of Birth: November 15

This character is brave, courageous and deeply religious. A life filled with adventures is indicated. Maturity brings a quieter time with the end of life around the age of fifty. You are filled with an undauntingly enterprising applying your energy and enthusiasm to fulfilling your goals. Sexually, few obstacles stand in the way of your self-assurance, and you are especially attracted to that which you feel is forbidden or hard to get.

Star Date of Birth: November 16

An independent personality which is unbendable is seen. In general, an unhappy life is indicated. You give your complete attention to your goals, knowing resourcefully how to make do on a little and how to turn what you have into more. Sexually, your resourcefulness turns situations into golden opportunities to enjoy the pleasures of life.

Star Date of Birth: November 17

This native possesses a temperament of a consummate fighter who is active, but moderately so. There is indicated a modest life with a decent amount of joy. Through chance and unstable partnerships your good fortune can turn to misfortune. You may give in to your urge to know all there is to know about your sexual partner, but accepting the good with the bad keeps you in the wrong relationship too long.

Star Date of Birth: November 18

A prying personality with an inclination to take goods that do not belong to him or her is noted. Success is threatened by catastrophe. Your self-confidence can make you proud and vain leading you to expect others to tend to your needs. Your sexual perceptiveness feeds your vanity, however, as others continue to find you attractive and appealing. And in this area of your life, you aim to please.

How to Find Your Soul-Mate, Stars, and Destiny

Star Date of Birth: November 19

A sober, taciturn personality is seen and a life with hard work is indicated. There may be delayed success. Conversely, for others a versatile life with real activity is noted but this individual may be scattered on too many planes. An existence sown with worries is indicated with late success. You have a lot of energy, but it is often diverted by others who oppose you. Sexually, you apply your strong will power into continuing a relationship whether it is advisable to do so or not. You strive to prove that all is fair in love and war whether or not it is to your benefit.

Star Date of Birth: November 20

Aggressiveness and more aggressiveness is indicated. Worries, corruption, and complete ruin is indicated for some. You feed your ego by collecting a long list of friends and associates. You feed your strong sex drive by your successful sexual conquests, being especially attracted to people who are at ease in large groups and who respond to your temptation to be alone with you.

Star Date of Birth: November 21

This native possesses great skills of persuasion. This native gains success through this gift. A life full of happiness is indicated. Your inquisitive and exploring nature leads you to investigate secrets, especially those related to the occult or to any subject centering on mystique. Sexually, the ho-hum experience is not for you, and you thrive on that added ingredient of ecstasy in your sexual encounters.

Colors:

The natives of Scorpio are best enhanced with all shades of crimson and blue while some of these individuals may prefer shades of burgundy, maroon, and black.

BIRTHSTONES:

The birthstones for Scorpio are the opal, turquoise, ruby, and the topaz.

POWER STONES:

The power stones for the sign of Scorpio include the obsidian, citrine, and the garnet.

FLOWERS:

Favorable flowers for Scorpio natives are those with dark red blooms and the chrysanthemum and rhododendron.

KEYWORD: "I DESIRE"

POSITIVE TRAITS:

Energetic; powerful; active; passionate; optimistic; fearless; devoted; patient; kindly; warm hearted; ambitious; tenacious; penetrating; discerning; subtle; persistent; daring; bold; dauntless; purposeful; pleasant; eloquent; and imaginative; intense; ingenious.

NEGATIVE TRAITS:

Jealous; possessive; revengeful; severe; callous; resentful; stubborn; obstinate; pessimistic; sarcastic; suspicious; destructive; vindictive; shrewd and cunning; overly secretive; addictions to drugs, alcohol, or sex; controlling; blunt; tyrannical; envious.

How to Find Your Soul-Mate, Stars, and Destiny

Scorpio

Personal Self-Expression and Mental Tendencies

1. Force, Energy, Courage, Activity, Hot, Dry, Masculine
2. Ambitions, Desires, Destructive, Individual, Vibrations
3. Constructive or Destructive Ability, Burden, Staunch
4. Dignified, Courageous, Venturesome, Strong, Daring, Keen
5. Aggressive, Fearless, Passionate, Appreciates Sensuality
6. Strong Characteristics, Keen Judgement, Tending to Violence
7. Critical, Suspicious, Skeptical, Enterprising, Sensual Nature
8. Determined, Secretive, Fond of Luxuries, Economical
9. Travel - Especially on Water, Admires Grandeur and Nature
10. Attends to Own Affairs in Business, Makes Trouble for Others
11. Speech Plain, Blunt, Sarcastic, and Forceful, Plots, Attainments,
12. Politics or Law, Original, Scientific, Secretly Sadistic, Antipathies
13. Sagacious, Daring, Creative, Success, Bold Enterprises, Sarcastic
14. Stingingly Quick-Witted, Power to Visualize, Double-Edged
15. Quick in Speech, Action, Alert, Positive, Often Blunt, Skilled
16. Possesses Grit, Reaches High, Seemingly Fond of Contest
17. Motivated, Vital Temperment, Accomplish Their Purposes
18. Revivals of Forgotten Enmity, Onslaught of Fresh Foes
19. Enjoys Travel, Investigates Mysteries and Things of the Occult
20. Can Be Very Frugal and Economical, Stinging, Brusque,
21. Muscular Skill, Aggressive Enterprises, Optimistic, Friends
22. Penetrating Mind, Self-Reliant, Bold, Fixed Views, Abrupt
23. Subtle Mind, Hard to Influence, Not Easily Imposed Upon
24. Willful, Othertimes Indolent, Angry when Provoked
25. Vigorous, Strong Willed, Determination, Practical Ability
26. Firm, Self-Confident, Gains Success in Undertakings
27. Fond of Pleasure and Comfort, Desire to Satisfy the Tastes
28. Independent, Masterful, Not Tolerant of Imposition
29. Purpose by Opposition, Often Sacrifices a Great Deal

30. Mysterious in Nature, Assists in Carrying Out Revolutinary Ideas
31. Changes, Employees Sarcasm or Satire, Ardent in Love
32. Attachments or Attrctions in Difficulties With the Opposite Sex
33. In Harmony in the Marriage State, Dangers in Voyages
34. Obstinate, Reckless Nature, Desirous of Gaining Knowledge
35. Partial to Opposite Sex and Company for Pleasure-Seeking
36. Many Disappointments, Occult, Different -ologies and -isms
37. Very Carefule with Personal Interests, Curious, Mistrustful
38. Mesmeric Ability, Suggestive Mental and Healing Qualities
39. Mental Resourcefulness, Fertility, Free, Quick, Pragmatic
40. Lavish in Expenditures, Gain by Gifts or Legacy, Partnership or Marriage
41. Emotional, Giving, Loves Sensation, Demonstrative in Affection
42. Disagreement or Jealousy, Attacks Honor, Death of Partner
43. Trouble or Failure in Social Affairs, Occult Tendencies
44. Friendships of Doubtful Repute, Unhappy Alliances
45. Promotes Development, Perceptive, Observant
46. Capacity to Work Hard and to Accomplish Much
47. Good Executive Power, Inventive, Mechanical Skill,
48. Matter of Fact Manner, Seemingly Cold or Unconscious
49. Disregard for the Feeling of Others, Selfish, Rash, Revengeful
50. Mind is Acute, Sharp, Keen; Diplomatic; Quick, Secret Missions
51. Capable in Government, Work of a Peculiar Nature
52. Employment With Confederates or Associates, Liquids, Tools
53. Projects with Intensity of Purpose and Action
54. Produce Results, Fondness for Hazardous Enterprises
55. Liable to Accidents, Sudden or Violent, Severe Illness, Operations
56. Engaged in Psychical Research, Likelihood to Gain by Marriage
57. Ship Experiences, Long Journeys and Voyages, Tends to Express
58. Unsociable, Ungrateful, Quarrelsome, Animal Nature,
59. Powerful Will, Deep Emotions. Ardor, Generous
60. Mind Active, Resolute, Fruitful, Loves Sex, Splendid
61. Analytical, Lofty, Proud, Hidden and Dangerous Enemies
62. Professional Secrets and Information, Open to Criticism
63. Intrigued With Superiors, Strange Adventures Abroad
64. Unafflicted, Gain, Arbitration, Legacy and Public Investments
65. Afflicted, Powerful Enemies, Misfortune, Ingenious
66. Loss Questionable or Unsound, Speculation, Securities
67. Sudden Resolutions, Violent Temper, Self-Willed

68. Acquistive, Inquistive, Cautious, Strength of Will
69. Profoundly Intellectual, Love Affairs, Secret Alliances
70. Domestic Difficulties, Psychic Ability, Chemistry or Geology
71. Persistence, Cleverness After Many Difficulties and Obstacles
72. Strength of MInd, Concentration, Tenacious, Intrigues,
73. Spirit Cannot Be Brokenby Resistance, Compulsive, Capable
74. Sharp-Spoken, Acute, Shrewd, Reserved, Rebellious
75. Frequently at Variance With Accepted Opionions, Intensifies Activity
76. Self-Advancement, Personal Gain, Self-Mastery
77. Industrial Chemistry, Drugless Healing Methods
78. Felled by Firearm Wounds, Explosions, Electrical Devices
79. Well Aspected, Intensifies Feelings and Emotions, Gives Greater Scope
80. Spiritual Transcendence, Reserved Secrecy, Beverages
81. Not Easily Fooled or Offended, Calculating, Treachery
82. Benefit to Humanity, Restless, Returns Kindnesses
83. Complex, Practical, Mystical, Lusty, Diurnal Day
84. Nocturnal, Intense, Vindictive, Prone to Extremes, Repressed
85. Stubborn, Loyal, Insensitive, Dictatorial, Compulsive
86. Arrogant, Self-Indulgent, Manipulative, Lost Legacy
87. Torrid, Asexual, Manically Possessive, Nonconforming, Inhibited
88. Iconoclastic, Leader, Lonely, Guilty, Self-Destructive
89. Unusual Destiny, Undergoes Changes and Turning Points
90. Emotional Death, Power User, Death and Rebirth in Life
91. Fascinates or Frightens, Endowed Powers
92. Willfulness, Paranoia, Vibrations, Used
93. Obsession With Power and the Use of Sex to Obtain It
94. Transformation Results in New Self and Lifestule, Comfortable With Less
95. Many Levels, Impulsive, Money Making
96. Fanactic Sexual Involvements, Manipulation of Individuals or Groups
97. Personal Power at th Expense of Others
98. Strong Hypnotic Aura, Commanding, Emotional Peace
99. Prevents Change, Demands Secrecy, Talented, Resourceful
100. Craves Understanding, Seldom is Understood, Excess

How to Find Your *Soul-Mate, Stars,* and *Destiny*

Celebrity Birthdays

October Scorpio

23	Dwight Yoakum Freddie Marsden Adlai Stevenson Weird Al Yankovic	Michael Chrichton Perola Negra Pele Johnny Carson	Diana Dors Jim Bunning Pele
24	Y. A. Tittle David Nelson Moss Hart	Jerry Edmonton Jackie Coogan	B.D. Wong Chester Marcol
25	James Carville Dan Issel Pablo Picasso Glen Tipton	Jon Anderson Helen Reddy Tony Franciosa Adm Richard Byrd	Minnie Pearl Johann Strauss Mathias Jabs George Bizet
26	Cary Elwes Leon Trotsky Mahalia Jackson Bob Hoskins	Pat Conroy Hilary Clinton Ivan Reitman Keith Strickland	Mike Hargrove Jaclyn Smith Keith Hopwood Pat Sajak
27	Lee Greenwood Terry Anderson John Cleese Sylvia Plath	Ruby Dee Carrie Snodgress Theodore Roosevelt Niccolo Paganini	Dylan Thomas Nanette Fabray John Gotti Marla Maples
28	Julia Roberts Telma Hopkins Edith Head Evelyn Waugh	James Cook Hank Marvin Jane Alexander Jonas Salk	Joan Plowright Bill Gates Suzy Parker Bowie Kuhn
29	Winona Ryder Denny Laine Joseph Goebbels Bill Mauldin	Ralph Bakshi Fanny Brice Melba Moore James Boswell	Kevin Dubrow Richard Dreyfuss Kate Jackson
30	Henry Winkler Ruth Gordon Ezra Pound Otis Williams	Todd Sand Pres John Adams Grace Slick Gordon Parks	Harry Hamlin Mickey Rivers Gavin Rossdale

How to Find Your *Soul-Mate, Stars,* and *Destiny*

October — Scorpio

31	Randy Jackson	Deidre Hall	Ethel Waters
	Sally Kirkland	Vermeer	Dale Evans
	John Keats	Dan Rather	Jane Pauley
	Lee Grant	Barbara Bel Geddes	Michael Landon

November

1	Robert Foxworth	Bill Anderson	Lyle Lovett
	Rick Allen	Barbara Bosson	Dan Peek
	Betsy Palmer	Eddie MacDonald	Jane Pauley
	Larry Flynt	Keith Emerson	Ronald Bell
2	Alfre Woodard	Marie Antoinette	k.d. lang
	Brian Poole	Bruce Welch	Burt Lancaster
	Luchino Visconti	Benvenuto Cellini	Pres James Polk
	Daniel Boone	Pres Warren G. Harding	
3	James Reston	Roseanne Arnold	Adam Ant
	Gary Sandy	Charles Bronson	Larry Holmes
	Dolph Lundgren	Dennis Miller	Lulu
	Bob Feller	Mike Evans	James Prime
4	Ralph Macchio	Art Carney	Walter Cronkite
	Markie Post	Loretta Swit	Chris Difford
	Gig Young	Yanni	Will Rogers
	Mike Smith	Bob Considine	Martin Balsam
5	Paul Simon	Bryan Adams	Elke Sommer
	Art Garfunkel	Andrea McArdle	Peter Noone
	Tatum O'Neal	Roy Rogers	Sam Shepard
	Vivian Leigh	Eugene V. Debs	Ike Turner
6	Ethan Hawke	Lori Singer	Maria Shriver
	James Jones	Mike Nichols	John Candelaria
	Glenn Frey	Sally Field	Ray Coniff
	George Young	John Philip Sousa	Doug Sahm
7	Joni Mitchell	Dean Jagger	Archie Campbell
	Marie Curie	Al Hirt	Johnny Rivers
	Billy Graham	Joan Sutherland	

… How to Find Your *Soul-Mate, Stars,* and *Destiny*

November Scorpio

8	Rickie Lee Jones June Havoc Morley Safer Alan Berger	Bonnie Bramlett Bonnie Raitt Patti Page Katherine Hepburn	Terry Lee Miall Alain Delon Roxana Zal Roy Wood
9	Lou Ferrigno Phil May Joe Buchard Hedy Lamarr	Anne Sexton Ed Wyann King Edward VII Carl Sagan	Mary Travers Bob Gibson Alan Gratzer Spiro Agnew
10	Ann Reinking Greg Lake Jack Scalia MacKenzie Phillips	Friedrich Schiller Dave Loggins Richard Burton Willaim Hogarth	Glen Buxton Roy Scheider Martin Luther Donna Fargo
11	Demi Moore Jonathan Winters Bibi Andersson Pat O'Brien	Barbara Boxer Kurt Vonnegut Jr. Fyodor Dostoevsky Sam Spiegel	Ian Marsh Gen George Patton Abigail Adams Paul Cowsill
12	Richard Whiting Charles Manson Nadia Comaneci Wallace Shawn	Kim Hunter David Schwimmer Rodin Princess Grace	Harry Blackmun Errol Brown Stephanie Powers Neil Young
13	Whoopi Goldberg Joe Montegna Jean Seberg Oskar Werner	Hermione Baddeley Richard Mulligan Nathaniel Benchley Robert Louis Stevenson	Chris Noth Louis Brandeis Linda Christian
14	McLean Stevenson Prince Charles Freddie Garrity Alexander O'Neal	Laura San Giacomo Mamie Eisenhower Robert Ginty Brian Keith	King Hussein Frankie Banali Claude Monet Aaron Copeland
15	Carol Bruce Ed Asner C.W. McCall Sam Waterston	Beverly D'Angelo Frida Lyngstad Daniel Barenboim Georgia O'Keefe	Yaphet Kotto Petula Clark Tony Thompson Gen Rommel
16	Elizabeth Drew Lisa Bonet Zina Garrison Chi Coltrane	George S. Kaufman Burgess Meredith Emperor Tiberius Jim „Fibber McGee' Jordan	Dwight Gooden Eddie Condon W.C. Handy

November Scorpio

17	Alexei Urmanov	Martin Scorsese	Lauren Hutton
	Gordon Lightfoot	Lorne Michaels	Tom Seaver
	Ronald DeVoe	Danny DeVito	Martin Barre
	Bob Gaudio	Dino Martin	Rock Hudson
18	Elizabeth Perkins	Kevin Nealon	Hank Ballard
	Brenda Vaccaro	Margaret Atwood	Kim Wilde
	Dorothy Collins	Johnny Mercer	Eugene Ormandy
	George Gallup	Alan Shepard	Linda Evans
19	Jody Foster	Roy Campanella	Dick Cavett
	Meg Ryan	Tommy Dorsey	Calvin Klein
	Indira Gandhi	Martin Luther	Larry King
	Jenny Meno	Clifton Webb	Ted Turner
20	Veronica Hamel	Dick Smothers	Art Ruchwald
	Robert F. Kennedy	Kaye Ballard	Richard Masur
	Estelle Parsons	Judy Woodruff	Gene Tierney
	Alistair Cooke	Emilio Pucci	Bo Derek
21	Harold Ramis	Goldie Hawn	Jim Bishop
	Marlo Thomas	Lonnie Jordan	Lorna Luft
	Harpo Marx	Juliet Mills	Martha Deane
	Eleanor Powell	David Hemmings	Voltaire

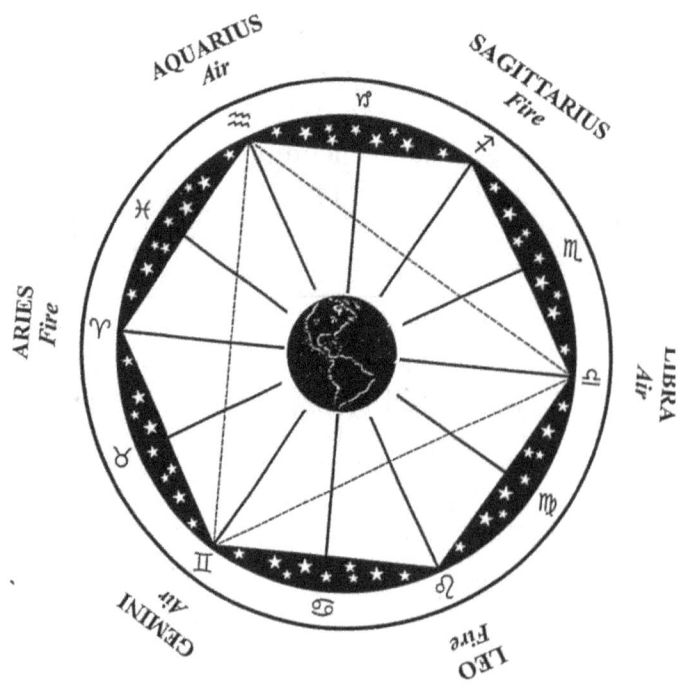

How to Find Your *Soul-Mate, Stars,* and *Destiny*

Date With Destiny

Share With Me Your Fantasy

How to Find Your *Soul-Mate, Stars,* and *Destiny*

Date With Destiny

Share With Me Your Fantasy

How to Find Your *Soul-Mate, Stars,* and *Destiny*

SAGITTARIUS

November 22 - December 20
Man - Woman - Child - Character - Relationships - Compatibilities - Love Signs

How to Find Your *Soul-Mate, Stars, and Destiny*

Sagittarius is the ninth Sun of the Zodiac and is symbolized by the Archer (or the Centaur). Its name is based on the Latin word for arrow, and Sagittarius is pictured as the Archer forever shooting its arrows in different directions. Sagittarius is the optimistic, happy-go-lucky idealist who is blessed with good luck at just the right moment. They are humanitarian philosophers who offer a new slant on their observations and who may express themselves energetically throughout a lifestyle of their own making. They love to travel, to see the world, to meet new people, and most of all to be exposed to new and exciting experiences. The dullness of routine does no appeal to these freedom-loving individuals who traipse the world hoping to find the perfect adventure. Versatile, adaptable, and sociable, they may be guilty of shooting their arrows in too many directions, scattering them to the winds, before deciding to settle down to a more permanent life of career and family. Pleasure seeking and fun-loving, these natives take to romance and sex quite readily and seek to gather new experiences throughout life. If they impulsively marry young, they may grow impatient and unhappy, wishing for the ultimate adventure to set them free. The Sagittarius personality is most noted for a forthright, honest, direct, and outspoken way with words even to the point of offending others. Their quick wit and love of a good joke helps them to laugh off these embarrassing moments, but it does little to improve their rapport or their relationships. It is their giving and kind nature that serves them the best, and their ability to put a philosophical slant on any situation. The challenge for Sagittarius natives is to harness their abundant energy and to focus it on a given direction. Then, of course, with their intelligence and abilities, they become successful and productive. Their greatest challenge, however, is to learn not to depend too heavily on their star-granted luck. Independent, progressive, and born to wander, these natives do best when they discover an interest that attracts their intellects. Then their acute mental energies and alert curiosity become geared to seeking answers to the most complex questions.

These characteristics of the Sagittarius Sun sign can be made stronger by the Moon sign, Ascendant, and the placement of the Planets, or they can be made more subdued by specific influences. It is by ascertaining these various influences that one can more fully understand the Sagittarius individual being studied, or, more importantly, one can more fully understand one's self.

The Zodiac sign of Sagittarius corresponds to that time of year when the first snow flakes fall to the ground. Nature wraps itself in its white coat allowing Earth a well deserved rest at the end of the working year. This is the eve of the coming holidays when there can be found both joy and joviality abounding everywhere.

Sagittarius, the ninth sign of the Zodiac, is known as the Archer. The Archer is a Centaur, half man and half horse, who in mythology was Chiron, the confidante of both gods and men. It is referred to as the Archer because the man half of this being is shooting an arrow from a bow. Only a part of this constellation is found in the sky: the bow, half of the arrow and the left hand. The rest of the figure is found in the southern hemisphere. Between the legs of the Centaur sparkles the Southern Crown and other important stars including Antares, the Dragon, Hercules, and the Snake.

How to Find Your Soul-Mate, Stars, and Destiny

Sagittarius is a masculine sign and a Mutable Fire sign, and it is the most temperate of the Fire signs of the Zodiac. The Archer is not dominating as is Aries, nor authoritarian like Leo. This native is energetic, bright and enthusiastic. Physically, this person is agile, active, and energetic. The Archer is optimistic and strong, but in comparing it to the other Fire signs, this sign possesses unique personal qualities. Neither ruled by only intellect nor by pleasure, these natives display a strong, philosophical spirit.

The sign of Sagittarius is ruled by Jupiter, the planet of luck, wealth, common sense, optimism, expansion and abundance. And like Jupiter, the natives are oriented, just like the Archer who is aiming the arrow infinitely toward idealism. The expression associated with this sign is "I see." Jupiter endows the natives of this sign with many lavish and desirable gifts including unusual mental powers and a highly developed sense of discrimination which produces a lofty perception of justice, foresight and wisdom. Natives born to Sagittarius are executive, fearless, and determined in all their endeavors. If the influence of Jupiter is positive, it endows the natives with riches and honors and a sincere and wise character. But if the influence is negatively inclined, it makes these natives too proud, arrogant, and hypocritical with a tendency toward gambling.

Sagittarius is a secure sign for an ascending existence. The person is honest with a strong inclination for administrative activities. The native is kind, athletic and polite. He is very scrupulous in all of his activities. The symbol of this sign, the Arher who is half man and half horse, indicates two sides to the individual. One side is idealistic, philosophical and possesses aspirations for the infinite. The other side is closer to the Earth and is more materialistically inclined. In other words, there may well be found a double character - a realistic person involved with the world and an abstract nature which focuses on the ideals.

Sagittarians are known for being on the go and involved with pursuits which are far-ranging. On top of that, they are lucky people. With the enthusiasm of the Fire sign but with it the restless mutable qualities, and the joviality of Jupiter, these natives possess an expansive personality which is free roaming and cannot be confined. They find it difficult to stay in one place or one position for too long, and they find good fortune wherever they go and in whatever they do. This is the successful speculator who purchases a remote cabin in the desert just to discover it is sitting on an abandoned gold mine.

The natives of Sagittarius possess a free, adventurous nature that thrives on motivations, new ideas and a constant change of scene. The intensity of the Fire sign bestows these natives with a strongly independent nature that slows down for no one.

The greatest quality of these natives is sincerity, and the greatest defect is superficiality. Generally, these are courageous people who are honorable, outspoken, active, energetic, and versatile. They are also known to be high-spirited and congenial people who have a high regard for their freedom and space. And they manage to achieve all they do with a spirit of humor and good will. An active, restless spirit, they ask of others what they themselves most want and desire: freedom, independence, and the opportunity to seek new adventures. Granted the expression of their inner most drives and desire, Sagittarius natives strive toward and most often find successful avenues of accomplishment.

Sagittarius Personality

The symbol of the Archer suggests a double meaning in the native's personality. The Centaur is a being that is half man and half horse thus presenting itself with two natures: (1) the animal and (2) the profound, idealistic human.

The human side of this person represents those persons who rise to the highest peaks of spirituality and who cast the arrow of their aspirations over their infinity. They are humanitarians who possess a respect for laws and for morality. They live as law-abiding citizens. It is this type of individual who may become a priest or enter the field of law. These are the people who belong to that sphere of activity known as prophecy, and they are forever peering into the future.

The other side of this nature produces a person who is inclined toward the animal nature. That is, the person is worldly and seeks distractions and pleasures. These individuals develop profound interests in games and gambling such as on the horses. A joyful exuberance for life is very well developed. The desire for mobility is so great, and the person is so active, that companions may suffer. The great desire for freedom and expansion often develops from some guilt over wrong doings or harm caused to others.

These two sides to the Sagittarian personality take turns dominating the individual, and that is why it is said that this sign produces two types of people. One who is primitive and worldly and one who is an humanitarian with an elevated nature.

The Sagittarius native who is not well developed, the primitive type, is often immoral and may have problems with the law. The extreme of this type may become a revolutionary or a political or religious fanatic. Others may be inclined to join cults or to follow extreme ideas. Negative influences compel this person toward arrogance, impatience, and an exaggerated suspicious and jealous nature. This person can be not only jealous but envious and possessive in personal relationships with others. This individual is inclined to be argumentative and to have a violent temper. These people are sharply critical of even the good intentions of others, and they can be harshly derogatory in their comments and conversations. Many of these individuals are stingy and self-centered. Some become selfishly ambitious and often seek government positions where they strive to attain positions and titles. Not only are they snobs, but many become hypocrites and bigots. They possess a strong inclination to exaggerate, to lie, to misrepresent, or simply to be inaccurate in their statements. Many are found to be careless in their work and tactless in their conversations. Needless to say, these individuals will seek material possessions and quite often will realize that goal.

The well developed Sagittarius individual is the person who possesses a natural feeling of justice. This is the humanitarian who gives to charity and those in need. This is a genuine and sincere person who hates hypocrisy. This individual strives not to interfere in the affairs of others, and goes to great lengths not to cause any harm to other people. This native has a highly developed intuitive ability that enhances the personal life as well as the professional life. Not easily led, this person remains independent in nature.

How to Find Your Soul-Mate, Stars, and Destiny

Generally speaking, native Sagittarians are genuinely happy and have an optimistic outlook on life. They appear to have a wonderfully uninhibited and impulsive nature. These people are not known for being repressed or for suffering from neuroses. Free of anxieties and fears, these natives experience life as much as possible to the fullest. Not being repressed or fearful, they are open to new ideas and new methods. They are also compassionate and receptive to new people and new experiences. In fact, easy-going and open-minded, they seek these aspects of life. Extroverted and filled with wanderlust, this native appears completely free of malice. These are generous people who are always doing favors for others. Apparently, the only thing that these natives asks of others is not to tie them down with obligations. While they are enterprising in their professional lives, they may not confine themselves to one pursuit throughout life. When these people realize success, they are motivated to attempt success in another field. It is important for them to be allowed freedom in making their own decisions and personal choices.

Believe it or not many of these natives are also conservative and conventional. They are known for the promptness of their decisions and for their precise natures when in command of a situation. And the only problem many of these natives may experience is deciding between their impulse and intuition and what is considered conventional and correct.

Many of these natives possess a pioneering spirit and seek adventure and new fields of endeavors. This is the exploring pioneer who conquered the New World. This is the inventive personality that intuitively discovers new fields of endeavors or new thoughts that lead in innovative directions. In addition to that, these are versatile people who are capable of completing one task and then moving in a completely different direction.

Sagittarius natives are daring risk takers. Their boldness, however, differs from that of the Scorpio native who is more than a little competitive. The Archer directs its natives' energies toward actions and noble inspirations. Sagittarius is the sign of the pioneering spirit and of noble adventurers. Their actions are directed toward difficulties that arise in their path and not toward competition for competition's sake. These persons do not give up easily. Experiencing defeat, this native learns a lesson that instructs him or her in life and which prepares the person for new roads and new experiences and most importantly for new avenues leading to success. However, these natives frequently appear to be visionaries, forecasting and predicting the outcome of projects and pursuits with amazing accuracy.

The natives of Sagittarius possess active minds and although they are fond of engaging in frequent and compelling discussions and even in a good argument occasionally, they are generally good humored, well meaning, and original and creatively independent in thought. Being both morally and mentally brave, they can be daring in their conversations and fearless of the opinions of others. This person is inclined toward being firm and sometimes fixed in his or her personal opinions, and while expressing ideas which are positive, these ideas may not agree with the accepted opinions and beliefs of others.

Found among the Sagittarius natives is the person who possesses the inclination toward prophecy. This person peers into the future, seeking new truths, insights and wisdom. By being thoughtful and leading a serious life, this person develops inner gifts and a truly spiritual insight. The more attuned and gifted native may actually commune with the spirit world, developing this gift and becoming inspirational to society.

Often considered dreamers by others, these natives have the ability to focus their concentration. The immediate situation receives their constant and undivided attention. This trait coupled with the philosophical, abstract nature leads many of these individuals to explore insightfully the original and creative thought processes necessary to discern and understand the laws, rules, new methods, or principles inherent in everyday life or in serious studies in the various fields of science.

These individuals attain the greatest heights when they cultivate their numerous and various natural gifts. These insightful people, blessed with the luck of the stars, find success in any endeavor which requires them to utilize their inner natures and to perceive and find the answers, however complex, to the pursuits and tasks at hand.

Sagittarius Character

The symbol for the Zodiac sign of Sagittarius is very significant to its characteristics. The Archer represents the Centaur with its arrow pointed toward the infinite, toward an ideal. This is the sign of the explorer and of the philosopher, forever seeking wisdom, insight, and knowledge while in pursuit of unique experiences.

The natives of this sign are gregarious and possess qualities which enhance interpersonal relationships. They are capable of humorous, quick and convincing speech, and a willingness to participate and converse with others. They have a clear and perceptive intelligence and a pronounced intuition. Their minds are so quick, in fact, that they often complete the sentences or thoughts of others, add the punch line, offer the story ending, or attempt to solve the problem under discussion. They appear to understand situations in general rather than paying close attention to details. There is found an ease of verbal expression, but there is also noted a tendency to argue and to stick stubbornly to their point of view. It is difficult to change the mind of the Sagittarian. There is noted also some impatience, and these natives can be overly decisive and outspoken in their conversations. On occasion, there is a tendency to speak too sharply or too harshly which may offend others, but generally these natives make good and loyal friends and are seldom envious or insincere. Generosity highlights the characteristics of Sagittarius.

Obvious in the nature of the Sagittarian native is a tendency to be impulsive. They may often think, act and speak without thinking the situation through. But for the most part, they have good intentions. Being that they are positive people known for being honest, blunt and outspoken, they don't always consider that what they say may offend others. Therefore, they say the first thing that comes to their minds regardless of the beliefs or ideas of others. Being so impulsive, on occasion the individual may speak too quickly, without thinking, and make an erroneous statement or contradict something already said. But this proud person seldom admits to an error or misjudgment of this sort.

These individuals will follow an idea to its completion. They are hard working, and seldom seem to tire until taken over by exhaustion. They will concentrate all their attention on the immediate task at hand. While they are exceptionally impatient, they do not allow themselves to become discouraged. These are honorable people, but this may be dependent on whether they feel others are confident in their work, ideas and diligence.

How to Find Your Soul-Mate, Stars, and Destiny

These people handle their finances well and are known for being thrifty and economical, if not down right lucky. These natives appear to learn early on that financial well being allows for freedom and independence. They know to waste not means to want not. They are prudent without being stingy or tight, but they seem to recognize that handling money well allows them to take care of themselves and to look out for others. This person is always planning for the future.

These are mentally and physically active people. The basic sense of motion is pronounced. This is not the person to sit still or to be inactive for long periods of time. In fact, being inactive or immobile is like a torture to this person. And being self-determined, the Sagittarius native sees nothing wrong with having a bad case of wanderlust or an adventure-seeking inner drive. There is found an innately restless, curious nature that desires travel, excitement and a touch of the daring adventure as well as meeting and getting to know any number of new and interesting people. These natives are as free and independent in their physical activities as they are in their speech. And whatever or wherever their enterprising nature leads them, they retain their basic happy and jovial disposition.

It takes a special kind of courage to love travel, adventure, new places and new people. This is the kind of courage found in seeking, curious individuals. But it also requires a strong self-confidence. This person is outgoing and extroverted. Insecurities and fears do not preoccupy their minds. Neither are anxieties or nervousness a major concern for them. Their happiness is quite simply based on their ability to learn and to see, to sample and to taste, and most importantly to meet others who share this zest for life. These are not slow, prodigious thinkers who ponder a question to death seeking details. Rather, these are intuitive people who jump to the conclusion, find the answer to the puzzle, and know immediately the right path to take. In fact, in an emergency, this person doesn't panic, but jumps to action to solve the problem.

Other people may have difficulty understanding the apparently fervent activity that marks the nature of the Sagittarius native. And conversely, the natives have difficulty understanding why others aren't as feverishly active as they are. This is not the quiet, calm individual found in other signs of the Zodiac.

These natives are impatient with others who are either secretive or misleading. These individuals are direct and honest, and they respect that in other people. They are known for being congenial and warm-hearted while at the same time being frank, outspoken and to the point. This person is honest and honorable and can be brutally truthful. They recent all deceptions or deceits in others. They also possess the ability to perceive or to discern the truthfulness of others. They will subtly question another person, until the truth or the most private thoughts of the other person is divulged. They can also perceive a falsehood, and hate prevarication, deception, shams, and underhanded methods. And facing this type of opposition arouses the hasty temper of these natives. At the same time, this person is not overly curious or nosy about the affairs of others and has a tendency to mind his or her own business rather than to pry into the lives of other people. The Sagittarius native doesn't have the time to be a gossip.

These are active, outdoor people who crave both constant activity and the companionship of others. They excel at sports and other group activities. They are lively competitors always looking for the daring risk and the jovial adventure in whatever they do. Their feverish pace is contagious and they can lead their team to victory on their enthusiasm alone.

This is a complex individual, and others will have trouble truly understanding the nature of the Sagittarian. They are loyal, but they love their freedom. They don't want to be fenced in or controlled. And they can be stubborn in this regard. Their joyous congeniality attracts many people, but the complexity of their natures can offend others and it puts some people off. Then too, the very intensity and changeability of these natives leads them to extremes in many areas of their lives. These people either make strong and loyal friendships or, on the other hand, harsh adversaries.

The natives of Sagittarius are born during the time of year when the days are short and the nights are long. This may portend for them a diverse and constantly changing nature that is self-possessed, intense, strong, and above all else free to face the challenges of life. This is the person to laugh in the face of danger and to dance from dawn to dark. Jupiter grants these natives the imagination to find joy and mirth in all their endeavors. Their congenial spirits remain as long as their freedom and independence is allowed to roam uninhibited about the Earth. These are remarkable and unique people who are naturally gifted with many talents. They possess a great wisdom and perceive the world and its societies from their own perspectives. This sign has produced many famous, accomplished and successful people.

Sagittarius Destiny

The nature of the Sagittarius native is ambitious but sincere. This person is just and generous, but very independent and at times even rebellious with inclinations for being rash and impulsive. When the natural gifts are developed, the mind becomes prophetic, wise and philosophical. These individuals are strongly inclined toward freedom of thought, speech and action. They are very energetic and active both mentally and physically and while they are changeable, they are also progressive in their thoughts. There is found an appreciation for nature and wildlife as well as an affinity for domestic animals and pets. In addition to this love of the out-of-doors, there is a strong attraction and affinity for travel. These individuals also have a love for the home and family. Many Sagittarians are involved in sports or related activities. These persons possess a strong appreciation for authority. There may well be found an intense inclination toward the development of the intellect through the study of philosophy, religion, science, law or medicine.

Jupiter in rulership of this sign grants the natives, if well-aspected, a significant amount of good luck and good fortune. There is found reverence, reason, determination and ambition for these persons. They will be noted for their visions of the future, dreams, inspirations and even mystical experiences. Many appear to possess an uncanny insight into business, art, science, theologies, international affairs, literature and psychic research. Many of these individuals attain positions of dignity and power in business and in society. In fact, there often is more than one career endeavor.

If Jupiter is poorly aspected, the native is found to be restless and indecisive with a tendency to be adversely affected through rash judgments, impulsive speculations, and unfortunate investments. There is an exaggerated affinity for change and for travel. The emotions may well be overly sensitive. These individuals can be vague and uncertain and troubled by annoying dreams or visions. This destiny may see difficulties in foreign countries or adverse conditions through religious or political sentiments.

Financial gains may be realized through two sources rather than one endeavor. There is strong indication of gains realized through business endeavors associated with horses, shipping, traveling, sports, speculation, investments, legacy or an affiliation or a partnership. The early life is fortunate but may see reversals related to the positions of the parents. While there are numerous obstacles to overcome in life, success and good fortune is indicated. These natives generally succeed in time through the persistence of their own diligent natures and hard work related to their careers. There is some indication for inheritance.

The Sagittarius native is attracted to and susceptible to the opposite sex. There is an indication for more than one marriage or serious relationship and also a relationship with a person from another country. One of these relationships may cause a reversal for the position of the native. The passions of these individuals are numerous and ardent, but are most often controlled by reason.

These natives have many good friends. There is seen relationships with influential persons as well as with in-laws or friends attained through the family and through marriage. Also numerous associations are found with those affiliated with education, science, theology, and with others involved in careers related to travel. Friends prove loyal and useful to the native, but a friend may attempt unsuccessfully to cause trouble. There is also seen an enemy or enemies who attempt to cause harm or reversals to the native. An influential lady will benefit the native at a most opportune time, perhaps during a crisis. Generally, the relations with family are good although there may be seen some adversity with a parent or in-law which can lead to restraints on the native's freedoms.

These individuals are known for their frankness and remain fearless, but kind and obliging. They develop humanitarian views and are always available to offer help or assistance to society or to their community, friends and associates. There is an intuitive understanding of conditions which may lead to insights to either the welfare of society or to scientific discoveries. Oppositions, disagreements, arguments and restraints offend this native, and this resentment can hinder and prevent the attainments of desired successes, positions, or accomplishments. The development of problems associated with public affairs or the native's public reputation may occur. This individual must strive to create an individual dignity based on the merit of ability, skill and diligent hard work. Success is realized by combining the natural gifts and good luck with which these natives are generously and abundantly endowed.

Sagittarius Occupation

The Sagittarius natives possess a pioneering drive and strive to seek and to excel in new fields of endeavor. The impulse is to explore and to avoid well-used paths and methods. These people require a free rein to encounter and pursue challenging and demanding enterprises. People of action, the personal intuition and perception provides the necessary guidance, direction and discipline needed for success. These individuals are not well suited for overly dull or monotonous, routine duties or work. They most enjoy change, travel, or challenge. There is a strong inclination to pursue positions which offer expansion, growth, freedom, and opportunity for success through hard work.

Found among these natives are the most adventuresome and adept financiers, bankers, and traders. Individuals so inclined show no hesitancy in making the necessary quick decisions to realize a successful gain. Their insights and natural luck propel them to positions requiring enterprise. These are astute business professionals many of whom will prefer to go into business for themselves. Businesses requiring speculation attract many of these natives. These professions, for example, might include real estate, building contractors, and other forms of investments. These natives possess strong administrative abilities if the position allows for independent decision making, autonomy, and initiative. Others are most adept in public relations, promotional activities, advertising, and as talent agents. Careers in writing, publishing or journalism may fill your need for challenge and provide an outlet for your opinions.

Many of these natives prefer careers in the travel industry, and they appear to be born navigators, pilots, flight attendants, guides, travel industry experts, and truck drivers. They excel at sales which offer the opportunity not only to travel but to meet new and interesting people from varied backgrounds. Sagittarians can be found in government positions many of which allow for travel or relocation. Positions with oil companies or other businesses requiring its employees to travel to remote areas are also highlighted. In addition, there will be found a large number of these natives who are drawn to creative pursuits in the fields of art or music. This sign has influenced a large number of talented musicians who performed remarkably creative, imaginative, and forceful interpretations as well as original renditions and performances. In any of these career choices, it is the native's energy and enthusiasm combined with ability and a perceptive personality that gains this person promotions, advancements, and successes.

There are any number of Sagittarians who discover fulfillment in careers related to environment, nature, wildlife and animals. These people make excellent veterinarians, ranchers, biologists, natural scientists, parks and wildlife employees, and persons involved with animal husbandry. The travel involved in training and showing animals may appeal to this person.

Any number of these individuals will be drawn to fields involved with sports, sports training or other vocations involved with such activities. Racing and not only the risk but the speculation associated with it attracts numerous natives of this sign.

It goes without saying that many Sagittarius are drawn to the humanitarian fields of sociology, theology, and any field requiring an interest in the overall social welfare of others. The highly developed native more than likely will also be a forceful and inspiring speaker. Positions related to the law or politics are also favorable. Other individuals become competent and talented counselors and psychologists. Many feel at home in an academic setting which offers the opportunity for new learning and for self-expression.

Sagittarius should never cease to be actively engaged either in physical or mental pursuits. For them, this inactivity would lead to an overwhelming despondency. Their natural instincts lead them to strive for the greatest possible opportunities for development, enlightenment, achievement and success. While physically energetic and active, these natives enjoy remaining cognitively active as well. Generally speaking, they are well organized and efficient, that is, as long as the tasks at hand are not boring or monotonous. These individuals are ingenious and inventive. They love to devise new methods of convenience or efficiency both at home and in the office. Then too, there are others who discover their own personal systems which may not appear all that well organized to others.

Luck and drive propels the Sagittarius natives. Give these individuals room to roam, space for expansiveness and abundant opportunity for creating and seeking new avenues and interests. Their pursuits will be numerous and varied, and often enough more staid and conventional individuals will be amazed at their successes.

Sagittarius Marriage

Jupiter, the ruling planet of this sign, in many instances indicates problems and inharmonious situations related to the domestic affairs of these natives. Unfortunately, many of these natives jump into marriage impulsively. It is not unusual for them to marry young and for the marriage not to last. Many natives will marry more than once. Other natives, too proud to admit any marital problems, or invariably too conventional to seek legal assistance, or too stubborn to benefit from counseling, will hide behind the pretensions of a harmonious marital relationship. This will invariably lead to unhappiness and unfulfillment.

It is most important for these individuals, known for their care free and freedom loving ways, to select partners carefully. The natural tendency for the Sagittarius native is to be loyal, devoted and faithful. In many there are found rather profound and definite ideals along this line. The problem arises, however, with the difficulty these natives find in expressing their emotions and repressing their restless nature which in some instances can lead to infidelities. For success in this area of your life, your marriage partner must be understanding. You require a person with a strong sense of humor and joy in life. Someone who tries to tie you down, break your spirit and control you will only succeed in harming you. Your partner should be independent and emotionally secure. Secure enough to allow you your wings and then wait patiently to see if you return. This type of person is difficult to find, but they do exist. And most often they are talented, creative and ambitious in their own pursuits and have every wish for you to lead your life and fulfill your dreams.

You may well find the most suitable marriage partners in the sign of Gemini which is your opposite sign. The opposite signs are known to possess complimentary personalities. Gemini (May 21-June 21) natives are known for pursuing change, challenges, and new endeavors in a creative manner. They are lively, sociable, imaginative and fun loving. A Gemini may well be the perfect compliment for the Sagittarius native.

Leo (July 23-August 22) and Libra (September 23-October 22) natives may also possess many compatible traits. Leo natives are independent and love travel, adventure and meeting new people. And the Sagittarius sense of humor may grace you with the ability to deal with Leo's vain ego. Sensual Libra may well know how to slow down your roaming fancy, and at any rate, this native is tolerant and won't explode over passing trivialities. Some astrologers forecast success with another Sagittarius native, but both of these individuals must be well developed. Also, it is felt that Aquarius (January 20-February 18) natives are equally fun loving, idealistic and innovative.

Take special care with Aries (March 21-April 20) who will make every attempt to cage you in, and Taurus (April 21-May 20) and Scorpio (October 23-November 21) who can be overly controlling. Cancer (June 22-July 22) is too sensitive, Pisces (February 19-March 20) too emotionally dependent, and Capricorn (December 21-January 19) too demanding, and there's little sense in mentioning serious Virgo (August 23-September 22).

It goes without saying that for the Sagittarius individual to find harmony in marriage there is required of the two partners involved an equity in development, and shared interests and values. You are a most delightful person, and the right person will adore your many positive and expansive traits. Life with you promises to be filled with adventure, new experiences and new avenues of thought. Choose carefully a mate who appreciates all the many gifts which you possess that you would love to share with a special and deserving person.

The Sagittarius Man

The Sagittarius man is most generally optimistic, jovial and capable of discovering a special joy to living. He may well be the ultimate risk taker who enjoys adventures on all planes of life. He is known for his generosity in dealing with his friends, family and associates. It is quite possible that this man will possess lofty ideas, be perceptive and possess an insightful vision of the future. He is most likely athletic and pursues with great energy a number of various sports and associated activities. He has the capability for swiftness of thought, movement, and perceptions. It is noted that he may well be the person to have around in times of emergencies for he acts quickly and decisively, knowing intuitively the right move to make.

It might be noted that you perceive your world from a personal vantage point, and you possess a unique outlook and perspective on life and human nature. You appear able to immediately grasp the situation at hand or the problem being discussed or analyzed.

You are futuristic and ponder with an intuitive nature the realms of possibilities existing in the human condition. Yours is the humanitarian sign, and the philosophical nature of being holds a special significance for you. Emotionally, also, you may discover yourself on another plane of existence wondering what others are making such a great fuss over. For you, life, while requiring insight and thought, was designed to be enjoyed and lived to the fullest.

This man is virile and secure within himself, knowing that all of life's needs will be met. He loves freedom and sampling life and all that life has to offer. This man may well be involved in any number of romantic affairs which may be brief but entertaining. Upon becoming involved in a more serious relationship, he is protective, affectionate and tender, but that doesn't mean that he is necessarily faithful. While he may be a productive and supportive husband, he may be prone to infidelities. However, these are seldom serious and often are found to be just passing fancies. It is important that this man is appreciated for himself, and whether he admits it or not, he needs to be complimented, praised and respected. He is a bit more sensitive in this respect than he shows the world.

You may be considered conservative and dignified or, just the opposite, an impulsive risk taker who is seeking the most adventuresome activity available. Either way, you are most likely loyal to your friends and associates and generous in your nature. This person is considered for the most part thrifty and wise and unbelievably fortunate and lucky in any and all speculations.

There will be obstacles, difficulties and many times sad experiences in the lives of these natives, but this man most likely attempts to overcome them. You pursue success through diligence and hard work using your insights and natural gifts to better your position in life and to find fulfillment and success in your many endeavors. You may marry more than once, and all indications are that you will have more than one successful career in your life. You will face uphill climbs and will meet with success.

You most generally possess a high expectation for yourself and for others and at times this can be the cause of creating obstacles in your own life. You have a tendency to be a bit impatient with others when they don't meet up to your standards or understand your logic. This can lead to you being somewhat self-righteous in your stubborn demand that you are right. This tendency is easily enough overcome if you consciously attempt to be more tolerant and understanding of the positions and perspective of others. Your usually strong interpersonal skills can only improve with this effort.

It goes without saying that the poorly developed man of this sign possesses the negative traits of being possessive and jealous in relationships. This man has a tendency to be too harsh and critical of others and can be very demanding. Some will be too involved in seeking the pleasure and thrill of the adventure rather than developing the diligence required for success. The instant success of the gambler who speculates on life and on fortune is most desired. Hypocritical, selfish and many times lazy or unmotivated, this man may not be the person to place your trust in. On the other hand, the poorly aspected man can be arrogantly bigoted and suspicious of others, and will at the same time seek to attain a good position in life even if it means stealing, lying or cheating. If this person discovers he possesses the luck of Jupiter, he will no doubt use it to better his position in life, and as has been noted, quite often he will succeed.

There will be any number of obstacles faced by the well-aspected Sagittarius man, and whatever obstacles come your way, they will find you with a smile on your face willing and able to persevere and to continue upward in life. Yours is the quest for the inner development that is necessary to sustain you in life and to successfully produce the results which you most want to attain. Not afraid of striving, of taking the necessary risk to achieve, yours will be anything but a dull life. Your natural talents and inclinations will carry you far, and you will realize any number of successes on the road of life. Always the humanitarian, this man will strive to improve himself, his knowledge, and his insights into the world not only for his own personal use but for the betterment of society in general. His prophetic nature will inspire him as well as others to strive for a better existence and for the improvement of social institutions.

THE SAGITTARIUS WOMAN

This woman is sparkling, witty and entertaining. She loves the company of others and seeks social occasions and group gatherings in order to glow in the presence of others. She also possesses a keen and well developed intellect which she isn't afraid of showing off. This woman more than likely possesses a strong appreciation for the beauty and wonder of nature and is drawn to outdoor activities. She may well be the female athlete who inspires the team to victory. She is proud and determined and has a profound love for her freedom of movement and thought.

You possess a strong humanitarian nature and have a deep and concerned interest in the well being of others. You also have a generous nature. You are loyal and sincere to family, friends and associates. This is not the woman inclined to be the gossip or to be found prying into the affairs of others. You wish no ill will on other people. The chances are that your life is so busy, your schedule so full with daily activities, that there is no time for idle past times.

It would be remiss not to mention that the Sagittarius woman is inclined to be rash and impulsive. But then we all have negative traits to work on. You may also display a temper on occasion and this may in part be due to an impatience. Your moods know the heights of happiness and at other times the melancholy of sadness. This woman wants to carry on, to get on with life, to see what adventure she is possibly missing out on. More seriously-inclined people may need to move out of the way, and let this lady pass. You can size up a situation or a person in a flash and keep on moving. At times, others may find your comments too harsh, but that could be their problem as much as yours.

If poorly developed, the women of this sign are fretful to the point of endless crying spells in attempts to gain what they want. They are often lazy and lack motivation and can be demanding, stubborn, and jealous.

On the other hand, a well developed Sagittarius, you love life and move through relationships with the flair and ease of a skilled romantic. It isn't that you aren't serious in your relationships, but you possess an insatiable curiosity and an urge to meet new people and to sample new adventures. You are sensitive to admiration and without it, love has no meaning to you.

When this woman does settle down and marry, it is best she find an understanding and compatible mate. Preferably, someone who is enthralled with her charm and appeal. She then devotes herself to loving and caring and providing a warm home atmosphere. She adores being admired by her husband and will prefer an unconditional love. She loves to help her husband be successful and will sacrifice to make the home life successful as well. The Sagittarius female is generally more faithful in marriage then the male of this sign. They possess an intense love of home and family and even if unhappily married will strive to turn it into a success. If this woman becomes fretful, it is because she lacks enough outlets for her abundant energies, drives, and ambitions or because she isn't receiving enough love and affection. And if she finds herself tied to a truly unfit spouse, this woman shows no remorse in taking away his throne and finding another more suitable relationship.

HOW TO FIND YOUR SOUL-MATE, STARS, AND DESTINY

You find yourself forever striving to overcome your current limitations in order to reach beyond your present situation or understanding. Under the rulership of Jupiter, you strive to discover answers to the many questions that perpetually pop into your mind. Forward looking and forever seeking, you quite often become impatient not only with others but with the very pace of life, especially when you perceive that situations, for example, fail to live up to your ideals. The lure of travel entices your ever-seeking mind and learning a new language for just that prospect of future travel may appeal to you. Or you may discover that your yearning for new knowledge makes you a life-long student, if not in an academic setting, than in your personal life. And through it all, you strive for a fuller understanding and a connection to a spiritual enlightenment and may seek to attain a higher consciousness. If you feel discontent and frustrated at times, it may well be that you are actually experiencing the limitations of being only human.

You too may find that you need to guard against being a bit self-righteous and feeling that your ideas are best and you know what is right. This natural impatience and stubbornness can easily be redirected toward positive understandings and furthering your own personal goals. Through improving your meditative spirit, and by continuing to study, travel, write or teach others, you can become inspiring to others. By overcoming any dogmatic thinking, you can learn to harmonize and to balance your actions and thoughts with your higher thinking abilities. You can develop a strong sense of personal power when you realize and fully understand that your natural gift of freedom of expression can lead you to greater potentials.

The Sagittarius woman is endowed by Jupiter with a loving and jovial nature. With the many gifts granted the women of this sign, and possessing the remarkable gift of good luck, you will seek and most often find success in many areas of your life. Your inner nature moves you forward not only in your domestic situation, but with your friends and associates. You make an ideal friend. You are the social person, but you also strive toward success and fulfillment in your career or financial life. You make your mark on life and keep on moving.

Sagittarius Love Life

The influence of Jupiter in the sign of Sagittarius influences these natives to be fortunate. These individuals take an optimistic outlook on life, and even when difficulties are encountered, they tend to find the bright side to the situation. Disliking monotony and routine, these pleasant people are drawn to variety. Their natural vivaciousness, generosity and warm-hearted nature draws and attracts other people to them. They are forward-looking and know that the future holds new and delightful experiences for them. They can be idealistic people in their relationships with the opposite sex, striving to find the perfect companion and being at times somewhat difficult to please. Life in the present doesn't necessarily always appeal to the philosophical Archer. And in this person's drive to be open-minded and honest, there can be found also a trait that leans toward being blunt, frank, and out-spoken. Naturally independent and freedom loving, these natives require another person who is just as strong and secure and who loves life.

The libido appears quite normal in these individuals, and the number of their affairs isn't based on being over-sexed. It is more likely due to an overwhelming desire to sample as much of life and as much variety in life as is humanly possible. A great deal of affection, amiability and friendship is found in the relationships of Sagittarians. These are well meaning people who simply love to be involved with others. They are impulsively pulled to the excitement and passion of being involved with others. These natives are the perfect playmates, loving affection and attention, praise and fun. Each new encounter becomes a learning experience from which can be drawn lessons for future encounters. Sagittarius natives love to flirt and covert, to flaunt their charms and fun-loving ways. And like the other Fire signs, Aries and Leo, there is a strong tendency to be impulsively caught up by your strong passions.

A relationship with either Leo (July 23-August 22) or Aries (March 21-April 20) may leave you panting and electrically charged. You may find that the slower pace of Taurus (April 21-May 20) is enduringly satiable but somewhat too unwieldy. Gemini (May 21-June 21) is sweetly charming and intensely magnetic and may well satisfy your desire for excitement. Cancer (June 22- July 22) entices your need for sensuality and romantic creativity, but the moodiness of this person may wear on your jovial nature. Virgo (August 23-September 22) can be so warm and loving, but their domestic nature may limit your freedom loving ways. Libra's flair for fun and tolerant acceptance of your worst qualities, you find endearing. You may also find yourself swept away by the intensity of Scorpio (October 23-November 21) so be sure to hold on to your heart. Another Sagittarius native will best share an understanding of your mutual natures and you can talk endlessly about your ideals of life over candle lit dinners. Capricorn (December 21-January 19) may catch your curiosity but will be too serious for you. Aquarius (January 20-February 18) and you share a drive to be original and creative and this would be a fun relationship. Also, the imagination of Pisces (February 19-March 20) fires your own creative spirit although the two of you may never truly understand one another.

To find that special ecstasy you seek, search for an open minded person who won't immediately begin installing limitations in your life. The other person in your life must be willing to accept you the way you are. And you love above all else your freedom of thought, movement and expression. Attempts to change you will only lead to endless efforts, discussions and at times arguments. In any relationship, you will maintain a strong preference for preserving your independence. Perhaps it is best to attempt to make the other person feel secure by instilling in your relationship that sense of who you are and what you want. Establishing a loving and caring friendship as well as a passionate sexual relationship will help to create an accepting atmosphere.

You are interested and drawn to ideal human potentials and to any and all possibilities for enhancing the limits of experience, and by doing so you gain knowledge and perceptions that lead you through life. And this knowledge also includes a desire to delight in the companionship of others who also enjoy the grand adventure of life. Your buoyant nature is enhanced by the attractions and attentions of the opposite sex, and you find yourself delighting in love and that glamorous feeling that surrounds your amorous nature when you meet a special person who inspires those feelings in you. Take heed Sagittarius. Many a romantically inclined person will seek you out and enjoy all which you have to offer.

SAGITTARIUS CHILDREN

These young natives are extroverted, gregarious and kind. Born to the sign of Sagittarius, they are influenced to be affectionate and sensitive. They possess a normal active and restless nature and a slight tendency to be quick tempered. These children desire to be appreciated for their kind and affectionate natures. They love to receive understanding and praise from the adults in their lives.

Encouraged by understanding and acceptance, these children become devoted to activities, tasks and chores which make life for everyone in the family more pleasant. This is by nature an unselfish child who loves to please others. The personality is pleasant and pleasing, and this child will strive to maintain an ambiance of good will toward family and play mates. Cruelty is not normally a part of their nature. There may well be found a strong love of nature, animals and also physically active games and sports. And others may love to read in order to be involved with educational activities whether it be a craft, hobby, skill or intellectual endeavor.

Exposed to unacceptance or a restraining, unpleasant environment, this child will become taciturn and restless. A warm and loving home life is most important for this child to develop well. It is possible that without these necessary aspects of life, this child may withdraw within himself or on the hand become particularly rebellious.

Being fun loving and gregarious young people, it is important that guidance be available to steer these children into positive and constructive past times. An abundance of pleasant social activities should be planned as well as a number activities that also provide for the development of this child's curious intellect. Theirs is a naturally sunny disposition and the nice temperament and cheerfulness of these children will be best enhanced if they are provided outlets for their abundant energy, both mental and physical. While guidance is being provided, remember that these children also require a great deal of freedom of choice and need to be included in the planning and selecting of entertainment and activities. Be careful not to carry this to an extreme, however, because this very quality of loving freedom can also lead to irresponsibility or a certain laziness. It might appear necessary to make work seem interesting and more like fun to attract this child's attention. A guiding hand in these matters can best lead these children to make good decisions in choosing their past times and pursuits.

This is also an intuitive child who, with proper guidance, can learn to develop his or her natural gifts of perception. And these are strong skills that benefit these children in wise decision making. These children also exhibit strong abilities to concentrate and to discern the topic of discussion. Again input from concerned parents and educators should be focused on helping these children to learn to be thorough and to complete the tasks they have started. Like all children, the Sagittarius born child can be careless and impulsive. Attracted to the companionship of others, they may have a tendency to be overly involved in activities outside the home. And at times this child may appear to be too candid, critical or harsh in his or her remarks or opinions. Guidance and supervision is necessary in this aspect of the child's life in order to be certain that their activities are acceptable and beneficial to the child's well being. And, of course, good manners and tact are learned by positive role models who exhibit just those traits. Over time, patience can also be fostered and learned, and again this is often something that is learned through the positive examples of others.

A positive, loving and accepting environment will most benefit this child. Criticism and discipline should be presented in the most beneficial and positive manner possible. This will require a parent who is both a talented diplomat and a good care provider. A true and loving concern for the welfare of this child will produce a particular strength of character and nature. And whatever the life choices of this child, it is important that the family remain loving, accepting and emotionally supportive throughout life. As a parent, you will find the experience much more enjoyable if you accept and love this child and foster an environment of tolerant understanding.

This joyful child will bring much happiness and warmth to the home life, pleasing the entire family with his or her kind and loving nature. This child's natural gifts may well see him or her through a childhood filled with pleasant and endless pursuits, surrounded by friends, companions and family members.

Relationships with Other Signs

Sagittarius energy and drive provide others with the ability to perceive the thrill of adventurous experience. These individuals can be found pursuing the thrill of sports and athletics to chasing around the world exploring and meeting new people and making new friends. Their encounters with others are prodigious. They seek others who are responsible, reliable and who share a loving need for fun and amusement. At the same time, these natives can be philosophical and idealistic and will discuss at length their notions pertaining to the meaning of life. These individuals may well be the rugged people found climbing the highest peak or camping in the wilderness. In order not to overly generalize, it should be noted that there is also the Sagittarius native who is conservative and reserved and who prefers to adopt a steadier pace in their daily lives. But this native also shares the love of knowledge and his or her curiosity regarding life is just as strong.

Be that as it may, these natives have gained a reputation for being pleasant, cheerful, optimistic and likable. Yes, they make enemies too, but these are often people who are offended by their outspoken, candid, and sometimes blunt speech habits. Then again, like many other people, these natives possess a quick temper which can result in harsh words. But given a moment to relent, the native will most probably come out with an enduring and kind remark.

The Sagittarius native are sincere and honest, to the point of being frank, and they possess a generous, caring and giving nature. They can make persevering and dependable friends or associates.

Relations and associations with Aries are good as this person also possesses a driving energy. Taurus may be too temperamental, but you will admire this person's tenacious tendencies. Strong affinities can exist with Gemini individuals who may share mutual interests. You may discover sincere and lasting friendships with Cancer natives and this sign is good for productive professional relations. You and Leo are both sincere, impulsive and loyal and share a mutual flair for fully savoring life. Good friendships and work relations can be established with the fair-minded Libra native who also values the humanitarian aspects of life, and you will find a mutual respect between yourself and Scorpio natives. Advantageous relationships may well exist between you and other native Sagittarians as well as with Capricorn individuals. Both you and Aquarius are active and dynamic, but Pisces may be too demanding on your time and energy.

Your most favored relationships will be realized with individuals born between March 18 to April 30, or July 24 to August 30, and from May 18 to June 25. Beneficial relationships can also be developed with other Sagittarius natives who share your intuitive perception of life.

As a Fire sign, Sagittarius influences it's natives with the positive qualities of enthusiasm, a self-propelled energy, and an inner drive that relentlessly pushes this person. These individuals challenge the more timid, the fearful, the introverted, and the insecure to sample the more fruitful and joyous aspects of life. Life can be a grand adventure full of surprises, highs and lows, experiences that are either good or at other times painful, and numerous obstacles. With all of that in mind, Sagittarius natives continue to strive to encounter and fully experience as much of life as possible. This is often displayed in your humorous and demonstrative nature which offers others a small sampling of what life could be if we lived it to the fullest.

At the same time, you encourage social awareness and the investigation of ideas and values. It is your very expansive nature which seeks new places and experiences that provide you with the needed insights and perceptions to offer intuitive and informative observations on people, social problems and cultural needs. It is this very aspect of your personality, that is, your humanitarian inclination that others find admirable. And being both well-informed and gregarious, you are admired by your friends and associates and discover numerous outlets for your overly abundant energy and drives. Add to that your love for being outdoors and physically active, and you find that you are surrounded by other people who appreciate these activities too. Fresh air and open spaces draw you almost as much as the possibility of meeting and sharing the experience with others. Plan many excursions, but remember that others will appreciate this aspect of your personality, so include your friends as well.

You are a person who can succeed at life and at any number of endeavors while at the same time winning the loyalty and devotion of friends and associates. Seek other people in life who appreciate and love not only the same things that you do, but who admire you for who you are and for what you believe in. You will no doubt discover any number of people who want to get to know you and to become long lasting friends.

Sagittarius Sexuality

That subject which interests us all: our own personal sexuality. Why does a person feel the way they do? Why does he or she like a certain person and not another? What arouses a person and why? On some level, these questions influences one and all. Like all aspects of our lives and lifestyles, the public attitude toward sex is ever changing and evolving. From the restrictive taboos of the Victorian Age, through the revitalization of the Industrial Age, to the make love not war of the 1960s to the commercialism of the 1980s and the 1990s, sex is always on our minds. Will the Age of Information or the Age of Aquarius bring new insights?

The American culture is not only influenced by popular trends and thought but by its unique cultural diversity as well. To the newcomer or newly arrived, American society can appear perplexing. What is difficult to understand is that in this freedom-based culture, the individual is literally free to be whoever he or she decides. And the gamut runs from the most traditional, reserved, cautious, and sexually repressed individuals to others who flaunt their sexuality, centering their lives around their sexual habits. Perhaps it is because of this very diversity that our culture makes some attempt not to be overly offensive to the sensitivities of some while giving a tolerant nod to the liberties of others. We are totally free, within the guidelines of laws, to seek divine enlightenment or to destroy ourselves with pleasures. Americans have the freedom to choose, individually, what importance their sexual behavior will play in their lives.

How to Find Your Soul-Mate, Stars, and Destiny

That being the case, sex is recognized by every serious discipline--from psychologists to scientists to astrologers--as being a central focus on individual lives. Freud saw sex as an influence on every aspect of the individual life. And from the sexist boys in the locker room to the most enlightened of intellectuals, sex remains a fundamental part of life that cannot be ignored. Get two friends together and the subject eventually turns to sex, romance, or marriage. One can blame it on the media, but sooner or later discussing the stock market gets boring, but sex never does.

There are those who hold to the theory that the primary function of sex is to have children and any other consideration is secondary. There are others for whom sex is an integral part of life, providing one of the greatest stress relievers ever invented. That all other living species procreate seasonally points to the reasoning of the second theory. But all pleasures (or temptations) in life also promote the possibilities of problems and health concerns unless a little logic is also applied.

Astrologically, the sexual nature has been examined from the Garden of Eden to the lives of contemporary celebrities. And what every serious astrologer will say is that how the individual relates to sexuality is not based on the Sun sign alone. The entire chart must be examined because each person is a unique combination of Sun, Moon, Ascendant, planets, Houses and aspects. A comparison of two charts often sheds light on compatibility. Compatibility between two people is often found when the Sun sign is in the same sign as their lover's Ascendant, or vice versa. Opposite Sun signs or an opposite Sun sign and Ascendant may also blend well together.

In a woman's chart, the placement of Venus is indicative of her sexuality while the position of Mars and the Sun indicates what kind of man she is attracted to. In a man's chart, the position of Mars tells how he relates to women, and the position of Venus and the Moon indicates what type of woman arouses him. In comparing two charts, look for the aspects of conjunction, sextile, square, trine, and oppositions. Remember that oppositions can blend. The square brings differences but much energy while conjunctions can be beneficial. The sextile and trine bring harmony. When a person's Venus and their lover's Mars are in the same sign, there is a strong attraction even if differences of opinions occur. When Venus and the other person's Ascendant are in the same sign, it adds to the sexual compatibility. Venus in the lover's sun sign brings a mutual interest while Mars in the lover's Moon sign is emotionally intense.

There is a vast variety of people found within each Sun sign, but basic characteristics and traits do exist. However, generalizations are just that and a fuller picture of the individual is reflected by the complete chart. The following section deals with Sun sign sexuality in a general manner. While the importance of sex remains the same in each Sun sign, the focus and attitudes vary.

SAGITTARIUS SEXUALITY - MAN

Have no doubts that a Sagittarius man thoroughly enjoys the novelty of the chase and the eventual conquest. The philosopher of the Zodiac gathers information by observing and asking question after question, but when it comes to his sexuality he will prefer to gather his information first hand. The symbol of Sagittarius is the Archer, half horse and half man, and it is said that with his bow and arrow, he is always on the hunt. And being that he is so lucky with love and romance, he has been called the Don Juan of the Zodiac. This may have something to do with his philosophical nature as opposed to the emotional nature of other signs. Generally speaking, Sagittarius is not in a big hurry to settle down to the ties that bind as in marriage. There may be those impulsive Sagittarius who marry young, but as a rule, Sagittarius prefers to take his time, gather plenty of experiences, and look around at what's available before taking that final leap. And this man will travel far and wide in search of experiences. On the lighter side, he likes jokes and pranks and may be prone to exaggerate which can also mean that he has gathered plenty of useful and successful lines. Add to that his natural persuasiveness and what woman stands a chance against his winning ways? Many a Sagittarius will use the luck of Jupiter, his ruling planet, to gamble or speculate, and he isn't afraid of taking a chance on romance either. But, as he prances through the sexual act, he can depend too heavily on luck and get himself into sticky circumstances. That he is ever ready for romance but hesitant about serious relationships, gets him into hot water with any number of woman, but this rarely slows down his meandering.

This man can be cheerful, optimistic and enthusiastic, and sex is another avenue for enjoying life to its fullest. The fact that so many people take sex so seriously rather than enjoying its many pleasures may confuse him. If it wasn't meant to be so enjoyable than why, he may ask, is it so enjoyable. That kind of logic can be difficult to argue with especially when he is so available to prove his point.

Philosophical and unconventional Sagittarius was probably the first to introduce the naturalness of masturbation and self play. And finally modern psychology caught on to this profound bit of knowledge and told the rest of the Zodiac that this is perfectly healthy even for children. It is now accepted that if grandma spanked your hand and told you not to touch yourself there, she was being old-fashioned and should have said not in public dear. With that convention out the window, anyone and everyone is now at liberty to enjoy the same degree of freedom as Sagittarius. This man is not about to allow any restrictions or limitations to his personal freedoms.

He adores the beauty, energy and openness of youth which matches his own outgoing and outspoken nature, and he may prefer younger sexual partners. In fact, it may have been a profound Sagittarius who termed the phrase, "get them young and train them right". He likes plenty of fun and laughter in his relationships as well, and may prefer to have two or three relationships going on at the same time. Jupiter grants opportunities along with luck, and this man is one to take advantage of every opportunity that comes his way. He has a wide range of interests, loves to socialize, and has a natural affinity for the outdoors all of which provides him with a wide basis of finding attractive partners who share his interests. He much prefers change, variety, novelty, and adventure, and this isn't a man to easily allow himself to be controlled by another.

There's no question that Sagittarius will shoot his arrows far and wide and with his penetrating interest in sex he will forever be on the hunt experimenting and sampling the pleasures offered by one and all. There's every chance that he will prance his clumsy way through the entire Zodiac before stumbling over that perfect female who throws a loop around his meandering and slows his pace to a steady halt.

Sagittarius is a true sportsman and a good sport who gives as well as he takes. While many of his personal preferences are actually quite healthy, more serious-natured people can be offended by his casual attitude toward his sexuality. But as profound Sagittarius will tell anyone willing to listen, that is their problem and not his. He is quick-witted, freedom-loving, and farsighted, and if others can't keep up with his logic, he may not have the time to slow down and explain himself. His alert mind is always moving on to the next opportunity, or conquest as the case may be, and his physically active body is only too happy to cooperate. This is a man who knows how to have a good time and is only too happy to share that experience with another.

Sagittarius Sexuality - Woman

Woman are culturally, historically, and socially told that they are suppose to grow up and get married and to want to do just that. The free-spirited Sagittarius woman may go against her intuition and her nature and impulsively succumb to this social conditioning at an early age only to wonder why she feels so confined and unhappy. It is just as likely that a Sagittarius woman will go against the dictates and conventions of society and wait until she is good and ready before she gives up her liberties and freedoms. She is a little struck by wanderlust and wants to see and experience a great deal of life before she settles down to home and family. Like the male Sagittarius, this precocious female may have begun her sexual exploration at an early age and sees nothing wrong with that at all. More intuitive than the male, she instinctively views sex as a natural and fun part of life. After all, humans are sexual beings so what is the point of repressing that facet of life. Of course, she learns early that what is socially acceptable for a man is not socially acceptable for a woman, and she may learn to wear a conventional mask and to keep her sexual adventures to herself. She also learns to be somewhat wary of men because no matter how casual they claim to be, they can suddenly become possessive and controlling. Because of this, this woman may develop a greater insight and fear of consequences than is present in the male Sagittarius. And she may learn to pick and choose carefully from among the only too willing and eager available men. In fact, the sophisticated Sagittarius woman may decide upon a convenient arrangement with a suitable partner which provides for a mutual sexual outlet without the dangers of promiscuity. Whatever her decisions in this matter, her sexual preference is for entertaining, fun, and pleasurable sexual affairs which satisfy both partners involved. Her casual attitude may upset the heavy-breathing types, but it suits her just fine. And if her partner attempts to pin her down to explanations of why she is the way she is, this may be the cue for her to take her leave and find her sexual fulfillment somewhere else with someone else.

Being profoundly philosophical herself, this woman is drawn to intellectual discourse and is even more pleased when those conversations are with mefi. Women, she finds, have a tendency to girl-talk rather than to fully discuss the more important matters of life. Sooner or later, she may discover that most of her friends are men. Whether or not this leads to the opportunity for sex depends greatly upon the individual female involved. Of course, with men the opportunity is always there, but she may become somewhat discerning and prefer that particular man who can maintain a casual relationship without reading more into it than is actually there.

What she needs, of course, is a truly liberated man who is willing to allow her the freedom to live her own lifestyle whether that means a career or a move to the other side of the country. When she's free within a relationship to have her own personal preferences and is not hemmed in by a confining relationship, then she finds happiness. If this doesn't happen, and she finds herself in a less than satisfying relationship, she can turn into a very unhappy and unpleasant woman. And that can last until she determines that it isn't her partner who is necessarily doing anything wrong, but it is simply her who is unhappy with the confinement of the relationship.

Of course, there are different types of Sagittarius women, and one type may be that female who has waited out a long list of admirers only to be swept off her feet by an overly aggressive type who, once he has her for his own, becomes not only domineering but abusive. Another type is the Sagittarius woman who in all this waiting has figured out that as long as she is waiting she may as well look for partner who is as financially healthy as he is physically fit for sex. It is only logical to assume that it is just as easy to love a wealthy man as a poor one, and no one has ever accused Sagittarius of not being smart enough to figure this out. There is also that Sagittarius female who is all heart, and when her adventurous nature has been satiated, she is more than willing to fall in love and settle down with the man of her dreams. Of course, it helps if that man has a healthy interest in sexual activities.

This is a lively and lovely woman who is looking for experiences including those of a sexual nature. She is adventurous and daring and willing to use her opportunities and good luck to her advantage. And needless to say, there is something to learn from her carefree ways.

Sagittarius Health

The Zodiac sign of Sagittarius rules the hips, thighs and liver, and Jupiter, the ruling planet, governs the liver. Some astrologers also associate Jupiter with the pituitary gland which regulates hormone production and some aspects of physical growth. Overall, Sagittarius are noted for being strong and healthy individuals.

Being active and full of energy, Sagittarius natives may experience more accidents than illnesses. Especial care should be taken to strengthen the back, hip and leg muscles in an effort to prevent strain or injury to the sciatic nerve which runs from the hip down the legs. Some natives are prone to fractures, sprains, pulled muscles or torn ligaments. Others may suffer from bruises, swelling or vericose veins in the legs. Proper footwear and clothing goes a long way in preventing sports accidents or other injuries to active people.

Those natives with a sensitive liver may find themselves susceptible to hepatitis. And of course these natives need to take care not to over indulge in alcohol which over a period of time can cause irreversible damage to the liver. It is found that any number of these natives suffer from rheumatism. Others may be prone to infections and problems with the throat, ears and bronchial tubes. In some, there is a tendency for skin infections and other afflictions of the skin. Some natives develop a tendency to gain weight with age which can lead to any number of associated problems. It is found that there are those Sagittarius natives who appear to suffer from nervous disorders perhaps brought on by running on nervous energy alone. And many of these natives have a tendency to overwork or to be over active in their daily lives which can, for some, wear the body down over time.

The temperament of these individuals requires activity and to remain active throughout life requires an adequate health regime. As with other natives, the Sagittarius individual must take the time to establish a healthy diet, and in this case it should be one which provides the necessary energy to maintain an active lifestyle. Each individual should evaluate his or her lifestyle and then plan an appropriate diet. Needless to say, green and leafy vegetables, fruits and grains and an appropriate amount of carbohydrates and proteins are necessary for an athletic or active life. Some caution must be taken not to eat in too much haste which can cause stomach problems for some people.

Remember that adequate exercise prevents weight gain, but also that exercise should be determined by age and condition. Conditioning your body may also prevent accidents. Rather you choose walking, jogging, weight lifting or aerobics, take care to plan your time and activities carefully. And the more active sports minded athletes among you should take the time to be well conditioned and prepared for whatever activity is planned. Being well informed about health and fitness, and knowledgeable and attuned with your body is more than likely the best approach for the Sagittarius native.

Your personal health and fitness will see you through the upcoming years, and it is up to you to plan for your body, your health and your welfare. An active life, a full schedule and all those new experiences you desire are contingent upon your health. More than likely, you are introspective as well as intuitive, and developing your meditative abilities can only enhance your overall life.

History of Sagittarius

The Archer, the symbol for the sign of Sagittarius, represents the famous centaur, Chiron. Chiron was a famous prophet, doctor and scholar trained in the arts of medicine, hunting, sports and music. He became the famous instructor of many outstanding Greek heroes of mythology including Castor, Pollux, Jason, Achilles, Peleus and Hercules. Perhaps the message here is that being a famous educator who was half horse, people must learn to control their worldly natures.

As the story goes, Hercules accidentally shot Chiron in the knee with an arrow. Because Chiron was an immortal, he could not die, but his suffering from this injury was great. Hercules journeyed to find Death to release Chiron from his agony. He came across Prometheus who was being punished by Jupiter by being chained to a boulder where an eagle ate at his liver. Jupiter's curse provided that if anyone would volunteer to suffer in his place, Prometheus could be released. Hercules volunteered Chiron to take Prometheus' place and the curse was fulfilled, freeing Prometheus and allowing Chiron to die. As a reward for Chiron's noble character, some say Jupiter, some say Zeus placed Chiron among the stars as the constellation of Sagittarius.

The ancient Babylonians pictured Sagittarius as a scorpion beneath the stomach of a horse. Other depictions present the symbol as a man with a scorpion's body and tail, but with human legs. These mythical creatures guarded the gateway to the underworld. Also, the Babylonian creature was depicted with two heads. One was human and faced forward, and the other head was a beast that looked backwards. The early astrologers of the Alexandrian period referred to this as a royal sign because the human head wore a crown. Both the crown and the backward seeking second head were abandoned over time.

In Jewish mythology, the Archer was associated with Ephriam and Manasseh, and was once referred to as a pictorial prophecy of the messiah. In Christian mythology, the symbol is referred to as the emblem of St. Matthew.

The sign of Sagittarius was historically perceived as granting its natives an interest in hunting, sports, law, religion, philosophy, science and medicine. And while Libra may be seeking balance, the Archer who is forever aiming his arrow into the sky is striving for variation and new things or experiences to shoot or aim toward. New challenges are explored, and this native sets his goal on achieving with the straight forwardness of purpose of mind. There is an indication for the persons of this sign to meet obstacles in life, but these can be readily overcome with strength, perseverance, and hard work.

How to Find Your *Soul-Mate, Stars,* and *Destiny*

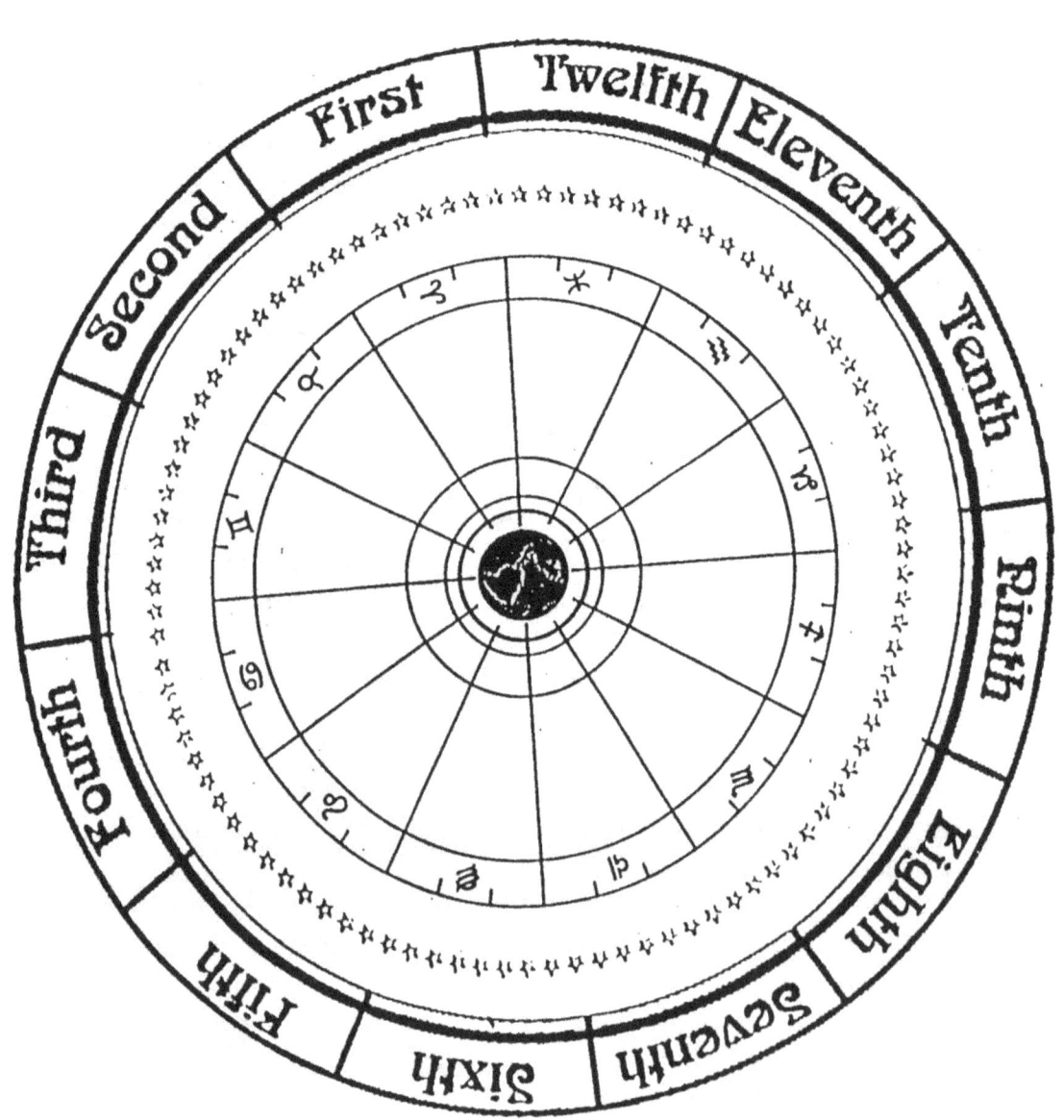

Sagittarius

November 22 -- December 20
The Thebaic Calendar
Character, Personality, and Destiny

The old civilizations and calendars once provided a daily character sketch and destiny. While this is more tradition than science, it was based on observations recorded over the years. This calendar is intended for a quick reference to the nature of individuals as indicated by their horoscope. The Thebaic Calendar represents the daily notes that the ancient astrologers wrote on burnt stones or papyrus. This is an easy and fast way to find information pertaining to your birth date. The native will often find his characteristics and destiny around his date of birth.

Whether Sagittarius is the person's Sun sign, the Ascendant, on the cusp, or found in a House, the characteristics of this sign become evident. As one of the three Fire signs, Sagittarius indicates radiant energy, magnetism, and enthusiasm. As the Mutable Fire sign, the natives of Sagittarius adapts this energy and enthusiasm to explore and discover life, wanting to sample as much as possible a long the way. Sagittarius is the sign of philosophy and represents the exploration of new ideas and thoughts, higher learning, and abstract concepts. There is an indication for leadership potential, but what is most expected when Sagittarius is found in a person's horoscope is the area of life where the native has the ability to enhance the philosophic, spiritual, and greater understanding of theology, law, or education. This is the area of life where the individual becomes most concerned with the meaning of life and the quality as well as the ideas upon which society is built.

DUALITY: Masculine   **ELEMENT:** Fire   **QUALITY:** Mutable   **RULER:** Jupiter

As a masculine sign, Sagittarius can be direct, and as a Fire sign, these natives can be forceful when necessary. But remember, this is also a Mutable sign, which means that these natives more than likely apply more thought to their forcefulness and their actions. Their directness is most observable in their speech patterns for Sagittarius natives are best known for being blunt, outspoken, and direct in their conversations. In fact, they are infamous for saying whatever thought pops into their heads, often putting their foot in their mouths with inappropriate remarks. That they are so quick with a phrase and possess somewhat of a quirky sense of humor only adds to this dilemna. They are as outspoken and frank as a person can be, and they need little help in being so. Sagittarius can take the intiative in a conversation with little or no outside motivation or stimuli. Fortunately, for these natives, they are blessed and endowed with the luck and good fortune of Jupiter, a luck that is known at times to swoop down and rescue them from sticky situations.

Sagittarius is that person who is liked and accepted for being who they are, quirky sense of humor and all, and for having their own outlook on life which again can be creative, original, and bordering on the unique. There is generally nothing run of the mill about this individual. Jupiter bestows upon Sagittarius, along with luck, the thought patterns of expansion, advanced study, and the willingness to chance speculative ventures. This native is most noted for being optimistic, positve, and enthusiastic about life and living. They possess a kind and generous nature with a strong sense of justice and an equally strong compassion. They are noted for a flair for sports, an apitude for languages, well directed intellectual abilities, and a breadth of vision that often astounds other people. When Jupiter is found in the sign of Sagittarius, all of the positive traits are emphasized allowing the native to fully develop his or her intellect and mental capacity.

It is, however, the thought process of expansion that most marks these Sagittarius natives. Not only are their thoughts and ideas prone to expansion, but their very lives as well. The Archer shoots its arrows in many directions, looking for whatever may come. This is not a person who adheres to being tied down, directed, restricted, or kept under limitations. They yearn for their freedom and liberties. They mean the best for one and all, but they most desire to retain their own personal freedoms. And their personal powers, productivity, intuition, and potential are realized only when they have the personal freedom necessary for them to expand and to explore their lives and their world. Tied to conventionality and harnessed to the will of another, this native can loose not only their drives and desire, but their luck as well. Through freedom and independence, this native strives to express himself or herself through their creativity which is rich with imagination and originality.

The First Decan

The First Decan occurs from 0 degrees to 10 degrees of Sagittarius and applies to those individuals born between November 22 and December 1.
Those natives born on the cusp of Scorpio may find that they possess characteristics of both signs. This First Decan, however, compels the native to aspire to wisdom as influenced by Jupiter. They are forever setting or thinking about new ideas and goals, many of which are lofty, exciting, and inspiring. These people are compelled to be students of human nature, wanting to broaden their understanding of life and people. They are both optimistic in their outlook and positive with an enthusiasm that is forever leading them to look for new opportunities and a brighter and better future. They are fond of travel, new experiences, and meeting new and different people from whom to learn or to broaden their exposure to all there is in life. They possess an expansive philosophical nature.

The Second Decan

The Second Decan occurs from 10 degrees to 20 degrees of Sagittarius and applies to those individuals born between December 2 and December 11. These individuals most strongly exhibit the characteristics of the sign of Sagittarius. They possess a courageous and generous spirit with an optimistic nature, a self-confident drive, and an intiative to be expansive and to seek all the opportunities available to them. They are drawn not only to adventure but to the excitement of experiencing life to its fullest. They are persuasive and often use this ability to influence, lead, and inspire others to listen to and consider their ideas. Whatever difficulties come their way, they turn a humorous and cheerful face to the world, and tackle their problems with a knowledge that all can be overcome. Their unique humor and turn of words allow them to speak their minds openly and frankly. They are in turn themselves lead to be independent thinkers who protect and respect their own personal freedoms.

The Third Decan

The Third Decan of Sagittarius occurs from 20 to 30 degrees of this sign and includes those born between December 12 and December 20. Those natives born on the cusp of Capricorn find that they are more determined to achieve their goals in life. And this determination is marked by their strong optimistic outlook which leads them to aspire to all that they dream and want in life. Their vitality, magnetism, and courage is combined with an intellect that knows few boundaries. And they turn their intellect and cheerfulness to their humor as well which grants them a pleasing personality and a charm that entreats and draws other people to them. They have a tendency to want to broaden their knowledge through travel to exotic and foreign places, by meeting and getting to know those from other cultures, and from careful study of the ideas and thoughts of others.

First Decan of Sagittarius:

November 22 - December 1 -
First Ten Days

Character, Personality, and Temperament:

The natives of Sagittarius born during the First Decan are courageous, nobel, optimistic, benevolent, and generous. This Decan accords a happy nature and character in individuals who are communicative and pleasant.

Mutable Element:

Fire: They are adaptable and changeable, and capable of using their enthusiasm to their best advantage.

Destiny:

These natives are not blessed in destiny, but they are well placed for opportunities, lucky situations, and good providence. The native earns a good reputation because of his many positive traits and good qualities.

Star Date of Birth: November 22

This person possesses a profound, clear-sighted spirit. There may be found a danger from sudden and unexpected accidents which can cause death. You may risk it all on a gamble or a legal dispute, counting on your good luck. And your luck does hold in romance as you gain philosophical insight from each affair of the heart. Travel provides opportunities to meet new people who are attracted to your enthusiasm.

How to Find Your *Soul-Mate, Stars,* and *Destiny*

Star Date of Birth: November 23

This individual may develop a suspicious character which ruins the possibility of positive activity. You resolve things from time to time. Unless the nature is improved, this native will only find success now and then. You are not truly happy until you discover your true soul mate with whom to share not only romance but lasting love. Those who have something to teach you inspire your mind and curious intellect, and in return you want to hold them close and dear to your heart.

Star Date of Birth: November 24

This native possesses a well-balanced, steady, and uniform character. There is found luck in avoiding danger. You are an achiever when involved in projects that promise a quick return. Your luck in love surrounds you with glamorous types who respond to your sexual allure and cheerful nature, even when it's understated. Your sexuality is unquestionable.

Star Date of Birth: November 25

The native born on this date will possess a very independent personality. There will be seen alternate success and failure with eventual successes in life. You have any number of great ideas but may not find yourself able to pursue them all. Sexually, you win the hearts of others easily, but your lovers may become less than pleased with your casual attitude toward relationships. But once your heart is hooked, you become a one and only.

Star Date of Birth: November 26

This individual possesses an excessive taste for taking risks. A lack of substantial wealth is seen and there is an indication for a sudden, unexpected death. You dally from one romantic relationship to another, but are prone to give your heart to the wrong partner and to stay in the relationship long after you should have left. Sexually, you can be a tease, tempting others with your alluring charm and disarming manner.

Star Date of Birth: November 27

This individual possesses a temperament ready for battle, to fight whether in love or war. A very agitated existence is seen. The pleasures of life may lead you to become addicted to romance and sexual encounters, always wanting a new experience to compare to the others. You know how to turn an opportunity to your advantage, and you know when the chase is right for you. This native has no trouble, though, going to the altar to say, "I do," because they follow their heart for happiness.

Star Date of Birth: November 28

The natives born on this date are inclined toward excessive trust in those close by and possess a tendency to give of themselves completely both body and soul. There is seen the possibility of danger because of a bad environment which the native frequents. Your patience and loyalty wins you respect, especially among the fashionable and well connected or influential members of your community. Your pleasing attitude blends well with your sexual allure and in this department you have no inhibitions about making the first move.

Star Date of Birth: November 29

The native displays a stubborn character. There is an inclination for success achieved relatively easy. Your curiosity and willingness to test your luck results in you being in the right place at the right time. Your sexuality is active and alive, but there again you have problems turning down what may turn out to be more excitement than you anticipated.

Star Date of Birth: November 30

The character of this individual is indecisive. Success is found in life in subordinate roles. You look to your relationships to bring enlightenment, and if that fails, you may turn to probing your spirituality through religious research. Once in love, however, you are willing to make any sacrifice necessary to further the relationship and fulfill your heart's desire.

Star Date of Birth: December 1

The temperament becomes more difficult to understand because of inertia. The life is calm and the talents and gifts of the native remain useful. Your public relations skills are impeded only by your outspoken and off-the-cuff remarks which earn you the reputation of having a quick wit. You only improve with the years, and it may well be that a lost love returns to fulfill your dreams and sexual desires for fulfillment.

Second Decan of Sagittarius:

December 2 - December 11 - Second Ten Days

Character, Personality, and Temperament:

This Decan extends a poetic tonality. The native knows what they want and are focused toward a dream or an ideal. The spirit of adventure is much more cerebral and philosophical.

Mutable Element:

Fire: Adapts enthusiasm, energy, and magnetism toward exploring life and reasoning.

Destiny:

The destiny is agitated, seeking, and with much love of traveling, always on the go; there is a driving nostalgia. These natives most like to have all their life an atmostphere of romance and sexual adventure. They like to embrace the shadow and to think fondly of their romantic dream life.

Star Date of Birth: December 2

This native possesses a vain and pretentious personality. Ruin may well be seen after a futile search for a better fate. Your luck is with you, but if you take too long to make a decision, you may miss that golden opportunity you've been anticipating. Your enthusiasm is side-tracked by your romantic encounters which can occur on the spur of the moment and with impulsive quickness.

Star Date of Birth: December 3

A versatile personality and temperment are seen for the natives born on this date. There is an indication for deceptions which are more of a romantic nature than material. Once you harness that wisdom you're so well known for, your luck brings you financial security. You adapt so well to new people and new situations that there seems to be no end to the opportunities to indulge your sexual fantasies, but you may find yourself wandering from one to another.

Star Date of Birth: December 4

This individual possesses a great power of assimilation. Life is full of riches. Your good natured self-confidence is enhanced by your ability to predict upcoming trends and fashions. Sexually, you are drawn to those who react to your allure the first time you meet. Your positive charm is only dampened by what can turn into biting sarcasm.

Star Date of Birth: December 5

There is indicated that the native born on this date will be inclined toward impassivity, credulity, and a weakness for the opposite sex. A useful life is seen with some suffering due to a lack of resources. You are so discreet that you do not confide in anyone, but this lack of trust does nothing to deter from your love life. Your sexual allure remains highly attractive, and you spread the philosophy of enjoying sex to its fullest for both you and your partner.

Star Date of Birth: December 6

This native is inclined toward a vast spirit which is imaginative but which can also be wasted on worthless pursuits. A life of toil is indicated which may proceed in nonproductive ways. You are highly distracted by your numerous ambitions and shoot your arrows in several different directions. You enjoy sex for the sake of sex and your partner may complain about a lack of more meaningful affection, but your mind drifts to other matters.

Star Date of Birth: December 7

An excessive belief in one's self and an overconfidence is seen for this individual. Rapid success in indicated, but it is fleeting and the native is always compelled to start things over. You are even tempered and do not see the need to become overly concerned about emotional matters, and others may complain you do not pay enough attention to this aspect of life. Sexually, you enjoy the thrills of romantic encounters, but your mind may be on your next adventure.

Star Date of Birth: December 8

This individual is inclined toward a strong independence with a lack of affection or closeness to home. This life may well be sown with bad luck, and loneliness and solitude is seen toward the end of life. You are ambitious to achieve your aims in life and count on your luck to see you through difficult moments. You want to share your happy-go-lucky attitude with your romantic partners, and indeed your self-assurance turns easily into an inticing sexual allure.

Star Date of Birth: December 9

A strong intelligence is noted for this person with a sense of moderation. A calm life is seen for the person who doesn't become upset or excited easily. You learn from experience that mistakes can erode your good luck, and you are concerned that others learn this lesson as well. Sexually, you are attracted to those who are faced with difficulties and who come to depend on you for your good will.

Star Date of Birth: December 10

Cunning and imprudence are shown for the native born on this date. Success is seen through cleverness and luck. Your spirituality makes you open-minded about the possibilities in life, especially metaphysics. Sexually, your enthusiasm and enjoyment is shared with your romantic partners, and you are attracted to the quiet, shy types who respond to your good nature.

Star Date of Birth: December 11

This individual possesses a desire to confide and to lean on others who are close. There may be experienced difficulties caused by the parents. When trusted to return in love, you are loyal and devoted to your partner. Sexually, you are attracted to those who share your outlook on life, and are put off by the overly egotistical types who need constant affirmation of your affections.

The Third Decan of Sagittarius:

December 12 - December 20 - Third Ten Days

Character, Personality, and Temperament:

These individuals possess a unique wisdom and intelligence which slows an inborn spontaneity. Egotism is often diminished or is completely avoided.

Mutable Element:

Fire: An enterprising enthusiasm that focuses energies on exploring opportunities and success.

Destiny:

The life is most successful on an intimate level sometimes distracting the native from being successful socially - usually destined for Sagittarian.

How to Find Your *Soul-Mate, Stars,* and *Destiny*

Star Date of Birth: December 12

A jealous and anxious nature is seen for this individual. Trials and hardships at home are indicated. You may have good intentions, but your outspoken bluntness can turn sarcastic and expose your mean streak and inability to consider the feelings of others. Sexually, you easily become bored if the relationship falls into a routine, leaving you thirsting for new experiences.

Star Date of Birth: December 13

This native is inclined to have a clever personality which is both cunning and sly. Success for this native is based on a friendly perseverance in his or her efforts. Your optimism renews your enthusiasm no matter what difficulties you face. Sexually, you aim to please both yourself and your partner and are most satisfied when your partner has fully enjoyed the experience. You may ramble a bit, but you find your thoughts returning to a former love.

Star Date of Birth: December 14

Often a childish nature is seen for this person and an attraction to unimportant things. An average career is indicated with the possibility of failure. What you may think is an unique philosophy, others may view as criticism and carping, but you usually save the day with your quick wit. A globe-trotting wanderer, your teasing and flirting ways bring you new sexual encounters through your travels.

Star Date of Birth: December 15

An impetuous and aggressive nature is indicated for this individual. There is seen a life clouded by numerous dangers and enemies. You are ambitious, but you strive most for a peaceful and contented life through your achievements. Your sexuality provides you with your greatest moments of ecstasy and the mental relaxation that is derived through physical exertion--and you adore the partner who can share this.

How to Find Your *Soul-Mate, Stars,* and *Destiny*

Star Date of Birth: December 16

This native has a tendency toward sensual pleasures which are sometimes excessive. There is indicated certain satisfactions in life but with bitter profits. You bask in the differences of exotic cultures and foreign lifestyles, being open minded and adaptable to changing circumstances. And sex is just another avenue of exploration, leading you to explore far and wide what is available for your delight.

Star Date of Birth: December 17

An unflinching will power and perseverance is indicated for this native. Success is seen and the native obtains his or her goals. In your quieter moments, your thoughts probe your personal philosophical observations about mankind and how you fit into the picture. Your luck bides you well in love and romance and influential and financially successful types are drawn to your allure.

Star Date of Birth: December 18

The individual possesses a great deal of initiative closely followed by a lot of judgment. A lasting success of good quality is indicated, but it takes time to acquire. You form strong opinions which you openly express, but you are also open to listening to the opinions of others. Luck bides you well in love and romance, and you are happiest when you have found the soul mate who wants to share your life, but you may also be drawn to a second life to satisfy your sexuality and pleasure.

Star Date of Birth: December 19

This native is inclined toward a restless temperament and is nervous, anxious and lacks confidence. Accidents are indicated. In life, obstacles are noted for those who are not prepared. You are unswerving in sticking to your opinion, but you are also more likely than most to win acclaim by proving yourself worthy. Sexually, you take nothing for granted and are inspired by those who know how to love strongly and to express emotions physically.

Star Date of Birth: December 20

An optimistic personality is noted for this individual but it is an optimism that is based on false judgment. Frequent misunderstandings with others are indicated. You guard your reputation and social standing, always concerned with what is best in any given situation. Sexually, you apply your energies to the physical aspect of sexual release and are not one to become overly emotional or wordy about what you want and feel.

Colors:

The most suitable colors for the native of Sagittarius are shades of purple, violet and mauve. Royal blue also favors these natives.

Birthstones:

The birthstones for Sagittarius natives are the amethysts, sapphires, and turquoise and topaz.

Power Stones:

The power stones for this sign include the lapis lazuli, the azurite, and the sodalite.

Flowers:

Favorable flowers for Sagittarius individuals include the narcissus, holly, and a number of wild flowers and wild plants including the dandelion.

Keyword: "I See"

Positive Traits:

Philosophical; adaptable; tolerant; enthusiastic; compassionate; sincere; jovial; fun; optimistic; honest; frank; outspoken; just; generous; prophetic; buoyant; enduring; persevering; sound judgment; good luck; well meaning; dependable; independent; freedom loving; logical; charitable; scrupulous; caring; kind; protective; loyal; wisdom; inspiring; truthful; exuberance; humanitarian; trusting.

Negative Traits:

Over confident; egotistical; exaggeration; tells tall tales; boisterous; rash judgment; selfish; self-centered; changeable; blunt; sarcastic; aggressive; defiant; tactless; restless; rash; careless; unrationally optimistic; irresponsible; unfaithful; whimsical; capricious; proud; stubborn; obstinate; insincere; lies; inconsiderate; gambles; two-faced; arrogant; immoral; jealous; hypocritical; superficial; impatient; suspicious; untrustworthy; and possessive.

How to Find Your *Soul-Mate, Stars,* and *Destiny*

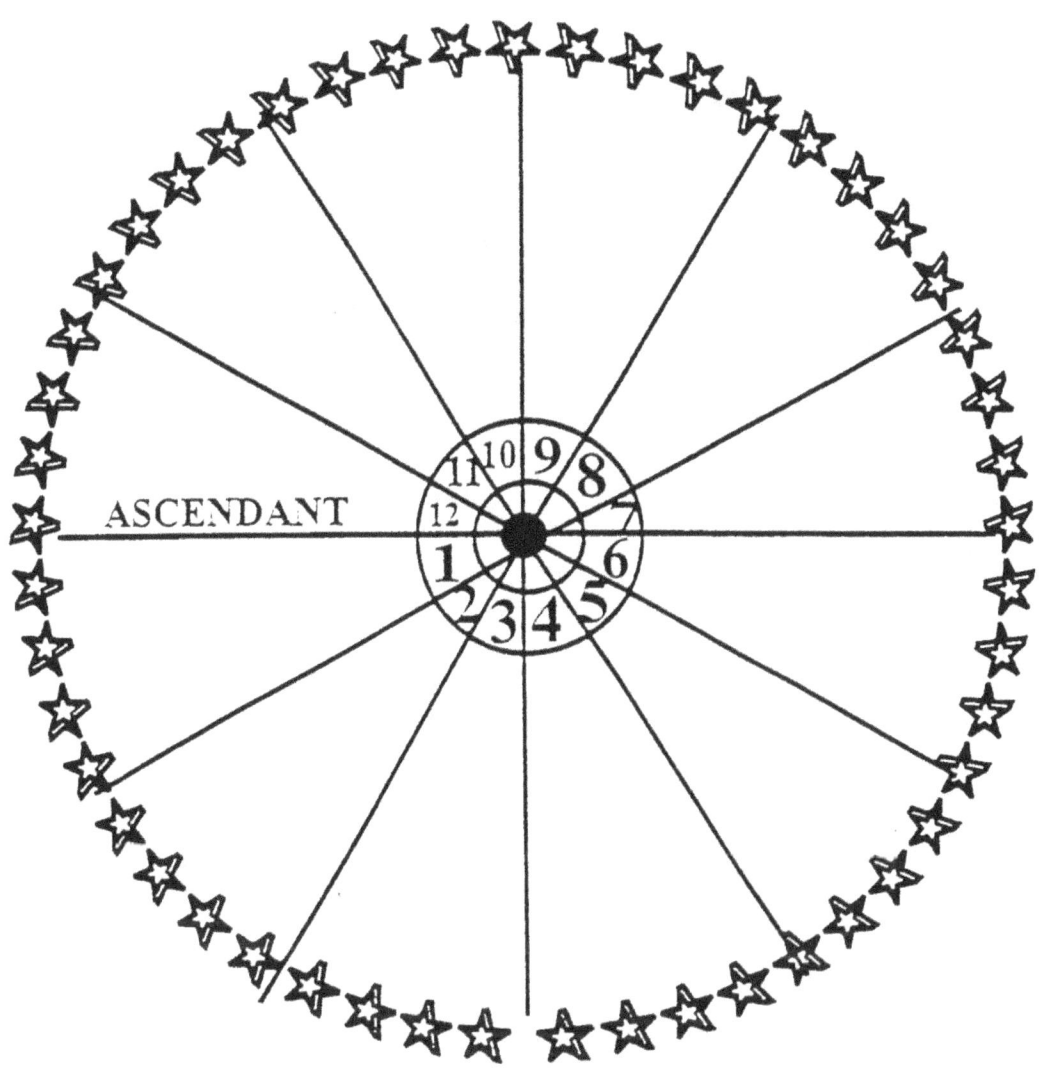

Sagittarius
Personal Self-Expression and Mental Tendencies

1. Jovial, Bright, Hopeful, Generous, Charitable, Dishonest
2. Self-Reliant, Active, Enterprising, Frank, Outspoken, Honest
3. Ambitious, Persevering, Not Easily Discouraged, Loves Liberty
4. Freedom, Out-of-Doors Sports, Dislikes Misers, Intuitive
5. Strong Willed, sincere, Honorable, Earnest, Aspiring, Energetic
6. Shows Reverence for Philosophy and Science, Good at Calculations
7. Foresight, Prophetic Outcomes, Movements, Enterprises, Eccentric
8. Hopeful, Independent, Dislikes a Master, Good Humored
9. Fearless, Impulsive, Demonstrative, Nervously Energetic
10. Quick to Arrive at Conclusions, Sympathetic and Loving
11. Possesses Foresight, Prophetic, Forceful, Straight to the Point
12. Often Appears Blunt or Abrupt, Bewitchment, Perverse Mind
13. Misses the Mark in Their Deductions, Restless, Over-Anxious
14. High-Strung, Respects Religious Customs, Enjoys Traveling
15. Aspiring, Takes Advantage of Opportunity to Consummate Business
16. Consummate Business Arrangements, Definitely Peculiar, Aggressive
17. Goes Straight to the Point, Aims Directly, Premeditated Acts
18. Likes Wholesale, Big Business, Large Financial Undertaking
19. Mental Temperament, Good-Hearted, Good-Tempered
20. Tendency t Stamp or Scrape the Feet, Mentally Stimulating
21. Cheerful, Friendly, Active, Humane, Ominous Forebodings
22. Impulsive, Traveling, Voyaging, Exercises, Occult
23. Benevolent, Humanitarian, Kind-Hearted, Wisdom
24. Sociable, Quickly Angered, Obstacles, Downfall, Setback
25. Forgiving, Promise, Danger of Imprisonment in Foreign Lands
26. Shows Love of Beauty, Harmony, and Sports; Develops Slowly
27. Unsettled Manner Either in Mind, Body, or Both; Free
28. Changes the Place of Residence Frequently, Self-Willed

29. Quick Walker or Worker, Very Philosophical, Prophet
30. Ingenious, Ability for Science, Significance of Inheritance
31. Rebellious, Just, Rash, Impulsive, Wise, Impressionable
32. Mentally or Physically Changeable but Progressive, Antiquarian
33. Change and Travel of Home and Family, Likes Authority
34. Mental Development for Philosophy, Religion, Science, Law, or Medicine
35. Likes Animals, Psychic Experiences, Refines Nature, Light-Hearted
36. Imaginative, Loyal Intentions, Romance, Complicated Affairs
37. Justice, Mystical or Spiritual Nature, Unexpected
38. Intellectual work, Philanthropy, Imprudent Action
39. Harmony Involving Higher Attributes of the Mind, Impulsive
40. Legacy, Partnership, Speculative Investment, Patriotic
41. Very Attracted to the Opposite Sex, Self-Development
42. Enthusiastic, Speech and Action, Argument is Usually
43. Morally and Mentally Brave, Daring and Fearless
44. Opinions of Others, Firm, Fixed, Positive, Ready,
45. Travel and Adventure, Particularly Inspirational
46. Ingenuity; Love of Pleasure, Marriage, Legacy, Voyages
47. Likelihood, Risk, Over-Estimation, Miscalculation, Exaggeration
48. Disagreement, Indisposed, Dual Experiences, Extravagant
49. Endowed, Courteous, Affable, Tolerant, Humorous, Noble
50. Merciful, Compassionate, Sincere, Good Fortune, General Success
51. Success in Enterprises, Receives Honors, Joyous, Pompous
52. Social Affairs, Speculation, Gambling, Danger of Nervous Tension
53. Kind, Obliging, Inventiveness, Visions, Premonition, Slapdash
54. Loves Science, Passing Events, Scientific, Inventions
55. Adventuresome, Enthusiastic, Expansive, Always in Motion
56. High-Spirited, Trustworthy, Gullible, Eager, Imbalance
57. Optimistic, Lucky, Giving Enchanting, Charming, Flashy
58. Exhibitionist, Adaptable, Versatile, Scholarly, Explorer
59. Musical, Good Judgement, Cultural Patron, Progressive
60. Far-Out, Inspirational, Spiritual, Animal Energy, Beverages
61. Idealistic, Lusty, Conquistador, Exciting, Intriguing
62. Rearranging, Seldom Satisfied, Self-Worth, Conservative
63. Vibrations, Historical, Brilliant, Life-Giving Energies
64. Simultaneous Relationships, Provocative, Self-Deception
65. Abusive, Unwittingly Blunt, Tactless, Progressive
66. Exploration, Dramatically Different Friends and Lifestyle

How to Find Your Soul-Mate, Stars, and Destiny

67. Many Acquaintances, Few Friends, Claustrophobic
68. Brilliantly Sarcastic, Violent Temper, Boredom, Exotic Flair
69. Eccentric Way of Life, Determination, Tendencies, Courage
70. Illumination, Obedience, Neglects Human Needs, Sexual Appetite
71. Obsessed With Power, Gallivanting, Boisterous, Obnoxious
72. Unwitting, Capable of Betrayal, Useful, Jealous
73. Suspicious, Mistrustful Lover, Disillusioned, Vindictive
74. Surface, Shy, Repressed, Indirect, Expresses Irritation
75. Glorious Sex Life, Powerful, Blind Selfishness
76. Struggle for Challenge, Fabulous Host or Hostess, Entertains
77. Domain, Capricious, Often Very Exotic, Self-Confidence
78. Enthusiastic, Warm, Curious Personality, Natural Leadership
79. Fantastic Mind, Physical Activity, Superficial Knowledge
80. Pedantic, Pompous, Opinions, Challenged, Methodology
81. Future-Oriented, Unheard of Passion, Atomic Waste, Pride
82. Transcendent, Comprehension of Reality, Stratosphere
83. Integrated, Organized, Buoyant, Undemanding, Ecstatic
84. Handles Business Arrangements, Left Behind, Intelligence
85. Excitement, Sophistication, Love is Sex, Romance is the
86. Sex is Completely Religion; Loss of Money, Property, and Credit
87. Manipulation, Bloodhound, Vanish, Surprises, Demands
88. Adventurous Sex, Sensual Magnets, Master-Slave Dynamic
89. Denotes Farsightedness, Love for Change, Vague
90. Indefinite, Over Sensitive, Political Sentiments
91. Marriage Brings Prosperity, Financially Well Off, Affairs
92. Public Nature; Psychism From a Religious, Scientific Standpoint
93. Confident, Mental Improvement, Risky Ventures
94. High Ideals, Desires Hard to Materialize, Disappointments
95. Hindrance Through Perversity, Good Counselor
96. Recognition, Responsible Undertakings, High Ideas
97. Courageous, Vigorous in Defense of Justice
98. Danger of Violence, Distressful Dreams or Fantasies
99. Career Possibly in Armed Forces or Allied Professions
100. Dangers and Sorrows, Evil and Dangerous Tendencies

Celebrity Birthdays

November Sagittarius

22	Boris Becker Billie Jean King Tina Weymouth Doris Duke	Jamie Lee Curtis Mariel Hemingway Floyd Sneed Rodney Dangerfield	Tom Conti Terry Gilliam Benjamin Britten Floyd Sneed
23	Bruce Hornsby Boris Karloff Charles Berlitz Louis Tiant	Susan Anspach Pres Franklin Pierce Billy the Kid	Vin Baker Jerry Bock Erte
24	Dale Carnegie Howard Duff David Bing Garson Kanin	Geraldine Fitzgerald Chen Lu Dwight Schultz William F. Buckley Jr	John Squire Toulouse-Lautrec Donald Dunn Scott Joplin
25	Carry Nation Steve Rotherby Arthur Schwartz John Larroquette	John F. Kennedy Jr Christina Applegate Andrew Carnegie Joe DiMaggio	Percy Sledge Amy Grant Spinoza Murray Schisgal
26	Shawn Kemp Eric Sevareid Charles Schulz Robert Goulet	Cyril Cusack Alan Henderson Michael Butler Eugene Ionesco	Norman Hassan Rich Little Tina Turner John McVie
27	Caroline Kennedy Charlie Burchill Jimi Hendrix Bob Smith	Eddie Rabbitt Fisher Stevens David Merrick Alfred Gwynne Vanderbilt	Robin Givens Jaleel White Bruce Lee
28	Randy Newman Beeb Birtles Judd Nelson Brooks Atkinson	Rita Mae Brown Natalia Makarova Gloria Graham Anton Rubinstein	Gary Hart Hope Lange William Blake Ed Harris
29	C.S. Lewis Vince Scully Suzy Chaffee Busby Berkeley	Jonathan Knight Denny Doherty Andrew McCarthy Louisa May Alcott	Howie Mandel Diane Ladd Garry Shandling John Mayall

November — Sagittarius

30 Dick Clark / Shirley Chisholm / Richard Barbieri
Ben Stiller / Mandy Patinkin / Abbie Hoffman John
Robert Guillaume / Sir Winston Churchill / Clements

December

1	Woody Allen / Charlene Tilton / Richard Pryor / Diane Lennon	Bette Midler / Gilbert O'Sullivan / John Densmore / Mary Martin	Treat Williams / Eric Bloom / Sandy Nelson / Cyril Ritchard
2	Cathy Lee Crosby / Ted Bluechel Jr / Julie Harris / Tracy Austin	Tom McGuinness / Michael McDonald / Rick Savage / Stone Phillips	Howard Stern / Alexander Haig / Maggie Smith / Adolph Green
3	Mary Alice / Maria Callas / Joseph Conrad	Andy Williams / Ozzy Osbourne / Jean-Luc Godard	Katarina Witt / Brian Bonsall / Ferlin Husky
4	Marisa Tomei / Tyra Banks / Chris Hillman / Lillian Russell	Michael Ovitz / Wink Martindale / Jeff Bridges / Gary Rossington	Bob Mosley / John Cale / Freddy Cannon / Deanna Durbin
5	Little Richard / Nunnally Johnson / Strom Thurmond / Jim Messina	Joan Didion / Gen. George Custer / Charles Lane / Morgan Brittany	Walt Disney / Otto Preminger / Jim Plunkett / Jeroen Krabbe
6	Janine Turner / Lynn Fontanne / Agnes Moorehead / Ira Gershwin	Steven Wright / Joyce Kilmer / Dave Brubeck / ‚Baby Face' Nelson	Peter Buck / Wally Cox / Ben Watt / Tom Hulce
7	Ellen Burstyn / Johnny Bench / C. Thomas Howell / Harry Chapin	Priscilla Barnes / Eli Wallach / Mary, Queen of Scots / Tom Waits	Ted Knight / Madame Tussaud / Larry Bird / Eli Wallach
8	Kim Basinger / Flip Wilson / Bobby Elliott / Sammy Davis Jr.	Gregg Allman / Teri Hatcher / Phil Collen / Paul Rutherford	David Carradine / Maximilian Schell / Sinead O'Connor / Jerry Butler

DECEMBER SAGITTARIUS

9	Beau Bridges John Malkovich Caryn Kadavy Hermione Gingold	Joan Armatrading Morton Downey Jr. Douglas Fairbanks Jr. Dick Van Patten	Kirk Douglas Dina Merrill Neil Innes Dick Butkus
10	Dorothy Lamour Morton Gould Susan Dey Walter Orange	Kenneth Branagh Emily Dickinson Chet Huntley Johnny Rodriguez	Chad Stuart Ace Kefford Frank Beard Raven-Symone
11	Donna Mills Brenda Lee Booker T. Jones Teri Garr	Jermaine Jackson Christina Onassis Rita Moreno David Gates	Nikki Sixx Hector Berlioz Carlo Ponti J-L Trintignant
12	John Osborne Frank Sinatra Connie Francis Paul Hornung	Mayim Bialik Bob Barker Dionne Warwick Jennifer Connelly	Eric Millot Cathy Rigby Terry Kirkman Ed Koch
13	Ted Nugent Dick Van Dyke Carlos Montoya Johnny Whitaker	Johnny Whitaker Richard Zanuck Mary Todd Lincoln Christopher Plummer	Randy Owen Dick Haymes John Davidson Tom Verlaine
14	Hal Williams Patty Duke Astin Morey Amsterdam Cynthia Gibb	Spike Jones Lee Remick Nostradamus Dee Wallace Stone	Cliff Williams Charlie Rich Mike Scott Dan Dailey
15	Don Johnson Tim Conway Gladys Shelley Jerry Wallace	Carmine Appice Paul Simonon Reginald Hudin Nick Buoniconti	Dave Clark Helen Slater Surya Bonaly J.Paul Getty
16	Steven Bochco Jane Austen Margaret Mead George Schaefer	Lesley Stahl George Santayana Billy Gibbons Noel Coward	Ben Cross William Perry Liv Ullmann Tony Hicks
17	William Saffire Tommy Steele Sarah Dallin Art Neville	Samuel Crompton Arthur Fiedler Bob Guccione Eddie Kendricks	Erskine Caldwell Paul Rodgers Eugene Levy Dave Dee

DECEMBER   SAGITTARIUS

18	Steven Spielberg	Kiefer Sutherland	Paul Klee
	Keith Richards	Gillian Armstrong	Brad Pitt
	Ramsey Clark	Betty Grable	Ray Liotta
	Elliot Easton	Leonard Maltin	Ossie Davis
19	Jennifer Beals	Robert MacNaughton	Zal Yanovsky
	Ford Frick	Sir Ralph Richardson	Alberto Tomba
	Reggie White	Cicely Tyson	Robert Urich
	David Susskind	Alyssa Milano	Tim Reid
20	Billy Bragg	Pamela Austin	Jenny Agutter
	Irene Dunne	Little Stevie Wright	Harvey Firestone
	Anita Baker	George Roy Hill	John Hillerman
	Chris Robinson	Max Lerner	Uri Geller

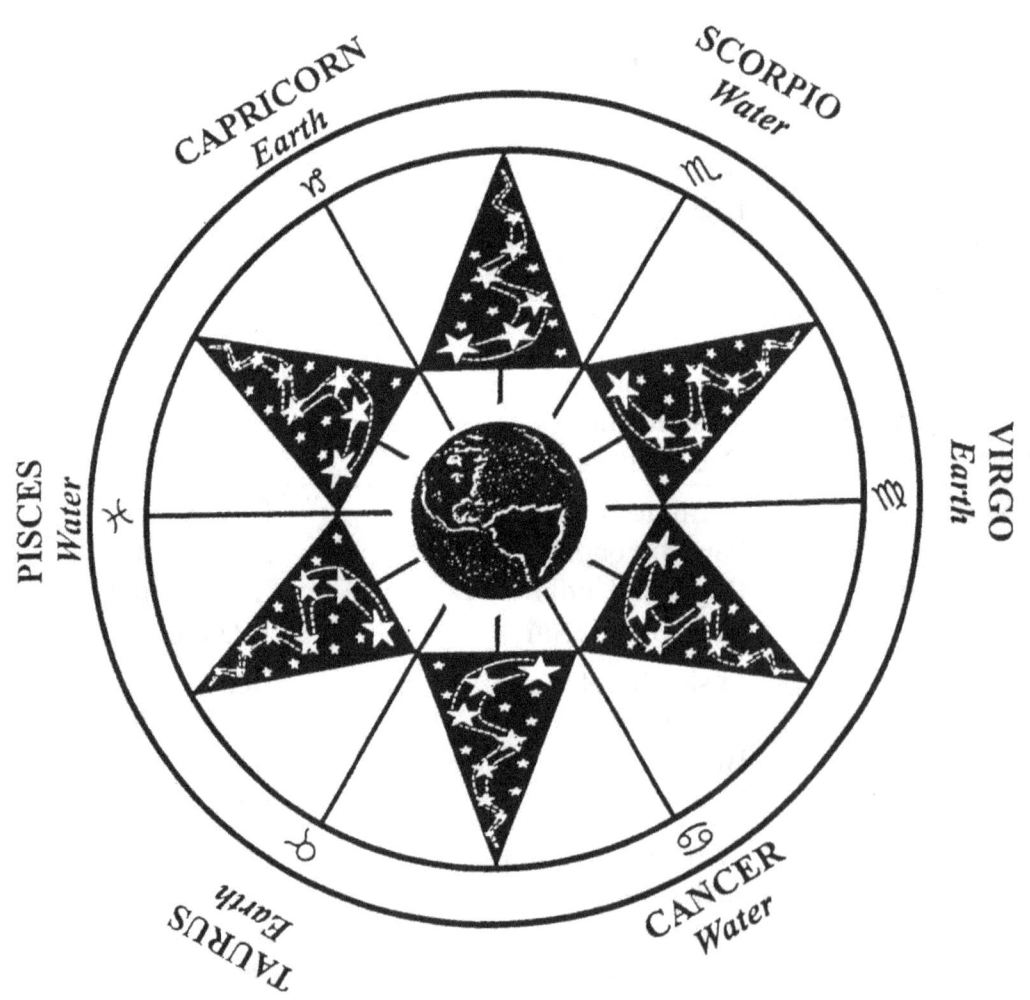

LIGIA BALU
www.ligiabalu.com

Astrological Books:

A Complete Compilation of ancient and modern reflections **on the individual zodiac signs.** Learn how to chart your **PERSONAL DESTINY**, understand your **SEXUALITY**, discover your **COMPATIBILITY WITH YOUR SOUL-MATE**, determine the **DESTINY OF YOUR SOUL-MATE**, find your **STARS**, and gain other information about your **FUTURE**. **Complete astrological information on Love Signs, Sun Signs, Moon Signs, Planets, Houses, Numerology**, as well as the complete **Astrological Tables for the Years from 1900 to 2025 and instruction on how to cast your very own Chart**.

Order the book for your specific Zodiac sign or the COMPLETE ASTROLOGY book series which contains information on *ALL TWELVE SIGNS* - from **ARIES** to **PISCES**. Each book contain over 550 pages.

Individual Zodiac Books

Individual Love Signs, Sun Signs, Moon Signs, Planets, Houses, Astrological Tables, Numerology, Relationships With Other Signs and a lot more in each book.

Astrology - Aries
HOW TO FIND YOUR SOUL-MATE, STARS AND DESTINY
ISBN: 0-9651186-2-2   Price: $49.95

Astrology - Taurus
HOW TO FIND YOUR SOUL-MATE, STARS AND DESTINY
ISBN: 0-9651186-3-0   Price: $49.95

Astrology - Gemini
HOW TO FIND YOUR SOUL-MATE, STARS AND DESTINY
ISBN: 0-9651186-4-9   Price: $49.95

Astrology - Cancer
HOW TO FIND YOUR SOUL-MATE, STARS AND DESTINY
ISBN: 0-9651186-5-7   Price: $49.95

Astrology - Leo
HOW TO FIND YOUR SOUL-MATE, STARS AND DESTINY
ISBN: 0-9651186-6-5   Price: $49.95

Astrology - Virgo
HOW TO FIND YOUR SOUL-MATE, STARS AND DESTINY
ISBN: 0-9651186-7-3   Price: $49.95

Astrology - Libra
HOW TO FIND YOUR SOUL-MATE, STARS AND DESTINY
ISBN: 0-9651186-8-1   Price: $49.95

Astrology - Scorpio
HOW TO FIND YOUR SOUL-MATE, STARS AND DESTINY
ISBN: 0-9651186-9-X   Price: $49.95

Astrology - Sagittarius
HOW TO FIND YOUR SOUL-MATE, STARS AND DESTINY
ISBN: 1-892530-00-7   Price: $49.95

Astrology - Capricorn
HOW TO FIND YOUR SOUL-MATE, STARS AND DESTINY
ISBN: 1-892530-02-3 Price: $49.95

Astrology - Aquarius
HOW TO FIND YOUR SOUL-MATE, STARS AND DESTINY
ISBN: 1-892530-01-5 Price: $49.95

Astrology - Pisces
HOW TO FIND YOUR SOUL-MATE, STARS AND DESTINY
ISBN: 1-892530-03-1 Price: $49.95

True - Stories:

Believe In Your Dreams, Not In Your Fears
Is the inspiring and unforgettable story of a young girl who possessed an **INDOMITABLE SPIRIT** that r5efused to give up no matter what life gave her. I*n her own brutally honest words, **Ligia Balu** paints a haunting picture of her life. She tells how she survived not only the **ABUSE** of her family, but also a man who took **ADVANTAGE** of her, and finally a government that wanted to **IMPRISION** her. **RISKING HER LIFE**, she **ESCAPED** two communist countries and finally found freedom for herself and her daughters in America. "Running from the **WOLVES** and finding the **BIG BAD BEARS**"
ISBN: 0-9651186-0-6

American Dream Made Me Cry and Scream

Is Ligia Balu's INCREDIBLE TRUE STORY of arriving in America and finding the AMERICAN DREAM THAT MADE HER CRY and SCREAM? Once in America, Ligia became ENTRAPPED and VICTIMIZED by the POWERFULL BUREAUCRACY that RAPED, BETRAYED. EXTORTED, and ROBBED.. She was abused by the greed fro money of the BUREAUCRACTIC JUNGLE. She was DISCRIMINATED against, and her CHARACTER was ASSASSINATED. The PAIN, SUFFERING, MANIPULATION, DISAPPOINTMENT, and ISOLATION inflicted upon her by the justice system and her legal advisors were unbelievable. She found that only those who have the power have the rights and the freedom. What kind of system would robe her DREAM and make her CRY and SCREAM? You have to read the book to believe it.\
ISBN: 1-892530-04-X

Adult Romantic Fiction:

Talk Dirty To Me
is a collection of light-hearted adult SATRICAL FANTASIES of MODER N SEXUALITY. Each story is filled with WILD, UNIHIBITED, and INTIMATE SEXUAL DISIRES and PLEAURES.
ISBN: 1-892530-05-8   Price: $39.99

Order Online

To order or learn more about Ligia Balu's books, visit
www.ligiabalu.com

www.ingramcontent.com/pod-product-compliance
Lightning Source LLC
Chambersburg PA
CBHW080453110426
42742CB00017B/2873